Meeting the Challenges to Measurement in an Era of Accountability

Under pressure and support from the federal government, states have increasingly turned to indicators based on student test scores to evaluate teachers and schools, as well as students themselves. The focus thus far has been on test scores in those subject areas where there is a sequence of consecutive tests, such as in mathematics or English/language arts with a focus on grades 4–8. Teachers in these subject areas, however, constitute less than 30 percent of the teacher workforce in a district. Comparatively little has been written about the measurement of achievement in the other grades and subjects.

This volume seeks to remedy this imbalance by focusing on the assessment of student achievement in a broad range of grade levels and subject areas, with particular attention to their use in the evaluation of teachers and schools in all. It addresses traditional end-of-course tests, as well as alternative measures such as portfolios, exhibitions, and student learning objectives. In each case, issues related to design and development, psychometric considerations, and validity challenges are covered from both a generic and a content-specific perspective.

The *NCME Applications of Educational Measurement and Assessment* series includes edited volumes designed to inform research-based applications of educational measurement and assessment. Edited by leading experts, these books are comprehensive and practical resources on the latest developments in the field.

The NCME series editorial board is comprised of Michael J. Kolen, Editor; Robert L. Brennan; Wayne Camara; Edward H. Haertel; Suzanne Lane; and Rebecca Zwick.

Henry Braun is Boisi Professor of Education and Public Policy, and Director of the Center for the Study of Testing, Evaluation, and Education Policy in the Lynch School of Education at Boston College, USA.

Meeting the Challenges to Measurement in an Era of Accountability

Edited by Henry Braun

Routledge
Taylor & Francis Group

NEW YORK AND LONDON

First published 2016
by Routledge
711 Third Avenue, New York, NY 10017

and by Routledge
2 Park Square, Milton Park, Abingdon, Oxon OX14 4RN

Routledge is an imprint of the Taylor & Francis Group, an informa business

Library of Congress Cataloging-in-Publication Data
Names: Braun, Henry I., 1949– editor of compilation.
Title: Meeting the challenges to measurement in an era of accountability /
edited by Henry Braun.
Description: New York : Routledge, 2016. | Series: The NCME applications
of educational measurement and assessment book series | Includes
bibliographical references and index.
Identifiers: LCCN 2015025922| ISBN 9780415838603 (hardback) |
ISBN 9780415838610 (pbk.) | ISBN 9780203781302 (ebook)
Subjects: LCSH: Education—United States—Evaluation. | Educational
tests and measurements—United States. | Academic achievement—United
States—Evaluation. | Teacher effectiveness—United States—Evaluation. |
Education—Standards—United States. | Schools—United States—Evalution.
Classification: LCC LB3051 .M4634 2016 | DDC 371.26—dc23
LC record available at http://lccn.loc.gov/2015025922

ISBN: 978-0-415-83860-3 (hbk)
ISBN: 978-0-415-83861-0 (pbk)
ISBN: 978-0-203-78130-2 (ebk)

Typeset in Galliard
by Book Now Ltd, London

Printed and bound in the United States of America by
Edwards Brothers Malloy on sustainably sourced paper

To my grandchildren Gabriel, Eitan, Gideon, Asher, Matan, Liat, and Eden who, I hope, will encounter through their school years assessments that provide useful guidance and meaningful markers of progress along each of their learning trajectories.

Contents

Foreword

The National Council on Measurement in Education (NCME) is pleased to sponsor this volume, *Meeting the Challenges to Measurement in an Era of Accountability*, in its *Applications of Educational Measurement and Assessment* book series. Henry Braun, the editor of this volume, has been at the forefront in studying the use of educational measures in educational accountability systems. Using tests and assessments in educational accountability is a major challenge, and this volume addresses design and psychometric considerations to help ensure the validity of their use for accountability purposes. This volume focuses on curriculum areas that are often not included in educational accountability systems.

The NCME book series is intended to increase understanding and to inform research-based applied educational measurement and assessment, as well as furthering NCME's mission to advance measurement science. Intended audiences include NCME members, graduate students, and professionals in related fields engaged in measurement and assessment.

Acknowledgments

I would like to thank the NCME Editorial Board for offering me the opportunity to serve as the editor of this volume, the second in the *NCME Applications of Educational Measurement and Assessment* series. The Board provided useful input on the focus of the volume and suggested the authors for some of the chapters. I am particularly appreciative of the support and encouragement that Professor Michael Kolen, chair of the Editorial Board, provided during the more than three years that it took to bring this volume to fruition. I would be remiss if I did not also express my thanks to the many reviewers who read early drafts of all the chapters, made many useful suggestions, and whose constructive criticism contributed to the quality of the volume. Their names are included at the end of the book. Of course, my greatest thanks goes to the many authors who labored mightily through many drafts to produce 13 chapters that constitute a significant milestone to the literature on assessment.

1 The Challenges to Measurement in an Era of Accountability

Introduction and Overview

Henry Braun

Introduction

Among the many aspects of public education that spark debate, few are as contentious as high-stakes assessments: those cumulative end-of-year or end-of-course tests that contribute to decisions about students (with regard to promotion or graduation) and now, increasingly, to evaluations of schools, principals, and teachers. Although such tests have always been a fixture of American education, more and more, state-mandated, externally developed, standardized assessments are the norm across subjects and grades. Their current uses as a basis for comparisons across districts and as instruments of educational reform, as well as significant sources of evidence about the efficacy of schools and educators, have led to increased scrutiny and criticism.

In the main, the focus of these debates has been on the subjects and grades specified in the No Child Left Behind Act (NCLB); that is, English/Language Arts (E/LA) and Mathematics in grades 3–8 and one high school grade. (NCLB also requires testing science once in each grade span, but that has not occasioned as much discussion.) It has been well documented, however, that the teachers who come under the NCLB mandates typically constitute only 25–30 percent of the teachers in a state. Nonetheless, many states are now demanding that test-based indicators be employed in the evaluation of all teachers—and even all school personnel. Education officials are scrambling to comply by bringing the other 70–75 percent of educators under the accountability tent.

These teachers are often said to be teaching in "non-tested subjects and grades" (NTSG). This is a misnomer as there often are associated tests. In fact, the situation varies widely from state to state: In some subjects and grades, there is a statewide end-of-course test; in others individual districts purchase or develop end-of-course tests; and in few others there is no test available. Obviously, the public credibility and legal defensibility of the accountability system, as it applies to all educators, including those in the NTSG, will depend on the technical quality of the assessments that are employed, how the different indicators are combined to yield an overall rating, and the consequences tied to each rating.

Yet, in comparison to the subjects/grades that are the focus of NCLB, comparatively little has been invested in, or written about, the summative measurement of achievement in the NTSG. This dearth of resources exacerbates the challenges confronting states as they seek to meet aggressive deadlines.

The present volume begins to remedy this imbalance by bringing together experts in educational measurement, as well as those steeped in the disciplines, to provide a comprehensive and accessible guide to the measurement of achievement in a truly broad range of subjects and grades. The volume covers both more traditional end-of-course tests and such alternatives as portfolios, exhibitions, and student learning objectives (SLOs). It tackles a number of topics, including design and development, psychometric considerations, and validity challenges.

Although the focus is on summative assessment, there is also considerable attention to formative assessment. The volume is divided into two parts: Part I, with six chapters, addresses these topics from more general perspectives, and Part II, also comprising six chapters, addresses them from discipline-specific perspectives.

It is appropriate to note that as this chapter was being written (June 2015) Congress has been working on the reauthorization of the Elementary and Secondary Education Act. It is possible, and perhaps even likely, that federal requirements for test-based accountability will be weakened or even entirely eliminated. Were that to be the case, it would surely have some impact on states' test-based accountability policies. Nonetheless, it is reasonable to expect that many states would continue on their present course, if only because their accountability policies are written into law! Irrespective of the evolution of states' NTSG-related accountability policies, I am quite confident that these chapters will retain their value for years to come—the rich, comprehensive treatment of the subject matter, often including important historical background, as well as insights into key issues in assessment design and development, whether more general or more specific, ensures that readers will be well rewarded for delving into the volume.

The intended audience is quite broad. It includes those with responsibilities for testing policy and/or test implementation at the district, state, or federal levels; those actually working on test design and development; and those concerned more generally with policies related to assessment and accountability. I anticipate that measurement professionals will benefit particularly from the multiple viewpoints and rich information provided by the chapters in Part II.

Some Background

The passage of NCLB in December 2001 ushered in the current era of test-based accountability for schools. Since 2010, with pressure and support from the U.S. Department of Education, many states began to revamp their teacher accountability systems to include, among other factors, one or more indicators based on student test performance. Under the Department's Waiver Program, states have been able to shift away from the status-based indicator of "Percent Proficient" of NCLB and toward indicators derived from value-added models and student growth percentiles. The latter type is intended to capture aspects of student progress and as such are most appropriate when there is a sequence of consecutive tests in a subject area. Consequently, they are generally employed in the evaluation of teachers of mathematics or E/LA in grades 4–8. Their application to other subject and grade combinations is at best problematic, if not completely infeasible.

Regardless of the subject and grade, the tests in use today were designed to elicit evidence of a student's knowledge and skills in relation to the relevant content standards. Testing guidelines are issued periodically under the auspices of the American Educational Research Association, the American Psychological Association, and the National Council on Measurement in Education (AERA/APA/NCME). The most recent edition (AERA/APA/NCME, 2014) details the work that must be done to validate tests employed for interpretations and decisions about students. However, the degree to which the *validity argument* (Kane, 2013) is actually carried out varies enormously.

The results of these same tests are now being used to construct indicators that are part of an educator accountability system. Of course, the employment of tests for purposes other than those for which they were originally designed and (possibly) validated requires further examination and validation. This is made clear in the testing guidelines, and in the current edition (AERA/APA/NCME, 2014), the case of their use for educator accountability is specifically addressed. Thus, one challenge is how to factor this new purpose into the design process so as to provide some support for the validity argument. Indeed, one can reasonably ask whether and to what extent assessment designers have responded to this challenge.

Test Design

Any design task can be thought of as *an exercise in optimization under constraints*. In the case of test design, the primary goal is to generate evidence about student learning with respect to the full set of content standards established for the particular grade and subject. This is usually termed *construct validity*. Auxiliary goals might encompass such psychometric criteria as score reliability or classification accuracy. The usual constraints involve time and cost—namely, the amount of time allocated to test administration and the costs associated with the testing process, including design, development, administration, scoring, analysis, and reporting. (Of course, there are other, more distal, costs often associated with high-stakes testing, such as the narrowing of the curriculum and time spent on test preparation. Important as they are, these considerations are beyond the scope of the present volume.) Optimization is the attempt to attain the goals while respecting the constraints. The quality of the assessment is then judged by the degree to which optimization has been achieved. Of course, in the real world, design necessarily involves various trade-offs.

As Braun (2005) noted more than a decade ago, the task of the test designer has become more challenging as the goals have become more demanding and constraints have multiplied. In plying their craft, test designers are forced to make difficult compromises among competing requirements. This necessitates finding a reasonable balance between construct validity and the various constraints that, in turn, depends on setting priorities among goals and constraints. Of course, one may ask if these constraints can be weakened or circumvented, and with what consequences.

For example, in many disciplines new content standards have been promulgated that focus on deeper learning that requires modifying test blueprints to reduce the use of traditional multiple choice items and increase the use of various types of constructed response or performance items. Such a shift is intended to improve construct validity but has implications for score reliability, administration time, and test costs.

Similarly, a transition to computer-based delivery can substantially expand the range of item types that can be employed and, through adaptive testing, minimize differences in measurement error across the score scale. It can also reduce scoring costs through the use of expert systems to replace human graders. At the same time, the required infrastructure costs are substantial and ongoing. Moreover, new issues of fairness arise due to the plethora of devices available, as well as the differences in computer familiarity among various student groups. These are the issues that, in various combinations, are addressed by the teams that have authored the chapters in this volume.

Part I: General Perspectives

Chapter 2, by Ferrara and Way, begins with a survey of the current landscape of assessment in the NTSG. This is followed by a succinct review of issues in the design, development, administration, and maintenance of conventional end-of-course or end-of-year assessments. The account is structured by the assessment design strategy favored by Pearson, Inc., and is enriched by the integration of relevant psychometric considerations, as appropriate. In particular, they argue that the intended interpretations and purposes of the test results should strongly influence the design process. However, they do note some potential conflicts between the use of test scores to make inferences about student performance with respect to certain predetermined thresholds and the use of aggregate test scores for educator accountability. They acknowledge that finding an appropriate balance between these two goals is challenging from both technical and policy perspectives.

Chapter 3, by Marion and Buckley, addresses the design issues that arise with performance assessments, as well as with other non-traditional assessments, such as portfolios and exhibitions.

They deal explicitly with the implications of using assessment results for accountability purposes. The chapter offers considerable coverage to SLOs, which are being used in many districts and states to generate student outcome data that can be used to satisfy legislative requirements regarding the amount and types of evidence for educator evaluation. Of course, the hope is that the conscientious and sustained implementation of SLOs will lead directly to better instruction and improved student learning.

Chapter 4, by Lane and DePascale, complements the previous chapter by focusing on the psychometric issues that arise with performance assessments and the like. In particular, the authors demonstrate how psychometric concepts and tools can help designers enhance the utility, comparability, and validity of such assessments, recognizing the tensions inherent in seeking assessments that can both inform instruction and contribute to educator accountability. Without minimizing the challenges inherent in achieving adequate levels of quality with respect to traditional psychometric criteria, they argue that the instructional and evidential value of well-constructed performance assessments is too great for such item types to be treated as an afterthought in the assessment design process.

G. Haertel and the team at SRI International authored Chapter 5, which offers an accessible introduction to evidence-centered design (ECD). ECD, developed by R. Mislevy and colleagues at the Educational Testing Service, is a now widely used approach to what is generally termed *principled assessment design*. The key idea is that the intended interpretations and uses of the assessment results should shape test design and development, thereby enhancing the likelihood of being able to validate those interpretations and uses. Although this strategy seems quite commonsensical, carrying it out in realistic settings demands considerable thought and effort, as the chapter clearly demonstrates. The benefits, however, are substantial—especially if the templates established are reused to build and maintain item pools, as well as to support a family of assessments serving a variety of purposes.

Chapter 6, by Sireci and Soto, directly addresses the problem of validating the use of aggregate assessment results for school and educator accountability. They highlight the differences between such uses and the more traditional uses involving decisions about individual students. Drawing, in part, on the most recent AERA/APA/NCME standards (2014), they are quite critical of the current state of test validation and propose some directions for both measurement professionals and policymakers to consider.

Briggs' chapter wraps up Part I with a commentary that uses Campbell's Law (1976) to frame a discussion of threats to validity that largely arise from the high-stakes uses of test results. The threats discussed are cheating, narrowing of the curriculum, and teacher-led coaching. Drawing on the different chapters in Part I, Briggs suggests that there are design-based strategies that can, to some degree, mitigate these threats to validity. In the validation context, Briggs asserts the importance of distinguishing between measurement and evaluation. In particular, he argues that the validity of an accountability system must ultimately rest on evidence that it has accomplished its goals and done so in a manner that is more effective and efficient than other feasible alternatives.

Part II: Disciplinary Perspectives

The second part of the volume opens with the chapter by Shuler et al. that discusses assessment-related issues in the arts domain, including music, visual arts, dance, and theater. In light of the relative lack of attention to arts assessment by the measurement community, the chapter begins with an historical overview of assessment in the arts, including some of the pioneering work conducted under the auspices of the National Assessment of Educational Progress. It also offers a compendium of assessments, both formative and summative, in current use. It is heartening to learn how the organizations representing teachers in the various arts domains, sometimes supported by one or more states, have been active in developing rigorous content standards and, building on those standards, issuing recommendations for curriculum and assessment. With the advent of outcomes-based accountability for all teachers, issues of assessment have become more salient in arts communities. The authors point out some of the challenges in devising teacher accountability systems that are fair, in view of the striking variation in contact time and available resources across domains and across districts, and even schools within districts. Although technology cannot remedy many of these difficulties, the authors do note that technology, when properly deployed, can facilitate instruction and instructional assessment, as well as the construct validity and reliability of summative assessments.

Chapter 9, by Malone and Sandrock, addresses assessment issues in world languages. The authors make clear that the models for proficiency in a foreign language have become more elaborated over the last decades, grounded in the notion of communicative competence in a variety of contexts and utilizing different modalities. Of course, this has resulted in concomitant changes in pedagogy and assessment. An important contribution of the chapter is an overview of the assessment landscape, along with exemplars of the kinds of tests, both formative and summative, that are now available. It is striking to see the many parallels between the situation in world languages and that in the arts domains: the heterogeneity in classroom contexts and student preparation, differences in resources and opportunity to learn, the inability to make substantively and psychometrically meaningful comparisons of proficiency across the country, and the pressing need for developing teachers' assessment literacy. The authors also examine some of the connections between the Common Core State Standards (CCSS) in E/LA and world languages and their implications for both pedagogy and assessment. Finally, they address some of the challenges posed by the new, state-level accountability mandates.

The next chapter, by Ercikan et al., discusses developments in the assessment of history and serves as a proxy for assessment in the social sciences generally. Innovation in this domain is being driven by a shift in learning goals from the mastery of isolated facts and predigested narratives to what has been termed *historical thinking*, a concept that embodies both the perspectives and procedures employed by professional historians to understand the past and the capacity to communicate those understandings to different audiences. Understandably, with regard to assessment, such a shift entails a greatly diminished role for selected response items and a greater role for tasks demanding more complex responses. The main body of the chapter comprises an informative description of the application of ECD (Haertel et al., this volume, Part I) to the redesign of the College Board's AP History examination. Both the benefits and challenges of employing ECD are elucidated, along with the trade-offs inherent in assembling a high-stakes assessment under manifold constraints. The chapter ends with a brief discussion of the possible impact of the CCSS in E/LA and writing on the assessment of history both in E/LA courses and in history courses.

Chapter 11, by G. Haertel et al., explores assessment in the life sciences from the standpoint of ECD. In particular, they explicate how following the ECD protocol for assessment design and development provides a solid foundation for establishing the validity of the intended inferences based on student performance. With the release of the Next Generation Science Standards (NGSS Lead States, 2013), there is a greater imperative to implement strategies to support the design and development of assessments that provide evidence with respect to "hard-to-assess" constructs. The chapter presents *design patterns* and *task templates* for a number of interesting constructs in the life sciences. Design patterns display in a specific format all the information needed to design extended assessment probes aligned to a set of standards and guidelines for the development of such assessments. The task templates further elaborate the guidelines to support the development of multiple instantiations of the assessments, possibly for different purposes. The chapter concludes with an argument for the importance of a principled approach to assessment design in the present context of high-stakes accountability, as well as proliferating demands on assessment designers.

The following chapter by Brown et al. considers the challenges to assessment in the physical sciences in light of the 2012 National Research Council report, *A Framework for K–12 Science Education: Practices, Crosscutting Concepts, and Core Ideas*, and the NGSS. They assert that adoption of these seminal documents necessitates profound shifts in instruction and assessment, with both grounded in a model of cognition that provides focus and coherence. In this context, the chapter presents a principled approach to assessment design and development, termed *construct modeling*, that, it is argued, is particularly well suited to generating evidence regarding student progress along a well-defined learning trajectory. A variety of exemplars, with accompanying scoring rubrics, are described across a range of topics in physics, as well as earth and space sciences. Chapters 10 and 11 together offer a rich introduction to forward-looking approaches to science assessment.

The final chapter, by Klag and Kluempen, tackles the assessment of high school mathematics. Strictly speaking, mathematics falls outside the purview of this volume. However, many of the issues raised in the other chapters of Part II are relevant, *mutatis mutandis*, to high school mathematics, so its inclusion here seems appropriate. The authors also adopt the ECD perspective on design and development and illustrate their argument through numerous examples. Of special interest is their discussion of how technology impacts assessment, with particular attention to the promises and pitfalls posed by the wide range of calculator functionalities now available in classrooms. The question of how the availability of powerful computational and visualization tools should be reflected in the conceptualization of mathematical proficiency, with concomitant changes in instruction and assessment, will only be answered in the years to come. The present chapter helps to chart the course.

Coda

Reading through these chapters, one is struck by the broad recognition of the need to adopt more systematic approaches to the design and development of assessment systems, if the goal of optimization is to be reasonably addressed. Although ECD appears to be a favored methodology, the chapters by Ferrara and Way and by Brown, Maderer, and Wood in this volume remind us that other approaches to principled assessment design are in play as well. This augurs well not only for the current crop of assessments but also for those in succeeding generations, as the different strategies become refined through further use and as developers become both more comfortable with their demands and more cognizant of their benefits.

The title of the volume is meant to signify that the challenges to measurement are not confined to those that arise because of accountability uses of assessment results. Certainly the specter of accountability haunts many of the efforts described in the various chapters. Over the years, Koretz (2015) has repeatedly reminded us that high-stakes uses of test results, especially those from an annual assessment system, can lead to score inflation and misleading test results. Briggs (this volume) makes an even broader point.

Nonetheless, if the chapters here are any indication, the current focus in the disciplines is, first, on developing new, more rigorous content standards and, second, on building assessments with greater construct representation and lower construct-irrelevant variance. Although the issues raised by Koretz, Briggs, and others certainly merit attention, they do not appear to be front-burner issues at present.

At the same time, it is refreshing to see that states, districts, and disciplinary associations are devoting substantial attention and resources to educator professional development with respect to assessment literacy—how to develop pedagogically useful assessments, how to interpret assessment results to inform classroom strategies, and how to make best use of the outcomes of external assessments. One can only hope that over time teacher preparation programs will see the wisdom in devoting more curricular attention to assessment literacy. In the long run, it is only through productive partnerships among test specialists, assessment savvy teachers, and psychometricians that assessment systems will more consistently and constructively contribute to improved student learning.

Acknowledgment

The author would like to thank Michael Kolen for helpful comments on an earlier draft of this chapter.

References

American Educational Research Association (AERA), American Psychological Association (APA), & National Council on Measurement in Education (NCME). (2014). *Standards for educational and psychological testing.* Washington, DC: AERA.

Braun, H. I. (2005). A post-modern view of the problem of language assessment. In Anthony John Kunnan (Ed.), *Studies in Language Testing 9: Fairness and validation in language assessment* (pp. 227–263). Cambridge, UK: Cambridge University Press.

Campbell, D. T. (1976, December). *Assessing the impact of planned social change.* The Public Affairs Center, Dartmouth College, Hanover, New Hampshire.

Kane, M. (2013). Validating the interpretations and uses of test scores. *Journal of Educational Measurement, 50*(1), 1–73.

Koretz, D. (2015). Adapting the practice of measurement to the demands of test-based accountability. *Measurement: Interdisciplinary Research and Perspectives, 13*, 1–25.

NGSS Lead States. (2013). *Next generation science standards: For states, by states.* Washington, DC: National Academies Press.

Part I

2 Design and Development of End-of-Course Tests for Student Assessment and Teacher Evaluation

Steve Ferrara and Denny Way

Introduction and Background

Over the last 10 years or so, high school end-of-course tests have begun to supplant broad surveys of reading and mathematics skills in some state high school testing programs. More recently, encouraged by federal education initiatives like *Race to the Top* (RTTT) and the *Teacher Incentive Fund* (e.g., Buckley & Marion, 2011), state policies and legislation have begun requiring local school systems to evaluate teachers annually, using classroom observations and other measures. In many states, these other measures include indicators based on student achievement on statewide end-of-course tests (e.g., average growth scores, student growth percentiles, or value-added scores).

The purpose of this chapter is to highlight the issues associated with the design, development, and implementation of end-of-course tests that are used for both student assessment and teacher evaluation. We begin with a brief description of current end-of course testing programs and teacher evaluation models that employ indicators based on student achievement data. Next, we review the major steps involved in designing and developing end-of-course tests. We describe a traditional, sequential approach because it reflects how most current end-of-course tests are developed. However, we also have added steps within the design process that may not be part of traditional practice in order to reflect the comprehensive, evidence-based steps of approaches such as Evidence-Centered Design (ECD; Haertel et al., this volume) and Principled Design for Efficacy (PDE; Nichols, Ferrara, & Lai, 2015). Finally, we address several of the more general trade-offs and challenges related to end-of-course tests, particularly those arising from the sometimes competing purposes of student assessment and teacher accountability.

The Current State of Affairs

As of February 2015, as many as 27 states required administration of at least one end-of-course test (see Table 2.2 for details). Of these states, 13 require students to pass end-of-course tests in order to graduate (see also Domaleski, 2011, Table A2) and two require students to "complete" the tests. This is an increase from two states in 2002 (Domaleski, 2011; Zinth, 2012).[1] The most frequently reported end-of-course tests appear to be in English I and II, Algebra I, Geometry, Biology I, and U.S. History. Other end-of-course test domains include English III, Writing, Algebra I, World History, Chemistry, and World Geography (see Table 2.2; see also McIntosh, 2012, Table 1-B).

What are end-of-course tests? Generally, they are tests that are intended to assess student mastery of course content, at or near completion of that (high school) course. For purposes of discussion, we have adopted Domaleski's (2011) definition: end-of-course tests are "state required, standardized exams administered at or near the completion of a term of instruction" (p. 1) that provide a "measure of student achievement with respect to the key knowledge and skills associated with each course" (p. 2). Typically, satisfactory performance on end-of-course tests is interpreted to indicate mastery of course content at the minimum level required to pass a course.

Ten of the 18 states with end-of-course tests include short or extended constructed response items (Domaleski, 2011, Table A3). Typically, states report that they include constructed response items to guide instruction and to target the full range of knowledge and skills that students are expected to learn. Constructed response items are kept to a minimum or excluded entirely, primarily to control scoring costs and to meet the timelines required to produce student score reports in time for course final grades (Domaleski, 2011, pp. 6–7), as well as the indicators needed for teacher evaluation. It is possible to trade off some student-level test score reliability (e.g., by reducing the number of multiple choice items to make room for constructed response items) to achieve greater construct representation and yet still achieve adequate reliability for mean scores for as few as 25 students (see Hill & DePascale, 2003, Table 1). The need to include constructed response items to cover important end-of-course learning outcomes is an important consideration in designing end-of-course tests for student assessment and teacher evaluation, as we make clear below (see also Marion and Buckley, this volume).

How many high school teachers teach courses that may be accompanied by end-of-course tests? More to the point, how many teachers teach in courses other than those most often accompanied by end-of-course tests (i.e., English I and II, Algebra I, Geometry, Biology, and U.S. History; see above)? Achieving convergence across reports is challenging. One report states that the "majority of teachers do not teach in test subjects or grades and as such standardized student achievement data is not available to be used in their ratings" (McGuinn, 2012, p. 47; based on interviews with state administrators and experts, P. McGuinn, personal communication, April 19, 2013). This statement applies to all grades and academic content areas. Another report that focuses on high school end-of-course tests asserts that the "overwhelming majority" of teachers (Domaleski, 2011, p. 19) do not teach tested courses. Buckley and Marion (2011), citing other estimates that indicate that NCLB required testing in English language arts and mathematics in grades 3–8, provide adequate data for calculating value-added scores for only 25–35 percent of teachers. According to another report, only 18 states and the District of Columbia have "the most ambitious evaluation designs" that address how to measure student achievement in non-tested grades and content areas (National Council on Teacher Quality, 2013, pp. vi and 32; see Marion and Buckley, this volume, for an extended discussion). We chose to take a different approach to provide yet another estimate.

According to the *Digest of Education Statistics* for the 2011–2012 school year (U.S. Department of Education, 2013), an estimated 1,108,191 high school teachers taught high school courses in English, mathematics, sciences, social studies, and other course areas. We have reproduced the 2011–2012 school year data in Table 2.1. Of those teachers, an estimated 224,178 (20 percent) taught English I or II, Algebra I or Geometry, Biology, or U.S. History courses. The remaining estimated 884,013 (80 percent) taught other English, mathematics, science, social science, and other high school courses. Consequently, according to our estimate, approximately 80 percent of high school teachers teach courses for which end-of-course tests currently are not offered.[2] So, according to this estimate, at best, one-fifth of high school teachers teach courses currently covered by end-of-course tests; end-of-course student achievement data are not available for evaluations for the other four-fifths.

How many states administer end-of-course tests? As before, evolving policies and practices make this determination challenging. Two reports provide a starting point. A Center for Education Policy report on high school exit examinations (McIntosh, 2012) identified 16 of 26 responding states with at least one current or imminent high school end-of-course test (Table 2.2). Nine of those states required that student state achievement test data be used as part of teacher evaluation

Table 2.1 Numbers (and Row Percentages) of Public High School Teachers (Grades 9–12) Who Reported Their Main Subject Area Teaching Assignment (2011–2012 School Year) and Estimated Numbers Teaching Courses with and without the Most Common End-of-Course Tests

	All Teachers	*Estimated Numbers of Teachers*	
		Courses with End-of-Course Tests	*Courses without End-of-Course Tests*
English	165,960	82,980 (50)	82,980 (50)
Mathematics	152,824	76,412 (50)	76,412 (50)
Sciences	132,900	33,225 (25)	99,675 (75)
Social sciences	126,246	31,562 (25)	94,685 (75)
Foreign languages	74,032	–	74,032
Arts and music	87,269	–	87,269
Health and physical education	65,619	–	65,619
Special education	130,293	–	130,293
Vocational/technical	125,595	–	125,595
All other	47,453	–	47,453
Total	**1,108,191**	**224,178 (20)**	**884,013 (80)**

Note: Data from the *Digest of Education Statistics*, Table 209.50. Percentage of public school teachers of grades 9 through 12, by field of main teaching assignment and selected demographic and educational characteristics: 2011–2012. Retrieved February 3, 2015 from http://nces.ed.gov/programs/digest/d13/tables/dt13_209.50.asp

Here, courses with end-of-course tests include English I and II, or an estimated 50 percent of all English teachers (the other 50 percent are assumed to teach English III and IV); Algebra I and Geometry, or an estimated 50 percent of all mathematics teachers (the other 50 percent are assumed to teach Algebra II, Calculus, and other mathematics courses); Biology, or an estimated 25 percent of all science teachers (the other 75 percent are assumed to teach Chemistry and other science courses); and U.S. History, or an estimated 25 percent of all social sciences teachers (the other 75 percent are assumed to teach World History and other social sciences courses). Sums across columns and rows may be affected by rounding.

determinations. And a recent survey of statewide summative assessments in grades 3–12 by the Education Commission of the States (Salazar, 2014) indicates that, as of October 21, 2014, 22 states have end-of-course tests. We searched the websites of states identified in these reports and found that 27 states have policies in place that require administration of end-of-course tests in a range of content areas (see Table 2.2).

Determining how many states require or allow use of end-of-course test scores as part of teacher evaluation is complicated by the ongoing evolution of those policies and practices. The National Council on Teacher Quality, in its State of the States 2013 report on teacher evaluation policies and practices, found that, as of October 2013,

- Forty-four states and the District of Columbia require classroom observations of instruction to be incorporated in teacher evaluations. (pp. ii and 1)
- Twenty-seven states require, "without exception," annual evaluations of all teachers. (p. 1)
- Thirty-five states and the District of Columbia require student achievement as "a significant or the most significant factor" in teacher evaluations. (p. 1)

In a policy analysis report, Steele, Hamilton, and Stecher (2010) cite two challenges to incorporating student test scores into teacher evaluation systems: (a) generating valid estimates of teacher contributions to student learning and the limitations of current models in doing so, and (b) generating student test scores in evaluations of teachers in typically untested grades and content areas. A RAND public fact sheet expands on these limitations by adding that important knowledge and skills can be underrepresented or even excluded in current student achievement

Table 2.2 States with End-of-Course Tests: Stakes for Students and Role of Student Achievement Data in Teacher Evaluation

EOC Tests	Stakes for Students	Role of EOC Test Scores in Teacher Evaluation[3]
Alabama[1,2]		
ACT Quality Core EOC tests: English 10 and Algebra I; others to be determined (Retrieved January 13, 2015 from http://www.alsde.edu/ sec/sa/Pages/assessmentde tails.aspx?AssessmentName= ACT%20QualityCore& navtext=ACT%20QualityCore)	Apparently, no stakes for students; previous Alabama High School Graduation Examination requirements were rescinded for the class of 2014 (Retrieved from http:// www.alsde.edu/sites/ boe/_bdc/ALSDEBOE/ BOE%20-%20Resolutions_4. aspx?ID=2041)	Teachers are required to use student test scores in their Professional Learning Plans; summative test scores will be used to evaluate teachers, planned to be in full effect by 2020 (Retrieved January 16, 2015 from https://www2. ed.gov/policy/eseaflex/ approved-requests/ alapprovalattach.pdf)
Arkansas[1]		
Algebra I, Geometry, and Biology for 2014–2015 To be supplanted by PARCC Algebra I and Geometry EOC tests beginning in 2015–2016 school year (Retrieved January 13, 2015 from http://www.arkansased. org/divisions/learning-services/ assessment/parcc-assessments)	"Results of the examinations will be … used as the basis for instructional change" (Retrieved January 19, 2014 from http:// www.arkansased.org/ divisions/learning-services/ assessment/end-of-course- exams)	"The teacher and evaluator shall choose the summary growth statistic associated with the state-mandated assessment for the tested content area as one (1) of the external assessment measures" (Retrieved January 16, 2015 from http://www.arkansased. org/public/userfiles/HR_ and_Educator_Effectiveness/ TESS/TESS_Statute.pdf)
California[2]		
California High School Exit Examination (CAHSEE): Algebra I (Retrieved January 13, 2015 from http://www.cde.ca.gov/ ta/tg/hs/)	Students must pass CAHSEE ELA and Algebra I in order to receive a high school diploma	Test scores may be used as part of a formative evaluation to make decisions for professional development and to enhance teaching practices (Retrieved January 16, 2015 from http://mauralarkins. com/EvaluatingTeachers. html)
Connecticut[2]		
Beginning with the graduating class of 2020, EOC tests in Algebra I, Geometry, Biology, American History, grade 10 English (Retrieved January 27, 2015 from http://www.casciac. org/pdfs/CT_Graduation_ Requirements.pdf)	No school system "shall permit any student to graduate from high school or grant a diploma to any student who has not satisfactorily completed" each of these tests (Retrieved from http://www.casciac.org/ pdfs/CT_Graduation_ Requirements.pdf)	Student growth and development based on student learning outcomes (45 percent) (Retrieved January 27, 2015 from http://www.connecti cutseed.org/?page_id=440)

Florida[1,2]

Florida State Assessments: Algebra 1, Algebra 2, and Geometry (Retrieved January 13, 2015 from http://www.fldoe.org/core/fileparse.php/5423/urlt/FSAEOCFS2014-15.pdf) Biology 1, Civics, and U.S. History EOC tests (Retrieved January 13, 2015 from http://www.fldoe.org/accountability/assessments/k-12-student-assessment/end-of-course-eoc-assessments/

Passing each test is a graduation requirement for the class of 2015[1]

Student performance data is one part of a multifaceted teacher evaluation system, which includes value-added modeling (Retrieved January 16, 2015 from http://www.fldoe.org/teaching/performance-evaluation)

Georgia[1,2]

Georgia Milestones Assessment System EOC tests in eight courses: Ninth Grade Literature and Composition, American Literature and Composition, Coordinate Algebra, Analytic Geometry, Physical Science, Biology, United States History, and Economics/Business/Free Enterprise (Retrieved January 13, 2015 from http://www.gadoe.org/Curriculum-Instruction-and-Assessment/Assessment/Pages/Georgia-Milestones-Assessment-System.aspx)

20 percent of course final grade (Retrieved January 13, 2015 from http://www.gadoe.org/Curriculum-Instruction-and-Assessment/Assessment/Pages/Georgia-Milestones-Assessment-System.aspx)

The Teacher Effectiveness Measure comprises three components, including "student growth and academic achievement" (Retrieved January 19, 2015 from http://www.gapsc.com/GaEducationReform/Downloads/PPEM_FAAQs_October_2013.pdf)

Hawaii[2]

Algebra I, Algebra II, Biology I, Expository Writing I, and U.S. History (Retrieved January 13, 2015 from http://www.hawaiipublicschools.org/TeachingAndLearning/Testing/EndOfCourseExam/Pages/home.aspx)

EOC tests are used to measure student proficiency of course content standards, inform instruction, and standardize course expectations (Retrieved January 13, 2015 from http://www.hawaiipublicschools.org/TeachingAndLearning/Testing/EndOfCourseExam/Pages/home.aspx)

Teachers receive feedback, support, and evaluation on four components, including student growth percentiles from the Hawaii Growth Model (Retrieved January 13, 2015 from http://www.hawaiipublicschools.org/TeachingAndLearning/EducatorEffectiveness/EducatorEffectivenessSystem/Pages/home.aspx)

Illinois[2]

PARCC EOC tests corresponding to English III, Algebra II, and Integrated Mathematics III courses (Retrieved January 13, 2015 from http://www.isbe.state.il.us/assessment/parcc.htm)

In the immediate future, no negative consequences if a student does not meet proficiency levels (Retrieved January 16, 2015 from http://www.isbe.net/assessment/pdfs/parcc/parcc-pta-guide-0214.pdf)

In the Model Teacher Evaluation System, an overall student growth rating is a component in the overall teacher practice rating (Retrieved January 16, 2015 from http://www.isbe.net/peac/pdf/guidance/13-9-te-model-summ-rating.pdf)

(Continued)

Table 2.2 (Continued)

EOC Tests	Stakes for Students	Role of EOC Test Scores in Teacher Evaluation[3]
Indiana[1]		
ISTEP+ EOC Assessments: English 10, Algebra I, Biology I (Retrieved January 14, 2015 from http://www.doe.in.gov/ sites/default/files/assessment/ iapm-1415-chapter-02-ecas.pdf)	Passing the test is a graduation requirement (except Biology) (Retrieved from http://www. doe.in.gov/sites/default/ files/assessment/iapm-1415- chapter-02-ecas.pdf)	None; the teacher evaluation system focuses on planning, instruction, leadership, and core professionalism (Retrieved January 16, 2015 from http://www.doe.in.gov/ sites/default/files/evaluations/ rise-handbook-2-0-final.pdf)
Kentucky[2]		
ACT Quality Core tests: English II, Algebra II, Biology, and U.S. History (Retrieved January 14, 2015 from http://education.ky.gov/ AA/Assessments/Pages/ EOC.aspx)	Kentucky Board of Education recommends 20 percent of course grade; school systems can opt for a lower percentage (Retrieved from http:// education.ky.gov/AA/ distsupp/Documents/ Linking%20Scores%20to%20 Letter%20Grades%20-%20 EOC.pdf)	Student growth percentiles used in teacher evaluation for grades 4–8 only (Retrieved January 19, 2015 from http://education. ky.gov/teachers/PGES/ TPGES/Pages/TPGES- Student-Growth-Percentile- Medians.aspx)
Louisiana[1, 2]		
English II and III, Algebra I, Geometry, Biology, and U.S. History (Retrieved January 14, 2015 from http://www.louisianabe lieves.com/assessment/end-of- course-tests)	15–30 percent of course grade (Retrieved from http:// www.louisianabelieves.com/ assessment/end-of-course- tests)	50 percent based on student growth using a value-added model as part of the Compass System (Retrieved January 16, 2015 from http://www. louisianaschools.net/lde/ uploads/20118.pdf)
Maryland[1]		
High School Assessments (HSA): Biology and Government PARCC EOC tests: English 10 and Algebra (Retrieved January 14, 2015 from http://www.msde.state. md.us/w/Top5HSTesting0214. pdf)	Passing the HSA is a graduation requirement The PARCC EOC tests are not a graduation requirement for first-time takers in 2015–2016 (Retrieved from http:// www.msde.state.md.us/w/ Top5HSTesting0214.pdf)	50 percent based on student growth measures, including EOC test scores (Retrieved January 16, 2015 from http://marylandpublic schools.org/MSDE/ programs/tpe/docs/ StateTeacherEvaluation Model_6.6.13.pdf)
Massachusetts[1]		
Massachusetts Comprehensive Assessment System tests in grade 10 English language arts, grade 10 mathematics, biology, chemistry, introductory physics, technology/engineering (Retrieved January 14, 2015 from http://www.doe.mass. edu/mcas/graduation.html)	Passing the English language arts and mathematics tests or achieving a compensatory composite score is a graduation requirement; passing one of the science/ technology/ engineering tests is a graduation requirement	Multiple measures, including MCAS student growth percentiles (Retrieved January 16, 2015 from http://www.doe.mass. edu/lawsregs/603cmr35. html?section=all)

(Retrieved from http://www.doe.mass.edu/mcas/graduation.html)

Mississippi[1]

PARCC EOC tests corresponding to courses English II and Algebra I (Retrieved January 14, 2015 from http://www.mde.k12.ms.us/student-assessment/parcc-assessments-%28mct3-and-satp3%29) Subject Area Testing Program, 2nd ed. tests in Biology I and U.S. History (Retrieved January 14, 2015 from http://www.mde.k12.ms.us/student-assessment/student-assessment-satp2)

PARCC EOC tests provide information on college and career readiness (Retrieved from http://www.mde.k12.ms.us/student-assessment/parcc-assessments-%28mct3-and-satp3%29) Passing biology and history tests is a graduation requirement (Retrieved from http://www.mde.k12.ms.us/student-assessment/student-assessment-satp2)

Teachers are expected to use test scores to guide instruction (Retrieved January 16, 2015 from http://www.mde.k12.ms.us/ms-college-career-standards/parcc)

Missouri[2]

EOC tests in English I, English II, Algebra I, Algebra II, Geometry, Biology, Physical Science, American History, and Government (Retrieved January 14, 2015 from http://dese.mo.gov/college-career-readiness/assessment/end-course)

Students must complete EOC tests in English II, Algebra I, Biology, and Government prior to high school graduation, for accountability (Retrieved from http://dese.mo.gov/college-career-readiness/assessment/end-course)

"The evaluation process should use student growth in learning as a significant contributing factor … using a wide variety of student performance measures" (Retrieved January 16, 2015 from http://dese.mo.gov/sites/default/files/CSR20-400-375-Final.pdf)

Nevada[2]

EOC exams in ELA I, ELA II, Math I, Math II, and Science (Retrieved January 14, 2015 from http://www.doe.nv.gov/Assessments/Reso/)

Students in the class of 2019 must pass the four ELA and mathematics EOC tests to graduate (see http://www.doe.nv.gov/Standards_Instructional_Support/Director_Meetings/2014/Notes_for_District_Directors_-_February_13_2014/)

50 percent of teacher evaluation based on growth on standardized tests (Retrieved January 16, 2015 from http://www.lasvegassun.com/news/2013/jun/14/teacher-evaluation-changes-being/)

New Mexico[1, 2]

EOC tests corresponding to English III, Algebra II, Integrated Mathematics III, Biology, Chemistry, and U.S. History (Retrieved January 14, 2015 from http://ped.state.nm.us/ped/PEDDocs/EoCFAQ2012.pdf)

Students must pass the English III/Writing and U.S. History EOC tests or local tests to graduate, in addition to High School Graduation Assessments in other content areas (see http://ped.state.nm.us/ped/PEDDocs/EoCFAQ2012.pdf)

50 percent based on student test scores in value-added models (Retrieved January 16, 2015 from http://www.abqjournal.com/470012/news/moratorium-urged-on-using-test-scores-in-teacher-evals.html)

(Continued)

Table 2.2 (Continued)

EOC Tests	Stakes for Students	Role of EOC Test Scores in Teacher Evaluation[3]
PARCC end-of-year assessments will replace the NM Standards Based Assessment system (Retrieved January 19, 2015 from http://www.ped.state. nm.us/Assessment Accountability/Assessment Evaluation/2014/ PartnershipfortheAssessment ofReadinessofCollegeand Careers%28PARCC%29 AssessmentsUpdaterev.pdf)		
New York[1,2]		
High School Regents Examinations correspond to courses in high school English, languages other than English, mathematics, science, and social studies (Retrieved January 14, 2015 from http://www.nysedregents. org/)	Students pass Regents examinations in Comprehensive English, mathematics, science, global history and geography, and U.S. history and government (Retrieved from http://www. p12.nysed.gov/ciai/gradreq/ 2011gradreqdetails.html)	Student growth percentiles (Retrieved January 16, 2015 from https://www.engageny. org/sites/default/files/ resource/attachments/appr-field-guidance.pdf)
North Carolina[2]		
READY EOC tests in English II, Mathematics I, and Biology (Retrieved January 14, 2015 from http://www.ncpublic schools.org/accountability/ testing/eoc/)	Local school system decision (Retrieved from http:// www.ncpublicschools. org/docs/accountability/ policyoperations/ exitstandards/gatewayfaq. pdf)	Teacher performance evaluation includes scores, weighted 70 percent for student growth value for the teacher's students, 30 percent for the student growth value for the entire school (Retrieved January 19, 2015 from http://www.ncpublic schools.org/docs/effectiveness-model/ncees/instruments/ teach-eval-manual.pdf)
Ohio[2]		
For class of 2018, EOC tests corresponding to English I, English II, Algebra I or Integrated Math I, Geometry or Integrated Math II, Physical Science or Biology, American History, and American Government (Retrieved January 19, 2015 from http://education.ohio. gov/Topics/What-s-Happening-with-Ohio-s-Graduation-Requirement/Graduation-Requirements-2018-Beyond)	Beginning in 2015–2016, school systems can use the EOC tests to replace teacher final exams as part of the course grade (Retrieved from http:// education.ohio.gov/ Topics/What-s-Happening-with-Ohio-s-Graduation-Requiremen/Graduation-Requirements-2018-Beyond)	Student growth rating is 50 percent of the teacher evaluation, or a new framework that weights teacher performance and student growth at 42.5 percent and an optional component at 15 percent of the total (Retrieved January 19, 2015 from http://education.ohio. gov/Topics/Teaching/ Educator-Evaluation-System/ Ohio-s-Teacher-Evaluation-System)

Oklahoma[1,2]

End-of-instruction secondary level tests for English II, English III, Algebra I, Algebra II, Geometry, Biology I, and U.S. History
(Retrieved January 14, 2015 from http://www.ok.gov/sde/sites/ok.gov.sde/files/Testing%20Calendar%20-%202014-2015%20-%20Revised%2011-20-14.pdf)

Students must "demonstrate mastery of the state academic content standards" in English II and Algebra I and two of the other five areas
(Retrieved from http://www.ok.gov/sde/sites/ok.gov.sde/files/documents/files/SUCCESS%20brochure%202014-15.pdf)

35 percent based on student academic growth using standardized test data
Retrieved January 16, 2015 from http://ok.gov/sde/tle-quantitative-components

Pennsylvania[2]

Keystone EOC Exams: Literature, English Composition, Algebra I, Algebra II, Geometry, Biology, Chemistry, U.S. History, World History, and Civics and Government
(Retrieved January 14, 2015 from http://www.portal.state.pa.us/portal/server.pt/community/state_assessment_system/20965/keystone_exams/1190529)

Students in the class of 2017 must pass EOC tests in Literature, Algebra I, and Biology
EOC test requirements increase for the classes of 2019 and 2020
(see http://www.portal.state.pa.us/portal/server.pt: press release September 12, 2013)

15 percent of teacher evaluation based on building-level data, which includes student test scores; 15 percent based on teacher-specific student achievement and growth, which includes test scores
(Retrieved January 16, 2015 from http://www.psea.org/uploadedFiles/Publications/Professional_Publications/Advisories/Advisory-TeacherSpecificData-Sept2014.pdf)

South Carolina[1,2]

End-of-Course Examination Program tests: English 1, Algebra 1/Mathematics for the Technologies 2, Biology 1/Applied Biology 2, and U.S. History and the Constitution
(Retrieved January 13, 2015 from http://www.ed.sc.gov/agency/programs-services/41/)

20 percent of the course final grade
(Retrieved from http://www.ed.sc.gov/agency/programs-services/41/)

Teacher evaluation includes a teacher value-added component
(Retrieved January 16, 2015 from http://ed.sc.gov/agency/lpa/documents/Proposed_SC_EdEval_Guidelines_06252012.pdf)

Tennessee[2]

English I, English II, English III, Algebra I, Algebra II, Biology I, Chemistry, and U.S. History
(Retrieved January 13, 2015 from http://www.tn.gov/education/assessment/high_school.shtml)

25 percent of the second semester grade
(Retrieved from http://www.tn.gov/education/assessment/high_school.shtml)

50 percent based on student achievement data, including 35 percent based on student growth data, and 15 percent based on other measures of student achievement
(Retrieved January 16, 2015 from http://team-tn.org/evaluation/overview/)

(Continued)

Table 2.2 (Continued)

EOC Tests	Stakes for Students	Role of EOC Test Scores in Teacher Evaluation[3]
Texas[1,2]		
State of Texas Assessments of Academic Readiness (STAAR) EOC tests: English I, English II, Algebra I, Biology, and U.S. History; phasing in English III and Algebra II (Retrieved January 14, 2015 from http://tea.texas.gov/ student.assessment/staar/)	As of January 2015, students must pass STAAR EOC tests in English I, English II, Algebra I, Biology, and U.S. History (Retrieved January 14, 2015 from http://www. yourhoustonnews.com/ eastex/news/new-high-school-graduation-requirements-passed-in-texas/article_86ad78f4-2341-5312-834a-e1f19b6d1360.html)	Beginning in 2015–2016, will base 20 percent on student growth data on standardized tests (Retrieved January 16, 2015 from http://www. texastribune.org/2014/ 07/23/texas-delays-roll-out-new-teacher-evaluations/)
Virginia[1,2]		
Standards of Learning EOC tests: Reading, Writing, Algebra I, Algebra II, Geometry, Biology, Chemistry, Earth Science, Virginia and U.S. History, World History and Geography to 1500, World History and Geography after 1500, World Geography (Retrieved January 19, 2015 from http://www.doe.virginia. gov/testing/sol/standards_ docs/english/index.shtml and from http://www.doe.virginia. gov/instruction/graduation/ approved_courses.pdf)	Students must earn at least six verified credits by passing EOC tests or other assessments approved by the Board of Education (Retrieved from http:// www.doe.virginia.gov/ instruction/graduation/ standard.shtml)	40 percent based on student growth percentiles (Retrieved January 16, 2015 from http://www.doe. virginia.gov/teaching/ performance_evaluation/ teacher/index.shtml)
Washington[1,2]		
EOC tests: Algebra I/Integrated Mathematics 1, Geometry/ Integrated Mathematics 2, and Biology (Retrieved January 14, 2015 from http://www.k12.wa.us/ assessment/StateTesting/)	Students must pass the Algebra I/Integrated Mathematics 1 or Geometry/ Integrated Mathematics 2 EOC tests and the Biology EOC test (see http://www.k12.wa.us/ assessment/StateTesting/ default.aspx)	Student growth percentiles recommended for local use as a component in teacher evaluation in 2016–2017 (Retrieved January 19, 2015 from http://tpep-wa.org/ student-growth-overview/ student-growth-percentiles/)

Note: Information in this table is as up-to-date and accurate as possible. Locating information on state department of education websites sometimes is difficult, and EOC testing programs and teacher evaluation policies are evolving. EOC = end-of-course.

1 Some EOC information based on responses from 26 states in McIntosh (2012), Table 1-B.
2 Some EOC information on 2014–2015 school year based on website searches (personal communication, T. Salazar, January 13, 2015) and reported in Salazar (2014).
3 Some teacher evaluation information in National Council on Teacher Quality (2012), Appendix B.

tests (see *Tests and the Teacher*, http://www.rand.org/content/dam/rand/pubs/corporate_pubs/2012/RAND_CP693z3-2012-09.pdf). There is little debate that student test scores used in teacher evaluations should be reliable and should cover the range of knowledge and skills specified in the content standards, including higher order thinking skills (e.g., Domaleski, 2011; Herman, Heritage, & Goldschmidt, 2011).

Intended Interpretations and Uses of End-of-Course Test Scores

Generally speaking, end-of-course tests are designed to contribute to the determination of whether students have reached a level required to pass a course and/or achieved a standard of proficiency that has been externally mandated. Indicators based on end-of-course test scores may serve as a (weighted) component of the course final grade; alternatively, passing the test may be a conjunctive requirement for passing a course and for earning a high school diploma. Weights for end-of-course test scores in final grades range from 10 percent to 33 percent (Domaleski, 2011, Table 1). Six states declare that they use performance on end-of-course tests to signal college or career readiness to students (see Domaleski, 2011, p. 11).

Aggregated end-of-course test results are also employed, in various ways, for school accountability reporting. Only recently have they come into use in teacher evaluation. Aside from the policy reports cited above, little has been written about the psychometric design principles that have guided the design and development of end-of-course tests (e.g., score reliability targets, classification consistency and accuracy targets, test information targeting) that are relevant to all their intended uses. Early in the writing of this chapter, we located technical reports for five of the sixteen state programs with end-of-course tests listed in Table 2.2. Three program technical reports indicate that the primary psychometric goal in assembling test forms was to match test characteristics and standard error curves as closely as possible to those of a baseline test form or scale. No information was provided on the psychometric characteristics of the baseline forms and scales. One program did not provide information about the psychometric targets for test construction. The fifth program's technical report appears to suggest that the primary psychometric goal was to minimize standard errors uniformly across the score scale in order to optimize accuracy of predictions of scores on external tests with college readiness benchmarks. In some cases, test characteristics, standard error curves, and cut score locations are presented. These and other displays indicate that, contrary to stated primary psychometric goals, test designs are intended to maximize precision around the cut scores.

End-of-Course Tests in the Context of Teacher Evaluation Models

Under the American Recovery and Reinvestment Act of 2009, the president and Congress invested unprecedented resources in the improvement of K–16 education in the United States. As part of that investment, the $4.35 billion RTTT fund focused on a state-level competition for educational reform support. One of the assurance criteria for RTTT funding involved the evaluative differentiation of teachers and principals according to effectiveness. Not surprisingly, the states and districts that won initial RTTT grants proposed using student achievement as a significant factor in teacher and principal evaluations and also proposed incorporating these evaluations into decisions regarding hiring, firing, tenure, and compensation. The RTTT notice recognized two types of student achievement: one "for tested grades and subjects" (Race to the Top Fund, 2009, p. 37811) based on scores earned on states' annual summative tests as required under the NCLB legislation; another "for non-tested grades and subjects" (p. 37811), defined as:

An alternative measure of student performance (e.g., student performance on interim assessments (as defined in this notice), rates at which students are on track to graduate from high school, percentage of students enrolled in Advanced Placement courses who take Advanced Placement exams, rates at which students meet goals in individualized education programs, student scores on end-of-course exams).

What are the possible roles of end-of-course test scores in a teacher evaluation system? Because RTTT emphasizes student growth (defined as the change in achievement for an individual student between two points in time), teacher evaluation models involving end-of-course tests would require data collection designs and measures that enable desired inferences about growth or progress. Different data collection designs and different intended interpretations about growth can lead to the use of different statistical models. Castellano and Ho (2013) provide an excellent introduction to the variety of available growth models and the primary interpretations they support. In the context of end-of-course test scores, several approaches to data collection might be used. Each approach has distinct challenges.

For example, one could use an end-of-course test administered to students at the end of the previous year as the pretest, the end-of-course test administered in the current year as the posttest, and measure the year-to-year growth between them. The resulting data would support the application of gain-based or conditional status growth models, as described by Castellano and Ho (2013). Although gain-based growth typically depends upon the existence of a vertical scale over time, end-of-course testing is not conducive to the use of vertical scales. At the high school level, this would be most viable in subject areas where the end-of-course tests measuring the same or similar content are administered to the same students in consecutive years, perhaps English language arts or history. However, in mathematics and science, end-of-course tests given in consecutive years, such as Algebra and Geometry or Chemistry and Physics, typically measure different constructs. As an alternative to formal vertical scales, transitions across performance-level boundaries are sometimes treated as gains. Interpretation of the transition tables that summarize student growth across performance levels in adjacent school years requires meaningful linkages between cut scores and performance levels from one end-of-course test to another. Procedures for establishing meaningful linkages of cut scores and performance levels across grade levels—or vertical articulation—are addressed in a special issue of *Applied Measurement in Education* (Cizek, 2005; see also Cizek & Agger, 2012). Conditional status growth models also can be applied to data obtained from year-to-year end-of-course tests. They include analyses of residual gains and student growth percentiles (Betebenner, 2011). However, one possible complication to using these models with end-of-course tests administered from year to year is that different high school students may follow different course-taking patterns (Buckley & Marion, 2011).

A second approach would be to administer a pretest at the beginning of the course and a posttest at the end of the course. This would ensure that growth was measured using parallel forms at two appropriate points in time, albeit with an additional burden on test development, since two parallel forms would be needed each year. Both gain-based and conditional status models could be applied to the resulting data. A formidable challenge with this approach, especially given the high-stakes nature of teacher evaluation, is susceptibility to gaming, since it would be easy to depress pretest scores artificially in order to maximize student growth as measured by the posttest at the end of the year (Baker, 2010; Baker, Oluwole, & Green, 2013).

A third approach that is feasible when more sophisticated value-added models are employed is to use multiple scores from previous grade levels in another subject or subjects to adjust statistically for prior academic achievement. For example, several years of past scores on reading, mathematics, and science tests, if available, could be used as conditioning variables in value-added analyses of scores on an end-of-course biology test. While this multivariate conditioning approach is in wide practice, it has disadvantages in that the predictor tests control only for general prior achievement rather than subject-specific performance (Buckley & Marion, 2011). Researchers generally recommend using multiple years of student achievement data in value-added estimation (e.g., Steele et al., 2010; see also Lockwood & McCaffrey, 2007 on bias compression). A fourth approach involves using student learning objectives for teacher evaluation. Marion and Buckley (this volume) address that approach.

When end-of-course tests are used as part of a system in which performance evaluation, compensation, and even dismissal decisions are made about educators, a high level of technical quality is necessary (Buckley & Marion, 2011). Herman et al. (2011) present a validity argument for justifying the use of tests for teacher evaluation that involves five propositions—namely, that (a) content standards clearly define what students are expected to learn, (b) instruments are designed to address accurately and fairly what students are expected to learn, (c) scores accurately and fairly measure what students have learned, (d) student assessment scores accurately and fairly measure student growth, and (e) growth scores that are based on the tests can be accurately and fairly attributed to the contributions of individual teachers.

End-of-course test design can influence student growth scores and impact the operating characteristics of a (teacher) value-added analysis. For example, test forms that are designed to maximize information around cut scores may exhibit floor and ceiling effects on student score distributions. The restriction of range at the top and bottom of the test score scale can, in turn, obscure substantial improvement in test performance of students at the low and high ends of the scale. Such gains will not enter the value-added analysis and, consequently, not be credited to teachers. Test design matters in teacher evaluation as do the statistical model itself and the predictors used in the model. There is much work to do in the area of test design effects on results from teacher evaluation models.

End-of-Course Test Design and Development

A fundamental defining feature of principled test design, development, and implementation is that planning and execution starts with explicit statements about intended interpretations and uses of test scores (e.g., Bejar, Braun, & Tannenbaum, 2007; Downing, 2006; Schmeiser & Welch, 2006). All subsequent steps are designed and executed to produce examinee responses and summary test scores that provide evidence to support the intended interpretations and uses.

In this section, we describe seven key steps in the design, development, and implementation of an end-of-course testing program: (a) explicate intended inferences and uses; (b) design the test, including selecting item types and creating psychometric plans, given program constraints; (c) develop the items for the test; (d) pilot test and field test the items; (e) implement the operational testing program; (f) set performance standards; and (g) continue ongoing operation of the program. In discussing these steps, we consider what a state or local testing program director would need to do differently, depending upon whether the end-of-course test results were to be used primarily for course grades, other inferences about student achievement, or for teacher evaluation.

Step 1: Explicate Intended Inferences and Uses

A principled approach to test design and development requires thorough explication of the interpretations that test users are intended to make from test scores and the actions users can appropriately take based on those interpretations. These can be broad statements about the purposes of end-of-course tests: what inferences and claims test score users should be able to make about what students know and can do after completing a high school course and obtaining a test score, how the test scores can be used to make decisions about students, and whether and how the scores may be used for teacher evaluation. Further, test score interpretation and use statements signal the role that end-of-course tests are expected to play in improving the rigor of high school courses. Thus, these decisions should be made by policymakers and educational leaders. Seeking participation and advice from test designers, psychometricians, and test users (e.g., teachers, principals) is certainly advisable. These decisions delineate, at a high level, the parameters and constraints governing test design and development, psychometrics, implementation, and score reporting. Accordingly, we refer to them as testing program policy decisions. The intended interpretations and uses should be described using terminology and language appropriate for communication to various stakeholders, as well as the general public. Nonetheless, the intended interpretations and uses of end-of-course test scores must be framed using measurement terminology in order to guide assessment designers, developers, and researchers conducting validation research.

Stating Intended Interpretations and Uses of End-of-Course Test Scores

The primary consideration in creating end-of-course tests should be the stated purposes. Purposes can be stated generally as intended interpretations about the level of mastery of course content and, subsequently, the intended uses of those scores. For example, students who pass the ISTEP+ English 10 Graduation Exam "display proficient understanding when approaching grade-level text, and they demonstrate satisfactory skills in writing, including adequate word usage, organization, and appropriate tone. Pass students identify literary devices and draw conclusions using text-based support" (Indiana Department of Education and Questar Assessment, 2010, p. 20, available from the Indiana Department of Education).

When an end-of-course test is intended for use in teacher evaluation, intended interpretations must be consistent with the teacher evaluation model. For pre-post statistical models, student learning gain is defined in terms of the amount of course material mastered by the end of the course in comparison to that at the beginning of the course (which is presumed to be low). For annual growth models, achievement growth is determined by comparing performance on the current end-of-course test to performance on the previous end-of-course or end-of-year test. Conditional models create expectations for end-of-course test performance based on past test scores. For multivariate models, performance on multiple measures administered over two or more prior years provides the basis for interpretations of (relative) improvement in achievement.

Unfortunately, these complex and subtle interpretations are often unstated or only partially stated. Nonetheless, they are part of the chain of inferences based on end-of-course tests and should be explicated before test design and development for teacher evaluation begins. Further, these decisions may appear to be the responsibility of test designers when, in fact, they represent policy decisions that should guide all subsequent test design and development, as well as operational use decisions.

Using end-of-course tests for student assessment sometimes may require establishing the proportion of the course grade determined by the test score and/or whether students must pass the test as well as meet other course requirements in order to pass the course. In some cases, passing both the end-of-course test and the course are independent determinations, with both required to meet high school graduation requirements (e.g., Florida, Indiana, New Mexico, New York; see Table 2.2). Average student scores, percentages of students in each proficiency level, and percentages of students who pass the end-of-course test then can be aggregated to the classroom (i.e., teacher), school, district, and state level for accountability reporting. In contrast, the role of end-of-course test scores in teacher evaluation models is part of the statistical modeling process, which should be made explicit before test development begins.

Announcing Intended Interpretations and Uses of Test Scores

When end-of-course tests are used for student assessment, it is common practice to develop proficiency level descriptors (PLDs; see, for example, Egan, Schneider, & Ferrara, 2012) that are meant to communicate intended score interpretations. Typically, one level is designated to represent proficiency with respect to course content. If test performance is to play a role in the course grade, in determination of passing or failing the course, or meeting a graduation requirement, then those roles must be made explicit as well. When test scores are to be used for teacher evaluation, publicity and controversy ensue (e.g., Layton, 2014).

Step 2: Decide on Overall Test Design, Item Types, and Psychometric Plans

Many end-of-course test design considerations do not depend on the particular interpretations or uses. This is so because end-of-course tests used for teacher evaluation must accurately and fairly assess what students are expected to learn in the course and the test scores must accurately and fairly measure what students actually have learned (e.g., Herman et al., 2011). However, some design decisions do depend upon the interpretations and uses, particularly those governing psychometric targets for test form assembly. At this step, test designers must make decisions about the numbers and types of items to include in a test form and document those decisions in test blueprints and related design documents. These decisions should support the intended interpretations and uses of test scores, with attention to construct representation, content coverage, and score reliability, recognizing test administration time constraints and other time and cost constraints (e.g., scoring). Because design is the heart of the assessment process, there are multiple aspects to the work of this step. The discussion that follows includes initial design considerations, such as the course content and cognitive targets to assess, the capabilities and needs of the target test takers, test content, item types and formats, test difficulty and the rigor of the performance standards, universal design for accessibility and accommodations, and technical documentation, psychometric desiderata, and considerations related to test administration, scoring, and reporting.

Course Content and Cognitive Assessment Targets

Practical limitations typically require test designers to identify a subset of objectives in the state content standards or a course syllabus. Usually, the number of state content standards exceeds the number that can be assessed in a test that must be administered in one or two 45-minute class periods. In addition, more ambitious content standards, such as those related to collaborative problem solving, cannot be assessed feasibly in traditional end-of-course tests (see Domaleski, 2011, Table A3). For those reasons, test designers and course content experts must identify the key content standards that can feasibly be assessed and, thus, be represented in test blueprints. Some content standards will be assessed annually, while others may be sampled across multiple years. Further, decisions must be made as to which types of items and response formats will be used to assess each content standard. Koretz (2013) has shown that sampling of content standards (e.g., only 58 percent of all standards over three years in one state) and narrowing of test content by highly similar item response demands become known and predictable and that with this predictability "test scores can become inflated … and [research] has shown that in some instances, the resulting bias has been quite large" (p. 4).

Designers must also identify cognitive targets so that test items elicit evidence of the intended level of cognitive demand. This can be particularly challenging for higher levels (e.g., reasoning from evidence in reading passages, modeling in mathematics). It is now fairly standard to focus on Depth of Knowledge (DOK) targets (see Web Alignment Tool training materials at http://wat.wceruw.org/index.aspx). It appears that content experts can make DOK judgments for state test items with high degrees of agreement (e.g., Yuan & Le, 2012). Unfortunately, there is little evidence to support the use of DOK-level judgments as proxies for actual examinee cognitive processing. Further, evaluations of current state tests conclude that they generally focus on lower levels of cognition. A recent RAND study (Yuan & Le, 2012) indicates that the majority of test items in elementary, middle, and high school tests in 17 states assess the lowest DOK level—level 1 (i.e., items that test recall, as in using a dictionary to find the meaning of a word). Other frameworks focus on the kinds of questions or cognitive tasks that items pose to examinees (e.g., application and explanation questions; see Ferrara & Duncan, 2011) or the cognitive complexity of items (Ferrara et al., 2014).

Whichever conceptual or empirical framework is selected, the goal must be a close match of the evidence elicited by the items to content and cognitive targets. Specifically, items that target higher order thinking course objectives (e.g., reasoning from evidence) must elicit higher order thinking skills, not lower order proxies (e.g., simply identifying relevant evidence in a reading selection). For fairness reasons, this is a particularly crucial requirement for end-of-course tests that are incorporated into student course grades or are a graduation requirement. Adequate coverage of content and cognitive targets is essential for making defensible interpretations about student mastery of course content. Similarly, adequate coverage is essential for teacher evaluation, in accordance with the validity argument proposition (b), that tests address accurately and fairly what students are expected to learn.

Capabilities and Needs of the Target Examinees

The capabilities and needs concern age- and grade-appropriateness of test material, educational background of target examinees, and accessibility and test administration accommodation needs of all target examinees, including students with disabilities, English language learners, and other struggling students (e.g., students reading below grade level). For example, an end-of-course test in Algebra I might include items with complexity and difficulty targeted for a broad range of students who intend to complete basic mathematics course graduation requirements—including all struggling students—as well as students who will pursue higher level mathematics during high school. This broad targeting is a significant challenge to item development and test assembly. Instead, narrowly focused test targeting seems to be the current practice in end-of-course programs (see above) and consideration of struggling students often is addressed in setting cut scores. Nonetheless, it is relevant in the design and development phase to ensure that test design is aligned with and supports intended interpretations explicated as policy decisions. It addresses the accuracy proposition for validity arguments for using student scores in teacher evaluation models (see proposition [d]).

Similarly, work in this step involves consideration of factors such as excessive reading load, obstacles to accessibility, and other sources of construct-irrelevant variance. In fact, test administration accommodations typically required for subgroups of target examinees should be identified at this step so that all students who take a course are able to understand, process, and respond appropriately to the requirements of the end-of-course tests. This is essential to establishing the validity of the assertion that student performance accurately and fairly indicates achievement or growth and a justification for using the test results for teacher evaluation.

Item Types and Formats

Ideally, test designers select item types that are most appropriate for eliciting evidence about examinee mastery of the full content and cognitive targets, without regard to practical constraints. We already have referred to time and cost constraints and alluded to a third constraint (i.e., relying solely on multiple choice, short constructed response items, and, perhaps, essay prompts or other extended constructed response items). These item types are not suitable for eliciting evidence with respect to certain content standards (e.g., speaking and listening) and cognitive targets (e.g., reasoning and argumentation). Thus, such content standards and cognitive targets are typically not addressed by the test blueprint or targeted by selected response items as proxies. These limitations constrain inferences and claims about what students know and can do in relation to course objectives, as well as the contributions of teachers' instructional efforts to students' achievement of those objectives.

To address intended purposes and interpretations most effectively, development of scoring criteria should occur simultaneously with that of both selected and constructed response items. The focus for selected response items is on the roles of the response options (e.g., to represent common errors and misconceptions, to identify levels of mastery of a concept or skill). The focus for constructed response items is on scoring rubrics, especially considerations of relevance, completeness, or correctness of the response, numbers of score levels, as well as training requirements for scorers (e.g., Johnson, Penny, & Gordon, 2009, chapters 6–8).

Test Difficulty and Rigor of Performance Standards

The intended range of difficulty of items included in a test form and the stringency of the performance standards often do not receive explicit attention during the design of end-of-course tests, although they are important for both policy and psychometric reasons. (This assertion applies to other grade-level tests, as well.) Principled assessment design approaches demand that PLDs be defined and made public in the policy decision stage (Bejar et al., 2007; Plake, Huff, & Reshetar, 2010). Thus, the expectations for student mastery are more transparent and guide psychometric decisions regarding overall test difficulty. Tests that are too difficult for many students provide less precise estimates of student mastery of course content than tests for which difficulty is targeted to provide maximal psychometric precision for key ranges of the score scale (e.g., at the pass/fail cut score). Imprecision in student scores, in turn, exacerbates imprecision in growth scores or value-added scores that may be used to evaluate teachers. Moreover, when tests are too difficult for many students, standard setting panels may be reluctant to set stringent performance standards (i.e., high cut scores), because of the resulting low passing rates and high percentages of examinees in the lowest performance levels.

Further, policymakers may hesitate to implement end-of-course tests as part of course or graduation requirements because of low pass rates (e.g., McIntosh, 2012, p. 4). The Maryland High School Assessment program illustrates this point. Development of specifications for high school end-of-course tests in English, mathematics, science, and social studies began in 1997. Field testing was planned for spring 1998, with implementation as graduation requirements in spring 1999 for the class of 2002. Concerns about field test pass rates led to delays in implementing the graduation requirements, though annual administrations continued. In spring 2003, only 45 percent of students passed the English 1 test, 52 percent the Algebra/Data Analysis test, 54 percent the Biology test, and 57 percent the Government test (see http://www.msde.state. md.us/publications/HSIUpdateOct03.pdf). In August 2003, the State Board of Education implemented the four end-of-course tests as high school graduation requirements for the graduating class of 2009 (see http://www.msde.state.md.us/publications/HSIUpdateOct03.pdf), then suspended the requirements only to reinstate them beginning in the 2013–2014 school year (see http://hsaexam.org/img/HSATop10_012013.pdf). Alternatively, states may develop relatively easy tests and set less rigorous performance standards. For example, McIntosh (2012) reports that the percentage of students who pass high school exit exams—meaning general content area surveys, not necessarily end-of-course tests—"generally ranges from 70% to 90% with few exceptions" (p. 2).

Content and Format Specifications Documents

Good testing practice as well as generally accepted testing guidelines (e.g., the Standards for Educational and Psychological Testing, chapter 7; see AERA, APA, & NCME, 2014) require comprehensive documentation of specifications for end-of-course tests to support the intended interpretations. This is particularly important when the use of test scores for teacher evaluations is challenged in legal proceedings. In such situations, a chain of evidence is required to support claims that the test reflects course content, student scores reflect current student status, and these can be employed to infer growth in student achievement. Detailed content and item format specifications documents, with rationales for numbers and types of items and evidence of their alignment with high school course content and cognitive targets, are essential components of this chain of evidence.

Universal Design and Accommodations Specifications

The principles of universal design for tests (Thompson, Johnstone, & Thurlow, 2002) are intended to minimize impediments to full participation of students with learning disabilities or perceptual impairments, English language learners, and other struggling students (e.g., students reading below grade level) by addressing their needs early in the test design process. Universal design principles such as reducing unnecessary, construct-irrelevant reading load and other accessibility impediments also optimize conditions for all examinees to demonstrate what they know and can do in relation to course content. At this step, test administration accommodations typically required by subgroups of target examinees must be specified. These include modifications of standard test administration procedures such as reading mathematics items to examinees or conditions such as small testing groups. Both design choices and post-design accommodations are essential to supporting valid interpretations of the degree of mastery of course content and growth for all examinees. A number of recent publications have addressed accommodations and accessibility in the context of computer-based testing (Thompson, Thurlow, & Moore, 2003; Thompson, Thurlow, Quenemoen, & Lehr, 2002; Thurlow, Lazarus, Albus, & Hodgson, 2010). The Common Core tests designed in the early 2010s also included a particular focus on testing accommodations and accessibility tools for students with disabilities (see Laitusis, Buzick, Stone, Hansen, & Hakkinen, 2012). One emerging challenge for computer-based tests is the need to support test-takers in using preferred assistive technologies. For example, visually disabled students may utilize a variety of devices in the classroom, such as screen readers, screen magnifiers, auditory and tactile devices, and braille printers. Advocates for these students demand that these same assistive devices should be available in computer-based tests as well.

Psychometric Considerations and Design Decisions

Psychometric considerations in the design of end-of-course tests are primarily the same ones that are relevant to most educational tests. These include psychometric specifications for test form assembly (e.g., distribution of item difficulties, target score reliabilities), decisions about score reporting scales, and designs for field testing new items and for equating successive test forms. Many test design decisions are strongly influenced by constraints that are psychometric in nature. For example, while it may be desirable to report subscores on an end-of-course test in addition to an overall total score or pass/fail decision, such reporting is not advisable if the subscores are insufficiently distinct or precise or if the added value of subscores cannot be demonstrated (Haberman, 2008; Sinharay, 2010; Sinharay, Puhan, & Haberman, 2011).

Psychometric considerations for end-of-course tests typically include the selection of an item response theory (IRT) model or other procedures for item calibration, scaling, and equating. An extensive literature on IRT supports practical applications (e.g., Hambleton & Swaminathan, 1985; Wright & Stone, 1979; Yen & Fitzpatrick, 2006). Unidimensional IRT models are commonly used for tests that are intended to measure course content that is expected to conform to a unidimensional construct. For dichotomously scored items, the most general form of an IRT model in common use is the three-parameter logistic (3PL) model, which models the probability of success on an item in relation to student proficiency as a function characterized by three parameters: item discrimination, item difficulty, and a lower asymptote often referred to as the pseudo-chance level to account for guessing on multiple choice items. Various simplifications of the 3PL model exist: the two-parameter logistic (2PL) model does not model the pseudo-chance level, and the Rasch model assumes all items to be equally discriminating and also does not model guessing. IRT models have also been developed for polytomously scored items (i.e., constructed response items on which students might earn one of three or more scores). The use of mixed IRT models that can simultaneously calibrate dichotomously and polytomously scored items has become commonplace, although research using these models for score equating is still quite active (e.g., Kolen & Lee, 2011).

For large-scale educational testing programs in the United States, including end-of-course tests, the 3PL and Rasch models are most commonly used. These models are typically combined with specific polytomous IRT models: the 3PL model with the Generalized Partial Credit (GPC) model (Muraki, 1992) and the Rasch model with the Rasch Partial Credit (RPC) model (Masters, 1982). There are trade-offs in model choice: the 3PL/GPC model will typically provide better fit to item response data but is more complex, requires larger sample sizes, and is more likely to encounter problems with parameter estimation. The Rasch/RPC model is based on a philosophy of measurement as well as a set of statistical assumptions that are typically violated, to some degree, in practice. However, from a data analysis perspective, the model is simpler, easier to use, and can be applied with much smaller sample sizes.

Psychometric test specifications may differ depending upon whether the end-of-course test is used for student assessment or if it is also used for teacher evaluation. If the primary purpose is to assess student learning, the ideal test form design would provide the most accurate measurement at the cut score that separates masters from non-masters, or at other relevant thresholds. However, if the end-of-course test also is used for teacher evaluation and student growth is of interest, then a test that yields scores that are reasonably precise over a wide range of the score scale is more appropriate.

Figures 2.1 and 2.2 illustrate this point by presenting sets of item characteristic curves (ICCs) and conditional standard errors of ability estimates for two 30-item tests, assuming the Rasch model and dichotomously scored items. The 30 ICCs for the test in Figure 2.1 correspond to a set of items with difficulties that are approximately normally distributed and clustered around ability level (theta) 0.0. By contrast, the 30 ICCs for the test in Figure 2.2 correspond to a set of items with difficulties that are approximately uniformly distributed around a theta value of 0.0. Roughly equivalent numbers of ICCs for the test in Figure 2.2 appear at all levels of the ability range. The thick dashed lines in each graph show that the standard error curve for the test with difficulties clustered around theta = 0.0 is much lower than the test with the uniformly distributed item difficulties in the ability range around theta = 0.0, but much greater at higher and lower ability levels.

Now, suppose the purpose of the end-of-course test was to assess student mastery with respect to a cut score of 0.0 on the theta scale. Clearly, the test in Figure 2.1 will be more precise for that purpose. For example, given a true ability of a ±0.3 unit from the cut score, the test in Figure 2.1 would be predicted to be about 6 to 7 percent more accurate than the test in Figure 2.2 in correctly classifying pass/fail status.[3] However, if the purpose of the test is to measure student growth across the range of ability, then the test in Figure 2.2 may be preferred because it measures students in a broad range of ability reasonably precisely.

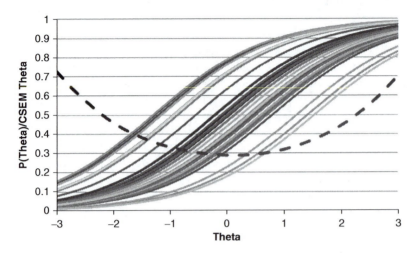

Figure 2.1 ICCs and the conditional standard error of measurement (CSEM) curve for a 30-item test with item difficulties normally distributed around theta = 0.0.

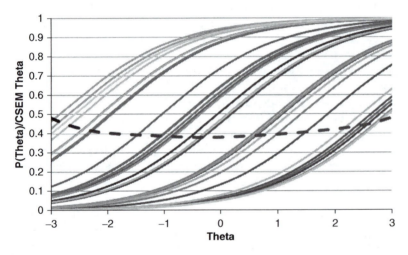

Figure 2.2 ICCs and the CSEM for a 30-item test with item difficulties uniformly distributed around theta = 0.0.

In addition to helping shape a test's psychometric specifications, the intended uses and interpretations should influence decisions about how to scale the test. For example, if the end-of-course test is used only for student assessment, there may be no need for a vertical score scale, as student performance can be compared primarily to the pass/fail cut score for each grade. However, a problem arises when the end-of-course test is to be used to assess student growth and as part of teacher evaluation. (We described earlier the limitations on creating vertical scales for some end-of-course test areas; see the section "End-of-Course Tests in the Context of Teacher Evaluation Models.") Indeed, some (but not all) growth models (e.g., gain score models) require student test scores from at least two time points obtained from tests aligned to a common scale (Castellano & Ho, 2013). Accountability program managers may select teacher evaluation models that do not require vertical scales (e.g., gain score and trajectory models;

see Castellano & Ho, 2013, Table 1.5). Even these models do not provide a simple solution, as variations in high school course selection patterns result in different combinations of end-of-course tests for use in the models.

Psychometric Considerations and Design Decisions for Computerized Adaptive Testing

The increasing use of computers to deliver end-of-course tests invites considerations of alternate test design and delivery models, such as computerized adaptive testing (CAT; van der Linden & Glas, 2010; Wainer, 2000). The basic premise of CAT is well known: In order to maximize the precision of the examinee's test score, the computer successively selects items (or sets of items) with (average) difficulties that are close to the current estimate of the examinee's theta, which is based on responses to the previous items. By such tailoring of questions, CAT can shorten testing time, increase measurement precision, as well as reduce measurement error due to boredom, frustration, and guessing (Wainer, 2000).

Furthermore, when supported by a sufficiently robust pool of items, CAT can improve the precision of scores for test takers at extreme ability levels, in comparison to conventional testing. This feature is particularly attractive for end-of-course tests because it can provide adequate measurement for both pass/fail decisions and for the evaluation of student growth. Thompson (2008) used simulated data to compare the precision of growth scores based on conventional and adaptive testing. In his simulations, the ability of a CAT to reduce the standard error of measurement of scores at the high and low end of the ability scale resulted in lower and less variable CSEM for gain scores compared with traditional, fixed form testing. For example, the simulated paper test indicated CSEMs for gain scores that were above 0.6 and as high as 1.1 for 20 to 30 percent of lower grade and upper grade ability combinations. In comparison, the simulated CAT gain score CSEMs were between 0.2 and 0.4 for most combinations of lower grade and upper grade abilities, and never were higher than 0.6.

One drawback to the use of CAT for end-of-course tests is that it is most effective when utilized with discrete, objectively scored questions. As noted by Way et al. (2010), innovative, multipart, stimulus-based, and constructed response items that are envisioned for next-generation tests require changes to the standard CAT item-by-item approach. These alternate approaches may include the use of flexi-level or multi-stage testing designs (e.g., Hendrickson, 2007; Lord, 1971; Luecht & Nungester, 1998; Wainer & Kiely, 1987) or other branching schemes that present specified content or item types at certain points in the testing process. For example, an alternate adaptive system might be designed so that item types that require human scoring (e.g., multistep performance tasks) are administered only after the computer obtained a reasonably accurate estimate of a student's ability from previously administered items that are objectively scored. This would permit choosing among some number of performance tasks calibrated through previous human scoring, administering the easier ones to lower performing students and the more difficult ones to higher performing students. These more sophisticated adaptive testing designs will likely prove attractive in the future and will be made even more attractive once expert systems capable of scoring various types of constructed response items (e.g., essays, math expressions) are more widely utilized in operational, high-stakes testing situations.

Performance Reporting and Feedback Plans

End-of-course tests used for student assessment primarily fulfill summative reporting functions, so score reports typically provide such information as the total test score, perhaps content sub-domain scores, and, where relevant, an indication of whether the examinee passed or failed the test and the proficiency level that corresponds to the total test score (see Goodman & Hambleton, 2004). Ryan (2006) reported research that indicates that "many educators have difficulty interpreting score reports from large scale assessment programs" (p. 705). More recently, Zenisky and Hambleton (2012) reported that additions to the psychometric literature, as well as recent advances in reporting practices, have facilitated improvements in score report interpretability. Subdomain scores are likely to be the only feedback to students regarding areas of strength or weakness in course content. Subdomain scores may or may not be informative (e.g., Feinberg & Wainer, 2014; Haberman, 2008; Sinharay, 2010, 2013). For tests used for teacher evaluation, the requirement is a test score or proficiency level determination with sufficient technical quality to support interpretation and use in the evaluation model.

Administration and Operational Requirements and Constraints

Given the summative function of end-of-course tests, test administration conditions should enable all examinees to perform optimally. This is true when end-of-course tests are used also for teacher evaluation, as both teachers and students are interested in being judged at their best. Plans for maximizing accessibility for all students and accommodations for students with disabilities and English language learners can be implemented as test administration requirements. Similarly, because stakes can be high for both students and teachers, the integrity of test data must be maintained. Thus, test security must be protected before, during, and after test administration from threats outlined in Fremer and Ferrara (2013, Table 2.1).

Step 3: Develop the Test Items

Current test development practices, whether or not following approaches like ECD and PDE, involve standard steps and activities (e.g., Downing, 2006, Table 1.1; Schmeiser & Welch, 2006). These include hiring professional item writers; training them on the target content standards, item specifications, and item writing procedures, guidelines, and requirements; and multiple review and revision steps that focus on content alignment, bias and sensitivity, and accessibility and accommodations needs. These steps are common practice because, drawing on long experience, they enhance item quality, minimize item problems, and provide "procedural validity" evidence (Braun, 2008).

Test Item Reviews, Refinement, and Approval

Item reviews for alignment to target content standards (e.g., the Achieve, Surveys of Enacted Curriculum, and Webb approaches), bias and sensitivity, and accessibility for special populations are standard operating procedures for end-of-course tests and other achievement tests. No special review considerations unique to tests used for teacher evaluation appear necessary. However, assuring and documenting that end-of-course test items are closely aligned to course content is a critical component of a validity argument that end-of-course test items accurately and fairly address course content.

Alignment to Course Content

Evidence of the alignment of end-of-course tests to course content is a primary validity consideration (and essential for all NCLB-required tests under peer review guidelines; see U.S. Department of Education, 2007). The Webb and Achieve alignment models (see http://programs.ccsso.org/projects/Alignment_Analysis/Models/) are used to demonstrate alignment of state test content to state content standards. The Surveys of Enacted Curriculum approach (see https://secure.wceruw.org/seconline/secWebHome.htm), which considers alignment among standards, assessments, and instruction, may be the most appropriate approach for evaluating alignment of end-of-course tests and course content. Evidence of curricular validity—that is, that the required course content actually has been taught—is a particularly important validity consideration for end-of-course tests required for high school graduation tests and a requirement established in the landmark Debra P. case in Florida (i.e., *Debra P. vs. Turlington*; see http://www.fldoe.org/asp/hsap/hsap1983.asp; Phillips & Camara, 2006, p. 735). Of course, course content and exposure to the course content standards can differ considerably across schools and classrooms. Strict alignment between course and test content is required for fairness to students, for whom the stakes can be high, and for their teachers in order to address validity argument propositions (b), (c), and (d) above.

NCLB requires alternate assessments of alternate achievement standards for students with significant cognitive disabilities for all courses where end-of-course tests are required. Current designs for these alternate assessments include portfolio assessments, standardized performance tasks, and rating scales (see Ferrara, Swaffield, & Mueller, 2009, Table 6.1) which will be supplanted by alternate assessment designs of the Dynamic Learning Maps consortium and National Center and State Collaborative; for details see http://www.k12center.org/publications/alternative.html.

Step 4: Pilot Test and Field Test the Items

Many large-scale operational testing programs are implemented within a year or two of authorization. The implementation timelines and funding often do not enable small-scale tryouts (e.g., cognitive labs) of items before initiating development and field testing of large numbers of items. This is not particularly risky for traditional achievement tests because developers generally know how to build well-functioning multiple choice and constructed response items. Small-scale pilot tests are advisable for end-of-course tests with alternative designs (see Marion & Buckley, this volume), technology-enhanced items which are now emerging in operational, online tests, and for examinee subpopulations with unique needs (i.e., students with disabilities, English language learners, and other struggling students). Pilot tests can focus on item quality, comprehensibility and accessibility for all students, and the feasibility of scoring responses from constructed response and technology-enhanced items. Item quality is equally important for end-of-course tests used for student achievement and teacher evaluation, of course. Instructional sensitivity of test items (e.g., Polikoff, 2010) may be an important consideration when a test is intended for use to assess achievement growth. We address this issue at step 5, in a discussion of evaluating and selecting field-tested items for operational use.

Additional Design and Development Considerations

Timelines for operational implementation and budget constraints typically permit only a single large-scale field test prior to operational implementation. In situations without these constraints, or when operational implementation is postponed (e.g., as in the Maryland example above), other possibilities arise. These can include small-scale studies of the construct relevance of the items (e.g., cognitive lab think-aloud studies), examinee usability considerations (e.g., studies of the effectiveness of test administration accommodations, logistics, and efficiency of online delivery of tests), and scoring and reporting systems (e.g., automated scoring of constructed response items, usefulness of the information in score reports). There also may be an opportunity to address issues unique to the use of end-of-course tests for teacher evaluation. Perhaps it is most important to investigate whether the fourth proposition in the Herman et al. (2011) validity argument is supportable: that student scores accurately and fairly measure student growth.

Field Testing the Items

As in all large-scale testing programs, field testing test items is necessary to evaluate and select psychometrically sound items and to estimate item parameters. Typical concerns include obtaining a generally representative sample of students, assuring student opportunity to learn the course material prior to field testing, and examinee motivation in a no-stakes testing situation. Limited opportunity to learn (e.g., Moss, Pullin, Gee, Haertel, & Young, 2008) course content and low examinee motivation generally are the norm for standalone field tests, and these factors can degrade the psychometric quality of IRT model item calibration and ability estimation (see Wise & DeMars, 2005, 2006). They also undermine the trustworthiness of performance data for setting performance standards. These concerns are important for assessing student achievement and, perhaps, more worrisome for selecting items for vertical scaling to support student growth interpretations.

Information from field tests enables assembly of test forms that are psychometrically parallel (to reduce the dependence on equating) and meet test information function targets. We discuss below consideration of test information targeting for end-of-course tests used for student achievement and teacher evaluation in Assembling Operational Test Forms.

Step 5: Implement the Operational Test

Evaluating and Selecting Items for Operational Use

Field testing supports test development activities by providing content experts with an additional opportunity to review item quality using item statistics (e.g., p values, item-total correlations, differential item functioning, or DIF). Other statistics available may include summaries of performance on multiple choice distractors, frequencies of the most popular responses to open-ended items, and summaries of item response time for tests administered by computer. In addition to informing final item review, these statistics also help to guide assembly of operational test forms.

Instructional sensitivity of test items (e.g., Polikoff, 2010; Popham, 2007) has been under debate in recent years as an important test development consideration (although it has a history that stretches back at least to the late 1960s). Instructional sensitivity "represents the degree to which students' performances on that test accurately reflect the quality of the instruction that was provided specifically to promote students' mastery of whatever is being assessed" (Popham, 2007, p. 146). The intent is that test items should reflect what is taught in classrooms, not learned outside of school. Enthusiasm for the use of instructional sensitivity as a criterion for evaluating test items is reflected in a recent conference, The First-Ever International Conference on Instructional Sensitivity (see https://aai.ku.edu/first-ever-international-conference-instructional-sensitivity-0), and a recent report, *Criteria for High-Quality Assessment* (Darling-Hammond et al., 2013). The report proposes using "items that are instructionally sensitive and educationally valuable" (pp. 11–12) as one of five criteria. Others propose caution and question whether instructional sensitivity can be measured reliably (e.g., Way, 2014) because instructional sensitivity item statistics, instruction-focused methods, and expert judgment methods are susceptible to confounding with other explanatory variables and measurement error (Polikoff, 2010).

Further, the logic of instructional sensitivity may be more consistent with using end-of-course tests for teacher evaluation but less so with their use for assessing student achievement. Instructionally sensitive items provide evidence for the validity argument in Herman et al.'s (2011) propositions 4 and 5 (regarding individual teachers' contribution to student achievement growth). However, items that support intended interpretations of mastery of course content, rather than growth in achievement, align with the definition of end-of-course tests in Domaleski (2011, pp. 1–2).

Assembling Operational Test Forms

Assembly of test forms involves attempting to achieve the design goals while respecting the constraints governing the testing program. Design goals include covering as much course content as possible, apportioning numbers of items to subdomains and to specific course objectives as delineated in the test blueprint, and ensuring reasonable decision consistency and accuracy at key cut scores (e.g., the pass/fail cut score). Unfortunately, these goals can be in conflict; for example, meeting all goals for content coverage and proportional allocation of items may limit the extent to which decision consistency and accuracy can be maximized for student assessment. In contrast, the goals for end-of-course tests intended for use in teacher evaluation models may be to cover as much content as possible (i.e., as in proposition 2) and to ensure growth scores that are as accurate as necessary (proposition 4) to support causal attributions about teacher contributions to student growth (proposition 5). As previously illustrated, these different purposes lead to different psychometric targets for test form assembly. Our interpretation of the Thompson (2008) study above suggests that, in comparison to fixed test forms, computer adaptive versions could provide a better balance between content coverage and the decision consistency and accuracy goals, as well as the growth score precision goal for teacher evaluation.

Administering the Operational Test

There are no special considerations for distributing and administering end-of-course tests used for teacher evaluation. However, the motivations for various forms of security breaches and cheating on end-of-course tests (e.g., Fremer & Ferrara, 2013) could differ for tests used for student assessment, for high-stakes decisions about students, and for teacher evaluation. For example, teacher motivation to cheat may be negligible when the stakes are high only for students. Teacher motivation to cheat could be quite high when end-of-course tests are used for school accountability (as in the Atlanta, Georgia cheating scandal; see Strauss, 2013), and especially so for teacher evaluation.

Step 6: Set Performance Standards

Establishing Plans to Collect Validity Evidence to Inform Performance Standard Setting

End-of-course tests are intended to assess student mastery of course content, help determine student course grades or course pass/fail status, and to determine eligibility for high school graduation. Pass/fail cut scores and other performance standards can be established for end-of-course tests using judgmental methods, without regard to criteria beyond examinee performance and standard setting panelist judgments. However, in this era of educational reform, there is some interest in setting performance standards in reference to external indicators of achievement (see, e.g., standard setting plans for the Smarter Balanced and Partnership for Assessment of Readiness for College and Careers assessment consortia at http://www.smarterbalanced. org/achievement-levels/ and http://www.parcconline.org/ccrd). In *benchmarked performance standard setting* (Ferrara et al., 2011; Phillips, 2012), performance standards on an end-of-course test would be benchmarked to external criteria such as performance levels on national or international assessments or to readiness for college or career (e.g., SAT or ACT scores). In *evidence-based standard setting* (McClarty, Way, Porter, Beimers, & Miles, 2013), sources of evidence external to the end-of-course test are selected to represent levels of performance (e.g., a grade of B or better in community college pre-calculus courses; see figure 2.1 in McClarty et al., 2013; see also O'Malley, Keng, & Miles, 2012) associated with levels of performance on the end-of-course test. Plans for collecting external benchmarks and evidence to support these methods for setting performance standards for an end-of-course test should be made so that, if possible, data collection can be conducted as part of field testing. For example, if relatively complete field test forms can be given to test takers and SAT or ACT scores for these same test takers can be obtained from an administration just before or just after the field test, relationships between field test performance and performance on the external measures can be estimated. Such relationships may need to be interpreted with caution because students taking field tests are typically not motivated to perform their best and some newly written items or tasks in the field test may be flawed.

Developing PLDs

PLDs serve the dual purpose of articulating policy aspirations for student achievement (e.g., Egan, Schneider, & Ferrara, 2012, p. 79) and describing levels of student achievement on end-of-course tests in relation to the content of high school courses. We proposed above that these descriptors should be articulated prior to test development as part of the process of establishing intended score interpretations and uses and, consequently, to guide subsequent design and development decisions.

The content and rigor of PLDs can depend on test purpose. For example, descriptors for student assessment might be quite different if the intended interpretation is about mastery of course content to determine pass/fail status rather than mastery that is intended to indicate readiness for college or for the workplace. Also, PLDs for separate grade-level scales and cross-grade, vertical scales are likely to define proficiency differently. However, once those distinctions are determined, PLDs are not likely to be different for teacher evaluation.

Conducting Empirical Studies to Support Standard Setting

Recent publications have presented the case for the use of empirical studies involving external criteria to support standard setting. For example, evidence-based standard setting (EBSS; McClarty et al., 2013) is a way of approaching standard setting that integrates content-centered judgments by appropriate experts with the best available evidence from research on external indicators of college or career readiness. The EBSS process involves planning, implementation, and follow-up which can be summarized by the following broad steps:

1   Define the outcomes of interest (e.g., college readiness).
2   Develop research, data collection, and analysis plans.
3   Synthesize the research results.
4   Conduct standard-setting meeting with panelists.
5   Continue to gather evidence in support of the standard.

In a similar vein, Ferrara et al. (2011) proposed using an external criterion to benchmark performance standards for achievement tests. They illustrated the steps for benchmarking the Mastery cut score for the West Virginia Biology end-of-course test to West Virginia performance on state NAEP in science. They set the benchmarked Mastery cut score through the following four steps:

1   Identify a cut score target on the end-of-course testing by linking statistically to the external criterion.
2   Write proficiency descriptors that are benchmarked to the target cut score.
3   Train standard-setting panelists to undertake the standard-setting method's cognitive judgmental task (e.g., Bookmark).
4   Calculate final cut scores using panelist recommendations and document final content-based rationales for the recommendations.

For a high school end-of-course test, the external criterion might be an indicator of mastery of course content (e.g., the end-of-course test scores of students who achieved a course grade of B or higher in previous years), a college and career readiness standard on another test or cross-grade scale, or some future outcome such as performance on a college admissions test or freshman year course placement test.

A recent example of using empirical studies to inform standard setting is the American Diploma Project (ADP) Algebra II exam (see McClarty et al., 2013). In fall 2005, a consortium of states created the ADP Algebra II exam to, among other things, provide an indicator of college readiness for entry-level college mathematics courses. In order to set performance standards that signaled students were prepared to earn a B or better in college algebra and pre-calculus courses without remediation, the consortium conducted several empirical studies. The studies included linking the ADP Algebra II exam to state tests, SAT, ACT, PSAT, college outcomes, and judgments by college faculty. The resulting analyses were summarized in a briefing book and presented to a policy committee to recommend the standards (see Haertel, Beimers, & Miles, 2012).

Conducting a Standard-Setting Workshop

Once empirical studies supporting standard setting are completed and the results synthesized, the standard-setting workshop can be conducted. The workshop follows essentially the same steps of a traditional standard setting: an introduction to standard setting and an overview of the tasks to be completed, shared understanding of key concepts, multiple rounds of cut score recommendations, and discussion of feedback after each round. However, to the extent that appropriate empirical studies are available, review and discussion of the research results becomes a more prominent feature of the workshop. For example, McClarty et al. (2013) described an elaborate presentation and consideration of empirical research that was considered in setting standards for the ADP Algebra II exam.

Gathering Evidence to Support the Validity of Performance Standards

Once an end-of-course testing program is implemented, the same type of research studies that were conducted to support initial standard setting should be conducted again to evaluate the original (intended) interpretations of performance standards. Other types of studies can be conducted as well. One type focuses specifically on interpretations of college and career readiness. The plan is to follow students who took the end-of-course test as they progress to college and technical training and document how well those who met the readiness standards actually performed.

Another possibility is that scores on end-of-course tests will increase with greater familiarity with the test format and demands. Therefore, it is important to continue to review the data and possibly revise the performance standards, or even modify the assessment, as the testing program matures.

Considerations Related to Standard-Setting Methodology

Considerations related to choice of standard-setting methodology for an end-of-course test are generally similar to those for other achievement tests. The extent to which empirical evidence is available could influence selection of a standard-setting methodology. Most content-based standard-setting methods (e.g., modified Angoff, Bookmark, Body of Work) tend to minimize the influence of data involving external criteria. Thus, modifications to the processes traditionally followed with these approaches may be needed. Another consideration is the extent to which constructed response or complex, technology-enhanced items are included in the tests. Some methods are better suited for tests comprising multiple choice items. If the test contains a large number of partial credit or polytomously scored items, modifications to the traditional methods may be necessary. One possibility is to use them in combination with more flexible methods such as Body of Work.

Procedures for achieving vertical moderation or articulation of performance standards across proficiency levels and tests in different grades and content areas is now a standard consideration (e.g., Cizek & Agger, 2012). Whether performance standards should be articulated across end-of-course tests (e.g., English 1, Algebra I, Algebra II) is a policy matter that should be decided as part of planning for setting performance standards.

Step 7: Continue Operation of the Program

Once an end-of-course testing program has been established, a number of activities are part of ongoing operations. These include (a) analyzing operational data collected over time, (b) refreshing item pools, (c) developing multiple test forms over time, (d) establishing and maintaining procedures for consistent response scoring across administrations, (e) designing and implementing ongoing validity studies, and (f) reviewing performance standards set for the program. Each of these topics is discussed briefly below.

Analyzing Operational Data

Post-administration analysis of end-of-course test data is a critical step in evaluation and provides supporting documentation for the testing program, as well as a basis for test improvements. These analyses are intended to confirm that student performance on the test is consistent with expectations driving test design and development. Test analyses include summaries of student performance (e.g., scaled score distributions, percentages of students passing or falling within proficiency categories), both for the overall sample of students and for all relevant subgroups. Item-level statistics calculated on operational data include difficulty and discrimination, analysis of selected response options, differential item functioning, new or updated IRT statistics, and, for tests administered online, summaries of item response times. For constructed response items, test analyses also should summarize the distributions of students across score categories and provide statistical summaries of the reliability or consistency of human scoring. Statistical analyses of operational data are important components of the documentation that is typically required by contract and used to support a testing program when evaluated or challenged by external parties. Such documentation should be collected for each administration and compiled at least annually.

Test score inflation due to reallocation of instructional emphasis to selected substantive test content and to coaching on non-substantive test features (e.g., item styles, scoring rubric details; see Koretz, 2013, p. 6) can influence test performance in ways that "bias inferences about achievement" (p. 3). It is easy to imagine teachers and students focusing inordinate attention on strategies to pass end-of-course tests as opposed to striving to achieve the learning goals of the course. Inflated end-of-course test scores are especially pernicious when they are included in teacher evaluation models, as increases in student scores may be misinterpreted as teacher effects on core course content rather than construct-irrelevant, non-substantive test features.

Refreshing Item Pools

A key element in maintaining a viable testing program is the continuing development and field testing of items to be incorporated into new test forms. There are a variety of approaches to field testing items and related activities (see, e.g., Kirkpatrick & Way, 2008; Schmeiser & Welch, 2006). The most common approach is to embed the new items in operational test forms. This is minimally intrusive since it does not require additional test administrations, although additional test administration time may be needed. When many items must be field tested, they can be (purposefully) divided into unique subsets that are spiraled with a single operational test form.

An important related activity is maintaining the program's test item bank, which typically contains digital representations of the items and all relevant metadata (i.e., both content codes and item statistics). Item banking systems support item authoring and review, provide inventorying and automated tools to assist with test form assembly, and facilitate the integration of metadata with the text, graphics, media objects, and interactions that comprise the items. Challenges abound in maintaining an item bank large enough to support ongoing, operational testing. Occasionally, item writers are not able to generate enough items targeting a specific content standard or content standard–difficulty level combination. The result can be that the small number of items that do exist are overused in multiple test forms.

Attempts to meet these challenges include item cloning (i.e., manipulating content response demands in an item to produce many items) and automatic item generation (i.e., generating many items as variants of an item model via computer algorithms; Gierl & Haladyna, 2013). In addition, introducing new item types (e.g., technology-enabled versions of selected response items that use hot spots and drag-and-drop computer capabilities) requires analyses to ensure that the items are reasonably consistent with the target achievement construct and do not violate the unidimensionality of the item pool. Recent efforts in developing technology-enhanced item types have focused on the use of templates to describe the interaction between a test-taker and the item or task presented, the response data that result, and the approach for scoring the responses (Haertel, Cheng, Cameto, Fujii, Sanford, Rutstein, & Morrison, 2012; Parshall & Harmes, 2007). Such templates hold promise for fostering efficiency and consistency in the development and scoring of technology-enabled items.

Finally, improving overall item quality is informed by psychometric analyses of operational test data, which includes (but not limited to) traditional and IRT analyses of item performance, estimates of test reliability, test equating, DIF analyses, analyses of scoring consistency, summaries of score distributions, and the proportions of test-takers classified in various performance levels. These analyses can point to the need to refine item development procedures or the need for certain classes of items.

Developing Multiple Test Forms

Most end-of-course testing programs involve secure administrations, necessitating the development of multiple test forms over years. For statewide end-of-course tests, there is an additional need to offer tests at multiple times during the school year. For example, some high schools follow block schedules, in which some courses are semester-long rather than year-long. Finally, students who miss a regularly scheduled administration must have an opportunity to sit for the test at another date. Consequently, testing programs must develop multiple test forms for administration over the school year. Of course, the different forms must be equated so that scores can be reported on a common scale. However, equating test forms and maintaining scale stability through time is more challenging when different administrations involve qualitatively different samples of examinees. For example, most students participate in the spring end-of-course administration, whereas relatively small numbers of students, with somewhat different demographic characteristics and academic preparation, participate in other administrations (see Holland & Dorans, 2006, pp. 212–213 for population sensitivity to equating functions).

Establishing and Maintaining Consistent Scoring Procedures

When end-of-course tests include performance tasks (e.g., essay prompts or open-ended problems), it is important to maintain consistent scoring procedures. Although the specifics may vary by domain, certain procedural components are nearly universal. These include rubric development, range finding, scorer selection, scorer training and qualification, and scorer monitoring. Rubric development for constructed response items is typically done at the outset. Depending upon the content and type of rubric (i.e., holistic or analytic), a single rubric for all items or item-specific rubrics may be developed. Once constructed response items or tasks have been developed and field tested, range finding can be conducted. The range-finding process determines how the rubric is to be applied to examinee responses to a particular item or task; therefore, it establishes the standards that are used in scoring the items. The process may also identify the responses associated with each score point and characterize the threshold between score points. The process is typically conducted by a committee and there are aspects of range-finding meetings that are similar to those of standard-setting meetings.

Scorers typically are recruited based on requirements developed in conjunction with the test sponsor, usually a state department of education. Depending on the setting and the test, specific educational and experience requirements are established (e.g., having a college degree in a relevant domain and/or experience as a classroom teacher). Scorers are trained using materials developed by the test vendor and that which are approved by the test sponsor. In most large-scale scoring operations, scorers must pass a qualifying test for the prompts they will score.

Scorer accuracy and consistency are monitored throughout the scoring process in a variety of ways (see, e.g., Johnson, Penny, & Gordon, 2009, chapter 8). In most programs, at least a sample of constructed responses is scored twice, providing the basis for the calculation of a number of statistics related to interrater reliability (e.g., perfect agreement, perfect plus adjacent agreement, Spearman correlations, kappa statistics). In addition, scorers may be monitored using back-reading; that is, a scoring leader rescores papers that have been marked by scorers who may be performing at a marginal level of accuracy. The scoring leader can provide specific feedback or additional training before scorers are allowed to continue scoring. Finally, papers previously marked by expert scorers can be distributed to scorers in validity check sets, providing data for validity indices that are similar to the interrater reliability statistics. Validity papers may be chosen because of certain features that, for example, can be used to evaluate whether scorers are consistently applying the rubric to borderline papers. These and other practices are critical to maintaining scoring accuracy over multiple test administrations.

Consistent scoring decisions can be assured using automated, computer-based scoring systems for essays and other items, where those capabilities exist (see, e.g., Williamson, Mislevy, & Bejar, 2006; and Williamson, Xi, & Breyer, 2012).

Conducting Validity Studies

Validity refers to an integrated, overall judgment about the extent to which empirical evidence and theoretical rationales support the soundness of interpretations, decisions, and actions based on test scores (e.g., Cronbach, 1988; Kane, 2013). Sources of validity evidence relevant to end-of-course tests are described in the *Standards for Educational and Psychological Measurement* (AERA et al., 2014) and include analyses of test content, response processes, internal structure, relations to other variables, and consequences of testing (see pp. 13–21). The conceptual framework for conducting validity studies for end-of-course tests is no different than that for any other test. That is, validation can be viewed as a process of proposing claims and evaluating evidence and arguments with respect to those claims (i.e., the intended interpretations of test scores and their relevance to proposed uses).

Evidence based on test content documents the degree of alignment with course content standards. The extent to which examinee processing of test item demands conforms to the intended cognitive targets provides construct-relevant evidence (e.g., Ferrara & Duncan, 2011). For example, if a claim associated with an Algebra II test is that students display appropriate mathematical reasoning by constructing viable arguments and/or critiquing the reasoning of others, it is essential to determine whether successful test-takers employ reasoning processes when responding to such items, rather than simply applying a generic rule or algorithm. Analyses of internal structure, such as factor analyses, IRT-based dimensionality analyses, and structural equation modeling, can provide additional information about whether the test measures the target construct. Empirical studies of the relationships of the test results with other variables can also provide useful evidence, especially if they are conducted periodically.

Finally, investigation of the consequences of end-of-course tests, broadly conceived, is important to address fully the validity of the end-of-course testing program. This is especially challenging when the end-of-course test results are employed for teacher evaluation: It can be difficult to disentangle traditional validation arguments concerning test score interpretations with respect to students from validation arguments about teacher effectiveness indicators based on test results, as well as from the properties of the accountability model that is intended to indicate teacher effectiveness (e.g., AERA et al., 2014, p. 206; Hill, Kapitula, & Umland, 2011).

Reviewing the Appropriateness of Performance Standards for Students and for Implementation in Teacher Evaluation Models

For end-of-course tests, an important aspect of validity evidence relates to the appropriateness of the performance standards for high-stakes decisions about students. Therefore, it is necessary to revisit performance standards after the end-of-course test has been in use for some time. Ideally, this review would be part of a planned series of studies to support the program over time.

Similarly, it is both reasonable and prudent to consider when in the life of an end-of-course testing program it might be appropriate to use end-of-course test results for teacher evaluation. Relatively large increases in aggregate student performance in the early years of a new testing program are quite common (e.g., Linn, 2000). They are both celebrated and viewed with skepticism, especially when the rates of improvement flatten. Koretz (2013, p. 6) argues that these early increases should be seen as score inflation due to two influences: (a) the unbalanced allocation of instructional time to tested content standards, to the detriment of other valued standards (i.e., "reallocation," p. 6); and (b) focusing instruction on narrow, incidental attributes of a test, such as item formats (i.e., "coaching," p. 6). These early increases can wreak havoc in interpreting individual student growth and in inferring teacher contributions to that growth. With these concerns in mind, it would be advisable to include in an educator accountability system indicators based on student scores from a new end-of-course testing only after the program has stabilized. Unfortunately, this sort of caution is at odds with the short time horizons typical of political demands.

Summary and Conclusions

In the previous section we provided considerable detail on the design, development, and implementation requirements for end-of-course tests for student assessment and teacher evaluation. In Table 2.3, we summarize differences for the two intended uses of end-of-course tests. Table 2.3 highlights activities and requirements within each of the seven steps in design, development, and implementation.

As Table 2.3 indicates, some end-of-course design, development, and implementation decisions and activities for student assessment and teacher evaluation uses are incompatible.

Table 2.3 Summary of Similarities and Differences in the Design, Development, and Implementation of End-of-Course Tests for Student Assessment and Teacher Evaluation

End-of-Course Tests for Student Assessment	*End-of-Course Tests for Teacher Evaluation*
Step 1. Explicate intended inferences and uses	
Designed to support status interpretations (assuming no need for vertical linking)	Designed to support status, growth, and value-added interpretations
Interpretations of test scores focus on mastery of course content, pass/fail status, their component weight in a course grade	Interpretations of student scores focus on how much students grew or how much growth is attributable to the influence of the teacher

Design and development differences: Different interpretations hold implications for design and development, as discussed in subsequent steps

Step 2. Decide on overall test design, item types, and psychometric plans	
Focus on total score reliability and especially classification consistency and accuracy	Focus on score total reliability, classification consistency and accuracy, and especially the amount of error in growth scores
Provide adequate coverage of testable course content standards	Provide adequate coverage of testable course content standards
Select items to target cut score and local score range	Select items to target uniform coverage of score scale to support growth measures throughout the scale
Focus on equating of parallel test forms, most likely with embedded equating anchors	Focus on equating of parallel test forms with equating anchors and slots for vertical linking items
Provide annual constructed response scoring stability	Provide annual constructed response stability and cross-grade scoring stability (for vertical linking items)

Design decision differences: Different test targeting strategies (i.e., item selection), focuses for equating, and concerns for scoring constructed response items require different strategies for item pool development

Step 3. Develop the test items	
Align items to on-grade, targeted content standards and cognitive demands	Align items plus cover off-grade standards and cognitive demands to support vertical linking, where it's used
Item development: Target cut score area to maximize classification consistency and accuracy	Item development: Target full proficiency range to support measurement of growth and growth interpretations
Determination of "comparability of" to "equivalence (i.e., equating) of"	Comparability and fairness issue for teachers, as well

Design and development differences: Different considerations for coverage of grade-level content standards and scale ranges

Step 4. Pilot test and field test the items	
Concerns about field test data for establishing a base scale and setting performance standards: student effort, wide participation	In addition to concerns about establishing a base scale for inferences about student achievement, concerns about making interpretations about student growth for teacher evaluation

Development differences: Concerns about evaluating and selecting field-tested items for interpretations about student achievement may be particularly acute for making student growth interpretations for teacher evaluation

Step 5. Implement the operational test

Assemble operational test forms to maximize classification consistency and accuracy for the pass/fail cut score

Assemble operational forms to maximize precision for the entire score scale to support precision of growth scores

Security concerns focus on cheating by students and teachers to increase student scores and passing the test

In addition, security concerns focus on teachers manipulating student scores to manipulate student achievement growth

Implementation differences: Different psychometric targets for assembly of subsequent operational test forms and sources of concern about test security

Step 6. Set performance standards

Pass/fail cut score; possibly multiple proficiency levels

Pass/fail cut score; need for multiple proficiency levels for teacher evaluation models based on status growth

Reasonable benchmarks are available to guide setting cut scores (e.g., Ferrara et al., 2011; McClarty, Way, Porter, Beimers, & Miles, 2013)

What benchmarks for amounts of growth for teacher evaluation models? Or use normative benchmarks, as in student growth percentiles

Design and development differences: Item selection to support test-targeting strategy; benchmarks for standard setting

Step 7. Continue ongoing operation of the program

Focus on scale stability so that passing standard is comparable from year to year for student fairness and to evaluate course effectiveness

Focus on scale stability so that passing standard is comparable from year to year for teacher evaluation interpretation and uses

Differences in course-taking profiles (i.e., which course taken prior to the end-of-course test) almost irrelevant; goal is to maximize test information around the cut score

Differences in course-taking profiles important for data needed for teacher evaluation models

Design, development, and implementation differences: Concerns about score stability arise for different reasons; course-taking patterns matter for teacher evaluation models

---

For example, as noted above, the ideal test information targeting strategies are quite discordant, and thus a compromise is required. One such compromise involves selecting items to provide reasonable score precision across the entire score scale, but with some emphasis in the neighborhood of the cut score. This is suboptimal for both purposes but is unavoidable in almost any design effort, which can be characterized as an exercise in optimization under constraints (H. Braun, personal communication, April 4, 2014). Thus, the compromise design typically involves *satisficing* (i.e., the combination of satisfying and sufficing; see Simon, 1956, pp. 129, 136). Another compromise could focus on optimizing outcomes for a particular test feature (e.g., maximizing test information around a cut score) while at the same time providing adequate measurement across the score scale and respecting pragmatic constraints (e.g., limits on testing time and scoring costs).

An alternative is to add satisficing requirements to the test design rather than simply adding on new uses to an existing design. Current practice seems to be to design end-of-course tests for student achievement, then to make a policy decision to use the resulting student achievement data in teacher evaluation models. A better approach would be to design end-of-course tests for both intended uses simultaneously. Of course, this could result in longer tests—that is, optimizing score precision at the cut score for student assessment purposes and optimizing precision throughout the scale for teacher evaluation purposes—which would be widely unpopular, given the growing opposition to standardized testing. In addition, it is unlikely to be practically feasible without CAT.

Ordinarily, a chapter like this would end with a call for additional research. As measurement researchers and psychometricians, we, of course, support the need for more research on end-of-course tests and their uses in assessing student achievement and evaluating teachers. In addition, and equally important, we call for explicit attention to intended score interpretations and uses during the design phase and throughout the development and implementation process for end-of-course tests and all educational achievement tests. Ball-peen hammers are designed for banging metal into shape, claw hammers for banging in nails. End-of-course tests should be designed for their specific, intended uses.

Acknowledgment

We thank Joan Herman and Henry Braun for their excellent advice on the content and organization of this chapter, and Susan Trent and Kaitlyn Stover for their important research support.

Notes

1 Twenty-five states require students to pass high school "exit exams" (McIntosh, 2012, p. 2) to receive a diploma, including the states that require end-of-course tests. Inconsistencies in numbers of states with end-of-course tests in the Domaleski (2011), McIntosh (2012), and Zinth (2012) reports are due to differences in focus (i.e., end-of-course tests versus high school exit exams), period of data collection, states that responded, and test use categorization decisions.
2 And this is an underestimate, as it does not account for the states that do not have end-of-course tests in all six courses and the 23 states and the District of Columbia which have no end-of-course tests (see Table 2.2).
3 The 6–7 percent difference is an estimate of the percentage of times an incorrect pass/fail classification would occur, given a cut score of 0.0, the item parameters used in Figures 2.1 and 2.2, and the standard error of Rasch ability estimates at true abilities equal to –0.3 and +0.3.

References

American Educational Research Association (AERA), American Psychological Association (APA), & National Council on Measurement in Education (NCME). (2014). *Standards for educational and psychological testing*. Washington, DC: AERA.

Baker, B. D., Oluwole, J. O., & Green, P. C. (2013). The legal consequences of mandating high stakes decisions based on low quality information: Teacher evaluation in the race-to-the-top era. *Education Policy Analysis Archives*, 21(5), 1–65.

Baker, E. (2010, August). *Problems with the use of test scores to evaluate teachers* (Briefing Paper No. 278). Washington, DC: Economic Policy Institute.

Bejar, I. I., Braun, H. I., & Tannenbaum, R. J. (2007). A prospective, progressive, and predictive approach to standard setting. In R. Lissitz (Ed.), *Assessing and modeling cognitive development in school* (pp. 1–30). Maple Grove, MN: JAM Press.

Betebenner, D. W. (2011). *New directions in student growth: The Colorado growth model*. Paper presented at the National Conference on Student Assessment, Orlando, FL. Retrieved from http://ccsso.confex.com/ccsso/2011/webprogram/Session2199.html

Braun, H. (2008). *Vicissitudes of the validators*. Invited keynote presentation at the 2008 Reidy Interactive Lecture Series, Portsmouth, NH.

Buckley, K., & Marion, S. (2011, June 2). *A survey of approaches used to evaluate educators in non-tested grades and subjects*. Retrieved from http://www.nciea.org/publications/Summary%20of%20Approaches%20for%20non-tested%20gradesKBSM2011.pdf

Castellano, K. E., & Ho, A. D. (2013). *A practitioner's guide to growth models*. Washington, DC: Council of Chief State School Officers. Retrieved from http://www.ccsso.org/Documents/2013GrowthModels.pdf

Cizek, G. J. (Ed.). (2005). Vertically moderated standard setting (Special issue). *Applied Measurement in Education*, 18(1), 1–115.

Cizek, G. J., & Agger, C. A. (2012). Vertically moderated standard setting. In G. J. Cizek (Ed.), *Setting performance standards: Foundations, methods, and innovations* (2nd ed., pp. 467–484). New York, NY: Routledge.

Cronbach, J. J. (1988). Five perspectives on the validity argument. In H. Wainer & H. I. Braun (Eds.), *Test validity* (pp. 3–17). Hillsdale, NJ: Lawrence Erlbaum.

Darling-Hammond, L., Herman, J., Pellegrino, J., Abedi, J., Aber, J. L., Baker, E., . . . Steele, C. M. (2013). *Criteria for high-quality assessment.* Stanford, CA: Stanford Center for Opportunity Policy in Education. Retrieved from https://edpolicy.stanford.edu/publications/pubs/847

Domaleski, C. (2011). *State end of course testing programs: A policy brief.* Paper commissioned by the Council of Chief State School Officers Technical Issues in Large Scale Assessment State Collaborative on Assessment and Student Standards, Washington, DC. Retrieved from http://www.ccsso.org/Documents/2011/State_End-of-course_Testing_Programs_2011.pdf

Downing, S. M. (2006). Twelve steps for effective test development. In S. M. Downing & T. M. Haladyna (Eds.), *Handbook of test development* (pp. 3–25). Mahwah, NJ: Lawrence Erlbaum Associates.

Egan, K. L., Schneider, M. C., & Ferrara, S. (2012). Performance level descriptors: History, practice, and a proposed framework. In G. J. Cizek (Ed.), *Setting performance standards: Foundations, methods, and innovations* (2nd ed., pp. 79–106). New York, NY: Routledge.

Feinberg, R. A., & Wainer, H. (2014). A simple equation to predict a subscore's value. *Educational Measurement: Issues and Practice, 33*(3), 55–56.

Ferrara, S., Dogan, E., Glazer, N., Haberstroh, J., Hain, B., Huff, K., . . . Piper, C. (2014). The PARCC cognitive complexity code frameworks: Development, application, and validation evidence. In D. Sundre (Chair), *Developing and establishing validity evidence: In theory and practice.* Paper session in the annual meeting of the American Educational Research Association, Philadelphia, PA.

Ferrara, S., & Duncan, T. (2011). Comparing science achievement constructs: Targeted and achieved. *The Educational Forum, 75*(2), 143–156.

Ferrara, S., Lewis, D. M., Mercado, R., Egan, K., D'Brot, J., & Barth, J. (2011). Setting benchmarked performance standards: Standard setting workshop procedures, panelist judgments, and empirical results. In K. Egan (Chair), *Innovations in standard setting.* Invited symposium at the annual meeting of the National Council on Measurement in Education, New Orleans, LA.

Ferrara, S., Swaffield, S., & Mueller, L. (2009). Conceptualizing and setting performance standards for alternate assessments. In W. D. Schafer & R. W. Lissitz (Eds.), *Alternate assessments based on alternate achievement standards: Policy, practice, and potential* (pp. 93–111). Baltimore, MD: Paul Brookes Publishing.

Fremer, J. J., & Ferrara, S. (2013). Security in large scale, paper and pencil testing. In J. A. Wollack & J. J. Fremer (Eds.), *Handbook of test security* (pp. 17–37). New York, NY: Routledge.

Gierl, M. J., & Haladyna, T. (2013). *Automatic item generation: Theory and practice.* New York, NY: Routledge.

Goodman, D. P., & Hambleton, R. K. (2004). Student test score reports and interpretive guides: Review of current practices. *Applied Measurement in Education, 17*(2), 145–220.

Haberman, S. (2008). When can subscores have value? *Journal of Educational and Behavioral Statistics, 33,* 204–229.

Haertel, E. H., Beimers, J., & Miles, J. (2012). The briefing book method. In G. J. Cizek (Ed.), *Setting performance standards: Foundations, methods, and innovations* (2nd ed., pp. 283–300). New York, NY: Routledge.

Haertel, G. D., Cheng, B. H., Cameto, R., Fujii, R., Sanford, C., Rutstein, D., & Morrison, K. (2012). *Design and development of technology enhanced assessment tasks: Integrating Evidence-Centered Design and Universal Design for Learning frameworks to assess hard-to-measure science constructs and increase student accessibility.* Paper presented at the ETS Invitational Research Symposium on Technology Enhanced Assessments, Princeton, NJ. Retrieved from http://www.k12center.org/rsc/pdf/session1-cameto-cheng-haertel-paper-tea2012.pdf

Hambleton, R. K., & Swaminathan, H. (1985). *Item response theory: Principles and applications.* Boston, MA: Kluwer-Nijhoff.

Hendrickson, A. (2007). An NCME instructional module on multi-stage testing. *Educational Measurement: Issues and Practice, 26,* 44–52.

Herman, J. L., Heritage, M., & Goldschmidt, P. (2011). *Developing and selecting assessments of student growth for use in teacher evaluation systems.* Los Angeles, CA: University of California, National Center for Research on Evaluation, Standards, and Student Testing (CRESST). Retrieved from http://www.cse.ucla.edu/products/policy/shortTermGrowthMeasures_v6.pdf

Hill, H. C., Kapitula, L., & Umland, K. (2011). A validity argument approach to evaluating teacher value-added scores. *American Educational Research Journal, 48*(3), 794–831.

Hill, R. K., & DePascale, C. A. (2003). Reliability of No Child Left Behind accountability designs. *Educational Measurement: Issues and Practice, 22*(3), 12–20.

Holland, P. W., & Dorans, N. J. (2006). Linking and equating. In R. L. Brennan (Ed.), *Educational measurement* (4th ed., pp. 187–220). Westport, CT: American Council on Education/Praeger.

Johnson, R. L., Penny, J. A., & Gordon, B. (2009). *Assessing performance: Designing, scoring, and validating performance tasks.* New York, NY: Guilford Press.

Kane, M. T. (2013). Validating the interpretations and uses of test scores. *Journal of Educational Measurement, 50*(1), 1–73.

Kirkpatrick, R. K., & Way, W. D. (2008). *Field testing and equating designs for state educational assessments.* Paper presented at the annual meeting of the American Educational Research Association, New York, NY.

Kolen, M. J., & Lee, W. (2011). Psychometric properties of scores on mixed-format tests. *Educational Measurement: Issues and Practice, 30*(2), 15–24.

Koretz, D. (2013, December 5). *Adapting the practice of measurement to the demands of test-based accountability.* Retrieved from http://projects.iq.harvard.edu/files/eap/files/adapting_the_practice_of_measurement_12.5.13_wp_2.pdf

Laitusis, C., Buzick, H., Stone, E., Hansen, E., & Hakkinen, M. (2012, June). *Smarter balanced consortium: Literature review of testing accommodations and accessibility tools for students with disabilities.* Retrieved January 10, 2015 from http://www.smarterbalanced.org/wordpress/wp-content/uploads/2012/08/Smarter-Balanced-Students-with-Disabilities-Literature-Review.pdf

Layton, L. (2014, May 13). Good teaching, poor test scores: Doubt cast on grading teachers by student performance. *The Washington Post.* Retrieved January 1, 2015 from http://www.washingtonpost.com/local/education/good-teaching-poor-test-scores-doubt-cast-on-grading-teachers-by-student-performance/2014/05/12/96d94812-da07-11e3-bda1-9b46b2066796_story.html

Linn, R. L. (2000). Assessments and accountability. *Educational Researcher, 29*(2), 4–16.

Lockwood, J. R., & McCaffrey, D. F. (2007). Controlling for student heterogeneity in longitudinal models, with applications to student achievement. *Electronic Journal of Statistics, 1,* 223–252. Retrieved March 2, 2015 from http://projecteuclid.org/download/pdfview_1/euclid.ejs/1181334321

Lord, F. M. (1971). The self-scoring flexilevel test. *Journal of Educational Measurement, 8,* 147–151.

Luecht, R. M., & Nungester, R. J. (1998). Some practical applications of computerized adaptive sequential testing. *Journal of Educational Measurement, 35,* 229–249.

Masters, G. N. (1982). A Rasch model for partial credit scoring. *Psychometrika, 47,* 149–174.

McClarty, K. L., Way, W. D., Porter, A. C., Beimers, J. N., & Miles, J. A. (2013). Evidence-based standard setting: Establishing a validity framework for cut scores. *Educational Researcher, 42*(2), 78–88.

McGuinn, P. (2012, November). *The state of teacher evaluation reform: State education agency capacity and the implementation of new teacher-evaluation systems.* Washington, DC: Center for American Progress. Retrieved from http://www.americanprogress.org/press/release/2012/11/13/44660/release-the-state-of-teacher-evaluation-reform/

McIntosh, S. (2012). *State high school exit exams: A policy in transition.* Washington, DC: Center on Education Policy, George Washington University. Retrieved from http://www.cep-dc.org/displayDocument.cfm?DocumentID=408

Moss, P. A., Pullin, D. C., Gee, J. P., Haertel, E. H., & Young, L. J. (Eds.). (2008). *Assessment, equity, and opportunity to learn.* New York, NY: Cambridge University Press.

Muraki, E. (1992). A generalized partial credit model: Application of an EM algorithm. *Applied Psychological Measurement, 16,* 159–176.

National Council on Teacher Quality (NCTQ). (2012, October). *State of the states 2012: Teacher effectiveness policies, area 3, at a glance.* Washington, DC: NCTQ. Retrieved from http://www.nctq.org/stpy11/reports.jsp

NCTQ. (2013, October). *State of the states 2013 connect the dots: Using evaluations of teacher effectiveness to inform policy and practice.* Washington, DC: NCTQ. Retrieved from http://www.nctq.org/dmsStage/State_of_the_States_2013_Using_Teacher_Evaluations_NCTQ_Report

Nichols, P. D., Ferrara, S., & Lai, E. (2015). Principled design for efficacy: Design and development for the next generation of assessments. In R. Lissitz & H. Jiao (Eds.), *The next generation of testing: Common core standards, Smarter Balanced, PARCC, and the nationwide testing movement.* Baltimore, MD: Paul Brookes Publishing.

O'Malley, K., Keng, L., & Miles, J. (2012). From Z to A: Using validity evidence to set performance standards. In G. J. Cizek (Ed.), *Setting performance standards: Foundations, methods, and innovations* (2nd ed., pp. 301–322). New York, NY: Routledge.

Parshall, C. G., & Harmes, J. C. (2007). Designing templates based on a taxonomy of innovative items. In D. J. Weiss (Ed.), *Proceedings of the 2007 GMAC conference on computerized adaptive testing.* Retrieved January 10, 2015 from http://iacat.org/sites/default/files/biblio/cat07parshall.pdf

Phillips, G. W. (2012). The benchmark method of standard setting. In G. J. Cizek (Ed.), *Setting performance standards: Foundations, methods, and innovations* (2nd ed., pp. 323–345). New York, NY: Routledge.

Phillips, S. E., & Camara, W. J. (2006). Legal and ethical issues. In R. L. Brennan (Ed.), *Educational measurement* (4th ed., pp. 734–755). Westport, CT: American Council on Education/Praeger.

Plake, B. S., Huff, K., & Reshetar, R. (2010). Evidence-centered assessment design as a foundation for achievement levels descriptor development and for standard setting. *Applied Measurement in Education, 23,* 307–309.

Polikoff, M. S. (2010). Instructional sensitivity as a psychometric property of assessments. *Educational Measurement: Issues and Practice, 29*(4), 3–14.

Popham, W. J. (2007). Instructional sensitivity of tests: Accountability's dire drawback. *Phi Delta Kappan, 89*(2), 146–150.

Race to the Top Fund; State Fiscal Stabilization Fund Program. (2009, July 29). Federal Register, 74(144).

Ryan, J. M. (2006). Practices, issues, and trends in student test score reporting. In S. M. Downing & T. M. Haladyna (Eds.), *Handbook of test development* (pp. 677–710). Mahwah, NJ: Lawrence Erlbaum Associates.

Salazar, T. (2014). *Fifty ways to test: A look at state summative assessments in 2014–15.* Retrieved January 13, 2015 from http://www.ecs.org/clearinghouse/01/16/06/11606.pdf

Schmeiser, C. B., & Welch, C. J. (2006). Test development. In R. L. Brennan (Ed.), *Educational measurement* (4th ed., pp. 307–353). Westport, CT: American Council on Education/Praeger.

Simon, H. A. (1956). Rational choice and the structure of the environment. *Psychological Review, 63*(2), 129–138.

Sinharay, S. (2010). How often do subscores have added value? Results from operational and simulated data. *Journal of Educational Measurement, 47,* 150–174.

Sinharay, S., Puhan, G., & Haberman, S. J. (2011). An NCME instructional module on subscores. *Educational Measurement: Issues and Practice, 30*(3), 29–40.

Steele, J. L., Hamilton, L. S., & Stecher, B. M. (2010). *Incorporating student performance measures into teacher evaluation systems.* Retrieved from http://www.rand.org/pubs/technical_reports/TR917.html

Strauss, V. (2013, March 30). Atlanta's former schools chief charged under law used against Mafia [electronic version]. *The Washington Post.* Retrieved from http://www.washingtonpost.com/blogs/answer-sheet/wp/2013/03/30/atlantas-former-schools-chief-charged-under-law-used-against-mafia/

Thompson, S. J., Johnstone, C. J., & Thurlow, M. L. (2002). *Universal design applied to large scale assessments* (Synthesis report 44). Minneapolis, MN: University of Minnesota, National Center on Educational Outcomes. Retrieved from http://education.umn.edu/NCEO/OnlinePubs/Synthesis44.html

Thompson, S. J., Thurlow, M., & Moore, M. (2003). *Using computer-based tests with students with disabilities* (Policy Directions No. 15). Minneapolis, MN: University of Minnesota, National Center on Educational Outcomes. Retrieved from http://education.umn.edu/NCEO/OnlinePubs/Policy15.htm

Thompson, S. J., Thurlow, M. L., Quenemoen, R. F., & Lehr, C. A. (2002). *Access to computer-based testing for students with disabilities* (Synthesis report 45). Minneapolis, MN: University of Minnesota, National Center on Educational Outcomes. Retrieved from http://education.umn.edu/nceo/OnlinePubs/Synthesis45.html

Thompson, T. D. (2008). *Growth, precision, and CAT: An examination of gain score conditional SEM.* Iowa City, IA: Pearson Research Report.

Thurlow, M., Lazarus, S. S., Albus, D., & Hodgson, J. (2010). *Computer-based testing: Practices and considerations* (Synthesis report 78). Minneapolis, MN: University of Minnesota, National Center on Educational Outcomes.

U.S. Department of Education. (2007, December 21). *Standards and assessments peer review guidance: Information and examples for meeting requirement of the No Child Left Behind Act of 2001.* Retrieved from http://www2.ed.gov/policy/elsec/guid/saaprguidance.pdf

U.S. Department of Education, National Center for Education Statistics. (2013). *Digest of education statistics, 2013 tables and figures.* Retrieved February 3, 2015 from http://nces.ed.gov/programs/digest/d13/tables/dt13_209.50.asp

van der Linden, W. J., & Glas, C. A. W. (Eds.). (2010). *Elements of adaptive testing.* New York, NY: Springer.

Wainer, H. (Ed.). (2000). *Computerized adaptive testing: A primer* (2nd ed.). Mahwah, NJ: Erlbaum.

Wainer, H., & Kiely, G. L. (1987). Item clusters and computerized adaptive testing: A case for testlets. *Journal of Educational Measurement, 24,* 185–201.

Way, W. D. (2014, August 15). *Memorandum on instructional sensitivity considerations for the PARCC assessments.* Retrieved from http://parcconline.org/assessments/test-design/research

Way, W. D., Twing, J. S., Camara, W., Sweeney, K., Lazer, S., & Mazzeo, J. (2010). *Some considerations related to the use of adaptive testing for the common core assessments.* Retrieved from http://www.ets.org/s/commonassessments/pdf/AdaptiveTesting.pdf

Williamson, D. M., Mislevy, R. J., & Bejar, I. I. (Eds.). (2006). *Automated scoring of complex tasks in computer-based testing.* Mahwah, NJ: Lawrence Erlbaum Associates.

Williamson, D. M., Xi, X., & Breyer, F. J. (2012). A framework for evaluation and use of automated scoring. *Educational Measurement: Issues and Practice, 31*(1), 2–13.

Wise, S. L., & DeMars, C. E. (2005). Low examinee effort in low-stakes assessment: Problems and potential solutions. *Educational Assessment, 10,* 1–17.

Wise, S. L., & DeMars, C. E. (2006). An application of item response time: The effort-moderated IRT model. *Journal of Education Measurement, 43*(1), 19–38.

Wright, B. D., & Stone, M. H. (1979). *Best test design.* Chicago, IL: MESA Press.

Yen, W. M., & Fitzpatrick, A. R. (2006). Item response theory. In R. L. Brennan (Ed.), *Educational measurement* (4th ed., pp. 111–154). Westport, CT: American Council on Education/Praeger.

Yuan, K., & Le, V.-N. (2012, November). *Estimating the percentages of students who were tested on cognitively demanding items through the state achievement tests.* RAND report WR-967-WFHF. Retrieved January 16, 2015 from http://www.rand.org/content/dam/rand/pubs/working_papers/2012/RAND_WR967.pdf

Zenisky, A. L., & Hambleton, R. K. (2012). Developing test score reports that work: The process and best practices for effective communication. *Educational Measurement: Issues and Practice, 31*(2), 21–26.

Zinth, J. D. (2012). *End-of-course exams.* Denver: Education Commission of the States. Retrieved from http://www.ecs.org/clearinghouse/01/01/27/10127.pdf

3 Design and Implementation Considerations of Performance-Based and Authentic Assessments for Use in Accountability Systems

Scott F. Marion and Katie Buckley

Introduction

This chapter explores the challenges and implications of designing authentic assessments for accountability purposes. Educational accountability takes many forms, from student-level certification for high school graduation to district-level accreditation to ensure that students are being provided with appropriate learning opportunities. Accountability systems are designed to instantiate policy values to lead to certain ends (e.g., 100 percent of students proficient in reading and math). Essentially all accountability systems involve collecting data, analyzing those data according to specific rules to transform the data into accountability indicators, classifying the indicators into various levels of performance (e.g., exemplary to failing), and attributing the results to appropriate individuals or organizations. Many current educational accountability systems have stated goals of promoting deeper learning for students for a variety of reasons, including, among other goals, improving college and career readiness. This chapter takes the position that performance-based and -related assessment approaches must be meaningfully incorporated into accountability systems—by serving as at least one key source of "input" data—if we are to do more than pay lip service to these policy goals. This chapter focuses on design considerations for performance-based assessments for use in accountability systems. This is a broad topic. In order to provide more than a superficial discussion, we focus much of the chapter on the use of performance-based assessments in educator evaluation systems, although the chapter includes brief discussions of school and student accountability systems as well. We do not focus on combining the results of performance-based or other open-response tasks with more traditional selected-response items into a single assessment score for use in any of these accountability determinations. This is clearly an important issue, but beyond the scope of this chapter.

We first provide an exposition of the various terms—authentic, direct, alternative, performance, and portfolio—and describe key design features of each. We contend that "performance-based" assessments should be used as the umbrella term as long as certain design principles are met and then describe how performance-based assessment designs may differ depending on the specific accountability use. Next, we offer a rationale for using performance-based assessments in accountability systems and discuss how they can and are incorporated into a variety of accountability systems. We then articulate both general and specific design principles that must be considered when incorporating authentic assessments into educator accountability systems. We focus on key technical criteria, including construct validity, generalizability, and comparability, from the standpoints of both design and evaluation. We conclude by addressing the potential for corruptibility of authentic assessments in accountability systems.

Our discussion of performance assessments as part of teacher accountability systems highlights the truism that all test design, especially for accountability purposes, is an exercise in optimization under constraints. In other words, test designers must consider technical, political, fiscal, and capacity constraints when trying to craft an assessment that best meets the design goals. Incorporating test-based indicators derived from value-added analyses or student growth percentile (SGP) models applied to state test score results (e.g., Braun, Chudowsky, & Koenig, 2010) is challenging; more challenging still is determining how to include valid documentation of student performance for the 70 percent or more of teachers in the "non-tested subjects and grades" (NTSG).

To further illustrate the challenges with incorporating performance-based assessments into educator evaluations, we focus much of the chapter on student learning objectives (SLOs), a key component of many teacher evaluation systems. We could have included a discussion of the various types of performance-based or authentic assessment designs for accountability systems ranging from student to district level. However, we chose to focus on SLOs precisely because they are intended to provide greater coherence between teacher instructional improvement and teacher accountability, and to do so, as we argue below, performance-based assessments are needed. The current debates regarding using test-based measures in teacher evaluation makes this a timely topic. Further, the issues of SLO assessment design for educator evaluation will likely generalize to other types of accountability.

What's in a Name? Some Definitions and Examples of Commonly Used Terms

Adjectives such as *direct*, *authentic*, and *alternative*, among others, are used to describe the assessments that are intended to provide a more realistic measure of student learning than tests comprised largely of selected-response or other short-answer items. In this sense, alternative is the broadest term in that it just indicates that the assessment is different from the more ubiquitous selected-response test. However, the term alternative may have a somewhat negative connotation in that it suggests that the assessment referred to is not the "real" assessment, and because of the nature of the subject matter or for some other reason, we are forced to use an "alternative."

Terms such as *direct* and *authentic* have found favor with those promoting the use of such assessments because they imply that such assessments are not simply proxies for the behavior of interest; they represent (or at least are closely related to) the knowledge and skills we want students to demonstrate. The problem, of course, is that calling something direct or authentic does not make it so—nor does it make it appropriate for the target construct (Braun, 2012; Messick, 1994). Empirical evidence is necessary to support claims of authenticity and/or directness. One can think of examples of performances that are convincingly authentic, such as a painting or music performance, but in more conventional academic content areas such as math and science, the task is often constrained to fit the logistics of a school structure (e.g., students must complete the investigation with specific resources in a 45-minute class period). Therefore, these performances are really proxies for the "authentic" behavior they intend to represent and evidence is required to evaluate the quality of the match between the proxy and the authentic activity. Regardless of the choice of label, it is important to remember that assessments are valuable to the extent that they lead to the types of interactions between the student and the task that generates evidence that is necessary to support desired inferences. As such, we settle on "performance-based" because we contend that it carries less inferential baggage and simply describes assessments that require students to produce or perform something. Nevertheless, we urge caution with any label that implies that the quality of the inferences follow simply from the mode of the assessment and not from the interaction it promotes among the student, task, and content (this point is further elaborated later in the chapter).

Types of Assessment

There are many types of "alternative" assessments, but they are often classified into two main categories: performance assessments and portfolios. We add one more category, exhibitions, that

Table 3.1 Summary of Key Performance-Based Formats

Assessment Form	Timing	Dimensionality	Status/Progress	Example
Performance-based assessment (PBA)	Throughout units and courses, as well as at the end of instruction	May be unidimensional, but most complex PBAs are multi-dimensional	Each PBA is a measure of status at a point in time	Designing, conducting, and reporting on a scientific investigation
Portfolio	Designed to cover an extended period such as a semester, course, or even multiple courses	May be unidimensional if purposefully focused on a narrow, single strand (e.g., development of an appropriate argument structure in writing), but will often be multi-dimensional as a result of multiple and varied portfolio entries	Individual entries can be considered status measures, but the portfolio is usually intended to provide evidence of progress	Writing portfolio to allow students and teachers to judge the changes (improvements) in writing over time
Exhibition	Generally at the end of a designated time period such as a course, series of courses, and/or terminal grade (e.g., 12)	Multi-dimensional	If intermediate products are collected, could be a measure of progress, but primarily a measure of achievement (status)	End of high school graduation exhibition

some might argue is an extension of performance assessments, but we include them separately for the role that they might play, especially in student accountability systems, particularly for high school graduation determinations. We summarize many of the key features in Table 3.1.

Performance assessments are generally multi-step activities ranging from quite unstructured to fairly structured. The key feature of such assessments is that students are asked to produce a product or carry out a performance (e.g., a musical performance) that is scored according to prespecified criteria, typically contained in a scoring guide or rubric.[1] In fact, the rubric is a critical component in establishing the validity of the score inferences since it is the bridge between student work and resulting score, the basis for the inference. Occasionally, performance assessments target key processes or skills, such as communicating with diverse audiences, engaging in critical thinking, and listening to diverse viewpoints that students employ when wrestling with a problem or participating in an event such as a debate or a mock presentation to a simulated (or real) city council. Like "authentic assessments," performance assessments suffer from definitional problems in that this one term can encompass many different types of assessments. For example, a performance assessment could range from 15–20-minute tasks (i.e., quite short) to multi-day activities with many scorable units. Both multi-state assessment consortia—PARCC[2] and Smarter Balanced[3]—plan to include complex performances and other open-response tasks as a significant component of their summative assessment designs.

A portfolio is a collection of work accumulated over longer time periods such as a term or school year. Portfolios typically include a reflection component that provides students with an opportunity for self-assessment, so there is a dynamic relationship between assessment and student learning such that participating in the assessment itself is an opportunity to influence learning. In principle, the entries in the portfolio can comprise a variety of assessment forms, but most are usually performance-based. The scoring protocols for the portfolio should be designed to reflect how the assessment results are intended to be used in the accountability system. For example, different rubrics might be used depending on whether the accountability determinations were based on growth or status metrics. While a similar argument could be made about rubrics for performance tasks, portfolios, because of the extended time frame for amassing evidence, are better suited to considerations of student progress (or growth). Therefore, rubrics that focus solely on the end of portfolio could unintentionally leave information "on the table."

Exhibitions are extended, often interdisciplinary performance tasks typically used as culminating or capstone experiences by certain school districts and states as part of student graduation determinations. They generally take place over a substantial period of time (e.g., several weeks or even a full school term) and often require students to do independent work outside of school. Exhibitions are typically considered extensions of "performance-based" assessments.

Why Performance-Based Assessment?

There are many challenges to the high-stakes use of performance and portfolio assessments, including factors such as psychometric information per unit time and scoring costs; both are discussed in greater detail below. Therefore, it is important to justify the use of such assessments. Among the reasons put forward for using such assessments are:[4]

- the **only** way to measure the intended construct,
- a **better** way to measure the intended construct,
- to produce **instructional information** in addition to accountability information,
- to provide both **learning** and **assessment** opportunity for students, and
- to **signal** the types of instructional tasks many would like to see in classrooms.

We explore each of these justifications for authentic assessments in more detail below.

Only Way to Measure the Construct

For many content areas such as art, music, and physical education, performance tasks or related assessment approaches appear to be the only way to measure the intended construct because the construct is defined to include the physical demonstration (i.e., performance) of a particular knowledge or skill. Additionally, many have argued (Linn, 1993; Resnick, 1996; Shepard, 1996; Wolf, Bixby, & Glenn, 1991) that to measure many other domains well (e.g., science, writing), performance assessment must be included. There is little doubt that certain aspects of each of these domains can be assessed with selected-response items, but if the construct is defined in ways that involve demonstrating a skill, creating something, or signaling deep understanding, then performance assessments (including such forms as open-response essay-type questions) or even exhibitions must be employed.

A Better Way to Measure the Intended Construct

There is no clear distinction between the *only* way to measure the construct and a *better* way to measure the construct. What distinction there is depends on one's perspective on the nature of the domain to be measured. For example, many current science exams use short-answer questions and, in some cases, include a limited number of extended-response or performance tasks. If the target construct includes doing "real" science and reasoning with evidence to construct scientific explanations, then designers of current assessments must acknowledge that these tests cannot measure the full depth of the intended construct, even though they are measuring important aspects of science, such as knowledge of key concepts and facts. For example, if the Next Generation Science Standards (NGSS Lead States, 2013) constitute a comprehensive representation of science learning targets, then full alignment of an assessment cannot be accomplished without measuring students' capability to conduct scientific investigations or other types of inquiry (NRC, 2014). Further, the NRC Committee on Developing Assessments of Science Proficiency in K–12 argued that assessments must measure the integrated or blended nature of science learning in order to legitimately assess the intended learning targets (NRC, 2014). Therefore, performance-based assessments are critically important for measuring such complex learning targets.

There has been a long-standing debate in the educational measurement community about the value of performance or authentic assessments in comparison to selected-response items or other similar formats. There is ample evidence that the results of tests comprising only selected-response items generally correlate well with more complex performance assessments, but such correlations cannot substitute for evidence of construct validity (Linn, Baker, & Dunbar, 1991). Measuring the full, intended construct requires using measures of complex performance (e.g., Resnick & Resnick, 1992; Shepard, 2000), with the potential additional benefit of useful instructional information (e.g., Delandshere & Petrosky, 1998; Parkes, 2000; Pearson & Garavaglia, 1997).

To Produce Instructional Information in Addition to Accountability Information

Performance assessments provide windows into students' thinking in ways that selected-response items cannot. We know that techniques such as item mapping can be useful for yielding instructional feedback, but they do not provide the same level and quality of instructional information at the student level that one can get from examining student work derived from complex tasks. Rich performance tasks, especially when closely linked to curriculum, offer teachers insight into students' thinking as part of formative assessment activities (Shepard, 2000). Performance tasks can serve formative purposes only if administered when there is still time to adjust instruction, but even if tasks are administered during an end-of-year summative assessment, they can still provide useful insights for evaluating the overall effectiveness of curriculum and instructional programs.

To Provide Both Learning and Assessment Opportunity for Students and Teachers

One of the major purported benefits of performance assessment is that simply participating in the assessment constitutes an instructional experience, as well as yielding assessment information. Research has documented the learning benefits of participating in assessment because it helps students encode information into long-term memory (Rohrer & Pashler, 2010). Therefore, participating in a well-designed performance assessment can serve both as a productive instructional episode and as an assessment event (see, e.g., Sabatini, Bennett, & Deane, 2011).

Shepard (2000) and others have argued that high-quality tasks and assessments provide teachers and students the opportunity to learn more about the content being assessed. Additionally, good assessments, especially performance tasks in which students have to generate solutions and reveal and/or explain their thinking, can provide opportunities for teachers to develop sophisticated understandings about the nature of student learning in a particular domain (see also NRC, 2014). Although such insights are not impossible to obtain with selected-response items, they are more likely to emerge from examining student work associated with complex performance tasks. To be sure, there are challenges associated with having assessments, even high-quality performance-based ones, serve both learning and accountability purposes—an issue to which we will return later.

To Signal the Types of Instructional Tasks Many Would Like to See in Classrooms

We subscribe to the view that assessment should be coherent with curriculum and instruction—a view that has its roots in the performance assessment movement of the 1990s that asserted that high-quality performance assessments should be indistinguishable from the rich tasks used for instruction. Resnick and Resnick (1992) argued that it would be appropriate to teach to high-quality, rich tasks because they would be a worthwhile focus of instruction and would signal the types of instructional and assessment tasks that should be used in classrooms. On the other hand, some authors expressed concern about "teaching the test" (Shepard, 2000) with this sort of initiative and potentially narrowing of the curriculum (e.g., Koretz, 2008). While it is important to attend to such potential unintended negative consequences, using rich assessment tasks can be an important signal to schools.

Despite the efforts of standards writers, content standards do not usually paint a clear picture of the intended learning expectations for students in ways that are specific enough to guide instruction. This has been true for most state content standards, and while the Common Core State Standards[5] are an improvement over previous standards in many ways (including the amount of supplemental information produced), it is still difficult for educators and others to fully understand the expectations until they see them instantiated in tasks. For this reason, many states release both sample and operational items and tasks. Both PARCC and Smarter Balanced[6] have released sample items/tasks. Releasing a task or set of tasks communicates to educators the specific knowledge and skills required of students with respect to a standard or set of standards more effectively than simply reading the standard itself, especially when the tasks are accompanied by scoring rubrics and exemplars of student work.

Of course, when coupled with accountability requirements, the instructional signal may become diminished because the pressure from accountability demands can lead teachers and school leaders to undermine the instructional value of such tasks unintentionally (or intentionally) in order to maximize score gains in the time available. Experimental psychologist Donald Campbell (1976) noted this challenge many years ago in what has become known as "Campbell's Law":

> The more any quantitative social indicator (or even some qualitative indicator) is used for social decision-making, the more subject it will be to corruption pressures and the more apt it will be to distort and corrupt the social processes it is intended to monitor.
>
> (p. 49)

Performance-Based Assessments in Accountability Systems

Performance-based assessments are used in a variety of accountability systems. There are important features of such systems that should be understood in order to properly contextualize the discussion of how performance-based assessments can support accountability determinations. Some of the key features and design challenges associated with school, educator, and student accountability systems are discussed below. However, we provide a more extensive treatment of educator accountability since it is the focus of much of the remainder of the chapter.[7]

School Accountability

School accountability systems attempt to characterize, document, and evaluate many aspects of school quality. However, proposals for school accountability reforms as part of the secretary's flexibility waivers under NCLB (Erpenbach & Domaleski, 2013; U.S. Department of Education, 2011) still rely heavily on measures of student achievement, as status (point in time) and/or growth metrics based on state assessment scores rather than incorporating results from rich performance-based measures. This is often the case because in many states the statutes authorizing accountability systems limit the indicators to data that are already collected by the state. In many school accountability systems, data related to indicators of readiness, achievement, growth, and equity are collected and combined to produce an overall judgment (Erpenbach & Domaleski, 2013).

Assessments used for school accountability systems are often state-required assessments purportedly designed to measure the full breadth of the relevant state content standards. Several states over the past 20 years (e.g., Kentucky, Nebraska, Wyoming, Maine, Vermont) have explored using locally developed assessments as part of their school accountability systems. These local assessments were not always constituted solely from performance-based tasks, but, in many cases, performance tasks were an important component. However, the incorporation of performance assessments in state accountability had mixed results, both technically and politically (National Research Council, 2010). Concerns have been raised about the technical quality of performance assessments for accountability purposes (e.g., Koretz, Klein, McCaffrey, & Stecher, 1993). These concerns have not always been justified, because the criticism focused primarily on the reliability of individual student scores despite the fact that the accountability system required aggregated student scores. Hill and DePascale (2003b) illustrated quite conclusively that assessments with less-than-acceptable levels of individual reliability often can provide quite reliable accountability indicators at the aggregate level, assuming a large enough sample size. Unfortunately, this finding was not always enough to offset strong political and stakeholder opposition to performance assessment initiatives in several states (e.g., Kentucky, California) that often capitalized on these misunderstandings of the relationship between individual and aggregate reliability.

There has been a renewed interest in reforming school accountability systems, both as part of the next round of federal waivers to NCLB and independently of the waiver process. For example, states such as New Hampshire and Kentucky are encouraging efforts among districts to implement competency-based education programs. These graduation competencies are often a complex constellation of key content in the discipline, along with important cross-cutting knowledge and skills. Rich performance assessments must be included as part of the assessment system if such competencies are to be validly assessed.

Similarly, the recent focus on improving students' rates of college and career readiness (e.g., Conley, 2007) has led to calls for more authentic means of evaluating readiness. This is especially true for readiness such as critical thinking, analysis, metacognition, and self-regulation. Determinations of readiness are also being included in reformed school accountability systems in states other than the two noted above. Although it is difficult to assess such knowledge and skills, even with high-quality performance assessments, it is impossible to do so relying on tests comprising multiple-choice items, because of the well-documented limitations of multiple choice for assessing complex content and thinking skills (Conley, 2013). If policymakers are serious about credibly evaluating students' readiness for college and careers, then performance and other authentic assessment formats must be part of the assessment system (Conley, 2007; Darling-Hammond et al., 2013).

Student Accountability

Approximately half of the states have high school graduation requirements that involve assessments of one sort or another, often using a single set of graduation exams, administered toward the end of high school and designed to determine whether students have the requisite knowledge and skills. These exams, almost all of which make extensive (if not exclusive) use of multiple-choice items, have been criticized for communicating low expectations (Achieve, 2004). A handful of other states, such as Georgia, North Carolina, and Louisiana, use a series of end-of-course exams and employ various rules for combining the results of these exams to determine if students are eligible to receive a high school diploma (Domaleski, 2011). Very few states require more authentic demonstrations of competence to determine graduation eligibility. Rhode Island's Proficiency-Based Graduation Requirements is the most ambitious, with requirements involving complex performance tasks and a culminating self-directed exhibition (http://www.ride.ri.gov/Instruction/curriculum/rhodeisland/assessment/diploma.aspx). Other states such as Wyoming, Maine, Vermont, and Oregon have, at times during the past 20 years, required the use of complex performance tasks, portfolios, and/or exhibitions as part of high school graduation requirements. Unfortunately, only Oregon and Wyoming still retain any elements of these systems and these are considerably weaker than they were in their heyday, having succumbed to political and financial pressures or capacity constraints (NRC, 2010). However, if states' graduation requirements begin to include the types of college and career-ready skills called for in the CCSS and related standards documents in order for students to graduate, then more authentic demonstrations of competence will have to become part of states' and/or districts' student assessment systems.

Educator Accountability

Educators have long been formally evaluated by their principals or other supervisors. It is only recently, however, that such evaluations are expected to be implemented systematically for all educators. Further, student assessment results must now play a significant role in educator evaluations. There is a rapidly growing literature both extolling the virtues of and, more often, critiquing the use of test-based indicators for educator effectiveness determinations, particularly with respect to value-added models (VAMs) and SGP models (see, e.g., Baker et al., 2010; Braun et al., 2010; Briggs, 2013). For the most part, this literature is focused on the so-called tested grades—those grades and subjects with a state test as well as state test in the same subject area in the prior grade. However, most educators—generally between 60–80 percent, depending on the state—teach in NTSG (Prince et al., 2009). Of course, that does not mean there are no measures of student performance in these courses; rather, it signifies that there are no state test data of two years available for calculating value-added scores or other growth metrics with which to attempt to document teacher contributions to student learning.

Assessment for NTSG

There has been a rush to identify valid approaches for documenting educators' contributions to student learning in these NTSG. In essentially all current educator evaluation systems, the student performance results are combined in some way with measures of teacher practice (usually based on classroom observations and other aspects of teachers' professional activities), as well as student and parent surveys or other forms of evidence, to produce an overall effectiveness rating. While much of the concern with using test-based indicators in teacher evaluations has focused on questions of reliability, there are validity issues associated with using state standardized test scores in teacher evaluation. Such concerns have focused on the technical quality of individual student scores, but the more significant validity threats relate to using aggregations of individual results. Threats to validity, particularly construct underrepresentation and construct-irrelevant variance, are often cited.[8] Teachers are sometimes held accountable for changes in scores on tests that may be only weakly related to their instructional practices and responsibilities. The performance-based assessments that are the focus of this chapter could play a significant role in improving the validity of educator evaluation systems for educators in non-tested (and tested) subjects and grades.

In an analysis of winning states' Race-to-the-Top (RTTT) grant proposals, we characterized approaches for incorporating the results of student performance into educator evaluations in NTSG (Buckley & Marion, 2011). In general, in order to measure teachers' contributions to student learning, states and districts have been considering the following types of assessments: norm-referenced assessments, interim assessments, and end-of-course assessments, along with school- or teacher-developed measures of student performance administered at the classroom level.

Analytic Issues

The validity of individual-level inferences from assessment scores is only part of the work that must be done to fully evaluate the validity of test-based indicators used for accountability purposes, especially teacher evaluation (see Bell et al., 2013; Hill, Kapitula, & Umland, 2011). Administering high-quality assessments for measuring student learning at a particular point in time is not nearly enough to ensure that appropriate analytic techniques will be used to convert such assessment results into metrics and/or indicators to support accountability determinations (see Marion, DePascale, Domaleski, Gong, & Diaz-Bilello, 2012). Current approaches for transforming assessment scores into accountability indicators include simple gain score models (with or without a vertical score scale), VAMs with very limited prior score information and perhaps none from the same subject, SGPs, and other approaches to document "growth" or "progress." Previous work (Braun, 2012; Marion et al., 2012) discussed the challenges associated with most of these approaches, reinforcing the fact that even with high-quality assessments the inferences about teacher effectiveness are dependent on much more than the nature of assessments. The properties of different analytic approaches are as significant a threat to the validity of current educator evaluation systems as assessment quality.

Attribution

Attribution is another major challenge to test-based approaches for educator evaluation. Causal attribution of current scores or changes in scores of a group of students to an individual teacher can rarely be supported by the available evidence and logic due to the influence of other (and often unobserved) factors on student test performance (Braun et al., 2010; Rothstein, 2010). Further, most students are instructed by multiple educators, directly or indirectly, so that properly connecting the performance of a particular student to the actions of a specific educator is a huge challenge. While some jurisdictions propose determining the "dosage" of educators' contributions based on such statistics as the proportions of instructional contact time, there are significant issues with obtaining accurate data to create such a metric.

Although analytics and attribution constitute significant threats to the validity of educator evaluation systems that rely on student performance results, it is beyond the scope of this chapter to address these issues in greater depth. Consequently, in the following sections, the focus is on the assessments used for educator accountability, specifically the assessments used to measure student learning in the NTSG. A primary goal is to measure student performance well at a single point in time, recognizing that assessments designed for use in educator evaluations likely must facilitate the determination of student progress or growth.

Designing and Using SLOs for Educator Evaluation

Defining SLOs as an Accountability Tool

In the rush to find methods for documenting student learning for teachers in NTSG, many state leaders initially viewed SLOs as the "last option" when more "rigorous" or "standardized" approaches were not available (Buckley & Marion, 2011). However, as the instructional potential of SLOs became more evident, they were increasingly seen as a first choice for NTSG and are now used in upwards of 30 state and district teacher evaluation systems across the United States. In fact, many states and districts are requiring, or at least making optional, the use of SLOs to supplement the information derived from standardized approaches in the tested subjects and grades (see Hall, Gagnon, Thompson, Schneider, & Marion, 2014; Lachlan-Haché, Cushing, & Bivona, 2012; Lacireno-Paquet, Morgan, & Mello, 2014; Slotnik & Smith, 2013).

SLOs provide a framework for defining and measuring content- and grade/course-specific learning objectives that can be used to document student learning over a defined period of time. The active involvement of the teacher throughout the process, including establishing learning goals and assessing the degree to which students achieve these goals, is a key advantage of the SLO approach over traditional test-centered approaches to accountability. When designed correctly, SLOs constitute an instructional improvement process for teachers in all grades and subjects while also providing important accountability information. Of course, the claim that SLOs positively contribute to instructional improvement must be supported by evidence.

SLOs include the following key components:

- learning goal(s),
- instructional strategies which facilitate students' achievement of the goal,
- targets for student and teacher performance, and
- assessments used to evaluate the learning goals.

We discuss each of these components below and use an illustrative example to make these concepts more concrete.

Clear and Meaningful Learning Goals

SLOs should reflect the relevant content standards and the corresponding curriculum to describe what students will be able to do at the end of the course/grade, or at least over a reasonably long period of instruction (e.g., a semester). The term "learning goal" is used purposefully instead of "objective" to reflect the deeper learning targets intended for SLOs, rather than the lower cognitive levels usually targeted by discrete objectives.

The learning goal(s) generally will be established by a group of teachers in the same grade and/or subject area and overseen by the district or school leadership. Typically, expectations or students' performance targets associated with the SLOs are designed to vary in concert with the current achievement levels of individuals or groups of students, but the content and skills defined by the learning goal should not vary for students in the same course/grade, much in the same way that all students are expected to learn all relevant content standards for a given grade. The learning goal for an SLO should reflect high leverage knowledge and skills of the discipline (or interdisciplinary), often referred to as a "big idea" of the discipline, and may encompass several key content standards. The learning goal may be related to an overarching school improvement goal (e.g., improvement in writing in all content areas) or may focus exclusively on the content and skills of the specific course. Multiple teachers could (and often should) be working on the same learning goals and, depending on the way in which instruction is structured (e.g., students are "shared" across multiple teachers), the results from the same SLO implemented by multiple teachers may be shared among them.

The following is an example of a learning goal from high school social studies:

> Students will independently use primary and secondary sources to explain and analyze current civics and/or political issues. Students will do so through the use of a written and oral argument that reflects an accurate and in-depth characterization of the relationship between the contemporary issue and historical precedent.

The learning goal represents key ideas in the study of history and civics, but is still somewhat general. The addition of assessments and student targets helps make the SLO more specific in terms of performance expectations.

Targets for Both Student Performance and Aggregate Targets for Educator Performance

Student Targets

The student target is the expected level of performance at the end of the instructional period. Targets may differ for students and should be appropriate, given the interval of instruction, for the whole class and for special populations (e.g., ELL, SWD). Those proposing SLOs should ensure that the student targets are both ambitious and realistic (a challenging design task). Several have suggested that teachers set targets using available baseline information to help contextualize the learning targets for individuals or groups of students (e.g., Lachlan-Haché et al., 2012; Marion et al., 2012). A description of a set of targets for the learning goal described above follows:

> These targets are based on the argumentative writing rubric scores for the teacher created tasks, as well as the three (3) formal performance tasks administered in this course over the entire school year. This is not an average of scores, but rather an evaluation of students' demonstrated consistent improvement over time in the criteria of the rubric. Since there is no state assessment for grade 12, these target grouping decisions are based on the evaluation of each of the criteria in the rubric for argumentative writing, across both teacher created and formal performance tasks throughout the school year.

- Approximately 75 percent of the 21 students starting in the low performing group at the beginning of the year will reach the proficient level on the majority of the rubric's criteria across both teacher created and formal performance tasks. The remaining students in the low performing group (5 students) will score at the nearing proficiency level on the majority of the rubric's criteria across both teacher created and formal performance tasks.
- Approximately 10 percent of the 33 students in the average performing group at the beginning of the year will score at the advanced level on the majority of the rubric's criteria. The other 30 students who started in the average performing group will score at the proficient level on the majority of the rubric's criteria with some demonstration of performance at the advanced level across both teacher created and formal performance tasks.
- 100 percent of the 6 students starting in the high performing group at the beginning of the year will score at the advanced level on the majority of the rubric's criteria across both teacher created and formal performance tasks.

This example presents one way of establishing SLO targets; setting ambitious and reasonable targets for SLOs is one of the most challenging aspects of SLO design and implementation. This has been the focus of several recent national meetings as states wrestle with how to approach this in fair and valid ways.[9]

Instructional Strategies

Instructional strategies comprise the approaches and tools that teachers use to help their students meet the learning goals. These can include differentiating instruction for students based on base-line and ongoing assessment information, as well as employing specific interventions if students are failing to make adequate progress. In theory, employing these instructional strategies should help teachers to improve their practice through a more concentrated focus on student progress toward meeting the learning goals. Further, linking these instructional strategies to the SLO will provide teachers with assessment evidence to evaluate how well the instructional strategies are working and what adjustments might be needed.

Teacher Targets

Teacher targets specify how the student aggregate scores (results) will be used to determine the degree to which the teacher has met the SLO targets and whether these results will be employed directly or transformed into an indicator for use in accountability determinations. In some cases these targets are set by the state, but more typically by the district in conjunction with school leaders. Ideally, school leaders will tailor the targets, in consultation with teachers, to account for specific classroom contexts. Typically, teacher targets and the corresponding performance rating are classified into three or four levels. For example, a teacher may be classified under "not meeting" if less than 50 percent of the students reach their target, "meeting" if 51–85 percent of the students reach their target, and "exceeding" if more than 85 percent of the students reach their target. Obviously, the appropriateness of these targets is contingent upon the learning goal, assessments, and student targets. It will take several years of data collection and analysis to evaluate the appropriateness of these targets.

Assessments Used to Evaluate Students' Achievement of the Learning Goals

The assessments used to evaluate the degree to which students have achieved the learning goals should be of high quality; that is, they should be designed to provide credible evidence of student learning of the specific learning goal. First, if the learning goals are of the rich form described above—our preference if they are to motivate high-quality instruction—it is unlikely that they will be measured well with just a single assessment. Multiple assessments will be required, and we argue that a performance or other authentic assessment must be part of the assessment system designed to evaluate the learning goal. An example of a prompt for a task related to the learning goal presented earlier follows. This example calls on students to engage in key practices of histor-ical reasoning by using primary and secondary sources to analyze current events in the context of historical events. Further, the example exemplifies the extended nature of this task as well as the instructional scaffolding that may be necessary for students to fully engage in the summative tasks.

> The current civil war in Syria, with well over 100,000 casualties, has prompted calls from world leaders for either intervening on the side of the rebels or otherwise imposing a cease-fire. However, the American people and their legislative leaders, as seen in the results of many opinion polls and the lack of legislative action to authorize military action in Syria,

appear opposed to entering another foreign conflict. This is far from the first time that the U.S. populace has opposed foreign action. Analyze the situation with U.S. views toward Syria and other Middle East hotspots in light of American attitudes prior to WWI and WWII. What is similar? What is different? Use primary and secondary sources to document and support your views. The responses to this task will be scored with a multi-dimensional rubric focused on historical analysis, argumentative writing, use of sources, and quality of writing and presentation.

Additionally, students will have monthly opportunities to demonstrate their ability to use various identified texts (primary and secondary sources) to respond to informal and formal teacher developed prompts requiring them to form an argument regarding a civic/government concept. At least three times during the year students will respond to a prompt on a formal assessment.

Role for Performance-Based Assessments in SLOs

As noted above, assessing rich learning goals requires that performance-based or other direct/ authentic measures must be part of the assessment mix, if not the main assessment tool. However, as discussed elsewhere in this chapter, and as Messick (1994) pointed out, performance assessments are not valid for the intended uses simply because they are called performance (or direct or authentic) assessments. Messick argued that calling something a performance or authentic assessment is a "promissory note" for validity, but the name alone does not constitute validity evidence. Further validating assessments for high-stakes accountability uses is a major undertaking (e.g., Herman, Heritage, & Goldschmidt, 2011; Kane, 2006), and users should devise appropriate strategies and develop the capacity for this purpose. In the section that follows, we discuss design considerations for performance assessments linked to SLOs so that such assessments may be more than a "promissory note."

Design Considerations for Assessments Used with SLOs

Principled Assessment Design

The design considerations for assessments used to evaluate SLOs should follow the same basic principles as the design of other high-quality assessments. SLOs, however, are intended to serve both instructional and accountability purposes. This dual purpose creates a greater design challenge than is the case for an assessment created for a single purpose. SLOs may help address this issue, but the real promise from SLOs is derived from the tight linkage between learning goal and assessment, which is hard to achieve with more distal, standardized assessments. The intentional connection among learning, instruction,[10] and assessment makes SLOs particularly well suited to using a principled approach to design such as Evidence-Centered Design (ECD; Mislevy, 1994) or following the assessment triangle as articulated in Knowing What Students Know (Pellegrino, Chudowsky, & Glaser, 2001). In its simplest formulation, the core of the ECD framework comprises a student model, an evidence model, and a task model. The student model describes the intended construct(s) or learning outcome(s); the evidence model, which links task and student models, describes the nature of the evidence that would convince one that the students mastered the intended knowledge and skills associated with the construct; and the task model describes the types of assessments that will elicit the desired evidence. The SLO design team should specify the student model, which operationalizes the intended construct, and make explicit the nature of the evidence needed to support the claim that the student has achieved the learning goal. Finally, the design team must create the tasks that can elicit the required evidence.

Specific Design Requirements for SLOs

Most state laws, the federal RTTT initiative, and the NCLB flexibility waiver regulations require the use of student growth measures for all teachers, for both tested and non-tested subjects and grades. Although the challenges to such a broad-based requirement have been described elsewhere (Baker et al., 2010; Marion et al., 2012), there is still a reasonable expectation that SLOs should be able to document some aspects of student progress. Pretest–posttest models, including those that employ complex analytic models, are generally not appropriate for SLOs because of the technical challenges described above, but also because of insufficient sample sizes and assessment information necessary for complex models.[11] Even though many states and districts using SLOs attempt to employ some type of pretest/posttest design to support simple growth models, this is problematic for both technical and practical reasons; in particular, it requires validating both tests as well as evaluating the degree to which the derived score (e.g., gain score, VAM score) is technically defensible. Moreover, the greater measurement error associated with simple gain scores is well known (Linn, 1981). A further challenge to the pretest/posttest design is the corruptibility of such designs, which is particularly true of SLOs since those who will be evaluated on the assessment results are often the ones scoring the assessments (Marion et al., 2012).

Nonetheless, SLOs do require some form of conditioning on baseline performance, so that students are held to expectations appropriate to their initial achievement levels (Marion et al., 2012). To be fair, this can introduce additional opportunities for corrupting SLOs because teachers may be incentivized to document lower levels of baseline performance than is actually the case. Further, the task(s) presented to the students must have the capability of eliciting a range of student performances so that the assessment generates useful information along a continuum of proficiency.

Validity Considerations in the Design of SLOs

A full exploration of technical issues related to performance assessments is the focus of the next chapter; however, here we address some key issues, especially how they should be taken into account during the design phase. Messick (1989, 1994) identified construct-irrelevant variance and construct underrepresentation as two major threats to validity and, as with all assessments, both are significant concerns in the design and evaluation of assessments associated with SLOs. Lack of generalizability and comparability are two additional, but related, threats to the validity of the assessment components of SLOs that assume greater importance in the context of accountability.

Construct-Irrelevant Variance

Construct-irrelevant variance—the need to rely on knowledge and skills other than those associated with the specific construct/learning goals—is a threat to the validity of inferences from complex performance assessments (Linn et al., 1991). For example, many performance assessments are language-intensive both in terms of setting up or contextualizing the problem and in requiring students to respond in writing or other forms of representation. This can be problematic, especially for second language learners and many students with disabilities. Although it might make sense for literacy-based assessments, many commentators have expressed concerns that performances in subjects such as mathematics or the sciences may include language demands that are "irrelevant," or at least not central, to the target construct (Dolan & Hall, 2001).

In this respect, there is much to be learned from efforts to promote Universal Design for Learning (UDL) and related approaches for promoting fair assessment and learning opportunities for all students (e.g., Dolan & Hall, 2001; Thompson, Johnstone, & Thurlow, 2002). The UDL work has prompted assessment designers to consider the construct-relevant and -irrelevant aspects of tasks at the outset. In the case of SLOs, designers must always specify the knowledge and skills required for successful attainment of the learning goal. For example, the SLO learning goal should describe the extent to which written explanation (e.g., proof) is necessary for the successful demonstration of target mathematical competencies. The assessment task(s) should then be designed with a focus on the learning goal and avoid, to the extent possible, requiring extraneous competencies.

Meeting this design challenge requires careful delineation of the relevant facets of the construct, as well as extensive analysis of student work. In this regard, cognitive laboratories, among other approaches that seek to elicit students' thinking and reasoning processes, are necessary to evaluate whether the designers have been successful. Even after doing such work, there are still disagreements whether or not a particular skill is part of the intended constructs or whether it may contribute to construct-irrelevant variance. These difficulties are exacerbated because teachers are often the designers of SLO assessments and most lack the expertise to recognize and properly address the assessment issues discussed here. Therefore, advocates of SLOs should provide tools and learning opportunities to help educators meet the design challenges discussed here. We offer some specific suggestions later in the chapter.

Construct Underrepresentation

In the context of SLOs, Messick's second major threat, construct underrepresentation, operates on two levels. To evaluate construct underrepresentation, one must consider the extent to which the assessment task(s), or, more precisely, the responses to the tasks, fully represent the intended facets of the learning goal. This is critical to the determination of the validity of the assessment component of the SLO and, ultimately, of the full SLO itself. However, SLOs not only yield student-level score inferences but also, for purposes of accountability, aggregate student performances are used to characterize the extent to which teachers have contributed to improving student learning.

Therefore, in addition to construct underrepresentation of a specific SLO, one must consider the extent to which the collection of SLOs proposed by the teacher fully represents the "construct set" of a course. For example, a particular task may be very well matched to an SLO goal, but that single SLO represents only a portion of the target domain. In that case, what inferences can be made about a teacher's contribution to student learning at the class level? In designing assessments to evaluate SLOs, one must first consider the degree to which the task (or tasks) can generate appropriate evidence with respect to the claim (or claims) associated with each individual SLO. Equally important, designers should determine if the collection of SLOs for the course fully represents the relevant content standards and then whether the assessments linked to each SLO are capable of eliciting evidence of competency.

An analogy that might help in understanding this issue is the relationship between test items and test forms. Each item might be high quality and well aligned to the target, but when the set of items is assembled into a test form, one might find that the construct is not well represented by the test form. At least in the early years of implementation, when it is rare that teachers are required to implement more than two SLOs, it appears that this second level of construct underrepresentation will indeed threaten the validity of the central inference—that teachers have (or have not) successfully contributed to improvements in student learning. Therefore, when there are a limited number of SLOs, the learning goals should target the most important aspects of the course and/or discipline.

Generalizability

Many researchers, working within a generalizability framework, have raised concerns about the number of complex performance tasks necessary for achieving a stable measure of performance (e.g., Cronbach, Linn, Brennan, & Haertel, 1997; Shavelson, Baxter, & Pine, 1992), with the often repeated recommendation from Shavelson et al. (1992) that 6–12 performance tasks are required to obtain a stable estimate of student performance. The generalizability of performance assessments is critical for understanding the degree to which inferences about student proficiency in a target domain can be supported by their responses to a limited number of performance tasks. In classical reliability theory, score variance is partitioned into true variance and error variance, whereas in generalizability theory, analysis of variance techniques are marshaled to estimate proportions of variance in a set of scores that can be attributed to different sources of variation such as time, tasks, persons, and raters (Brennan, 1992; Shavelson & Webb, 1991). Generalizability theory provides an analytic framework to help evaluate the extent to which the scores based on a sample of the relevant facets (e.g., items, raters) may generalize to a score drawn from the universe of all possible items, raters, and other relevant facets (Brennan, 1992; Cronbach et al., 1997).

The main challenges to the generalizability of the scores yielded by performance tasks have been attributed to person-by-task ($p \times t$) interaction and person-by-task-by-occasion-by-rater ($p \times t \times o \times r$) interaction. These interaction effects can influence proficiency estimates depending on how the assessment system is designed. When many tasks and/or items are used, the main effect (i.e., person achievement) dominates the interactions, but it is not often practical to incorporate many extended performance tasks in a given assessment.

This is not just an academic argument. It has had significant practical implications over the past 20 years. For example, Koretz and colleagues (Hambleton et al., 1995; Koretz, Klein, McCaffrey, & Stecher, 1993) authored several critiques that contributed to eliminating or curtailing several ambitious performance assessment initiatives such as the Vermont Portfolio System and the Kentucky mathematics and writing portfolios.

Unfortunately, in our view, the critics were correct about the wrong thing. They focused on the generalizability of individual student scores. This is not surprising since most reliability and generalizability studies to that point had investigated the consistency and dependability of individual scores. However, the policies around the performance assessment projects discussed above were focused on school-level inferences such as those designed to support school accountability designs. Hill and DePascale (2003a) demonstrated quite conclusively that school accountability determinations can be quite reliable even when the individual student scores that comprise the school scores may fall below what many consider to be acceptable levels of individual reliability.[12] This is germane to our discussion of the ways in which authentic assessments as part of SLOs are used to support inferences about teacher quality and not individual students. There is no question that assessments should be as reliable as possible (or practical) for students. Nonetheless, for inferences about teachers, the number of students being measured by the SLO has a greater influence on the reliability of the inference of interest. This may mean pooling students across multiple teachers using the same SLO to get a more stable estimate of overall performance and having the teachers "share the attribution" of all of the students in the sample.[13]

Fortunately, much has been learned over the last two decades about the design of performance tasks to yield improved generalizability (e.g., Herman, Aschbacher, & Winters, 1992; Wiggins & McTighe, 2005; Yen & Ferrara, 1997). These include more tightly defined tasks and scoring rubrics, along with improved methods of training and monitoring raters. However, if a single task is used to evaluate the learning associated with a SLO, it is highly unlikely that the inferences associated with the student results will meet acceptable levels of reliability/generalizability. This limitation can be addressed by adding more tasks or designing tasks with multiple, scorable dimensions to help stabilize estimates of performance. We note that adding more dimensions to the same task will typically not have the same beneficial effect on generalizability as adding more independent tasks, but still yields some improvement over tasks scored on a single dimension (Yen & Ferrara, 1997). However, this approach adds to the already heavy responsibilities faced by school personnel as they attempt to meet the SLO development requirements imposed by many states.[14]

Further, as in the case of construct representation, SLO designers need to be clear about the target domain for generalization. The first level of generalization focuses on student responses to the task (or tasks) associated with a specific SLO. The second level is from the results of a set of SLOs to a characterization of student proficiency in the course. This second level of generalization, when aggregated over students, leads to the decision inference (Kane, 2006) that, in the context of teacher evaluation, relies on an assumption of causal attribution. The problems of causal attribution in contexts with notable selection forces have been well documented (e.g., Braun et al., 2010; Rothstein, 2010), but we do not address the issue of causal attribution in this chapter as it involves much more than performance on SLOs.

Designers must attempt to support both levels of generalization. The first level is a necessary but not sufficient condition for generalizability at the second level. By attending to the design phase at the second level of generalization, designers have the opportunity to explore alternative strategies for improving the generalizability at the course and, ultimately, the teacher level. This relationship between SLO assessments to generate individual student scores and the set of SLOs to make inferences regarding teaching effectiveness highlights the way that accountability systems (should) influence the design of SLOs and related assessments. If the major purpose of assessments associated with SLOs is to provide defensible information at the aggregate level, systems designs may include more tasks distributed over a larger number of students than if the desire was to achieve comparable results for all students. However, there are practical limitations with such a suggestion.

Unfortunately, there are still many unknowns. For example, are the results of multiple assessments associated with a single SLO more or less generalizable than having multiple SLOs, each with a single assessment? It is likely that the answer is contingent, at least in part, upon the nature of learning goals associated with the SLOs. A related question concerns the "grain size" of learning goals. Many SLO designers favor a "Goldilocks" criterion (not too big, not too small), which is based implicitly on considerations of both generalizability and appropriate targets for learning (Lachlan-Haché et al., 2012; Thompson & Marion, 2013). Would a larger grain size SLO that was fully evaluated with a range of assessment evidence lead to more generalizable inferences about student learning in the course in comparison to several smaller grain size SLOs each with its own specific assessment? This is an important area for investigation as SLOs become more prevalent components of teacher evaluation systems and as relevant data is generated on a large scale.

One of the challenges, as well as a major strength of SLOs, is that the design should be carried out by those with the most knowledge of the intended learning outcomes. This must include teachers, preferably working collaboratively with content and assessment experts, but often it will be individual teachers, or small groups of teachers, working on their own. The design challenges discussed here are typically beyond the competence of those without expert knowledge in assessment and accountability. However, such experts, working with practitioners, can craft a set of design exemplars and guidance documents, along with other training and disseminated materials, to encourage more technically defensible approaches for the design of SLOs and associated assessments.[15]

Comparability and Accountability

Comparability is mentioned frequently as a critical aspect of technical quality for assessments, particularly when assessments are used for accountability purposes. What is comparability and why is it so important? In the context of accountability, it is linked to the notion of fairness. If many individuals (e.g., teachers) are expected to adhere to the same rules and be subjected to the same requirements, then generally there is an expectation that the same or similar processes and approaches are followed in making judgments about each of the individuals. This is especially important in educator accountability systems because there is an assumption that a teacher's rating should not be contingent upon the subject, grade, or even the school where they happen to teach.[16] Although the goal of full psychometric invariance is clearly out of reach, it is still important to design systems so that stakeholders feel confident that all social studies teachers, for example, are being held to a similar standard. At the next level of the system, the challenge of holding all the teachers in a school, district, or state to a similar standard is likely impossible to meet. In trying to promote comparability, designers typically try to create highly standardized (i.e., common) assessment experiences. On the other hand, such standardization may undermine the validity of score inferences because some students will be administered assessments that are not closely related to their learning experiences.

This trade-off between flexibility and standardization is not new and is certainly not unique to SLOs. Flexibility (or standardization) is not necessarily good or bad in terms of assessment quality. Having a high-quality assessment or set of assessments is critical to evaluate student learning in relation to a specific learning goal. There is great value in having common assessments across teachers working on the same learning goals, but commonality and standardization should not be the deciding factor if that means that students are administered assessments that are either not closely related to their learning opportunities or at a level far above or below their level of proficiency.

Authentic assessments, particularly in specialized and/or elective courses, may need to vary in the degree of standardization required to support the intended inferences and accountability uses. It would be counterproductive to administer the same assessment to all students in an art class, for example, who have entered the class with a wide range of skills and experiences. Similarly, with the push toward individualized learning opportunities in many schools and courses, it may be inappropriate to require all students to take the same assessment. This is not an argument against common assessments. Rather, it is an argument against clinging to standardization at all costs.[17]

Fortunately, we can draw from recent experiences with designing assessments for students with the most significant cognitive disabilities who participate in alternate assessments based on alternate achievement standards (AA-AAS), as well as work with Advanced Placement Studio Art (Myford & Mislevy, 1995). Rather than conceptualizing the degree of standardization along a unidimensional scale, Gong and Marion (2006) devised a framework comprising the multiple dimensions on which AA-AAS may vary from highly standardized to highly flexible or idiosyncratic. Although the specific dimensions of flexibility/standardization along which performance-based assessments for teacher evaluation vary will be somewhat different than what Gong and Marion (2006) outlined for AA-AAS, the important point is to stipulate a priori that the dimensions along which assessments for SLOs or other accountability mechanisms should be allowed to vary. SLOs, for example, can vary with respect to the learning goals, assessments, student performance targets, and aggregate teacher targets.

Rigid adherence to strict comparability may unintentionally interfere with the instructional goals associated with SLOs—goals that arguably are more fundamental than strict comparability. Furthermore, European and Australian measurement specialists have shown that there are alternative approaches for accomplishing the key goals of comparability. For example, the Queensland Studies Authority's (2010) social moderation methods have been well documented for achieving moderate comparability among school-based assessments across an entire Australian state.

From our examination of state educator evaluation plans (Buckley & Marion, 2011; Hall et al., 2014), as well as through interactions with state policymakers, we find that there is a widespread assumption, or at least a hope, that systems can be designed to ensure comparability of teacher evaluation ratings across schools and districts. However, since many aspects of SLOs will have to vary due to differences in curriculum and other relevant dimensions, we have found it helpful to conceptualize a comparability gradient, ranging from micro to macro levels of an educational system:

1   across students for the same teacher;
2   across teachers in the same school and same content area;
3   across teachers in the same school and different content areas;
4   across teachers in different schools and the same content area; and
5   across teachers in different schools and different content areas.

We note that achieving comparability is difficult, even if all teachers are using SLOs. In many cases, however, the challenge is greater because some teachers will be evaluated with SLOs and others with scores derived from VAM or SGP models. In fact, in many schools, some teachers will be evaluated with multiple approaches, so even obtaining a single composite score for these teachers is not a trivial exercise.

Strict psychometric comparability across students, for the same teacher, may not be achievable if students are permitted to complete the assessment at markedly different times or if the assessment includes different ancillary materials that depend on student interest and/or achievement. However, it appears that at present most SLOs are being designed to require the same assessment(s) for students who share the same goal. The expected performance targets may vary depending on students' initial achievement, but students in the same class/course are generally participating in the same or very similar assessment.

Earlier discussions of SLOs (e.g., Marion & Buckley, 2011) suggested that SLOs generally would be constructed by individual teachers in the context of their own classes. However, the lack of curricular and assessment capacity for creating high-quality SLOs at classroom and school levels has led to the more prevalent approach of having district- or even state-created SLOs. This is also due to the understandable desire on the part of the state to ensure a reasonable degree of comparability across schools, within the district or the state. Often, individual teachers in conjunction with school leaders are allowed to modify these "common" SLOs, or at least modify the performance targets for students and teachers, to reflect the considerable differences in student populations. Such adaptation is certainly a threat to comparability in a strict sense. But if the goal is to determine the degree to which the teacher has contributed to student learning over the course of a year, it is counterproductive to use an SLO and its associated assessment that is either too easy or too difficult for students. These considerations certainly influence the strict comparability of SLO results for teachers in the same content area at the same grade level (#2 and #4 from the list above). When students participate in the same curriculum, the challenge to comparability will be less than when students participate in different curricula, even within the same school or district.

Most current teacher evaluation systems are designed as policy instruments based on implicit theories of action about how to improve teaching quality and student learning. As such, there is often an explicit or implicit goal to hold all teachers to the same standard in terms of the various dimensions of teacher quality. One of the goals in employing SLOs is to achieve comparable levels of rigor and equivalent expectations of performance for teachers regardless of the subject and grade. This is especially important within a school to minimize competition and conflict among teachers who, ideally, should be working collaboratively toward a common set of goals. At this point, there is very little empirical information regarding the extent of comparability in various settings, but it is an important area of study in the near future. A step in the right direction would be to employ a common design template and rubric for evaluating the quality of SLOs.

For example, measurement specialists acknowledge that state reading and math test scores cannot be truly compared. Nonetheless, because they share similarities in design, development, administration, and psychometric processes, most stakeholders do not question the comparability of the results from these two sets of tests at the student and, by extension, the teacher level. At this juncture, SLOs generally do not have the empirical and procedural documentation associated with state assessments, so there is a need for evidence regarding the assertion that all teachers are being held to similar levels of expectations.

As noted above, the state of Queensland has established a multi-layered approach for establishing comparability of results despite differences in the assessments (Queensland Studies Authority, 2010). In Queensland, "senior secondary exams" are designed, administered, and scored by local school personnel and are used to evaluate student learning at the end of a two-year high school course of study and for the high-stakes determination of eligibility for admission to postsecondary institutions. Queensland has implemented a hierarchal review process based on social moderation procedures used by the British Office of the Qualifications and Examinations Regulator (Newton, 2007) and by others: Student work and assessment scores are first reviewed within school and then at the district, region, and state levels. Although such an approach might be too elaborate and labor-intensive for already burdened educators working feverishly to implement new evaluation systems, the use of common criteria to evaluate the quality of SLOs and associated assessments may help provide some assurance that educators and their students are being held to similar expectations. An example of such a rubric developed by our colleagues at the Center for Assessment (Thompson & Marion, 2013) is contained in Appendix A.

Assuring comparability of expectations using this judgmental approach will likely work better within smaller units such as schools or perhaps even districts where shared understandings of quality can be developed. It may be possible in larger units if a formal peer review process is used. Although such judgmental approaches can help to provide some level of credibility for the assessments and targets associated with SLOs, technical designers and advisors need to be frank with policymakers about the severe limits on comparability of inferences across teachers. Further, states and districts should plan to monitor the SLO system and identify areas where procedures need to be modified.

Corruptibility and Accountability

We have argued that SLOs may be used appropriately for supporting inferences regarding educators' contributions to student learning as part of teacher evaluation systems. However, we would be remiss if we did not return to the discussion of potential unintended negative consequences, particularly with regard to cheating and other forms of corruption, and how these threats must be addressed in the design of the SLO package.

Outright cheating, which can certainly occur, clearly undermines SLO validity. But there are also more subtle threats. High-stakes uses of SLO results can lead to a narrowing of the curriculum with a focus on the knowledge and skills for which teachers will be held accountable. Although SLOs should identify the highest priority learning goals for a course, these are likely not the only learning goals. Consequently, care should be taken to make sure that other important goals are not neglected. This can be accomplished by requiring multiple SLOs for each teacher so that each of the learning goals targets highly important but different aspects of the curriculum. Additionally, states and districts can require SLOs to be refreshed over time to avoid having teachers fall into a curricular rut. Further, SLOs may be supplemented with more conventional end-of-course assessments to support the inferences drawn directly from SLO assessments. Of course, including additional assessments will require thoughtful approaches for combining the multiple assessment results.

It could be argued that having rich assessments (to match rich learning goals) designed to evaluate deeper learning and from which students have to generate complex responses constitutes a "test worth teaching to." Such a claim must be substantiated with empirical evidence. One strategy for evaluating the validity of the SLO could involve the use of an "audit" assessment to provide a basis for comparing the performance of students on the SLO assessments. The externally designed audit assessment may produce noticeably discrepant results, such as very low correlations and weak classification consistency, which should trigger additional investigations.

A related strategy would include using SLOs in tested grades where the SLO results could be compared to SGP or VAM results. In fact, one team of researchers proposed using the subsequent VAM score predicted from the NTSG approach as a way to evaluate the validity of the NTSG method (Croft et al., 2011). If the SLO score, for example, predicted the subsequent year VAM score similarly to the degree to which VAM in one year predicted VAM in a subsequent year, one could be confident that SLOs were at least as accurate as VAM. While we disagree with some of the methodological approaches proposed by these authors, the general framework could provide useful information for evaluating the quality and corruptibility of SLOs. The results of the two different measures would not be expected to be the same, but they should not be widely discrepant. Given the small sample sizes associated with many teachers, it would not be unreasonable to see results that appear inconsistent for individual teachers, but across many teachers, it seems reasonable to expect moderate correlations, limited by the reliability of multiple measures.

In an accountability context, there will likely be considerable pressure to lower both student and teacher performance targets associated with SLOs in order to have more teachers receive high (effective) ratings. Since SLO targets for students and teachers are generally established by teachers in concert with their school administrators, this is a distinct possibility. On the other hand, there is little evidence at this point that teachers and administrators have the necessary expertise to establish realistic and ambitious targets. Lowering the performance targets for students runs counter to the policy goal of preparing students for college and careers, but could occur due to the personal relationships among teachers and administrators. We note that this type of pressure is similar to the challenges of providing honest and critical feedback (including lower ratings than teachers might like) on classroom observations. Accountability system designers should assume that these pressures will exist and take them into account in the design and implementation phases.

Finally, employing a peer review process like the Queensland system (QSA, 2010) described above could provide feedback to schools and districts about the relative rigor of their SLOs and provide an audit mechanism for the state. Samples of SLOs, including assessments, targets, and student work, could be reviewed against agreed-upon criteria. Such reviews could help determine the degree to which the pressure to lower targets or use less rigorous assessments has been manifest in some schools and districts.

Given these potential threats, why should one expect that SLOs linked to authentic assessments will lead to positive outcomes overall? First, when designed and implemented as described in this chapter, SLOs should fit seamlessly into the existing curriculum and instructional program with the added benefit of making more explicit the long-term learning goals for students. Although we support strategies of gradual implementation with only one or two SLOs required for each teacher, we believe that the instructional and accountability benefits will really accrue when teachers are implementing more SLOs—on the order of four or more—covering varying time spans (e.g., full year, a semester). Because of the promise of more strongly tying accountability to instruction, SLOs offer hope for creating a more constructive accountability and improvement system than the "drop-from-the-sky" externally mandated assessments and complex analytic models (see Hargreaves & Braun, 2013 for a detailed exposition of data-driven improvement and accountability). Circling back to the beginning, we argue that SLOs incorporating performance-based assessments are more likely to achieve these policy aims than SLOs employing tests targeted toward lower cognitive levels. Beyond the learning benefits associated with performance-based assessments, such assessments generate a record of student work products that make it less likely that educators will succumb to the temptation to lower student and teacher targets than is the case when the work consists of responses to a computer-administered multiple-choice test.

Closing Thoughts

The principal focus of this chapter has been the design of performance-based assessments for use in the context of high-stakes teacher evaluations, particularly through the use of SLOs. SLOs are a "package deal," so that the quality of assessments must be evaluated in light of the associated learning goals and performance targets. We argued that a principled approach to assessment design, such as ECD, is well matched to SLOs, where the student, evidence, and task models are a natural fit with the design of the SLO goals, student and teacher performance targets, and assessments used to evaluate the learning. SLOs offer a potential advantage over other approaches for evaluating teachers in NTSG, as they should have instructional value in their own right. This supports the ultimate goal of educational accountability—enhancing student learning through improved teaching and school quality (Elmore, 2004; Hargreaves & Braun, 2013).

As we have noted throughout, much more empirical evidence is needed to evaluate the assertions and hopes put forth in this chapter. Mandates for incorporating evidence of student learning in teacher evaluations have contributed to the proliferation of SLOs in many states and districts, even though districts could have mounted such efforts without tying the results to teacher evaluations. The policy pressure for new forms of evaluation has created an opportunity for widespread adoption of SLOs. We have argued that SLOs will be more likely to fulfill the intended aims of improvements in learning and instruction if they are accompanied by rich, performance-based assessments. Nonetheless, more research is needed to better understand the consequential impact of various types of assessments for use in educator effectiveness systems and accountability systems in general.

Appendix A: A Rubric for Evaluating the Quality of SLOs (Thompson & Marion, 2013)

This rubric is for use by teachers, school administration, and district administration to evaluate the quality of SLOs prior to being used for teacher performance ratings.

	Acceptable Quality	*Quality Needs Improvement*	*Insufficient Quality*
Learning Goal A description of what students will be able to do at the end of the course or grade based on course- or grade-level content standards and curriculum. • Acceptable Quality • Quality Needs Improvement • Insufficient Quality	Appropriately identifies and thoroughly describes an important and meaningful learning goal, with a clear explanation of: • the big idea and the standard(s) that are thoughtfully aligned to and measured by the learning goal,	Identifies and provides a description of a learning goal that is either too specific or too general, with a weak explanation of: • the big idea and/ or standards that minimally align to the learning goal,	Identifies and provides an unclear description of a learning goal that is vague, trivial, or unessential, with: • the big idea and/ or standards not aligned to the learning goal,

	• the critical nature of the learning goal for students in the specific grade/course, • how the learning goal allows students to demonstrate *deep* understanding of the content standards within the identified time span, and • specific and appropriate instruction and strategies used to teach the learning goal.	• the importance of the learning goal for students in the specific grade/course, • how the learning goal allows students to demonstrate *adequate* understanding of the content standards within the identified time span, and/or • some generic instruction and strategies used to teach the learning goal.	• lack of information of the importance of the learning goal for students in the specific grade/course, • little to no description of how the learning goal allows students to demonstrate understanding of the content standards in the identified time span, and/or • questionable and/or vague instruction and strategies used to teach the learning goal.
Assessments and Scoring Assessments should be standards-based, of high quality, and be designed to best measure the knowledge and skills found in the goal of this SLO. They should be accompanied by clear criteria or rubrics to determine student learning from the assessment. • Acceptable Quality • Quality Needs Improvement • Insufficient Quality	Appropriately identifies and clearly describes: • documented high-quality assessment(s) used to measure the learning goal, • rubrics that appropriately and thoughtfully differentiate student performance, and • progress-monitoring measures that will be used, including how instruction will be differentiated for all learners based on this information.	Identifies and provides some description, which may lack specificity, of the: • assessment(s) and partial explanation of how the quality has been established, • rubrics that partially differentiate student performance, and/or • progress-monitoring measures used with little detail in how instruction will be differentiated based on this information.	Identifies and provides an unclear, insufficient, or confusing description of the: • assessment(s) with minimal or no reference to how the quality has been established, • scoring rubrics with minimal or no reference of how student performance has been differentiated, and/or • progress-monitoring measures used with minimal or no reference to the differentiation of learners based on this information.

(Continued)

(Continued)

	Acceptable Quality	*Quality Needs Improvement*	*Insufficient Quality*
Targets Identify the expected outcomes by the end of the instructional period for the whole class as well as for different subgroups, as appropriate. • Acceptable Quality • Quality Needs Improvement • Insufficient Quality	Clearly and thoroughly explains how the data are used to define teacher performance, including: • the baseline data/information used to establish and differentiate these targets, and • rigorous targets that are realistic and attainable for each group of students.	Broadly, without specificity, explains how the data are used to define teacher performance and may include: • unclear baseline data/information used to establish and differentiate these targets, and/or • targets that are imprecise, somewhat realistic, and/or attainable for each group of students.	Provides an unclear, insufficient, or confusing explanation of how the data are used to define teacher performance and may include: • baseline data/information not aligned to the SLO, and/or • arbitrary or unattainable targets for each group of students.

Notes

1 *Products* are sometimes thought of as a separate category of assessment form, but we argue that products are really one possible outcome or piece of evidence derived from a performance assessment.

2 Partnership for Assessment of Readiness for College and Careers; see http://www.parcconline.org/

3 Smarter Balanced Assessment Consortium; see http://www.smarterbalanced.org/smarter-balanced-assessments/

4 We acknowledge that there may be other reasons, but we contend these are the most important.

5 See http://www.corestandards.org/

6 See http://www.parcconline.org/ and http://www.smarterbalanced.org/smarter-balanced-assessments/, respectively.

7 District accountability systems were more commonplace prior to the focus on schools ushered in with the NCLB. While many states still employ some forms of district accountability, the major focus of accountability systems in current policy is on the school, educators, and students, which is where we focus our discussion.

8 The other primary validity issue related to test use for teacher accountability is that of causal attribution, which we discuss later in the chapter.

9 This topic could fill an entire chapter, but for now see Marion et al. (2012) and Reform Support Network (2014).

10 The instructional strategies associated with SLOs are included in many SLO templates, and if part of a well-designed educator evaluation system, the SLO can also provide evidence related to teacher practices. Using SLOs to bridge the two major aspects of educator evaluation—teacher practices and student learning—is discussed in Marion (2014).

11 Many of these models are "data hungry," requiring hundreds or, better, thousands of students in the sample. However, even high school teachers rarely have more than 180 students or so, while elementary teachers generally have less than 35 students.

12 Most measurement professionals, including the critics noted above, would like to see individual student-level reliabilities of at least 0.9, but Hill and DePascale (2003b) demonstrated that acceptable levels of reliability of accountability determinations can be made when student-level reliability is much lower: "For example, if a school has 50 students, the reliability of a school mean will be higher if the reliability of student results is .60 than when a school with 25 students and the reliability of individual student results is .90" (Hill & DePascale, 2003b, p. 3).

13 While "shared attribution" ameliorates several problems (e.g., reliability, potential competition among educators), it may also introduce threats to the validity of the system as well (e.g., masking poor-performing teachers). Therefore, system designers will need to weigh the advantages and disadvantages of shared attribution carefully in the design of their systems.

14 In spite of the practical challenges, states and districts will have to—over time—conduct validity evaluations of their educator evaluation systems that should include generalizability studies to help understand the issues raised here and perhaps modify the system designs in light of this technical information.

15 See, for example, the Center for Assessment's SLO Toolkit at http://www.nciea.org

16 Although we know that factors like subject, grade, and types of students, along with many others, can make a big difference in how teachers and their students perform.

17 For example, many recognize the advantages of the way that computer adaptive testing tailors each test to the achievement level of each individual student within certain constraints.

References

Achieve. (2004). *Do graduation tests measure up? A closer look at state high school exit exams.* Washington, DC: Achieve.

Baker, E. L., Barton, P. E., Darling-Hammond, L., Haertel, E., Ladd, H. F., Linn, R. L., . . . Shepard, L. A. (2010, August). *Problems with the use of student test scores to evaluate teachers.* EPI Briefing Paper #278. Washington, DC: Economic Policy Institute.

Bell, C. A., Gitomer, D. H., McCaffrey, D. F., Hamre, B. K., Pianta, R. C., & Qi, Y. (2013). An argument approach to observation protocol validity. *Educational Assessment, 17*(2–3), 62–87.

Braun, H. (2012, September). Paper presented at the Reidy Interactive Lecture Series, Portsmouth, NH.

Braun, H., Chudowsky, N., & Koenig, J. A. (2010). *Getting value out of value-added: Report of a workshop.* Washington, DC: The National Academies Press.

Brennan, R. L. (1992). *Elements of generalizability theory.* Iowa City, IA: American College Testing Program.

Briggs, D. C. (2013). Making value-added inferences from large-scale assessments. In M. Simon, K. Ercikan, & M. Rousseau (Eds.), *Improving large-scale assessment in education: Theory, issues and practice.* London, UK: Routledge.

Buckley, K., & Marion, S. F. (2011). *A survey of approaches used to evaluate educators in non-tested grades and subjects.* Retrieved from http://www.nciea.org/publications/Summary%20of%20Approaches%20for%20non-tested%20gradesKBSM2011.pdf

Campbell, D. T. (1976, December). *Assessing the impact of planned social change.* The Public Affairs Center, Dartmouth College, Hanover, New Hampshire, USA.

Conley, D. (2007). *Redefining college readiness.* Eugene, OR: Educational Policy Improvement Center.

Conley, D. (2013). *Getting ready for college, careers, and the Common Core: What every educator needs to know.* San Francisco, CA: Jossey-Bass.

Croft, M., Glazerman, S., Goldhaber, D., Loeb, S., Raudenbush, S., Staiger, D., & Whitehurst, G. J. (2011, April). *Passing muster: Evaluating teacher evaluation systems.* Washington, DC: The Brookings Brown Center Task Group on Teacher Quality. Retrieved from http://www.brookings.edu/reports/2011/0426_evaluating_teachers.aspx

Cronbach, L. J., Linn, R. L., Brennan, R. L., & Haertel, E. (1997). Generalizability analysis for performance assessments of student achievement or school effectiveness. *Educational and Psychological Measurement, 57*, 373–399.

Darling-Hammond, L., Herman, J., Pellegrino, J., Abedi, J., Aber, J. L., Baker, E., . . . Steele, C. M. (2013). *Criteria for high quality assessment.* Stanford, CA: Stanford Center for Opportunity Policy in Education. Retrieved from https://edpolicy.stanford.edu/publications/pubs/847

Delandshere, G., & Petrosky, A. R. (1998). Assessment of complex performances: Limitations of key measurement assumptions. *Educational Researcher, 27*(2), 14–24.

Dolan, R. P., & Hall, T. E. (2001). Universal design for learning: Implications for large-scale assessment. *IDA Perspectives, 27*(4), 22–25.

Domaleski, C. S. (2011). *State end of course tests: A policy brief.* Paper commissioned by the Council of Chief State School Officers Technical Issues in Large Scale Assessment State Collaborative on Assessment and Student Standards, Washington, DC. Retrieved from http://www.ccsso.org/Documents/2011/State_End-of-course_Testing_Programs_2011.pdf

Elmore, R. F. (2004). Moving forward: Refining accountability systems. In S. H. Fuhrman & R. F. Elmore (Eds.), *Redesigning accountability systems for education* (pp. 276–296). New York, NY: Teachers College Press.

Erpenbach, W. J., & Domaleski, C. (2013). *ESEA flexibility request—A study of states' requests for waivers from requirements of the No Child Left Behind Act of 2001.* Washington, DC: Council of Chief State School Officers.

Gong, B., & Marion, S. F. (2006). *Dealing with flexibility in assessments for students with significant cognitive disabilities* (Synthesis Report 60). Minneapolis, MN: University of Minnesota, National Center for Educational Outcomes.

Haertel, G. D., Vendlinski, T. P., Rutstein, D., DeBarger, A., Cheng, B. H., Snow, E. B., D'Angelo, C., Harris, C., Yarnall, L., & Ructtinger, L. (2015). General introduction to evidence-centered design. In H. Braun (Ed.), *The challenges to measurement in an era of accountability.* New York, NY: Routledge.

Hall, E., Gagnon, D., Thompson, J., Schneider, C., & Marion, S. (2014). *State practices related to the use of student achievement measures in the evaluation of teachers in non-tested subjects and grades.* Dover, NH: National Center for the Improvement of Educational Assessment. Retrieved from http://www.nciea.org/publication_PDFs/Gates%20NTGS_Hall%20082614.pdf

Hambleton, R. K., Jaeger, R. M., Koretz, D., Linn, R. L., Millman, J., & Phillips, S. E. (1995). *Review of the measurement quality of the Kentucky instructional results information system, 1991–1994.* Report prepared for the Office of Educational Accountability, Kentucky General Assembly.

Hargreaves, A., & Braun, H. (2013). *Data-driven improvement and accountability.* Retrieved from http://nepc.colorado.edu/publication/data-driven-improvement-accountability

Herman, J. L., Aschbacher, P., & Winters, L. (1992). *A practical guide to alternative assessment.* Alexandria, VA: ASCD.

Herman, J. L., Heritage, M., & Goldschmidt, P. (2011). *Developing and selecting assessments of student growth for use in teacher evaluation systems (extended version).* Los Angeles, CA: University of California, National Center for Research on Evaluation, Standards, and Student Testing (CRESST).

Hill, H. C., Kapitula, L., & Umland, K. (2011). A validity argument approach to evaluating teacher value-added scores. *American Educational Research Journal, 48*(3), 794–831.

Hill, R. K., & DePascale, C. A. (2003a). Reliability of No Child Left Behind accountability designs. *Educational Measurement: Issues and Practices, 22*(3), 12–20.

Hill, R. K., & DePascale, C. A. (2003b). *Reliability of No Child Left Behind accountability designs.* Paper presented at the annual meeting of the National Council of Measurement in Education, Chicago, IL.

Kane, M. T. (2006). Validation. In R. L. Brennan (Ed.), *Educational measurement* (4th ed., pp. 17–64). New York, NY: American Council on Education/Macmillan.

Koretz, D. (2008). *Measuring up: What educational testing really tells us.* Cambridge, MA: Harvard University Press.

Koretz, D., Klein, S., McCaffrey, D., & Stecher, B. (1993). *Interim report: The reliability of Vermont portfolio scores in the 1992–93 school year* (CSE Technical Report 370). Santa Monica, CA: RAND; Los Angeles, CA: Center for Research on Evaluation, Standards and Student Testing, UCLA.

Lachlan-Haché, L., Cushing, E., & Bivona, L. (2012). *Student learning objectives as measures of educator effectiveness: The basics.* Washington, DC: American Institutes for Research.

Lacireno-Paquet, N., Morgan, C., & Mello, D. (2014). *How states use student learning objectives in teacher evaluation systems: A review of state websites* (REL 2014–013). Washington, DC: U.S. Department of Education, Institute of Education Sciences, National Center for Education Evaluation and Regional Assistance, Regional Educational Laboratory North-east & Islands. Retrieved from http://ies.ed.gov/ncee/edlabs

Linn, R. L. (1981). Determining pretest–posttest performance changes. In R. A. Berk (Ed.), *Educational evaluation methodology: The state of the art* (pp. 84–109). Baltimore, MD: The Johns Hopkins University Press.

Linn, R. L. (1993). Educational assessment: Expanded expectations and challenges. *Educational Evaluation and Policy Analysis, 15*(1), 1–16.

Linn, R. L., Baker, E. L., & Dunbar, S. B. (1991). Complex performance-based assessment: Expectations and validation criteria. *Educational Researcher, 20*(8), 15–21.

Marion, S. F. (2014). *Using common assignments and an SLO framework to support educator effectiveness in Kentucky and Colorado.* Dover, NH: National Center for the Improvement of Educational Assessment.

Marion, S. F., & Buckley, K. (2011). *Approaches and considerations for incorporating student performance results from "non-tested" grades and subjects into educator effectiveness determinations.* Retrieved from http://www.nciea.org/publications/Considerations%20for%20non-tested%20grades_SMKB2011.pdf

Marion, S. F., DePascale, C., Domaleski, C., Gong, B., & Diaz-Bilello, E. (2012, May). *Considerations for analyzing educators' contributions to student learning in non-tested subjects and grades with a focus on Student Learning Objectives.* Retrieved from http://www.nciea.org/publication_PDFs/Measurement%20Considerations%20for%20NTSG_052212.pdf

Messick, S. (1989). Validity. In R. L. Linn (Ed.), *Educational measurement* (3rd ed., pp. 13–103). New York, NY: American Council on Education and Macmillan.

Messick, S. (1994). Alternative modes of assessment, uniform standards of validity. *ETS Research Report Series, 1994*, i–22. doi:10.1002/j.2333-8504.1994.tb01634.x

Mislevy, R. J. (1994). Evidence and inference in educational assessment. *Psychometrika, 59*, 439–483.

Myford, C. M., & Mislevy, R. J. (1995). *Monitoring and improving a portfolio assessment system* (Center for Performance Assessment Research Report). Princeton, NJ: Educational Testing Service.

National Research Council (NRC). (2010). *State assessment systems: Exploring best practices and innovations: Summary of two workshops.* Washington, DC: The National Academies Press.

NRC. (2014). *Developing assessments for the Next Generation Science Standards.* Washington, DC: The National Academies Press.

Newton, P. (2007). Comparability monitoring: Progress report. In P. Newton, J. Baird, H. Goldstein, H. Patrick, & P. Tymms (Eds.), *Techniques for monitoring the comparability of examination standards* (pp. 452–476). London, UK: Qualifications and Curriculum Authority (QCA).

NGSS Lead States. (2013). *Next generation science standards: For states, by states.* Washington, DC: The National Academies Press.

Parkes, J. (2000). The relationship between the reliability and costs of performance assessments. *Educational Policy Analysis Archives, 8*(16), 1–14.

Pearson, P. D., & Garavaglia, D. R. (1997, August). *Improving the information value of performance items in large scale assessments.* Paper commissioned by the NAEP Validity Studies (NVS) Panel, Palo Alto, CA.

Pellegrino, J. W., Chudowsky, N., & Glaser, R. (2001). *Knowing what students know: The science and design of educational assessment.* Washington, DC: National Academy of Sciences.

Prince, C. D., Schuermann, P. J., Guthrie, J. W., Witham, P. J., Milanowski, A. T., & Thorn, C. A. (2009). *The other 69 percent: Fairly rewarding the performance of teachers of nontested subjects and grades.* Washington, DC: Center for Educator Compensation Reform. Retrieved from http://www.maine.gov/education/effectiveness/other69Percent.pdf

Queensland Studies Authority (QSA). (2010). *Comparability processes for authority subjects: Systemic consistency and reliability.* Queensland, Australia: QSA. Retrieved from http://www.qsa.qld.edu.au

Reform Support Network (RSN). (2014). *Student learning objectives work group approaches to setting targets for student learning objectives.* Retrieved from https://rtt.grads360.org/#communities/slo/slo-library

Resnick, L. B. (1996, June). *Performance puzzles: Issues in measuring capabilities and certifying accomplishments* (CSE/CRESST Technical Report 415). Retrieved from http://cse.ucla.edu/products/reports/TECH415.pdf

Resnick, L. B., & Resnick, D. P. (1992). Assessing the thinking curriculum: New tools for educational reform. In B. R. Gifford & M. C. O'Conner (Eds.), *Changing assessments: Alternative views of aptitude, achievement and instruction*. Boston, MA: Kluwer Academic Publishers.

Rohrer, D., & Pashler, H. (2010). Recent research on human learning challenges conventional instructional strategies. *Educational Research, 39*, 406–412.

Rothstein, J. (2010, January). Teacher quality in educational production: Tracking, decay, and student achievement. *Quarterly Journal of Economics, 125*(1), 175–214.

Sabatini, J. P., Bennett, R. E., & Deane, P. (2011). *Four years of cognitively based assessment of, for, and as learning (CBAL): Learning about throughcourse assessment (TCA)*. Paper presented at the Invitational Research Symposium on through course summative assessments, Princeton, NJ: ETS. Retrieved from http://k12center.org/rsc/pdf/TCSA_Symposium_Final_Paper_Sabatini.pdf

Shavelson, R. J., Baxter, G. P., & Pine, J. (1992). Performance assessments: Political rhetoric and measurement reality. *Educational Researcher, 21*(4), 22–27.

Shavelson, R. J., & Webb, N. M. (1991). *Generalizability theory: A primer*. Thousand Oaks, CA: Sage.

Shepard, L. A. (1996). *Measuring achievement: What does it mean to test for robust understanding? The Third Annual William H. Angoff Memorial Lecture*. Princeton, NJ: Educational Testing Service Policy Information Center.

Shepard, L. A. (2000). The role of assessment in a learning culture. *Educational Researcher, 29*(7), 4–14.

Slotnik, W. J., & Smith, M. D. (2013). *It's more than money*. Boston, MA: Community Training and Assistance Center. Retrieved from http://www.ctacusa.com/wp-content/uploads/2013/11/MoreThanMoney.pdf

Thompson, J., & Marion, S. F. (2013). *The student learning objective toolkit*. Retrieved from http://www.nciea.org/slo-toolkit

Thompson, S. J., Johnstone, C. J., & Thurlow, M. L. (2002). *Universal design applied to large scale assessments: Synthesis Report #44*. Minneapolis, MN: National Center on Educational Outcomes.

U.S. Department of Education. (2011, September). *ESEA flexibility*. Washington, DC: U.S. Department of Education.

Wiggins, G., & McTighe, J. (2005). *Understanding by design: Expanded 2nd edition*. Alexandria, VA: ASCD.

Wolf, D., Bixby, J., & Glenn III, J. (1991). To use their minds well: Investigating new forms of student assessment. In G. Grant (Ed.), *Review of research in education* (Vol. 17, pp. 31–74). Washington, DC: American Educational Research Association.

Yen, W. M., & Ferrara, S. (1997). The Maryland school performance assessment program: Performance assessment with psychometric quality suitable for high-stakes usage. *Educational and Psychological Measurement, 57*, 60–84.

4   Psychometric Considerations for Performance-Based Assessments and Student Learning Objectives

Suzanne Lane and Charles DePascale

Introduction

Performance-based assessments are considered an effective tool for educational reform because of their instructional value and have been used in assessment-based accountability systems in the United States since the 1980s (Linn, 1993). For the purpose of this chapter and to be consistent with Marion and Buckley (this volume), we use the term *performance-based assessments* to encompass the following forms of assessments: assessments that consist of a set of performance tasks, portfolios of student work, and exhibitions. It is important to note that portfolios in some content areas such as science or mathematics may not be entirely performance-based in that they may include selected-response items as well as performance tasks, whereas in other content areas such as studio art and performing arts, they are entirely performance-based in that they include student products or performances only.

There is ample evidence that performance-based assessments also serve as powerful professional development tools, particularly if teachers are engaged in the design of assessments and the scoring of student products. Performance-based assessments are well aligned to the learning goals in all academic disciplines. As an example, art and music teachers may require students to demonstrate skills through performance. To accomplish this, art students may create a portfolio that provides evidence of mastery and progress of certain skills (as determined at the start of the course), and music students may give live performances or submit recordings that are evaluated. In social science, physical science, or life science classrooms, teachers may require students to demonstrate applied learning skills such as critical thinking, perspective taking, problem solving, research, communication, reflection, and self-evaluation through extended research projects, experiments, and inquiry tasks. These performance-based assessments may also require collaboration and adjustment of plans in response to new information that embodies extended strategic thinking over a longer period of time (Webb, 2002).

Those very features that enhance the instructional value of performance-based assessments and make them a valuable tool for education reform, however, pose significant psychometric challenges to their use in summative assessments for purposes of accountability. The Race to the Top initiative requires that alternative measures of student performance and learning for non-tested grades and subjects are "rigorous and comparable across classrooms" (U.S. Department of Education, 2012). The comparability of results across students and across classrooms is one of the psychometric requirements or constraints that must be considered when performance-based assessments are used in accountability systems. Reliability and generalizability of assessment results, as well as precision of measurement across the score scale, are additional critical psychometric considerations that impact the validity of using performance-based assessments to make high-stakes accountability decisions. Further, design criteria, including alignment to content standards and content representativeness, will have an impact on the psychometric quality of performance-based assessments and the validity of score interpretations and uses. These challenges were well documented in the 1990s when several states attempted to incorporate performance-based assessments into their large-scale assessment and accountability systems (Koretz, Stecher, Klein, & McCaffrey, 1994; Linn, 1993).

In this chapter we consider the tension between instructional and accountability uses of performance-based assessments that occurs due to practical constraints in the design of assessment and accountability systems, but more importantly, we address how psychometrics can play a valuable role both in delineating student learning objectives (SLOs) (see Marion & Buckley, this volume, for a discussion on the design of SLOs) and in designing performance-based assessments that can be used for student and educator accountability purposes while maintaining their instructional value. The use of psychometric procedures and tools, as well as criteria for psychometric quality, in the design of these assessments can contribute to the validity of score inferences and the appropriateness of actions taken based on those inferences, as well as imposing some constraints in their design. The chapter is divided into six main sections:

1   Design of assessments in the era of accountability;
2   Design and implementation features that affect psychometric properties;
3   Comparability;
4   Brief introduction to measurement models;
5   Reliability, generalizability, and classification accuracy;
6   Validity of score inferences about student proficiency and progress.

In the first section, "Design of Assessments in the Era of Accountability," we provide an overview of the issues associated with using performance-based assessments for accountability purposes, with particular attention to the conflicts in the design and use of performance-based assessments as instructional tools in classrooms and as indicators of educator effectiveness. The second section, "Design and Implementation Features that Affect Psychometric Properties," contains an in-depth discussion of the manner in which an interpretative and validity argument can provide a framework that will identify, perhaps implicitly, how psychometrics can be used to accomplish the goals of assessment and accountability systems by enhancing psychometric quality throughout the design and implementation process. The focus of the third section, "Comparability," is on describing the meaning and importance of comparability and the multiple contexts in which comparability must be considered (i.e., comparability across tasks, time, students, administration conditions, and raters). The tension between the needs for standardization and flexibility in the design of performance-based assessments is addressed across these areas. In the fourth section, we provide "A Brief Introduction to Measurement Models." In addition to introducing key concepts and terms associated with the three major measurement models (classical test theory, generalizability theory, and item response theory [IRT]), our goal in this section is to briefly describe how those models can be used during the design phase to improve the psychometric quality of performance-based assessments and enhance the validity of score interpretations and use in accountability systems. In the final two sections, "Reliability, Generalizability, and Classification Accuracy" and "Validity of Score Inferences about Student Proficiency and Progress," we address several ways in which an awareness and understanding of the intended uses of assessments, including the inferences and claims to be made about student performance, can inform design decisions that will improve the psychometric quality of the assessments. Given our belief that the question is not *whether* but *how best* to use performance-based assessments as a component of accountability systems, we conclude the chapter with a summary of the major issues that impact the use of performance-based assessments in accountability systems and a discussion of how an understanding of those issues can enhance the design, implementation, and evaluation of those assessments.

Design of Assessments in the Era of Accountability

In the context of teacher accountability for non-tested grades and subjects, it has been argued that "measuring the effectiveness for the 'other 69 percent' is probably the most challenging aspect of including student achievement growth as a component of teacher evaluation" (Goe & Holdheide, 2011, p. 1). In the design of performance-based assessments in this era of account-ability, consideration needs to be given to their use in student, teacher, school, and district accountability, as well as their use in informing instruction and in improving student learning. There is an inherent conflict between the goals of instruction and accountability, and although psychometrics provides us with tools to design high-quality assessments, certain constraints will arise that inevitably lead to trade-offs in achieving the different goals of assessment and account-ability systems. As an example, the standardization of content, administration, and scoring of performance-based assessments to help ensure comparability of scores across students and over time may lead to fairness issues as well as instructional value issues. To better understand the trade-offs and to make informed decisions about assessment designs for particular uses, an explicit delineation of the multiple purposes of assessments (e.g., instructional support and guidance; student, teacher, or school accountability) and varying psychometric considerations for each of these purposes (e.g., reliability, generalizability, classification accuracy, comparability) should be undertaken. In addition, in the design and evaluation of performance-based assessments, to ensure the validity of test score inferences and uses, a balance must be maintained between the psychometric (e.g., comparability and reliability) and design criteria (e.g., coverage of content standards), as well as other considerations such as local capacity and resources needed to design, implement, and score these assessments. In summary, to help alleviate the tension between school instructional improvement and accountability, Hargreaves and Braun (2013) suggest that there needs to be a "collaborative involvement in data collection and analysis, collective responsibility for improvement, and a consensus that the indicators and metrics involved in DDIA [data-driven improvement and accountability] are accurate, meaningful, fair, broad and balanced" (p. 1).

To ensure a sustainable assessment system, consideration needs to be given to the level at which it will be designed (i.e., state or local level); time, money, and other resources allocated to its design; and how it will be maintained, monitored, and evaluated over time. In addition to the assessment itself, thought should be given to establishing and maintaining a data management system and how the results of the assessment will be recorded, submitted, and verified. Decisions also must be made about how often assessment data are collected, when and who collects it, and how much data are needed to support the claims about student achievement and progress.

Definition of Performance-Based Assessments

An important feature of performance-based assessments, as compared to tests composed of selected-response items, is that they have high fidelity for the goals of instruction in that they have the potential to provide more direct evidence of what a student knows and can do within an academic discipline. As described by Messick (1994), the directness of a performance-based assessment relies on the extent to which the assessment measures what is intended and "is not unduly broad because of added method variance" (p. 21). Assessments consisting of a set of performance tasks, portfolios, and exhibitions, all forms of performance-based assessment, are addressed in this chapter.

An important characteristic of performance-based assessments is the close correspondence between the performance that is assessed and the performance of interest. As indicated in the *Standards for Educational and Psychological Testing*, performance assessments "require examin-ees to demonstrate the ability to perform tasks that are often complex in nature and generally require the test takers to demonstrate their abilities or skills in settings that closely resemble real-life situations" (AERA, APA, & NCME, 2014, p. 77). Typically performance-based assessments require students to perform a task such as conduct a science investigation or play a musical instrument, or to construct an original product or response such as a painting or a persuasive essay. They are intended to emulate the conditions in which the knowledge and skills are ultimately applied in real-life situations.

Portfolios, one form of performance-based assessments, are "systematic collections of work or educational products, typically gathered over time" (AERA et al., 2014, p. 78), and they usually include self-reflections and student descriptions of the submitted work. Portfolios may be composed of performance tasks as well as other types of tasks; they may reflect representative student work, best work, or document student progress. An example of a large-scale portfolio assessment that has been sustained over time is the Advanced Placement (AP) Studio Art assessment (Myford & Mislevy, 1995). For the 3D Design assessment, students are required to submit a specified series of images of their 3D artworks that are evaluated independently according to their quality (form, technique, and content), breadth (visual principles and material techniques), and concentration (depth of investigation and process of discovery). The assessment is standardized in terms of its design and scoring to help ensure comparability of scores. Students are provided with detailed instructions that delineate the specific requirements for the artworks and with scoring rubrics that describe what is expected for each of the areas being assessed. Further, art educators score the submitted images of the artworks using well-delineated scoring rubrics for each of the three areas.

Exhibitions or capstone projects involve students creating original work, reflecting real-world situations and issues, as well as important disciplinary knowledge and skills, and are presented to a panel that uses predetermined scoring rubrics and procedures to evaluate them. These types of performance-based assessments allow for the demonstration of a wide range of skills within a discipline and are similar to the "merit badge" approach. They typically serve as summative assessments.

For the purpose of this chapter, a performance-based assessment that may be used for high-stakes purposes is designed to more closely reflect the performance of interest, require standardized directions and administration conditions, allow students to construct or perform an original response that reflects important disciplinary knowledge and/or skills, and the student work or performance is evaluated by predetermined scoring criteria.

States' Performance-Based Assessment Designs and Use of SLOs

The history of performance-based assessment designs for large-scale use is characterized by the reduction of big ideas to small realities. Plans to integrate performance-based assessments into state assessment and accountability systems often begin with grand visions of lengthy research projects culminating in written, oral, and multimedia presentations by students describing and defending their work. Almost immediately, these grand visions are viewed through the lens of the current assessment and accountability frameworks that embody inherent constraints. Over a short period of time, a combination of practical and psychometric concerns chips away at the planned assessments until they fit into the existing framework. The most common outcomes of this process in large-scale assessment settings are:

- on-demand writing tasks that require students to produce a single draft in response to a prompt or text;
- small, short-term "research" tasks or simulations that can be completed in one or two test sessions; and
- "portfolios" consisting of a collection of student work from a series of standard assessments containing multiple-choice or short constructed-response items administered over a period of time.

Current examples of this reduction process can be seen in newly implemented teacher accountability systems and the initial design requirements for SLOs that will be used to measure a teacher's impact on student learning. Although housed in the classroom and designed to reflect growth (i.e., student learning) over an extended period of time, the requirements imposed by many state systems effectively reduce SLOs to a summative, end-of-year assessment that may be developed locally rather than by a state or commercial vendor.

Use of Performance-Based Assessments and SLOs for Accountability Purposes

The use of performance-based assessment designs in accountability systems depends far more on a reimagining of assessment and accountability systems than it does on the design features and psychometric properties of performance-based assessments. The natural tension between the flexibility of performance-based assessments and the standardization of accountability systems will always exist. In a world in which accountability is limited to the aggregation of student scores derived from common, external assessment(s), there will be no more than a limited role for performance-based assessments.

What is needed to accompany performance-based assessments is an alternative concept of accountability that (a) recognizes the strengths and limitations of both standard and performance-based assessments, and (b) attempts to make maximum use of the strengths of each. Such a conception of accountability is likely to lead to tiered or layered evaluation approaches to accountability (that existed, or were under development in some states prior to NCLB) and foster innovative approaches to assessment.

There are a number of states and districts that have designed performance-based assessments for non-tested grades and subjects. As an example, Tennessee, which was awarded over $500 million in the Race to the Top Competition in 2010, developed the Fine Arts Growth Measures System that employs a portfolio approach to document student growth in the arts (Memphis City Schools, 2011). The portfolio includes representative teacher-collected student work samples. Guidelines are provided to teachers indicating the requirements such as a minimum of five student work samples assessing three of four domains (Perform, Create, Respond, and Connect). Teachers score their own students' work samples and then the portfolio. Subsequently, a teacher-completed scoring rubric and a teacher-completed form explaining the nature and process of the collected evidence are submitted to a blind peer review committee of content-specific expert art teachers. Two members of the peer review committee score each artifact and determine student growth using discipline-specific scoring rubrics.

South Carolina uses a combination of multiple-choice and performance tasks for student assessments in music and visual arts (Paul et al., 2012). Analytic rubrics have been developed for music and a detailed holistic rubric is used for visual arts. A web-based training procedure was developed for the raters, and approximately 50 percent of the visual arts assessments are double-scored, and 20 percent double-scored for music. A person-by-rater generalizability study yielded dependability coefficients ranging from .68 to .94; however, no information is provided regarding the interchangeability or comparability of the performance tasks.

Minnesota adapted a model for school-based arts assessment and accountability originally developed in Queensland, Australia (http://www.pcae.k12.mn.us/pdr/21stlearning.html; Queensland Studies Authority, 2009). In this model, assessments designed by individual teachers or schools are aligned with state-level standards and criteria. A state-level committee approves the schools' work plan and evaluates the assessment program. The accumulated student projects are evaluated locally and then schools submit their assessment program and samples of student portfolios to the state. The state-level committee verifies the local scoring of submitted portfolios and determines the degree of agreement between the schools' and the state's standards.

Although many of these examples are within the arts and music disciplines, the current zeitgeist has encouraged many other districts and states to begin using performance-based assessments in these and other disciplines and to require teachers and administrators to set SLOs at the school or classroom level, including public schools in the District of Columbia; Austin, Texas; Houston, Texas; Denver, Colorado; Indiana; New York; and Rhode Island. The specification of SLOs may vary in terms of level of detail, number of SLOs for students, whether they are schoolwide or teamwide SLOs, who crafted the SLOs such as a team of teachers or district- or state-level staff, and the weight that is given to the attainment of SLOs for teacher evaluation. As an example, in the Austin Independent School District, every year each teacher develops two SLOs for the year that are aligned to the state standards and campus improvement plans and must be approved by the principal. One SLO must address all students and be achieved by 75 percent of the students in a class, and the other SLO can be targeted to a subgroup of students. An SLO team uses a rubric to evaluate the rigor of the SLOs.

Most of the assessment approaches described above are in the initial stages of design and implementation. Like previous efforts to use performance-based assessments on a large scale for accountability purposes, their long-term success depends on the ability to account for psychometric and practical constraints while maintaining the essential characteristics of the assessment. Ultimately, it will be a policy decision as to whether the benefits of performance-based assessments outweigh their limitations for use in accountability systems. Ideally, that decision will be based on the use of assessments that best contribute to meeting the goals of the assessment and accountability system.

Forces that Support the Use of Performance-Based Assessments and SLOs

In spite of the many challenges and still unresolved issues in designing assessments in the era of accountability, it appears that we are on the threshold of yet another opportunity to integrate performance-based assessments into state accountability systems. There are several reasons to account for this resurgence of interest in performance-based assessments. There are also reasons to be cautiously optimistic that this attempt might be more successful than previous efforts.

As a starting point, the two main arguments at the heart of the last significant push for assessments with greater fidelity that took hold in the late 1980s are just as relevant today:

- the overreliance on selected-response items has unintended consequences that extend well beyond the assessment and accountability system; and
- performance-based assessments such as portfolios, exhibitions, and products are better suited to measure higher order thinking skills than conventional selected-response items.

Those arguments were first challenged by psychometric concerns in the 1990s (Koretz et al., 1994; Linn, 1993) and then overwhelmed by the assessment requirements and budget crises of the NCLB era. They are being renewed at this time by a confluence of forces which are shaping this *next generation* era of education reform:

- the development and nearly universal adoption of the Common Core State Standards with their emphasis on higher order thinking skills, research, collaboration, and the long-term retention and successful application of securely held knowledge;
- the impetus for all students to be college- and career-ready when they graduate from high school;
- the concerns with the performance of students in the United States on international assessments as compared to students in other countries;

- the increased focus on teacher evaluation and its redesign to include measures of student learning;
- emerging technology that has the potential to alleviate many of the practical and psychometric issues related to large-scale implementation of performance-based assessment; and
- an expanded view of assessment beyond end-of-year summative assessment combined with a richer view of the role that assessment results can play in improving instruction.

None of these forces individually guarantees the use of performance-based assessments for accountability, but in the aggregate they create a compelling argument for their use.

As described earlier in this chapter, and in the chapter by Marion and Buckley (this volume), the use of performance-based assessments in accountability systems introduces additional design considerations above and beyond those that would be required for their use in a lower-stakes environment. An increased need for comparability of results and heightened concerns for corruptibility often lead to actions designed to increase security and reliability through standardization of content, administration procedures, and scoring procedures. The psychometric quandary that results is that the very actions designed to increase the suitability of performance-based assessments for use in accountability systems are often the biggest threat to their effective and valid use.

The challenge, therefore, is to recognize that many of the features of performance-based assessments that appear to threaten their reliability and suitability for use in accountability systems are, in fact, essential elements of those assessments and the validity of inferences drawn from their results. As Wiggins (1993) noted, "this validity-versus-reliability dilemma must never be construed as an either-or choice, however, but as a design problem to be carefully negotiated on the basis of better guidelines for balancing the concerns." That is the prism through which the psychometric considerations provided in this chapter should be viewed.

The remaining sections of this chapter focus on design and implementation features that affect the psychometric properties of performance-based assessments as well as critical steps that can be built into the design, development, and implementation processes to optimize those assessments for use in accountability systems. We will discuss psychometric properties and constraints common to the use of these forms of assessment in any valid accountability system, but there will not be an effort to impose additional constraints upon the assessments to force their fit into existing accountability systems built around standard, summative, end-of-year assessments.

Design and Implementation Features that Affect Psychometric Properties

In this section, we argue that psychometrics has a valuable role in ensuring the quality of performance-based assessments used for state assessment and accountability purposes. In the design of performance-based assessments for accountability purposes, an argument-based approach to validity should be adopted to ensure that the multiple purposes and uses of performance-based assessments are clearly delineated. Once the claims that one wants to make about students, teachers, and schools are articulated, psychometric principles, procedures, and criteria are used in the design of assessments that will support such claims.

Psychometrics as a Tool to Accomplish the Goals of Assessment and Accountability Systems

Psychometrics in educational assessment and accountability is most often associated with technical procedures and activities that occur following the development of items and the administration of the assessment. Psychometric tasks such as calibrating items, developing scales, and equating assessment forms within and across years are well known, if not well understood. Analyses to determine the psychometric properties of assessment and its constituent items such as reliability, standard error of measurement, item and test information, and differential item functioning are also widely known. Becoming more visible with the growth of adaptive testing, but critical in the development of all educational assessments, is the role that psychometrics plays in the item development and test construction process. Many of the same types of analyses applied to the completed large-scale assessment following administration can be, and typically are, used to inform item development and selection. Often not considered, however, when one thinks of psychometrics, is the way in which attention to psychometric criteria (even without technical analyses) can support a principled approach to assessment design such as evidence-centered design (see Haertel et al., this volume).

In this section, we address several design decisions in the development of assessments for accountability systems and describe how consideration of psychometric principles can help ensure that appropriate decisions are made. Principles such as identifying the purpose of the assessment and delineating a validity argument, comparability, reliability and generalizability, and the validity of score inferences will be discussed in relation to how performance-based assessments can best be used as a component of accountability systems. Beginning with contextual questions such as "What is the purpose of the assessment?," "What claims do we want to make about student performance?," and "How will the results be used?" is the key to the consideration of psychometric principles and constraints in the development of educational assessments. In general, there are no generic or universal black/white or right/wrong answers to questions about comparability, reliability, etc. The answers depend on the purposes, claims, and uses.

- A level of reliability or classification accuracy that is adequate when an assessment is one of many components within a relatively low-stakes accountability system may be wholly insufficient when the same assessment is the sole or principal indicator of student learning in a high-stakes accountability system.
- For some accountability purposes, comparability might be necessary at the school or district level, but not across districts statewide. For other purposes, however, statewide or even cross-state comparability may be essential.
- Similarly, the factors that must be comparable (e.g., content, score, both content and score) will vary based on context.

A straightforward answer to questions about whether a particular form of assessment can or should be used is also rare. Again, consideration of claims and uses, as well as a balancing of practical and psychometric concerns, should inform decisions about how best to use—or not use—a particular assessment in a given situation.

Importance of Delineating an Interpretive/Use Argument and Validity Argument

Validation entails constructing and evaluating coherent arguments for and against proposed test interpretations and uses (Cronbach, 1971, 1988; Kane, 1992, 2013; Messick, 1989). To ensure that the multiple, and potentially competing, purposes and uses of performance-based assessments are clearly articulated, an argument-based approach to validity can be adopted. It entails an interpretive/use argument that explicitly identifies the proposed interpretations and uses of test scores and a validity argument that provides a structure for evaluating the interpretive/use argument requiring the accumulation of evidence to support the appropriateness of the claims (Kane, 2006, 2013). This necessitates the specification of score inferences, claims and uses, evaluation of the proposed inferences and their supporting assumptions using evidence, and the consideration of plausible alternative interpretations. To help prioritize what should be the focus, Shepard (1993) proposed three questions to guide validation efforts: "What does the testing practice claim to do?, What are the arguments for and against the intended aims of the test?, What does the test do in the system other than what it claims, for good or bad?" (p. 429). The delineation of a validity argument will help identify the psychometric considerations in the design of an assessment and accountability system.

Threats to Validity of Interpretations, Claims, and Uses

As described by Messick (1989, 1994), two sources of potential threats to the validity of score interpretations and uses are construct underrepresentation and construct-irrelevant variance. Construct underrepresentation occurs when the assessment is not representative of the targeted domain or covers only a portion of the targeted domain. Construct-irrelevant variance occurs when one or more irrelevant constructs are being assessed in addition to the intended construct (i.e., there are sources of score variance unrelated to the target construct).

The extent to which the assessment is not representing or underrepresenting the targeted domain will have an impact not only on the fidelity of the assessment but also on the generalizability of the assessment results—that is, the extent to which inferences and claims based on scores from the assessment can be applied across other tasks, administration conditions, raters, or over time (Messick, 1989, 1994). Achieving generalizability may be less problematic if the target of a performance-based assessment comprises specific important skills within a discipline, such as reasoning and critical thinking, as opposed to a focus on discipline-specific content. For example, the claim of student proficiency in sixth-grade mathematics would require an assessment that adequately covers the entire targeted domain (i.e., the grade 6 mathematics content standards). A claim of the student's ability to demonstrate mathematical reasoning and problem solving in the context of sixth-grade mathematics might be supported by tasks drawn from, but not completely covering, the grade 6 mathematics content standards. Of course, limiting claims and constraining the target domain to offset the construct underrepresentation of a particular assessment instrument is not a long-term course of action.

Sources of construct-irrelevant variance in performance-based assessments may include task wording and context, response mode, and, in some cases, students' prior experience with or knowledge of the task. Other sources of construct-irrelevant variance may include differential levels of support by teachers (or others) during the administration of the assessment or construction of the product, differences in grading standards across teachers or other raters, and, even when the grading standards are the same, raters' attention to irrelevant features of performances and products.

Evidence to Support Claims

To provide evidence to support the articulated claims when using performance-based assessments, content representativeness, cognitive complexity, transfer and generalizability, fairness, and consequences need to be examined (Linn, Baker, & Dunbar, 1991; Messick, 1994). These are closely intertwined to sources of validity evidence proposed by the *Standards for Educational and Psychological Measurement* (AERA et al., 2014): evidence based on test content, response processes, internal structure, relations to other variables, and consequences of testing. Appropriate test use and sound interpretations in a complex educational system necessitate the accumulation of evidence from multiple sources to support the assessment results.

An analysis of the extent to which the knowledge and skills reflected in the assessment represent the target knowledge and skills provides important validity evidence. Alignment procedures developed for large-scale assessments over the last two decades to accomplish this task (e.g., CCSSO, 2010) can also be applied to performance-based assessments with the caveat that there must be a clear understanding and explication beforehand of what is meant by the target knowledge and skills. Evidence is also needed regarding the extent to which the scoring rubrics are capturing the intended knowledge and skills. An examination of the coherence among the tasks, assessment criteria, scoring rubrics and procedures, and the target domain in terms of both knowledge and skills provides evidence to support the validity of score inferences and uses. With respect to fairness, evidence is needed to support the meaningfulness, appropriateness, and usefulness of the test score inferences and uses for all relevant subgroups of students. Validity evidence for assessments that are intended for students from various cultural, ethnic, and linguistic backgrounds, as well as students from various disability groups, needs to be collected systematically as assessments are being developed and implemented.

A critical validation consideration for performance-based assessments used in models to evaluate educators is instructional sensitivity, as these models assume that student learning that is attributable to educators is being captured (National Research Council, 2010). Popham (2007) argues that "an instructionally *sensitive* test would be capable of distinguishing between strong and weak instruction by allowing us to validly conclude that a set of students' *high* test scores are meaningfully, but not exclusively, attributable to effective instruction.... In contrast, an instructionally *insensitive* test would not allow us to distinguish accurately between strong and weak instruction" (pp. 146–147). As described by Polikoff (2010), researchers have investigated instructional sensitivity using item and test statistics, expert judgment, and instruction-focused methods. As an example, Stein and Lane (1996) examined the relationship between presence of reform features in mathematics instruction and student performance on a mathematics performance assessment. Extensive observations throughout the school year were conducted in the classrooms to examine the quality of mathematics instruction and student engagement in the "doing of mathematics." The analyses of instruction focused on the cognitive demands of instructional tasks as represented in the instructional material, as set up by the teacher in the classroom, and as implemented by students. Evidence was provided for the instructional sensitivity of the assessment in that the greatest student gains on performance assessment were observed for those classrooms where the instructional tasks were set up and implemented with high levels of cognitive demands. Students in these classrooms were engaged in using multiple solution strategies and multiple representations and were adept at explaining their mathematical thinking. The classroom teachers encouraged non-algorithmic forms of thinking associated with the doing of mathematics. Whereas, the smallest gains were observed in classrooms where instructional tasks were procedurally based and could be solved by a single, easily accessible strategy and required little or no mathematical communication. Niemi and his colleagues (2007) also examined the relationship between students' opportunity to learn (OTL) the knowledge and skills assessed on a language arts performance assessment and student performance on the assessment. They found that student performance was sensitive to different types of language arts instruction: students who received instruction on literary analysis were significantly better able to analyze and describe conflict in literature than students who received instruction on either the organization of writing or English languages art instruction selected by the teacher. Results like these stress the need to ensure alignment among content standards, curriculum, instruction, and assessment. For assessments to have optimal instructional sensitivity, there needs to be a required level of score precision and comparability across the score scale to accurately capture changes in student performance over time.

To provide validity evidence for performance-based assessments, states may require committees composed of expert teachers at the district level to rate the rigor of the assessment, its alignment to important or priority standards within the state content standards, and the extent to which components of the assessment contribute to the intended score-based inference. In disciplines or courses for which there are no established state standards, states such as

Rhode Island have required districts to align assessments with standards developed or adopted by national associations of teachers within the discipline. The committees could also review teacher-submitted evidence about the assessment rigor and alignment to standards. Moreover, committees could also review evidence provided by teachers about the rigor and alignment of their instruction to both content standards and assessment. For this to be effective the district or state would need to provide training and training materials to ensure the teacher committees are well qualified.

In examining student progress and evaluating educators, changes in student performance need to be attributed to actual changes in acquired knowledge and skills, rather than to familiarity with tasks or inappropriate support that undermines the validity of the inferences. Research has shown that practices that lead to inflated scores may be due to reallocation of resources, such as shifts in instructional time, from non-tested content to tested content (Koretz & Hamilton, 2006).

An important impetus for the next generation of assessments is to improve the educational opportunities afforded to students so as to improve their learning. As a result, integral to the validation of these assessment and accountability systems are the consequences of decisions made based directly on information provided by assessment scores as well as on decisions that have no direct dependence on the information provided by the scores, but are linked to the purpose(s) of the assessment. As E. Haertel (2013) indicated, the former relates to the direct effects of educational assessments, such as instructional guidance for students and educational management (e.g., the use of assessments to help evaluate the effectiveness of educators or schools), that rely directly on the information that assessment scores provide about the assessed construct or domain. Whereas, the latter relates to the indirect effects of assessments, such as directing student effort, focusing the system (i.e., curriculum and instruction), and shaping public perceptions, that have no direct dependence on the information provided by the scores, but are linked closely to the purpose(s) or claims of assessment (Haertel, 2013). These indirect mechanisms of action, which are key components of interpretive/use arguments for assessment and accountability systems, are critical in the evaluation of the consequences of these systems. Further, the potentially negative, unintended consequences tend to be embedded within these indirect effects (Haertel, 2013). As Linn (1993) has argued, the need for consequential evidence in support of the interpretive and validity argument is "especially compelling for performance-based assessments … because particular intended consequences are an explicit part of the assessment system's rationale" (p. 6). Both positive and negative consequences of assessment and accountability programs typically have different impacts on different groups of students and in different schools, and these impacts need to be examined as part of the validity argument (Lane & Stone, 2002).

Issues Related to the Design of Each Type of Performance-Based Assessment

A clear articulation of the content and/or skills to be assessed by performance assessments, portfolios, and exhibitions will provide a basis for gathering relevant validity evidence to support the stated claims. In some disciplines, such as reading and history, inferential and critical evaluation skills may be of primary importance and the content or nature of the text is secondary. Whereas in other disciplines such as mathematics and science, content as well as thinking and reasoning skills are typically of importance. The assessment of skills within these disciplines may be prioritized over discipline-specific content. As an example, for science or mathematics exhibitions, students may choose to work on different content areas within the discipline but would be required to demonstrate the same skills. This may allow for generalizations to a skill domain within a discipline. Evidence should be collected that demonstrates the skills can be reproduced across disciplinary content and across occasions (i.e., transfer), as well as evidence to demonstrate growth in skills such as critical thinking or artistic performance over time.

To assess student learning over a year, portfolios can include student work that provides indicators of progress instead of representative products or a student's best work. As an example, an SLO in reading may require students to demonstrate their skill in taking a critical stance on an author's ability to provide a persuasive argument. A student's portfolio could include entries that demonstrate the skill at the beginning, middle, and end of the year, and scoring rubrics could capture the extent to which a student's critical thinking skills progressed over the year. To better assess student learning, learning progressions may help inform the design of portfolios (National Research Council, 2006). Portfolios that are designed to reflect learning progressions that describe successively more sophisticated ways of problem solving and reasoning in a discipline have particular value in monitoring student progress. To examine student growth in performance subjects (e.g., music, art, and physical education), students can perform or create a product on multiple occasions during the year, necessitating the design of scoring rubrics that capture key aspects of student growth.

When using portfolios and exhibitions, it is essential that the evaluation criteria closely reflect instructional goals because the instruction should be preparing students in the design of their portfolios and exhibitions. Scoring rubrics for exhibitions will need to be specific enough to ensure consistency within and across raters, but they will also have to accommodate variation in the specific content areas addressed by students. Higher rates of rater consistency require more standardized portfolios with common task expectations, strong training in both design and scoring of portfolios, and the use of clearly articulated analytic rubrics (e.g., Koretz et al., 1994). To address some of the validity concerns, trained committees can be used to evaluate the assessment tasks and procedures as well as scoring rubrics. The design and implementation of performance-based assessments will require professional development and support at both local and state levels.

Districts and states should consider adopting multiple measures that are aligned to the targeted content standards (including performance assessments, portfolios, and exhibitions) so as to enhance the validity, fairness, and generalizability of score inferences. If performance-based assessments are designed and implemented at the state level, the state should consider online delivery and data transmission, as well as remote scoring of performance assessment tasks, similar to the South Carolina Arts Assessment Program (Paul et al., 2011).

Comparability

To monitor the progress of individual students or cohorts of students across time or to make inferences about the relative performance of different students or the effectiveness of different teachers, it is important that the scores used to draw those inferences are comparable (see also Marion & Buckley, this volume). In order for scores from performance-based assessments to be comparable within and across schools as well as over time, some level of standardization of the assessment design, including the selection of content and skills assessed, administration conditions, scoring rules and procedures, and level of results reported, is required. Departures from standardization resulting from common design features of some forms of performance-based assessments, such as extended time periods, collaborative work, choice of tasks, and the use of ancillary materials, however, pose challenges to the comparability of the results. Flexibility in choosing or modifying the assessment components and the weighting of components to better reflect the goals of instruction may be needed, but assessment criteria should be developed by the state or district that specify what features need to be standardized and what features can be altered, including guidelines for altering assessment features, to help obtain the desired level of comparability.

In making those decisions about what features need to be standardized and what features can be altered to achieve the desired level of comparability, there are two critical factors that need to be taken into account. The first is what we refer to as a *desired level of comparability* because it is useful to consider where two assessments fall along a continuum of comparability rather than to render a simple dichotomous decision that the two assessments are comparable or not (Winter, 2010). The similarity between assessments in terms of content and skills assessed may range from the same content area (e.g., reading or mathematics) to the same set of content standards, to the same set of items. The level of content similarity sets a limit on the level of comparability that might be expected in results across the assessments, ranging from consistency in a "pass/fail" decision to the interchangeability of raw scores between the two assessments. The second factor is that determining the necessary level of comparability is impacted by claims made about performance across the two assessments or the intended use of assessment results. Within status- or improvement-based accountability contexts based on student proficiency, it has been more critical that assessments produce results closer to the "proficient/not proficient" end of the comparability continuum than it is that they produce interchangeable raw scores or scaled scores. However, an increased emphasis on progress or growth over time could change the required level of precision and, therefore, comparability needed.

Fairness is also an important comparability consideration for any assessment and is contingent on the interpretations and uses of the assessment results. OTL may not impact the accuracy of assessment results estimating student proficiency on a selected set of content and skills, but may have a profound impact on the interpretation and use of those assessment results in an accountability system. Similarly, students need to have the same opportunity to demonstrate their knowledge and skills to produce comparable results. In many cases, standardizing some of the assessment features will allow for equal opportunity; however, in other cases, such as for students with disabilities, flexibility rather than standardization in terms of the availability of accommodations will better allow for equal opportunity (Gong & Marion, 2006).

An attempt to design performance tasks, as well as assessment criteria and guidelines for portfolios and exhibitions, as comparable as possible within and over years, helps ensure comparability and will allow for more valid inferences regarding student progress (Haertel & Linn, 1996). Moreover, comparability of performance-based assessments across students and over time will be important in the models used for evaluating educators. It should be noted, however, that in the beginning years of a new performance-based assessment program, achieving high levels of comparability and reliability is challenging because it requires time for participants to develop the necessary expertise in assessment design and scoring as well as to reach consensus on design and scoring criteria. Students also need time to become familiar with different assessment formats and features.

The implementation of performance assessments and portfolios by states over the last few decades has provided valuable information that can inform the design and use of the next generation of performance-based assessments. A lack of standardization in the selection of tasks, scoring rubrics that were not well articulated, and insufficient rater training and calibration in Vermont's portfolio assessments in the early 1990s was found to contribute to inconsistency in scoring (Klein, McCaffrey, Stecher, & Koretz, 1995; Koretz et al., 1994). For the next generation of performance-based assessments, standardization of portfolios, including the collection of the same performance (content and/or skills) or well-specified criteria for submitted products (as is the case for AP Studio Art Portfolios), adherence to rules regarding guidance by teachers and others, and standardized criteria for scoring work products, will improve the comparability and hence their psychometric quality, as well as the validity and fairness of assessment results and uses.

For performance assessments and exhibitions, standardizing the assessment administration time period and the amount of time that is allocated for students to demonstrate competency helps ensure that no student is unfairly advantaged or disadvantaged. For portfolios that are constructed over the instructional year, standardizing when each student entry is submitted within a classroom and across classrooms that have the same instructional sequence will help ensure comparability and fairness. Of particular importance is that differences in student performances are not due to irrelevant sources of variance, such as differences in the amount of guidance and support provided to students in preparing their portfolios within a classroom and across classrooms. Providing specifications on what should be included and determining whether guidelines are consistently adhered to within classrooms and across classrooms will guard against some earlier problems exhibited with large-scale portfolio assessment programs. An evaluation of local assessment design, administration, and scoring procedures for quality by the district or state prior to implementation and a process for monitoring and auditing consistency during implementation will foster appropriate implementation.

This combination of detailed specifications combined with an established process of evaluation and auditing can be seen in the current development of guidance and implementation procedures for SLOs by states such as Rhode Island, Indiana, Connecticut, and New York. A similar approach was applied to the development of local graduation portfolios and performance exhibitions in Rhode Island. With funding from the Bill and Melinda Gates Foundation, the Rhode Island Department of Education and The Education Alliance at Brown University collaborated to develop a set of toolkits to support local districts in the development of local assessment systems required for student graduation (RIDE & The Education Alliance, 2005).

Districts and states can be guided with respect to score comparability by the *Standards for Educational and Psychological Testing* (AERA et al., 2014, pp. 95–101). The *Standards* indicate that "a clear rationale and supporting evidence should be provided for any claim that scale scores earned on alternate forms of a test may be used interchangeably" (p. 105). The *Standards* also acknowledge that, for complex item types, "score linking is sometimes conducted through judgments about the comparability of item content from one test to another … writing prompts built to be similar, where responses are scored using a common rubric, might be assumed to be equivalent in difficulty" (p. 99). Such judgmental appraisals of comparability should be evaluated with empirical data when it becomes available. Therefore, it is essential that the desired level of comparability among assessments (both performance-based and other assessments) be determined a priori and that principled design, administration, and scoring decisions be made to help achieve that level of comparability.

Comparability across Performance Tasks

Variability resulting from tasks occurs because typically only a few tasks are included in a performance assessment. Student–task interactions tend to average out over a set of multiple-choice items because the set usually contains relatively large numbers of items. However, student–task interactions have a greater impact on assessments comprising performance tasks because there are usually fewer tasks (Haertel & Linn, 1996). For example, Lane and her colleagues (1996) showed that task sampling variability was the major source of measurement error for mathematics performance assessments. Between 42 and 62 percent of the total score variability was accounted for by the person × task interaction, indicating that persons were responding differently across tasks due to task specificity and potential sources of construct-irrelevant variance. Shavelson and his colleagues (Shavelson, Baxter, & Gao, 1993; Shavelson, Ruiz-Primo, & Wiley, 1999) provided evidence that the large task sampling variability in science performance assessments was due to variability both in the person × task interaction and the person × task × occasion interaction. The person × task interaction accounted for 26 percent of the total score variability, whereas the person × task × occasion interaction accounted for 31 percent of the total score variability. The latter suggests that there was a tendency for students to change their approach to each task from occasion to occasion. Although students may have approached the tasks differently on different testing occasions, once the data were aggregated over the tasks, their aggregated performance did not vary across occasions (Shavelson et al., 1999). Consequently, assessment design must take into account the context of the task, directions, and materials, as well as other potential sources of construct-irrelevant variance, so as to minimize student–task interactions and to help foster fairness of the assessment (Bond, Moss, & Carr, 1996).

The use of evidence-centered design (Haertel et al., this volume; Mislevy, Steinberg, & Almond, 2003) can help promote comparability of assessment scores by clearly articulating the cognitive demands of the tasks and the necessary content and skills that provide evidence of students' understanding. The designs of both task models and scoring models are fundamental components of evidence-centered design, and building assessments using these models can help achieve the level of standardization that is needed to compare scores across students and over time. Aggregating scores across performance tasks can help alleviate some but not all of the comparability concerns at the level of individual tasks (Haertel & Linn, 1996). If performance tasks are to be used, a field test to evaluate prompts with respect to their difficulty and their interchangeability will help in the design of assessments that are comparable.

Comparability across Student Populations

Construct-irrelevant sources of variance may adversely affect the performance of some subgroups of students. Examples include task features such as language complexity and context, as well as student motivation to perform their best. With regard to the latter, differences in student motivation will most likely occur across classes and schools if there is variation in the use of assessment results in the grading process. To help alleviate the effect of language demands on tasks, Abedi and his colleagues (Abedi, 2010; Abedi & Lord, 2001) have developed methods to simplify the linguistic demands, such as reducing the complexity of sentence structures and replacing unfamiliar vocabulary with familiar vocabulary, and found that these methods resulted in a significant improvement in scores of both ELL and non-ELL students in low- and average-level mathematics classes (Abedi & Lord, 2001). This approach can be used in the design of performance assessments to help ensure a valid, fair, and comparable assessment not only of English language learners but also of other students who may have difficulty with reading. However, when applying such methods to simplify linguistic demands or determine what other types of accommodations might be allowable and appropriate, it is important again to consider the construct being measured and the claims being made about the results of the assessment.

Comparability in Human Scoring

It is critical that the scoring procedures employed by human raters are consistent within and across schools and districts. Accuracy and consistency in scoring can be jeopardized by the raters' interpretation and implementation of the scoring rubric and features specific to the training of raters and how they are monitored over time (Lane & Stone, 2006). Human raters may differ in the extent to which they implement the scoring rubric, the way in which they interpret the scoring criteria, the extent to which they are severe or lenient in scoring, their understanding and use of scoring categories, and their consistency in rating across examinees, scoring criteria, tasks, and over time (Bachman & Palmer, 1996). Training of the raters on how to apply the scoring rubrics to student work should include feedback to raters on their scoring accuracy and raters should demonstrate their accuracy prior to scoring actual work. Experiences from scoring statewide assessments have demonstrated that carefully designed scoring rubrics, training materials, and training procedures will help guard against low inter-rater reliability. To help ensure comparability over time, the same scoring rubrics, training procedures, training materials, calibration checks, and rater drift procedures should be used within schools and districts and perhaps across districts (Herman, 1998). Throughout the scoring process it is essential to evaluate the accuracy of raters in assigning scores and the extent to which they may drift in their accuracy in assigning scores.

Additionally, audits are needed to ensure that the implementation of training is consistent within and across districts within a year and over time. A moderation or audit process in which a panel of trained experts verifies the scores promotes fairness and reliability of scoring as well as providing relevant information to teachers to improve their scoring.

Providing benchmarks or anchors, examples of student work at each scoring level, allows for teachers, students, and raters to have a shared understanding of what student work looks like at each level of achievement and has implications for the validity and fairness of the assessment. It also meets Linn's (1994) criterion of transparency of the assessment process, allowing for a common understanding of what constitutes quality work, and therefore also has implications for instruction. The use of task-specific rubrics that were developed based on a general rubric may also lead to increased rater accuracy.

When possible, particularly when high stakes for students and teachers are involved, student work should be evaluated by trained raters/teachers who have no stakes in student performances; teachers should not evaluate their own students' work because of the risks of score corruption (Koretz, 2008). If the teachers do rate their own students' work, it is particularly important for schools and districts to require evidence, perhaps through an audit process, of the quality of scoring procedures and resulting scores.

Although two raters could independently score the student work, blind double-scoring has not proven to be practical for performance-based assessments within local districts. Nonetheless, as stakes increase, it may be prudent to double-score certain student assessments, such as those near a cut-score. In general, the burden and costs of double-scoring all assessments tend to outweigh gains in comparability above and beyond those achieved by the design, training, and monitoring procedures described above.

There are various formats that schools, districts, and states can use for training raters such as online and in-person training. A study that examined the effects of distributed online, regional online, and in-person training for raters of writing performance assessments concluded that these three groups of raters were comparable in terms of qualification rate, rating quality, and rater perceptions (Wolfe, Matthews, & Vickers, 2010). The major difference between these groups was that online training was considerably faster.

In addition to design considerations and implementation procedures intended to enhance consistency in human scoring, there are also analyses, such as generalizability studies (Brennan, 2001), that can be conducted to evaluate the actual consistency of scoring and its impact on results. Assuming adequate training of the raters, researchers have shown that rater inconsistency for science (e.g., Shavelson et al., 1993) and mathematics performance tasks (Lane et al., 1996) tends to be smaller than for writing assessments. Further, task sampling variability, in comparison to rater sampling variability, is a greater source of measurement error in science, mathematics, and writing performance assessments. Consequently, increasing the number of tasks, in comparison to increasing the number of raters, has a greater impact on the extent to which one can generalize from the obtained score to the larger domain.

Comparability of Administration Conditions

If administration conditions for performance-based assessments differ across classes, schools, and districts, score comparability will be jeopardized. Thus, it is important to standardize the conditions for administration of performance-based assessments. As an example, portfolio assessment guidelines can state the type of work to be included, the number of pieces of work to be included, and scoring criteria. Portfolio guidelines such as those developed by the College Board for the AP Studio Art course also routinely include a detailed description of the conditions under which the content for the portfolio can be generated (e.g., allowable interactions among the student, other students and teachers, and others outside of the school), as well as statements of ethics and proper administration that are to be read and/or signed (The College Board, 2011). The standardization of administration conditions, including materials, equipment, and time, within and across administration sites and years, promotes comparability. This requires training for teachers and other educators on administration procedures, such as when and how often evidence should be collected, the nature and extent of assistance that is allowed, and how to record assessment results.

Brief Introduction to Measurement Models

To help establish the comparability of performance-based assessments as well as to investigate other psychometric characteristics of assessments, various measurement models can be employed. Measurement models provide a mechanism to enhance the psychometric quality of the assessment and as a result the validity of score inferences and uses. Classical test theory, generalizability theory, and IRT facilitate both the design of assessments and the interpretation of student work products. Depending on the question being answered and the nature of assessment, assessment programs typically will use measurement models derived from one or more of these test theories.

Classical Test Theory

Classical score reliability statistics, such as coefficient alpha, provide information on the extent to which students are consistent in responding to different tasks in an assessment. Such internal consistency reliability coefficients, however, provide an incomplete evaluation of score reliability, as it is also affected by the occasion of administration (i.e., stability of scores) and the raters who are scoring student work. Interrater reliability is an important consideration for performance-based assessments that are being evaluated by human scorers because one wants to minimize the extent to which a student's score on the assessment is affected by the idiosyncrasies of the raters who evaluated the student's work. Intrarater consistency is also important because variation in scoring within a rater across time will affect the accuracy of the scores. This is particularly true for complex performance tasks which may involve multiple components and tasks such as portfolio entries which may be scored over extended periods of time. Classical test theory rater reliability indices include percent agreement and correlation coefficients between rater pairs such as Cohen's kappa that adjusts for chance agreement. Correlations, however, only provide information about the stability of relative rankings, and thus are not sufficient for absolute score interpretations, that is, criterion-referenced score interpretations. Furthermore, classical test theory cannot distinguish among different sources of error (Brennan, 2011).

Generalizability Theory

For a performance-based assessment that is composed of several performance tasks, generalizability theory is an important psychometric tool that can aid in the design and evaluation of the assessment. Generalizability theory provides a comprehensive framework for evaluating the extent to which results of performance-based assessments can be generalized to an intended domain and provides information regarding the precision of scores (Brennan, 1996, 2001, 2011; Cronbach, Gleser, Nanda, & Rajaratnam, 1972; Cronbach, Linn, Brennan, & Haertel, 1997). It is particularly relevant for the evaluation of performance-based assessments because it is able to distinguish and quantify the contributions of different sources of error, such as tasks, raters, and administration occasions. Modifying tasks or procedures based on the results of a generalizability analysis can promote the generalizability and validity of score inferences.

As previously discussed, measurement error due to tasks occurs because there are only a small number of tasks typically included in a performance assessment. Generalizability theory uses analysis of variance procedures to estimate a variance component for the object of measurement (e.g., student, class) and variance components that reflect errors in measurement such as error due to rater inconsistency and to task sampling variability. Examination of the estimated variance components provides information about the relative contribution of each source of measurement error. This information is then used to improve the assessment design so as to support more accurate relative and/or absolute score interpretations.

For performance assessments, portfolios, and exhibitions, the breadth of content standards will not be fully represented; rather, targeted standards will be represented in greater depth, and, therefore, it is necessary to clearly delineate the relevant content standards to be assessed in the domain of generalization. The results of generalizability studies on performance-based assessments have indicated that clearly articulated assessment specifications and scoring rubrics, trained raters, and periodic checks of rater performances can together reduce score variance and increase the generalizability of scores (Lane, Liu, Ankenmann, & Stone, 1996; Lane & Stone, 2006; Shavelson, Baxter, & Gao, 1993).

Item Response Theory

IRT denotes a class of mathematical models that are used to analyze test results in terms of latent, stable characteristics of persons that are presumed to underlie both student performance and psychometric characteristics of tasks. IRT enables the estimation of precision of an obtained test score and provides information about how each task functions across the ability or achievement scale. Models that have been developed for the polytomous scoring of tasks (e.g., assigning a score of 0, 1, 2, or 3), as would likely be needed for performance-based assessments, include the graded response model (Samejima, 1969), the generalized partial credit model (Muraki, 1992), and the many-facet Rasch measurement model (Linacre, 1989). In addition to the unidimensional models listed above, increasing complexity in the design of standard assessments combined with advances in technology suggests that multidimensional IRT models which may be more appropriate for complex performance-based assessments could be widely available in the near future.

IRT-Based Information

IRT-based conditional standard error of measurement curves provide information on the precision of scores along the score scale, providing a visual display of the precision near the performance level cut-scores (AERA et al., 2014). Consequently, IRT can be used to develop and refine assessments in order to maximize, for example, the precision of assessment near important cut-scores that mark the borders between adjacent classifications. The conditional standard error of measurement curve also provides evidence of how well the assessment can differentiate among students across the score scale. This information is important in the design of assessments and in the interpretation of assessment results for use in educator evaluation systems. For this purpose, it is essential that assessments are designed to provide precision not only near important cut-scores but also across the score scale, especially for students scoring at the upper and lower ends of the score scale. This is particularly important for the use of performance-based assessment results in accountability systems based on class means and those that incorporate individual student growth within or across years.

At a minimum, the review of IRT-based conditional standard error of measurement curves provides information on the precision of score estimates at various points along the score scale, which can be used to inform decisions about the appropriateness of using the assessment for particular accountability purposes. IRT-based information evidence can also inform the selection of items in the construction of new test forms with more desirable psychometric properties, such as increased precision near important cut-scores. For example, items that provide more information or measure student ability with more precision around the cut-score can be considered for inclusion in the assessments. Ultimately, over time and items, IRT can also provide item-level information on how particular characteristics appear to impact the difficulty and discriminating power of performance-based assessment tasks, resulting in efficiencies in the item development process. Although IRT cannot be used for all forms of assessments, it can be used for assessments that consist of a relatively large number of performance tasks or for assessments that consist of both selected-response items and performance tasks. It is important to note that, in classical test theory and generalizability theory (e.g., Brennan, 1998), methods have been developed to estimate conditional standard errors of measurement and, therefore, classical test theory and generalizability theory can also be used to maximize precision at particular regions on the score scale.

Modeling Rater Effects

While generalizability studies are important for the design of performance-based assessments and quantifying sources of error, measurement models that incorporate rater effects and behavior into the estimation of performance can be applied to performance-based assessments. Linacre's work (1989) was the first attempt to model rater effects using IRT models, and his approach enables test developers to compare the difficulty of tasks in relation to student proficiency and rater severity. It allows for estimating effects and identifying unusual patterns for particular raters, tasks, and rater/task combinations, thereby providing information to improve an assessment system. As an example, an interaction effect can be incorporated into the model to evaluate whether the score scale properties are invariant over raters or over tasks and raters. If time facets are included in the model, interaction effects involving the item facet and the rater facet can be used to examine rater drift over time. One type of informative output is a variable map, a graphic display that summarizes information about each facet and examines the fit between the students' proficiency and difficulty of the tasks, severity of the raters, and the consistency of score levels over tasks. In addition to information on the match between the distribution of student proficiency and task difficulty, information is provided on the extent to which each rater uses all the points on the score scale and if some raters overuse the middle points and avoid the extremes. The extent to which raters are consistent in their application of the criteria provides information on the reliability of student scores. If rater variance is large compared to the variance among students, calibrating raters and adjusting scores may improve the reliability of ratings by removing some of the noise associated with raters. If states or large districts are designing performance-based assessments, the many-facet Rasch model can be adopted to inform assessment design and scoring (see, e.g., Engelhard, 2013).

Reliability, Generalizability, and Classification Accuracy

It is important to clearly delineate the psychometric requirements of assessments such as reliability, generalizability, and classification accuracy for each intended purpose and use—student, educator, district, and state accountability. Schools, districts, and states then need to develop the infrastructure necessary for collecting, analyzing, and integrating different types of information about the assessment system so as to inform its design and implementation and to provide evidence of its quality and fairness for each intended purpose, claim, and use. A detailed evaluation plan should consider psychometric methods and criteria, as well as reflections and feedback from parties involved who can provide information on the actual implementation of designed features of the assessment such as administration procedures, training of raters, and the application of scoring criteria (i.e., any factors that might be considered sources of error that would impact the use of scores from the assessment). Analyses can provide information on the sources of error, but in advance of analyses it is important to identify the potential and likely sources of error and then obtain information on them to inform analyses such as generalizability studies.

Reliability and Generalizability

A challenge in the design and use of performance-based assessments is obtaining sufficient reliability and generalizability of the assessment scores. As suggested by Kolen (2011), one approach for increasing the reliability of performance-based assessments is to develop tasks that can be scored separately. In the design of assessment criteria for portfolios and performance assessments, if the tasks are specified to be independent, reliability could be estimated using composite scores as described in Haertel (2006).

Generalizability Studies

When examining the generalizability of a performance-based assessment, the facets that can be considered include tasks, rater, administration occasion, rater occasion, measurement method, and scoring method. As discussed earlier, in the design of performance-based assessments, perhaps the two most important facets that will affect the precision of scores are tasks and raters. Generalizability studies can be conducted to provide information on the number of tasks and number of raters needed to ensure sufficient reliability. Task sampling variability, which has been shown to be a greater concern than rater variability (Lane et al., 1996; Shavelson et al., 1993), can be examined with a student × task design, providing information on the inconsistency of persons responding across tasks as well as the number of items that are needed to provide reliable scores. A more comprehensive design, student × task × rater, allows for the estimation of multiple error variances, including the student × task, student × rater, and student × task × rater interactions. This design provides information on both the number of tasks and number of raters needed to provide reliable scores. For exhibitions that are scored holistically by two or more raters, a person × rater design could provide information on the number of raters needed to provide reliable scores on the exhibitions. To help determine the type of rubric (e.g., analytic or holistic) that provides the most reliable scores, a person × (rater:rubric) design could be used in which some raters use one rubric to score the student work and other raters use the other rubric to score student work. The use of these types of generalizability studies in a field test will inform the design of performance-based assessments.

Reliability of Aggregate Scores for Educator Accountability

In previous sections, we have discussed classical test theory, generalizability theory, and IRT approaches to estimating the reliability, consistency, or precision of individual student scores obtained from an assessment. There is no question that the reliability of individual student scores is important, particularly for accountability systems that are based on status measures of student performance or on estimating student progress or growth over time. In the context of educator, school, and district accountability, however, the reliability of aggregate scores is at least as important and must also be computed. Concerns regarding the reliability of school accountability scores were raised at the outset of NCLB (Hill & DePascale, 2003; Kane & Staiger, 2002;

Linn & Haug, 2002), and although those concerns were addressed to some extent through the use of confidence intervals and minimum sample size requirements, additional attention needs to be given to using test scores to measure school and educator performance over time. Hill and DePascale (2003) demonstrated that systems built to meet the assessment and accountability requirements of NCLB could not provide the reliability or precision necessary to support the fundamental decisions and inferences about school quality that were required by the law. Using a reliability-based approach, Kane and Staiger (2002) demonstrated the volatility of using test scores for measuring change at the school level. Rogosa (2003), however, argued that the reliability-based approaches used by Kane and Staiger (2002) as well as Linn and Haug (2002) were not appropriate for examining the volatility in school test scores; instead he demonstrated that growth curves for individuals or groups are more appropriate for measuring change at the school level. Research is needed for examining how best to use assessment scores for evaluating educator effectiveness and changes in performance over time. Such use of assessment scores is more challenging given that in most cases educator effectiveness scores are based on many fewer students than the number of students contributing to school scores; the construct of educator effectiveness is more complex and measures of it are less understood than the percent proficient metric used in school and district accountability; and more precise measurement is required under proposed models of educator effectiveness than the simple pass/fail decisions applied to school and district accountability systems under NCLB.

The consideration of measurement error is needed for performance-based assessments that are used for educator accountability. Measurement error tends to be much higher at the ends of the score scale than in the middle, and therefore a class mean score based on students who score at the lower end of the scale most likely will have more measurement error than a class mean based on students scoring in the middle of the distribution (National Research Council, 2010). Consequently, class composition with respect to performance level will affect the reliability of educator evaluation measures such as gain scores (National Research Council, 2010). Class performance level will also affect value-added estimates in that a class composed of low-performing students will result in less stable student estimates and consequently highly variable teacher value-added estimates. In Braun's (n.d.) thoughtful evaluation of psychometric and validity issues related to the use of value-added estimates and gain scores for educator accountability, he concluded:

> if we regard the estimation of teachers' relative effectiveness as an instance of measurement, then the validity of that measurement process is critically dependent on the quality of the test instruments that produce the raw data, the psychometric analyses that follow, and the strength of the argument supporting the causal interpretation of the output of the value-added model.

It is important that a performance-based assessment is designed to target all regions of the score scale. This may be difficult to accomplish by using performance tasks only; therefore, the use of selected-response items in addition to performance tasks may be preferable for some subject domains such as science and social studies. The use of evidence-centered design can result in more reliable measures for all students. Districts and states can also use generalizability theory to examine the dependability of class and school mean scores prior to their use in educator evaluation measures.

Classification Accuracy

Although generalizability theory can inform the design of performance-based assessments, accuracy of classification is imperative for standards-based assessments that assign students to performance levels (Rogosa, 1994). Classification consistency refers to whether students would receive the same classification if they took the same or a parallel form of assessment on a different occasion. Classification accuracy provides information on the extent to which a student classified using one assessment would be classified in the same way based on his/her "true" score (i.e., in theory, the average of performance on all possible forms of that assessment). There are a number of methods for estimating classification accuracy and consistency (see, e.g., Huynh, 1976; Livingston & Lewis, 1995).

Classification accuracy depends on the number of proficiency levels, as well as the measurement precision, especially around the cut-scores. Variation in measurement accuracy along the score scale results in variation in classification accuracy for students of different levels of proficiency: The closer the student is to the cut-score, the likelihood of a classification error increases and, as the number of proficiency levels increases, the number of students who are misclassified increases. Ercikan and Julian (2002) demonstrated that classification accuracy decreased as the number of proficiency levels increased, and this was of greater concern when the measurement precision (i.e., reliability) decreased. They provide guidelines for the minimum required reliabilities for a desired level of classification and number of proficiency levels.

Validity of Score Inferences about Student Proficiency and Progress

The use of test-based indicators in an accountability system usually requires additional layers of psychometric or statistical processing as well as additional interpretations regarding student proficiency and/or progress beyond those needed to produce the basic assessment results on which those indicators are based. Student proficiency is usually described by classifying student performance relative to several established performance-level thresholds, with one of those thresholds representing the lower bound for an adequate level of proficiency for the specific purposes of the accountability system (i.e., the same assessment results may be used to produce different proficiency thresholds for high school graduation, college- and career-readiness, or school accountability). Student progress, often referred to as growth, is described by a variety of methods ranging from simple gain scores, computed as the difference between two test scores on the same reporting scale, to the application of complex statistical procedures. As they have developed in conjunction with accountability systems, the operational definitions of both student proficiency and progress are tied closely to the large-scale state assessments on which they are based. This presents some unique challenges to attempts to draw valid inferences about student proficiency and progress or school or teacher effectiveness on the basis of student results on local performance-based assessments.

Student Proficiency—Performance-Level Classification

Since the shift from norm-referenced to criterion-referenced score interpretations, and especially with the advent of accountability requirements of NCLB, the primary reporting metric for educational assessments has been performance levels. That is, student performance is classified in relation to some previously established performance standards describing levels of performance such as Basic, Proficient, and Advanced. The use of performance-based assessments presents some unique challenges with regard to classifying student performance. Similarly, the role that performance-level classifications play in establishing performance targets for SLOs used in teacher accountability systems also requires careful consideration.

In general, for both standard and performance-based assessments, performance-level classifications create additional concerns about the validity of inferences regarding student proficiency or progress. The labels associated with performance-level classifications (e.g., Proficient, Basic,

Advanced) carry connotations and generate interpretations of student performance only loosely related to actual performance. In designing performance-based assessments for accountability systems, it must be considered whether the benefits gained from reporting performance in terms of performance levels outweigh the costs.

Specifying Performance Levels When Using Performance-Based Assessments

Reporting student results on performance-based assessments in terms of performance levels presents a variety of design and psychometric issues. The first set of issues stems from the fact that it is likely that there are no existing district or state performance standards for most of the courses in which performance-based assessments would be offered (i.e., courses for which there is not a corresponding state assessment). Although for most disciplines content standards have been proposed by national organizations composed of content experts, those standards are simply a starting point in the development of an assessment-based accountability system. Many of those content standards have not taken the additional step of establishing performance standards similar to those developed by states in reading and mathematics, and additional work is required to use content standards as a basis for assessment design, including further delineation of the claims to be made about student performance and evidence to support such claims. When performance standards do exist, the challenge is to ensure that the assessments provide evidence consistent with the claims made directly or implied in the language of the performance standards and to ensure that the evidence is sufficient to support a classification of student performance.

There are issues related to comparability as well as other technical and policy challenges associated with developing performance-level cut-scores for assessments in courses in which there are no established state performance standards (and perhaps no statewide content standards). Although the end result might make the process seem very easy (e.g., a score of 70 percent on the test = Proficient; or a score of 4 on the 6-point rubric = Proficient), the process of arriving at performance-level cut-scores is quite complex. Done improperly, the likely outcome is the arbitrary assignment of a figure like 70 percent or a score of 4 on the 6-point rubric as a cut-score for Proficient with little to no regard for the content of the test and its relation to a performance standard. The time, costs, and technical challenges associated with developing detailed performance standards and determining performance-level thresholds for each assessment (or set of assessments) administered in each course would be prohibitive for virtually all districts and many states. Whether performance standards are established at the state level or district level, comparability across grades, content areas, and individual courses is also an important consideration. The desired level of comparability claimed in the meaning of Proficient across courses and grades must be specified, and if a strong claim of comparability is made it would be necessary to evaluate that claim after performance standards were established. Although it probably would not be a desirable outcome to have multiple definitions of Proficient performance for the same course within a district, it may be less important to claim comparability across districts throughout the state.

A decision to establish statewide performance standards in all courses within a particular discipline (e.g., music, American history) would raise its own set of psychometric considerations. In theory, performance standards are independent of a particular assessment (i.e., performance standards should not be confused with the cut-scores on the reporting scale of the tests that delineate the standards) and it should be possible to establish performance standards that could be applied across a variety of performance-based assessments. An initial challenge in this case will be to determine the extent to which the performances (potentially) elicited by the assessment match the performances described in the performance standards. Does the performance-based assessment elicit the full range of content described in the performance standard, or does it focus more in depth on a limited range of content? Is the depth of knowledge or level of thinking skills elicited by the performance-based assessment consistent with the performance standards? Do the performance standards and the assessment both describe performance with respect to the same time frame (e.g., a fixed point in time versus growth or average performance over a period of time)? Each of these questions and surely others would have to be addressed in developing or selecting assessments to match previously established performance standards.

A final challenge commonly associated with performance-based assessments is related to sufficiency, that is, the amount and adequacy of evidence on which to base a judgment of proficiency. A common criticism of performance-based assessments is that although they may measure complex skills and cover content in depth, they produce limited results (perhaps a single score) which cannot be generalized across tasks. This is particularly true for large performance tasks or exhibitions which may be administered only once per year and produce a single score. However, even with performance-based assessments such as portfolios that contain a number of entries that are combined to produce a proficiency rating, the scope and nature of the evidence collected must be examined. When designing an assessment to be used in an accountability system, whether it be a collection of performance tasks or an exhibition, it will be necessary to consider how the results of the assessment will be used in the system, whether the assessment provides sufficient evidence, and how that sufficiency can be demonstrated.

Performance-Level Classifications and SLO Performance Targets

As a carryover from content areas and grade levels in which a state assessment is administered (aka, the tested grades and content areas), there is a temptation to define performance targets for an SLO in terms of the percent of *Proficient* students, where Proficient refers to a specific, established performance level. There are many reasons why this appears to be a reasonable approach. It may be desirable for consistency and ease of use and interpretation within the accountability system to report results from all grades and content areas in terms of "percent proficient." There may also be instructional benefits to using the same standards-based concepts and terms across all content areas. With many SLOs focused on performance on an end-of-year assessment, proficiency seems a logical target for student performance.

There are also several reasons, however, to proceed cautiously in attempting to tie SLO performance targets to a performance-level classification such as Proficient. Primary among these, of course, are the issues listed above related to defining and establishing performance levels in courses for which there is not an established state standard and the appropriateness of classifying student performance on the basis of the assessment(s) administered. There are also issues to consider related to determining the appropriate percent proficient performance target for a particular course or section (i.e., class) within a course. Unless the expected target is that all students within a grade level will be proficient (i.e., 100 percent proficient—which presents its own set of problems), it may be more appropriate to establish percent proficient targets for a teacher across classes within a grade level than within particular classes. For example, if a middle school English teacher is assigned to teach five sections of seventh-grade English, there are technical advantages to designating a goal such as 70 percent of students Proficient across the five sections as opposed to 70 percent of students Proficient within each section. In addition, the use of performance-level classifications to evaluate educator effectiveness is not sensitive enough to measure changes in student performance.

Related to the percentage of Proficient students in a particular class, there are cases in which a performance target of Proficient might not be appropriate at all. Consider that SLOs are used to document growth in student learning during the instructional process and are tied to specific teachers and groups of students. For students in an AP class or a remedial class, a performance target of Proficient might be too low or too high, respectively.

Student Progress—Growth

The practice of measuring progress or growth as part of large-scale educational accountability systems is certainly not new. For many years, normal curve equivalent (NCE) gains on successive Spring–Spring administrations or Fall–Spring administrations of norm-referenced standardized tests were a primary indicator of the success of Title 1 programs. Although admittedly crude, NCE gains contained the key element of all definitions of student progress—change. Central to the concept of student progress is a change in absolute performance and/or in relative standing. Another formulation of student progress for accountability systems is change in relation to what might be expected or predicted based on prior performance and (possibly) student characteristics.

The inclusion of student progress in school accountability systems and now in teacher accountability systems has spawned the development of a variety of so-called *growth models*—although some popular models make no attempt to measure or model growth directly in terms of the amount of change in performance. Rather, they construct indicators of progress in terms of current status conditioned on prior performance. Efforts to describe and evaluate growth models used in state accountability systems have identified four main classes of growth models: gain score, regression, value-added, and normative (Braun, 2012; Castellano & Ho, 2013; Goldschmidt, Choi, & Beaudoin, 2012). Despite the fact that there are key differences across model types with respect to how they define growth or progress, the type of results that are reported, and the inferences that they support, all are inextricably linked to the state's large-scale assessment system. Although, with regard to status-based measures such as performance-level classifications, performance-level descriptions are closely tied to the content and skills demonstrated through the standard state assessment, it is possible to apply those descriptions directly to, or to extrapolate from them, the knowledge and skills measured through the performance-based assessments even in other grade levels and content areas. Typically, performance-level descriptions provide general statements about the knowledge and skills required at each level so that extrapolations by subject matter experts is possible. With regard to growth, however, the measure, the metric, and its interpretation are all defined in terms of the state assessment and cannot be applied easily, if at all, to performance-based assessments or to an SLO. For example, a student growth percentile in Massachusetts, a value-added score on the 1.0 to 4.0 scale in Washington, DC, or a NCE on the Tennessee Value-Added Assessment System scale in Tennessee do not contain any content-based descriptions of growth or progress that can be applied to make comparable classifications of "growth" or progress on performance-based assessments in those states.

Defining Progress on Performance-Based Assessments

Although it is unlikely that many of the growth indicators developed for standard assessments can be applied directly to performance-based assessments, psychometrically sound evaluations of student progress can be derived from performance-based assessments for the purposes of accountability. Moreover, the unique, one-time nature of some forms of performance-based assessments, such as performance tasks or exhibitions, does not preclude drawing valid inferences regarding student progress. When developing the SLOs and selecting performance-based assessments that will be used as evidence that performance targets embedded in the SLOs have been met, it is essential to clearly define student progress and to specify the inferences about student progress that will be made as part of the accountability system.

Apart from the statistically based definitions of growth that accompany the growth models developed for accountability systems, there are fundamentally different conceptual definitions of growth. Gong (2010) proposed four concepts of growth that can be applied to performance-based assessments:

- Growth is increase in performance on the same thing, toward mastery.
- Growth is learning one topic and then learning a more advanced topic in a sequence of content.
- Growth is increase in expertise on the same thing (e.g., a more powerful mental model, increased fluency, greater independence).
- Growth is increase in integration across content and skills.

Each of these conceptions has implications for the design of an assessment system, but each can be built into the design of performance-based assessments such as portfolios, exhibitions, and performance tasks. Unlike standard assessments, many performance-based assessments incorporate time into their design; that is, they require performance over a period of time. Through well-designed portfolios, exhibitions, and performance tasks, it is possible to track and evaluate student progress over time in terms of one or more of those concepts of growth. Even if student proficiency is based on an evaluation of a final product or presentation, certain types of student progress can be determined through an evaluation of artifacts produced during the project.

Extended duration, however, is not a requirement for measuring student progress through performance-based assessments. In some cases, such as in the successful completion of an AP course, student progress is implicit in the assumption that virtually all students enrolled in the course did not enter the course with the knowledge and skills necessary to succeed on the summative assessment. In other words, the claim of growth is based on an inference from status. Similarly, in cases where the performance-based assessment is designed to directly measure critical or higher order thinking skills, a baseline level of student performance on those skills can be established through evidence from indirect measures of those skills on standard forms of assessment. Although it may not be possible to distinguish among degrees of progress in these examples, it may be feasible to determine adequate or sufficient levels of progress based on student status on a culminating assessment. This is one of the reasons that a solid description of baseline performance is built into the design requirements for many state-level SLOs used for teacher accountability systems.

Summary of Major Issues that Affect Psychometric Properties of Performance-Based Assessments and SLOs

The major issues that today affect the psychometric properties of performance-based assessments used as summative assessments and in educator accountability systems are the same as those identified by Koretz et al. (1994) in their evaluation of the Vermont Portfolio Assessment Program:

> We believe that the tensions between the instructional and measurement goals is fundamental and will generally arise in performance assessment systems that either embed assessment in instruction, rely on unstandardized tasks, or both. This appears not to be a problem that can be fully resolved by refinements of design; rather, policymakers and program designers must decide what compromise between these goals they are willing to accept.

> Validation will require clear statements of the inferences that the assessments are designed to support, including the levels of aggregation at which scores are to be reported and the metrics that will be used to report them. Firm validation of the results will also require clear delineation of the domains that the new assessments are designed to tap...

(p. 15)

The psychometric properties discussed in this chapter—comparability, reliability, generalizability, and classification accuracy—each must be viewed in terms of the conflict between instructional and measurement goals of assessment and accountability systems with a primary focus on the validity of inferences and uses that assessments and accountability systems are designed to support. Attention during the design phase to instructional sensitivity, comparability across tasks, rater and rating considerations, and factors that introduce construct-irrelevant variance, as well as areas in which standardization supports rather than threatens validity, will certainly enhance the quality of performance-based assessments and resulting score inferences. Clear statements of claims and intended inferences along with precise definitions of the domains being assessed will also make it easier to distinguish between factors that introduce construct-relevant variance and those that introduce construct-irrelevant variance as well as to identify areas of standardization that threaten the validity of inferences and decisions based on those inferences. For example, dependent upon the claims that will be made on the basis of assessment results, factors such as collaboration, use of external resources, and limited control of time spent on the assessment project could be either an important aspect of the construct being measured or a source of construct-irrelevant variance.

An appreciation of the difficulties related to achieving adequate levels of reliability, generalizability, and comparability of performance-based assessments should not serve as a reason not to include performance-based assessments in accountability systems. Rather, examination of these issues can serve to strengthen the design of such assessments by clarifying which claims can be made or which inferences and uses can be supported on the basis of a particular design. Incorporating the results of these investigations into the design process (rather than using analyses of reliability, generalizability, and comparability purely for summative evaluation purposes) puts the power of psychometrics to work in support of the design, development, and evaluation of performance-based assessments for use in accountability systems while maintaining their value for instructional purposes.

Acknowledgments

The authors would like to thank Henry Braun, the editor of this volume, Robert Brennan, and Courtney Bell for their constructive comments and suggestions that greatly improved this chapter.

References

Abedi, J. (2010). Linguistic factors in the assessment of English language learners. In G. Walford, E. Tucker, & M. Viswanathan (Eds.), *The Sage handbook of measurement.* Oxford, England: Sage.

Abedi, J., & Lord, C. (2001). The language factor in mathematics tests. *Applied Measurement in Education, 14*(3), 219–234.

American Educational Research Association (AERA), American Psychological Association (APA), & National Council on Measurement in Education (NCME). (2014). *Standards for educational and psychological testing.* Washington, DC: AERA.

Bachman, L. F., & Palmer, A. S. (1996). *Language testing in practice: Designing and developing useful language tests.* New York, NY: Oxford University Press.

Bond, L., Moss, P., & Carr, P. (1996). Fairness in large-scale performance assessment. In G. W. Phillips (Ed.), *Technical issues in large-scale performance assessment* (pp. 117–140). Washington, DC: National Center for Education Statistics.

Braun, H. (2012). *The many facets of growth modeling.* Paper commissioned by PARCC, Washington, DC.

Braun, H. (2013). Value-added modeling and the power of magical thinking. *Ensaio: Evaluation of Public Policies in Education* [Brazil], *21*, 115–130.

Braun, H. (n.d.). Magical thinking and the use of value-added models for educator accountability (unpublished article).

Brennan, R. L. (1996). Generalizability of performance assessments. In G. W. Phillips (Ed.), *Technical issues in large-scale performance assessment.* Washington, DC: National Center for Education Statistics.

Brennan, R. L. (1998). Raw-score conditional standard errors of measurement in generalizability theory. *Applied Psychological Measurement, 22,* 307–331.

Brennan, R. L. (2001). *Generalizability theory.* New York, NY: Springer-Verlag.

Brennan, R. L. (2011). Generalizability theory and classical test theory. *Applied Measurement in Education, 24*(1), 1–21.

Castellano, K. E., & Ho, A. D. (2013). *A practitioner's guide to growth models.* Washington, DC: Council of Chief State School Officers.

Council of Chief State School Officers (CCSSO). (2010). *Models for alignment analysis and assistance to states.* Retrieved from http://programs.ccsso.org/projects/Alignment_Analysis/Models

Cronbach, L. J. (1971). Test validation. In R. L. Thorndike (Ed.), *Educational measurement* (2nd ed., pp. 443–507). Washington, DC: American Council on Education.

Cronbach, L. J. (1988). Five perspectives on validity argument. In H. Wainer & H. I. Braun (Eds.), *Test validity* (pp. 3–17). Hillsdale, NJ: Erlbaum.

Cronbach, L. J., Gleser, G. C., Nanda, H., & Rajaratnam, N. (1972). *The dependability of behavioral measurements: Theory of generalizability of scores and profiles.* New York, NY: Wiley.

Cronbach, L. J., Linn, R. L., Brennan, R. L., & Haertel, E. H. (1997). Generalizability analysis for performance assessments of student achievement or school effectiveness. *Educational and Psychological Measurement, 57*(3), 373–399.

Engelhard, G. (2013). *Invariant measurement: Using Rasch models in the social, behavioral, and health sciences.* New York, NY: Routledge.

Ercikan, K., & Julian, M. (2002). Classification accuracy of assigning student performance to proficiency levels: Guidelines for assessment design. *Applied Measurement in Education, 15*(3), 269–294.

Goe, L., & Holdheide, L. (2011, March). *Measuring teachers' contributions to student learning growth for nontested grades and subjects.* Washington, DC: National Comprehensive Center for Teacher Quality. Retrieved from http://www.tqsource.org/publications/MeasuringTeachersContributions.pdf

Goldschmidt, P., Choi, K., & Beaudoin, J. P. (2012). *Growth model comparison study: Practical implications of alternative models for evaluating school performance.* Washington, DC: Council of Chief State School Officers.

Gong, B. (2010, June). *Using growth data to improve learning, teaching, and school functioning.* Presented at the annual CCSSO National Conference on Student Assessment, Detroit, MI.

Gong, B., & Marion, S. (2006). *Dealing with flexibility in assessments for students with significant cognitive disabilities* (Synthesis Report 60). Minneapolis, MN: University of Minnesota, National Center on Educational Outcomes.

Haertel, E. H. (2006). Reliability. In R. L. Brennan (Ed.), *Educational measurement.* Westport, CT: American Council on Education & Praeger.

Haertel, E. H. (2013). How is testing supposed to improve schooling? *Measurement: Interdisciplinary Research and Perspectives, 11*(1–2), 1–18.

Haertel, E. H., & Linn, R. L. (1996). Comparability. In G. W. Phillips (Ed.), *Technical issues in large-scale performance assessment* (NCES 96–802). Washington, DC: U.S. Department of Education.

Hargreaves, A., & Braun, H. (2013). *Data-driven improvement and accountability.* Boulder, CO: National Education Policy Center. Retrieved from http://nepc.colorado.edu/publication/data-driven-improvement-accountability

Herman, J. L. (1998). The state of performance assessment. *School Administrator, 55*(1), 17–18.

Hill, R. K., & DePascale, C. A. (2003). Reliability of No Child Left Behind accountability designs. *Educational Measurement: Issues and Practice, 22*(3), 12–20.

Huynh, H. (1976). On the reliability of decisions in domain-referenced testing. *Journal of Educational Measurement, 13,* 253–264.

Kane, M. T. (1992). An argument-based approach to validity. *Psychological Bulletin, 12*(3), 527–535.

Kane, M. T. (2006). Validation. In R. L. Brennan (Ed.), *Educational measurement.* Westport, CT: American Council on Education & Praeger.

Kane, M. T. (2013). Validating the interpretation and uses of test scores. *Journal of Educational Measurement, 50*(1), 1–73.

Kane, T. J., & Staiger, D. O. (2002). Volatility in school test scores: Implications for test-based accountability systems. In D. Ravith (Ed.), *Brookings papers on education policy 2002* (pp. 235–260). Washington, DC: Brookings Institution.

Klein, S. P., McCaffrey, D. F., Stecher, B. M., & Koretz, D. (1995). The reliability of mathematics portfolio scores: Lessons from the Vermont experience. *Applied Measurement in Education, 8*(3), 243–260.

Kolen, M. (2011). *Generalizability and reliability: Approaches for through-course assessments.* Princeton, NJ: Educational Testing Service.

Koretz, D. M. (2008). *Measuring up: What education testing really tells us.* Cambridge, MA: Harvard University Press.

Koretz, D. M., & Hamilton, L. S. (2006). Testing for accountability in K–12. In R. L. Brennan (Ed.), *Educational measurement.* New York, NY: American Council on Education & Praeger.

Koretz, D. M., Stecher, B., Klein, S., & McCaffrey, D. (1994). The Vermont portfolio assessment program: Findings and implications. *Educational Measurement: Issues and Practice, 13*(3), 5–10.

Lane, S., Liu, M., Ankenmann, R. D., & Stone, C. A. (1996). Generalizability and validity of a mathematics performance assessment. *Journal of Educational Measurement, 33*(1), 71–92.

Lane, S., & Stone, C. A. (2002). Strategies for examining the consequences of assessment and accountability programs. *Educational Measurement: Issues and Practice, 21*(1), 23–30.

Lane, S., & Stone, C. A. (2006). Performance assessments. In R. L. Brennan (Ed.), *Educational measurement.* New York, NY: American Council on Education & Praeger.

Linacre, J. D. (1989). *Many-facet Rasch measurement.* Chicago, IL: Mesa Press.

Linn, R. L. (1993). Educational assessment: Expanded expectations and challenges. *Educational Evaluation and Policy Analysis, 15,* 1–16.

Linn, R. L. (1994). Performance assessment: Policy promises and technical measurement standards. *Educational Researcher, 23*(9), 4–14.

Linn, R. L., Baker, E. L., & Dunbar, S. B. (1991). Complex performance assessment: Expectations and validation criteria. *Educational Researcher, 20*(8), 15–21.

Linn, R. L., & Haug, C. (2002). *Stability of school building accountability scores and gains* (CSE Technical Report 561). Los Angeles, CA: Center for the Study of Evaluation.

Livingston, S., & Lewis, C. (1995). Estimating the consistency and accuracy of classifications based on test scores. *Journal of Educational Measurement, 32*(2), 179–197.

Memphis City Schools. (2011). *TN Arts Growth Measures System.* Retrieved from https://www2.ed.gov/programs/racetothetop/communities/tle2-tn-arts-system.pdf

Messick, S. (1989). Validity. In R. L. Linn (Ed.), *Educational measurement* (3rd ed., pp. 13–104). New York, NY: American Council on Education and Macmillan.

Messick, S. (1994). The interplay of evidence and consequences in the validation of performance assessments. *Educational Researcher, 23*(2), 13–23.

Mislevy, R. J., Steinberg, L. S., & Almond, R. G. (2003). On the structure of educational assessments. *Measurement: Interdisciplinary Research and Perspectives, 1*(1), 3–62.

Muraki, E. (1992). A generalized partial credit model: Application of an EM algorithm. *Applied Psychological Measurement, 16,* 159–176.

Myford, C. M., & Mislevy, R. J. (1995). *Monitoring and improving a portfolio assessment system* (Center for Performance Assessment Research Report). Princeton, NJ: Educational Testing Service.

National Research Council. (2006). System for state science assessment. In M. R. Wilson & M. W. Bertenthal (Eds.), *Board on testing and assessment.* Washington, DC: National Academies Press.

National Research Council. (2010). Getting value out of value-added: Report of a workshop. In H. Braun, N. Chudowsky, & J. Koenig (Eds.), *Committee on value-added methodology for instructional improvement, program evaluation, and educational accountability.* Washington, DC: National Academies Press.

Niemi, D., Wang, J., Steinberg, D. H., Baker, E. L., & Wang, H. (2007). Instructional sensitivity of a complex language arts performance assessment. *Educational Assessment, 12*(3–4), 215–238.

Paul, K. A., Lewis, A., Zhu, M., Zhang, X., Burgess, Y., & Tinson, J. (2011). *South Carolina arts assessment program 2011: Technical report prepared for the South Carolina department of education.* Columbia, SC: University of South Carolina, Office of Program Evaluation.

Paul, K. A., Lewis, A., Zhu, M., Zhang, X., Burgess, Y., & Tinson, J. (2012). *South Carolina arts assessment program 2011*. Retrieved from http://scaap.ed.sc.edu/documents/SCAAP1011Tech nicalReport.pdf

Polikoff, M. S. (2010). Instructional sensitivity as a psychometric property of assessments. *Educational Measurement: Issues and Practice, 29*(4), 3–14.

Popham, J. (2007). Instructional insensitivity of tests: Accountability's dire drawback. *Phi Delta Kappan, 89*(2), 149–155.

Queensland Studies Authority. (2009). *The arts: Learning area*. Queensland, Australia: Queensland Studies Authority. Retrieved from http://www.qsa.qld.edu.au/downloads/senior/yr10_guide_learning_areas_arts.pdf

Rhode Island Department of Education (RIDE) & The Education Alliance at Brown University. (2005). *Rhode Island Diploma System: Local Assessment Toolkits*. Retrieved September 9, 2015 from http://www.ride.ri.gov/TeachersAdministrators/EducatorEvaluation/OnlineModules.aspx

Rogosa, D. (1994). *Misclassification of student performance categories*. Unpublished manuscript, Stanford University, Stanford, CA.

Rogosa, D. (2003). *Confusions about consistency in improvement*. Retrieved from http://statweb.stanford.edu/~rag/api/consist.pdf

Samejima, F. (1969). *Estimation of latent ability using a response pattern of graded scores* (Psychometric Monograph No. 17). Richmond, VA: Psychometric Society.

Shavelson, R. J., Baxter, G. P., & Gao, X. (1993). Sampling variability of performance assessments. *Journal of Educational Measurement, 30*(3), 215–232.

Shavelson, R. J., Ruiz-Primo, M. A., & Wiley, E. W. (1999). Note on sources of sampling variability. *Journal of Educational Measurement, 36*(1), 61–71.

Shepard, L. (1993). Evaluating test validity. In L. Darling-Hammond (Ed.), *Review of research in education* (Vol. 19, pp. 405–450). Washington, DC: AERA.

Stein, M. K., & Lane, S. (1996). Instructional tasks and the development of student capacity to think and reason: An analysis of the relationship between teaching and learning in a reform mathematics project. *Educational Research and Evaluation, 2*(1), 50–80.

The College Board. (2011). *Studio art: Course description*. Retrieved from https://secure-media.collegeboard.org/ap-student/course/ap-studio-art-2d-3d-studio-art-drawing-2011course-exam-description.pdf

U.S. Department of Education. (2012). *Race to the top program*. Retrieved from http://www.ed.gov/programs/racetothetop/resources.html

Webb, N. L. (2002, April 1–5). *Assessment literacy in a standards-based urban education setting*. Paper presented at the annual meeting of the American Educational Research Association, New Orleans, Louisiana. Retrieved from http://facstaff.wcer.wisc.edu/normw/AERA%202002/Assessment%20literacy%20NLW%20Final%2032602.pdf

Wiggins, G. P. (1993). *Assessing student performance*. San Francisco, CA: Jossey-Bass.

Winter, P. C. (2010). Introduction. In P. C. Winter (Ed.), *Evaluating the comparability of scores from achievement test variations*. Washington, DC: Council of Chief State School Officers.

Wolfe, E. W., Matthews, S., & Vickers, D. (2010). The effectiveness and efficiency of distributed online, regional online, and regional face-to-face training for writing assessment raters. *The Journal of Technology, Learning, and Assessment, 10*(1). Retrieved from http://escholarship.bc.edu/jtla

5 General Introduction to Evidence-Centered Design

*Geneva D. Haertel, Terry P. Vendlinski,
Daisy Rutstein, Angela DeBarger, Britte H.
Cheng, Eric B. Snow, Cynthia D'Angelo,
Christopher J. Harris, Louise Yarnall,
and Liliana Ructtinger*

For over a decade, educators have been confronted by urgent demands for evidence of improved instruction and increased student learning. These demands emerged in an era marked by new understandings about learning and cognition, previously unimagined technologies, and advancements in the statistical methods needed to model psychological constructs. This same era has yielded sobering evidence that U.S. students' proficiency and enthusiasm for learning, especially STEM learning, has flagged (National Research Council, 2005, 2007, 2011a).

The President's Council of Advisors on Science and Technology (PCAST, 2010) report presents evidence that less than one-third of U.S. students demonstrated proficiency in science and math on the National Assessment of Educational Progress (NAEP). With regularity, reports are published documenting the mediocre and sometimes dismal performance of U.S. students. For example, in 2009, when U.S. students were compared with their counterparts in other nations on the Programme for International Student Assessment (PISA) in science, math, and reading, they were placed near the middle of the score distribution within each respective content area (Walker, 2011). The National Research Council (2011b, p. 3), in its report on education, quoted from *Rising above the Gathering Storm, Revisited: Rapidly Approaching Category 5* (Augustine et al., 2010): "The U.S. ranks 6th among developed nations in innovation-based competitiveness, 11th in percentage of young adults who graduated from high school, 15th in science literacy among top students, and 28th in mathematics literacy among top students." Evidence of students' disengagement from science learning, in particular, is also provided by the meager numbers of African-Americans, Hispanics, Native Americans, and women undertaking careers in science (PCAST, 2010). Finally, the National Research Council (2011b) reflected on the weak achievement of the nation's students and posited several interacting factors as likely to contribute to their current status—poor teaching, limited educational resources, and school experiences that are overly focused on high-stakes accountability tests. Thus, educators, assessment designers, and policymakers are called on to conceive of instructionally valid, consequential large-scale assessments of deep learning that can provide students, parents, teachers, school and district administrators, and state and national policymakers with useful information that will spur learning and support engagement in all content disciplines.

Design Challenges for Large-Scale Assessment

Mislevy and Haertel (2006) point out that "long-established assessment practices did not evolve to deal with interactive tasks, multidimensional proficiencies, and complex performances" (p. 6), and yet these are the very types of assessments that educational practitioners, as well as other stakeholders, are now demanding. Progress in addressing these shortcomings, however, is well underway. Today's assessments are intended to address "hard-to-assess" constructs that are multidimensional and based on understandings from the learning sciences (Mislevy & Haertel, 2006).

In science, assessment designers are required to measure not only knowledge and skills but science inquiry processes as well (Opfer, Nehm, & Ha, 2012). In mathematics, assessment designers operationalize not only measures of algebra, geometry, and number and operations but also mathematical processes such as mathematical reasoning, modeling, and argumentation (Knudsen et al., 2013). The measurement of complex English language arts skills is being required, including the extraction of information from informative and literary passages; explanation of the interactions among a story's characters, plot, and setting; and the ability to write logical arguments based on substantive claims, sound reasoning, and relevant evidence.

In addition, these "hard-to-assess" constructs often require the use of complex multi-step procedures and processes, such as the construct of "expertise" in DNA sequencing. Furthermore, increasingly rigorous content and practice standards are being put forth by professional education associations (National Governors Association, 2010a, 2010b; NGSS, 2013). Computer technologies provide the means for being able to assess these complex understandings on a large scale in ways previously unimagined (Bennett, Persky, Weiss, & Jenkins, 2007; Quellmalz & Pellegrino, 2009) and to deliver these assessments for both classroom-based and large-scale assessment purposes.

Huff and her colleagues, in designing and implementing the next generation of Advanced Placement (AP) program examinations, have broken new ground in the application of Evidence-Centered Design (ECD) to an assessment system intended to measure highly complex content domains (Huff, Steinberg, & Matts, 2010). The design of the AP exams challenged the content specialists and assessment designers to tackle the measurement of deep conceptual understandings and complex reasoning skills through the use of multiple choice and constructed response item formats. Huff and her colleagues used ECD to assist in the specification of a measurement model and evidence rules that would ensure comparability of scores within and across years. ECD supported the detailed item writing and form assembly that was required to ensure form-to-form comparability. Having applied ECD, Huff and her colleagues were then able to articulate a validity argument to support meaningful and comparable inferences. Such an approach would have been a challenge before the mid-1990s, when Mislevy and his colleagues at ETS formalized the ECD approach to assessment design (Mislevy, Steinberg, & Almond, 2003; Mislevy, Steinberg, Almond, & Lukas, 2006; Steinberg et al., 2003).

In this chapter, large-scale assessment is described with particular attention to the advancements in assessment design and development described above. These include the use of ECD to guide the articulation of comprehensive assessment arguments, the application of technology to create innovative interactive computer tasks (ICTs), the application of findings from the learning sciences and cognition to measure "hard-to-assess" constructs, and the explosion of item/task formats available for use in measuring these constructs.

Applying ECD to Large-Scale Assessment

In this section, the work and processes of ECD are briefly presented and illustrated. Organized in five layers, ECD-informed processes include (1) Domain Analysis, (2) Domain Modeling, (3) Conceptual Assessment Framework (CAF) Articulation, (4) Assessment Implementation, and (5) Assessment Delivery. Greater depth is provided about two of the layers—Domain Modeling and the CAF—as these two layers yield design documents, Design Patterns and Task Templates, that are the hallmarks of the ECD approach. (Examples of each of these documents are presented below.) Table 5.1 displays the five ECD layers and presents each of their roles, key concepts used in each layer, and the knowledge representations commonly associated with each layer.

Although the layers of ECD are presented sequentially and give the appearance of being linear in nature, the practice of designing assessments using ECD is iterative. In practice, the assessment revision process requires cycling among three layers—the CAF (layer 3), Assessment

Table 5.1 The Five Layers of ECD

Layer	Role	Key Concepts	Selected Knowledge Representations
Domain Analysis	Gather substantive information about the domain of interest that has implications for assessment; how knowledge is constructed, acquired, used, communicated	Domain-specific concepts, terminology, tools, knowledge representations, analyses, situations of use, patterns of interaction	Representational forms and symbol systems used in domain (e.g., algebraic notation, number lines, graphing conventions, sentence diagrams, literary genres, style conventions, the Periodic Table, Punnett squares, food webs, phylogenetic trees, computer program interfaces, content standards, concept maps)
Domain Modeling	Express assessment argument in narrative form based on information from Domain Analysis	Specifications of knowledge, skills, or other attributes to be assessed; features of situations that can evoke evidence; features of items and tasks that convey evidence	Design patterns; "big ideas"; Toulmin and Wigmore diagrams for assessment arguments; assessment blueprints, ontologies, generic rubrics
CAF	Express assessment argument using psychometric structures and specifications for tasks and tests, evaluation procedures, measurement models, descriptions of work products	Student, evidence, and task models; student, observable, and task variables; rubrics; measurement models; test assembly specifications; task templates and task specifications	Algebraic and graphical representations of measurement models; task templates and task specifications; item generation models; generic rubrics; rules of evidence; algorithms for automated scoring
Assessment Implementation	Implement assessment, including presentation-ready tasks and calibrated measurement models	Task materials (including all materials, tools, affordances); pilot-test data to hone evaluation procedures and fit measurement models	Coded algorithms for rendering tasks and interacting with examinees and evaluating work products; tasks as displayed; IMS/QTI representation of materials; APIP formats for presenting assessment materials for students with disabilities; ASCII files of item parameters
Assessment Delivery	Coordinate interactions of students and tasks: task and test-level scoring; reporting	Tasks as presented; work products as created; scores as evaluated	Renderings of materials; numerical and graphical summaries for individuals and groups; specifications for results files

Source: Adapted from Mislevy and Haertel, 2006.

Implementation (layer 4), and Assessment Delivery (layer 5). Once a final version of the assessment is designed, the amount of iteration is greatly reduced and future versions of the assessment can be done in a fairly linear fashion by using existing Design Patterns and Task Templates to create new items and forms of the assessment.

ECD Layer 1: Domain Analysis

As the first stage, *Domain Analysis* is about marshaling substantive information about the content domain. Assessment designers use this substantive information to understand and organize the knowledge, skills, and abilities (KSAs) people use in the domain of interest, the representational forms they employ, the characteristics of good work, and key features of situations. All of the information used in the Domain Analysis has important implications for assessment design, although usually most of the source materials are neither originally created to support assessment nor presented in the structure of an assessment argument. For example, the National Council of Teachers of Mathematics Standards and Focal Points (http://www.nctm.org/standards/default.aspx), the Common Core State Standards for Mathematics (National Governors Association, 2010b), and some state mathematics standards are good content sources for designing a large-scale mathematics assessment. These standards can serve as a Domain Analysis and contribute to organizing the relevant mathematics content for the purposes of large-scale assessment design and development. These documents provide standards for each grade level or grade band. For example, a middle school grade band would include standards for grades 6, 7, and 8. Thus, the Domain Analysis is able to accommodate the need for standards at specific grades or grade bands. In addition to standards documents, key substantive reports such as the National Research Council publication *Taking Science to School: Committee on Science Learning, Kindergarten through Eighth Grade* (2007) provide information that is useful in analyzing a content domain. A thorough analysis of the content domain of interest is prerequisite for generating a design pattern, which is the product of the work that is conducted in the next layer of ECD. For specific examples of the work conducted in a Domain Analysis, see Knudsen et al. (2013) and Cheng, Ructtinger, Fujii, and Mislevy (2010), and for a description of the Domain Analysis process used in the revision of the AP tests, see Ewing, Packman, Haman, and Thurber (2010).

ECD Layer 2: Domain Modeling

In the Domain Modeling layer, information identified in Domain Analysis is organized along the lines of an assessment argument. According to Baxter and Mislevy (2005),

> An assessment argument lays out the chain of reasoning from evidence (what students say or do in particular situations) to inference (what we wish to say about students' abilities more generally). The key elements of an assessment argument—what is important to know, what constitutes evidence of knowing, and in what ways this evidence can be elicited from students—are explicated in design patterns (see below for examples). Making substantive considerations explicit from the onset serves to place appropriate boundaries on subsequent design decisions. Because assessment design is inevitably iterative, a process of inquiry itself, design decisions always can be revisited in light of reflection and empirical feedback. The point is to ensure that the designed assessment is (a) consistent with the developer's goals/intentions and (b) internally coherent (i.e., evidence is gathered and interpreted in ways that bear on the underlying knowledge and purposes the assessment is intended to address).

(p. 5)

Table 5.2 Key Attributes of a Design Pattern

Design Pattern Attribute	Attribute Definition	Assessment Argument Component
Focal KSAs	The primary KSAs targeted by this Design Pattern	Claim
Rationale	Nature of the KSAs of interest and how it is manifest	Warrant
Additional KSAs	Other KSAs that may be required by tasks motivated by this Design Pattern, but not the target of the assessment	Claim, if relevant; alternative explanation, if irrelevant
Potential Work Products	Things students say, do, or make that can provide evidence about the Focal KSAs	Data concerning a student's actions
Potential Observations	Qualities of Work Products that encapsulate evidence about Focal KSAs	Data concerning a student's actions
Potential Rubrics	Ways of evaluating Work Products to produce values of observations	Warrant
Characteristic Features	Aspects of assessment situations likely to evoke the desired evidence	Data concerning situation
Variable Features	Aspects of assessment situations that can be varied in order to control difficulty or target emphasis on various aspects of KSAs	Data concerning situation

Source: Adapted from Mislevy and Haertel, 2006.

Drawing heavily on the work of Toulmin (1958), the assessment argument provides terminology describing how substantive theories and accumulated experience can be used to reason from particular data to a particular claim. A claim is a proposition that is supported with data. Inferences about student performance are justified by a warrant. A warrant is defined as a generalization that justifies the inference from the particular data to the particular claim. Warrants can be "backed" by empirical studies, prior research findings, theory, and experience. In any particular assessment argument, the designer reasons back through the warrant and may need to qualify the inferences drawn, if there are alternative explanations for student performances.

Without getting enmeshed in the technical details of assessment design, this layer requires researchers to clarify what is to be assessed and how and why to do so. Design Patterns (Mislevy, Hamel, et al., 2003) support work in the Domain Modeling level of ECD by helping the assessment designer think through the key elements of an assessment argument in narrative form. Key attributes of Design Patterns are briefly described in Table 5.2. In addition, we specify the role the attribute plays in the assessment argument.

Focal KSAs

A Design Pattern is organized around Focal KSAs. Focal KSAs can be cast in terms of one of many perspectives of capabilities—behavioral, trait, information processing, or sociocultural (Mislevy, 2003). The Design Pattern helps designers conceptualize and create tasks from one or more of those perspectives. The Observational Investigation (Mislevy et al., 2009) and Experimental Investigation (Colker et al., 2010) Design Patterns in Appendices A and B reflect the "science as inquiry" stance taken in the National Science Education Standards (National Research Council, 1996).

Focal KSAs are central to the claims that a family of assessment tasks is meant to support, although there may be other KSAs that are included in the target of inference. For example, in addition to a student's proficiency with observational investigations (a science practice), science content knowledge might also be included in the target of inference. Thus, the

Design Pattern can support multidimensional assessment task design as well as the design of unidimensional tasks.

Rationale

The rationale provides background into the nature of the Focal KSAs and the kinds of things that a student will be asked to do in given situations in order to provide evidence with respect to the Focal KSAs. Rationales reported in Design Patterns are often drawn from research in the specific domain and the underlying philosophy of science. Key references for citations to the research, theory, and underlying philosophy may be included.

Additional KSAs

Additional KSAs play several roles in assessment design. Initially, task designers need to identify the Focal KSAs that are necessary to include as targets of inference (i.e., construct-relevant with respect to validity) for the assessment of interest. Then, they must identify which KSAs are required for success on the assessment task, but are not construct-relevant, and those that might influence student performance resulting in an invalid inference about a student's performance. The Additional KSAs that assessors *do* want to include as targets of inference are part of the claim. For example, if an assessment task is intended to test the ability of a student to formulate a scientific model in an investigation, he or she needs content knowledge of the scientific phenomenon being modeled (e.g., Mendel's laws). In this case, the skills of model formation are the primary target of inference, but the content knowledge about Mendel's laws is a construct-relevant KSA. If the student does not possess adequate content knowledge of Mendel's laws, his or her performance on the modeling task will be degraded. The Additional KSAs that assessors *do not* want to include as targets of inference introduce alternative explanations for poor performance, which would blur the claim assessors want to make about students. For example, if a student has to use a mouse to respond to a technology-enhanced assessment task, but does not possess good "mousing" skills, he or she may perform poorly on the science task, but not because they do not understand the science content knowledge and skills. Prerequisite skills are often Additional KSAs, as they are background knowledge that is required for successful performance, but not the specific KSAs being targeted in the items and tasks being designed. A strength of ECD is that it enables, if not forces, assessment designers to acknowledge and model Additional KSAs.

This latter role of Additional KSAs is especially important for assessing special populations (Hansen, Mislevy, Steinberg, Lee, & Forer, 2005). To minimize the contributions of irrelevant factors on student performance, such as poor vision or attention-deficit disorder, task designers should conduct their work using the principles of Universal Design for Learning (Cameto, Haertel, DeBarger, & Morrison, 2010) with due attention to the appropriate accommodations and modifications for students with special needs.

Additional KSAs can be related to Variable Features and Work Products as a means for providing support and scaffolding for a student's performance (Haertel et al., 2010). Specifically, a Design Pattern can provide direction about how to support or circumvent particular construct-irrelevant Additional KSAs by offering design choices regarding how and what information will be presented to a student, how the student will interact with the tasks, and how responses will be expressed and captured.

Potential Work Products

Assessment designers use Work Products to capture performances—a selected response, a procedure, a constructed model, an essay, a drawing, etc.

Potential Observations

Potential Observations highlight the qualities of Work Products that contain evidence about the Focal KSAs. They produce data that will be used to summarize a student's Work Product in ways that can be leveraged as evidence regarding a claim.

Potential Rubrics

Potential Rubrics are the scoring rules for evaluating Work Products.

Characteristic Features

Characteristic Features of assessment tasks are intended to elicit evidence required for the valid measurement of Focal KSAs. For example, a task designer using the Observational Investigation Design Pattern might build an assessment task around the "emergence of an invasive species, the Burmese Python, in the Florida Everglades over the past decade." Examinees would be presented with a table in which data collected about the prevalence of Burmese Pythons is presented for each year from 2004–2013. This table would be a characteristic feature of tasks designed to elicit evidence about the Focal KSA: "Ability to formulate conclusions, create models, and appropriately generalize results from observational, non-experimental results."

Another example of a Characteristic Feature is drawn from a mathematics assessment task titled Roadtrip. This task was designed to measure a student's ability related to linear functions. In the task, the student is given a scenario-based assessment in which a family goes on a road trip with two other families. One of the Focal KSAs that is included in this assessment task is "Ability to translate between graphs, tables, equations, and words for a single linear function." One example of a Characteristic Feature related to this Focal KSA is that a task must have multiple interrelated representations of one or more linear functions. This Characteristic Feature must be present in any task developed from this Design Pattern focused on linear functions.

Variable Features

Variable Features of tasks can be used to increase or decrease the difficulty of the assessment task. Reducing the demand for Additional KSAs is an effective way to avoid alternative explanations for a student's performance. Some Variable Features can prompt designers to be aware of how they might match features of tasks with the characteristics of a student such as his or her interests, familiarity with the content, and prior instruction.

One enhancement to the Domain Modeling process that some assessment designers use is the specification of Achievement Level Descriptors (ALDs) (Hendrickson, Ewing, Kaliski, & Huff, 2013; Huff & Plake, 2010). ALDs, which were implemented as part of the ECD-driven redesign of the AP examination, identify what students are expected to know and to do at each level of cognitive complexity. Through the use of this process, ALDs contribute substantially to the articulation of task models (Hendrickson, Huff, & Luecht, 2010; Huff, Alves, Pellegrino, & Kaliski, 2013).

The process of specifying ALDs begins with the use of exemplar claims to generate preliminary ALDs in narrative form. These ALDs define characteristics of the performance levels associated with claims or evidence statements. The process of generating the ALDs is iterative, and the emergence of new or refined claims or evidence statements may point to the need to generate new or refine existing ALDs. These ALDs extend the chain of reasoning in terms of the validity argument from pairs of claims and evidence to the intended score interpretation. In other words, the claims and evidence pairs are mapped to the score scale. The ALDs are used to inform item and task development, contribute to form assembly specifications, and inform the setting of cut scores—all of which provide validity evidence and buttress the underlying validity argument. Along with the advances surrounding the use of ALDs in task models, ECD has stimulated the conceptualization of cognitive complexity as a way of creating task models that are more aligned to the range of abilities that must be elicited to validly measure a student's performance on a given claim.

According to Hendrickson et al. (2013, p. 6), cognitive complexity addresses:

a   the skills, processes, and/or practices that we value in this content area;
b   how these factors change as students become more proficient; and
c   the nature of the interaction with content vis-à-vis cognitive demand.

When task models are being specified, the level of cognitive complexity of a claim is identified first and, from this initial specification, the level of the cognitive complexity of the task models is established. Levels of cognitive complexity can be expressed using a variety of terms—in the AP redesign, the cognitive complexity of claims was expressed using levels of proficiency, such as "basic." Once the cognitive complexity of the task model is established, the assessment designer then identifies the features that impact the complexity of the tasks that will yield evidence for a given claim (Kaliski, Huff, & Barry, 2011; Schneider, Huff, Egan, Tully, & Ferrara, 2010). Below, an example of six manipulable features of cognitive complexity are presented from an AP biology task model that focused on cell division (Hendrickson et al., 2013, p. 12):

(1) type of cell division (mitosis is simpler than meiosis); (2) number of steps in the process (mitosis has fewer steps than meiosis); (3) type of statement alternative (definition is less challenging than explanation); (4) use of vocabulary particular to cell division will increase complexity: ploidy, tetrads, synopsis, crossing over, sister chromatids, homologous chromosomes, segregation, equatorial plate, cytokinesis; (5) phase of cell division in question; the events in some phases are more conceptually difficult than the events of other phases; (6) making a comparison (more challenging) vs. selecting a true statement (less challenging).

The six manipulable features provided in the example above are comparable to the Variable Feature attribute in Design Patterns.

The work of Huff and her colleagues in identifying and prescribing the development of ordered task models (task models associated with a particular claim or evidence statement are nested within an achievement level) provides a method that can help advance the use of ECD and overcome some of these challenges. The process of producing robust task models is challenging, and researchers have identified specific issues that make building such models difficult. Among those issues are (1) finding the right grain size for the expression of claims and the production of a manageable amount of evidence; (2) determining whether the task model is complete; (3) determining whether the task model can generate the number of items needed; and (4) identifying the evaluative criteria applicable to judging the quality of a task model.

In sum, Design Patterns are key documents in the ECD process. They provide the minimum level of specification needed to initiate the ECD process and are essential for subsequent item and task design. In some cases, projects and clients begin with Design Patterns and proceed to develop Task Templates and other forms of documentation to support the item/task design process. In many cases, Design Patterns alone serve to conceptualize the design of the item and task families. Thus, the actual writing of items and tasks flows from the ideas conceptualized in the Design Patterns. Design Patterns express the underlying idea of an assessment argument in a manner that is readily accessible to those charged with designing the assessment without heavy reliance on psychometric and statistical concepts. The Design Patterns that are yielded by the Domain Modeling process are more of a conceptualization process of a content domain rather than a technical implementation of the assessment task design. The process of ECD through the Domain Modeling phase is useful in developing a curriculum framework and instructional lessons without going through the process of the development of assessment items and tasks.

ECD Layer 3: Development of the CAF

The Student, Evidence, and Task Models comprise the CAF (Messick, 1994; Mislevy & Haertel, 2006; Mislevy, Steinberg, et al., 2003). Figure 5.1 displays a schematic representation of each of these models and their interrelationships. Each model has its own internal logic and structures and is linked to the others through key elements called Student Model Variables, Observable Variables, Work Products, and Task Model Variables. The three models are relevant to assessment design, regardless of the content domain being assessed.

The relationships among the Student, Evidence, and Task Models are further clarified through the work of Michael Kane. Kane (2006) asserts that validating an assessment involves two distinct types of arguments—an interpretative argument and a validity argument. Specifically, Kane (2006, p. 27) describes the interpretative argument as follows: "Initial inference in a quantitative interpretative argument is to be from a record of performance on some task (datum) to a score (the claim)." The process of using ECD to establish and to relate claims and evidence includes an explicit rationale explaining why specific tasks were designed for use in the test under development; that is, claims are linked to evidence and relate to particular tasks and test specifications. Thus, the specificity required by ECD, as the test designer moves from Domain Analysis (identification, organization, and prioritization of content and skills) to the work of Domain Modeling (claims, evidence, and ALDs are articulated) and finally to the specification of the CAF (psychometric information), enhances the robustness of the validity argument underlying test score interpretation (Ewing et al., 2010).

In specifying the CAF, the assessment designer makes the decisions that give shape to the actual assessment that will be generated. Details about task features, measurement models, and stimulus material specifications are expressed in terms of representations and data structures that will guide the implementation and ensure their coordination for assessment development in the content domain of interest.

Paraphrasing Levy (2013), three principles are used to guide the articulation of the measurement model to be used in the CAF for scenario-based tasks. Popular unidimensional IRT models may be sufficient if the CAF targets a single broad proficiency of performance on which students will be differentiated and the proficiency can be characterized as a "cross-sectional picture" that is operationalized as a single student model variable which contains many discrete tasks that will then produce one dichotomous observable variable that corresponds to the correctness of the answer which is conditionally independent.

When dealing with scenario-based tasks, the line of evidentiary reasoning may be more complex. There may be multiple student model variables that have to be related in complex ways. Several observable variables may be generated from a single task. These observable variables may reflect performance at the end of the task and performance during the process which leads to the observable variable. There may be behaviors that occur at the end of the performance that depend on performances that occur earlier in the assessment task. Finally, complex relationships may exist among the performances (e.g., conjunctive, compensatory). Levy states that "These OVs [observable variables] are then entered into a unidimensionable measurement model characterized by a single latent SMV [student model variable], which is our representation of student used to make inferences and decisions about the student" (p. 204). The differences between

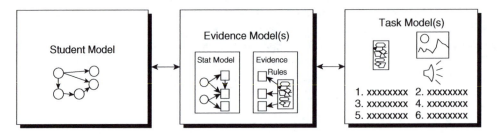

Figure 5.1 Schematic representation of the Student, Evidence, and Task Models.

the articulation of the CAF for scenario-based assessments and non-scenario-based assessments have to do with (1) the large space of possible behaviors and performances that can occur in scenario-based tasks; (2) the complexity of the inferences that need to be drawn; (3) the use of new and less familiar item formats; (4) the need to model observable variables with dependencies; and (5) the contextualized nature of the task presentation required to assess multidimensional student models.

In the Principled Assessment for Design in Inquiry (PADI) online assessment design system, task templates are where users of the PADI do this work. Appendix C displays the summary page of the task template for generating BioKIDS/Ecology Life Science tasks. Some of the more detailed objects the template contains are discussed below.

Student Model

The Student Model represents the student proficiencies an assessment designer wants to measure (Mislevy, Steinberg, et al., 2003). The number, character, and granularity of these proficiencies, as well as their interrelationships, are determined by the purpose of the assessment. For example, a single Student Model variable can be used to characterize a student's overall proficiency in a domain of tasks for a graduation/placement decision, whereas a multidimensional Student Model variable can be used to sort out patterns of proficiency from complex performances that can provide more detailed feedback. The proficiencies being specified in the Student Model are connected to those Focal KSAs and Additional KSAs identified in the Domain Modeling layer. BioKIDS/Ecology uses a multidimensional Student Model to track aspects of both content knowledge in Ecology and inquiry skills such as making hypotheses, generating explanations, and analyzing and interpreting data. These multidimensional Student Model variables were first introduced in the Design Patterns that the BioKIDS project developed when they were working at the Domain Modeling layer.

Task Model

The Task Model describes an assessment setting in which students say, do, or make something to provide evidence (Mislevy, Steinberg, et al., 2003). In designing the Task Model, an assessment designer specifies the directives, stimulus materials, and the features of the presentation environment. A key design decision is specifying the Work Product(s) that will capture student performances. For example, one may decide to capture students' Work Products using an image-enhanced selected response, an essay, an interactive computer task, a specimen slide, or excerpts from a laboratory notebook. The Full Option Science System (FOSS) project, for example, designed a series of simulations of science phenomena to assess the science content and inquiry processes covered in the FOSS modules. The type of Work Products derived from these simulations, such as a table of results, a text explanation of a scientific phenomenon, a series of graphs, and an associated mathematical formula, can be used with many different tasks generated from the same Task Model.

For example, FOSS asks students to conduct an experiment using a computer-based simulation to gather evidence of the relationship between the number of times a wire was coiled around a rivet and the number of washers the rivet could attract when a student applied an electric current to the wire. Students recorded their results in a data table within the simulation. After running the simulation several times, the students used a dynamic Cartesian graphing tool to plot the results of their experiment. This graphing tool allowed students to label the vertical and horizontal axes and to plot and connect the points resulting from their experiment. This graphing tool and its associated Work Product can be reused with other science tasks with different content, stimulus materials, and activity patterns. Decisions about the Characteristic and Variable Features in the Task Model are guided by the Domain Modeling conducted in the second layer of the ECD workflow.

Behrens, DiCerbo, and Ferrara (2012) discuss ways to think about possible spaces of examinee–task interactions that are relevant for the development of innovative item types. They point out that "the ECD model opens one's understanding to the broad range of possible interactions and activity, but it remains silent on specific conceptualization of tasks and, therefore, how one may consider simulations from a psychosocial or activity framework" (p. 9). They address this gap by identifying four aspects of task design that are relevant to a student's assessment experience: problem space, tool space, solution space, and response space. Each of these is described below.

- Problem space: An assessment task includes a goal that leads each examinee to the conceptualization of the problem he or she is going to solve. This goal steers the examinee to a set of constrained actions. The problem to be solved may be informational or procedural. Sometimes the problem space is clear; in other cases it is left purposely ambiguous.
- Tool space: The mechanisms used to solve the assessment task. Sometimes the tools are the intellectual capabilities of the examinee. In other cases, the tools are technology affordances that can enhance the performance of the individual beyond what he or she could accomplish without the tools. These tools may provide visual, auditory, or temporal representations, illustrations, or manipulations that improve the examinee's comprehension of complex information. Examples of tools include dynamic graphs and tables, chat experiences, word processing, and spreadsheets.
- Solution space: The set of possible activities that can be used to attain a goal. In open-ended and performance assessment tasks, a wide variety of activities can be supported. Assessment designers can control the size of the solution space in several ways, including tools that are made available to the examinee or the specific form of a solution that is requested.
- Response space: Activities that result in the Work Product to be evaluated (a table representing data from an experiment or a selection of an option in a multiple choice item).

An assessment designer using ECD might specify the Task Model with reference to one or more of these four "spaces" which an examinee would then consider when solving the assessment task. The performance of the examinee in each of these four spaces needs to be considered when designing innovative items and tasks.

Evidence Model

An Evidence Model bridges the Student Model and the Task Model. The Evidence Model consists of two components: the Evidence Rules and the Measurement Model. These components correspond to two steps of reasoning. The Evidence Rules detail how the relevant features of the student work are used to obtain values for the Observable Variables and how they are evaluated. Evaluation procedures can be algorithms for automated scoring procedures, or rubrics for human scoring. The Measurement Model specifies how the evidence generated by the Evidence Rules will be assembled and combined to generate one or more student scores.

Messick's (1994) representation of the CAF illustrates the relationships among the Student, Evidence, and Task Models as three separate modules—a characterization that facilitates reuse. For example, different evaluation procedures could be used to extract different observable variables from the same Work Products when the assessment tasks are used for different purposes. For example, a task that asks a student to produce an essay describing the contribution of a U.S. president may be scored using different rubrics specified within an Evidence Model. The rubrics specified should be aligned to the student model of interest. One rubric may examine how well the student applied grammatical rules, how many words they misspelled, and how accurately he or she applied punctuation rules in his or her essay. This rubric would be aligned with a student's knowledge and ability to apply the norms and conventions of Standard English usage. A second rubric may focus on the quality of information the student presents, the relevance of that information to the topic, and the conclusions that are drawn based on that information. This rubric would be used to measure a Student Model aligned to a student's ability to use relevant and significant evidence to support conclusions. Depending on the purpose of the assessment and which Student Models are being measured in the assessment, one or both of these rubrics could be applied. The CAF for a given assessment may specify multiple Student, Evidence, and Task Models which could be used to design several assessments. A critical decision that an assessment designer must make is the identification of which of the related Student, Evidence, and Task Models represent the goals and purpose of the particular assessment that is being designed. The assessment designer uses the CAF to chart a pathway through the development process, making use of the conceptual and technical specifications presented in each of the three models.

One advantage of ECD is that the relationships among a sequence of related tasks and a corresponding measurement model can be articulated (Embretson, 1998). Evidentiary relationships in complex tasks and multivariate Student Models can be expressed in reusable Measurement Model fragments.

The capability of the CAF to model such relationships is well illustrated when assessing scientific investigations involving several components of science inquiry or practice. Assessing scientific investigations requires the ability to model the interdependencies among several components of the investigative activity (e.g., posing a question, designing an investigation, selecting tools and procedures, collecting data, analyzing and interpreting data, and drawing a conclusion). Many times assessment designers are expected to generate several scores which represent multidimensional constructs that may cross science content knowledge with scientific inquiry and practices. For example, the BioKIDS project models the conditional dependencies between their Claim and Explanation tasks in a modular way (Gotwals & Songer, 2006), using the same "bundled" structure (Wilson & Adams, 1995) to model structurally similar responses from the many tasks that can be generated from their summary task template (see Appendix C). Using the BioKIDS PADI Task Templates, assessment task authors create unique complex tasks but know ahead of time how to score them.

The modularity and reusability of the CAF are especially important for computer-based tasks that are costly to author and implement, such as interactive simulations (see, e.g., Niemi & Baker, 2005, on task design; Mislevy, Steinberg, Breyer, Almond, & Johnson, 2002, on measurement models; Luecht, 2002, on authoring and assembly; and Stevens & Casillas, 2006, on automated scoring). Bringing down the costs of such tasks requires exploiting every opportunity to reuse arguments, structures, processes, and materials specified in the CAF.

ECD Layer 4: Assessment Implementation

The Assessment Implementation layer of ECD is about constructing and preparing all of the operational elements specified in the CAF. This includes authoring tasks, finalizing scoring rubrics or automated scoring rules, estimating the parameters in measurement models, and producing fixed test forms or algorithms for assembling tailored tests. Following the ECD approach requires specifying these implementation processes and is especially useful in content areas where complex interrelated procedures and processes need to be assessed. In the past decade, many new types of assessment tasks have emerged, including ICTs, hands-on tasks (HOTs), video game-based assessments, and computer simulations. Additionally, interest has developed in the integration of content and practice, resulting in the formation of more diagnostic variables which can be used to better identify gaps in learning and point to avenues of remediation.

For example, items and tasks can be created which involve the integration of domain-specific content and a particular skill. These items and tasks can then be scored in such a way that the student's knowledge of the content can be assessed separate from his or her ability to apply the skill or practice. Thus, the item or task reveals whether the student lacks specific content knowledge or the ability to apply a skill based on that knowledge, or both. The demand to use novel assessments in new ways requires careful attention to, and specification of, the processes needed to produce these products. ECD supplies a language, tools, and structure for fulfilling these demands. When ECD principles are not systematically applied, the possibility of introducing construct-irrelevant variance increases, which can result in invalid inferences about what a student knows or can do.

Another process that is part of Assessment Implementation is the specification and compilation of test forms. In particular, test assembly is the process of taking content and psychometric specifications associated with the overall assessment and specific items and tasks that are being developed and using them as evaluative criteria to allocate items and tasks to test forms. This process is used to support the argument that the forms are equivalent in some sense (Spray, Lin, & Chen, 2002). This process of test assembly assumes that more than one form of a test is being developed and that the test developer has psychometric information at the level of entire tests and individual items and tasks (e.g., for tests being developed using classical test theory, the information would likely include mean item difficulties and standard deviations; for tests being developed using IRT, the information might include plots of test response functions) available in an item or task bank. In this process, items are allocated from an existing item bank and assigned to one of several forms being developed with the intended goal of having each form achieve the desired content and psychometric characteristics in the domain being assessed. Spray et al. (2002) provide an example of how following these item allocation procedures can confer efficiency to the test development process while maintaining the technical qualities of the test being developed:

> For example, if the psychometric specifications refer to the first and second moments of target difficulty and variability for each individual examinee, the constructed test forms would be parallel if all of the psychometric specifications were met across all of the test forms. The result is that a single passing standard or score could be used across forms, eliminating the need for post-administration equating or the establishment of separate passing scores for each form.
>
> (p. 1)

Evaluative criteria that might be used to allocate items include:

- conformity to test assembly constraints in terms of test length and content emphases;
- test equivalence as determined by the psychometric properties of items and tasks;
- average test item overlap; and
- distribution of item response rate.

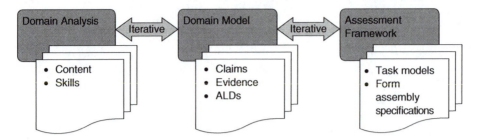

Figure 5.2 Form assembly specifications in the ECD process described by Hendrickson et al.
Source: Adapted from Huff et al. (2010).

This process of allocating items and tasks to achieve equivalence would be accomplished during the fourth layer of the ECD process—Assessment Implementation—as described in Table 5.1. Figure 5.2, presented by Hendrickson et al. (2013), illustrates the iterative flow of ECD processes in the design of the AP tests. Note that "Form assembly specifications" (p. 3) is called out as occurring in the third layer of the ECD work—Conceptual Assessment Framework. There is no discrepancy between the two papers in terms of the layers of ECD in which these types of work would be done. As Hendrickson et al. indicate, the specifications are articulated during layer 3 when the Student, Evidence, and Task Models are designated. The actual allocation of the items to forms, as described by Spray et al. (2002), would be accomplished in layer 4.

As online delivery of tests becomes increasingly common, the automated assembly of multiple test forms can result in a saving of time without resulting in a reduction in the test's technical qualities. In addition, the use of automated assembly with minimal test overlap can contribute to ensuring test security. ECD specifications articulated in the CAF can be used to support human or automated test item or task allocation to forms. Once the specifications are articulated in the CAF, they can be easily deployed for use in the Assessment Implementation layer of ECD.

ECD Layer 5: Assessment Delivery

Finally, the Assessment Delivery layer is where students interact with tasks, their performances are recorded, stored, and evaluated, and feedback and reports are produced. Here again, assessments can be delivered using an increasingly diverse set of modalities. These modalities range from conventional paper–pencil assessments, portfolio assessments, HOTs, ICTs, and game-based assessments. The delivery requirements must be considered in light of the need to ensure that the inferences based on the assessment are accurate and auditable. In addition, the application of ECD to large-scale assessments must adhere to the practical limitations associated with time, delivery mode (technology-enhanced versus paper–pencil), and cost (each student tested versus matrix sampling of students). In the future, assessments will exploit these new means of delivery; thus, ECD's requirement for delivery specifications becomes a critical step in the process of assessment design and development.

Selecting Item Types and Supporting Their Design Using ECD

An ECD process can be used to design and develop both constructed response and selected response items, whether or not they are stand-alone, discrete items, or integrated within a larger assessment task, as in scenario-based assessments. Information in the ECD documents can help an item writer select the most appropriate format, align the item with the KSAs of interest, write rubrics for constructed response items, and generate response options for selected response items. In addition, ECD is particularly well suited to support the design of scenario-based tasks that measure multi-step, complex performances and other "hard-to-assess" constructs.

Challenges in Item Development

Development of items and tasks that can measure "hard-to-assess" constructs for diverse students using a wide range of delivery modalities is the challenge set before today's assessment specialists. These challenges can be addressed through advances in the richness of the assessment situations presented, the creation of new technology-enhanced item types, and the advent of new delivery and scoring methods. The following paragraphs highlight key challenges in item development.

When item writers are given an assignment, they are often told the desired item format and medium (paper-and-pencil or computer-based) in which the item will be presented. Beyond these initial requirements, there are many additional decisions required in order to produce a "good" item. Numerous guidelines have been published to assist item writers in generating "good" selected response items (e.g., Haladyna, Downing, & Rodriguez, 2002). These guidelines typically identify pitfalls associated with poorly written items, such as use of distractors including "none of the above" and "all of the above," item interdependence, using multiple choice formats to assess high-level thinking, and phrasing distractors negatively. For a selected response item, the writer must determine how to format the stem and response options.

Likewise, guidance has been provided to support item writers in developing "good" constructed response items (Bennett & Ward, 2009). For example, when writing a constructed response item, the developer must make sure the item is at the correct grain size to allow the student to display his or her competency with respect to the construct of interest. In addition, for constructed response items, the preparation of scoring rubrics often poses a significant challenge. The scaffolding of constructed response items and tasks requires that careful distinctions be made between prerequisite knowledge that all students are expected to know and background knowledge that is needed to familiarize students with the context of the item or task. Time constraints, amount of space allocated to response capture, and the clarity of steps a student must follow when responding to an open-ended question are all significant challenges that item writers continue to face in designing good assessment questions.

Developing Items for New Testing Modalities

While much assessment is still done in paper-and-pencil format (National Research Council, 2012), efforts are underway to include more HOTs and ICTs in large-scale assessment. For example, the NAEP has developed both HOTs and ICTs that will be administered along with more traditional, stand-alone, multiple choice, and constructed response items in future administrations of NAEP assessments (National Research Council, 2012). Some states also use ICTs in their standardized tests; for example, Minnesota, Nevada, Connecticut, Massachusetts, North Carolina, Utah, and Vermont have incorporated ICT items in their online science assessment (Quellmalz, Timms, Silberglitt, & Buckley, 2012). The use of ECD facilitates the specification of the complex Evidence and Task Models that are required in both performance tasks, especially those requiring computer delivery.

Sireci and Zenisky (2006) and Scalise (2012) have identified a range of new item types that have been developed to take advantage of computer-based testing. Some of these new item types blur the boundaries between selected response and constructed response items. For example, one innovative item type is graphical modeling in which examinees are asked to create a bar graph from data (Sireci & Zenisky, 2006). The range of response options given to a student can determine where on the "selected response–constructed response continuum" the item falls. Although graphical modeling is typically regarded as a constructed response item, technology may impose limitations that make this essentially a selected response item. The Variable and Characteristic Features in the ECD process, in particular the Task Model, provide design specifications that can be used by software developers and assessment designers to make the authoring, rendering, and delivery of computer-based tasks more efficient than traditional methods using storyboards.

Technology can be used to breathe new life into traditional item formats. For example, Scalise (2012) and Scalise and Gifford (2006) present 28 interactive, technology-enhanced item types which can be used in both discrete items and scenario-based tasks. Scalise's taxonomy is represented using a two-dimensional matrix. The first dimension ranges from most constrained item types (e.g., multiple choice and selection/identification) to least constrained (e.g., construction and presentation). The second dimension ranges from less complex items (e.g., true/false) to more complex (e.g., multiple choice with new media distractors). Among the more innovative item types are those that are found along the lower right hand side of Scalise's display: essay and automated editing, cloze procedures, figural constructed response, open-ended multiple choice, concept maps, and demonstrations and experiments. Examples of Variable Features that might be identified when using ECD to design a technology-enhanced assessment are type of item format, degree of item "openness," number and type of computer tools needed to complete an item or task, use of supporting diagrams and illustrations, use of rollovers to support vocabulary, and availability of calculators and equation editors. This level of specification is particularly useful for software developers making these items and tasks.

In sum, today's item writers have available an abundance of item and task types that can be used to measure knowledge and skills in a variety of disciplines using paper–pencil, hands-on, and technology-enhanced assessment modalities. The item writer is challenged to select the item type that best aligns with the knowledge and skills they are trying to assess while managing other considerations such as the time allotted for students to complete the task, the scoring guide, and accessibility.

In the last decade, assessment designers have begun to use even more innovative methods for capturing student data, some of which make use of unobtrusive measures such as eye-tracking (Mayer, 2010), mouse clicks (Vendlinski & Stevens, 2002), and telemetry data (Murray et al., 2012; Shute, Ventura, Bauer, & Zapata-Rivera, 2009). These "stealth" methods enable assessment designers to acquire information about complex student performances without interfering with students' engagement in cognitively demanding tasks.

In developing computer-based items and tasks, writers must determine what needs to be presented to students. Using current technologies, dynamic models of systems and data can be presented in ways that differ radically from the kinds of assessment environments used in the past. Early technology-enhanced learning environments such as NetLogo, GenScope, IMMEX, and Biological inspired the development of assessment tasks in which students could model systems, collect, manipulate, and transform data, view multiple representations of phenomena, engage in pattern finding, and solve interactive, complex scientific investigations. These new forms of assessment are nicely represented in the SimScientists assessments in which inquiry skills are tested that involve multiple steps requiring students to demonstrate several KSAs that interact in complex ways (Quellmalz & Pellegrino, 2009).

Applying Design Pattern Attributes to Select an Item Type

The Focal KSAs, Potential Observations, and Potential Work Products, which are all Design Pattern attributes and are presented in design patterns, provide information to support an item writer's decision about the type of item/task type to use. For example, if the Focal KSA requires a student to identify or recognize a fact, principle, or phenomenon, then a selected response item may be appropriate. If the Focal KSA is about the ability to explain or describe, then a constructed response item type may be appropriate. Not all Focal KSAs provide clues as to which item/task type is most appropriate. For example, Focal KSAs that begin "knowledge that..." could be measured by an item in which students must select an answer or they may have to construct the answer. When the Focal KSA does not point to the use of a particular item type, then the item writer can turn to the use of Potential Observation(s) and Potential Work Product(s) to determine the item type(s) that are appropriate. Thus the various Design Pattern attributes may suggest or provide guidance about what type of item/task could be used.

The Additional KSAs can be used to check whether additional non-construct-relevant KSAs have been introduced by the use of a particular item type. For example, in one of the released HOTs from the NAEP, the task requires a student to use a stopwatch. The ability to use a stopwatch is then an Additional KSA (as this is not the focus of the task). In order to support this Additional KSA, the task includes specific instructions on how a student needs to use the stopwatch. If the item writer is not able to provide supports for tool use, then the use of a HOT is inappropriate. Thus, the Additional KSAs can provide information on whether certain item types should be excluded from consideration.

When several item types can be used to measure a given construct, an item writer unfamiliar with the different item types might not choose the most appropriate format to measure the construct of interest. In ECD, Work Products are often stated as item types (e.g., selected response, HOTs, drag and drop, essay). The specification of Potential Work Products can make item/task writers aware of the range of formats available and help them to select an appropriate item/task type. See Appendix D for examples of a HOT and an ICT assessment task and the use of Design Pattern attributes to relate the Focal KSAs, Potential Observations, and Potential Work Products used when designing items and tasks.

Applying Design Pattern Attributes to Prompt and Rubric Development

ECD can be used to aid the development of constructed response items/tasks. The attributes of a Design Pattern can support not only the development of prompts but also rubric development. In fact, it is recommended that both the item/task and the rubric be developed at the same time to ensure that the item prompt provides the student with enough information to answer the item/task as intended. The strategy of developing both the item/task and the rubric simultaneously also helps support the coherence of the validity argument since the assessment designer is more likely to develop prompts that require the student to provide all relevant information specified in the evidence rules of the rubric.

For example, an item prompt might ask a student to compare two models. If the rubric requires that the student's response include three individual comparisons and the student only provides two comparisons, the student who responds by providing only two comparisons would likely earn a lower score. In this situation, the prompt needs to include directions for the student to include three comparisons in his/her answer. Without such specific directions, it is unclear whether the student did not provide the third comparison because he or she could not specify a third comparison or thought that two comparisons were sufficient. A well-designed prompt aligns to the scoring rubric and supports the validity of the claims made from the scoring of the item/task. By designing the prompts and scoring rubrics simultaneously, the test designer is more likely to reduce sources of construct-irrelevant variance that would lead to an invalid inference about a student's performance than if the prompt and rubric were designed separately.

The Potential Observations specified in the Design Pattern can also provide clues about the construction of the rubric. The Potential Observations specify the qualities of the Work Products that will be examined in order to make judgments about the student's responses. The Potential

Rubrics then further define these judgments and specify how the item/task should be scored. For example, if the Potential Observation is the "accuracy with which the student describes the results of an investigation," then the rubric would specify the levels of accuracy to be distinguished and the score points assigned to each level.

Applying Design Pattern Attributes to Development of Stems and Response Options/Distractors

ECD can also be used to aid the development of selected response items. A selected response item comprises the stem and a set of response options (the correct answer and the distractors). The choice a student makes among the different response options can be caused by the different knowledge or skills the student draws on or by the misconceptions he or she holds about the content. An item writer can use the Focal KSAs, Additional KSAs, and Potential Observations to guide their item writing to help ensure that the stem and response options measure the construct of interest. In ECD, an item writer documents the reasons that particular options or distractors were included. It is inappropriate to include implausible or "tricky" distractors as part of an item. Good ECD practice requires that the distractors support the inference or claim on which the student is being assessed. Thus, all the distractors need to be plausible and present alternative but incorrect answers to the question. Even in large-scale assessment, distractors can be used to indicate a student's instructional needs in a subject area and thereby contribute to the development of a focused intervention plan. King, Gardner, Zucker, and Jorgensen (2004) discuss the distractor rationale taxonomy as an approach to enhancing selected multiple choice items.

Benefits of Using ECD to Develop Item/Task Types

There are numerous benefits conferred by the use of ECD. In particular, the ECD process helps item/task writers select item/task types that are appropriate to the Focal KSAs being assessed and the desired Potential Observations; ensure that the prompt and rubric in constructed response items are aligned; and properly align stems and distractors in selected response items. Because of the way that ECD is used to model content domains (e.g., Focal KSAs, Potential Observations, Task Features, and Work Products), item writers are often better able to exploit the affordances of technology in the design and selection of item/task types.

Illustrations of ECD for Challenging Assessments

Below are three examples of assessment projects that tackle difficult design challenges. The first describes how ECD was used to measure "hard-to-assess" constructs beyond the measurement of domain-specific knowledge and skills. The second example describes the use of a four-step design process that included articulation of the ALDs. The third example describes the use of a reverse engineering methodology to permit the extension of an existing formative assessment for use in additional assessment contexts, including large-scale applications. Both these examples illustrate the versatility of the ECD process and its power as a design framework that can be tailored to a variety of assessment purposes and situations.

Example of an ECD Assessment Measuring "Hard-to-Assess" Constructs

The initial two layers of ECD, Domain Analysis and Domain Modeling, provide the essential foundation for this process. For example, in freshman and sophomore college biology, students are exposed to a dizzying volume of domain-specific content, and there are many available assessments that are focused on the recall of specific content. There are not any assessments, however, that measure how a college student learns to reason with such rich content in college. This was the goal for one ECD assessment design effort, Domain-Specific Assessment (DSA) (Yarnall, Gallagher, Haertel, Lundh, & Toyama, 2012).

To illustrate the process, the DSA team began with the ECD Domain Analysis phase. The team needed to identify biology content that was covered in enough detail to permit students to develop reasoning skills during the first two years of college. To do so, the team referred to the "big ideas" taught in college. The design team identified these through discussions with college and industry experts and a review of the literature, including life science benchmarks (AAAS, 2001), syllabi of college biology, and relevant cognitive research into biology learning (Corcoran, Mosher, & Rogat, 2009; Lawson, Alkhoury, Benford, Clark, & Falconer, 2000; Lawson, Clark, et al., 2000; National Research Council, 2003; Songer & Mintzes, 1994). The team identified three initial foundational big ideas and the problems students had learning them. The big ideas were energy flow/matter cycling, evolution, and the nature of scientific inquiry, all of which are commonly taught in high school and college.

In the Domain Modeling phase, the DSA team further specified types of reasoning with content by using some ideas of schematic ("knowing why") and strategic knowledge ("knowing how") identified by Shavelson, Ruiz-Primo, Li, and Ayala (2003). The Design Patterns clarified the attributes of assessments that would measure these kinds of knowledge and skills. The Design Patterns described the kinds of assessment scenarios that would require students to use such knowledge and skills, what this type of reasoning looks like when done well, and some initial ideas of how to score student performances. Eventually, the DSA team designed 41 scenario-based tasks. A sample Design Pattern using biological scientific principles to predict outcomes is presented in Appendix E.

To test the assessment's validity, the pilot biology assessment was administered in paper–pencil form to 296 community college students and compared with two other tests—a traditional biology test and a critical thinking test. A content validity study rated the newly developed DSA items as measuring more conceptually complex content knowledge and more forms of model-based reasoning than the comparison biology test. The new assessment also was instructionally sensitive to what students were learning in college. A correlational study and cognitive analysis showed that the DSA test went beyond the measurement of declarative knowledge and was assessing knowledge judged to be schematic and strategic in nature. The correlational study showed, as expected, that the pilot biology test had a moderate relationship with the traditional biology test ($r = 0.52$) and a somewhat weaker positive relation with the critical thinking test ($r = 0.25$). Coupled with the content validity findings above, these results suggest that the newly developed biology test went beyond the measurement of declarative knowledge and was assessing knowledge judged to be schematic and strategic in nature. Subsequent cognitive labs suggested that strategic knowledge is not simply a more complex form of schematic or declarative knowledge, but may operate in tandem with them. These forms of knowledge appear to function differently.

Although this study focused on the post-secondary context, the procedures and processes could be applied to the assessment of knowledge at the high school level. Studies of science instructors' priorities have consistently found, however, that high school teachers emphasize memorized content knowledge more than their post-secondary counterparts, who place a higher priority on reasoning skills (ACT, 2009, 2013).

An Example of an ECD Placement Examination Using ALDs

For example, in the College Board's AP program, ECD was used to guide the revision of the large-scale biology placement examination (Ewing et al., 2010). The ECD approach used

Table 5.3 ECD Activities and Resulting Artifacts Used in Revision of the College Board's AP Examination

ECD Activity	Resulting Artifact
Analyzing domain	Prioritization of content and skills to facilitate curriculum and assessment design
Modeling the domain	Pairs of claims and corresponding evidence, i.e., learning objectives
Articulating ALDs	Specification of what students know and can do at each level of ALDs
Construct assessment framework	Task models and form assembly specifications

included four design activities, each of which is briefly summarized below. Each design activity and its resulting artifacts are identified in Table 5.3.

- Analyzing the domain which resulted in prioritization of content and skills, organized conceptually to facilitate curriculum and assessment design to support deep understanding.
- Modeling the domain which resulted in claims and corresponding evidence. Claims and evidence emerge directly from the content and skills produced by the Domain Analysis. (Claims are also referred to as Learning Objectives in AP publications.)
- Articulating the ALDs that identify what examinees at each of the achievement levels are expected to know and be able to do.
- Constructing the assessment framework that resulted in task models, in some content areas, and form assembly specifications.

An Example of Using ECD to Reverse-Engineer a Formative Assessment for Purposes of Large-Scale Assessment

The design of facet-based diagnostic assessments is based on an impressive foundation rooted in instructional practice and incorporation of knowledge about student cognition and learning into physics (Minstrell, 2001; Minstrell, Anderson, Kraus, & Minstrell, 2008). These assessments are designed to reveal not only whether a student falls short of mastery, but also the particular nature of a student's problematic understanding and hence the type of additional learning experiences needed. Seventeen facet clusters, constellations of learning goals, and common problematic ideas related to fundamental physics concepts are the conceptual underpinnings of the online Diagnoser Tools, a classroom formative assessment system (http://www.diagnoser.com). The diagnostic questions are intended to help teachers distinguish among different facets of student thinking. Because facet-based physics assessments diagnose and distinguish normative and problematic ways of thinking and reasoning and are easy to administer, they have potential applications beyond the classroom (e.g., for large-scale formative assessment purposes). Yet the design principles underlying these assessments are not transparent. Thus ECD was applied using a reverse engineering methodology to make explicit these design principles. By applying the ECD approach, the Diagnoser assessment designer will be able to reuse and extend the reverse-engineered design documents for application in other assessment situations. Reverse-engineered question sets were instantiated into PADI Design Patterns and a PADI Task Template.

Each Design Pattern (see Table 5.4) focused on defining the assessment argument for a facet cluster. Because questions evaluate both normative and non-normative ideas, the Focal KSAs represent both goal and problematic understandings. Accordingly, evidence, in the form

Table 5.4 Design Pattern Attributes, Definitions, and Corresponding Messick Components

Design Pattern Attribute	Attribute Definition	Messick Assessment Argument Component
Focal KSAs	The primary KSAs targeted by the design pattern	**Student Model/claim:** What construct (complex of student attributes) should be assessed?
Additional KSAs	Other KSAs that are required but not targeted	
Potential Observations	Qualities of student performances that constitute evidence of KSAs	**Evidence Model/actions:** What behaviors should reveal the construct?
Potential Work Products	Products produced by students	
Characteristic Task Feature	Aspects of assessment situations that are necessary in some form to elicit desired evidence	**Task Model/situation:** What tasks should elicit those behaviors?
Variable Task Features	Aspects of assessment situations that can be varied in order to shift difficulty or focus	

of Potential Observations, was described to illustrate goal and problematic student responses. Characteristic Features were identified broadly across all of the questions targeted in a facet cluster. An example of a Characteristic Feature was that each item's context should include features that are associated with the goal facet and one or more problematic facets. Because facets are elicited in contexts or scenarios presented to students, Variable Features were described as the types of contexts implemented in items (e.g., types of objects, whether objects are moving, representations used).

The PADI Task Template reverse-engineered for the Diagnoser Tools specified details about the structures of facet-based assessments. A "general" Task Template sufficed, in contrast to templates specific to facet clusters, because the structure of the facet-based assessments is largely parallel across all 17 facet clusters. The Task Template identified measurement models, evaluation procedures, work products, details about how items would be presented, and task model variables. For more details about this reverse-engineering process, see DeBarger, Werner, Minstrell, and DiBello (2013).

Use of ECD for Formative Purposes

Although this chapter has focused on the use of ECD to design large-scale assessments developed outside the classroom setting, most student assessments conducted in U.S. classrooms are not large-scale, high-stakes assessments for accountability purposes. Rather, most educational assessments are designed and implemented by classroom teachers for the purposes of assigning grades, predicting student performance on future assessments, or for informing instructional interventions. While these first two purposes are summative in nature, the third serves a more formative purpose. As Wiliam and Black (1996) note, given the central role of teacher-developed assessment in both grading and instruction, both summative and formative assessments that support the valid and reliable inferences of classroom teachers are critical to the educational enterprise. Often, advocates of ECD say that a full-blown ECD analysis may not be the best choice, for example in one-off classroom assessment such as a spelling quiz. Certainly thinking in terms of evidence, alternative explanations, and the like is useful, but the stakes may not warrant the investment in a full-blown ECD process. In terms of classroom assessments for formative purposes, it makes sense to invoke ECD procedures when the construct to be measured is of significant import (Newton's three laws), will be taught in multiple classes, and reused in subsequent years.

Benefits and Limitations of Using ECD for Assessment Design

Practical experience based on numerous implementations of ECD suggests a number of key benefits that flow from this design approach. The most valued benefits include the ability to:

- better reflect and measure what is taught and valued in the classroom and resulting score inferences that are strongly supported by an evidentiary argument (Hendrickson et al., 2013);
- design a variety of assessments for multiple purposes including summative, formative, classroom-based, large-scale, diagnostic, interim, benchmark, placement, certification, capstone, exit, etc.;
- identify the most appropriate item types to be included in the assessment given its purpose;
- design a wide range of item types, including selected response, constructed response, HOTs, ICTs, essays, drawings, cloze procedures, simulations, assessments embedded in games, etc.;
  - support the articulation of item stems and task prompts;
  - support the articulation of rubrics, response options, and distractors;

- design assessments based on different psychological and theoretical perspectives (e.g., cognitive, trait, behavioral, situational);
- reduce sources of construct-irrelevant variance resulting in increased construct validity as compared to the original assessment;
- develop construct representation which is a broader form of validity than establishing content validity alone and diminishes the need for post hoc content alignment investigations (Messick, 1994; Mislevy, 2007);
- conceptualize and document the assessment argument at a narrative level;
- specify the psychometric and technological requirements for valid inferences;
- reuse design documents (i.e., Design Patterns and Task Templates) to generate new items and tasks (i.e., clones and variants), thus reducing costs of future design and development efforts;
- support rendering and delivery of costly technology-enhanced assessment items and tasks; and
- support the integration of other design frameworks, such as Universal Design for Learning and 21st Century Skills.

Here again, experience with the ECD model suggests two possible limitations. These include:

- a steep learning curve for assessment designers and developers who are "new" to ECD; and
- substantial upfront costs (time and money) associated with the creation and production of Design Patterns and Task Templates enroute to item and task development.

Conclusions

The chapter identifies several limitations of long-established assessment practices and addresses how ECD helps to mitigate them. These challenges include:

- the need to measure "hard-to-assess" constructs required for the measurement of state-of-the-art, domain-specific content and practices; constructs that go beyond the measurement of recall and recognition and probe for evidence of deep knowledge, including conceptual, schematic, and strategic understandings;
- the use of technology-enhanced tasks to present complex stimuli and capture not only whether the student answers the items/tasks correctly but also the process they used to arrive at their conclusion;

- the ability to measure student knowledge and skills associated with interdependent practices (e.g., phases of scientific inquiry, steps in mathematical problem solving, and processes used in writing and speaking);
- the need to produce complex assessments efficiently at scale;
- the need for assessments with high levels of technical quality (e.g., validity and reliability); and
- the need for comprehensive, defensible validity arguments that relate the abilities and skills to be assessed, to observations of what students can do, to the features of tasks that elicit those performances.

Some advocates of ECD argue that a thorough ECD analysis may not be the best choice for formative assessment purposes; it may be beyond what is needed for designing a "one-off" classroom assessment. Invoking ECD for formative classroom assessments makes sense when the construct to be measured is of significant import, will be taught in multiple classes, and reused in subsequent years.

In sum, this chapter introduces basic understandings of the ECD process used to assess what students know, say, and can do. ECD tools and processes enable multidisciplinary groups of subject matter and assessment experts to develop rigorous assessment arguments to target more complex student performances and types of KSAs. ECD is evolving rapidly and has been adopted as a requirement in the development of new assessments for the Common Core State Standards in Mathematics and English Language Arts as well as being used in the development of the mathematics and science strands of the NAEP, including the design of science ICTs. Further, ECD enables the design of assessments with built-in flexibility, for example to adapt the measure to better assess English language learners and students with disabilities.

The successive refinement and reorganization of knowledge about the domain of interest and the purpose of the assessment being implemented proceed from a general substantive argument to an increasingly specific argument that identifies the elements and processes needed to operationalize the assessment. Consequently, ECD can be used to design assessments in any content domain, for the entire range of assessment purposes, for diverse learners, and for students at all grade levels. Its fundamental role in identifying and mitigating construct-irrelevant variance makes it a likely candidate to transform the state of practice in assessment design.

Appendix A

| Design Pattern for Observational Investigation | Design Pattern 2167 | | [ ] Delete | View: | View (vertical) ⇕ | |

Title	[Edit]	Design Pattern for Observational Investigation
Overview	[Edit]	This design pattern supports the writing of tasks that address scientific reasoning and process skills in observational (non-experimental) investigations. Observational investigations differ from experimental investigations. In experimental investigations, it is necessary to control or manipulate one or more of the variables of interest to test a prediction or hypothesis; in observational investigations, variables typically cannot be altered at all (e.g., objects in space) or in a short time frame (e.g., a lake ecosystem). This design pattern may be used to generate groups of tasks for any science content strand.
Use	❶ [Edit]	U1. This design pattern supports the construction of tasks that address observational investigations - that is, investigations where experimental methods are not appropriate (e.g., earth and space science, demography, paleoanthropology, physiology, ecology). In order for students to have a well-rounded understanding of the scientific method, they need to be familiar with the context and methods of observational investigations. details
Focal knowledge, skills, and abilities	❶ [Edit]	Fk1. Ability to analyze why observational investigation methods are more appropriate than experimental methods for some phenomena/situations details
		Fk2. Ability to distinguish between observational and experimental methodology details
		Fk3. Ability to generate or evaluate predictions or hypotheses about scientific phenomena that are appropriate for observational investigation details
		Fk4. Ability to formulate conclusions, create models, and appropriately generalize results from observational investigations details
		Fk5. Ability to test predictions or hypotheses using observational methods details
		Fk6. Ability to plan a systematic collection of observational data based on a predicted relationship
		Fk7. Ability to collect, analyze, and interpret observational data with appropriate tools
Additional knowledge, skills, and abilities	❶ [Edit]	Ak1. Content knowledge (may be construct relevant) details
		Ak2. Prerequisite knowledge from earlier grades details
		Ak3. Data collection and analysis details
		Ak4. Representational forms (e.g., graphs, maps) details
Potential observations	❶ [Edit]	Po1. Appropriateness/strength of observational evidence to help confirm or disconfirm a prediction or hypothesis details
		Po2. Accuracy in identifying the effects of an observed active phenomenon and how these effects are consistent with a posited cause and effect relationship details
		Po3. Correctness of recognized pattern in data to support a prediction or hypothesis details
		Po4. Plausibility/correctness of explanation for observed findings details
		Po5. Accuracy in critiquing the observational investigation methods, evidence, and conclusions of others details
		Po6. Plausibility and systematicity of the data collection plan

		Po7. Correctness of selected tools and procedures for data collection
		Po8. Systematicity and appropriateness of collected data
		Po9. Appropriateness of measurement precision
Potential work products	❶ [Edit]	Pw1. Identification or generation of a prediction or hypothesis that is appropriate to an observational investigation situation details
		Pw2. Identification of observational settings where data could be collected to confirm or disconfirm a prediction or hypothesis details
		Pw3. Identification of additional source of data that could confirm or disconfirm a prediction or hypothesis supported by existing data details
		Pw4. Identification or generation of a replicable data collection process (e.g., repeated sampling over time or at several locations) details
		Pw5. Identification of potentially disconfirming observations
		Pw6. Filling in of a representational form (e.g., a graph, chart, or map) to show the relationship among variables relevant to a prediction or hypothesis details
		Pw7. Generation or selection of an explanation for observed findings details
		Pw8. Critique of flawed explanation based on observations
		Pw9. Peer critique (hypothetical in a standard assessment, real in classroom work) of the observational investigation methods, evidence, and conclusions details
Potential rubrics	❶ [Edit]	
Characteristic features	❶ [Edit]	Cf1. Scientific question not amenable to experimentation, because impractical, unethical, etc. details
		Cf2. Presentation of a real-world situation with patterns suggesting the relationship between at least two variables that can be observed systematically (but are not amenable to experimental investigation). details
Variable features	❶ [Edit]	Vf1. Content (strand) context details
		Vf2. Qualitative or quantitative investigations details
		Vf3. Number of variables and the complexity of their relationships details
		Vf4. Simple or complex investigations details
		Vf5. Type of data representation (e.g., patterns in geographically distributed phenomena via geospatial visualizations; patterns in data; similarities in specialized representations appropriate to the scientific phenomenon) details
		Vf6. Sufficient or insufficient data about an already established relationship details
		Vf7. Amount of scaffolding given to student to guide the presentation or representation of data collected details
		Vf8. Amount of observational data from which an analysis, explanation, or conclusion is to be drawn details
		Vf9. Completeness of model given from which predictions or hypotheses can be generated details
		Vf10.
		Vf11.
Narrative structure	❶ [Edit]	Cause and effect. An event, phenomenon, or system is altered by internal or external factors.

<u>Change over time</u>. A sequence of events is presented to highlight sequential or cyclical change in a system.

<u>Investigation</u>. A student or scientist completes an investigation in which one or more variables may be observed or manipulated and data are collected

<u>Specific to general and Parts to whole</u>. Specific characteristics of a phenomenon are presented, culminating in a description of the system or phenomenon as a whole.

National educational standards ❶ [Edit]		<u>NSES 8ASI1.1</u>. Identify questions that can be answered through scientific investigations. Students should develop the ability to refine and refocus broad and ill-defined questions. An important aspect of this ability consists of students' ability to clarify questions and inquiries and direct them toward objects and phenomena that can be described, explained, or predicted by scientific investigations. Students should develop the ability to identify their questions with scientific ideas, concepts, and quantitative relationships that guide investigation.

<u>NSES 8ASI1.2</u>. Design and conduct a scientific investigation. Students should develop general abilities, such as systematic observation, making accurate measurements, and identifying and controlling variables. They should also develop the ability to clarify their ideas that are influencing and guiding the inquiry, and to understand how those ideas compare with current scientific knowledge. Students can learn to formulate questions, design investigations, execute investigations, interpret data, use evidence to generate explanations, propose alternative explanations, and critique explanations and procedures.

<u>NSES 8ASI1.3</u>. Use appropriate tools and techniques to gather, analyze, and interpret data. The use of tools and techniques, including mathematics, will be guided by the question asked and the investigations students design. The use of computers for the collection, summary, and display of evidence is part of this standard. Students should be able to access, gather, store, retrieve, and organize data, using hardware and software designed for these purposes.

<u>NSES 8ASI1.4</u>. Develop descriptions, explanations, predictions, and models using evidence. Students should base their explanation on what they observed, and as they develop cognitive skills, they should be able to differentiate explanation from description, providing causes for effects and establishing relationships based on evidence and logical argument. This standards requires a subject knowledge base so the students can effectively conduct investigations, because developing explanations establishes connections between the content of science and the contexts within which students develop new knowledge.

<u>NSES 8ASI1.5</u>. Think critically and logically to make the relationships between evidence and explanations. Thinking critically about evidence includes deciding what evidence should be used and accounting for anomalous data. Specifically, students should be able to review data from a simple experiment, summarize the data, and form a logical argument about the cause-and-effect relationships in the experiment. Students should begin to state some explanations in terms of the relationship between two or more variables.

<u>NSES 8ASI1.6</u>. Recognize and analyze alternative explanations and predictions. Students should develop the ability to listen and to respect the explanations proposed by other students. They should remain open to and acknowledge different ideas and explanations, be able to accept the skepticism of others, and consider alternative explanations. |
| **State standards** ❶ [Edit] | | |
| **State benchmarks** ❶ [Edit] | | <u>MCA II: 6.I.A.2</u>. The student will explain why scientists often repeat investigations to be sure of the results.

<u>MCA II: 7.I.A.2</u>. The student will explain natural phenomena by using appropriate physical, conceptual and mathematical models.

<u>MCA II: 6.I.B.1</u>. The student will identify questions that can be answered |

through scientific investigation and those that cannot.

MCA II: 7.I.B.1. The student will formulate a testable hypothesis based on prior knowledge.

MCA II: 6.I.B.2. The student will distinguish among observation, prediction and inference.

MCA II: 6.I.B.4. The student will present and explain data and findings from controlled experiments using multiple representations including tables, graphs, physical models and demonstrations.

MCA II: 8.I.B.1. The student will know that scientific investigations involve the common elements of systematic observations, the careful collection of relevant evidence, logical reasoning and innovation in developing hypotheses and explanations.

MCA II: 8.I.B.2. The student will describe how scientists can conduct investigations in a simple system and make generalizations to more complex systems.

MCA III: 7.1.1.1.1. Understand that prior expectations can create bias when conducting scientific investigations. For example: Students often continue to think that air is not matter, even though they have contrary evidence from investigations.

MCA III: 7.1.1.1.2. Understand that when similar investigations give different results, the challenge is to judge whether the differences are significant, and if further studies are required. For example: Use mean and range to analyze the reliability of experimental results.

MCA III: 8.1.1.1.1. Evaluate the reasoning in arguments in which fact and opinion are intermingled or when conclusions do not follow logically from the evidence given. For example: Evaluate the use of pH in advertising products related to body care and gardening.

MCA III: 7.1.1.2.1. Generate and refine a variety of scientific questions and match them with appropriate methods of investigation, such as field studies, controlled experiments, reviews of existing work and development of models.

MCA III: 7.1.1.2.3. Generate a scientific conclusion from an investigation, clearly distinguishing between results (evidence) and conclusions (explanation).

MCA III: 7.1.1.2.4. Evaluate explanations proposed by others by examining and comparing evidence, identifying faulty reasoning, and suggesting alternative explanations.

MCA III: 8.1.1.2.1. Use logical reasoning and imagination to develop descriptions, explanations, predictions and models based on evidence.

MCA III: 7.1.3.4.1. Use maps, satellite images and other data sets to describe patterns and make predictions about natural systems in a life science context. For example: Use online data sets to compare wildlife populations or water quality in regions of Minnesota.

MCA III: 8.1.3.4.1. Use maps, satellite images and other data sets to describe patterns and make predictions about local and global systems in Earth science contexts. For example: Use data or satellite images to identify locations of earthquakes and volcanoes, ages of sea floor, ocean surface temperatures and ozone concentration in the stratosphere.

I am a kind of	❶ [Edit]	
These are kinds of me	❶ [Edit]	
These are parts of me	❶ [Edit]	
Templates	❶ [Edit]	

Exemplar tasks	❶ [Edit]	
Online resources	❶ [Edit]	
References	❶ [Edit]	

Tags [Add Tag]

(No tags entered.)

Appendix B

Experimental Investigation (used for the Marigold task) | Design Pattern 2298

[| Permit | Delete | View: View (vertical) ‖]

Title	[Edit]	Experimental Investigation (used for the Marigold task)
Overview	[Edit]	This design pattern supports the writing of storyboards and items that address scientific reasoning and process skills in experimental investigations. In experimental investigations, it is necessary to manipulate one or more of the variables of interest and to control others while testing a prediction or hypothesis. This contrasts with observational investigations, where variables typically cannot be manipulated. This design pattern may be used to generate groups of tasks for science content strands amenable to experimentation. details
Use	❶ [Edit]	U1. This design pattern supports the construction of tasks that address experimental investigations - that is, investigations where experimental methods are appropriate (as compared with investigations where only observations of phenomena are possible). In order for students to have a well-rounded understanding of the scientific method, they need to be familiar with the context and methods of experimental investigations.
Focal knowledge, skills, and abilities	❶ [Edit]	Fk1. Ability to distinguish between experimental and observational methodology
		Fk2. Ability to recognize that when a situation of scientific interest includes aspects that can be altered or manipulated practically, it is suitable for experimental investigation details
		Fk3. Ability to recognize that the purpose of an experiment is to test a prediction/hypothesis about a causal relationship details
		Fk4. Ability to identify, generate, or evaluate a prediction/hypothesis that is testable with a simple experiment
		Fk5. Ability to plan and conduct a simple experiment step-by-step given a prediction or hypothesis
		Fk6. Ability to recognize that at a basic level, an experiment involves manipulating one variable and measuring the effect on (or value of) another variable details
		Fk7. Ability to identify variables of the scientific situation (other than the ones being manipulated or treated as an outcome) that should be controlled (i.e. kept the same) in order to prevent misleading information about the nature of the causal relationship details
		Fk8. Ability to recognize variables that are inconsequential in the design of an experiment details
		Fk9. Ability to recognize that steps in an experiment must be repeatable to dependably predict future results
		Fk10. Ability to recognize that random assignment to treatment conditions (i.e. levels of the independent variable) is an important way to rule out alternative explanations for a causal relationship details
		Fk11. Ability to interpret or appropriately generalize the results of a simple experiment or to formulate conclusions or create models from the results
Additional knowledge, skills, and abilities	❶ [Edit]	Ak1. Content knowledge (may be construct relevant) details
		Ak2. Prerequisite knowledge from earlier grades details
		Ak3. Prerequisite experience assessing or conducting component steps of an investigation details
		Ak4. Ability to collect, organize, analyze, and present data details

		Ak5.	Familiarity with representational forms (e.g., graphs, maps) details
		Ak6.	Student needs based on UDL categories may be included (Perceptive, Expressive, Language and Symbols, Cognitive, Executive Functioning, Affective)
Potential observations	❶ [Edit]	Po1.	Accuracy in identifying situation suitable for experimental investigation
		Po2.	Plausibility of a measurable research question being raised
		Po3.	Plausibility of hypothesis as being testable by a simple experiment
		Po4.	Plausibility/correctness of design for a simple experiment
		Po5.	Correct identification of independent and dependent variables
		Po6.	Accuracy in identifying variables (other than the treatment variables of interest) that should be controlled (held constant) or made equivalent (e.g., through random assignment).
		Po7.	Plausability/correctness of steps to take in the conduct of an experiment
		Po8.	Plausibility of plan for repeating an experiment
		Po9.	Correctness of recognized data patterns from experimental data
		Po10.	Plausibility/correctness of interpretation/explanation of experimental results
		Po11.	Accuracy in critiquing the experimental design, methods, results, and conclusions of others
		Po12.	Generate a prediction/hypothesis that is testable with a simple experiment
Potential work products	❶ [Edit]	Pw1.	Selected response - students select the response (or responses) from a provided set details
		Pw2.	Constructed Response - students must generate their response given a prompt
		Pw3.	Drag and Drop - students drag and drop objects around the screen
		Pw4.	Dynamic branching - students are provided different choices depending on which option they select.
		Pw5.	Hot spots - students can move the cursor around the screen and an event happens when they click or move their curser
		Pw6.	Simulation - students can interact with a simulation, by providing inputs
		Pw7.	Interactive graphs - students can generate or manipulate graphs details
		Pw8.	Highlighting - students can highlight parts of the screen details
Potential rubrics	❶ [Edit]		
Characteristic features	❶ [Edit]	Cf1.	Focus on Nature of Science (Strand I in MCA) benchmarks that relate to experimental investigations at the appropriate grade level
		Cf2.	Presentation of situation of scientific interest where variables can be (or have been) practically altered to address a causal prediction details
		Cf3.	Presentation of situation requiring the design or conduct of a controlled experiment details
		Cf4.	Presentation or representation of an experimental design
		Cf5.	Presentation of observed result from an experiment requiring the development of explanations, conclusions, or models details
Variable features	❶ [Edit]	Vf1.	Content (strand) context details

	Vf2. Which one of multiple phases of experimental investigation will be addressed
	Vf3. Qualitative or quantitative investigation or a combination
	Vf4. Ease or difficulty with which the treatment (independent) variable can be manipulated
	Vf5. Are manipulated variables given or to be determined?
	Vf6. The number of variables investigated and the complexity of their interrelationships details
	Vf7. Number of variables that need to be controlled to unambiguously study the relationship between the manipulated variable and the outcome variable details
	Vf8. Length of time over which the experiment must be conducted in order to study the potential impact of the treatment variable
	Vf9. Data representations details
	Vf10. Variable features may be added to support student needs associated with UDL categories (Perceptual - Screen presentation will include variable font size, Option for altering screen contrast, Option for magnification or zoom, Optional text-to-speech; Expressive - Range of response options required (radio buttons, drag and drop), Range of student support for producing response (speech-to-text); Language and Symbols - Provision of multiple representations of symbols (linguistic labels for symbols, define abbreviations, etc.), Provide definitions of non-construct relevant terminology, Use of studentsÂ¢?? dominant language; Cognitive - Use of a concept map, Use of a response template, Use of context to heighten salience, Highlighting key terms and ideas; Executive Functioning - Breaking task into manageable units, Icons to encourage thinking and reflection, On-screen progress monitoring; Affective - Use of scenario or real-world context to heighten engagement, Age-appropriate materials -Interactive narrative (gaming), Affirmation of participation
Narrative structure ❶ [Edit]	Cause and effect. An event, phenomenon, or system is altered by internal or external factors.
	Investigation. A student or scientist completes an investigation in which one or more variables may be observed or manipulated and data are collected
	Change over time. A sequence of events is presented to highlight sequential or cyclical change in a system.
National educational standards ❶ [Edit]	NSES 8ASI1.1. Identify questions that can be answered through scientific investigations. Students should develop the ability to refine and refocus broad and ill-defined questions. An important aspect of this ability consists of students' ability to clarify questions and inquiries and direct them toward objects and phenomena that can be described, explained, or predicted by scientific investigations. Students should develop the ability to identify their questions with scientific ideas, concepts, and quantitative relationships that guide investigation.
	NSES 8ASI1.2. Design and conduct a scientific investigation. Students should develop general abilities, such as systematic observation, making accurate measurements, and identifying and controlling variables. They should also develop the ability to clarify their ideas that are influencing and guiding the inquiry, and to understand how those ideas compare with current scientific knowledge. Students can learn to formulate questions, design investigations, execute investigations, interpret data, use evidence to generate explanations, propose alternative explanations, and critique explanations and procedures.
	NSES 8ASI1.3. Use appropriate tools and techniques to gather, analyze, and interpret data. The use of tools and techniques, including mathematics, will be guided by the question asked and the investigations students design. The use of computers for the collection, summary, and display of evidence

is part of this standard. Students should be able to access, gather, store, retrieve, and organize data, using hardware and software designed for these purposes.

NSES 8ASI1.4. Develop descriptions, explanations, predictions, and models using evidence. Students should base their explanation on what they observed, and as they develop cognitive skills, they should be able to differentiate explanation from description, providing causes for effects and establishing relationships based on evidence and logical argument. This standards requires a subject knowledge base so the students can effectively conduct investigations, because developing explanations establishes connections between the content of science and the contexts within which students develop new knowledge.

NSES 8ASI1.5. Think critically and logically to make the relationships between evidence and explanations. Thinking critically about evidence includes deciding what evidence should be used and accounting for anomalous data. Specifically, students should be able to review data from a simple experiment, summarize the data, and form a logical argument about the cause-and-effect relationships in the experiment. Students should begin to state some explanations in terms of the relationship between two or more variables.

NSES 8ASI1.6. Recognize and analyze alternative explanations and predictions. Students should develop the ability to listen and to respect the explanations proposed by other students. They should remain open to and acknowledge different ideas and explanations, be able to accept the skepticism of others, and consider alternative explanations.

NSES 8ASI1.7. Communicate scientific procedures and explanations. With practice, students should become competent at communicating experimental methods, following instructions, describing observations, summarizing the results of other groups, and telling other students about investigations and explanations.

State standards	❶ [Edit]
State benchmarks	❶ [Edit]
I am a kind of	❶ [Edit]
These are kinds of me	❶ [Edit]
These are parts of me	❶ [Edit]
Templates	❶ [Edit]
Exemplar tasks	❶ [Edit]
Online resources	❶ [Edit]
References	❶ [Edit]

Tags [Add Tag]

(No tags entered.)

Appendix C

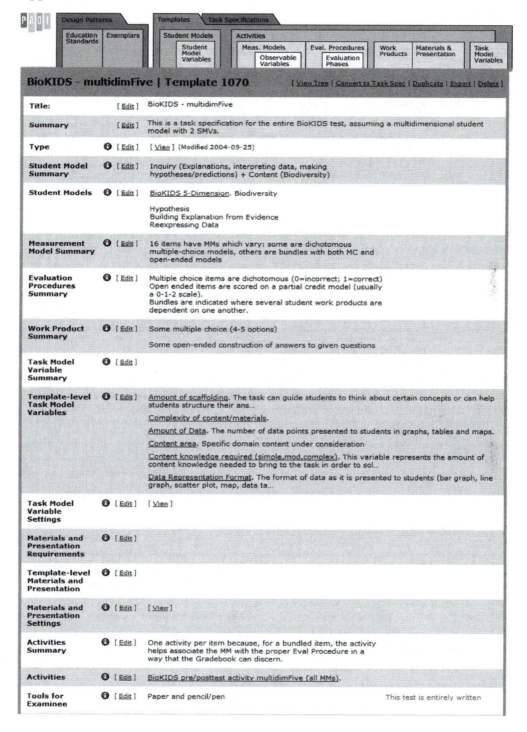

BioKIDS – multidimFive | Template 1070   [View Tree | Convert to Task Spec | Duplicate | Export | Delete]

Title:	[Edit]	BioKIDS - multidimFive
Summary	[Edit]	This is a task specification for the entire BioKIDS test, assuming a multidimensional student model with 2 SMVs.
Type	❸ [Edit]	[View] (Modified 2004-09-25)
Student Model Summary	❸ [Edit]	Inquiry (Explanations, interpreting data, making hypotheses/predictions) + Content (Biodiversity)
Student Models	❸ [Edit]	BioKIDS 5-Dimension. Biodiversity Hypothesis Building Explanation from Evidence Reexpressing Data
Measurement Model Summary	❸ [Edit]	16 items have MMs which vary: some are dichotomous multiple-choice models, others are bundles with both MC and open-ended models
Evaluation Procedures Summary	❸ [Edit]	Multiple choice items are dichotomous (0=incorrect; 1=correct) Open ended items are scored on a partial credit model (usually a 0-1-2 scale). Bundles are indicated where several student work products are dependent on one another.
Work Product Summary	❸ [Edit]	Some multiple choice (4-5 options) Some open-ended construction of answers to given questions
Task Model Variable Summary	❸ [Edit]	
Template-level Task Model Variables	❸ [Edit]	Amount of scaffolding. The task can guide students to think about certain concepts or can help students structure their ans... Complexity of content/materials. Amount of Data. The number of data points presented to students in graphs, tables and maps. Content area. Specific domain content under consideration Content knowledge required (simple,mod,complex). This variable represents the amount of content knowledge needed to bring to the task in order to sol... Data Representation Format. The format of data as it is presented to students (bar graph, line graph, scatter plot, map, data ta...
Task Model Variable Settings	❸ [Edit]	[View]
Materials and Presentation Requirements	❸ [Edit]	
Template-level Materials and Presentation	❸ [Edit]	
Materials and Presentation Settings	❸ [Edit]	[View]
Activities Summary	❸ [Edit]	One activity per item because, for a bundled item, the activity helps associate the MM with the proper Eval Procedure in a way that the Gradebook can discern.
Activities	❸ [Edit]	BioKIDS pre/posttest activity multidimFive (all MMs).
Tools for Examinee	❸ [Edit]	Paper and pencil/pen This test is entirely written

Appendix D: Examples of NAEP Science HOT and ICT

NAEP-Released HOT

See http://nationsreportcard.gov/science_2009/hot_g12_scoring.asp?tab_id=tab4&subtab_id=Tab_1#tabsContainer

Table D.1 contains an example of the relationship among Focal KSAs, Potential Observations, and Potential Work Products that might appear in a Design Pattern used to create the grade 12 Maintaining Water Systems Task (a released NAEP HOT).[1]

Within the HOT there are several different items. The item writer must decide what type of item format to choose for each individual item. For this task, the first item asks the student to decide which of the two town sites would have less contaminated water. This relates to the student's ability to make a prediction. A task developer could examine the Potential Work Products and see that they could use a multiple-choice item or a constructed-response item. They might then look at the Potential Observation and decide that they really care about the correctness of the prediction and that in this context they are interested in a student's ability to use a map to make the prediction about which town would have less contaminated water. Since the student is asked to choose between options, a multiple-choice format would be more appropriate.

For the second part of the question and the second Focal KSA, the task asks the student to support his or her prediction. Here the Work Product specifies that this should be a constructed response item, and so the item writer's only option is to use that type.

Part 2 of the task has the student testing the water samples, which is related to his or her ability to use a tool to collect data. Here one of the options for Potential Work Products is a table that the student completes. An item writer might decide that if what is important is the appropriateness of the data recorded, then it might be important to have all of the data the student records. The use of a table provides a student with a structured way in which to record his or her data, which then might make the item easier to score than an open-ended constructed response. Here thinking about the relationship among the Focal KSA, the Potential Work Products, and the Potential Observations might lead an item writer to choose the fill-in-the-table option.

In part 3 of the task, students are asked to use the data they collected to draw conclusions about the type of water contamination that might be more prevalent at each potential town site. Here again, an item writer could look at the Focal KSA, the Potential Observations, and the Potential Work Products and decide to use a combination of item types.

NAEP-Released ICT

See http://nationsreportcard.gov/science2009ict/mysteryplants/mysteryplants.aspx

Table D.2 contains an example of the relationship among Focal KSAs, Potential Observations, and Potential Work Products that might appear in a Design Pattern used to create the Mystery Plants Task (a released NAEP ICT).[1]

One of the foci of this task is on a student's ability to design an investigation (the second Focal KSA in Table D.2). The task uses an interactive item in which the student is asked to drag planters into the experiment and set variables for these planters. An item writer not familiar with the item types for computer-based assessments might not think of using a drag-and-drop item format. However, having it listed in the Potential Work Products would allow the item writer to think about this item type and how it can be used to support the Potential Observations.

Table D.1 An Example of the Relationship among the Focal KSAs, Potential Observations, and Potential Work Products Based on a Released NAEP HOT Task

Focal KSA	Potential Observation	Potential Work Products
Part 1 of Task		
Ability to make a prediction	Correctness of the prediction	Multiple Choice
	Appropriateness of the prediction	Constructed Response
Ability to support a prediction	Appropriateness of the data used to support a prediction	Constructed Response
Part 2 of Task		
Ability to use a tool to collect data	Appropriateness of the data recorded	Fill-in-the-Table
		Multiple Choice
		Constructed Response
Part 3 of Task		
Ability to draw conclusions	Appropriateness of the conclusion drawn	Multiple Choice
	Appropriateness of the support used for the conclusion	Constructed Response

Table D.2 An Example of the Relationship between the Focal KSAs, Potential Observations, and Potential Work Products Based on a Released NAEP ICT Item

Focal KSA	Potential Observation	Potential Work Product
Ability to pose a question	Appropriateness of the support provided for the question	Multiple Choice
	Appropriateness of the questions posed to the context of the task	Constructed Response
Ability to design an investigation	Appropriateness of the number of samples used	Drag-and-Drop
	Appropriateness of the levels of the variables chosen	Multiple Selection (being able to choose a variety of options)
	Whether or not the student controlled for exogenous variables	Constructed Response
Ability to draw conclusions	Correctness of the conclusions drawn	Multiple Choice
	Appropriateness of the support used for the conclusion	Constructed Response

Appendix E: Sample Design Pattern. Using Biological Scientific Principles to Predict Outcomes

Title

Using Biological Scientific Principles to Predict Outcomes

Summary

The Design Pattern generates assessment tasks that require students to use biological scientific principles to predict outcomes relating to personal and public health and/or environmental issues.

Rationale

It is important to practice applying biological science principles to predict outcomes because this is a form of reasoning that improves everyday decision making and policy making around issues of personal and public health and the environment.

Student Model

Focal KSAs (Grade Level Implicit)

Ability to articulate a hypothesis prior to predicting an outcome.

Ability to make logical or likely predictions based on the biological scientific principles of a personal health decision-making situation, public health policy-making situation, or an environmental policy-making situation (*schematic knowledge*).

Ability to understand scientific principles and represent them in tabular or graphical form and to know which tools should be used and which observations should be studied based on the question.

Ability to select the appropriate scientific principles that best frame specific personal and public health situations or environmental situations (*strategic knowledge*).

Knowledge about (*declarative knowledge*):

Environmental quality

- The understanding that all life on earth as we know it adapted because of the capacity of cells to, through photosynthesis, convert carbon dioxide into more complex forms and release oxygen from water. The related understanding that when organic matter is consumed or destroyed, the carbon released into the atmosphere in the form of CO_2 is generated by fungi, bacteria, and animals consuming or destroying the matter.
- The understanding that the environment is constantly changing and species are adapting to these changes. In natural selection, some members of a population will contain mutations that permit greater survival to these environmental changes. One method of environmental change is by humans, which usually occurs faster, and so species do not have time to adapt. The related understanding that evolution of living things is not teleological, but rather based on replication/reproduction that leads to an expanding diversity of genotypes and, therefore, phenotypes. Selection pressure acts on phenotypes.
- The understanding that when material goes into the soil, these materials transform into other forms because of metabolic processes of organisms.
- The understanding that studying how living things evolve specific functions for reproduction, development, homeostasis, environmental response, and energy consumption can inform the design of new technologies that can improve life.

Personal health

- The understanding that body functions are based on maintaining cellular health; exercise and food intake directly influence the life of cells, including their capacity to convert glucose to energy using oxygen. The cells need energy to perform a variety of functions which occur constantly during life. The related understanding that all cells in the body are self-replicating and engaged in a continual cycle of life. In other words, the cells we are born with in our body are not those we die with, but rather the descendants of those original cells.
- The understanding that body functions are based on hereditary and developmental factors that direct cells to engage in specialized functions. These cellular functions can be disturbed any time in the life of the organism because of problems relating to genetics, aging, poor lifestyle, or environmental toxins.
- The understanding that maintaining homeostatic internal balance and sensitivity to changing conditions in the surrounding environment is central to maintaining healthy cell functions. Disturbances in these functions can lead to health problems or death.
- The understanding that studying how living things evolve specific functions for reproduction, development, homeostasis, environmental response, and energy consumption can inform the design of new lifestyle and nutrition choices that can improve life.

Public health

- The importance of monitoring how the public uses drugs to fight pathogens (e.g., bacteria, viruses) because these are life forms that evolve and may adapt resistance to our drugs.
- The importance of promoting widespread public access to practices and procedures such as hand washing, vaccinations, healthy lifestyle, regular physical and dental checkups to monitor body functions and combat/prevent disease, vector control, maternal health practices, and genetic testing to maintain quality public health.
- The understanding that studying how living things evolve specific functions for reproduction, development, homeostasis, environmental response, and energy consumption can inform the design of new health treatments that can improve life.

Additional KSAs

- Familiarity with underlying declarative knowledge of cellular self-replication processes (i.e., a gene and a protein are not the same).
- Familiarity with underlying declarative knowledge of cellular metabolic pathways for living organisms (photosynthesis) (glycolysis prepares glucose for conversion via anaerobic or aerobic chemical processes; anaerobic is typically less efficient than aerobic).
- Familiarity with underlying declarative knowledge that genetic mutation occurs in replicating gene sequences and, over long periods of time, some of those mutations make a species more adaptable to environmental conditions.
- Familiarity with underlying declarative knowledge of osmosis and the basis of exchange through the cell membrane.
- Familiarity with underlying declarative knowledge of receptors on cell surfaces to permit delivery of key messages for cellular function and communication. These messages trigger reactions in the cell.
- Familiarity with the hierarchical organization of life.
- Basic skills of reading and writing.
- Ability to interpret graphical or tabular data.

- Basic computational and arithmetic skills.
- Understanding the steps of the scientific method.

Evidence Model

Potential Observations (Student Actions)

- Quality of appropriately applying biological scientific principles to a given situation.
- Quality of the thought process providing a correct, step-by-step rationale based on scientific principles leading up to the predicted result.

Potential Work Products (Artifacts)

- Multiple choice question (e.g., identify relevant scientific principle for a situation).
- Short answer response.
- Different teams share predictions with each other.
- Student-generated table or graph.

Potential Rubrics

3—Student identifies appropriate set of several key principles and provides elaborated and logical step-by-step rationale leading up to predicted result.

2—Student identifies appropriate set of several key principles and can provide major steps in the rationale leading up to predicted result.

1—Student identifies only one or two key principles and can provide some steps in the rationale leading up to predicted result.

0—Student fails to identify appropriate principle; illogical connections.

Task Model

Characteristic Task Features

- Task should include a simplified real-world situation that can be used to predict an outcome based on a set of biological scientific principles.

Variable Task Features

- Familiarity of real-world situation.
- Number of biological science principles invoked.
- Length of time given for solution work.
- Number of specific technical details of underlying declarative knowledge required (minor vs. major differences here).
- Genre of presentation (e.g., news article vs. scientific study).
- Data may be presented in textual, graphical, or tabular form.

Note

1 Note that the table was constructed to provide an example of the relationships among the Focal KSAs, Potential Observations, and Potential Work Products and are not necessarily representative of the KSAs designed to be measured by the task. In addition, this example does not provide a complete list of all of the Potential Observations and Potential Work Products that might be associated with the Focal KSAs included.

Acknowledgments

Research findings and assessment tasks described in this chapter were supported by the National Science Foundation under grants REC-0129331 (PADI Implementation Grant) and DRL-0733172 (An Application of Evidence-Centered Design to State Large-Scale Science Assessment), and a grant from the Institute of Education Sciences, U.S. Department of Education, R324A070035 (Principled Assessment Science Assessment Designs for Students with Disabilities).

We are grateful to Robert Mislevy at Educational Testing Service; Cathleen Kennedy and Mark Wilson at the BEAR Assessment Center, University of California, Berkeley; Nancy Songer, University of Michigan; Kathy Long at the Lawrence Hall of Science, University of California, Berkeley; Paul Nichols and Robert Dolan at Pearson; and David Rose and Elizabeth Murray at CAST for their participation and expertise in our project work. We also recognize the contributions of several anonymous reviewers for helpful suggestions on this chapter.

Disclaimer

Any opinions, findings, and conclusions or recommendations expressed in this material are those of the authors and do not necessarily reflect the views of the National Science Foundation or the Institute of Education Sciences, U.S. Department of Education.

References

ACT. (2009). *ACT National Curriculum Survey 2009.* Iowa City, IA: ACT.

ACT. (2013). *ACT National Curriculum Survey 2012.* Iowa City, IA: ACT.

American Association for the Advancement of Science (AAAS). (2001). *Atlas of science literacy.* Washington, DC: AAAS.

Augustine, N. R., Barrett, C., Cassell, G., Grasmick, N., Holliday, C., Hackson, S., . . . Zare, R. (2010). *Rising above the gathering storm, revisited: Rapidly approaching category 5.* Washington, DC: National Academy of Sciences, National Academy of Engineering, Institute of Medicine.

Baxter, G. P., & Mislevy, R. (2005). *The case for an integrated design framework for assessing science inquiry* (PADI Tech. Rep. No. 5). Menlo Park, CA: SRI International.

Behrens, J. T., DiCerbo, K. E., & Ferrara, S. (2012). *Intended and unintended deceptions in the use of simulations.* Princeton, NJ: Center for K–12 Assessment and Performance Management, Educational Testing Service.

Bennett, R. E., Persky, H., Weiss, A., & Jenkins, F. (2007). *Problem-solving in technology-rich environments: A report from the NAEP Technology-Based Assessment Project* (NCES-2007-466). Washington, DC: U.S. Department of Education. National Center for Education Statistics. Retrieved August 3, 2014 from http://nces.ed.gov/pubsearch/pubsinfo.asp?pubid=2007466

Bennett, R. E., & Ward, W. C. (Ed.). (2009). *Construction versus choice in cognitive measurement: Issues in constructed response, performance testing, and portfolio assessment.* New York, NY: Routledge.

Cameto, R., Haertel, G., DeBarger, A. H., & Morrison, K. (2010). *Applying evidence-centered design to alternate assessments in mathematics for students with significant cognitive disabilities* (Alternate Assessment Design–Mathematics Technical Report 1). Menlo Park, CA: SRI International.

Cheng, B. H., Ructtinger, L., Fujii, R., & Mislevy, R. (2010). *Assessing systems thinking and complexity in science* (Large-Scale Assessment Technical Report 7). Menlo Park, CA: SRI International.

Colker, A. M., Liu, M., Mislevy, R. J., Haertel, G., Fried, R., & Zalles, D. (2010). *A design pattern for experimental investigation* (Large-Scale Assessment Technical Report 8). Menlo Park, CA: SRI International.

Corcoran, T., Mosher, F. A., & Rogat, A. (2009). *Learning progressions in science: An evidence-based approach to reform.* Philadelphia, PA: Consortium for Policy Research in Education.

DeBarger, A. H., Werner, A., Minstrell, J., & DiBello, L. (2013). *Using evidence-centered design to articulate a facets-based assessment argument.* Menlo Park, CA: SRI International.

Embretson, S. E. (1998). A cognitive design system approach to generating valid tests: Application to abstract reasoning. *Psychological Methods, 3*, 380–396.

Ewing, M., Packman, S., Hamen, C., & Thurber, A. C. (2010). Representing targets of measurement within evidence-centered design. *Applied Measurement in Education, 23*(4), 325–341.

Gotwals, A. W., & Songer, N. B. (2006). *Cognitive predictions: BioKIDS implementation of the PADI assessment system* (PADI Technical Report 10). Menlo Park, CA: SRI International.

Haertel, G., DeBarger, A. H., Cheng, B., Blackorby, J., Javitz, H., Ructtinger, L., . . . Hansen, E. G. (2010). *Using evidence-centered design and universal design for learning to design science assessment tasks for students with disabilities* (Assessment for Students with Disabilities Technical Report 1). Menlo Park, CA: SRI International.

Haladyna, T. M., Downing, S. M., & Rodriquez, M. C. (2002). A review of multiple-choice item-writing guidelines for classroom assessment. *Applied Measurement in Education, 15*(3), 309–336.

Hansen, E. G., Mislevy, R. J., Steinberg, L. S., Lee, M. J., & Forer, D. C. (2005). Accessibility of tests within a validity framework. *System: An International Journal of Educational Technology and Applied Linguistics, 33*, 107–133.

Hendrickson, A., Ewing, M., Kaliski, P., & Huff, K. (2013). Evidence-centered design: Recommendations for implementation and practice. *Journal of Applied Testing Technology, 14*, 1–27.

Hendrickson, A., Huff, K., & Luecht, R. (2010). Claims, evidence, and achievement-level descriptors as a foundation for item design and test specifications. *Applied Measurement in Education, 23*(4), 358–377.

Huff, K., Alves, C., Pellegrino, J., & Kaliski, P. (2013). Using evidence centered design task models in automatic item generation. In M. Gierl & T. Haladyna (Eds.), *Automatic item generation: Theory and practice.* New York, NY: Informa UK Limited.

Huff, K., & Plake, B. (2010). Innovations in setting performance standards for K–12 test-based accountability. *Measurement: Interdisciplinary Research and Perspective, 8*(2), 130–144.

Huff, K., Steinberg, L., & Matts, T. (2010). The promise and challenges of implementing evidence-centered design in large-scale assessment. *Applied Measurement in Education, 23*(4), 310–324.

Kaliski, P., Huff, K., & Barry, C. (2011, April). *Aligning items and achievement levels: A study comparing expert judgments.* Paper presented at the meeting of the National Council on Measurement in Education, New Orleans, LA.

Kane, M. (2006). Validation. In R. L. Brennan (Ed.), *Educational measurement* (4th ed., pp. 17–64). Washington, DC: American Council on Education.

King, K. V., Gardner, D. A., Zucker, S., & Jorgensen, M. A. (2004). *The distractor rationale taxonomy: Enhancing multiple-choice items in reading and mathematics* (Assessment Report). San Antonio, TX: Pearson.

Knudsen, J., Vendlinski, T., Lara Meloy, T., Empson, S., Paek, P., Werner, A., & Haertel, G. (2013). *NAEP mathematics framework: DRAFT recommendations and literature review.* Menlo Park, CA: SRI International.

Lawson, A. E., Alkhoury, S., Benford, R., Clark, B. R., & Falconer, K. A. (2000). What kinds of scientific concepts exist? Concept construction and intellectual development in college biology. *Journal of Research in Science Teaching, 37*(9), 996–1018.

Lawson, A. E., Clark, B., Cramer-Meldrum, E., Falconer, K. A., Sequist, J. M., & Kwon, Y.-J. (2000). Development of scientific reasoning in college biology: Do two levels of general hypothesis-testing skills exist? *Journal of Research in Science Teaching, 37*(1), 81–101.

Levy, R. (2013). Psychometric and evidentiary advances, opportunities, and challenges for simulation-based assessment. *Educational Assessment, 18*, 182–207.

Luecht, R. M. (2002, April). *From design to delivery: Engineering the mass production of complex performance assessments.* Paper presented at the annual meeting of the National Council of Measurement in Education, New Orleans, LA.

Mayer, R. E. (2010). *Applying the science of learning.* Upper Saddle River, NJ: Pearson.

Messick, S. (1994). The interplay of evidence and consequences in the validation of performance assessments. *Educational Researcher, 23*(2), 13–23.

Minstrell, J. (2001). Facets of students' thinking: Designing to cross the gap from research to standards-based practice. In K. Crowley, C. D. Schunn, & T. Okada (Eds.), *Designing for science: Implications for professional, instructional, and everyday science.* Mahwah, NJ: Lawrence Erlbaum Associates.

Minstrell, J., Anderson, R., Kraus, P., & Minstrell, J. E. (2008). Bridging from practice to research and back: Tools to support formative assessment. In J. Coffey, R. Douglas, & C. Sterns (Eds.), *Science assessment: Research and practical approaches*. Arlington, VA: NSTA Press.

Mislevy, R. J. (2003). Substance and structure in assessment arguments. *Law, Probability, and Risk*, 2, 237–258.

Mislevy, R. J. (2007). Validity by design. *Educational Researcher, 36*, 463–469.

Mislevy, R. J., & Haertel, G. D. (2006). Implications of evidence-centered design for educational testing. *Educational Measurement: Issues and Practices, 25*(4), 6–20.

Mislevy, R. J., Hamel, L., Fried, R. G., Gaffney, T., Haertel, G., Hafter, A., . . . Wenk, A. (2003). *Design patterns for assessing science inquiry* (PADI Technical Report 1). Menlo Park, CA: SRI International. Also presented at American Education Research Association (AERA) in April, 2003.

Mislevy, R. J., Liu, M., Cho, Y., Fulkerson, D., Nichols, P., Zalles, D., . . . Hamel, L. (2009). *A design pattern for observational investigation assessment tasks* (Large-Scale Assessment Technical Report 2). Menlo Park, CA: SRI International.

Mislevy, R. J., Steinberg, L. S., & Almond, R. G. (2003). On the structure of educational assessments. *Measurement: Interdisciplinary Research and Perspectives, 1*, 3–67.

Mislevy, R. J., Steinberg, L. S., Almond, R. G., & Lukas, J. F. (2006). Concepts, terminology, and basic models of evidence-centered design. In D. M. Williamson, I. I. Bejar, & R. J. Mislevy (Eds.), *Automated scoring of complex tasks in computer-based testing* (pp. 15–47). Mahwah, NJ: Erlbaum.

Mislevy, R. J., Steinberg, L. S., Breyer, F. J., Almond, R. G., & Johnson, L. (2002). Making sense of data from complex assessments. *Applied Measurement in Education, 15*, 363–378.

Murray, J. M., Arns, D. C., Byrnes, J. J., Chow, E., Connolly, C., Dieterle, E. R., . . . Taylor, N. (2012, November). *Reynard VERUS final report*. Prepared by SRI International for the Air Force Research Laboratory (AFRL-RY-WP-TR-2012-0286), Wright-Patterson AFB, OH.

National Governors Association. (2010a). *Common Core State Standards for English language arts & literacy in history/social studies, science, and technical subjects*. Washington, DC: National Governors Association.

National Governors Association. (2010b). *Common Core State Standards for mathematics*. Washington, DC: National Governors Association.

National Research Council. (1996). *National science education standards*. Washington, DC: National Academy Press.

National Research Council. (2003). Identifying desired student learning outcomes. In R. A. McCray, R. L. DeHaan, & J. A. Schuck (Eds.), *Improving undergraduate instruction in science, technology, engineering, and mathematics: Report of a workshop*. Washington, DC: National Academy of Sciences.

National Research Council. (2005). Committee on high school science laboratories: Role and vision. In S. R. Singer, M. L. Hilton, & H. A. Schweingruber (Eds.), *America's lab report: Investigations in high school science*. Washington, DC: The National Academies Press.

National Research Council. (2007). Committee on science learning, kindergarten through eighth grade. In R. A. Duschl, H. A. Schweingruber, & A. W. Shouse (Eds.), *Taking science to school: Learning and teaching science in grades K–8*. Washington, DC: The National Academies Press.

National Research Council. (2011a). Committee on science learning: Computer games, simulations, and education. In M. A. Honey & M. L. Hilton (Eds.), *Learning science through computer games and simulations*. Washington, DC: The National Academies Press.

National Research Council. (2011b). *Successful STEM education: A workshop summary*. Washington, DC: The National Academies Press.

National Research Council. (2012). *A framework for K–12 science education: Practices, crosscutting concepts, and core ideas*. Washington, DC: The National Academies Press.

NGSS. (2013). *Next Generation Science Standards*. Retrieved August 3, 2014 from http://www.nextgenscience.org/next-generation-science-standards

Niemi, D., & Baker, E. L. (2005, April). Reconceiving assessment shortfalls: System requirements needed to produce learning. In F. C. Sloane & J. W. Pellegrino (Co-Chairs), *Moving technology up—design requirements for valid, effective classroom and large-scale assessment*. Presentation at the annual meeting of the American Educational Research Association, Montreal.

Opfer, J. E., Nehm, R. H., & Ha, M. (2012). Cognitive foundations for science assessment design: Knowing what students know about evolution. *Journal of Research in Science Teaching, 49*(6), 744–777.

President's Council of Advisors on Science and Technology. (2010). *Report to the president. Prepare and inspire: K–12 education in science, technology, engineering, and math (STEM) for America's future.* Retrieved August 3, 2014 from https://www.whitehouse.gov/sites/default/files/micro sites/ostp/pcast-stemed-report.pdf

Quellmalz, E. S., & Pellegrino, J. W. (2009). Technology and testing. *Science, 323,* 75–79.

Quellmalz, E. S., Timms, M. J., Silberglitt, M. D., & Buckley, B. C. (2012). Science assessments for all: Integrating science simulation into balanced state science assessment systems. *Journal of Research in Science Teaching, 49*(3), 363–393.

Scalise, K. M. (2012, May 7–8). *Using technology to assess hard-to-measure constructs in the Common Core State Standards and to expand accessibility.* Presented at Invitational Research Symposium on Technology-Enhanced Assessments (K–12 Center at ETS), Washington, DC.

Scalise, K. M., & Gifford, B. (2006). Computer-based assessment in e-learning: A framework for constructing "intermediate constraint" questions and tasks for technology platforms. *Journal of Technology, Learning, and Assessment, 4*(6). Retrieved from http://ejournals.bc.edu/ojs/index.php/jtla/issue/view/192

Schneider, C. B., Huff, K. L., Egan, K. L., Tully, M., & Ferrara, S. (2010, April). *Aligning achievement level descriptors to mapped item demands to enhance valid interpretations of scale scores and inform item development.* Paper presented at the annual meeting of the American Educational Research Association, Denver, CO.

Shavelson, R., Ruiz-Primo, M. A., Li, M., & Ayala, C. C. (2003). *Evaluating new approaches to assessing learning* (CSE Report No. 604). Los Angeles, CA: University of California, Center for the Study of Evaluation (CSE).

Shute, V. J., Ventura, M., Bauer, M., & Zapata-Rivera, D. (2009). Melding the power of serious games and embedded assessment to monitor and foster learning. In U. Ritterfeld, M. J. Cody, & P. Vorderer (Eds.), *Serious game: Mechanisms and effects* (pp. 295–321). New York, NY: Routledge.

Sireci, S. G., & Zenisky, A. L. (2006). Innovative item formats in computer-based testing: In pursuit of improved construct representation. In S. M. Downing & T. M. Haladyna (Eds.), *Handbook of testing* (pp. 329–347). Mahwah, NJ: Lawrence Erlbaum.

Songer, C. J., & Mintzes, J. J. (1994). Understanding cellular respiration: An analysis of conceptual change in college biology. *Journal of Research in Science Teaching, 31*(6), 621–638.

Spray, J. A., Lin, C.-J., & Chen, T. T. (2002). *Controlling item allocation in the automated assembly of multiple test forms.* Iowa City, IA: ACT, Incorporated.

Steinberg, L. S., Mislevy, R. J., Almond, R. G., DiBello, L. V., Chernick, H., & Kindfield, A. C. H. (2003). *Introduction to the Biomass project: An illustration of evidence-centered assessment design and delivery capability* (CRESST Technical Report 609). Los Angeles, CA: Center for the Study of Evaluation, CRESST, UCLA.

Stevens, R., & Casillas, A. (2006). Artificial neural networks. In D. M. Williamson, R. J. Mislevy, & I. I. Bejar (Eds.), *Automated scoring of complex tasks in computer based testing* (pp. 259–312). Mahwah, NJ: Erlbaum Associates.

Toulmin, S. (1958). *The uses of argument.* Cambridge, UK: Cambridge University Press.

Vendlinski, T., & Stevens, R. (2002). Assessing student problem-solving skills with complex computer-based tasks. *The Journal of Technology, Learning and Assessment, 1*(3), 1–20.

Walker, M. (2011). *PISA 2009 Plus Results: Performance of 15-year-olds in reading, mathematics and science for 10 additional participants.* Melbourne: ACER Press.

Wiliam, D., & Black, P. (1996). Meanings and consequences: A basis for distinguishing formative and summative functions of assessment? *British Educational Research Journal, 22*(5), 537–548.

Wilson, M., & Adams, R. J. (1995). Rasch models for item bundles. *Psychometrika, 60,* 181–198.

Yarnall, L., Gallagher, L., Haertel, G., Lundh, P., & Toyama, Y. (2012, April). *Using evidence-centered design to broaden the range of cognitive performances in college tests.* Paper presented at the annual conference of the American Educational Research Association, Vancouver, BC.

6 Validity and Accountability
Test Validation for 21st-Century Educational Assessments

Stephen G. Sireci and Amanda Soto

In educational and psychological testing, validity is often referred to as the most important criterion in evaluating the quality and appropriateness of a test. Its importance is inherent in the definition of validity provided by the *Standards for Educational and Psychological Testing*, an authoritative publication produced by a joint committee from the American Educational Research Association (AERA), the American Psychological Association (APA), and the National Council on Measurement in Education (NCME; AERA, APA, & NCME, 2014). The *Standards* define validity as "the degree to which evidence and theory support the interpretations of test scores for proposed uses of tests," and they claim validity is "the most fundamental consideration in developing tests and evaluating tests" (p. 11).

What does this definition mean for 21st-century educational assessments? At least two characteristics currently distinguish 21st-century educational assessments from their predecessors. The first is increased use of technology. Computerized adaptive testing, technology-enhanced item formats, and computerized scoring of responses constructed by examinees are becoming increasingly common. The second characteristic is the use of educational tests for accountability purposes, which is the principal focus of this chapter. Using tests for educational accountability often entails employing the test for purposes beyond which it was originally developed. Like the originally intended purposes, using test scores for accountability purposes also requires evidence and theory to justify their use.

Historically, educational tests have been designed to provide information about an individual examinee. However, in current accountability systems, examinees' test scores are also being used to make inferences about *other* people and systems that interact with the examinee—specifically, teachers, administrators, schools, school districts, and teacher preparation programs. The validation of test scores for these new purposes is difficult and raises concerns about tests being inappropriately used to answer systemic performance questions when they were designed to assess individual students' content knowledge.

The processes of validating test scores for accountability purposes and validating test scores used to make inferences about individual students can be quite different, largely due to the derivative nature of accountability data. For example, to estimate a school's performance, the performance of students and teachers must be measured and quantified. Accountability measures are being quickly developed and can vary widely in their design, statistical characteristics, and the way in which they represent student achievement. The greatest need in validation for accountability testing is further study of these derivative indicators and ongoing evaluation of their utility for providing valid information about teachers and schools.

These concerns are the focus of this chapter in which we (a) describe the fundamental aspects of validity and approaches to test validation, (b) discuss the issues involved in validating educational tests for accountability purposes, and (c) critique the current status of test validation for accountability purposes. In addition, we provide a discussion of future directions for developing and validating educational assessments for accountability purposes.

Validity Theory and Test Validation

Theories of validity and methods of test validation are almost as old as the practice of testing itself (Sireci, 2009). In the earliest days of modern testing, two definitions of validity were proposed, and both were influenced by statistical developments. The first definition adopted the correlation coefficient developed by Pearson in 1896 and described tests as being valid for anything with which they correlated (Kelley, 1927; Thurstone, 1932). The second definition defined validity as "the degree to which a test measures what it purports to measure" (Garrett, 1937; Smith & Wright, 1928), which was heavily influenced by the development of factor analysis by Spearman in 1904.

However, these definitions were eventually dismissed as being inadequate. The definition based on correlation was rejected due to problems in finding and validating relevant criteria (e.g., Jenkins, 1946), and the definition based on measurement of the intended construct was rejected because it failed to address the purpose and intended uses of the test and the resulting scores. As Rulon (1946) put it, "This is an unsatisfactory and not very useful concept of validity, because under it the validity of a test may be altered completely by arbitrarily changing its 'purport'" (p. 290).

Given the debates about what validity was and how tests should be validated, APA put forward a "preliminary proposal" of technical recommendations for tests that initiated the development of a consensus definition of validity. These *Technical Recommendations for Psychological Tests and Diagnostic Techniques: A Preliminary Proposal* (APA, 1952) led to the eventual joint committee representing APA, AERA, and NCME that produced standards for guidance in test development and validation and that defined validity in practical terms. Table 6.1 lists the different versions of these *Standards* and the nomenclature they used to describe validity. These validity terms are historically interesting and still appear in the literature. However, the current consensus is that validity should be described as a unitary concept, and validation should focus on the five sources of validity evidence stipulated in the 1999 and 2014 versions of the *Standards*.

A notable improvement in the current version of the *Standards* (AERA et al., 2014) is its emphasis on the need to validate inferences and actions made on the basis of *aggregate* test scores. This improvement is important because accountability systems use aggregated test scores to evaluate teachers, schools, and districts. As the *Standards* describe,

> Users of information from accountability systems might assume that the accountability indices provide valid indicators of the intended outcomes of education…, that the differences among indices can be attributed to differences in the effectiveness of the teacher or school, and that these differences are reasonably stable over time and across students and items. These assumptions must be supported by evidence.
>
> (p. 206)

Essentially, the *Standards* mandate that accountability indices based on aggregates of students' test scores "should be subjected to the same validity, reliability, and fairness investigations that are expected for the test scores that underlie the index" (p. 210).

The Standards' Five Sources of Validity Evidence

The current version of the AERA et al. (2014) *Standards* stipulates five sources of evidence "that might be used in evaluating the validity of a proposed interpretation of test scores for a particular use" (p. 13). These sources, which appear in Table 6.1, are validity evidence based on (a) test content, (b) response processes, (c) internal structure, (d) relations to other variables, and (e) consequences of testing. These sources must be considered when validating educational tests for accountability purposes.

Table 6.1 Evolution of the *Standards for Educational and Psychological Testing* and Validity Terminology

Publication	Validity Terminology
Technical Recommendations for Psychological Tests and Diagnostic Techniques: A Preliminary Proposal (APA, 1952)	*Categories*: predictive, status, content, congruent
Technical Recommendations for Psychological Tests and Diagnostic Techniques (APA, 1954)	*Types*: construct, concurrent, predictive, content
Standards for Educational and Psychological Tests and Manuals (APA, AERA, & NCME, 1966)	*Types*: criterion-related, construct-related, content-related
Standards for Educational and Psychological Tests (APA, AERA, & NCME, 1974)	*Aspects*: criterion-related, construct-related, content-related
Standards for Educational and Psychological Testing (AERA, APA, & NCME, 1985)	*Categories*: criterion-related, construct-related, content-related
Standards for Educational and Psychological Testing (AERA, APA, & NCME, 1999)	*Sources of evidence*: content, response processes, internal structure, relations to other variables, consequences of testing
Standards for Educational and Psychological Testing (AERA et al., 2014)	*Sources of evidence*: content, response processes, internal structure, relations to other variables, consequences of testing

Validity Evidence Based on Test Content

Validity evidence based on test content refers to traditional studies of content validity such as practice (job) analyses and subject matter expert (SME) review and rating of test specifications and items (Crocker, Miller, & Franks, 1989; Sireci, 1998), as well as newer methods for evaluating the "alignment" of educational tests, curriculum frameworks, and instruction (Bhola, Impara, & Buckendahl, 2003; Martone & Sireci, 2009). This form of evidence involves recruiting independent SMEs who are familiar with the subject areas tested and the testing purpose. These SMEs review test items and rate the degree to which they are adequately measuring their intended content areas, cognitive skills, or benchmarks (content standards). Such data can provide evidence that the test is adequately measuring what it intends to measure, which is fundamental for adequate score interpretation.

With respect to validating the use of educational tests for accountability purposes, validity evidence based on test content will be important to ensure tests are measuring the intended curricula (e.g., aligned with state curriculum frameworks). If such evidence is not provided, the test scores may not reflect students' achievement with respect to the intended curriculum and may not be valid for evaluating the degree to which teachers were teaching that curriculum. Again, borrowing from the AERA et al. (2014) *Standards*, "If a primary goal of an accountability system is to identify teachers who are effective at improving student achievement, the accountability index should be based on assessments that are closely aligned with the content the teacher is expected to cover…" (p. 206). Therefore, the design of the assessment, specifically which content standards (benchmarks or objectives) are assessed each year and in what proportions, should ensure the intended curriculum to be enacted by teachers is sufficiently represented by the assessment. In addition, the expectations for teaching the curriculum should be clear to the teachers. In essence, a fundamental assumption in the use of students' test performance to evaluate teachers is that the curriculum, instruction, and assessment are well aligned. Validity evidence based on test content is needed to evaluate that assumption.

Validity Evidence Based on Response Processes

Validity evidence based on response processes refers to "evidence concerning the fit between the construct and the detailed nature of performance or response actually engaged in by test takers" (AERA et al., 2014, p. 15). Examples of this type of evidence include interviewing examinees about their responses to test questions, systematic observations of examinees responding to test items, evaluation of the criteria used by judges when scoring performance tasks, analysis of item response time (chronometric analysis), tracking students' eye movements, and evaluation of the reasoning processes examinees use when solving test items (Embretson, 1983; Messick, 1989; Mislevy, 2009). This evidence is particularly useful for evaluating the degree to which tests tap higher order skills and for evaluating how well students in different subpopulations understand the test items. Given that many of the new content standards in the *Common Core State Standards* and emerging state curriculum frameworks emphasize higher level cognitive skills, evidence will be needed that the new tests aligned with these standards adequately measure these skills.

Validity Evidence Based on Internal Structure

Validity evidence based on internal structure refers to statistical analysis of item and sub-score data to investigate the primary and secondary (if any) dimensions measured by a test. Procedures for gathering such evidence include factor analysis (both exploratory and confirmatory), multi-dimensional scaling, and residual analysis (departure of test data from an item response theory model). In addition, analysis of differential item functioning, which is a preliminary statistical analysis to assess item bias, also falls under the internal structure category.

Internal structure evidence also evaluates the "strength" or "salience" of the major dimensions underlying an assessment, and this salience has a relationship to internal consistency reliability. Therefore, indices of measurement precision such as reliability estimates, conditional and unconditional standard errors of measurement, and test information functions can be classified as validity evidence in this category. Estimates of decision accuracy and consistency and generalizability coefficients are also relevant.

For accountability purposes, it is important to estimate the reliability of derivative indicators or aggregate scores. Derivative indicators include indices such as "value-added estimates" or "median growth percentiles" that have been proposed for use in teacher and school evaluation systems as "progress indicators." Other aggregate scores include percentage of students in a particular achievement level (referred to as a "status" indicator), mean scale scores, or difference scores that are tracked over time. Given that reliability sets an upper bound for validity (i.e., if test scores are unreliable, an examinee's score will fluctuate from one test occasion to another, even if the examinee's proficiency has not changed), evidence that these derivative and aggregate indicators are reliable is paramount in evaluating the validity of test-based accountability systems. Unfortunately, emerging research on these measures has not provided enthusiastic support. For example, Wells, Sireci, and Bahry (2014) estimated that a 68 percent confidence interval for a student's growth percentile can range up to 50 points (i.e., a reported growth percentile of 50 had a 68 percent confidence interval ranging from 29 to 78!). Such unreliability at the student level is likely to also be manifested at the aggregate level.

Validity Evidence Based on Relations to Other Variables

Validity evidence based on relations to other variables refers to traditional forms of criterion-related validity evidence such as concurrent and predictive validity studies, as well as more comprehensive investigations of the relationships among test scores and other variables such as multitrait-multimethod studies (Campbell & Fiske, 1959) and score differences across different groups of students (e.g., students who have taken different courses). These external variables can be used to evaluate hypothesized relationships between test scores and other measures of student achievement (e.g., test scores and teacher grades) to evaluate the degree to which different tests actually measure different skills and the utility of test scores for predicting specific criteria (e.g., college grades). In the context of accountability, the degree to which accountability indicators are congruent with other indicators of teacher or school effectiveness can be used to provide valuable validity evidence for aggregate or derivative indicators.

However, it should be noted that when students' performances on educational tests are used to evaluate teachers, the relevant data to correlate with a criterion of teaching performance are not the individual student's score but rather some aggregate measure based on the performance of a group of students (e.g., mean test score, average "growth" score, change in proportions of students meeting a standard). Thus, validity evidence based on relations of test scores with other variables should involve investigating the relationships of aggregate measures of students' test performance against other measures of teaching effectiveness associated with a teacher.

Admittedly, it is difficult to find external variables for validating accountability measures based on students' test performance, in part because current teacher evaluation systems have serious limitations. Existing evaluation methods like structured observations (Ho & Kane, 2013) are subject to sources of unreliability such as the chosen observation day(s), the ability of the observer to follow the observation rubric, data interpretation issues, and so forth. However, when the observation protocol and assessment instrument overlap to some degree in what they are targeting, observational data can be helpful for evaluating aggregated or derivative scores used in accountability systems (Grossman, Cohen, Ronfeldt, & Brown, 2014).

Validity Evidence Based on the Consequences of Testing

Validity evidence based on the consequences of testing refers to evaluation of the intended and unintended consequences associated with a testing program. This type of evidence is particularly important in considering the validation of tests for accountability purposes because accountability almost always involves consequences. With respect to accountability, the interpretations made on the basis of test scores can lead to rewards or sanctions for teachers, districts, and schools (e.g., availability of Title I/School Improvement Grant funds linked to school-level accountability measures). In addition, these rewards and sanctions may influence the numbers and types of teachers who teach different grades and subject areas, as well as the communities and schools in which they teach.

Accountability testing is required by federal educational policy and typically comes with a theory of action outlining the intended consequences for stakeholders. For example, using students' test results to evaluate teachers encourages teachers to teach the intended curriculum, and it is assumed that this more focused instruction will improve student learning with respect to that curriculum. The degree to which these intended consequences are realized and other unintended consequences (e.g., decreased teacher morale, narrowing the curriculum in a way that decreases student learning) are minimized is essential to investigating the validity of educational tests for accountability purposes.

An Argument-Based Approach to Validation

The aforementioned definition of validity provided by the AERA et al. (2014) *Standards* emphasizes that an evaluation of validity involves the justification of the use of a test for a particular purpose. Kane (1992, 2006, 2013), borrowing from Cronbach (1988), suggested that validating the use of a test for a particular purpose is tantamount to developing a sound and logical argument that use of the test for a particular purpose is justified. The *Standards* essentially adopted this perspective by claiming that the five sources of evidence should be coherently synthesized to support use of a test for a particular purpose. For example, they state: "A sound validity argument integrates various strands of evidence into a coherent account of the degree to which existing evidence and theory support the intended interpretation of test scores for specific uses" (AERA et al., 2014, p. 21).

Hill (2009) used Kane's argument-based approach to validation to evaluate the use of value-added models for teacher accountability. She proposed three assumptions inherent in the use of students' test scores in value-added models of teaching effectiveness: (a) students' test scores are valid indicators of teaching effectiveness, (b) teachers' value-added scores are reliable, and (c) teachers' value-added scores are free from manipulation. The research framework she used to evaluate these assumptions involved validity evidence based on relations with other variables, validity evidence based on test content, and studies of reliability and decision consistency. Based on these sources of evidence, she concluded teacher effectiveness scores represent "not only teacher quality but also bias due to student selection, the effect of other resources on student achievement, and a generous amount of measurement error" (p. 706).

To summarize how the five sources of validity evidence can be used to develop an argument to support the use of a test for a particular purpose, Table 6.2 crosses the *Standards'* five sources of validity evidence with five types of testing purposes. The first three purposes are described as "traditional," with the first two referring to interpretation of individual student scores and the third on the use of test results to improve instruction more generally. The fourth and fifth purposes refer to accountability purposes.

Several observations can be made from Table 6.2. First, validity evidence based on test content is relevant, and in fact required, to adequately validate all of the purposes listed. This requirement is due to the fact that both interpretations of student performance and evaluations of schools and teachers are intended to be linked to the content standards within state-mandated curriculum frameworks. Thus, the content of a test must be aligned with these frameworks for valid interpretations to be made for both traditional and accountability purposes. Another observation is the importance of reliability information (listed under Internal Structure) to support inferences related to students, teachers, and schools. However, when moving from traditional to accountability testing, the unit of analysis shifts from individuals' test scores to the aggregate or derivative measures. A third observation is the need to include external variables in the validation process to ensure the interpretations arrived via students' test scores are congruent with those obtained using other relevant data. Finally, educational assessments have consequences for students, teachers, schools, and others. Thus, validity evidence based on testing consequences is critical when the testing purpose involves broad goals such as improving instruction and student achievement.

The information provided in Table 6.2 indicates the types of evidence that *should* be collected to validate the use of a test for a particular purpose. For traditional testing purposes, in most cases, such evidence is typically available. However, the use of tests for accountability purposes has outpaced validity research to support such use. This has led to a gap in practice, with test scores being used for evaluative purposes, but research has not been done to validate those uses. This use of test scores for purposes for which validation evidence is lacking is unfortunate and is in violation of the AERA et al. (2014) *Standards,* which state:

> When test score information is released, those responsible … should provide interpretations appropriate to the audience. The interpretations should describe in simple language what the test covers, what scores represent, the precision/reliability of the scores, and how the scores are intended to be used.
>
> (p. 119)

Table 6.2 Use of Five Sources of Validity Evidence for Traditional and Accountability Purposes

Testing Purpose	Source of Validity Evidence				
	Content	Response Processes	Internal Structure	Relations to Other Variables	Consequences of Testing
Traditional: Assess student proficiency in a given subject	Content validity and alignment studies	Chronometric analysis, think-aloud studies	α, DA/DC	Correlations with other measures of subject area performance	Teacher surveys regarding the accuracy of information provided about students
Traditional: Measure student progress over time	Content validity and alignment studies		Reliability of change scores	Correlations with other measures of change	Analysis of dropout rates, achievement gaps
Traditional: Inform instruction	Content validity and alignment studies				Teacher surveys regarding use of test results and impact on teaching practices
Accountability: Evaluate teacher effectiveness	Content validity and alignment studies		Reliability of aggregate scores and derivative measures	Correlations of aggregate measures with other measures of teacher effectiveness	Surveys of teacher morale, dropout, adverse impact, improved feedback for teachers, changes in courses taught, etc.
Accountability: Evaluate school effectiveness	Content validity and alignment studies		Reliability of aggregate scores and derivative measures	Correlations of aggregate measures with other measures of school effectiveness	Changes in achievement gaps, graduation rates, teacher retention/ attrition, improvement in achievement at overall and subgroup levels, etc.

Note: α = reliability estimates, DA/DC = decision accuracy and decision consistency estimates.

In the next section, drawing on relevant research, we elaborate on some of the unique validity issues associated with the use of statewide educational tests to evaluate teachers and schools.

Validity Issues in Using Students' Test Performance for Accountability Purposes

The use of educational tests for evaluating teachers, districts, and schools is becoming widespread in the United States, with at least 20 states using student test scores for teacher accountability

(Baker, Oluwole, & Green, 2013) and all states using student test scores for school and district accountability. In most cases, students' test scores are aggregated to the classroom level (for teacher accountability) or the school level (for school accountability). Using students' test scores for this purpose requires at least three assumptions. One assumption is the test is measuring what teachers are supposed to be teaching. Evidence to support that assumption can come from content validity and alignment studies described earlier. A second assumption is that changes in students' test scores over time can be linked to the effectiveness of a teacher and, on a broader scale, generalized to teachers in a school. That assumption is harder to justify because there are many factors in addition to a student's teacher that affect a student's performance on educational tests and their academic achievement in general. A third assumption is that the "scores" assigned to a teacher or school are reliable. Evidence to support that assumption involves evaluating the consistency of the effectiveness estimate or other score assigned to a teacher over different samples of students, over different types of tests, and over time.

Evaluating these assumptions involves evaluating the validity of the practice of using students' test scores for accountability purposes. As the AERA et al. (2014) *Standards* state, "An index that is constructed by manipulating and combining test scores should be subjected to the same validity, reliability, and fairness investigations that are expected for the test scores that underline the index" (p. 210).

Thus, as with all uses of test scores, validity evidence is required to justify how test scores are used in each level of an accountability system. Earlier we described the five sources of validity evidence that can be used to support the use of test scores within an accountability system. However, there are also several threats to the validity that must be considered.

Threats to the Validity of Accountability Decisions Based on Test Scores

The term *validity* has meaning from both psychometric and educational research design perspectives, and both are relevant when evaluating the use of test scores in educational accountability. The psychometric definition, published in the AERA et al. (2014) *Standards*, was presented earlier, and it pertains to the validity of test score interpretations, which typically refer to interpretations about the students who took the test. Many current state-level accountability systems do not involve *teachers* taking a test, and so the validity of the extrapolated inference from student performance to teacher performance also requires consideration of *internal validity*. This concept differs from the "internal structure evidence" of validity that we described earlier and so it needs further explanation.

The concept of internal validity in educational research was introduced by Campbell and Stanley (1963) to refer to the soundness of conclusions made from experimental, quasi-experimental, and non-experimental research. Studies (and evaluations) with good internal validity control for extraneous factors that would otherwise qualify, or even invalidate, the conclusions made on the basis of the observed results. Clearly, the degree to which inferences about teaching effectiveness are based on analyses that control for extraneous variables should be a major consideration in judging the validity of teacher accountability systems. There is one particularly conspicuous extraneous variable to be addressed in teacher accountability—selection bias, which we discuss next.

Selection Bias

One of the most damaging threats to the internal validity of any research-based conclusion is *selection bias*. This type of bias occurs when the groups being studied are not equivalent before the study begins, and differences observed after the "treatment" are due, at least in part, to the non-equivalence of groups, rather than due to treatment differences. The use of value-added models to evaluate teachers, which is the most common form of teacher accountability currently in use (Baker et al., 2013), is essentially a model that infers a causal effect due to exposure to a teacher. That is, each teacher is essentially considered a "treatment" that causes (affects) students' test performance. However, because students are not randomly assigned to teachers, and models vary widely in how they attempt to control for students' backgrounds, previous teachers, and prior achievement patterns, there are many other "hidden" factors that can affect students' test performance. Given that these factors are typically not controlled for in accountability systems, selection bias is a significant threat to the internal validity of conclusions made about teachers in current accountability systems.

Selection bias may stem from some teachers within a school consistently having students who are more difficult to teach or who respond more slowly to effective teaching. This problem may exist at the school level when students are assigned to schools based on where their parents and guardians live. Across schools, students differ with respect to socioeconomic status, community resources, parental education, and peer and family support of academics, which can possibly impact student learning and performance on accountability measures (Ballou, Sanders, & Wright, 2004; Henderson & Mapp, 2002). These factors are generally beyond the school's control, but are likely to affect any "effectiveness" score based upon students' test performance.

The lack of control for non-equivalent student groups has been pointed out by several researchers. For example, Kupermintz (2003) simulated different conditions of student gains to evaluate the value-added teacher accountability model used in Tennessee. Zero, small, moderate, and large effects were simulated for teachers, and small to moderate effects were simulated for students. Three different scenarios were investigated. In the first, teacher effects were simulated to have no impact on students; in the second, effective teachers were assigned to weaker students; in the third, effective teachers were mixed with weaker and stronger students. The results indicated that the estimated teacher effect was highly related to the student achievement level, not the simulated teacher effect. For example, where the teacher effect was simulated to be zero, teachers of weaker students had large negative value-added estimates and teachers of stronger students had large positive estimates.

Similarly, Hill, Kapitula, and Umland (2010) found that value-added effectiveness estimates were correlated with not only the quality of a teacher's instruction but also with the socioeconomic status of the teacher's students. Although these estimates were validated by their relationships with other indicators of teaching effectiveness, they should be only weakly correlated with student characteristics if they are to be used for accountability purposes at the teacher or school level.

Reliability of Effectiveness Measures

With respect to the assumption that "effectiveness" or "value-added" scores assigned to teachers are reliable, research conducted thus far has not been particularly supportive (Baker et al., 2013). Value-added estimates vary depending on the form (and/or subtests) of the assessment used (Lockwood et al., 2007; Papay, 2011), and some studies found that a teacher classified as "effective" has up to a 50 percent chance of being classified as ineffective the following year (Haertel, 2011; Koedel & Betts, 2010; Papay, 2011). Corcoran (2010), for example, estimated that the margin of error around a value-added score can range up to 28 percentile points, while Baker et al. (2013) put the average margin of error at 35 percent. Braun (2013) noted that even when confidence intervals are provided for teachers' value-added estimates, those intervals are model-based and do not take into account biases outside the model (e.g., selection bias and other threats to internal validity). Given that reliability sets an upper bound for validity, this research alone should give us pause when considering the use of students' test performance for teacher accountability.

In addition to these reliability issues, there is the problem of variability in the classification of teachers into effectiveness categories. Kersting, Chen, and Stigler (2013) found that the number of students from which teacher effects were calculated greatly affected the consistency of teacher classifications, with 32 percent of teachers being classified into different effectiveness categories when the number of students in their class was reduced from 50 to 10 (based on using a four-year cohort to estimate for the large-n condition and then adjusting the standard errors based on the smaller sample size condition). Briggs and Domingue (2011) reanalyzed the data used to classify Los Angeles teachers into effectiveness categories and found that a revised model, which accounted for student characteristics, classified only 46 percent of the teachers into the same category using reading test scores and only 60 percent of the teachers using math test scores. Clearly, such variability makes it hard to justify using value-added estimates to reward or sanction teachers (or to publish them in newspapers!). Baker et al. (2013) described current effectiveness classifications as "arbitrary numerical cutoffs" and noted: "Placing an arbitrary, rigid, cut-off score into such noisy measures makes distinctions that simply cannot be justified especially when making high stakes employment decisions" (p. 6).

Instrumentation

Campbell and Stanley (1963) also discussed *instrumentation* as a threat to internal validity and described this problem as a change in the measurement instrument between pretest and posttest. This idea is relevant to the validity of teacher accountability systems because they typically involve measuring student gains across years, which involves two different tests. Prior year test performance is used to account for differences not related to the current teacher, but, as Martineau (2006) noted, what is taught and tested across grade levels often involves different knowledge and skills within a given subject area. For example, the overlap between the construct of math in the fourth grade and the construct of math in the fifth grade is incomplete, and in many subjects, construct overlap decreases as grade level increases. This problem of "construct shift" makes interpretation of teacher or school effects difficult, particularly when assessments in adjacent grades only partly overlap with respect to the construct measured. Validity evidence based on test content can help assess construct overlap and can also evaluate the alignment of testing and instruction. Such alignment studies should provide evidence regarding the degree to which construct shift may affect interpretations of teaching effectiveness.

Concerns about construct shift necessitate the evaluation of "vertical equating" whenever accountability models assume test scores are on a common scale across grades. Vertical equating is a process that involves placing scores from tests in different grades, and in the same subject area, on the same scale. When test scores are vertically scaled across grades, and there is adequate overlap in the construct measured across grades, students' progress across grades can be measured on the vertical scale. However, vertical scaling poses many measurement challenges, some of which can be accounted for through test design and careful test construction. However, Briggs and Weeks (2009) showed that different methods of vertical equating will produce different patterns of student gains, which will lead to different inferences about student gains and teacher effectiveness.

Although only some teacher accountability models assume test scores are reported on a vertical scale, all models used to estimate student progress rely on gains or deviations between expectations and observed performance, which require testing students at two or more points in time. The impact of construct shift and test–curriculum alignment is relevant in evaluating the validity of these models (see Culpepper, 2014 for further consideration of issues in using gain scores for teacher evaluation). A related issue is the degree to which test scores from any student assessment adequately possess interval scale properties, which is assumed in regression-based accountability systems that involve student gains (Briggs, 2013; Martineau, 2006).

Summary of Threats to Validity of Accountability Measures

In this section, we listed several factors that may seriously threaten the inferences that are derived from aggregate measures of students' test performance that are used to evaluate teachers, schools, and other levels of the educational system. These threats included selection bias, reliability, and instrumentation. Other factors such as the alignment of assessments and curriculum may also undermine causal inferences about teacher and school effectiveness based on students' test scores. Braun (2013) described policymakers' use of value-added estimates in the face of these problems as "magical thinking that the identified problems with value-added analysis will somehow cancel each other out or that they will be of little concern once the system is implemented" (p. 118). He went on to state that "magical thinking consists of believing that assertions accompanied by certain statistical incantations can overcome the deleterious effects of multiple serious threats to validity" (p. 126). As psychometricians who strive for fair and appropriate test use, we must steer policymakers away from such "magical thinking" and call for validity evidence to support the use of test scores for accountability purposes.

Additional Validity Issues

In addition to threats to the validity of inferences we make about teachers and schools, there are also other problems to be considered in using students' test scores as part of an accountability system. These issues include evaluating teachers who teach in subject areas that are not tested and providing due process for teachers.

Teachers of Untested Subject Areas and Grades

A problem in current teacher accountability systems is the evaluation of teachers who teach subjects that are not currently tested (Goldhaber, 2010; Marion & Buckley, 2011) or teachers who teach subjects at non-tested grade levels (e.g., kindergarten through second grade). Teachers of social studies, art, physical education, economics, humanities, and other subject areas may do a fine job adhering to statewide curriculum frameworks and helping students learn, but their effectiveness will not be documented in accountability models that use statewide test scores as the criterion of student progress. Goe (2010) estimated that up to three-quarters of teachers work in untested grades and subjects and do not have test data for their students. Lane and DePascale (this volume) and Marion and Buckley (this volume) describe how student learning objectives can be used to develop measures of teaching effectiveness in these subject areas.

In considering legal issues in teacher evaluation, Phillips (2009) pointed out: "There may be fairness issues if teachers who teach non-tested subjects are treated differently than those teaching tested subjects or if students' test scores for a content area are applied to a teacher with minimal or no responsibility for that content area" (p. 5). This is also an issue when school-based rewards are linked to measures of teaching effectiveness. These practices can exacerbate school politics about which teachers are assigned to tested (or untested) subjects and levels; teachers may also intentionally seek out students who may help increase their effectiveness score (especially in models that do not control for past teacher effects).

Teachers of some students with disabilities may also be less likely to have associated student test score data. Although all students with disabilities are to be included in assessments, some take alternate assessments that are not on the same scale as the general assessments, and others take assessments that are modified to such a great extent that they cannot be aggregated with scores from the general assessment. Although there is an ongoing debate about the usefulness of derivative scores for evaluating teachers in special education, there is a negative correlation between the proportion of students with disabilities a teacher teaches and the availability of student assessment data for accountability purposes, as well as potential complicating factors and differential impact on the value-added scores computed for special education teachers (Steinbrecher, Selig, Cosbey, & Thorstensen, 2014).

Due Process

Teachers who consistently receive low effectiveness scores in a teacher accountability system may face sanctions up to and including losing their job. Actions such as firing teachers require that states and districts follow "due process," which refers to rules for fair treatment in employment and other settings. In particular, the Due Process Clause of the 14th amendment of the U.S. Constitution forbids a governmental entity from depriving a person of a property or liberty interest without due process of the law. Given that public school teachers are government employees, due process should be incorporated into teacher accountability systems.

Recent events in teacher accountability practices suggest that due process protections are not in place. For example, in separate incidents in New York City (Gonen, 2012), the District of Columbia (Lewin, 2010), and Los Angeles (Felch, Song, & Smith, 2010), teachers were terminated or reassigned based on their value-added scores, and in some cases those scores were released to the public. In the case of Washington D.C., the IMPACT program results, based on a single year of student test score data, were used to support the dismissal of 241 teachers—representing 5 percent of the district teachers (Lewin, 2010). Whether these dismissals represent negative consequences or effective identification of substandard teachers is the ultimate validity issue.

In addition to due process concerns, other legal challenges to teacher accountability systems might be made based on whether teachers had the opportunity to learn how to teach to the new curriculum frameworks (e.g., Common Core State Standards) before they were evaluated based on students' test performance and whether the results from accountability systems have disparate impact. For these and other reasons, Pullin (2013) concluded that "there are strong reasons to suggest that high-stakes implementation of VAM is, at best, premature and, as a result, the potential for successful legal challenge to its use is high" (p. 17). If such cases are taken to court, history suggests the courts will use the AERA et al. *Standards* and look particularly closely at issues of content validity, reliability, and standard setting (Sireci & Parker, 2006).

Validating Educational Tests for Accountability Purposes: A Look to the Future

In this chapter, we discussed the concept of validity as it applies to educational assessments and educational research, and we described the process of validation, with a focus on validating tests for use in teacher accountability. A key theme was that validation focuses on the use of test scores for a particular purpose and requires multiple sources of evidence to develop a sound argument to justify a particular use. As we described validity issues specific to the evaluation of teachers based on their students' test scores, we reviewed literature that pointed out several problems, including:

- a lack of attention to selection bias, which threatens causal attributions to teachers;
- inconsistency of teacher classifications due to different assessments, statistical models, sample sizes of students, and time periods;

- a shift in the knowledge and skills measured across time from which student gains are estimated;
- the omission of teachers who teach in non-tested subject areas and grades; and
- an absence of provisions for due process.

For accountability systems to be valid, these problems will need to be addressed.

At the beginning of this chapter, we claimed that accountability testing is a distinguishing characteristic of 21st-century educational assessment. We believe that 21st-century problems deserve 21st-century solutions. Therefore, we propose that test development and accountability systems take advantage of advances in psychometrics and technology to help improve accountability efforts. Specifically, the use of computerized adaptive testing, matrix sampling of items and students, and interim assessments will likely lead to more valid accountability systems that focus on student achievement.

Accountability System Design

The use of educational tests for accountability should involve tests explicitly designed to provide information at a system level. Examples of tests that provide information at the system level include the National Assessment of Educational Progress, the Trends in International Mathematics and Science Study, and the Program for International Student Assessment. These programs report results at the group level only, such as at the state or country level, or subgroups within a state or country (girls, boys, etc.). Given this purpose, they use a matrix item sampling approach where, instead of taking all items, students are sampled to take only subsets of items that are eventually combined at the analysis stage to make inferences about group performance relative to the entire domain tested. This strategy could be applied to accountability efforts at the teacher and school levels within states, but solving the problem of motivating students to do well on these tests is a concern.

Unfortunately, current tests used for accountability in the United States are serving several purposes, with teacher and school accountability being secondary. Most of these tests are developed with the primary goal of determining the level of proficiency of the student in the subject area tested in accordance with the requirements of No Child Left Behind.

Therefore, to improve the validity of accountability testing, either tests must be designed specifically for accountability (e.g., matrix sampling to provide performance estimates at an aggregate level such as for a teacher or school), or the design must address the multiple purposes of student-level and accountability-level information. Furthermore, the design issues must be made at the *system* level rather than at the level of each individual test.

In addition to the use of matrix sampling, accountability systems should take advantage of computerized adaptive technology to reduce testing time and make tests more informative for each student. Furthermore, student gains should be measured *within* the school year rather than across years. As discussed earlier, comparing students' performance in one spring to their performance in a subsequent spring involves too many confounding factors (e.g., selection bias, instrumentation) to extract a teacher effect. Evaluating student gain *within* the school year when the teachers are actually teaching the students may make more sense. Rather than projecting a score for a student (as is done with SGPs or VAMs), each student becomes her or his own control, and gains throughout the school year become the focus of the analysis. This practice would also ameliorate the problems of construct shift, vertical equating, and attribution of test results to teachers, because all items would be relevant to knowledge and skills taught during the year by the specific teacher. This strategy will work best in those subject areas where pretesting early in the year makes sense (e.g., a pretest of math concepts taught the prior year, where those skills are relevant to the current year), but not for subject areas that are new to the student (e.g., first course in physics).

In addition to adaptive testing and within-year assessments, we recommend one other feature be incorporated into accountability systems designed for teacher accountability—criterion-referenced performance standards for teachers. Current teacher accountability systems are normative in that they relate teachers' effectiveness ratings to the average teacher. Instead, absolute criteria of how much gain students, or groups of students, should attain within a school year should be developed. All students should improve over the course of a year. Standard setting procedures could be used to determine how much improvement is associated with different levels of teaching effectiveness. Such performance standards would improve upon the current situation where teachers are evaluated relative to one another, rather than to a criterion of effective teaching based on demonstrated student progress in their subject area. Of course, like current systems, the reliability of teachers' classification decisions would need to be established.

Accountability System Validation

The purpose of this chapter was to describe validity issues for 21st-century educational tests, particularly tests that will be used for accountability purposes. Thus, the discussion of system design is a bit outside the scope of the chapter. Nevertheless, a system designed to serve multiple purposes, such as that described in the previous section, is more likely to generate positive evidence to support the actions and inferences that are made on the basis of test scores and will address several of the current problems we noted in the literature.

In addition to accountability assessment system design that uses adaptive technology and interim assessments, another design issue that has the potential to promote validity is *evidence-centered* (Mislevy, 2009; Mislevy & Riconscente, 2006) or *principled assessment* (Luecht, 2011) design. These approaches require the specification of "task models" that will generate the types of information specified in a testing purpose. This concept is beyond the scope of the present chapter and so readers are referred to the sources above and Haertel et al. (this volume). It is important to note, however, that work in evidence-centered design has focused on providing evidence at the student level, and so its impact on the validity of inferences at the group level, such as for teacher accountability, is unknown at the present time.

So, how should we go about the process of validating tests that are used for accountability purposes? Do the AERA et al. (2014) *Standards'* five sources of validity evidence provide an adequate framework for validating the use of test scores for accountability purposes? In our opinion, the description of validity in the *Standards* and the advice it provides on test validation hold for validating the uses of test scores for accountability purposes. Such validation efforts need to confirm the tests are measuring what they claim to measure, the scores and classifications assigned to teachers are reliable, students' performance on these tests is reflective of the effectiveness of teachers, and the accountability system is doing more good than harm. Sufficiently providing this information will involve all five sources of validity evidence. However, validity evidence based on testing consequences is particularly relevant to evaluating a testing *system* and forms the bridge between traditional, examinee-level test score validation and validating a testing system's *theory of action* (Sireci, in press).

Validating a Theory of Action

According to Bennett (2010), the concept of a theory of action comes from the field of program evaluation and describes the intended goals of a program. He noted that accountability testing is analogous to an educational program and so the concept of theory of action is relevant. As he put it, in educational accountability testing,... change *is* intended,... it seems appropriate to require a theory of action for such assessment programs, in addition to the more usual scientific evidence in support of instrument technical adequacy.

(p. 71)

Bennett's conclusion is similar to ours (and to Cronbach's 1971 conceptualization of validity as evaluation) in that accountability testing requires more than what we typically do to validate test score interpretations for individual students. He stated that a theory of action for an assessment *system* "might include the following elements:

- the intended effects of the assessment system
- the components of the assessment system and a logical and coherent rationale for each component...
- the interpretive claims that will be made from assessment results
- the action mechanisms designed to cause the intended effects
- the potential unintended negative effects and what will be done to mitigate them." (p. 71)

If assessment systems designed for accountability develop theories of actions with these elements, they will facilitate validation. Bennett's third bullet, the interpretive claims made from test results, has been the focus of this chapter. However, evaluating all elements in the broader sense of program evaluation will provide more complete information for evaluating the entire accountability system. Such an evaluation is consistent with the notion of gathering validity evidence based on testing consequences, which, as illustrated in Table 6.2, is important in any endeavor involving educational tests.

Concluding Remarks

In this chapter, we pointed out several problems in using students' test performance for accountability purposes. As we see it, the greatest need in validation for accountability testing is further study of the statistical properties of derivative measures and evaluating their utility for providing useful information about teachers or other educational units. As the studies we reviewed indicate, at this juncture, the test-based indicators used for teacher accountability have not demonstrated adequate reliability or validity for judging teacher effectiveness and so need the same cautions attributed to other measures of teaching effectiveness such as those based on classroom observation. This state of affairs for accountability measurement is disheartening, because we want policymakers to value the opinions and input of the psychometric community. If we promote accountability metrics that are not fully studied or supported by empirical data, our opinions will not be valued, and we will lose credibility.

Furthermore, the cost to society of using invalid measures of accountability could be dire. As Braun (2009) lamented, "we will do students and their families no favor if we impose an accountability system that unfairly penalizes schools that are contributing to student development broadly conceived, that hastens the departure of good teachers from the field and discourages prospective teachers from entering the field altogether" (p. 55). Therefore, we must do more to evaluate accountability indicators *before* they are used. We may be late on this issue, given that the use of metrics such as value-added estimates and student growth percentiles has occurred without sufficient research to support them. But it is better to be late than give up. As mentioned earlier, the AERA et al. (2014) *Standards* stipulated: "An index that is constructed by manipulating and combining test scores should be subjected to the same validity, reliability and fairness investigation that are expected for the test scores that underlie the index" (p. 210). In our view, if we rigorously gather and analyze data related to validity of the emerging accountability measures, we will learn a great deal about them, including what seems to work and which aspects need improvement or replacement.

One way in which educational accountability measures can be improved is in how the results are reported to various stakeholders. With respect to reporting the results of assessments, the AERA et al. (2014) *Standards* advised that "score reports for educational tests should be designed to provide information that is understandable and useful to stakeholders without leading to unwarranted score interpretations" (p. 194). Therefore, future research on the validity of accountability metrics should include the degree to which they are properly interpreted, and are resistant to misinterpretations, by key stakeholders.

Our review of the validity issues and the research associated with validating teacher accountability tests pointed out several problems with the current systems. However, by gathering the right types of validity evidence, we can help improve these systems. Twenty-first-century validation should provide more than summative data on the use of a test for assessing student knowledge and skills. Modern validation efforts should also provide data that can help to support and inform the laudable goals of accountability systems while incorporating new technological possibilities that allow for more complex sampling and scoring designs for state assessments. Twenty-first-century validation should also provide *formative* validation data to testing agencies so that testing systems can be improved as they evolve.

In this chapter, we discussed validity issues related to accountability testing and provided advice for how to go about (a) the process of evaluating the validity of these systems and (b) designing them to address potential validity threats. We hope our review and discussion of these issues helps improve future test design and validation efforts for tests used for accountability purposes.

References

American Educational Research Association (AERA), American Psychological Association (APA), & National Council on Measurement in Education (NCME). (1985). *Standards for educational and psychological testing.* Washington, DC: APA.

AERA, APA, & NCME. (1999). *Standards for educational and psychological testing.* Washington, DC: AERA.

AERA, APA, & NCME. (2014). *Standards for educational and psychological testing.* Washington, DC: AERA.

American Psychological Association (APA). (1952). Committee on Test Standards. Technical recommendations for psychological tests and diagnostic techniques: A preliminary proposal. *American Psychologist, 7*, 461–465.

APA. (1954). Technical recommendations for psychological tests and diagnostic techniques. *Psychological Bulletin, 51*, 201–238.

American Psychological Association (APA), American Educational Research Association (AERA), & National Council on Measurement in Education (NCME). (1966). *Standards for educational and psychological tests and manuals.* Washington, DC: APA.

APA, AERA, & NCME. (1974). *Standards for educational and psychological tests.* Washington, DC: APA.

Baker, B. D., Oluwole, J., & Green, P. C. III. (2013). The legal consequences of mandating high stakes decisions based on low quality information: Teacher evaluation in the race-to-the-top era. *Education Policy Analysis Archives, 21*(5). Retrieved March 15, 2013 from http://epaa.asu.edu/ojs/article/view/1298

Ballou, D., Sanders, W., & Wright, P. (2004). Controlling for student background in value-added assessment for teachers. *Journal of Educational and Behavioral Statistics, 29*(1), 37–65.

Bennett, R. E. (2010). Cognitively based assessment of, for, and as learning (CBAL): A preliminary theory of action for summative and formative assessment. *Measurement, 8*(2–3), 70–91.

Bhola, D. S., Impara, J. C., & Buckendahl, C. W. (2003). Aligning tests with states' content standards: Methods and issues. *Educational Measurement: Issues and Practice, 22*(3), 21–29.

Braun, H. (2009). Discussion: With choices come consequences. *Educational Measurement: Issues and Practice, 28*(4), 52–55.

Braun, H. (2013). Value-added modeling and the power of magical thinking. *Ensaio Avaliação e Políticas Públicas em Educação, 21*, 115–130.

Briggs, D. (2013). Measuring growth with vertical scales. *Journal of Educational Measurement, 50*(2), 204–226.

Briggs, D., & Domingue, B. (2011). *Due Diligence and the evaluation of teachers: A review of the value-added analysis underlying the effectiveness rankings of Los Angeles Unified School District teachers by the Los Angeles Times.* Boulder, CO: National Education Policy Center. Retrieved March 16, 2013 from http://nepc.colorado.edu/publication/due-diligence

Briggs, D., & Weeks, J. P. (2009). The impact of vertical scaling decisions on growth interpretations. *Educational Measurement: Issues and Practice, 28*(4), 3–13.

Campbell, D. T., & Fiske, D. W. (1959). Convergent and discriminant validation by the multitrait-multimethod matrix. *Psychological Bulletin, 56*, 81–105.

Campbell, D. T., & Stanley, J. C. (1963). *Experimental and quasi-experimental designs for research.* Chicago, IL: Rand McNally.

Corcoran, S. P. (2010). *Can teachers be evaluated by their students' test scores? And should they be? The use of value-added measures of teacher effectiveness in policy and practice* (Education Policy for Action Series). New York, NY: Annenberg Institute for School Reform. Retrieved June 6, 2011 from http://www.annenberginstitute.org/pdf/valueaddedreport.pdf

Crocker, L. M., Miller, D., & Franks, E. A. (1989). Quantitative methods for assessing the fit between test and curriculum. *Applied Measurement in Education, 2*, 179–194.

Cronbach, L. J. (1971). Test validation. In R. L. Thorndike (Ed.), *Educational measurement* (2nd ed., pp. 443–507). Washington, DC: American Council on Education.

Cronbach, L. J. (1988). Five perspectives on the validity argument. In H. Wainer & H. I. Braun (Eds.), *Test validity* (pp. 3–17). Hillsdale, NJ: Lawrence Erlbaum.

Culpepper, S. A. (2014). The reliability of linear gain scores as measures of student growth at the classroom level in the presence of measurement bias and student tracking. *Applied Psychological Measurement, 38*(7), 503–517. doi:10.1177/0146621614534763

Embretson (Whitley), S. (1983). Construct validity: Construct representation versus nomothetic span. *Psychological Bulletin, 93*, 179–197.

Felch, J., Song, J., & Smith, D. (2010, August 14). Who's teaching L.A.'s kids? *Los Angeles Times.* Retrieved June 19, 2013 from http://www.latimes.com/news/local/la-me-teachers-value-20100815,0,258862,full.story

Garrett, H. E. (1937). A rejoinder. *The American Journal of Psychology, 49*, 683–685.

Goe, L. (2010). *Teacher evaluation in transition: Using evaluation to improve teacher effectiveness.* Washington, DC: The National Comprehensive Center for Teacher Quality.

Goldhaber, D. (2010). *When the stakes are high, can we rely on value-added? Exploring the use of value-added models to inform teacher workforce decisions.* Retrieved May 23, 2012 from https://www.americanprogress.org/issues/education/report/2010/12/01/8720/when-the-stakes-are-high-can-we-rely-on-value-added

Gonen, Y. (2012). NYC makes internal ratings of 18,000 public school teachers available. *The New York Post.* Retrieved June 24, 2012 from http://www.nypost.com/p/news/local/nyc_makes_internal_ratings_of_public_4nzYXTN1L4LQXU17G2YktO#ixzz1okkfxFDT

Grossman, P., Cohen, J., Ronfeldt, M., & Brown, L. (2014). The test matters: The relationship between classroom observation scores and teacher value added on multiple types of assessment. *Educational Researcher, 43*, 293–303.

Haertel, E. (2011, April). *Using student test scores to distinguish good teachers from bad.* Paper presented at the annual conference of the American Educational Research Association, New Orleans, LA.

Henderson, A. T., & Mapp, K. L. (2002). *A new wave of evidence: The impact of school, family, and community connections on student achievement.* Institute of Education Sciences (ED). Retrieved September 8, 2014 from http://files.eric.ed.gov/fulltext/ED474521.pdf

Hill, H. (2009). Evaluating value-added models: A validity argument approach. *Journal of Policy Analysis and Management, 28*(4), 700–709.

Hill, H., Kapitula, L., & Umland, K. (2010). A validity argument approach to evaluating teacher value-added scores. *American Educational Research Journal, 48*(3), 794–831.

Ho, A. D., & Kane, T. J. (2013). *The reliability of classroom observations by school personnel* (MET Project Research Paper). Seattle, WA: Bill & Melinda Gates Foundation. Retrieved November 23, 2014 from http://www.metproject.org/downloads/MET_Reliability%20of%20Classroom%20 Observations_Research%20Paper.pdf.

Jenkins, J. G. (1946). Validity for what? *Journal of Consulting Psychology, 10,* 93–98.

Kane, M. (1992). An argument-based approach to validity. *Psychological Bulletin, 112,* 527–535.

Kane, M. (2006). Validation. In R. L. Brennan (Ed.), *Educational measurement* (4th ed., pp. 17–64). Washington, DC: American Council on Education/Praeger.

Kane, M. (2013). Validating the interpretations and uses of test scores. *Journal of Educational Measurement, 50*(1), 1–73.

Kelley, T. L. (1927). *Interpretation of educational measurement.* Yonkers-on-Hudson, NY: World Book Co.

Kersting, N. B., Chen, M., & Stigler, J. W. (2013). Value-added teacher estimates as part of teacher evaluations: Exploring the effects of data and model specifications on the stability of teacher value-added scores. *Education Policy Analysis Archives, 21*(7). Retrieved March 15, 2013 from http://epaa.asu.edu/ojs/article/view/1167

Koedel, C., & Betts, J. R. (2010). Value-added to what? How a ceiling in the testing instrument influences value-added estimation. *Education Finance and Policy, 5*(1), 54–81.

Kupermintz, H. (2003). Teacher effects and teacher effectiveness: A validity investigation of the Tennessee value added assessment system. *Educational Evaluation and Policy Analysis, 25,* 287–298.

Lewin, T. (2010). School chief dismisses 241 teachers in Washington. *New York Times.* Retrieved June 6 from http://www.nytimes.com/2010/07/24/education/24teachers.html

Lockwood, J. R., McCaffrey, D. F., Hamilton, L. S., Stecher, B., Le, V. N., & Martinez, J. F. (2007). The sensitivity of value-added teacher effect estimates to different mathematics achievement measures. *Journal of Educational Measurement, 44*(1), 47–67.

Luecht, R. M. (2011, March). *Assessment design and development, version 2.0: From art to engineering.* Invited, closing keynote address at the annual meeting of the Association of Test Publishers, Phoenix, AZ.

Marion, S., & Buckley, K. E. (2011). Approaches and considerations for incorporating student performance results from "non-tested" grades and subjects into educator effectiveness determinations. *Center for Assessment.* Retrieved December 20, 2011 from http://www.nciea.org/publications/ Considerations%20for%20non-tested%20grades_SMKB2011.pdf

Martineau, J. A. (2006). Distorting value added: The use of longitudinal, vertically scaled student achievement data for growth-based, value-added accountability. *Journal of Educational and Behavioral Statistics, 31,* 35–62.

Martone, A., & Sireci, S. G. (2009). Evaluating alignment between curriculum, assessments, and instruction. *Review of Educational Research, 4,* 1332–1361.

Messick, S. (1989). Validity. In R. Linn (Ed.), *Educational measurement* (3rd ed.). Washington, DC: American Council on Education.

Mislevy, R. J. (2009, February). Validity from the perspective of model-based reasoning (CRESST Report 752). Los Angeles, CA: National Center for Research on Evaluation, Standards, and Student Testing.

Mislevy, R. J., & Riconscente, M. M. (2006). Evidence-centered assessment design. In S. M. Downing & T. M. Haladyna (Eds.), *Handbook of test development* (pp. 61–90). Mahwah, NJ: Lawrence Erlbaum.

Papay, J. P. (2011). Different tests, different answers: The stability of teacher value-added estimates across outcome measures. *American Educational Research Journal, 48,* 163–193.

Phillips, S. E. (2009). Legal corner: Using student test scores to evaluate teachers. *NCME Newsletter, 17*(4), 3–6.

Pullin, D. (2013). Legal issues in the use of student test scores and value-added models (VAM) to determine educational quality. *Education Policy Analysis Archives, 21*(6). Retrieved March 15, 2013 from http://epaa.asu.edu/ojs/article/view/1160

Rulon, P. J. (1946). On the validity of educational tests. *Harvard Educational Review, 16*, 290–296.

Sireci, S. G. (1998). Gathering and analyzing content validity data. *Educational Assessment, 5*, 299–321.

Sireci, S. G. (2009). Packing and unpacking sources of validity evidence: History repeats itself again. In R. Lissitz (Ed.), *The concept of validity: Revisions, new directions and applications* (pp. 19–37). Charlotte, NC: Information Age Publishing Inc.

Sireci, S. G. (in press). A theory of action for validation. In R. Lissitz (Ed.), *The next generation of testing*. Charlotte, NC: Information Age Publishing Inc.

Sireci, S. G., & Parker, P. (2006). Validity on trial: Psychometric and legal conceptualizations of validity. *Educational Measurement: Issues and Practice, 25*(3), 27–34.

Smith, H. L., & Wright, W. W. (1928). *Tests and measurements*. New York, NY: Silver, Burdett & Co.

Steinbrecher, T. D., Selig, J. P., Cosbey, J., & Thorstensen, B. I. (2014). Evaluating special educator effectiveness: Addressing issues inherent to value-added modeling. *Exceptional Children, 80*(3), 323–336.

Thurstone, L. L. (1932). *The reliability and validity of tests*. Ann Arbor, MI: Edwards Brothers.

Wells, C. S., Sireci, S. G., & Bahry, L. (2014, April). *Estimating the amount of error in student growth percentiles*. Paper presented at the annual meeting of the National Council on Measurement in Education, Philadelphia, PA.

7 Commentary

Can Campbell's Law Be Mitigated?

Derek C. Briggs

If you are reading this book, it probably means you have a deep-seated interest in mitigating a rather resilient "law" first introduced by the social psychologist Donald Campbell in his report *Assessing the Impact of Planned Social Change.*

> The more any quantitative social indicator (or even some qualitative indicator) is used for social decision-making, the more subject it will be to corruption pressures and the more apt it will be to distort and corrupt the social processes it is intended to monitor.
>
> (1976, p. 49)

Campbell went on to provide a number of examples of distorted and corrupted social processes across a range of contexts: curtailing crime, increasing workplace productivity, and tracking success in a military operation. Writing in the mid-1970s, Campbell had anticipated the modern-day emphasis on quantitative indicators for educational accountability.

> In the Texarkana "performance contracting" experiment (Stake, 1971), supplementary teaching for undereducated children was provided by "contractors" who came to the schools with special teaching machines and individualized instruction. The corruption pressure was high because the contractors were to be paid on the basis of the achievement test score gains of individual pupils. It turned out that the contractors were teaching the answers to specific test items that were to be used on the final play-off testing ... [W]hen test scores become the goal of the teaching process, they both lose their value as indicators of educational status and distort the educational process in undesirable ways. (Similar biases of course surround the use of objective tests in courses or as entrance examinations.) In compensatory education in general there are rumors of other subversions of the measurement process, such as administering pretests in a way designed to make scores as low as possible so that larger gains will be shown on the post test, or limiting treatment to those scoring lowest on the pretest so that regression to the mean will provide apparent gains ... Achievement tests are, in fact, highly corruptible indicators.

One reaction to Campbell's Law is to accept its premise and conclude that testing for accountability is an enterprise that is doomed to failure from the outset. For those with this reaction, the chapters in this book are unlikely to be of much interest! However, those taking a more optimistic position can take heart in the fact that Campbell's Law does not state that the distortion and/or corruption of a social process is inevitable whenever a quantitative indicator is being used; only that the *potential* for distortion and corruption is inevitable. Indeed, in his writing, Campbell suggests that the proper response to his law was to anticipate such threats to validity in designing "social systems." In this regard, he favored the use of both multiple indicators and external auditing checks. It is in this spirit that the chapters from this section of the book can be best appreciated.

For example, it is rather easy to anticipate that if new tests are developed and administered by local education agencies to complement existing tests administered to all students in a state, and if there are consequences attached to the aggregate performance of students on these tests, then teachers will surely respond to this by making changes to their instruction. Koretz and Hamilton (2006) describe three types of responses that can lead to distorted inferences about year-to-year student gains and describe the resulting phenomenon as "test score inflation."

One possible response is outright cheating, which happens when teachers or administrators either provide students with answers to test questions or change their answers after the fact. The second is narrowing the curriculum, which happens when teachers reallocate time in the curriculum away from topics that (they believe) will not be covered on a test to topics that will be covered. The third is coaching, when teachers focus preparation on features of test item formats rather than the relevant knowledge, skills, and abilities the items are meant to elicit.

Collectively, the chapters in this section offer a variety of design-based strategies that can help to anticipate (and hopefully counteract) behavioral responses that would distort judgments about teacher or school effectiveness. To illustrate how these chapters are helpful in this regard, I begin by focusing on the threats to validity caused by cheating, narrowing the curriculum, and coaching as teacher responses to testing for high-stakes purposes. Inspired by one or more of the chapters, for each threat I suggest design-based strategies that could be taken to mitigate that threat and point to some challenges in implementing these strategies given constraints in time, personnel, and money. I then turn my attention to the controversial issue of using evidence of student growth in test scores as indicators in the evaluation of teachers. I argue that it is a mistake to conflate measurement—the goal when designing tests for students—with evaluation—the goal when choosing a set of indicators to support categorical decisions about teachers.

Cheating

The prevalence of outright cheating by teachers in response to the use of test scores for accountability purposes and the extent to which this has increased over time is difficult to ascertain. Although a few wide-scale cheating scandals have been detected and revealed to the public (cf. Jacob & Levitt, 2002; Jarvie, 2014), it seems plausible that many cases are detected within schools or school districts but kept confidential. One strategy for dealing with this threat is to establish rigorous test security protocols such that test forms are never handled or viewed by teachers before, during, and after student testing. However, not only is this rather draconian strategy difficult to implement, but the increasing use of computer-based testing will surely pose new and unanticipated challenges. For example, it may become easier to steal secure test items and then make them available commercially through test preparation materials marketed directly to schools and districts. There is also a notable tension here to the extent that test results are intended to serve both summative and formative purposes. The level of security that would be needed to protect test validity for summative purposes would also likely undermine formative uses of the test.

Nationally administered undergraduate and graduate entrance exams such as the SAT, ACT, GRE, and MCAT are prototypical examples of standardized tests with strong security protocols built into their administration. However, this is very costly and could place a serious strain on resources if applied across grades 3–12 in multiple courses. Just as importantly, maintaining a strict level of security may also be counterproductive if it leads to teachers to view the test as disconnected from their own local instructional and assessment practices. For example, Marion and Buckley (this volume) argue that beyond their alignment with the target constructs, performance-based assessments (PBAs) have great potential to provide instructional information and a learning opportunity for students, as well as to signal the types of instructional tasks that would be desirable in the classroom. For PBAs to be instructionally useful, the more that teachers can be involved in the scoring (and perhaps the development) of PBAs, the better.

Lane and DePascale (this volume) provide three examples of auditing strategies that antici-pate concerns about cheating without removing teachers from the testing process. In Tennessee, student achievement in fine arts is assessed using portfolios of student work samples assem-bled by teachers according to state guidelines. These teachers subsequently score their own students' work samples and submit a written rationale for their scoring. These artifacts are ulti-mately submitted for blind peer review to a committee of content experts, and this serves as the key auditing function. In South Carolina, music and visual arts teachers also play a direct role in the administration and scoring of assessment tasks, but some proportion of these tasks are double-scored. In Minnesota, assessments designed by individual teachers or schools are aligned with state-level standards and criteria. Student projects are evaluated within each school, but then samples are submitted to a state-level committee to ensure that there is a match between the state's standards and the way they have been implemented at the local level. The Minnesota approach can be traced to a model originally developed in Queensland, Australia, also discussed by Marion and Buckley (this volume).

Although some cheating is always to be expected, there are some good reasons to believe that it is likely to be rare, at least in any well-designed accountability system with annual testing. If a single teacher has cheated by making students appear higher achieving than they actually are, this would become apparent to their teachers in subsequent years, or to an attentive school prin-cipal, because these students' growth scores would drop in the following year, potentially quite dramatically. Maintaining the false impression of high growth would require some impressive coordination between multiple teachers across grades.

But perhaps more importantly, if schools are going to be successful, it requires a starting point of trust that everyone involved has the best interests of children at heart. If one designs an accountability system under the premise that teachers are guilty until proven innocent, then the well has already been poisoned from the start. There is likely greater damage to be done in treating all teachers as potential cheaters than there is involving them directly in the process of student assessment (cf., Hargreaves & Braun, 2013).

Narrowing the Curriculum

There is an ever-present concern that when teachers teach to the test, this will lead to a nar-rowing of the curriculum. Although empirical research on this topic over the past 15 years has been surprisingly limited, there is at the very least considerable anecdotal evidence that teachers and schools tailor their curricula to the content of high-stakes assessments (Nichols & Berliner, 2007), and this has been confirmed empirically in at least one large-scale mixed-methods study (Firestone, Schorr, & Monfils, 2004). The degree to which teaching to the test leads to a narrowing of the curriculum depends greatly on the extent to which there is good alignment between some agreed-upon set of learning objectives (i.e., standards), a curriculum that is estab-lished to achieve these objectives, and the test(s) in question.

It is here that the process of developing assessments according to the tenets of Evidence-Centered Design (ECD; Haertel et al., this volume) and Principled Design for Efficacy (Ferrara & Way, this volume) can provide some useful guidance. Since the approaches share many elements in common, I will focus on ECD. Consider, for example, the domain analysis and modeling layer of ECD as described by Haertel et al. (this volume). If the knowledge, skills, and abilities of interest in a content domain are made explicit in item design templates, then (in principle, at least) it should be evident if there is a disconnect between the intended use and the evidence that the assessments can plausibly generate. Indeed, in assembling evidence to support the validity of test score interpretations (see Sireci & Soto, this volume), it has become common for states to expect test vendors to produce items that are aligned to represent an underlying set of content standards, and alignment studies are typically conducted to establish the degree to which this has taken place.

An inherent challenge is that it is difficult to imagine a single assessment of a rich content domain that could be fully representative of the knowledge, skills, and abilities that comprise the domain. When "standards" documents are assembled, they often contain statements about learning objectives that are open to many different interpretations (e.g., creativity, collaboration). Or, they may focus on student attributes (e.g., critical reasoning, modeling, argumentation) that would require a very time-consuming sequence of open-ended tasks or projects to be properly assessed. It follows that if "higher order thinking skills" are part of the target domain, then one can predict that a standardized test consisting solely of multiple-choice items will be hard-pressed to elicit evidence that can accurately distinguish differences in students' depth of knowledge. In such a scenario, teaching to the test would indeed be tantamount to narrowing the curriculum, leading to the classic complaint of tests that are "a mile wide and an inch deep."

To a large extent, the Common Core of State Standards in mathematics and English language arts and the Next Generation of Science Standards can be viewed as a reaction to this state of affairs. Both sets of standards attempt to limit the breadth of content being described so that more attention can be placed on how students apply the content in an increasingly sophisticated manner. To this end, these documents provide starting points for nascent theories of learning progressions across grades, where a learning progression focuses on a "big picture" core concept (or concepts) and how student understanding becomes more sophisticated and interrelated with other core concepts over time. This provides support for the position taken by Marion and Buckley (this volume) that, in many instances, PBAs are not just an alternate way to measure a construct but may often be the best or only way to measure a construct.

The conundrum, as discussed in some detail by Lane and DePascale (this volume), is that the scores from PBAs seldom provide student-level scores that are sufficiently generalizable. The basic problem is that attributes such as reasoning and argumentation do not exist in a vacuum—rather, they are only evident in specific contexts. For example, a student in a U.S. History course may be able to develop a powerful argument about the causes of the Civil War, yet fall flat when asked to make an argument about the causes of the Great Depression. And when asked to score essays on these different topics, some teachers have a much easier time making distinctions in the quality of student responses across contexts.

One possible solution to this problem in the context of accountability testing would be to focus on grade levels as the unit of analysis rather than students and classrooms, in which case it might be possible to randomly administer (across classrooms and schools) some combinations of common and unique performance-based tasks that target the same focal skills, but may situate the unique tasks within a variety of different content. A drawback to this solution is that it would not produce scores that could be reported back to individual students (because no single student would take enough tasks to generate a reliable score), but it would provide generalizable information about students overall. This could be supplemented by low-stakes formative assessments that are embedded in weekly classroom activities. A selling point of this approach would be to decrease the amount of time devoted to testing for high-stakes purposes.

The recent proliferation of student learning objectives (SLOs) poses an interesting challenge. As noted by Marion and Buckley (this volume) and Lane and DePascale (this volume), SLOs for subjects that have not been traditionally assessed at the state level are most amenable to PBAs in the form of portfolios, projects, and exhibitions. From a perspective of "covering" the content of a course and avoiding a narrowing of the curriculum, it would be sensible to intentionally vary the breadth of content elicited by performance-based tasks. But from the perspective of providing teachers with diagnostic information that could be used to monitor students, provide feedback, and change instructional practice, it may well be more sensible to focus on just a few "big picture" aspects of the content domain that can be thoughtfully deconstructed and carefully connected to a series of mutually reinforcing instructional activities. That is, if the primary emphasis of an SLO were formative, it might be considered an acceptable trade-off to enact more tailored PBAs, if it could be proven that they do in fact lead to more educationally productive interactions among teachers and their students.

Fundamental to almost any theory of action behind the use of test-based indicators for educational accountability is the belief that the test outcomes on which they are based can drive productive changes in instructional practice that, in turn, can have positive effects on student learning. But this is likely to happen only when teachers view student assessment as providing authentic information that can inform everyday classroom activities. This is a very good reason to champion the use of PBAs because, to the extent that they more closely resemble day-to-day classroom activities, they have the potential to bring teachers to a deeper understanding of what their students know and can do than is usually possible when examining the results from a test comprised of selected-response items. Here we would be wise to appreciate the warning from Lane and DePascale (this volume):

> The history of performance-based assessment designs for large-scale use is characterized by the reduction of big ideas to small realities. Plans to integrate performance-based assessments into state assessment and accountability systems often begin with grand visions of lengthy research projects culminating in written, oral, and multimedia presentations by students describing and defending their work. Almost immediately, these grand visions are viewed through the lens of the current assessment and accountability frameworks that embody inherent constraints. Over a short period of time, a combination of practical and psychometric concerns chips away at the planned assessments until they fit into the existing framework … Current examples of this reduction process can be seen in newly implemented teacher accountability systems and the initial design requirements for SLOs that will be used to measure a teacher's impact on student learning. Although housed in the classroom and designed to reflect growth (i.e., student learning) over an extended period of time, the requirements imposed by many state systems effectively reduce SLOs to a summative, end-of-year assessment that may be developed locally rather than by a state or commercial vendor.

Through this example we appreciate the distorting force of Campbell's Law. If SLOs are viewed solely as a means of formalizing a feedback loop between teachers, students, and parents around the core ideas and skills that will truly prepare students for the future, then psychometric criteria for comparability and generalizability, though still important, become a more secondary concern. In contrast, if the primary use of an SLO is to provide an indicator of teacher effectiveness, then issues of comparability and generalizability rise in importance and will more likely lead to assessments that are externally developed, administered, and scored.

One possible mitigating strategy, whenever possible, would be to initially develop and implement SLOs with no stakes attached, keeping the emphasis firmly on the formative utility of the approach and keeping the bureaucratic process (and paperwork) to a minimum. The challenge would be to establish a support mechanism so that teachers were provided with the time to work in teams to develop common goals and assessments and to collaboratively engage with student work. If teachers and principals can be first convinced of the utility of a system of embedded student assessments, they may be more amenable to the kind of standardization that Lane and DePascale describe as a precondition for comparability.

Coaching

The form of teaching to the test that Koretz and Hamilton (2006) describe as coaching occurs when teachers place undue emphasis on anticipated test content and item format features for the sole purpose of increasing test performance. The distinction between coaching and instruction can be rather subtle. One relatively benign example of an activity that resembles coaching more than it resembles instruction is when teachers assign their students practice versions of end-of-year assessment items as an in-class activity or homework assignment, without situating the work within the broader curriculum and targets for student learning. The problem is not in using a practice test as an instructional tool, but in making performance on the end-of-year test the de facto learning goal. After all, even the best test can only provide a sample of the knowledge, skills, and abilities that comprise the domain of interest. The ideal in education, and the signal that true learning has occurred, is evidence of transfer—when the concepts and ideas apparently mastered by students in the context of classroom activities and homework assignments are successfully employed by them in other contexts. With this in mind, one hopes that students who perform better on an end-of-year assessment are also most likely to exhibit evidence of transfer (National Research Council, 2000, 2001). The more that teachers allocate instructional time to coaching, and the more that this coaching is effective, the more tenuous the link between test performance and learning.

Historically, a classic example of coaching for a large-scale, standardized test comes from the SAT preparatory courses offered by *The Princeton Review*. The SAT math and verbal sections have long been marketed as indicators of a student's readiness for college, and in earlier incarnations, each section included a variety of distinctive item formats (Lawrence, Rigol, Van Essen, & Jackson, 2004). For example, the verbal section contained items that required students to complete analogies and identify antonyms; the math section included items that required students to compare two quantities. Because these item formats were persistent and recognizable, *The Princeton Review* incorporated methods to "crack the code" of the SAT into its preparatory materials. Rather than reviewing or teaching the reasoning skills that the items were intended to elicit, *The Princeton Review* and its instructors marketed their ability to "beat the test." Indeed, the founder of *The Princeton Review*, John Katzman, has made little effort to conceal his disdain for the SAT as a measure of anything valuable[1] and professed such confidence in his methods that clients could be offered a "guaranteed" point increase. With the increase in standardized testing in K–12 settings over the past two decades, there has also been an increase in companies and organizations with off-the-shelf preparation materials or programs that do not brazenly claim to "beat the test" per se, but that promise a positive effect on large-scale assessment scores on the basis of rather dubious methods (e.g., "data-driven instruction"). If such effects are real, and if access to coaching is unequally distributed, this can serve to artificially widen perceived gaps in achievement.

Although no published research to date has evaluated the efficacy of coaching programs, materials, or practices on state-administered achievement tests, a large number of studies have been conducted over the years to evaluate the efficacy of commercial coaching programs on the SAT. It continues to come as a surprise to the general public (and apparently to John Katzman) to learn that in these studies the magnitude of the SAT coaching effect has generally been quite small—about 15–20 points on the math section and about 10 points on the verbal section (Briggs, 2001, 2004, 2009; Powers & Rock, 1999). These effects amount to roughly 10–20 percent of a standard deviation. By extension then, even if teachers respond to high-stakes consequences with coaching practices, there is no guarantee that it will have a significant impact on test performance. This is an area where there is a great need for further research, especially as (or if) educational accountability systems begin to stabilize in the coming years.

An emphasis on learning objectives, or content standards, that emphasize higher order thinking skills (e.g., Common Core State Standards, the Next Generation of Science Standards); the application of principled assessment design strategies (e.g., ECD) in the development of aligned assessments; and the liberal use of PBAs as a means for eliciting the relevant evidence may in combination mitigate the potential for coaching to have an effect on student achievement. That said, there is at least one "backdoor" challenge that will need to be monitored with some vigilance by test developers. Namely, a central product of the domain modeling stage of ECD is one or more design patterns that provide item writers with the recipe for the development of a bank of assessment tasks. An important innovation of design patterns is to be explicit about the characteristic and variable features of tasks—in other words, what features of the task are always present and what features can be varied to make the task more or less cognitively complex? The challenge is that this same recipe could also serve as the "code" that coaching companies would seek to explicitly crack (for more on this issue, see Koretz, 2015).

Auditing Results from Accountability Tests

There are a number of pragmatic steps that can be taken to monitor accountability tests for evidence that results are being distorted by some combinations of cheating, narrowing of the curriculum, and coaching. One approach is to use infrequently administered low-stakes assessments from the same content domain as an audit of the results on the high-stakes assessment in question. Examples of this approach have been reported by Koretz, Linn, Dunbar, and Shepard (1991), Koretz and Barron (1998), and Klein, Hamilton, McCaffrey, and Stecher (2000). A challenge with this approach is that there is no guarantee that the audit test has also been designed with the same focal knowledge, skills, and abilities firmly in mind—in the parlance of ECD, one would want to compare the respective domain models, domain analyses, design patterns, student models, and task models that led to each assessment to be sure that they were consistent. In addition, there may well be differential motivation when students are administered tests in high- and low-stakes conditions. Although the stakes are usually greater for teachers and schools than for students, students are more likely to perceive a sense of urgency when taking a state- or district-administered test than when taking a low-stakes assessment such as NAEP.

Dan Koretz (Koretz, 2015; Koretz & Beguin, 2010) proposed that high-stakes testing should be seeded with "audit items" that purposely vary construct-irrelevant features of commonly administered tasks to see whether performance on these tasks is consistent with performance on the test overall. Neal (2013) argued that the best way to avoid a narrowing of the curriculum and coaching is to administer separate tests for student and teacher/school-level inferences. The tests intended for teacher/school accountability would be less sensitive to coaching because there would be no need to maintain a common scale from year to year (i.e., that practice known among psychometricians as "horizontal test score equating"). In the absence of equating, there would be no need to maintain common items on test forms across years, and these common items are the ones that are most susceptible to coaching. Both of these ideas are intriguing, yet it is unclear if either would be practically or logistically feasible (e.g., Briggs, 2010 and Sinharay, Haberman, & Zwick, 2010 for critiques of Koretz's audit item proposal).

An alternative that might be more feasible when assessments have been designed according to ECD-style principles would be to use estimates of the cognitive complexity of tasks as a basis for hypotheses about which tasks should be more or less susceptible to distortion due to a narrowing of the curriculum or coaching. For example, it has become common for test developers to use Norman Webb's Depth of Knowledge (DOK) categories as a distinguishing feature of tasks. If this has been done successfully, then one would typically expect that performance on a

DOK 1 (Recall) task would be easier to inflate relative to a DOK 2 (Skill/Concept) or DOK 3 (Strategic Thinking) task, let alone a DOK 4 (Extended Thinking) task. If evidence is found that year-to-year gains are inversely related to DOK level, this would at least be consistent with what one might expect if Campbell's Law is being realized. On the other hand, it is also possible that gains in the higher order thinking skills reflected by DOK 3 and 4 items are simply harder to achieve, even in the presence of no coaching or curriculum narrowing, so one would need to be careful not to overinterpret evidence that is fundamentally correlational.

Measurement versus Evaluation

Sireci and Soto (this volume) argue that, when test scores are used as inputs in growth models with the intent to making value-added inferences about teachers (or schools), the resulting teacher-specific "scores" should be regarded as "measures" of teacher effectiveness in the same way that student-specific test scores are typically regarded as measures of student ability. If this analogy holds, then it follows that these measures should be submitted to the same scrutiny with respect to their validity implied by the most recent edition of the *Standards for Educational and Psychological Testing* (AERA, APA, & NCME, 2014). Hill (2009) and Haertel (2013) have suggested or embraced a similar perspective in recent years. But although this perspective can be a good way to promote debate and conversation, I worry that it may ultimately be misguided because it confuses the distinction between educational measurement and evaluation.

The most frequent definition of measurement provided in education (and the social sciences more generally) was first suggested by the psychologist Stevens (1946), who defined measurement as the assignment of numbers to objects or events according to rule. The more standard definition, as understood in the physical sciences, is the estimation of the magnitude of a quantity relative to a defined unit of the same quantity (Michell, 1999). In contrast, an evaluation is fundamentally about *making a judgment* about the amount, number, or value of something. The outcome from a measurement is a measure; the outcome(s) from an evaluation is one or more decisions. An important differentiating feature between a measure and a decision is that the quality of a measure can be established with respect to its precision, but the quality of a decision cannot. The aspiration of a measure is for objectivity, but by its very nature, an evaluative decision will be a blend of the objective and subjective.

In educational measurement, there is a reciprocal nature between the outcome (student measures) and the way that tests are designed. The chapters by Haertel et al. (this volume) and Ferrara and Way (this volume) provide good examples of a sequence of design principles that can be implemented in practice, and if these principles are followed, the likelihood of producing a defensible test will be increased. This test can be readily evaluated to determine if it is aligned to content standards and curriculum, if it can be modeled using item response theory, if it supports reliable classifications into achievement levels, and so on. If the test is not aligned, if it does not meet key assumptions of the item response theory model, if it does not support reliable classifications, etc., then test developers can make directed changes to improve the test (e.g., new items can be written that increase alignment, items that misfit an IRT model can be removed or an alternate model can be specified, more items can be selected to minimize measurement error at a desired performance level, etc.).

In contrast, there is very little that can be done to design a test to be more valid as a basis for "measuring" teacher effectiveness *beyond what would already be done to design the assessment to be a valid measure of student ability.* If conceptualized as a measure, teacher effectiveness scores depend first and foremost upon the statistical model that is being used to disentangle the role of the teacher or school from all the other factors that cause variability in student test performance, not on decisions being made about item writing or test form equating. The empirical research

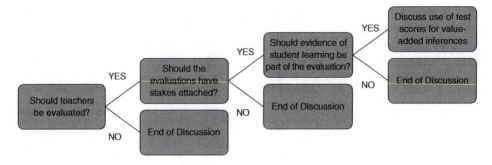

Figure 7.1 Flowchart for discussions about test score use in teacher evaluation.

literature has produced mixed results on this issue (for reviews, see Braun, Chudowsky, & Koenig, 2010; Briggs, 2012; Harris, 2009). If a state has decided that there is sufficient evidence to support the validity of student-level test scores as measures of some underlying construct (i.e., if they are willing to report the scores publicly), the next question is whether it is possible to get a valid estimate of the effect that teachers (and/or schools) have had on these test scores. One may very well argue that this is not possible in a statistical sense, but I worry that it muddies the waters to conceptualize a growth-based statistic as a measurement of a teacher's "ability" in the same way that one may conceptualize a test score as a measure of a student's ability.

When teachers are being evaluated, the end result is a decision, and the ideal is to bring as many relevant indicators to bear as possible in making this decision. How these indicators get combined to come to a summative evaluative decision is just as much a matter of negotiation and politics as it is a matter of statistics, psychometrics, or standards. This is true, by the way, whenever a person or institution is being formally evaluated. Every year as a faculty member at a university, my productivity is evaluated by a committee of faculty peers assembled by my dean, and the ratings that result are used to determine annual merit-based salary increases. In evaluating me, this committee examines indicators in three key areas: scholarship, teaching, and professional service. The process that they use to do this is systematic but hardly scientific, and were I to regard each indicator that figures into my final rating as "measures," I would no doubt find numerous violations of the *Standards*. However, the process is largely transparent and leads to salary decisions that my dean can justify and that I can appeal if I perceive the rating to be unfair.

In past discussions about the use of value-added indicators as part of teacher evaluation, I have taken to presenting the graphic depicted in Figure 7.1. The point of the graphic is that if one agrees that

1   teachers should be evaluated,
2   the evaluation should have stakes attached, and
3   that evidence of student learning should be part of the evaluation,

then it follows that the need for some sort of indicator that will be used to support inferences about value-added is unavoidable. The question in this case is not *whether* a statistic should be generated in support of this indicator, but *what* statistic should be generated. If the answer to the first two questions is yes but the third is no, then high-stakes decisions about teachers will rely solely upon direct observation of teaching practice, and all the concerns Sireci and Soto (this volume) raise in their chapter would apply in equal force if these were to be regarded as measures. If the answer to the first question is yes but the second is no, then the fundamental problem is not with the validity of using student test scores to support value-added inferences, but with the use of test scores for high-stakes decisions. I have a great deal of sympathy for this position, as there seems to be little evidence from a systems improvement perspective that the pros of high-stakes teacher evaluation are likely to outweigh the cons, but again, this points to a more fundamental concern with Campbell's Law than it does to a concern about the validity using value-added indicators as a basis for teacher evaluation.

Sireci and Soto (this volume) apply strict criteria from the *Standards* that would need to hold to justify the use of value-added indicators. However, if applied with equal stringency, many tests now under development that are the impetus for this book would also fail to meet all components of the *Standards*. A drawback to the conventional wisdom that validity is a matter of degree rather than a dichotomy is that the threshold for declaring that a measure is sufficiently valid cannot be objectively or unequivocally established. In this sense the blurring of distinctions between measurement and evaluation is not surprising, because the *Standards* themselves cast the process of test validation as synonymous with an ongoing process of evaluative inquiry.

It seems important to appreciate that in contrast to evaluating the validity of a test, the validity of a teacher evaluation system is always relative to some alternative. Given the constraint that teachers are to be evaluated with stakes attached, the question is not whether value-added indicators are valid "measures" according to the *Standards*, but whether the evaluative decisions that include these indicators are more justifiable than the decisions that would be made in their absence. And in the long term, the fundamental question about validity is whether the educational system as a whole has improved more because of the teacher evaluation system than it would have in its absence. The counterfactual argument is far more central to evaluation than it is to measurement.

Conclusion

The five chapters in this section represent a valuable contribution because they provide an accessible survey of design-based approaches to testing that could be used to mitigate Campbell's Law. The use of ECD (Haertel et al., this volume) and Principled Design for Efficacy (Ferrara & Way, this volume) can help to anticipate a misalignment between tested content and desired targets for inference that can lead teachers to narrow the curriculum. These approaches also require test designers to be explicit about task design and hypothesized differences in cognitive complexity. When tests are being designed to elicit information about higher order student practices such as defending claims with evidence, modeling, and reasoning, it will often be the case that PBAs are a necessary ingredient (Lane & DePascale; Marion & Buckley, this volume). PBAs have the potential to blur the boundary between the embedded assessments that exist in classroom activities and the formal assessment environment of a standardized test. In a best case scenario, it would be very difficult for teachers to coach students to high PBA scores by focusing on superficial features of the assessment, but this is an empirical question and will depend on the characteristics of the PBA. Finally, validity theory in general and categories within the *Standards* in particular can be used to design studies that may support or, alternatively, call into question key assumptions being made about a testing program (Sireci & Soto, this volume).

Note

1 The headline of an April 14, 2014 opinion article Katzman wrote for MSNBC was titled "I taught America how to beat the SAT. That's how I know it's useless." http://www.msnbc.com/msnbc/princeton-review-founder-the-sat-useless

References

American Educational Research Association (AERA), American Psychological Association (APA), & National Council on Measurement in Education (ACME). (2014). *Standards for educational and psychological testing*. Washington, DC: AERA.

Braun, H., Chudowsky, N., & Koenig, J. (2010). *Getting value out of value-added*. Washington, DC: National Academies Press.

Briggs, D. C. (2001). The effect of admissions test preparation: Evidence from NELS-88. *Chance*, *14*(1), 10–18.

Briggs, D. C. (2004). Evaluating SAT coaching: Gains, effects and self-selection. In R. Zwick (Ed.), *Rethinking the SAT: The future of standardized testing in university admissions*. New York, NY: RoutledgeFalmer.

Briggs, D. C. (2009). *Preparation for college admissions exams*. Arlington, VA: National Association of College Admissions Counseling. Retrieved January 5, 2009 from http://www.nacacnet.org/research/publicationsresources/marketplace/documents/testprepdiscussionpaper.pdf

Briggs, D. C. (2010). Validate high stakes inferences by designing good experiments, not audit items. *Measurement: Interdisciplinary Research and Perspectives, 8*(4), 185–190.

Briggs, D. C. (2012). Making value-added inferences from large-scale assessments. In M. Simon, K. Ercikan, & M. Rousseau (Eds.), *Improving large-scale assessment in education: Theory, issues and practice*. London, UK: Routledge.

Campbell, D. T. (1976, December). *Assessing the impact of planned social change*. The Public Affairs Center, Dartmouth College, Hanover, New Hampshire.

Firestone, W. A., Schorr, R. Y., & Monfils, L. F. (Eds.). (2004). *The ambiguity of teaching to the test: Standards, assessment, and educational reform*. Mahwah, NJ: Lawrence Erlbaum Associates.

Haertel, E. (2013). *Reliability and validity of inferences about teachers based on student test scores* (William H. Angoff Memorial Lecture). Princeton, NJ: Educational Testing Service.

Hargreaves, A., & Braun, H. (2013). *Data-driven improvement and accountability*. Boulder, CO: National Education Policy Center. Retrieved February 2, 2015 from http://nepc.colorado.edu/publication/data-driven-improvement-accountability

Harris, D. N. (2009). Would accountability based on teacher value added be smart policy? An examination of the statistical properties and policy alternatives. *Education Finance and Policy, 4*(4), 319–350.

Hill, H. (2009). Evaluating value-added models: A validity argument approach. *Journal of Policy Analysis and Management, 28*(4), 700–709.

Jacob, B. E., & Levitt, S. (2002). Rotten apples: An investigation of the prevalence and predictors of teacher cheating. *The Quarterly Journal of Economics, 118*(3), 843–877.

Jarvie, J. (2014, September 6). Atlanta school cheating trial has teachers facing prison. *Los Angeles Times*.

Klein, S. P., Hamilton, L. S., McCaffrey, D. F., & Stecher, B. M. (2000). What do test scores in Texas tell us? *Education Policy Analysis Archives, 8*(49), 1–22. Retrieved July 16, 2013 from http://epaa.asu.edu/ojs/article/view/440/563

Koretz, D. (2015). Adapting educational measurement to the demands of test-based accountability. *Measurement: Interdisciplinary Research and Perspectives, 13*(1), 1–25.

Koretz, D., & Barron, S. I. (1998). *The validity of gains on the Kentucky Instructional Results Information System (KIRIS)*. Santa Monica, CA: RAND.

Koretz, D., & Beguin, A. (2010). Self-monitoring assessments for educational accountability systems. *Measurement: Interdisciplinary Research and Perspectives, 8*(2–3), 92–109.

Koretz, D., & Hamilton, L. S. (2006). Testing for accountability in K–12. In R. L. Brennan (Ed.), *Educational measurement* (4th ed., pp. 531–578). Westport, CT: American Council on Education/Praeger.

Koretz, D., Linn, R. L., Dunbar, S. B., & Shepard, L. A. (1991, April). *The effects of high-stakes testing: Preliminary evidence about generalization across tests*. Paper presented at the annual meetings of the American Educational Research Association and the National Council on Measurement in Education, Chicago, IL.

Lawrence, I., Rigol, G., Van Essen, T., & Jackson, C. (2004). A historical perspective on the content of the SAT. In R. Zwick (Ed.), *Rethinking the SAT: Perspectives based on the November 2001 conference at the University of California* (pp. 57–74). Santa Barbara, CA: RoutledgeFalmer.

Michell, J. (1999). *Measurement in psychology: Critical history of a methodological concept.* New York, NY: Cambridge University Press.

National Research Council. (2000). *How people learn: Brain, mind, experience and school.* Washington, DC: National Academies Press.

National Research Council. (2001). *Knowing what students know: The science and design of educational assessment.* Washington, DC: National Academies Press.

Neal, D. (2013). *The consequences of using one assessment system to pursue two objectives* (NBER Working Paper No. 19214). Cambridge, MA: National Bureau of Economic Research.

Nichols, S. N., & Berliner, D. C. (2007). *Collateral damage: The effects of high-stakes testing on America's schools.* Cambridge, MA: Harvard Education Press.

Powers, D. E., & Rock, D. A. (1999). Effects of coaching on SAT I: Reasoning test scores. *Journal of Educational Measurement, 36*(2), 93–118.

Sinharay, S., Haberman, S. J., & Zwick, R. (2010). Issues with self-monitoring assessments: Comments on Koretz and Béguin. *Measurement: Interdisciplinary Research and Perspectives, 8*(4), 191–194.

Stake, R. E. (1971, June). Testing hazards in performance contracting. *Phi Delta Kappan, 52,* 583–588.

Stevens, S. S. (1946). On the theory of scales of measurement. *Science, 103*(2684), 677–680.

Part II

8 Arts Assessment in an Age of Accountability

Challenges and Opportunities in Implementation, Design, and Measurement

Scott C. Shuler, Timothy S. Brophy,
F. Robert Sabol, Susan McGreevy-Nichols,
and Mary J. Schuttler

Introduction

Decades of effort to develop assessment tools in arts education have yielded a growing array of measures that are useful for classroom assessment. The National Assessment of Educational Progress (NAEP) in the arts as well as several state initiatives have provided examples of how formal measurement of arts learning might work on a larger scale.[1] More recently, states have included arts educators in new teacher evaluation systems that require documentation of student learning and growth. This chapter describes the development of the field's assessment practices and systems, summarizes key measurement challenges, and identifies promising strategies and trends that address those challenges.

Although federal legislation has identified the arts as a core subject in schools for more than 20 years (103rd Congress, 1994), federal support has largely focused on reading and mathematics. Those federal policies that provide funding for specific subjects (U.S. Department of Education, 2010) have placed the arts in the "non-tested subjects" category. Federal appropriations for large-scale arts assessment have only supported those administered under the NAEP, which are infrequent and not regularly scheduled.

In the absence of federal funding, state education agencies and professional arts education associations have led most initiatives in arts assessment. These largely voluntary efforts, often motivated by advocacy needs as well as a desire to measure arts learning, have led to the development of a variety of arts assessment systems, sets of standards-based assessments available in individual publications and online, and some standardized measures. Assessment items (sometimes referred to as "tasks") in these systems are generally teacher-developed and require authentic demonstrations of artistic processes. They are prized by teachers both for their instructional utility and for the opportunity to collect evidence of student learning. However, these systems are loosely structured and often leave significant measurement-related decisions to teachers and school district personnel, raising questions about their use for accountability.

In the absence of the need for formal accountability for learning, arts educators have generally focused their assessment development and practices on low-stakes assessments for formative purposes. New teacher evaluation systems that require documentation of student learning and growth, such as through student learning objectives (SLOs), have raised the stakes for teachers and refocused attention on the measurement of arts learning, leading to the development of new measures and formal reviews of existing measurement tools.

We set the stage for this chapter with an overview of the multifaceted context for arts assessment in the United States. Next, we lay out the challenges to arts assessment, followed by a brief review of the status of arts assessment in music, dance, theater, and the visual arts. We then discuss selected states' arts assessment systems and the emerging national system of Model Cornerstone Assessments (MCAs). After a discussion of the relevant measurement issues, we close with our view of the way forward.

Arts Assessment in the United States: The National Context

The Evolution of Arts Assessment

Several arts achievement measures intended for large-scale use were developed in the late twentieth century, with most focused on music. The assessment and measurement of musical skills and knowledge has been addressed in some form for nearly 100 years. At the beginning of the twentieth century, psychologist Carl Seashore (1915, 1939, 1940, 1960) conducted scientific research on the measurement of musical talent. A series of early tests of musical skills subsequently emerged, followed by the development of music achievement tests based on knowledge and skills taught in the public school music curriculum. Seashore's early description of music as a combination of "capacity and mental attitudes" and "skill acquired in training" (1915, p. 129) influenced the later development of music aptitude and achievement tests.

Shuler (1991) identified the most important music achievement tests as Gordon's *Iowa Tests of Music Literacy* (1970), Simons' *Measurements of Music Listening Skills* (1976), and Colwell's *Music Achievement Tests* (MAT; 1967, 1969, 1970a, 1970b, 1970c) and *Silver Burdett Music Competency Tests* (1979). Each of these measures provided audio stimuli for at least some items and pioneered creative strategies to overcome the limitations of their pencil-and-paper, selected-response format. Colwell's tests stand out because they are among the only measures that were standardized ($N = 21,000$ for tests 1 and 2, and $N = 19,000$ for tests 3 and 4) and for which complete item analyses were conducted. Reliabilities were estimated using KR_{21} and were all above .90 "in school systems [with] a superior music program" (Colwell, 1970a, p. 73). Test–retest reliabilities were all at .87 and above.

Arts assessment development flourished during the early 1990s. Shuler and Connealy (1998) identified five factors that contributed to this trend:

- the general movement toward educational accountability in states;
- the growing political awareness and assertiveness of supporters of arts education;
- the development of National Standards in the Arts;
- the 1997 NAEP in the arts; and
- the State Collaborative on Assessment and Student Standards in the Arts (Council of Chief State School Officers, 2014).

Another factor that spurred arts assessment initiatives in many states was the 1994 Goals 2000 Act. As Herpin, Washington, and Li (2012) write in their history of national and state assessment in the arts,

> A major impetus for assessment of the arts at the national level came in 1994 when the *Goals 2000: Educate America Act* was signed into law. It stated that by the year 2000, students in grades 4, 8, and 12 would have to demonstrate competency in a number of subject areas, including the arts. (103rd Congress, 1994)

The release of the first set of National Standards for the Arts (MENC, 1994) provided assessment developers for the first time with a widely accepted, defensible basis for defining content domains in the arts (Shuler, 1996). Arts assessments could be linked to one commonly recognized set of national standards or to state standards that were based on those national standards. The original standards were a milestone that clarified the outcomes of arts education—and, indirectly, their assessment—at the national level for the first time. The original National Standards in Arts Education used the terms "*arts discipline* and *art form* to refer to Dance, Music, Theatre, and the Visual Arts, recognizing that each of these encompasses a wide variety of forms and sub-disciplines" (MENC, 1994, Preface). In the revised national standards, the National Coalition for Core Arts Standards (NCCAS) added standards for a fifth arts area, Media Arts, which combines elements of the other four arts disciplines in a technological context while also incorporating emerging genres such as animation (NCCAS, 2014).

NAEP Arts Assessment

The first national assessment of student learning in the arts (NAEP Arts) was administered in 1974; subsequent administrations occurred in 1978, 1997, and 2008. Early NAEP assessments also had some influence on assessment work at the state level. For example,

- the Michigan Department of Education developed music assessment items that were first administered in 1972 and expanded to include NAEP-inspired performance tasks in 1974 and 1978 (Roeber, 2013); and
- in 1980–81 the Connecticut and Minnesota education agencies readministered selected art and music items from the 1978 arts NAEP that included performance assessments (Vaughan, 1993).

The 1997 and 2008 NAEP arts assessments were designed to measure achievement of the national arts standards issued in 1994. These assessments were organized and reported based on the three Artistic Processes[2] of Creating, Performing, and Responding that collectively comprise the Artistic Process Model. Shuler (2011a) writes that the ultimate goal of arts education is to empower students to independently carry out these three Artistic Processes at increasing levels of knowledge, skill, and engagement. The processes may be defined as follows:

- *Creating* refers to the process of developing new artwork, such as through painting, music composition, play- or script-writing, choreography, or improvisation.
- *Performing* refers to the process of giving life to existing work through skillful interpretation.
- *Responding* refers to discerning the meaning in others' artistic creations and performances, i.e., in the role of an audience member or consumer.

The Artistic Process Model not only provided the organizational scheme for the 1997 and 2008 NAEP assessment in the arts but also underpins the arts frameworks of several states and nations (College Board, 2013) and provides the framework for the new national arts standards developed by NCCAS (National Coalition for Core Arts Standards, 2014). The NCCAS standards posit "Presenting" in visual arts and "Producing" in media arts as non-performing arts counterparts to the Performing process and add the process of Connecting.

The 1997 arts NAEP Assessment Framework (1996) was developed concurrently with, and was based upon, the 1994 arts standards. To strengthen that connection, some members of the NAEP development team also served on national standards writing teams. Assessment exercise blocks piloted for the 1997 NAEP included authentic tasks designed for grades 4, 8, and 12 that assessed knowledge and skills in Creating or Performing and Responding in music, theater/drama, dance, and visual art. The involvement of many arts educators and assessment personnel in the process of designing, scoring, and disseminating the results of the 1997 NAEP increased general interest and expertise in arts assessment.

Unfortunately, the NAEP format has inherent limitations as a measure of arts learning. Because Creating and Performing are multi-step processes that generally play out over time, the roughly 45-minute format for NAEP administration placed significant limitations on the complexity and authenticity of performance assessment items. The arts item types appropriate for timed tests are:

- Responding items in which any multimedia stimuli are of limited duration—i.e., short videos of dance or theater work, short audio recordings of music—and responses are provided in short-answer or selected-response mode. Such items have historically comprised the majority or entirety of standardized music assessments;
- Creating tasks in the performing arts that focus on improvisation (an item type included in the 1997 NAEP); and
- Performing tasks in music based on sight-reading, in which individual students (or, at some adjudicated festivals, entire ensembles) are given a limited amount of time to inspect a score before performing it for evaluation.

Although measures that incorporate these types of items address some important learning outcomes, those outcomes comprise only a small subset of the essential arts learning outlined in the national arts standards (Shuler, 2008). Any test limited to these item types, therefore, suffers from construct underrepresentation (Lane & DePascale, this volume). To prevent contractors from designing assessments for the 1997 NAEP composed primarily of selected-response items, the assessment specifications were written explicitly to limit the percentage of such items to no more than 20 percent (NAGB, 1994, p. 83).

Those specifications drove up the cost of item development, piloting, and administration, which contributed to NAGB's decision to focus the final 1997 NAEP solely on art and music items administered to a limited student sample in grade 8 (Persky, Sandene, & Askew, 1999). The representative probability samples of eighth-grade students from across the nation who participated included both students who were in arts education programs and those who were not. Each student participating in the 1997 or 2008 NAEP arts assessments completed one of several blocks of assessment items, but the music portion of the 2008 NAEP omitted all performance items, thereby limiting its scope to Responding and severely limiting its validity as a measure of music achievement (Shuler, Lehman, Colwell, & Morrison, 2009). The students also responded to a questionnaire that provided contextual information (e.g., demographic characteristics, school and community resources, qualifications of instructional staff).

SCASS/Arts

The State Collaborative on Assessment and Student Standards in the Arts (SCASS/Arts), an initiative launched in 1993 by the Council of Chief State School Officers, brought arts educators and assessment specialists from as many as 30 states together on a regular basis to work on standards-based arts assessment. The professional learning community created by sustained collaboration on this project contributed to the assessment expertise of state arts education personnel, as well as the arts interest of state assessment personnel (Shuler & Connealy, 1998).

State Department of Education personnel participating in SCASS/Arts were invited by the Educational Testing Service, the contractor for the 1997 NAEP, to convene groups of teachers in their states for the purpose of developing performance tasks in all four arts disciplines. Half of the tasks thus developed were turned over for use in NAEP, and the other half were reserved for use by SCASS/Arts and participating states. During the final years of its operation, SCASS/Arts transitioned from this focus on performance tasks to developing a pool of more traditional tasks, such as multiple-choice items.

The Authenticity Imperative

Because there have been few contemporary, commercially available standardized measures for assessing arts achievement, arts educators have followed their instinctive preference for authentic, performance-based assessments of students' capacity to create new artwork (i.e., Creating) or to give life to an existing work of music or theater through expressive performance (Performing). Such measures are "authentic" in that they emulate the practices of arts professionals and are highly engaging for students. These assessments also fall into the category of "alternative" assessments (Lane & DePascale, this volume), in that they are well aligned with learning goals and have considerable instructional value.

Numerous graduate theses in arts education include the development and application of performance measures for various student populations. Although many of these studies report acceptable levels of reliability, practicing arts educators have, in general, placed a higher priority on the degree to which assessments represent what artists do. Despite their instructional utility and value, these assessments raise a number of measurement issues. For example, authenticity alone does not guarantee that validity can be established, although Messick (1994) calls it a "promissory note."

Assessment as Advocacy

Most arts assessments administered in educational settings have been low-stakes formative instruments focusing on monitoring and improving achievement at the classroom level, generating data to inform individual teacher instructional practice and student reflection. As Shuler (2011) observed,

> We do need to provide assessment evidence to survive in today's data-driven school environment. However, the more important reasons we must assess are to improve our professional effectiveness as teachers, to improve student learning, and to help us advocate for excellent ... programs.
>
> (p. 10)

When arts assessment data have been shared outside the classroom, the purpose has typically been to advocate for programs by demonstrating to parents and policymakers that students have attained high levels of achievement in competitive or adjudicated settings such as large ensemble festivals, thespian events, or art contests. Arts educators leverage such external recognition to position their programs as centers of excellence and sources of community pride, similar to successful competitive sports programs. In an educational and fiscal environment where the arts are often treated as peripheral to the curriculum and students' opportunity to learn in the arts is threatened, attaining such "branding" helps arts teachers advocate for maintaining or increasing resources.

Opportunity to Learn and Arts Assessment

In a keynote address to the first International Symposium on Assessment in Music Education, Colwell (2008) remarked, "There is no point in getting excited about assessment if the student has not had an opportunity to learn the material" (p. 7). In a sense, without the opportunity to learn particular content, students will do poorly even if the content validity (with respect to the relevant standards) of the assessment has been established. Lehman (2014) remarked that "in the United States, we don't have an educational system; we have 13,809 educational systems" (p. 4), referring to the number of school districts across the country. The quantity and quality of arts instruction are influenced significantly by available arts opportunities, which must be taken into account when employing assessment data in high-stakes contexts such as teacher evaluation. Those opportunity-to-learn variables include, but are not limited to, (a) the number of minutes per week of instruction offered in the arts, (b) the expertise of the individual delivering arts instruction and assessing student work, (c) the existence and quality of arts curriculum supported by appropriate resources, and (d) the number of students and classes for which the arts teacher is responsible.

The 2001 reauthorization of the Elementary and Secondary Education Act, also named *No Child Left Behind (NCLB)* (107th Congress, 2001), raised the stakes on test scores in basic skills. One unintended consequence of this legislation was the reduction of the relative emphasis on, and resources allocated for, non-tested subjects, including the arts. The impact of this legislation on arts education has been documented in two recent reports.

The publication of *Arts Education in Public Elementary and Secondary Schools 1999–2000 and 2009–10* (Parsad & Spiegelman, 2012) provided information about the current status of elementary and secondary arts education in the United States. The most recent data were collected during the 2009–10 academic year using the Fast Response Survey System (FRSS). Approximately 6,000 school principals, arts education specialists, and classroom teachers from a representative, stratified sample of 3,400 elementary and secondary public schools were identified for participation. Participants received one of seven survey forms. Return rates were high (81.5 percent for classroom teachers, 85 percent or higher for all others). Findings for dance and theater were produced from information from school (i.e., principal) surveys, because dance and theater specialists were not surveyed. Issues addressed included (a) the extent to which students received arts instruction, (b) the facilities and resources available for arts instruction, (c) the preparation, work environments, and instructional practices of arts educators in school-based arts education programs, as well as their extracurricular arts activities, and (d) the presence of school–community partnerships in the arts.

The design of the 2009–10 FRSS study was sufficiently similar to previous FRSS studies in 1994–95 and, particularly, 1999–2000 to permit some analysis of trends during the era of NCLB. The number of elementary schools providing music instruction showed no change, remaining at 94 percent from 1999 to 2009. Schools reporting visual arts instruction declined from 87 percent to 83 percent, and those reporting dance and theater instruction dropped from 20 percent to 3 percent (dance) and to 4 percent (theater) for this period. Secondary school reports indicated that the overall percentage of schools offering music instruction rose from 90 percent to 91 percent between 1999–2000 and 2009–10. The percentage offering instruction in visual arts dropped from 93 percent to 89 percent, and dance and theater instruction from 14 percent to 12 percent during the same period.

Ultimately, successful assessment depends upon the expertise of those who design, devise validity arguments from available evidence, implement, score, analyze, and use the results of that assessment. Among elementary schools that provided instruction in the arts, the percentage in which arts specialists deliver that instruction declined in all four arts areas:

- in music from 91 percent in 1999–2000 to 89 percent in 2009–10;
- in visual arts from 84 percent in 1999–2000 to 72 percent in 2009–10;
- in dance from 57 percent in 1999–2000 to 38 percent in 2009–10; and
- in theater from 42 percent in 1999–2000 to 36 percent in 2009–10.

At the secondary level 97 percent of arts instructors were arts specialists.

The percentage of secondary schools reporting requirements of arts course work for graduation rose from 52 percent in 1999–2000 to 57 percent in 2009–10. The national trend toward offering credit or waivers for high school courses based on demonstrated competency— competency often developed outside the traditional school environment, such as in the community or online—increases the importance of defining essential outcomes and developing tools to measure their achievement in all subject areas, including the arts. The New England Secondary School Consortium (NESSC, 2014), which consists of five partner states, lists "proficiency-based graduation decisions" as one of its "three critical, high-leverage areas of schooling in the 21st century." Rhode Island's high school graduation requirement in the arts is based on competency rather than credit (Rhode Island Department of Education, 2013). This practice raises an important consequential validity issue (AERA, APA, & NCME, 2014). It is not clear that available validity evidence sufficiently establishes the degree to which the scores on the assessments used to determine proficiency warrant their use in fulfilling a requirement for graduation. Furthermore, the use of test scores for multiple purposes has implications for accountability (Koch, 2013).

Arts educators self-reported the following assessment practices: performance tasks or projects (98 percent), direct observation of student performance (96 percent), teacher-developed rubrics (85 percent), portfolios (76 percent), and assessments requiring short answers or essays (54 percent).

Differences in community wealth account for many differences in students' access to arts opportunities. For example, in all four art forms, low-poverty secondary schools were far more likely to offer five or more courses in that art form than high-poverty secondary schools. Similarly, students in low-poverty secondary schools were far more likely to have access to dedicated classrooms with specialized equipment for instruction. Dedicated arts classrooms are more likely to provide a number of elements conducive to arts assessment, such as storage space for long-term products, soundproof practice rooms where students can audio-record their performances, mirrored walls where young dancers can monitor and self-evaluate their movements, and a collection of resources (e.g., art tools, instruments, materials, printers, video and audio recording and playback equipment) appropriate for making, viewing, or listening to artistic work.

Federal policy has exacerbated opportunity-to-learn barriers to arts teaching and learning. Sabol (2010) conducted a national study that examined the impact of NCLB on visual art education programming in relation to staffing, teaching loads, workloads, enrollments, funding, scheduling, curriculum, instruction, assessment, and art educators' attitudes related to these variables. Sabol surveyed a stratified random sample (weighted by state) of 5,000 individuals who included art educators from all instructional levels. The 3,412 respondents (a 68 percent response rate) reflected the overall distribution of art teachers by instructional level in the United States: 34 percent taught at the elementary level, 32 percent taught at the secondary level, 22 percent taught at the middle school level, 7 percent taught in higher education, 3 percent were in art supervision and administration, and 2 percent taught in art museums (Sabol, 2001b).

Sabol's report identified several areas in visual art education across the nation that were impacted by NCLB. Those areas most negatively affected were scheduling, teacher workload, funding, and teachers' ability to focus on art learning. For example, 65 percent reported they had to decrease the time that students spent on studio work due to increased emphasis on NCLB content in their art classes. As a consequence, 75 percent reported diminished quality of student artwork because students did not have enough time to fully experiment, explore media, develop ideas, and develop personal expression in their work. They also reported increased submissions of unfinished work, reduced levels of creativity, increased dependence on stereotypical responses, and reliance on previously created responses at all instructional levels. On the positive side, 50 percent reported increasing emphasis on assessment in their art programs and 43 percent reported using more types of assessments.

Collectively, the FRSS and Sabol studies raise the issue of the consequential validity of the NCLB high-stakes tests and their unintended consequences for arts education. The continuing availability of music and visual arts instruction in most American schools confirms that arts education is valued. However, the budgetary impact of the economic downturn of the late 2000s, as well as the increased focus on high-stakes assessment in a small number of subject areas, has contributed to the erosion of arts education programming and decreased opportunity to learn across the country.

Challenges to Arts Assessment in the United States

In this section we present the challenges to the development and implementation of arts assessment. (We will address the measurement issues in a separate section, as they arise from the practices, contexts, and unique characteristics of arts education in the United States.) Some of these challenges—such as lack of access to readily available, high-quality measures, and the need to establish validity and reliability in performance assessments—are shared with other disciplines. Other challenges—including opportunity-to-learn barriers such as limited instructional time, infrequent instruction, large student–teacher ratios, the multimedia nature of artwork, and the need to measure success in creative work—are more specific to arts education.

In 2012, the National Endowment for the Arts (NEA) released *Improving the Assessment of Student Learning in the Arts—State of the Field and Recommendations* (Herpin et al., 2012). In 2005, the NEA commissioned WestEd to:

> examine current trends, promising techniques, and successful practices being used to assess student learning in the arts throughout the country, as well as identify potential areas in which arts assessment could be improved. Although the original intent of the study was to identify strong models of assessment practices that could serve as examples for possible replication, the study found that such models were not available and are in fact a need of the field.
> (Herpin et al., 2012, p. ii)

The conclusions of this study were as follows:

1   There is a lack of publicly available, high-quality assessment tools, how-to resources, technical reports, and informational documents.
2   There is a need for vetted, high-quality assessment tools and models.
3   There is a lack of understanding about what a rubric is and how to use one, and there is not always a clear distinction between knowledge and skills.
4   Survey respondents use a variety of assessment tools to collect data for multiple purposes.
5   Professional development is needed to improve the assessment of student learning in the arts.
6   Survey respondents reported needs of the field around four categories—guidance, trained professionals, making the case, and additional needs. (Herpin et al., 2012, pp. 88–91)

The NEA study identified several of the common issues and challenges in arts assessment. Additional challenges grow out of chronic resource issues, including large class loads and limited instructional time, and others out of the nature of artwork itself. In the next section, we discuss some of these challenges to the development and implementation of arts assessments.

Challenges to the Development and Implementation of Arts Assessments

Availability of Measures

Unlike the "tested subjects" (i.e., English/language arts, mathematics, and science), where vetted, high-quality assessment tools and models are available in the form of state- and commercially developed standardized measures, there are few state measures and even fewer commercially available measures of learning in the arts. State-developed arts measures that consist of selected-response items are typically proprietary and secure and therefore, with the exception of a handful of released items, unavailable to teachers. By contrast, performance assessments created by departments of education or statewide organizations in states such as Connecticut, Washington, Rhode Island, Michigan, Colorado, and Delaware are publicly available and have been widely disseminated.

Authentic Artwork Requires Time

Curriculum and instruction based on the Artistic Process Model engage students in complex projects and performances that can be developed only over extended periods of time. Language arts experts note strong similarities between Creating in the arts and process writing, which typically requires significant time over multiple class periods and/or outside class to complete. Although the timed impromptu writing tasks called for by standardized writing assessments provide some measure of competency, they do not fully reflect students' ability to organize and convey their ideas and, therefore, raise questions of validity. Similarly, arts assessments that seek to measure students' core understandings and proficiency in using artistic media to convey their ideas (arguably the primary purpose of arts education) must allow students time to organize, reflect upon, and refine their work.

Frequency and Amount of Instruction

The infrequent classes and limited instructional time available to many elementary and middle school arts teachers limit the extent to which they can ask their students to carry out the multiple steps (referred to in NCCAS arts standards as "Process Components") of the Creating and Performing processes. Brophy (2008) found that elementary music teachers in Florida averaged 38 minutes of instruction per week, and the range of instructional time varied among schools ($N = 106$) from no music classes at all to 45 minutes daily. In visual art, limited instructional time, limited storage space, and/or the absence of dedicated arts facilities lead some art teachers to assign their students "instant art" projects that can be completed in a single class period and carried home (Chapman, 1982), without retaining the work for scoring. The lack of student personal investment in such work renders it trivial in nature, diminishing its usefulness as an assessment of anything more than rudimentary skills and techniques.

Particularly at the elementary and middle school levels, where the frequency and quantity of instructional time are limited, authentic performance assessments can demand such a large percentage of available class time that they are necessarily designed as learning units or projects embedded into the basic curriculum. Most of the state-developed performance tasks mentioned elsewhere, as well as the MCAs currently under development by NCCAS, fall into the curriculum-embedded category. Embedding assessments within instructional units helps address authenticity issues associated with traditional standardized assessments, at the cost of reducing control over potential sources of construct-irrelevant variance such as the amount of time that students are given to prepare their work and the amount of assistance that students receive from peers or teachers.

Multimedia Stimuli

Artwork assumes a wide variety of forms, so exemplars and stimuli require a variety of media to present, and students' arts products require a variety of media to preserve.

Historically, the need for stimuli in the arts to be presented with appropriate fidelity has been an obstacle to reliable assessment and—to the extent that classrooms in underfunded schools are less likely to provide quality audio and video equipment—is a potential source of bias as well. Accurate reproduction of artwork—such as authentic color in a painting, high-quality film or video of a dance or theatrical performance, and high-fidelity audio in a sound recording—has been expensive and dependent upon the purchase of multiple copies of media that degrade over time (such as art prints, film, records, or tapes) and even more expensive equipment for presentation of those media (such as video players, audio playback equipment, and speakers). Students in classrooms where pristine media and high-fidelity equipment were provided were better able to perceive detail in the artwork, and therefore respond accurately, than were students in other settings.

State agencies explored creative, cost-effective solutions to these challenges. For example,

- Minnesota's State Board of Education began piloting music assessments for voluntary local use in 1971 and first administered a statewide visual arts assessment in 1981. To make in-depth content questions possible in the absence of mandated statewide curriculum and avoid copyright issues, for later versions of these assessments the Board distributed advance copies of public domain art prints and music examples on CD and encouraged participating districts to prepare their students by using those materials in instruction (Vaughan, 1993).
- Drawing and Responding items based on prints were included in the Arts and Humanities portion of the Maine Educational Assessment from 1992 until at least 1995. Test developers used the glossy cover included in the printer's specifications to present a color reproduction of visual art (Long & Moran, 1995).

By contrast, NAEP arts assessments prior to 1997 relied on simple line drawings for images such as musical instruments.

As discussed further below, ongoing improvements in technology are providing cost-effective means of presenting arts stimuli for assessment with consistent fidelity of reproduction.

Copyright Costs

Copyright issues pose another significant challenge when developing large-scale arts assess-ments, particularly when addressing the Artistic Processes of Responding and Performing. Costs and administrative work associated with obtaining permission to use non-public domain art-work have parallels in the testing of reading, where permission is needed to use passages from contemporary literature. In the performing arts, such challenges are further compounded by the need to obtain permission to use copyrighted performances. Some arts test developers have worked around some of these issues by creating or commissioning content specifically for the assessment, such as the music passages in the *Watkins–Farnum Performance Scale* (Watkins & Farnum, 1954) and Edwin Gordon's tests (Gordon, 1969); by obtaining permission from composers and other creative artists who want their work to circulate more widely (Vaughan, 1993); or by using public domain content such as artwork made available by public museums, high-quality performances by military and (with permission) university ensembles, and historic recordings archived at the Library of Congress.

Multimedia Student Work

Arts students produce work that only occasionally fits on traditional 8.5 × 11" paper, can be three-dimensional (e.g., sculpture) and fragile (e.g., collage), and often, particularly in the performing arts, occurs in real time. Preserving such work requires an investment of student and/or teacher time, which can be reduced but rarely eliminated through a variety of technologies, ranging from audio to video to multi-view photography and, increasingly, to holographic images of three-dimensional forms. These challenges to the collection, preservation, storage, and management of student work tend to increase assessment cost.

Large Class Size and Teacher Load

The difficulty of documenting student work is further exacerbated by the fact that many arts teachers are responsible for teaching large numbers of students (in the case of most elementary schools, the entire student population) and often teach large classes (such as bands, choirs, and orchestras).

Emerging Technology-Based Solutions

Improvements in online technology and reductions in the cost of local and cloud-based data storage have made innovative solutions to arts assessment challenges more feasible. Several state-sponsored systems suitable for large-scale assessment purposes have emerged that use digital technology to present arts stimuli and to retain and manage work, facilitate scoring, and store results. For example:

- The Rhode Island high school competency model employs a system in which student products are developed over time and only after completion are digitally uploaded for subsequent asynchronous review and scoring (Rhode Island Arts Learning Network, 2013).
- South Carolina's Arts Assessment System provides a web-based system to present arts stimuli and to facilitate uploading students' music improvisations and performances for scoring (Lovins, 2010).
- Tennessee's GLADiS Project (Tennessee Department of Education, 2014b) is designed to enable teachers to upload digital files to document student growth for purposes of teacher evaluation, as part of the state's Fine Arts Portfolio Model.
- Connecticut's upgrade to its CTcurriculum.org site, renamed MeasureSuccess.org (EASTCONN, 2015), enables any user or user group not only to post and disseminate performance tasks but also to benchmark student work, moderate scores, and calibrate scorers in an open-access environment (Shuler, 2015). The National Coalition for Core Arts Standards chose to use this site for piloting and benchmarking MCAs in all five arts areas.

Each of these systems stores student work and teachers' scores online, making them readily accessible for virtual asynchronous or summer peer review.

Commercially available technological tools are also emerging to help arts teachers meet these challenges. Currently available commercial products for storing and managing multimedia student artistic work include *Digication*, an online portfolio management system (Digication, 2014), and *SmartMusic* (SmartMusic, 2014), an online interactive learning system that not only facilitates the collection and management of student performances but can also score certain performances on pitch and rhythmic accuracy. Although the increasing availability of web-based solutions can facilitate the collection, storage, management, and scoring of the multimedia products produced by arts students, teachers must have ready access to broadband Internet and digital hardware in their classrooms to make use of such solutions. Fortunately, one positive unintended consequence of states' implementation of PARCC and Smarter Balanced tests is that they have compelled policymakers to provide more universal access to online connections, significant bandwidth, headsets, and multimedia computing devices necessary for administration of those assessments. Access to such technology not only makes performance assessment in arts classes more feasible but also provides a potential vehicle for delivering the multimedia arts stimuli that are essential for assessing students' ability to carry out the Responding process.

Assessing Creative Work

Issues and strategies associated with assessing creative work, which is a central focus of arts classes and comprises a large proportion of the student work they produce, would be too numerous and intriguing to address adequately even in a chapter devoted solely to this topic. Like assessors of writing who focus narrowly on the low-hanging fruit of spelling, punctuation, and grammar, assessors of Creating in the arts who privilege statistical considerations such as reliability over content authenticity tend to gravitate toward the assessment of technical dimensions, because such traits possess more readily identifiable degrees of "rightness" and are therefore easier to measure reliably. For example, the authors have observed that music teachers' classroom assessment of music composition too often focuses on whether students used the correct number of beats in each measure, and art teachers' assessment of portraits focuses on realistic reproduction of the face rather than on the more fundamental issues of whether students have conveyed their expressive intent or purpose.

There *are* useful parallels between more aesthetically based traits of writing and those of successful music compositions, dance choreography, and theatrical scripts. For example, common writing traits such as effective opening and closing passages and smooth transitions between sections also appear in some of the music composition scoring scales developed for Connecticut's Common Arts Assessments (CSDE, 2014b). Navigating the assessment of Creating also demands clarity about how that Artistic Process overlaps with, but differs from, the trait of "creativity."[3]

Professional Development to Improve Assessment of Student Learning

The need among arts educators for professional development "to improve the assessment of student learning" (Herpin et al., 2012) is one that is shared by teachers of other content areas. A case can be made, however, that arts educators must overcome greater obstacles than most of their peers. School leaders obsessed with raising standardized scores in tested subjects are, unfortunately, more likely to provide professional development focused on preparation for high-stakes testing than they are to bring in arts assessment experts or release arts teachers to attend arts assessment workshops. Even as new teacher evaluation systems have increased the need for precise measurement of student growth, the elimination of many district arts leadership positions has forced an increasing number of arts teachers to assume full responsibility for finding discipline-specific professional guidance and support.

The administration of embedded assessments inherently places the teacher in the dual role of learning facilitator and assessor, which in traditional assessment would be considered a conflict of interest and a barrier to accurate measurement. In the arts, this seems unavoidable. Teachers cannot help their students attain standards unless they have a thorough understanding of those standards and can apply them in their classrooms; hence, a strong case can be made that teachers *must* be engaged in scoring their students' work. Professional development that calibrates teachers to apply scoring standards consistent with predetermined benchmarks or anchor sets also empowers them to clarify those scoring standards to their students and deliver instruction that helps students attain those standards.

Assessment in the Arts Education Disciplines

In this section we provide a discipline-specific view of important assessment initiatives in music, visual art, dance, and theater/drama. These initiatives are contributing to the development of arts assessment systems at the state and national levels.

Music Education

As mentioned earlier, music is the art form which has seen the greatest progress in measurement and testing over the past century. However, a review of the *Mental Measurements Yearbooks* (Gutkin, 2000) reveals few published music tests are currently available in the United States; most are out of print. Two measures merit mention here, because of their continued use or influence. The *Watkins–Farnum Performance Scale* (Watkins & Farnum, 1954) provides instrumental music teachers with a "standardized, objective testing method for measuring performance and progress on a musical instrument" (p. 1). Although its passages are not musically satisfying, this measure is unique in providing a tool that measures technical performance on several common musical instruments in a statistically reliable manner and is therefore still in use by some teachers. The most thoroughly developed and analyzed test of music achievement is the MAT by Richard Colwell (1967, 1969, 1970a, 1970b, 1970c). Like the *Watkins–Farnum Performance Scale*, MAT employed then innovative measurement strategies that have been studied and often adapted by subsequent test developers.

In 2007, the Florida Music Educators Association supported the development, piloting, and field-testing of the fourth-grade *Florida Music Assessment* (FMA) (Brophy & Perry, 2007). Groups of trained music educators created a bank of 96 selected-response items designed to test achievement of a subset of the fourth-grade Grade-Level Expectations (GLEs) of Florida's Sunshine State Standards for Music at the state level. The questions were divided among four forms of the test, for a total of 30 questions on each test, with eight common items across all four forms. The test questions were presented on CD in four parts: listening; knowledge of music literature; symbol identification (these were the eight common items); and notation recognition. As students listened to the CD, they filled in an answer sheet to record their responses. There were no performance items on any form of the test. The FMA was administered by 126 classroom teachers to 9,473 fourth graders in 106 schools in 42 of Florida's 67 counties. CTT analysis of the four forms revealed KR_{20} reliabilities ranging from .61 to .68. The eight common items yielded difficulty levels of .41 to .68, item discriminations of .41 to .64, and point biserial correlations from .36 to .51.

The FMA was developed by trained teachers who focused on content validity, with the intention of creating a test for large-scale use. Because of funding loss and changing leadership, some components of the original project were suspended in 2008, but assessment development work continues under a grant to Polk County in a project discussed elsewhere in this chapter (Center for Fine Arts Education, 2014).

Two international assessment systems in music merit mention here. The system established by the Associated Boards of the Royal Schools of Music (ABRSM) is one of the most mature and highly respected music assessment systems in the world. The ABRSM has over 700 examiners in 90 countries.[4] The ABRSM rubrics present clear marking criteria for pieces, scales and arpeggios, and sight-reading, and aural tests for grades 1–8[5] (Associated Boards of the Royal Schools of Music, 2014). Scaife (2013) reports that these rubrics provide reliable international benchmarks for music performance; however, there are no technical reports available to support this claim. The International Baccalaureate (IB) program in music publishes clear assessment objectives for its standard and high-level programs, as well as specific markbands and markschemes (International Baccalaureate Program, 2014). Haaf (in press) reports that the curriculum and assessments are in revision. There are no technical reports available for the IB Music measures either (Brophy, personal communication, October 13, 2013), but the IB program and its assessments are used in schools scattered across the United States. ABRSM's assessments are largely ignored in the United States. The authors believe, however, that these graded exams represent a significant resource for assessment developers in the United States.

The International Symposia on Assessment in Music Education (Brophy, 2008, 2010; Brophy, Lai, & Chen, 2014; Brophy & Lehman-Wermser, 2013) are a series of conferences that specifically focus on assessment issues in music education. Brophy (2011) completed a topical analysis of the 109 papers published from the first three symposia. Results revealed that 82 percent addressed assessment methods and practice.[6] In that group, 40 percent addressed classroom music assessment, 13 percent addressed large-scale efforts, and 29 percent addressed assessment in music teacher education. This analysis and the ongoing work presented in this chapter make clear that the majority of music educators are still coming to terms with defining and implementing good practice in assessment at the classroom level.

Visual Art Education

In the field of visual art education, portfolios have been used for many years and are the single most widely used strategy for assessing student art production (Beattie, 1997; Dorn, Madeja, & Sabol, 2004; Sabol, 2001b; Sabol & Zimmerman, 1997). The College Board's Advanced Placement (AP) program includes what is perhaps the most widely known implementation of art portfolios in large-scale assessment in the United States. Since the Studio Arts Program first began in 1972 with a single portfolio, the number of arts AP courses and exams has gradually increased to include Music Theory; Art History; Studio Art: 2-D Design; Studio Art: 3-D Design; and Studio Art: Drawing. Portfolios are submitted in AP Studio Art: 2-D Design; Studio Art: 3-D Design; and Studio Art: Drawing (College Board, 2014).

The College Board routinely conducts curriculum surveys of colleges, universities, and art schools focusing on the content of courses that AP courses are intended to parallel (Sims-Gunzenhauser, 1999); the 2-D and 3-D portfolios were added in 1999 and a reconstructed Drawing Portfolio was released in 2002 (Myford & Sims-Gunzenhauser, 2004). In all AP courses except Studio Arts, students take an exam which consists of multiple-choice questions and an essay section. Studio Arts students complete a portfolio assessment. Items submitted in the portfolios usually represent the work of one year and are scored by visual arts teachers. Portfolios receive a score on a scale of 1 to 5, with 5 representing the highest ranking of "Extremely Well Qualified" (McElroy, 2009).

The 2-D Design Portfolio demonstrates the student's competency in the use of composition on a two-dimensional surface. Works in the 3-D Design Portfolio relate to design concepts, but are executed in three-dimensional space. The Drawing Portfolio includes works that demonstrate students' drawing abilities broadly defined, which can involve a variety of media and kinds of work. Each of the portfolios in Studio Arts includes three subsections: Quality, Concentration, and Breadth. *Quality* is the overarching value and figures into the success of the work in the other two sections. The *Concentration* section includes works that are unified by an underlying idea that has visual and/or conceptual coherence. The *Breadth* section requires that students demonstrate a range of abilities with technique, problem solving, and ideation (McElroy, 2009).

The IB program is also noteworthy for its use of assessment portfolios. In the arts, students may concentrate on subjects in music, theater, or visual arts. All students must complete a studio component and a research workbook. The IB program is unique in that it requires students to take responsibility for defining their own learning pathways. Independent research is expected in both studio and research components. Two fundamental requirements are that students demonstrate knowledge of more than one cultural context and that their studio and research notebooks be closely related through the investigations undertaken. IB assessments require that students exhibit portfolios of their work containing finished works and working pieces demonstrating the process of their research. An external examiner visits the school and conducts an interview with the candidate. Following the interview, the external examiner issues a holistic grade for the studio work using the following five criteria: Imaginative Expression, Purposeful Exploration, Meaning and Function, Formal Qualities, and Technical and Media Skills. The research workbook is evaluated using the following criteria: Independent Research, Critical Research, Contextual Research, and Visual Research.

A key aspect of IB assessment practice is the *moderation of grades.* This is a collaborative judgment process undertaken by teachers to ensure that equivalent work done by students in different classrooms and schools is rated equally. The purpose of moderation is to reduce variations of interpretations among differing examiners. The moderation process is dependent upon the practice of benchmarking. Benchmarks are samples of student work selected by moderators to exemplify specific levels of achievement. The work samples indicate the limits of performance within each level. Benchmarks typically take the form of actual examples of student work.

Teachers of AP and IB courses typically undergo substantial training to deliver the curricula. The success of their students on the examinations associated with those curricula naturally plays a role in the annual goals and evaluation of these teachers.

Portfolio Issues and Challenges

Historically, one challenge with managing the portfolio process was storage of the works generated. Digital technology has alleviated this problem somewhat. Improvements in digital photography and storage capabilities have enabled art students to create digital reproductions of their studio works for inclusion in digital portfolios. Electronic storage has also made digital portfolios more accessible and transportable.

Not surprisingly, the proliferation of digital portfolios has raised other questions. Art educators questioned whether their evaluations of digital or virtual portfolios would be consistent with their evaluations of the same portfolios in physical form (i.e., as a result of reviewing students' actual works). Dorn et al. (2004) suggested that when arts educators evaluate digital versions of students' portfolios, the holistic ratings they assign are very similar to their ratings of portfolios of those students' physical works. Dorn and Sabol (2006) investigated whether scores produced from art teachers' evaluations of digital copies of works of art were consistent with scores produced from evaluations of these same works in their physical forms ($n = 178$ secondary students, $n = 29$ secondary teachers). Using a one-group pre-test/post-test design, teams of three art teachers completed two holistic evaluations of students' portfolios at the midpoint and the end of the semester. The teams assessed four works of art at the midpoint adjudication; four additional works were added to each portfolio for the second adjudication. All portfolios were submitted in their physical and digital forms. The adjudications were blind-scored on a scale of 1 to 4, with 4 being high and 1 being low. To control for rater bias, each set of portfolios (digital and physical) was divided in half. Each team evaluated a different half of each set at the midpoint and final adjudications.

Evaluation data were compared using unmatched cases. The researchers examined intra-rater reliability using Hoyt's method (alpha) and the intra-class correlation based on an analysis of variance. Findings revealed no significant differences between the scores assigned to the digital versions of portfolios and those assigned to their original, physical versions; digital portfolio scores matched scores assigned to their physical counterparts in 95 percent of the cases. This finding suggests that the medium in which artwork is presented—i.e., digital or physical—does not affect how art educators are likely to evaluate portfolios. The findings also suggested that art teachers can be trained to use this process to produce reliable evidence of students' learning.

Currently, quantitative measures of learning are favored by the public, local school districts and by state and federal governments (Dorn et al., 2004; Kohn, 2000; McMillan, 2001; Popham, 2001, 2003; Sabol & Zimmerman, 1997). It appears that the portfolio evaluation process examined in this study can provide reliable and substantively meaningful indicators of learning in the art classroom. Moreover, these holistic evaluations produce data that can be easily stored and tracked over time and can become the basis upon which comparisons of achievement among classes and students and the progress of individual students can be made. As the availability and use of digital technology increases in the field, the use of these tools for evaluating arts achievement is likely to grow in importance as well.[7]

Dance Education

Large-scale assessments in dance are not as numerous as those developed for music and visual arts. There are fewer dance education programs in schools in comparison to the other arts education disciplines, although the dance education community continues to work toward achieving equal representation. The following challenges to dance education impact the assessment of learning in dance education programs in K–12 schools.

1   *Lack of appropriate teaching credentials/certificate at the state level.* There are 38 states in the United States that issue a K–12 teaching credential/certificate in dance. In other states, dance is taught within the Physical Education (P.E.) curriculum. This heterogeneity in the qualifications of the teachers who deliver dance content, the type of department to which dance education is assigned, and the amount and type of high school credit awarded for dance courses create great disparities in the quality and content of dance education available to students.

2   *Logistical pitfalls in obtaining a teaching credential/certification.* Dance educators often find it difficult to teach in states that do not grant dance certification, even if they hold credentials from other states. For example, some states require candidates to earn a second degree in P.E. and/or pass the P.E. Praxis exam. Hence, the very policies that are meant to prevent unqualified teachers from being hired often end up preventing qualified dance teachers from getting jobs or cause them to move to other states.

3   *Inadequate data collection at the federal level.* Because of the lack of national-level information on where dance education is offered, the identification and collection of assessment data in dance education is problematic. For example, dance items were developed and piloted for the 1997 arts NAEP, but were not administered in part because a viable sampling frame was not available. The exact number of dance education programs remains unknown.

4   *Lack of infrastructure to support dance as an art form.* It takes a while for change to happen in education. Dance found its way into the K–12 curriculum through P.E. In the *No Child Left Behind Act* (107th Congress, 2001), the arts—which include dance—were declared a core subject. However, Local Education Agencies (LEAs), districts, and schools can be slow to shift policies, make curriculum changes, and provide appropriate support for the arts.

Despite these challenges, large-scale dance assessments do exist. In January 2012, an e-mail survey of State Education Agency Directors of Arts Education (SEADAE) asked for a status report on statewide assessments in dance. Responses ranged from "we have assessments in dance" to "we do not have statewide assessments in the arts, but are interested in developing them at some point." Seven states (Rhode Island, Washington, North Carolina, Kentucky,

Illinois, New Jersey, and New York) reported having large-scale assessment systems in place that included dance as an art form. Additional research revealed two nationwide assessment initiatives in the United States (NAEP and SCASS/Arts) and five from other countries (New Zealand, England, Australia, Canada, and South Africa) (McGreevy, 2012).

Among U.S. arts assessment initiatives, the Rhode Island model (Rhode Island Department of Education, 2013) provides an example of a state-level assessment to determine students' qualifications for graduation. The assessment addresses the four traditional arts areas of dance, music, theater, and visual arts and promotes an integrated approach involving the preparation of a student portfolio, the administration of on-demand tasks, and end-of-course exhibitions. To earn a diploma under the Rhode Island Department of Education's Proficiency-Based Graduation Requirements (PBGR) model, students are required to demonstrate achievement of the state's high school grade span expectations in six core areas: English/language arts, mathematics, science, social studies, the arts, and technology.

The Rhode Island Arts Learning Network (2013) was formed to support the arts as one of the six core areas and successfully advocated for a requirement that each graduating student has demonstrated proficiency in at least one art form. The Network provides the structure, rubrics, and guidance for assessment in the arts; it is up to LEAs to implement and manage them. To further support this work, the Network created proficiency teams in the visual arts, dance, music, and theater. The teams began in January 2003 to define what proficiency for "all kids" might look like at graduation. In the case of dance and theater, where there are few certified professionals in the schools, the professional associations put together educator-community teams who are trained to judge proficiency. These teams of trained evaluators can be contracted by the districts and schools to evaluate student work and determine proficiency. Working with a Rhode Island Skills Commission consultant, the dance educator-community team created a handbook for individual students, as well as for both school-based and private sector teachers, that provides guidance in the process, common tasks, and rubrics. This unconventional assessment system allows for students who do not have an in-school dance program to meet proficiency in dance.

Rhode Island subsequently refocused its assessment efforts to align with the demands of the Common Core, and the state's arts assessment work was suspended to focus on high-stakes testing in reading, writing, and mathematics. While the PBGRs still exist, the authority to determine the level of achievement required for proficiency in the arts was subsequently delegated to school districts, schools, and individual certified arts educators. However, the Rhode Island model is promising for a number of reasons. For schools it makes learning more visible and encourages community buy-in and support. For teachers it supports student-centered instruction and relevant content beyond preparation to answer questions on a test. For students it provides clear expectations, authentic experiences, and a positive opportunity for them to follow their passion. For schools, districts, and states it provides a unique model that can be adopted or adapted to assess proficiency for graduation and to guide the development of digital portfolios designed to demonstrate student or teacher success. Reports indicate that numerous teachers are drawing on these assessment tools to fulfill their teacher evaluation requirements.

Theater Education

Arguably the most significant recent contribution to the assessment of student learning in theater was completed by the Colorado Content Collaboratives. In 2011–12, the Colorado Department of Education (CDE) commissioned a theater team to research current national and international drama and theater arts assessments that might ultimately inform the creation of similar assessments in Colorado. The first step was to find the most useful sets of standards available. They obtained standards documents from ten states (Connecticut, Florida, Indiana, Kentucky, Massachusetts, New Jersey, New York, Rhode Island, South Carolina [South Carolina Arts

Assessment Project], and Washington) and from nine countries (Singapore, Scotland, Australia [New South Wales], Canada, Ireland, the Netherlands, Finland, Sweden, and New Zealand). They also reviewed documents from the IB theater program and materials available from the Theatre Communications Group. After obtaining these standards documents, the team contacted these sources to determine whether aligned assessments were also available.

The team then evaluated the assessments based upon the extent to which each offered authentic assessment examples aligned with Colorado's Academic Standards and GLEs. Some of the assessments were outdated and required significant modification to meet Colorado's new standards, including the 21st-century learning and workforce readiness standards. In particular, the team identified a need for assessments that involved more open-ended inquiry and encouraged students to engage in creative thinking. As a result, some were reworked to go beyond the traditional emphasis on assessing basic skill attainment and recall of factual information (i.e., the focus on paper-and-pencil testing that produces easily quantifiable results but only requires that students exercise lower levels of cognition when responding to the items).

In the absence of readily available theater assessments from other sources, the Colorado assessment bank represents an important contribution to the field, as well as a centralized databank of vetted assessments to which educators in all art forms can refer.

State Arts Assessment Systems

In this section we describe briefly a select sample of state approaches to arts assessment. We use the term *system* to describe these efforts inasmuch as these systems comprise elements that work together to provide arts educators with assessment tools, tasks, and, in some cases, data on their students' progress. While many of these tools are being used or adapted by teachers to satisfy teacher evaluation requirements, at present no state arts assessment system is linked to school or district accountability systems.

Some states such as Kentucky and Washington developed assessment systems that were stimulated by state law or policy. Others such as Tennessee and Colorado have responded directly to the federal NCLB waiver policy (U.S. Department of Education, 2014) or have used Race-to-the-Top funds to enable state arts assessment development and implementation (U.S. Department of Education, 2010). Florida is a state that has engaged some field-initiated state-level assessment development in music (Brophy, 2008) but whose recent efforts arise from the federal policies associated with NCLB waivers. The Connecticut system, on the other hand, arose in response to demand from the field (CSDE, 2014b).

Kentucky

The Commonwealth of Kentucky implemented arts and humanities assessment for students in grades 5, 8, and 11 from 1992 through 2008, as part of a state-mandated battery of assessments that addressed several core content areas (Kentucky Department of Education, 1999). Because the unit of analysis was the school and not the individual student, the Kentucky Instructional Results Information System (KIRIS) was able to minimize the interruption of instruction by using matrix sampling, in which each student completed only one subset (form) of the full set of items designed to measure a content domain. The weighting of arts scores in the state's accountability system evolved over time and varied somewhat among grade levels, but by 2008 constituted between 5 percent and 7 percent of each school's overall index.[8]

Although Kentucky's assessment system was laudable in its sustained commitment to the measurement of arts learning and consequential weighting of that achievement in a school's index, the comprehensiveness of its arts items was constrained by their pencil-and-paper format, which was in turn dictated by limited resources. As a part of the Department of Education's planning process, assessable arts outcomes were sorted into three tiers, with the goal of evolving toward the capacity to measure more complex, authentic performance outcomes at Tier Three:

- Tier One: Outcomes assessable through pencil-and-paper stimuli and pencil-and-paper response—mostly Responding in the performing arts, with some potential for drawing in visual art and design work in theater;
- Tier Two: Outcomes assessable through multimedia stimuli and pencil-and-paper response—i.e., Responding across a richer array of artwork, including video and audio performances; and
- Tier Three: Outcomes assessable through multimedia stimuli and multimedia response—i.e., Creating or Performing.

Although Kentucky designed and implemented performance tasks across the state at the beginning of the assessment program in 1992, assessment environments were deemed too variable and scoring too unreliable to continue this effort. As a result, throughout the remainder of its existence, KIRIS was limited to Tier One assessment, using a pencil-and-paper format for both the presentation of stimuli and entry of student responses.

Kentucky's experience became an illustration of the unintended consequences for curriculum of construct underrepresentation in high-stakes arts testing. Because KIRIS results—including student performance on arts items—were linked to school evaluation, and the Tier One format limited arts items primarily to factual knowledge, many arts teachers reported pressure to refocus their curriculum on arts facts at the expense of Creating and Performing (Shepherd, 2013).

Tennessee

In Tennessee, arts educators spearheaded the development of a practical teacher evaluation system for teachers of "non-tested" subject areas. Public praise from the U.S. Secretary of Education, Duncan (2010), has focused considerable national attention on this approach and its developers (Shuler, 2012). Teachers collect evidence in portfolios documenting standards-based student growth in at least three of four domains that parallel the Artistic Processes: Create, Perform, Respond, and Connect.

Tennessee arts teachers select for their portfolios a small but varied sample of students whose growth they will monitor, thereby reducing the scope of assessment and the quantity of data to be managed. Teachers design and administer pre- and post-assessments to measure growth in relation to state standards and submit their scored portfolios of student work at the end of the year via digital upload, for review during summer institutes. The system emphasizes professional development to maximize consistency in scoring among teachers and calibrates moderators or peer reviewers to verify teachers' scoring during summer institutes (Tennessee Department of Education, 2014a).

Florida

Legislation and regulations in some states require that standardized assessments comprise a significant percentage of the evaluation of each teacher's overall success. In the absence of—or sometimes in addition to—the existence of formal arts measures, scores on statewide standardized English/language arts and mathematics assessments are factored into teachers' evaluations. To address the need for standardized arts measures, Florida is among the states that have initiated development of such tools.

In 2011, Florida's Department of Education issued a multimillion-dollar grant to the Polk County Public School District to develop the "Race to the Top" Florida Performing Fine Arts

Assessment for dance, music, and theater (Center for Fine Arts Education, 2014). Polk County involved teams of arts educators in each discipline, but subcontracted technical development to the American Institutes for Research. The Responding section of the Performing Fine Arts Assessment will be administered via an online test platform. The performance task portion, where the students will actively demonstrate mastery through performance, is currently under construction. The students will perform "prepared tasks" (note the similarity to Michigan's "performance tasks") and "on-demand tasks" (Michigan's "performance events") as well as creating works of their own through improvisation, writing, composing, or designing.

Washington

The State of Washington and Connecticut assessment initiatives share a number of similarities and are often cited together as examples of state-developed arts performance assessments intended for curriculum-embedded use.

In 2003 the Washington Office of Superintendent of Public Instruction (OSPI) formed assessment teams to assist in the development of classroom-based assessments that are now referred to as OSPI-Developed Performance Assessments for the Arts. The development of the Washington assessment tasks/items included:

- Reviews for content and bias/sensitivity—Assessments were reviewed by OSPI, teams of teachers, and community members from across the state.
- Pilot testing—Items were piloted across the state.
- Pilot range finding—Teams of teachers were trained to conduct range finding.
- Data review—Assessment responses were reviewed to ensure items assessed what was expected. Holistic rubrics developed and refined through piloting.
- Benchmarking—Student work was selected to illustrate levels of achievement in the rubrics.

In 2004, the legislature passed a bill that required districts to have in place assessments or other strategies at the elementary, middle, and high school levels to assure that students have an opportunity to learn the state standards in the arts and to report their implementation of these assessments annually through an implementation verification report. OSPI recommends that districts use the OSPI-developed assessments. If local assessments or other strategies are used to meet the requirements, it is strongly recommended that they are reviewed for quality and alignment to state standards, are based in research, and are able to measure individual student achievement. School districts are encouraged to develop policies and procedures that support the implementation of assessments in these areas, as well as the collection and retention of assessment data. In addition to the required reporting, which began in 2008, districts are asked to provide optional reporting information including which assessments were administered and at what grade levels (State of Washington OSPI, 2014).

As part of the state's educator evaluation system, the teacher and the evaluator decide which assessments are appropriate for demonstrating student growth. OSPI-developed performance assessments are on the list of possibilities, although there are no state requirements that these must be used. Some districts do have in place local requirements about which can be selected.

Connecticut

The Connecticut State Department of Education has been engaged in arts assessment training, development, refinement, and implementation for nearly two decades. As a result of this work, Connecticut's Common Arts Assessment initiative offers a comparatively mature set of arts performance tasks. Launched by the Connecticut State Department of Education in 2006 in collaboration with the Connecticut Arts Administrators Association, the task design and piloting process has subsequently been joined by educators from Massachusetts and New Hampshire.

The Common Arts Assessment initiative produces unit-embedded music and visual arts performance assessments for voluntary classroom and districtwide uses that:

1   gather data on student learning useful in improving instruction;
2   focus curriculum on key learning outcomes;
3   provide models of quality units with embedded assessment;
4   clarify standards through clear rubrics and benchmark student work;
5   reveal gaps among schools in students' opportunity to learn in the arts; and
6   promote professional learning communities among arts educators around instruction, assessment, and quality expectations.

Like Washington's OSPI-developed project (State of Washington OSPI, 2014), the Common Arts Assessment initiative has focused on the development of embedded performance assessments. In addition, the Connecticut tasks:

- are designed, piloted, refined, and benchmarked with anchor student work by practicing classroom teachers over a period of several years;
- provide varied types and combinations of analytic (multiple-trait) scoring tools, according to the dictates of each task; and
- are disseminated via CTcurriculum.org and MeasureSuccess.org, open-access, dynamic websites that enable teachers to "clone," edit, and adapt existing tasks and scoring scales, as well as share their own work by posting online (EASTCONN, 2015).

Connecticut's task development process began with a series of deep discussions and surveys to determine which content and skills called for by the 1994 arts standards are most central to student learning at each grade level. Multi-year, iterative cycles of piloting, revision, and repiloting enabled developers to:

- clarify and align each assessment with the constructs that were the foci of each task;
- minimize construct-irrelevant variance through experimentation with various types and degrees of scaffolding that minimize the degree to which below-level reading and writing skills impede students' written responses while maximizing the amount of useful information those responses provide;
- ensure feasibility of the tasks for use in a variety of classroom settings; and
- refine scoring tools to maximize the extent to which scorers arrived at the same scores for the same student work to strengthen inter-rater reliability.

Although measuring student growth and teacher accountability were not explicit goals for the project, a number of teachers and district leaders in Connecticut and other states report that they have adopted or adapted these assessments for such purposes.[9]

Michigan

The Michigan Arts Education Instruction and Assessment (MAEIA) project was developed by the Michigan Assessment Consortium for the Michigan Department of Education. The goal of MAEIA is to create and disseminate model resources for Michigan educators that foster high-quality arts programs. As of this writing, the student assessment phase of this project is still a work in progress. It is, however, worthy of mention because of its scope (dance, music, theater, and visual arts at all grade levels), the collaborative nature of the task development process, and ongoing efforts to subject each assessment item to appropriate psychometric review.

To encourage a supportive context for arts achievement and to provide a means for improving arts education programs, the project first produced two documents oriented toward opportunity-to-learn. The *Michigan Blueprint of a Quality Arts Education Program* (Michigan Assessment Consortium, 2013a), which defines a high-quality arts education for schools engaged in ongoing improvement processes, is supported with a compendium of research and recommendations (*Michigan Blueprint of a Quality Arts Education Program—Research and Recommendations*, Michigan Assessment Consortium, 2013b). A companion research-based tool, the *Michigan Arts Education Program Review Tool* (Michigan Assessment Consortium, 2015), can be used by local educators to analyze and improve school or district arts education programs, based on the criteria for high-quality arts education programs.

The *Model Michigan Arts Education Assessments* are designed to serve as interim benchmark assessments for use throughout the school year. Collectively, they span the four art forms in grades K–2, 3–5, 6–8, and 9–12. At the high school level, the assessments are divided into three levels, based on the number of years of high school-level arts course enrollment, in order to provide assessments for beginning students as well as those who are more advanced. Teachers may select performance assessments from this pool that match their curriculum, then use these assessments at the conclusion of instruction to document student learning and achievement. MAEIA leaders anticipate that teachers will use these assessments in their educator evaluation process to improve instruction and student learning.

More than 300 stand-alone performance "events" and "tasks" were developed for release and field testing. Performance events are one-day, on-demand assessments, while performance tasks are administered over multiple class periods and may involve homework. All items underwent content review and, as of this writing, are undergoing a process of field testing and further revision. Each item requires student reflection and is accompanied by teacher scoring rubrics. Although individual teachers are responsible for scoring, project leaders will be identifying benchmark (anchor) student work based on field testing to inform that scoring.

The performance assessments align with Michigan's grade-level arts content expectations, which were approved by the State Board of Education in 2011. However, because they are organized by three "strands" paralleling the Artistic Processes—create, perform, and respond—they reflect many of the National Core Arts Standards released in 2014 (Dewsbury-White & Roeber, 2015).

Colorado

Colorado's arts assessment initiative is presented last here because it uniquely attempted to compile the best of then existing arts assessments developed elsewhere and resulted in an online listing of vetted tasks widely used as a resource by educators in other states.

In 2012, the CDE implemented a "New Assessments" system in all content areas that was fully aligned with the Colorado Academic Standards. Due to the lack of readily available large-scale assessments in the arts that had sufficient validity evidence and reliability data to support their use in teacher evaluation, the CDE formed groups of Colorado teachers called the Colorado Content Collaboratives to participate in a comprehensive review of existing arts assessments, funded by a grant from the *Race to the Top* initiative (U.S. Department of Education, 2010). After receiving appropriate training and professional development, these groups reviewed performing arts assessments from a wide variety of sources. The search for arts assessments revealed that most readily available assessments were published on the Internet by practitioners or available from for-profit companies, usually as part of a software or textbook program (Colorado Department of Education, 2014b).

Colorado education officials directed the teachers in the Collaboratives to evaluate each arts assessment using a comprehensive Assessment Review Tool (Colorado Department of Education, 2014a). The tool was "designed to help Colorado educators rate an assessment's appropriate potential for measuring student academic growth aligned to the Colorado Academic Standards." During the research and review process, the Colorado arts assessment team leaders identified a need among arts educators for professional development in assessment literacy, including "validity and reliability, purposeful sampling, observational data collection for data-based decision making in instruction, [and] how to develop an authentic body of evidence" (Gates, 2014).

Based on these criteria, the reviewers used their professional judgment to recommend, partially recommend (i.e., the assessment was recommended for the Colorado Resource Bank only if modifications were made), or not recommend each assessment (Colorado Department of Education, 2014a) for its Resource Bank (2014b). The Collaboratives recommended 16 Music assessments, 5 Dance assessments, and 10 Drama assessments. The Collaboratives partially recommended 16 Music assessments, 11 Dance assessments, and 9 Drama assessments. A number of these tasks were selected from the Connecticut and Washington initiatives. At the time of this writing, no Visual Arts assessments were listed.

While the Resource Bank presents a good snapshot of available arts assessments that have been developed and vetted, no validity evidence is provided. The majority of the assessments reviewed by the Colorado teachers were not standardized and lacked information regarding reliability or validity; they involve the performance of specific tasks, sometimes related to the originating school district's standards, or at least to the individual teacher's interpretation of them in her/his classroom. Teachers and school districts are given the responsibility for determining the purpose of the assessment, how the assessment is to be used, and making any necessary adjustments to align the assessment to the intended purpose. The responsibility for developing validity arguments, therefore, lies with the user.

The Resource Bank assessments are presented as options for educators, and not as mandates. The guidance to educators indicates that they could be used as part of a body of evidence for teacher evaluation. It is up to the educator and his/her administrator to determine whether the assessment is aligned with and supports local curriculum and whether it is appropriate for use in evaluation. This raises a number of questions related to the expertise of the individuals making these decisions and the appropriate use of assessment results. Nevertheless, Colorado's online database of arts assessments provides a useful source of vetted tasks for the field.

Developing the Next Generation of Arts Assessments

With the exception of the Commonwealth of Kentucky's school evaluation system, there have been no high-stakes uses of arts assessment until the recent trend toward growth-based teacher evaluation and competency-based graduation systems. The absence of serious consequences and attendant legal defensibility issues has led arts leaders to develop assessments in an organic, grassroots fashion, with little policy impetus (with the exception of the 2011 NCLB waiver policy) or funding support. Arts assessment efforts have also been used for advocacy purposes, driven by the belief that measuring the extent to which arts educators are fostering student learning documents the value of the arts to the educational enterprise. As a result, arts assessment systems have focused on creating practical, authentic items and tasks, often with minimal consideration of psychometric issues.

We have asserted throughout this chapter that it is imperative for arts learning to be measured authentically. As Brophy (2014) stated, "In the arts we teach what we value, and we measure what we value most." The degree to which arts assessments simulate what artists do is a primary guiding framework for their development. We have described the rigorous authentic assessment development processes in the arts, and these processes continue to produce high-quality assessments that possess the instructional utility that is valued by teachers who have limited time with students.

These authentic assessments present several measurement challenges. First, educators must capture sufficient data to analyze the technical properties of the assessments. This challenge has been difficult to meet because of widely varied opportunities to learn in the arts. The MCAs are the first well-designed national models that can be adapted to the diverse opportunity-to-learn conditions in American public schools. The Music pilot and field test discussed below is groundbreaking for the arts because, for the first time, a diverse national K–12 data set will be captured and analyzed taking opportunity-to-learn variables into account; this model should be replicable with the visual art, theater, and dance assessments. Once the assessments meet current measurement standards, the next challenge will be to link authentic assessment data to accountability systems. Arts educators have much work ahead of them.

Although arts educators' focus on authentic performance assessment has enabled them to avoid the distortions of curriculum that have occurred as a result of high-stakes assessment systems in other content areas (with the exception of Kentucky's cautionary tale, mentioned above), the very fact that these tools have been developed without consideration of high-stakes accountability has minimized discussions of psychometric issues. Little information is, therefore, available on the technical properties of the measures used for arts performance assessments. There are, however, encouraging signs in recent studies such as Wesolowski, Wind, and Engelhard's (2015) examination of rater analyses of music performance assessment using the Many Facet Rasch model and in the planned examination of the technical properties of the MCAs.

In this chapter, we have laid out the development of arts assessment in the disciplines and have briefly described a few state arts assessment systems as well as plans for developing MCAs associated with the National Core Arts Standards initiative. In the process, we have highlighted several key development and measurement challenges associated with arts assessments. In the next section, we focus on the development of the new MCAs and address a number of validity concerns.

MCAs in the Arts

The new National Core Arts Standards released in June 2014 included, for the first time, a draft set of MCAs to

> illustrate how student learning can be assessed through rich performance tasks with clearly identified criteria … The term cornerstone is meant to suggest that just as a cornerstone anchors a building, these assessments should anchor the curriculum around the most important performances that students should be able to do (on their own) with acquired content knowledge and skills.
>
> (National Coalition for Core Arts Standards, 2014, pp. 9, 15)

The MCAs in all five art forms are written for three grade spans in grades PreK–8 (PreK–2, 3–5, and 6–8) and three levels for high school (Proficient, Accomplished, and Advanced); the music ensemble and harmonizing instruments strands will also include MCAs for two preparatory levels (Novice and Intermediate) roughly corresponding to grades 5 and 8, respectively. They are designed to "reflect genuine and recurring performances that become increasingly sophisticated across the grades" (National Coalition for Core Arts Standards, 2014, p. 16). For consistency across the art disciplines, the format of the MCAs is based on a common template (State Education Agency Directors of Arts Education, 2014) that closely parallels the template developed and refined over time for tasks in Connecticut's CTcurriculum.org website

(Connecticut State Department of Education, 2014a) and MeasureSuccess.org. Over an anticipated two- to three-year piloting period, benchmark student work (a.k.a., anchor sets) will emerge from piloting and refining these assessments, which will provide visual and aural illustrations of the expectations outlined in the standards.

The National Association for Music Education, National Art Education Association, Educational Theatre Association, and National Dance Education Organization have each assembled at least one discipline-specific team of researchers and practitioners to guide the MCA piloting and benchmarking process, so that when administered the resulting tasks will provide information regarding students' attainment of the skills and knowledge contained in the standards.

A Promising Example: The Development of Music MCAs

The development of each Music MCA is spearheaded by a research advisor. To ensure a balance between theoretical and practical considerations in the design and review process for each MCA, a research advisor—who is typically a university professor in music education—collaborates with practicing K–12 classroom teachers and program leaders who helped develop the National Core Music Standards for the relevant grade level or strand. The deliberate, utilitarian design of the assessments allows for their adaptation to a variety of instructional contexts, an essential characteristic for large-scale, authentic arts assessments.

Each MCA focuses on one Artistic Process and is designed to measure students' ability to carry out every component (step) of that process. For example, the Performing assessments provide assessment procedures to collect and score student work for the process components of select; analyze; interpret; rehearse, evaluate, and refine; and present. MCAs for each Artistic Process are designed to be parallel across grade levels, to facilitate tracking students' longitudinal growth within the categories of Creating, Performing, and Responding.

The primary purpose of the initial round of prepiloting is to assess and refine the utility of the instructionally embedded measures. Music MCAs prepiloted during the 2014–15 school year included Creating and Performing MCAs for general music in grades 2, 5, and 8; a Responding MCA for general music in grade 8; and a Performing MCA for the intermediate (grade 8) level in the ensemble strand.

The research advisor partners with a member of the National Core Arts Standards writing team to train and manage a group of music educator piloters. Pilot participants answered a nationwide call issued by the National Association for Music Education and were selected on the basis of documented assessment expertise and experience. The majority of participants are highly experienced teachers who collectively represent a variety of states and demographics and operate in a variety of opportunity-to-learn contexts. Teachers involved in the pilot receive instructional assistance, professional development, and training in scoring student work in order to improve score comparability across administration conditions, performance tasks, and student populations.

The data collected in the initial prepilot phase will include pre-, during-, and post-perception survey questions to gather participant perceptions of and suggestions for improving (a) the alignment of the assessment content with the National Core Arts Standards, (b) instructional strategies recommended in the MCAs, and (c) the practicality of administration of the MCAs under the teacher's particular opportunity-to-learn conditions. Planned data collection also includes (a) individual student analytic scores for each process component assessment, (b) at least one example of student work for each achievement level of each process component from each piloting teacher, and (c) teacher scores of student work, both of work that is submitted as a potential benchmark and entire class score sets. To facilitate examination of inter-judge reliability, teachers will not only score their own students' work but also blind-score samples of student work from other teachers.

Analyses of prepilot data will be both qualitative and quantitative. For example, research advisors will apply statistical analyses to establish intra- and inter-rater reliabilities and to identify needed refinements to assessment procedures and scoring tools. Content validity will be addressed comprehensively both within and across grade bands for all process component constructs. Context validity (Skinner, 2012) will be examined to identify factors that might influence a teacher's ability to administer the assessment and provide some evidence of external validity across a variety of settings, students, teachers, and contexts. The pilot will also provide evidence of consequential validity and the impact of the assessments on the participants' instructional time and responsibilities for producing performances and programs.

Validity

Throughout this chapter we have presented concerns regarding the lack of validity evidence in arts assessments. Lehman (2014) refers to the "case of the Mysterious Missing Validity" in the use of assessment in music teacher evaluation (p. 12); Colwell (2014) remarks that "validity is probably the most important concept in assessment and least understood" (p. 84). The development of validity arguments for arts assessments is a paramount concern for the field, especially when developing assessments for accountability purposes. We have documented that the field has increased arts assessment development in recent years, but validity arguments are often missing from the available materials.

We also find evidence of promising practices in some state systems that bear attention. For example, in Colorado, a bank of existing assessments developed for a variety of purposes has been reviewed by trained groups of teachers and recommended for consideration for a variety of different uses, including possibly as instruments for the measurement of student growth for teacher evaluation. The inferences from scores and ratings from arts assessments developed for one purpose may not be appropriate for another purpose. Koch (2013) points out that "interactions among any of the multiple uses of an assessment are a concern for the validation process" (pp. 8–9). Koch suggests that one way to address this concern is to begin the process of validation "by determining the multiple uses associated with a large scale assessment" (pp. 12–13). The Colorado model requires that individual teachers and districts determine the appropriate uses of the recommended assessments, opening the possibility for unsupported inferences from the results.

We have noted that arts assessment developers often equate validity with authenticity, based on the erroneous belief that if an assessment is authentic it is automatically valid. Arts assessments have also relied heavily on content validity and construct representation arguments, assuming that if the assessment covers the content taught it is valid by default. Alignment with the content taught does not necessarily provide evidence that the inferences made from the results comport with its intended use, although as Marion and Buckley (Chapter 3, this volume) acknowledge, "One can think of performances that are convincingly authentic, such as a painting or music performance." The key, they suggest, is "to remember that assessments are valuable to the extent that they lead to the types of interactions between the student and the task that generates evidence that is necessary to support desired inferences" (p. 50).

We are particularly encouraged by the validity examination built into the development process for MCAs in music. As the MCA pilot and field tests continue, we must bear in mind Kane's (2009) warning that confusion can occur if our validation process is not separated from the actual data interpretation.

Arts assessments are subject to many of the same validity threats as all assessments. For example, reading and writing skills required for certain arts assessments pose potential construct-irrelevant validity threats. Opportunity-to-learn conditions and their impact on arts learning and assessment have been discussed earlier in this chapter. Arts assessments that attempt to rely on pencil-and-paper stimuli and response modes (i.e., the "Tier One" level that limited the effectiveness of the arts items in Kentucky's annual assessments), and even assessments that provide authentic, media-rich stimuli but limit student responses to the pencil-and-paper format (termed "Tier Two" in the Kentucky model), inherently suffer from construct underrepresentation because they cannot measure students' ability to carry out the Creating and Performing Processes that comprise roughly two-thirds of arts curricula. The definition of assessment dimensions for the arts and the carefully considered design features of the MCAs have attempted to address these concerns a priori; the planned pilot and field testing described above provides assessment researchers with the opportunity to examine the extent to which construct underrepresentation exists in those measures.

A Way Forward

The purposes of this chapter have been to review the evolution of the measurement of arts learning, to describe key challenges in the current age of accountability, and to identify promising strategies that have emerged to address those challenges. We have outlined the philosophical, practical, logistical, and psychometric issues inherent in the assessment of students' performances of complex artistic tasks. To conclude, we address the broader national issues that continue to influence the development and implementation of arts assessment and propose a way forward to address those issues.

In the arts, we continue to argue that students learn from rich and engaging experiences, as well as from meaningful artistic interactions. However, the availability and depth of those experiences vary widely across schools and districts. Limited arts instructional time is the opportunity-to-learn issue that has the most impact on student learning, especially when compared to the amount of instructional time that districts allocate to other content areas that are the focus of current large-scale statewide testing. Challenging local conditions have not, however, deterred arts teachers from continuing to cultivate their students' artistic literacy and skill; from delivering a full, diverse, and rigorous curriculum; and from seeking effective ways to measure their students' learning.

For many years, individual classroom teachers have shouldered the entire burden of designing arts assessments to measure students' attainment of content knowledge and skills addressed in their curricula. Fortunately, high-quality measures are being developed and made accessible to practitioners and program leaders. We have described a number of state initiatives in which arts professionals have collaborated to create arts assessments that are based on nationally recognized standards and are designed to be used in multiple contexts and classrooms. These assessments provide an unprecedented array of thoughtfully designed and stakeholder-vetted assessment tools and materials that enable measurement of students' arts learning. Large-scale field testing is needed to identify unanticipated practical concerns related to varying opportunity-to-learn conditions in schools. The success of such initiatives will ultimately rely on partnerships between arts professionals and educational measurement specialists (such as members of the National Council on Measurement in Education).

Portfolios are well-established, authentic tools frequently used by professional artists and musicians. However, for the purpose of measuring arts learning among large numbers of students in public school settings, the logistics of managing collections of portfolios remains a concern. If portfolios are to be used on a large scale for measuring arts learning or growth, they must be facilitated by technology, meet acceptable standards for psychometric rigor, and be supported by convincing validity evidence. Indeed, because arts teachers in public schools often serve hundreds of students, the increasing availability of "smart" technological devices and sophisticated software programs for classroom assessment is already having a major positive impact on the collection, management, and objective interpretation of results from all forms of arts assessment.

There *is* a way forward with assessment in the arts that can meet the practical needs of educators who are working under highly diverse school conditions:

1   We must increase the assessment literacy of teachers. Preservice teacher programs should prepare teachers for classroom assessment; arts education program accreditation standards should include specific requirements for such training; and graduate programs that specialize in measurement in the arts are needed. In-service professional development for arts educators should include participation in rubric development and calibration to enable teachers to carry out assessment scoring in a rigorous, reliable, and valid manner. A teacher's ability to appropriately administer, score, and interpret results from arts assessments should become a condition of continued, or even initial, employment.

2   The profession must create banks of well-designed, professionally vetted, psychometrically sound items/tasks that are standards-based, adaptable to varying school conditions, and fair to all students. NCCAS and several states represented in SEADAE have agreed to make MeasureSuccess.org their common platform for the dissemination of high-quality performance tasks. This site is also designed to facilitate essential processes such as cloning and adapting tasks, benchmarking, calibration, and moderation. Indeed, arts educators' leadership in the development of MeasureSuccess.org serves as an excellent example of how innovations in arts assessment can pave the way for improved practices in other content areas, as the site is designed to facilitate performance assessment in any discipline.

3   Arts teachers working in high-volume arts programs should have access to technologically facilitated digital data collection software and electronic scoring tools to assist them in their efforts to assess students' learning.

4   Arts educators must partner with educational measurement specialists to design assessments that measure important outcomes of learning in the arts and to conduct appropriate analyses and validation studies. The synergies between research and practice that the SCASS/ Arts and NCCAS MCA initiatives achieved provide models worthy of emulation.

Controversies about what an increasingly large and vocal number of citizens deem to be American education's excessive emphasis on standardized assessments, especially in core subjects, have inspired vigorous discussions about how a more constructive convergence of curriculum, instruction, and assessment might be achieved. "Teaching to the test" supports learning when the test demands understandings and behaviors that are important, authentic, and curriculum-aligned. Such beliefs have inspired the Smarter Balanced Assessment Consortium and the Partnership for Assessment of Readiness for College and Careers to develop a new generation of assessments to measure students' attainment of the Common Core State Standards.

James W. Pellegrino, member of the technical advisory committees for both consortia, is among those who foresee a new day in educational measurement. In an *Education Week* article titled "The Coming Age of Instructionally Integrated Testing," he described how such new systems might work:

> I think we need to give a whole lot of thought and emphasis to the development of quality tools and materials that can support teachers in enacting assessment as part of a learning environment in the classroom. In other words, we need to spend less time being so preoccupied with the large-scale standardized accountability tests. We still need to have assessments that do that kind of monitoring, but I and a lot of other people in the assessment field think that we need to reverse the emphasis. We need to focus on assessment for learning at the classroom level …

Really good assessment of the type we're thinking about doesn't look all that different from really good instruction—or the kinds of tasks we would want students to engage in the classroom …

I don't think you can enact some of these more powerful uses of assessment at the instructional level without technology to help manage the process … so you don't put the entire burden on teachers.

(Rebora, 2014, questions 4, 5, and 6)

Arts teachers observe student performance, assess progress, and provide feedback in real time. We posit that the arts classroom is one place in the school where instruction and assessment are well integrated as a matter of standard practice. In the future, arts assessment should—and will—look different than current forms of standardized testing. Arts students will engage in rich, instructionally integrated performance tasks that have met professional and measurement standards and offer sufficient validity evidence to support their use for their intended purposes. Information thus gathered may be supplemented through efficient, psychometrically robust assessments that address areas of the arts curriculum—particularly Responding—that lend themselves to on-demand testing. All of these assessments will be delivered, scored, and the results interpreted by teachers who are assessment literate. They will have participated in standard setting and/or rater calibration sessions, and they will be adept at storing, managing, and monitoring their data digitally. They will receive expert feedback about their scoring from outside moderators, who will access and review their student work and scores remotely.

The arts classroom has always been a place where instruction and assessment meet seamlessly— where learning and its assessment are so closely related as to be nearly indistinguishable and where, as Colwell (2015) states, context *matters*. We concur with Pellegrino that this is the best model for all disciplines. The arts education profession is poised to lead the transition from overreliance on large-scale standardized testing practices to context-sensitive, rigorous measurements of student learning that assess the acquisition and application of content knowledge, skills, and processes throughout the instructional process. We believe this is the future of assessment, and the arts are in its vanguard.

Notes

1 There has been only one formal statewide accountability system for arts learning to date. The Kentucky Arts and Humanities Index was part of that state's accountability system from 1992 to 2008.
2 The capitalized words "Artistic Process" will be used to refer to this system of organizing arts learning, to distinguish it from other processes associated with artistic work. Similarly, the capitalized form of Creating, Performing, and Responding will be used throughout this chapter to refer to *Artistic Processes*, thereby distinguishing them from the simple action verbs of creating, performing, and responding. The same convention will apply to Presenting and Producing.
3 Examples of innovative, teacher-developed solutions to issues associated with assessing Creating in the arts, as well as examples of scored student artwork, can be found in Connecticut's Common Arts Assessments posted on CTcurriculum.org (Connecticut State Department of Education, 2014b) and MeasureSuccess.org.
4 There are no ABRSM examiners in the United States.
5 In the ABRSM system, grades 1–8 do not comport with U.S. grade levels. ABRSM grades are levels of skill and technical difficulty, starting with the easiest or lowest level of difficulty in grade 1 and progressing through grade 8, the most advanced level. Students progress to the next grade level when they pass the exams and performance assessments for their current grade level.
6 The rest of the topic breakdown was as follows: 7 percent addressed curriculum, 4 percent addressed law and policy, and 7 percent addressed the application of measurement theory.
7 For more information on the use of arts assessments, see Dorn et al. (2004) and Sabol (2001a, 2001b, 2004a, 2004b, 2006a, 2006b, 2009).

8 The authors were unable to locate any source to describe the formulae or processes for how the arts and humanities index was calculated.

9 A detailed description of the background, development process, and key learnings from this ongoing project are presented in *Connecticut's Common Arts Assessment Initiative: Helping Teachers Improve Learning in a Data-Driven School Environment* (Shuler & Wells, 2010).

References

103rd Congress. (1994, March 31). Goals 2000: Educate America Act. *Public Law 103–227(Section 102(3)(A))*, 3–5. Washington, DC: U.S. Congress.

107th Congress. (2001). House Resolution 1, Statute 115, 1425 2002 (enacted). *Public Law 107–110, No Child Left Behind Act of 2001 (short title) [Electronic Version]*.

American Educational Research Association (AERA), American Psychological Association (APA), & National Council on Measurement in Education (NCME). (2014). *Standards for educational and psychological testing*. Washington, DC: AERA.

Associated Boards of the Royal Schools of Music. (2014, August 25). *Graded music exam marking criteria*. Retrieved from http://us.abrsm.org/en/our-exams/information-and-regulations/graded-music-exam-marking-criteria

Beattie, D. (1997). *Assessment in art*. Worcester, MA: Davis.

Brophy, T. S. (2008). The Florida music assessment project: An association-driven model of large scale assessment development. In T. S. Brophy (Ed.), *Assessment in music education: Integrating curriculum, theory, and practice* (pp. 139–152). Chicago, IL: GIA Publications, Incorporated.

Brophy, T. S. (Ed.). (2010). *The practice of assessment in music education: Frameworks, models, and designs*. Chicago, IL: GIA Publications, Incorporated.

Brophy, T. S. (2011, September 15). *A topical analysis of papers presented at the International Symposia on Assessment in Music Education*. Presented at the 2011 Society for Music Teacher Education Symposium, Greensboro, NC.

Brophy, T. S. (2014, July). *A declaration of interdependence: A facets model of arts assessment leadership*. Keynote address presented to the SEADAE Arts Assessment Leadership Institute, Chevy Chase, MD.

Brophy, T. S., Lai, M.-L., & Chen, H.-F. (Eds.). (2014). *Music assessment and global diversity: Practice, measurement, and policy*. Chicago, IL: GIA Publications, Incorporated.

Brophy, T. S., & Lehman-Wermser, A. (Eds.). (2013). *Music assessment across cultures and continents: The culture of shared practice*. Chicago, IL: GIA Publications, Incorporated.

Brophy, T. S., & Perry, J. (2007). *The Florida music assessment (FMA) 2007 elementary phase 1 field test report*. Gainesville, FL: Unpublished report to the Florida Music Educators Association Executive Board.

Center for Fine Arts Education. (2014, August 19). *RTTT performing fine arts assessment project*. Retrieved from http://cfaefl.org/AssessmentProject/InnerPage.aspx?ID=7

Chapman, L. (1982). *Instant art, instant culture: The unspoken policy for American schools*. Reston, VA: National Art Education Association.

College Board. (2013). *International arts education standards: A survey of the arts education standards and practices of thirteen countries and regions*. New York, NY: College Board.

College Board. (2014, August 20). *Course home pages*. Retrieved from http://apcentral.collegeboard.com/apc/public/courses/teachers_corner/index.html

Colorado Department of Education. (2014a, August 18). *Assessment review tool, RT-6-2-2014*. Retrieved from http://www.coloradoplc.org/assessment/assessment-review-tool-0

Colorado Department of Education. (2014b, August 18). *CDE Resource Bank: Assessments*. Retrieved from http://www.coloradoplc.org/assessment

Colwell, R. (1967). *Elementary music achievement test administration and scoring manual*. Chicago, IL: Follett Publishing Company.

Colwell, R. (1969). *MAT Music Achievement Tests 1 and 2 interpretive manual*. Chicago, IL: Follett Education Corporation.

Colwell, R. (1970a). The development of the Music Achievement Test series. *Bulletin of the Council for Research in Music Education, 22*(Fall), 57–73.

Colwell, R. (1970b). *MAT Music Achievement Test 3 administration and scoring manual.* Chicago, IL: Follett Education Corporation.

Colwell, R. (1970c). *MAT Music Achievement Test 4 administration and scoring manual.* Chicago, IL: Follett Educational Corporation.

Colwell, R. (1979). *Silver Burdett music competency tests.* Morristown, NJ: Silver Burdett.

Colwell, R. (2008). Music assessment in an increasingly politicized, accountability-driven educational environment. In T. S. Brophy (Ed.), *Integrating curriculum, theory, and practice: Proceedings of the 2007 Symposium on Assessment in Music Education.* Chicago, IL: GIA Publications, Incorporated.

Colwell, R. (2014). The black swans of summative assessment. In T. S. Brophy (Ed.), *Music assessment and global diversity: Practice, measurement, and policy* (pp. 67–100). Chicago, IL: GIA Publications, Incorporated.

Colwell, R. (2015, February 18–21). Tergiversation today: Interpreting validity. In T. Brophy, J. Marlatt, & G. Ritcher (Co-chairs), *Connecting practice, measurement, and evaluation.* The 5th International Symposium on Assessment in Music Education, Williamsburg, VA.

Connecticut State Department of Education (CSDE). (2014a, August 25). *Task search.* Retrieved from http://www.ctcurriculum.org

CSDE. (2014b, August 18). *Arts—common arts assessment.* Retrieved from http://www.sde.ct.gov/sde/cwp/view.asp?a=2618&q=320840

Council of Chief State School Officers. (2014). *SCASS/Arts glossary of assessment terms.* Washington, DC: Council of Chief State School Officers.

Dewsbury-White, K. D., & Roeber, E. (2015). Unpublished correspondence with leaders of the Michigan Assessment Consortium, Lansing, MI.

Digication. (2014, March 27). *Digication assessment management system (AMS).* Retrieved from https://www.digication.com/k-12/assessment

Dorn, C. M., Madeja, S., & Sabol, F. R. (2004). *Assessing expressive learning.* Mahwah, NJ: Erlbaum.

Dorn, C. M., & Sabol, F. R. (2006). The effectiveness and use of digital portfolios for the assessment of art performances in selected secondary schools. *Studies in Art Education, 47*(4), 344–362.

Duncan, A. (2010). *Prepared remarks of U.S. Secretary of Education Arne Duncan on the report Arts Education in Public Elementary and Secondary Schools: 2009–10.* Retrieved from http://www.ed.gov/news/speeches/prepared-remarks-us-secretary-education-arne-duncan-report-arts-education-public-eleme

EASTCONN. (2015). MeasureSuccess.org

Gates, K. (2014, February). Interview regarding the Theatre Assessment Research Team results (M. Schuttler, Interviewer).

Gordon, E. E. (1969). Intercorrelations among Musical Aptitude Profile and Seashore Measures of Musical Talents subtests. *Journal of Research in Music Education, 17*(3), 263–271.

Gordon, E. E. (1970). *Iowa tests of music literacy.* Iowa City, IA: Bureau of Educational Research and Service, University of Iowa.

Gutkin, T. B. (2000). In A. E. Kazdin (Ed.), *Encyclopedia of psychology* (Vol. 1, p. xiv). Washington, DC: American Psychological Association; New York, NY: Oxford University Press. doi:10.1037/10516-192

Haaf, C. (in press). The impact of assessment design on teaching and learning in music. In T. Brophy, J. Marlatt, & G. Ritcher (Eds.), *Connecting practice, measurement, and theory: Proceedings of the 5th International Symposium on Assessment in Music Education.* Chicago, IL: GIA Publications, Incorporated.

Herpin, S. A., Washington, A. Q., & Li, J. (2012). *Improving the assessment of student learning in the arts—State of the field and recommendations.* Retrieved from http://www.nea.gov/research/ArtsLearning/WestEd.pdf

International Baccalaureate Program. (2014, August 25). *Diploma programme: Group 6, the arts.* Retrieved from http://www.ibo.org/en/programmes/diploma-programme

Kane, M. (2009). Validating the interpretations and uses of test scores. In R. W. Lissitz (Ed.), *The concept of validity: Revisions, new directions, and applications* (pp. 39–64). Charlotte, NC: Information Age Publishing, Incorporated.

Kentucky Department of Education. (1999, September). *Core content for arts and humanities assessment.* Retrieved from http://www.e-archives.ky.gov/pubs/Education/arthumanitiescc30.pdf

Koch, M. (2013, Winter). The multiple-use of accountability assessments: Implications for the process of validation. *Educational Measurement: Issues and Practice, 32*(4), 2–15.

Kohn, A. (2000). *The case against standardized testing: Raising the scores, ruining the schools.* Portsmouth, NH: Heinemann.

Lehman, P. (2014). How are we doing? In T. S. Brophy, M.-L. Lai, & H.-F. Chen (Eds.), *Music assessment and global diversity: Practice, measurement, and policy* (pp. 3–17). Chicago, IL: GIA Publications, Incorporated.

Long, S., & Moran, J. (1995). *Maine educational assessment.* Unpublished manuscript, Maine Department of Education, Augusta, ME.

Lovins, L. T. (2010). Assessment in the arts: An overview of states' practices and status. In T. S. Brophy (Ed.), *The practice of assessment in music education: Frameworks, models, and designs* (pp. 23–42). Chicago, IL: GIA Publications, Incorporated.

McElroy, P. (2009). *Evaluating the AP portfolio in studio art.* New York, NY: College Board.

McGreevy, S. (2012, January). Email survey for Colorado Department of Education.

McMillan, J. H. (2001). *Essential assessment concepts for teachers and administrators.* Thousand Oaks, CA: Corwin.

Messick, S. (1994). The interplay of evidence and consequences in the validation of performance assessments. *Educational Researcher, 23,* 13–23.

Michigan Assessment Consortium (MAC). (2013a). *Michigan blueprint of a quality arts education program.* Lansing, MI: MAC.

MAC. (2013b). *Michigan blueprint of a quality arts education program—Research and recommendations.* Lansing, MI: MAC.

MAC. (2015). *Michigan arts education program review tool.* Lansing, MI: MAC.

Music Educators National Conference (MENC). (1994). *National standards for arts education: What every young American should know and be able to do in the arts.* Reston, VA: MENC.

Myford, C. M., & Sims-Gunzenhauser, A. (2004). The evolution of large-scale assessment programs in the visual arts. In E. W. Eisner & M. D. Day (Eds.), *Handbook of research and policy in art education* (pp. 637–666). Reston, VA: National Art Education Association.

National Assessment Governing Board (NAGB). (1994). *1996 arts education assessment framework: Pre-publication edition and arts education assessment and exercise specifications for the 1996 National Assessment of Educational Progress (NAEP).* Washington, DC: NAGB.

National Coalition for Core Arts Standards (NCCAS). (2014, August 20). *National Core Arts Standards: A conceptual framework for arts learning.* Retrieved from http://www.nationalartsstandards.org/sites/default/files/NCCAS%20%20Conceptual%20Framework_4.pdf

New England Secondary School Consortium (NESSC). (2014). *Home page.* Retrieved March 27, 2014 from http://newenglandssc.org

New York State Education Department. (2014, February 16). *New York state district-wide growth goal setting process: Student learning objectives* (Rev. March 2012). Retrieved September 2015 from https://www.engageny.org/resource/student-learning-objectives

Parsad, B., & Spiegelman, M. (2012). *Arts education in public elementary and secondary schools: 1999–2000 and 2009–10 (NCES 2012–014).* Washington, DC: National Center for Educational Statistics, Institute of Education Sciences, U.S. Department of Education.

Persky, H. R., Sandene, B. A., & Askew, J. M. (1999). *The NAEP 1997 arts report card: Eighth grade findings from the National Assessment of Educational Progress.* Washington, DC: U.S. Department of Education, Office of Educational Research and Improvement, NCES 1999–486.

Popham, W. J. (2001). *The truth about testing: An educator's call to action.* Alexandria, VA: Association for Supervision and Curriculum Development.

Popham, W. J. (2003). Preparing for the avalanche of accountability tests. In Harvard Education Letter (Ed.), *Spotlight on high-stakes testing* (pp. 9–15). Cambridge, MA: Harvard Education Press.

Rebora, A. (2014, March 5). *The coming age of instructionally integrated testing.* Interview with James Pellegrino for *Education Week.* Retrieved from http://www.edweek.org/tm/articles/2014/03/05/ndia_pellegrinoqa.html

Rhode Island Arts Learning Network. (2013, August 26). *Arts proficiency FAQs.* Retrieved from http://riartslearning.com/proficiency/faq.php

Rhode Island Department of Education. (2013, August 26). *Instruction and assessment: Other subjects.* Retrieved from http://www.ride.ri.gov/InstructionAssessment/OtherSubjects.aspx

Roeber, E. (2013). *Michigan music assessments 1972–2014.* Unpublished manuscript obtained via correspondence.

Sabol, F. R. (2001a). *Reaching out to rural and urban art teachers in the western region of the National Art Education Association: Needs assessment and identification of new members.* Reston, VA: National Art Education Foundation.

Sabol, F. R. (2001b). Regional findings from a secondary analysis of the 1997 NAEP art assessment based on responses to creating and responding exercises. *Studies in Art Education, 43*(1), 18–34.

Sabol, F. R. (2004a). The assessment context: Part one. *Arts Education Policy Review, 105*(3), 3–9.

Sabol, F. R. (2004b). The assessment context: Part two. *Arts Education Policy Review, 105*(4), 3–9.

Sabol, F. R. (2006a). Identifying exemplary criteria to evaluate studio products in art education. *Art Education, 59*(6), 6–11.

Sabol, F. R. (2006b). *Professional development in art education: A study of needs, issues, and concerns of art educators.* Reston, VA: National Art Education Foundation.

Sabol, F. R. (2009). Stepping back: An objective look at the impact of assessment on art education. In F. R. Sabol & M. Manifold (Eds.), *Through the prism: Looking into the spectrum of writings by Enid Zimmerman* (pp. 139–150). Reston, VA: National Art Education Association.

Sabol, F. R. (2010). *No Child Left Behind: A study of its impact on art education.* Reston, VA: National Art Education Foundation, National Art Education Association.

Sabol, F. R., & Zimmerman, E. (1997). An introduction: Standardized testing and authentic assessment research in art education. In S. D. La Pierre & E. Zimmerman (Eds.), *Research methods and methodologies for art education* (pp. 137–169). Reston, VA: National Art Education Association.

Scaife, N. (2013, April 11). *The role of criteria in the assessment of instrumental performance: How graded exams provide reliable international benchmarks.* Paper presented at the 4th International Symposium on Assessment in Music Education, Taipei, Taiwan.

Seashore, C. E. (1915). The measurement of musical talent. *The Musical Quarterly, 1*(1), 129–148.

Seashore, C. E. (1939). Psychology of music. *Music Educators Journal, 26*(1), 31–33.

Seashore, C. E. (1940). Measures of musical achievement. *Music Educators Journal, 26*(4), 24, 70.

Seashore, C. E. (1960). *Seashore measures of musical talents* (Rev. ed.). New York, NY: The Psychological Corporation.

Shepherd, P. (2013). Message from former arts and humanities consultant in the Kentucky Department of Education describing the history of arts assessment in the state.

Shuler, S. C. (1991). The effects of Gordon's learning sequence activities on vocal performance achievement of primary music students. *The Quarterly, 2*(1–2), 118–129.

Shuler, S. C. (1996). The effect of standards on assessment practices (and vice versa). In S. C. Shuler, (Ed.), *Aiming for excellence: The impact of the standards movement on music education* (pp. 81–108). Reston, VA: Music Educators National Conference.

Shuler, S. C. (2008). Large-scale assessment of music performance: Some hows and whys for today's data-driven educational environment. In T. S. Brophy (Ed.), *Assessment in music education: Integrating curriculum, theory, and practice* (pp. 123–138). Chicago, IL: GIA Publications, Incorporated.

Shuler, S. C. (2011a). The three artistic processes—Paths to lifelong 21st-century skills through music. *Music Educators Journal, 97*, 9–13.

Shuler, S. C. (2011b). Music assessment part I: What and why. *Music Educators Journal, 98*(2), 10–13.

Shuler, S. C. (2012). Music assessment part II: Instructional improvement and teacher evaluation. *Music Educators Journal, 98*(7), 7–10.

Shuler, S. C. (2015). *Model cornerstone assessments: Clarifying standards, supporting learning.* Paper presented at the 5th International Symposium on Assessment in Music Education, Williamsburg, Virginia.

Shuler, S. C., & Connealy, S. (1998). The evolution of state arts assessment: From Sisyphus to stone soup. *Arts Education Policy Review, 100*(1), 12–19.

Shuler, S. C., Lehman, P., Colwell, R., & Morrison, R. (2009). Music assessment and the nation's report card: MENC's response to the 2008 NAEP and recommendations for future NAEP in music. *Music Educators Journal, 96*(1), 12–13.

Shuler, S. C., & Wells, R. (2010). Connecticut's common arts assessment initiative: Helping teachers improve learning in a data-driven school environment. In T. S. Brophy (Ed.), *The practice of assessment in music education: Frameworks, models, and designs* (pp. 43–55). Chicago, IL: GIA Publications, Incorporated.

Simons, G. M. (1976). *Simons measurements of music listening skills.* Chicago, IL: Stoelting Co.

Sims-Gunzenhauser, A. (1999). [Results of the 1998 Advanced Placement studio arts curriculum survey]. Unpublished raw data.

Skinner, C. H. (2012, December). Contextual validity: Knowing what works is necessary, but not sufficient. *The School Psychologist.* Retrieved from http://www.apadivisions.org/division-16/publications/newsletters/school-psychologist/2012/12/contextual-validity.aspx

SmartMusic. (2014, March 27). *Assessment.* Retrieved from http://smartmusic.com/onlinehelp/desktop/content/assessment.htm

State Education Agency Directors of Arts Education. (2014, August 20). *NCCAS MCA blank template 6-30-14.* Retrieved from http://www.nationalartsstandards.org/#

State of Washington OSPI. (2014, August 18). *OSPI-developed performance assessments for the arts.* Retrieved from http://www.k12.wa.us/Arts/PerformanceAssessments/default.aspx

Tennessee Department of Education. (2014a, June 22). *About the model.* Retrieved from https://sites.google.com/site/tnfineartsportfoliomodel/home/about-the-model

Tennessee Department of Education. (2014b, March 24). *The GLADiS project.* Retrieved from https://sites.google.com/site/tnfineartsportfoliomodel/home/gladis--the-online-portal

U.S. Department of Education. (2010, April 14). *Race to the top fund phase II applications CFDA 84.395A.* Retrieved from http://www.grants.gov/search/search.do?mode=VIEW&oppId=53746

U.S. Department of Education. (2014, July 20). *ESEA flexibility options.* Retrieved from http://www2.ed.gov/policy/elsec/guid/esea-flexibility/index.html

Vaughan, S. (1993). Evaluation of arts education in Minnesota: A description of Minnesota's arts assessment programs. In R. J. Colwell & R. J. Ambrose (Eds.), *Measurement and evaluation special interest group newsletter* (Winter 1993 ed., Vol. 14, pp. 5–15). Boston University.

Watkins, J. G., & Farnum, S. E. (1954). *The Watkins–Farnum performance scale.* Winina, MN: Hal Leonard Music, Incorporated.

Wesolowski, B., Wind, S., & Engelhard, G. (2015, February). *Rater analyses in music performance assessment: Application of the many facet Rasch model.* Paper presented at the 5th International Symposium on Assessment in Music Education, Fredricksburg, VA.

9 Assessment Issues in World Languages

Margaret E. Malone and Paul Sandrock

Introduction

In this era of accountability, assessment has taken center stage in education for teachers, students, administrators, parents, and community members. For many teachers, not only do assessment results demonstrate what their students are learning, these results also provide evidence that is increasingly being used as part of a state's system to evaluate teaching effectiveness. For world languages, a core subject according to the Elementary and Secondary Education Act (but one not mandated for annual testing), the public focus on national or state testing has been less than that in other subjects. Nonetheless, assessment initiatives from within the world language education community have positioned languages as a subject area that develops key competencies and frames a system for eliciting evidence to demonstrate these competencies. Broad national assessments may not be in place for world languages as they are for other disciplines, but rigorous content standards together with competency-based standards of performance provide strong support for local and state-level efforts to transition language learners from K–12 to post-secondary education and the workplace. The National World-Readiness Standards for Learning Languages represent a broad consensus of language professionals across languages (including a growing number of language-specific organizations customizing the National Standards to consider unique features of each language and the cultures of those who use it), as well as across grade and institutional levels (from pre-kindergarten through university/college level; NSFLEP, 2006, 2015).

With so much mandated testing, states and districts may be understandably reluctant to add yet other requirements. Although many districts and schools in the United States provide outstanding world languages programs, there is no current consensus that identifies a national test that would both measure proficiency and allow for comparisons across states, districts, and schools.[1] As a result, this chapter takes a different view than many of the others. Rather than examining only current assessment practices, we will provide an overview of the current diversity of approaches to assessing world languages and offer challenges and opportunities for the future of world language assessment.

Test design is an exercise in eliciting the best evidence about learning outcomes possible under a variety of constraints. Those constraints range from time and available equipment for administration to the availability of appropriately trained professionals to rate and report results. In other words, every test needs to provide results about what students have learned or mastered, and, for world language assessment, there are a number of constraints in simply eliciting this information, as well as in rating the results. For language assessment, the constraints are both similar to and different from those for other subjects.

For example, alignment to the National Standards is central to determining the degree of attainment of world languages content. This demonstration requires a great deal of evidence about students' competencies on a spectrum of proficiency; much of that evidence is relevant to student literacy attainment, as defined in the *Common Core State Standards for English Language Arts and Literacy* (Common Core). The Common Core standards have become increasingly important in state testing in other core areas. And thus connections have been made between world languages standards and the Common Core. In order to highlight the relevance of world language learning, Figure 9.1 shows the three modes of communication of the National Standards and the proficiency levels through which learners' progress is aligned with the four strands of the Common Core standards.

As represented in Figure 9.1, the Common Core standards in the reading strand match the assessment of the interpretive mode of communication in the National Standards for world languages. Similarly, the ten standards in the Common Core writing strand match the assessment of the presentational mode, as do standards four through six in the Common Core speaking and listening strand; the first three standards in the Common Core speaking and listening strand match the assessment of the interpersonal mode; and the six standards in the Common Core strand of language match the descriptions of the continuum of proficiency levels from the American Council on the Teaching of Foreign Languages (ACTFL) Proficiency Guidelines (ACTFL, 2012b): Novice, Intermediate, and Advanced.

These links with Common Core add value to the assessment of language performance, in which students demonstrate their developing literacy through authentic tasks, contexts, and materials in a non-native language. Simultaneously, the standards of Common Core provide a deeper understanding of how literacy skills develop through performances in each mode of communication. For example, Common Core Speaking and Listening Anchor Standards 1–3 emphasize comprehension and collaboration, underscoring in the interpersonal mode of the National Standards the importance of negotiating meaning through a collaborative process.

The Common Core standards, referenced frequently throughout this volume, highlight the importance of opportunities for students to demonstrate their knowledge and ability both in writing and orally. Both skills are important, but spoken language has a heightened importance in world language assessment compared with other subject areas (Lowe, 1988). While many learn a world language to read and write texts in that language, oral communication, including understanding and responding to spoken language, is often considered the hallmark of language proficiency. Designers of world language assessments have long struggled with ways to appropriately and efficiently test the variety of ways language is used, and testing oral language is a particular challenge. Perhaps the greatest constraint is the time necessary to elicit and rate spoken language. Writing can be elicited from a full class of students at the same time. Capturing student-to-student conversations presents unique logistic challenges. Assessments of spoken language may require technology to record the language with ease and clarity among dyads, as well as within an entire classroom.

As a result of being a core subject under No Child Left Behind (NCLB), but one that is not required to be tested under NCLB (Rosenbusch, 2005), world language instruction and assessment does not necessarily follow a standard path across the United States or even within a state or district. The elements of a first-year Spanish language class, for example, may vary widely depending on the teacher, the textbook, where it is being taught, and the background of the students who comprise the class. Therefore, students may enter into world language study and the assessment of their progress with different expectations; students who move from one state to another may find themselves behind or advanced in comparison to their new peers, with no standard assessment to document their previous experience or to help place them into an appropriate course. The variety of student experiences and skills is a hallmark of world languages and demonstrates the challenge of assessing world language outcomes.

Because there is no nationally adopted world language assessment or curriculum for world language learning, world languages have neither benefited from nor been disadvantaged by the testing pressure that has swept across K–12 education since 2001. One benefit

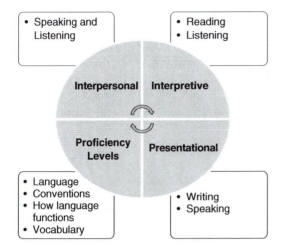

Figure 9.1 Model for aligning National Standards for learning languages with the Common Core
State Standards (ELA).

Source: ACTFL (2012c).

is that world languages have been able to develop classroom-based approaches to specifying
competency-based assessment outcomes without being subject to the public visibility and
assessment emphases that have influenced other disciplines. The assessment of languages has
benefited from more than two decades of experience at all levels of education in describing
proficiency outcomes (ACTFL Proficiency Guidelines, ACTFL, 1986) and learning outcomes
(Performance Descriptors for Language Learners, ACTFL, 2012a; NCSSFL-ACTFL Can-Do
Statements, NCSSFL-ACTFL, 2013). As a result, states, districts, and schools have created
numerous examples of connecting curriculum, instruction, and assessment around a common
set of standards. For this reason, although world languages suffer from a lack of consistent
implementation of instruction, as well as a lack of agreed-upon evidence of student outcomes,
the field has a valuable perspective to offer other subject areas in the realm of assessment while
also benefiting from the lessons learned in those areas.

The audience for this chapter is broad: policymakers who wish to understand the context for
world language assessment, the for-profit and not-for-profit organizations that develop language
assessments, colleagues in state and local education agencies, as well as preservice and in-service
teachers and teacher educators who need to understand the current state of assessment in world
languages. The goal is to help educators understand how their language assessment settings are
different or similar to others'. In addition, it explores how language assessment in instructional
settings links with the expectations of students, parents, teachers, administrators, and federal and
state education agencies.

To achieve these goals, the chapter first describes the opportunities and challenges of developing summative assessments for world languages. While no assessment instrument or battery
for language learners has attained national adoption or support, numerous promising examples
will be examined. Specifically, the chapter explores some current approaches to assessing world
languages, including formative and summative assessments. In this regard, the exploration of the
usefulness of existing assessments for young learners (elementary and middle school students)
and older learners (high school and post-secondary school students) outlines key issues concerning the assessment of constructs as complex as language, as well as ways to follow students'
progress in attaining language skills and proficiency. This analysis is followed by a report on the

results of a national survey of world language teacher assessment practices, which shows not only which assessments are available but also how teachers report using them in their programs. Following this survey, the chapter describes the potential impact of language assessments to provide motivation for students, to guide learners' self-reflection on their progress, and to inform educators' approaches to instruction and assessment, which, in turn, can inform their classroom strategies. The chapter also describes efforts to improve the assessment literacy of language teachers. It ends with reflections on future directions in world language assessment, as well as the challenges and opportunities facing developers and users of world language assessments.

Opportunities and Challenges in Assessing World Language Outcomes

Assessing language is a complex undertaking. Creating a summative assessment of a language learner's ability to use the language requires numerous decisions. Summative assessments based on the National World-Readiness Standards for Learning Languages (NSFLEP, 2006, 2015) need to incorporate means of collecting evidence that the language learner can use language in each of the three modes of communication: interpersonal, interpretive, and presentational. Each mode presents logistical issues that arise in tasks that seek to predict how well the learner may be able to function in authentic situations. Practical considerations include the need for efficient procedures to randomly pair students and record prompted conversations; identifying authentic selections for listening, reading, or viewing; providing age-appropriate tasks; and establishing contexts that require the learner to generate messages in different modalities (writing, speaking, visually representing).

Few assessments meet these criteria, due in part to the nature of language itself and in part to ongoing debates about what it means to know a language and some about an operational definition of language ability in a second language that is both widely accepted and amenable to the development of tasks that can be efficiently administered and rated. The difficulty of describing student performance, capturing it (via writing or recording), developing a system to rate the performance, and reporting the performance in a way that is understandable and meaningful to learners (and others) is an ongoing challenge.

These issues are relevant to both test reliability and validity. If student performance cannot be captured and rated consistently, then the test is not reliable and should not be used (Hughes, 2003). By contrast, test validity is a complex and never-ending challenge for test developers and test users. Validity is not a static property of a test; rather, it involves the evaluation of the appropriateness of the test with the interpretation and intended uses of the outcomes. Moreover, the argument that supports a test's validity at one point in time may not be acceptable as the test's uses and outcomes shift. Therefore, the assessment uses an argument model which differs from that used in previous decades, when validity was frequently described as a series of components—construct, content, criterion-related, face, internal and external, for example—rather than viewed from the standpoint of the test and its proposed uses as a whole (Bachman & Palmer, 2010; Cronbach, 1988; Harris, 1969; Hughes, 2003).

Generally, assessment is categorized as either formative (i.e., used as points-in-time checks to inform adjustments to instruction in the classroom setting, allowing for reflection on progress) or summative (i.e., administered at an end point, such as the unit, semester, or course, to measure acquisition of concepts or skills; Huhta, 2010). In assessing languages, as with all subject areas, it is desirable and important that what is being assessed (application of vocabulary, structures, and functions through differing modes of communication) is assessed the way it is taught (in this case, through a contextualized approach that allows for meaningful communication).

After designing engaging tasks and assembling them into an instrument that meets certain psychometric and logistic requirements, assessment designers must decide how the performances will be evaluated and what the reporting mechanism might be. If scored locally rather than at one central location, then raters need a deep understanding of the criteria for rating the language samples and extensive practice in understanding how to apply the criteria consistently. In language performance, rating goes far beyond counting errors; raters must consider how student performances show what they can do with the language, not just what they cannot do. If rated centrally by raters trained using standard procedures, factors such as cost and timeliness of receiving results become critical. Regardless of who evaluates the assessment performances, the audience using the results must be comfortable with the decisions made by the designer about how the performance was captured and how the results are rated and reported.

The development of summative world language assessments provides a number of opportunities for measuring language outcomes, and there are at least an equal number of challenges for test development. As recent surveys (ACTFL, 2010; Furman, Goldberg, & Lusin, 2007; Rhodes & Pufahl, 2011) show, Americans are studying a number of languages from kindergarten through university levels; in addition, world language programs in the United States follow a number of different models, varying greatly from the grade level at which instruction begins to the amount of time and the intensity devoted to language learning. Still the most prevalent program model is to offer world languages only in middle schools and high schools. Although an increasing number of schools and districts institute language learning in the elementary grades, programs' goals and results vary widely, ranging from two-way immersion (the goal of which is full academic fluency in two languages) to elementary school programs that provide students with some familiarity with a language and culture, mainly to instill some appreciation.

The wide variety of program models for providing instruction in world languages, coupled with the diversity of languages being taught, means that there are obstacles to having more than just a few nationally available approaches to determining student attainment of world language proficiency. Assessment instruments must be appropriate for the grade levels, program goals, languages, and cultures in which language learning is taking place. To further complicate the issue, as there is neither a mandated start time nor a specific language mandated for students to pursue (as in most European and Asian countries), world language assessments in the United States reflect a variety of approaches that may differ not only within a state but even from building to building in a school district. As a result, the lack of standard practices and shared tools may confuse all stakeholders, because different results are expected from different programs. Although national standards in all subject areas provide the broad outline of content for learning and assessment, world languages, unlike other subject areas, do not have an agreed-upon set of content objectives to serve as the focus for assessment. Instead, assessment of languages must indicate progress along a continuum of proficiency. The expected rate and level of growth will vary among learners, because the nature and length of their school experiences are so different. In addition, language learners bring their background to the language classroom, such as using the language at home, having lived in an area where the language is used, or being a heritage learner of the language. There is no single test or set of standards that all stakeholders use; therefore, not all language learners and teachers are working toward a single, or even similar, goal. Consensus on both standards and expected outcomes is essential to identify acceptable measures of performance.

Current Approaches to Assessing World Languages

At present, educators rely on a number of approaches to formative and summative assessment to measure student progress and attainment. As the focus of world language instruction shifted in the 1980s from the audio-lingual method to proficiency-based teaching, assessment slowly followed suit. However, testing the ability to communicate meaningfully is far more challenging than testing discrete points of grammar. Consequently, language educators required professional development and assistance in developing, administering, rating, and reporting the results of assessments, as well as generally incorporating new assessment approaches into their classrooms. Just as it took time for classrooms to move toward a communicative approach, that is, an emphasis on learning the language by using the language rather than by talking about the language and its grammatical forms, it has taken time for teachers to learn to assess student progress appropriately.

Understanding by design (UBD; Wiggins & McTighe, 2004) has gained popularity in teaching in general and language assessment in particular. This approach encourages language instructors to work deliberately to ensure that the assessments being used reflect the course goals and daily activities. In turn, such efforts mean that it is increasingly likely that summative assessments will better reflect classroom activities and outcomes, thus strengthening the alignment between summative and formative assessments. In assessing language outcomes, UBD allows test users to develop or select tests with different ranges of possible outcomes in mind.

The issue remains, though, of how world language educators understand, use, and apply National Standards in their teaching and assessment. As discussed earlier, the National Standards were first published in 1996. A recent survey was conducted through professional associations of language educators, resulting in 2,134 respondents representing language teachers, methods instructors, district supervisors/program chairs, or state supervisors. Seventy-eight percent of respondents indicated that they agreed or strongly agreed that the National Standards are reflected in their state standards or framework; 80 percent reported that their local or departmental curriculum or program of study is based on the National Standards and/or state standards (Abbott & Phillips, 2011). For the group surveyed, the professional development on implementing the standards had a tremendous influence on classroom instructional practices (85 percent of respondents), as well as the design of units and daily lessons (70 percent) and some impact on assessments (57 percent). However, these findings are limited to those who participated in the survey, namely those who had some connection to professional associations of language educators. Therefore, while the results of the survey provide data on a small sample of world language educators and their beliefs about the extent to which National Standards are reflected locally, these results cannot be generalized nationally to cover the national population of language educators at all levels (prekindergarten through post-secondary).

To illustrate an assessment designed explicitly around the National Standards (NSFLEP, 2006, 2015) to measure students' progress toward meeting those standards, we offer a description of the Integrated Performance Assessment (IPA). The IPA model was developed by ACTFL through a U.S. Department of Education International Research and Studies grant to help educators design effective assessments for each mode of communication (interpersonal, interpretive, and presentational) within the context of each classroom unit. The project goal was to model assessment of the standards, focused on the definition of communication and what it means to know a language, demonstrated in a meaningful context. The basic approach is to design an assessment for each mode of communication that can generate evidence commensurate with the expectations of performance in the context of a given thematic unit. The modes of communication are intended to emphasize the communicative purpose behind the use of language skills: interpersonal communication is the two-way spontaneous exchange of information, opinions, or emotions combining listening and speaking (or reading and writing as in text messaging); interpretive communication is understanding and analyzing the message that is heard, read, or viewed; and presentational communication is the creation of a message (spoken, written, or visually represented) for a specific audience and purpose. The assessment of the first mode can provide information or experiences that are linked to, or built upon, the second assessment (of another mode of communication). The assessment of the third mode of communication is also intended to build on the prior experiences and knowledge gained.

In principle, a thematically linked model can capture what students have learned and can do with the language—meaning that students are more likely to understand what is expected of them and where they should focus their efforts: that is, what would contribute most to improved performance. As a result, the IPA model is based on a thematic focus used in class (such as "healthy habits"). Each task cluster allows the student to build on his or her earlier performance and demonstrate proficiency in the context of the thematic focus and to carry out the task individually, in pairs, or in groups. The IPAs include sample rubrics to facilitate rating by instructors and enable them to relate student performance to ACTFL proficiency levels.

By focusing instruction on what is needed for students to improve their language performance and to be successful on the summative assessments, IPAs can help instructors to develop assessments consistent with their classroom goals. By implementing the IPA model, teachers and students can move from an emphasis on memorized vocabulary and isolated manipulation of grammatical structures to an emphasis on authentic application of language elements (vocabulary, structures, and functions).

Because this approach is still new, how it is used for various assessment needs across instructors, schools, districts, and states cannot be documented. Similarly, since the IPA is as much an approach to designing units of instruction as it is an assessment model, a validity argument consistent with Bachman and Palmer (2010) and other, more recent approaches to test validity has not yet been established. Therefore, although this approach shows some promise (Adair-Hauck, Glisan, & Troyan, 2013), a great deal of further research and analysis is needed.

The following section describes summative assessments available in the United States; the assessments are described according to the grade levels for which they have been developed.

Summative Assessments

To provide an overview of assessments currently available to pre-K–16 language instructors, we conducted a search of the Foreign Language Assessment Directory (FLAD), a free searchable directory of foreign language assessments hosted by the Center for Applied Linguistics (CAL) and supported by grants from the U.S. Department of Education. Updated annually, the FLAD provides information about foreign language assessments available in the United States as provided by test developers. An initial search of the FLAD revealed a number of assessments available for learners at different grade levels. For the purposes of this chapter, summative assessments take place after a period of teaching and learning to determine progress that has been made (Huhta, 2010).

Assessments for Young Learners

Although there are many world language programs for students in K–5 programs, there are few standardized assessments available to measure their progress. One assessment is the Early Language Listening and Oral Proficiency Assessment (ELLOPA; http://www.cal.org/ela/sopaellopa/). The assessment relies on paired interviews, or structured interactions between two students, facilitated by two trained interviewers. The format is designed to enable students to demonstrate their highest level of performance in oral fluency, grammar, vocabulary, and listening comprehension. The interviews include paired activities and age-appropriate manipulatives (such as puppets) that help elicit language. Interview tasks are developed to mirror the curriculum so that students are able to show what they have learned, which is particularly important for students with low levels of language proficiency (i.e., limited vocabulary in and experience with the language). Students interact not only with the interviewers but also with each other. The ELLOPA, developed by CAL, is available in Chinese, English, French, German, Japanese, Russian, and Spanish. Ratings are provided to schools and districts that use the ELLOPA via a written report that describes the proficiency levels attained by students within a grade level and compared to earlier results, when applicable. CAL provides local rater training as well as confirmatory ratings for school districts. Therefore, when school districts choose to use their own trained teachers or raters to assess students, districts can also ask for confirmatory ratings from CAL raters to track local rater accuracy.

Assessments for Older Elementary and Secondary Learners

There are a number of assessments available for learners above the second- and third-grade level. Some are designed specifically for learners in upper elementary or middle school, while others are available for learners at a range of grade levels. The most widely used instruments in the United States are described briefly below; we then comment on their applicability.

The ACTFL Assessment of Performance toward Proficiency in Languages (AAPPL; http://aappl.actfl.org) is an online assessment of the three modes of communication of the National Standards: interpersonal, interpretive, and presentational. The test taker is asked to help with a variety of functional tasks, such as rearranging a website by matching the sound clips with the appropriate photos on the webpage, responding to a blog to help foreign students learn more about the local school, or communicating via a simulated video chat with a foreign student to share information about the local school and community. The score report identifies for each mode selected where the test taker's performances are on a scale across the Novice and Intermediate ranges of performance. The score report also provides learners with specific strategies that will help the test taker move to the next higher level. The test is available in Arabic, Chinese, English, French, German, Portuguese, Russian, and Spanish. Approximately 17,000 students were assessed through AAPPL during January–May 2013. In 2014, approximately 30,000 students were assessed using AAPPL. AAPPL is considered appropriate for students in grades 4 through post-secondary. The score report is intended to serve as a useful diagnostic tool to help teachers of non-native speakers of languages, as well as heritage speakers, by identifying specific strengths and areas needing improvement for each mode.

AAPPL was used for a large-scale research project for the Flagship—Chinese Acquisition Pipeline (F-CAP), a consortium of programs mostly in Utah, Arizona, New Mexico, and Texas. Through the state departments of education and local districts in a total of 17 states, AAPPL was administered to gauge learners' progress toward the Flagship goal of reaching the advanced level by the end of high school. With the data from AAPPL for interpersonal, interpretive, and presentational modes of communication, F-CAP was able to determine whether students were making appropriate progress toward program goals based on information from learners in prior cohorts.

The Standards-based Measurement of Proficiency (STAMP4S) test is a computer-delivered test of discrete skills: listening, speaking, reading, and writing (http://avantassessment.com). Appropriate for students in grade 7 to university, the test is targeted at lower levels of proficiency, corresponding roughly to the ACTFL Novice and Intermediate levels. Available in Chinese, French, German, Hebrew, Japanese, Spanish, and Turkish, over 29,000 students in the United States and overseas took a STAMP test in the 2008–2009 school year (Avant Assessment, personal communication). The STAMP 4SE (formerly known as the National Online Early Language Learning Assessment) is similar to the STAMP; however, it was developed specifically for learners in grades 3–6. The STAMP 4SE is available in Chinese, French, Japanese, Korean, Russian, and Spanish.

Two additional tools, developed by CAL, were designed to measure student oral proficiency. These are the Student Oral Proficiency Assessment (SOPA) for grades 3–5 and the CAL Oral Proficiency Exam (COPE) for grades 6–12. Like the ELLOPA, the SOPA is a paired assessment of student oral proficiency and relies on activities administered by trained test administrators.

Like the ELLOPA, activities may combine manipulatives and puppets. The COPE is also a paired interview that relies on a trained administrator to elicit language; however, the COPE does not rely on manipulatives and puppets, because such objects are not appropriate for a middle school curriculum (http://www.cal.org/ela/cope/index.html). Similar to the SOPA and ELLOPA, score reports are provided in the form of a written report that describes the proficiency levels attained by students within a grade level and compared to earlier results, when applicable.

Tests for High School and Post-Secondary Students

There are a number of tests available for students at the high school and university levels that can be used to evaluate language competencies in any grade, for students transitioning from high school to post-secondary programs, and to provide high school and/or post-secondary credits. Several assessments are used for these purposes, but are not considered appropriate for younger students.

Commonly used in high school programs across the United States is the Advanced Placement (AP) Language and Culture Exam, currently available in Chinese, French, German, Italian, Japanese, Latin, and Spanish (http://apcentral.collegeboard.com/apc/public/courses/teachers_corner/index.html). Typically, students take the exam as the culminating summative assessment linked with the high school course. The exams for most languages have been recently revised to focus on the three modes of communication in the National Standards and a set of six broad themes. The AP exam is often used to grant college credit. In addition, each national organization devoted to a specific major language administers paper-and-pencil tests of language (the American Association of Teachers of Spanish and Portuguese administers its National Spanish Exam online). Finally, the International Baccalaureate (IB) program, gaining in popularity in the United States, currently provides in 800 schools the IB Diploma Programme (for ages 16 to 19) that requires students to study at least two languages and increase understanding of cultures, including their own. IB has tests for Arabic, Chinese, French, German, Japanese, Korean, Russian, and Spanish with paper-and-pencil materials and oral performance measures, engaging learners in a variety of comprehensive tasks (http://ibo.org/en/programmes/diploma-programme/assessment-and-exams/).

The ACTFL Oral Proficiency Interview (OPI) is a valid and reliable means of assessing how well an individual speaks a language (http://www.actfl.org/professional-development/assessments-the-actfl-testing-office/oral-proficiency-assessments-including-opi-opic). It is a 20- to 30-minute face-to-face or telephonic interview between a certified ACTFL tester and an examinee. The interview is interactive and continuously adapts to the interests and abilities of the speaker. The speaker's performance is compared to the criteria outlined in the ACTFL Proficiency Guidelines 2012—Speaking (ACTFL, 2012b) similar to the Inter-Agency Language Roundtable Language Skill Level Descriptors—Speaking (Interagency Language Roundtable, n.d.). The interview is double-rated and an Official ACTFL Oral Proficiency Certificate stating the candidate's proficiency level is issued to the candidate. Tens of thousands of ACTFL OPIs are conducted annually for academic, commercial, and government purposes in over 80 languages. The American Council on Education established recommendations for college credit to be awarded based on the proficiency level demonstrated through the official OPI rating. In addition, the ACTFL OPI is available in an online version (OPIc), where the test taker begins by completing a questionnaire of background information from which content is placed into the question templates asked by the onscreen avatar. Certified raters then evaluate the test taker's responses. A special K–12 OPIc is available to assess Novice Low through Advanced Low, the range of performance second language learners typically achieve in K–12 settings. In addition to the cap at advanced, the contexts and content areas of the K–12 OPIc are specific to language programs in elementary grades, middle schools, and high schools.

The Writing Proficiency Test (WPT; http://www.actfl.org/professional-development/assessments-the-actfl-testing-office/actfl-writing-proficiency-assessments), developed by ACTFL and administered and rated by Language Testing International, relies on standard prompts to elicit writing performances that are rated by trained and certified raters. The four to five prompts deal with practical, social, and professional topics across all levels of the ACTFL Proficiency Guidelines for Writing. Some language tests are available in an online format. While less commonly used than the ACTFL OPI, the WPT is administered to approximately 7,000 test takers annually, in 26 languages.

The Brigham Young University Web Computerized Adaptive Placement Exam (WebCAPE) is a placement test for Chinese, ESL, French, German, Italian, Russian, and Spanish commonly employed at the university level (http://www.perpetualworks.com/webcape/overview). Generally used for placement, this test is a tool to allow university programs to place students in appropriate university-level courses. Although it is nationally available, individual institutions must decide how to use the scores for accurate placement based on their program goals, textbooks, and expected outcomes.

In addition to telephonic tests of oral proficiency conducted in real time by trained interviewers, efforts have also been made to develop what are termed semi-direct approaches. These comprise a set of questions following a similar protocol, but are predetermined rather than adapted in response to the interviewee. In the 1980s and 1990s, CAL developed the Simulated Oral Proficiency Interview (SOPI) that relies on two tape recorders or a language lab and a test booklet to elicit language from examinees, rather than employing an interviewer (Stansfield & Kenyon, 1992). CAL has also developed a computerized oral proficiency assessment instrument, which begins with a self-assessment instrument to place students at an appropriate starting point in the test and to probe the highest level at which a student can perform in the language.

As this review of assessment measures has demonstrated, there are limited assessments available for children in elementary grades. Despite the availability of pre-K–5 programs, there are few instruments to assess student progress. In the present age of accountability, such a dearth may place teachers and administrators of such programs in a quandary: how can instructional or program effectiveness be documented without assessment results? In addition, many of the tests available, such as the ELLOPA and SOPA, can be administratively burdensome and expensive; at the same time, such tests, including AAPPL and STAMP 4SE, with their emphasis on oral production and comprehension, accurately mirror the kind of learning that occurs (and is valued) in early grades; in addition, teachers who learn to rate tests such as these can apply their knowledge of proficiency to lesson planning and formative assessment.

While the summative tests reported may help individual programs track progress toward their goals, the tests have not been used to demonstrate student outcomes on a national scale. In addition, only some of the assessments provide technical reports. For the OPI, and writing, listening, and reading proficiency tests, reports documenting construct validity, rater reliability, and technical reports are available at http://www.languagetesting.com/research. Five of the STAMP4S tests (Arabic, Chinese, French, Japanese, and Spanish) include publicly accessible technical reports that describe the processes by which the tests were developed and field-tested, as well as the measurement processes used to determine which items were included in final forms. The STAMP4S technical reports also describe the processes by which inter-rater reliability is determined. Therefore, programs selecting many of these described tests must do so without much of the information necessary to make an informed decision about test selection.

Language Test Use: A Survey of Programs

In 2006, ACTFL and CAL conducted and analyzed a nationwide survey of over 1,600 foreign language instructors' assessment needs and uses (Malone et al., 2008). The survey was sent to all members of ACTFL and language-specific associations and distributed via listserv. The purpose of the project was to investigate the current uses of assessments, as well as the kinds of assessments that were not available to foreign language instructors. The multi-part survey asked respondents to describe their current uses for assessments, as well as their assessment needs. In one part of the survey, respondents were asked to name their most commonly used assessments and distinguish between their use of internal and external assessments. To help guide respondents' decision making, the following definitions were provided: internal assessments were defined as "developed, administered, and/or scored within a school or district," while external assessments are "developed, rated, and/or validated by state, national, corporate, or non-profit organizations." Respondents described the types of assessments they used and classified each assessment as internal or external (Malone et al., 2008).

Respondents (N = 1,600) reported using a total of 2,427 assessments; 80.4 percent were classified as internal and 19.6 percent as external (Malone et al., 2008). Common types of assessments identified as internal included chapter and unit tests, semester mid-term and final tests, textbook tests, internally created vocabulary and grammar tests, and various project-based assessments. Commonly reported external assessments included the AP exams, the national language exams, the STAMP, the ACTFL OPI, the WebCAPE, and the IB language assessments (Malone et al., 2008).

The results of this survey demonstrate that these K–12 language teacher respondents, who fairly closely represented the population of language teachers in the 50 states, report using primarily internal and often self-made or locally developed assessments. As a result, these locally developed assessments may carry as much weight as do many national assessments in other subjects in awarding credit for learning or even in evaluating teacher effectiveness. Because there is no test which all language programs use to provide comparative data, considerable variation likely exists in how language learners' progress is rated and scored; in addition, there is likely to be considerable variation in how outcomes are reported and used for program decision making and learner evaluation.

It is also notable that many of the most commonly used external assessments test discrete skills, such as listening or reading, rather than the integrated skills emphasized by the National Standards for learning world languages (NSFLEP, 2006, 2015). Assessments such as the IPA and AAPPL assess all three modes, STAMP4S does so to some degree, and, since 2012, the AP language programs have begun to incorporate the three modes into their exams and accompanying curricula. Thus, while internal formative assessments for some time have attempted to reflect current classroom practices to implement the Standards' emphasis on the three modes of communication, large-scale, external summative assessments have only recently begun to move in this direction.

One disturbing survey finding was that respondents reported using tests for purposes other than those intended, offering further evidence of the need for professional development with respect to assessment literacy. Without a deeper understanding of how to match assessments to purposes, much of the potential positive washback effect of assessment on instruction is not realized. Consequently, the results of the survey emphasize the need for assessment literacy among language educators who generally receive minimal (if any) training on how to evaluate and classify students' performances.

There are a few post-secondary efforts to develop a system for assessing world language learning in a systematic way that allows for cross-institutional comparisons. For example, Stanford University has determined an expected outcome of Intermediate Mid in the commonly taught languages and Novice High in the less commonly taught languages for their first-year students (Stanford University, n.d.). This requirement includes listening, reading, writing, and speaking; Stanford has adapted CAL's SOPI for computerized administration via the university's intranet and assesses students in first- and second-year language classes. Stanford also has a writing test for first- and second-year students. Hundreds of universities use the ACTFL OPI for a variety of local purposes, including entrance, placement, and graduation requirements, as well as for program evaluation.

At Stanford, the positive impact of assessment on practice is demonstrated by the requirement that every teaching assistant who will be teaching in the undergraduate language programs must complete a language teaching methodology course and participate in an ACTFL Modified Oral Proficiency Interview workshop to understand the proficiency levels that guide instruction and assessment in each course.

Regardless of level of instruction (K–12 or university), one critical issue is instructors' understanding of the basic principles of assessment and the procedures and processes that must be used to reliably and validly assess students, that is, assessment literacy (Taylor, 2009). Recent research (Malone, 2013) on assessment literacy among small groups of world language instructors and administrators suggested that more work is needed to help instructors understand the principles of assessment and apply these principles to both the selection of tests for their students as well as to the development of tests for classroom use.

The Impact of New Assessment Models on Learners and Educators

Assessment can drive change, ideally change for improvement. Test results can be used to measure the effectiveness of teaching and learning and, therefore, provide feedback to teachers, students, and administrators about ways to improve instruction or maintain current, excellent instruction (Rudner & Schafer, 2002). When the assessment being used mirrors that of real-life usage (such as communicating with a native speaker and conducting daily transactions in the language), the ensuing discussion of assessment results demonstrates the power of real-world applications to motivate students' best performance in the assessment.

Assessment to Increase Learners' Motivation

Envisioning such new approaches to the assessment of world languages provides opportunities to engage students in understanding the expected performance, take responsibility for learning, analyze their own strengths and weaknesses, and identify strategies for improvement.

Traditionally, students identify test performance with grades. Students usually receive feedback as a score or grade, which becomes part of a calculation of a quarter or semester grade. Ordinarily, a test score or a grade does not provide learners with the feedback they need to improve their performance. Many of the formative and summative assessments described in this chapter describe a shift in grading in world languages from counting errors and subtracting that number from the maximum possible score, to providing substantive feedback on the student's performance. In this regard, the National Assessment Governing Board commissioned a report on high school students' motivation to do well on the NAEP assessments (Brophy & Ames, 2005), which concluded that high school students were not motivated to do their best on assessments that had no stakes for them, even when the tests had moderately high stakes for their states. When tests are unconnected to an impact on the individual, motivation to do one's best decreases (Braun, Kirsch, & Yamamoto, 2011).

The results of Brophy and Ames (2005) and Braun et al. (2011) suggest that students must be motivated in order to give their best performance. Therefore, when a student participates in an external assessment that may have little or no impact on the student's final grade, the likelihood that the student will do his or her best decreases. Pink (2009) argues that people are more likely to be motivated to be successful when they have a clear sense of what they want to accomplish and also why they want to accomplish it (Azzam, 2014). Motivation comes as much from enjoyment of the activity as the recognition that effort or practice will improve performance (Ericsson, Krampe, & Tesch-Römer, 1993). For assessment of languages, requiring students to perform real-life tasks (or at least to perform tasks that mirror those found in authentic language situations) may provide one way to motivate students. Therefore, performance tasks in end-of-unit or end-of-course summative assessments should reflect realistic language situations in order to increase the likelihood of motivation.

Motivating Learners through Self-Reflection on Assessments

For learners of world languages, the kinds of tasks that reflect authentic settings described earlier can allow students to find out how well they can perform in such settings. However, it is also important to not only assess students' performance but also provide a means by which they can reflect on their performance. The NCSSFL-ACTFL Can-Do Statements represent a new tool for educators and language learners to chart progress in reaching higher levels of language performance in the classroom. The concept of a language portfolio came from the Council of Europe as part of the implementation of the Common European Framework of Reference and was designed for citizens to evaluate their language ability, whether native language, heritage language (that of their background or family), or language for a specific purpose (such as travel or researching one's genealogy).

In the United States, the National Council of State Supervisors for Languages (NCSSFL) adapted the European Language Portfolio for K–12 language learners to create a Self-Assessment Grid (with statements to describe what students "can do" in each mode of communication at each of the ACTFL proficiency levels through Advanced Mid). Each statement begins with "I can" and is descriptive of both how and how well the learner can use language at each level in interpretive listening, interpretive reading, interpersonal speaking and listening, presentational speaking, and presentational writing.

In order to improve the original LinguaFolio, ACTFL and NCSSFL collaborated to create a new document that aligns "Can-Do" statements with the ACTFL Proficiency Guidelines 2012. The NCSSFL-ACTFL Can-Do Statements (NCSSFL-ACTFL, 2013) describe classroom performances that point toward the proficiency levels and sub-levels from Novice Low through Distinguished. The value of this document is that it illustrates performances arising in a classroom context. Educators and learners recognize the performances described with each "I can" statement and therefore gain insight into the corresponding proficiency level to which each performance points. Figure 9.2 shows examples of NCSSFL-ACTFL Can-Do Statements at the Intermediate Mid level. The full document describes a continuum of language learning, providing a common framework to document learner growth on a nationally recognized scale. This clear identification of competency-based learning targets is reflective of the language learning process.

LinguaFolio provides another opportunity for language assessment: student self-assessment. The Can-Do Statements that comprise LinguaFolio are designed for students to use to indicate their language learning progression. The statements provide a way for language learners to chart their progress through incremental steps, based on a wide variety of assessment evidence from the instructional setting.

Emerging research highlights the powerful potential impact on learners' progress in developing higher levels of language proficiency when they were involved in using the Can-Do Statements of the LinguaFolio to identify what they were able to do in each mode of communication. The more students are engaged in monitoring their learning trajectories, the more intrinsically motivated they become. A recent study shows that the ability of language learners to set goals is linked to increased student motivation, language achievement, and growth in proficiency (Moeller, Theiler, & Wu, 2012). When students thought about what and how they learned, their performance improved (Moeller et al., 2012). The NCSSFL-ACTFL Can-Do

INTERMEDIATE MID

I can participate in conversations on familiar topics using sentences and series of sentences. I can handle short social interactions in everyday situations by asking and answering a variety of questions. I can usually say what I want to say about myself and my everyday life.
I can start, maintain, and end a conversation on a variety of familiar topics.

☐   I can ask for information, details, and explanations during a conversation.
☐   I can interview someone for a project or a publication.

Figure 9.2 NCSSFL-ACTFL Can-Do Statements: Sample from Interpersonal Mode

Statements do not represent a formal assessment, but the document influences the assessment design while also providing a means for students to reflect on what they have learned and mastered. More research is needed to support these outcomes, but the emerging work shows promise. LinguaFolio and the NCSSFL-ACTFL Can-Do Statements are useful to educators as they design a variety of assessment tasks to indicate performance along the continuum of language proficiency.

Projects Using Assessments to Inform Instruction

These tools for the assessment of languages have influenced a number of projects. Below, current efforts to use Can-Do Statements in two states and two districts are described.

North Carolina Department of Public Instruction Assessment

To implement the new *North Carolina World Language Essential Standards: Classical Languages, Dual & Heritage Languages, Modern Languages,* the North Carolina Department of Public Instruction (NCDPI) initiated a project to assist districts in the evaluation of student progress in world languages (NCDPI, 2012). The NCDPI does not mandate assessment of world language and wanted to provide local school districts with examples of assessments that could offer reasonable levels of validity and reliability. At the core of the new standards are eight proficiency levels that form the learning targets for each course. Interestingly, the NCDPI identified for each mode of communication the exit proficiency expectations (Novice, Intermediate, Advanced, and their sublevels) based on the number of hours of instruction across each of the eight levels and differentiated by language: alphabetic languages (where each letter is associated with a particular sound or sounds), logographic languages (those using a character writing system), and visual languages (American Sign Language; NCDPI, n.d.). Sample exercises for classroom use are being developed and provided to local districts for use in creating appropriate assessments of language learners in each mode of communication at different levels of proficiency. Such guidance will help educators set realistic expectations for assessing language proficiency; that is, answering the question of what a learner in a particular type of program, learning a specific language, should be able to do with and through the target language, after different periods of instruction. In addition, by understanding what reasonable expectations for progress look like for their students, language teachers can align their goals to their student learning objectives (SLOs). In turn, such SLOs will soon comprise one part of an evaluation of teacher effectiveness.

New Jersey Department of Education Model Curriculum

Each unit in the model curriculum centers on the summative assessment of each mode of communication (New Jersey Department of Education, n.d.). The performance assessments in the interpersonal, interpretive, and presentational modes guide the design of each learning activity and all the language elements learned and practiced in the unit. Specific Can-Do Statements identify how students will demonstrate achievement of the SLOs for each unit. The Can-Do Statements are illustrated through responses to specific assessment tasks that identify the "how" and the "how well" of the expected performance. Such benchmarks allow teachers to develop shared understanding of expected performances.

Some districts have begun to implement collaboratively developed summative assessments to influence classroom instruction. For example, in Lexington School District One, the curriculum identifies for each unit of instruction (from elementary grades through high school) the performance assessment for interpersonal, interpretive, and presentational communication (Lexington School District One, n.d.). Implementation of this assessment model has provided structure for the language programs as they move away from traditional levels identified by grammar and vocabulary studied toward a focus on the performance expectations for each course. Because these approaches are new, no research has documented their long-term influence; however, such research is needed to help guide future attempts.

Focusing Professional Development on Assessment Literacy

These examples demonstrate how school districts have used assessments to influence programs, curriculum, and instructional practices. An important part of the use of assessment data was providing teachers in those districts with ample opportunities to discuss student learning. Professional development focused on increasing teachers' assessment literacy provides opportunities for teachers to develop better assessment practices, as well as a deeper understanding of assessment in general.

For example, promising practices with respect to levels of proficiency include specific attention to the characteristics of language proficiency and the type of language required to demonstrate performance at each level of proficiency. Understanding expectations for student performances at specific levels is often accomplished as teachers bring samples of student work and collaboratively evaluate and rate the samples, agreeing on what really counts as evidence of a specific level, and such understanding may also help instructors better achieve successful teaching and learning outcomes. Without such experiences, teachers typically overestimate what their students can do, often because they are recalling student work products that involved substantial teacher input such as heavily scaffolded activities, editing, and revising.

Language assessment literacy entails understanding the principles of good assessment of language for both formative and summative purposes (Malone, 2013). By better understanding the fundamentals of assessment, such as reliability and validity, as well as the elements of test design, teachers can create better assessments. For example, in constructing schoolwide or districtwide assessments, greater assessment literacy can result in more valid and reliable summative assessments.

Similarly, with greater assessment literacy, teachers can design more useful formative classroom assessments and, equally important, develop more appropriate and informative scoring rubrics. Without intensive discussion and debate regarding the criteria that characterize performance at each level, teachers typically have difficulty creating rubrics appropriate for the targeted level and applying such rubrics consistently. The rubrics also have to be detailed enough to provide information that will help students make gains along the continuum of proficiency. The ACTFL Performance Descriptors along with the NCSSFL-ACTFL Can-Do Statements provide guidance to develop unit-level rubrics or course-specific rubrics, accurately capturing the targeted proficiency level.

This focus on the teacher as the designer, and not just a user, of assessments is a promising development as states and districts move toward accountability measures of teacher effectiveness.

Valid evidence of the teacher's impact through standards- and performance-based instruction should be derived from appropriate assessment measures. As teachers collaboratively design the types of assessments of language performance that are linked to state and district expectations or SLOs, these assessments will provide stronger evidence of student learning. Teacher effectiveness measured by traditional chapter tests or classroom quizzes would lack both fidelity to the standards and appropriate links to the scale of proficiency levels. It is important that the standards used to assess student outcomes are aligned to the accountability measures for teachers. North Carolina's approach to measuring teacher effectiveness demonstrates consistency with such an alignment.

Helping teachers understand the basics of standards-based assessment can provide important background for teachers when they design and implement classroom-based assessments. When testing specialists who work with teachers to design and implement performance assessments, three goals are achieved. First, testing specialists, by working collaboratively with teachers, better understand the challenges and opportunities of the language classroom and improve their own understanding of what transpires in a language classroom. Second, teachers, by collaborating with test development specialists, can learn more productive ways of assessing their students. Third, by working collaboratively, testing specialists and teachers have the opportunity to understand the difficulties each group faces in developing assessments, and this understanding may have positive benefits for both testing specialists and teachers.

Conclusion

This chapter has addressed a number of issues related to the assessment of world languages, including the essential complexity of assessing language proficiency, the lack of nationally accepted reliable and valid language assessments, and insufficient understanding of performance assessments and how to administer, rate, and provide feedback on such measures.

First, few nationally accepted assessments are available for world languages, and, of equal importance, the assessments that exist are not in widespread use. The unfortunate lack of consistent use of assessments nationwide has resulted in an information gap; there is no way to document current language attainment by U.S. students. Without common language assessments, not only is there sporadic measurement of student outcomes, but also there is no way to compare student performances across schools, districts, and states. This lack of a common yardstick makes it very difficult to identify best practices in teaching. In addition, there is a lack of consensus around reasonable, shared expectations for student performances among the school community members and parents. How can students, their teachers, and parents credibly determine the students' learning unless there are agreed-upon measures to evaluate and report on progress toward achievement of mutually understood standards? Moreover, agreeing on the nature of the evidence required to gauge language learners' progress is essential to developing meaningful systems of educator accountability and effectiveness. Common districtwide assessments based on the three modes of communication of the National Standards and administered at key points of a program best capture learners' performance.

A second issue is the lack of assessment literacy on the part of language teachers, administrators, and students. The ACTFL survey conducted in 2006 (Malone et al., 2008) revealed that many language tests are being implemented in ways inconsistent with their stated purposes. Although the use of standards- and performance-based assessments such as AAPPL and IPA is increasing, at present it is still limited to a few states and districts. The dominant type of assessment in language classrooms is the use of assessments provided by the textbook program. Language educators have limited familiarity with standards-based assessments of performance, how to use or adapt different assessments, and how to use the resulting data generated by the assessment. Educators need more than mere awareness of different assessments; the existence of and use of good assessments is not sufficient since it is possible to use them in inappropriate ways. Professional development to expand educators' repertoire of formative and summative assessments is essential both for supporting reflective practice utilizing assessment information and for learners benefiting from the feedback provided by those assessments. Accountability has forced the question on assessment: do we have commonly used and valid measures to measure what we value? In other words, are there widely available, implemented, and understood measures of language performance on which teachers can evaluate their classroom outcomes? Although several promising approaches have been identified in this chapter, world language is not yet a part of state-level accountability systems.

Finally, in an era of increasing accountability through state- and district-level requirements for evaluating teacher effectiveness, appropriate assessment of world language learning is critical. This chapter has focused on efforts to develop assessments that reflect language use for teaching and learning. Proper assessment of language performance ought to reflect how language is used; that is, an assessment should incorporate an integrated approach to language in all its aspects. At present, such assessments are in short supply, and those in the market place are expensive to develop and score, although developments in technology may improve their cost-effectiveness. It is undeniable, however, that assessments based on authentic language use are essential in order to meet the real needs of language learners. As standards- and performance-based assessment models become widespread, educators will increasingly turn to assessments that truly support language learning, that is, assessments that reflect real-world applications of language. Such assessments provide both useful feedback to language learners and link to substantively meaningful milestones along the path to proficiency. Teachers analyzing the results of these assessments are likely to experience a positive washback effect, resulting in adjustments to their instructional strategies, as has been documented with the use of the IPA model (Adair-Hauck et al., 2013). In turn, this focus on performance leads to improvement of what learners demonstrate they can do with language that, in turn, leads to increased public support for learning languages.

At the same time, as noted earlier, although world languages have been identified as a core subject in the federal Elementary and Secondary Education Act (No Child Left Behind), their assessment is not required. As a result, world languages have not been included in the annual testing calendar to the same degree as science and social studies, and certainly not to the same degree as mathematics and English language arts. Consequently, language assessments developed during the past decade generally have not adhered to the rigorous test development procedures of these disciplines. In addition, most assessments developed for world languages lack the funding and scrutiny of high-stakes assessments.

Therefore, the assessment of world languages has both benefited and suffered from this lack of attention. On the positive side, assessments such as the IPA have been tried out and developed with input from committed world language teachers and learners. On the negative side, such assessments are generally used as classroom assessments and not regarded as assessments that can measure either student growth or teacher effectiveness. Testing of how well students are learning languages lags behind other content areas in both the quality of summative assessment and linkages between such assessments and formative classroom assessments. Until world language is accorded the same status as other content areas and held to the same high standards for testing, assessment of students in this content area will be inadequate to guide continuous improvement for each learner.

Note

1 In 1999, a consensus-building project to develop a framework for the National Assessment of Educational Progress—Foreign Language (NAEP-FL) was conducted. The NAEP-FL was developed and field-tested initially for Spanish with the intent to add other languages later, but the test was never operationalized. The framework for the NAEP-FL did reflect consensus among world language specialists at the turn of the century.

References

Abbott, M., & Phillips, J. (2011). *Decade of foreign language standards: Influence, impact, and future directions.* Alexandria, VA: ACTFL.

Adair-Hauck, B., Glisan, E. W., & Troyan, F. (2013). *Implementing integrated performance assessment.* Alexandria, VA: ACTFL.

American Council on the Teaching of Foreign Languages (ACTFL). (1986). *ACTFL proficiency guidelines.* Yonkers, NY: ACTFL.

ACTFL. (2010). *Foreign language enrollments in K–12 public schools: Are students prepared for a global society?* Alexandria, VA: ACTFL.

ACTFL. (2012a). *Performance descriptors for language learners.* Alexandria, VA: ACTFL.

ACTFL. (2012b). *ACTFL proficiency guidelines 2012.* Alexandria, VA: ACTFL.

ACTFL. (2012c). *Alignment of the national standards for learning languages with the Common Core State Standards.* Alexandria, VA: ACTFL. Retrieved August 25, 2014 from http://www.actfl.org/news/reports/alignment-the-national-standards-learning-languages-the-common-core-state-standards#

Azzam, A. (2014). Motivated to learn: A conversation with Daniel Pink. *Educational Leadership, 72*(1), 12–17.

Bachman, L., & Palmer, A. (2010). *Language assessment in practice.* New York, NY: Oxford University Press.

Braun, H., Kirsch, I., & Yamamoto, K. (2011). An experimental study of the effects of monetary incentives on performance on the 12th grade NAEP reading assessment. *Teachers College Record, 113*(11), 2309–2344.

Brophy, J., & Ames, C. (2005). *NAEP testing for twelfth graders: Motivational issues.* Washington, DC: National Assessment Governing Board.

Cronbach, L. J. (1988). Five perspectives on the validity argument. In H. Wainer & H. I. Braun (Eds.), *Test validity* (pp. 3–17). Hillsdale, NJ: Lawrence Erlbaum.

Ericsson, K. A., Krampe, R., & Tesch-Römer, C. (1993). The role of deliberate practice in the acquisition of expert performance. *Psychological Review, 100*(3), 363–406.

Furman, N., Goldberg, D., & Lusin, N. (2007). *Enrollments in languages other than English in United States institutions of higher education, Fall 2006.* New York, NY: MLA.

Harris, D. P. (1969). *Testing English as a second language.* New York, NY: McGraw-Hill.

Hughes, A. (2003). *Testing for language teachers.* New York, NY: Cambridge University Press.

Huhta, A. (2010). Diagnostic and formative assessment. In B. Spolsky & F. M. Hult (Eds.), *The handbook of educational linguistics* (pp. 469–482). Oxford, UK: Blackwell.

Interagency Language Roundtable. (n.d.). *Interagency language roundtable language skill level descriptions—speaking.* Retrieved December 18, 2013 from http://www.govtilr.org/Skills/ILRscale2.htm

Lexington School District One. (n.d.). *Assessment and grading in Lexington One's world language program.* Retrieved September 18, 2015 from http://lexoneworldlanguages.weebly.com/assessment-and-grading-in-world-languages.html

Lowe, P. L. (1988). The unassimilated history. In P. L. Lowe & C. W. Stansfield (Eds.), *Second language proficiency assessment.* Washington, DC: Center for Applied Linguistics.

Malone, M. E. (2013). The essentials of assessment literacy: Contrasts between testers and users. *Language Testing, 30*(3), 329–344.

Malone, M. E., Swender, E., Montee, M., Gallagher, C. M., & Wicher, M. (2008). *Study of assessment uses and needs in U.S. world language programs.* Unpublished manuscript.

Moeller, A., Theiler, J., & Wu, C. (2012). Goal setting and student achievement: A longitudinal study. *Modern Language Journal, 96*(2), 153–169.

National Council of State Supervisors for Languages (NCSSFL)–American Council on the Teaching of Foreign Languages (ACTFL). (2013). *NCSSFL-ACTFL Can-Do Statements: Performance indicators for language learners.* Alexandria, VA: NCSSFL-ACTFL. Retrieved December 18, 2013 from http://www.actfl.org/publications/guidelines-and-manuals/ncssfl-actfl-can-do-statements

National Standards in Foreign Language Education Project (NSFLEP). (2006). *Standards for foreign language learning in the 21st century.* Lawrence, KS: Allen Press.

NSFLEP. (2015). *World-readiness standards for learning languages.* Alexandria, VA: NSFLEP.

New Jersey Department of Education. (n.d.). *World languages framework project homepage.* Retrieved May 13, 2013 from http://www.state.nj.us/education/aps/cccs/wl/frameworks/wlo/index.html

North Carolina Department of Public Instruction (NCDPI). (2012). *AEs for world languages.* Retrieved September 18, 2015 from http://wlnces.ncdpi.wikispaces.net/AEs+for+World+Languages

NCDPI. (n.d.). *Unpacking standards.* Retrieved September 18, 2015 from http://wlnces.ncdpi. wikispaces.net/Unpacking+Standards

Pink, D. (2009). *Drive: The surprising truth of what motivates us.* New York, NY: Riverhead.

Rhodes, N., & Pufahl, I. (2011). *Foreign language teaching in U.S. schools: Results of a national survey.* Washington, DC: Center for Applied Linguistics.

Rosenbusch, M. H. (2005). The No Child Left Behind Act and teaching and learning languages in U.S. schools. *The Modern Language Journal, 89*(2), 250–261.

Rudner, L. M., & Schafer, W. D. (2002). *What teachers need to know about assessment.* Washington, DC: National Education Association.

Stanford University. (n.d.). *Language requirement.* Retrieved September 18, 2015 from https://web.stanford.edu/dept/lc/language/requirement/index.html

Stansfield, C. W., & Kenyon, D. (1992). The development and validation of a simulated oral proficiency interview. *The Modern Language Journal, 76*(2), 129–141.

Taylor, L. (2009). Developing assessment literacy. *Annual Review of Applied Linguistics, 29*, 21–36.

Wiggins, G., & McTighe, J. (2004). *Understanding by design.* Alexandria, VA: ASCD.

10 Use of Evidence-Centered Design in Assessment of History Learning

Kadriye Ercikan, Peter Seixas,
Pamela Kaliski, and Kristen Huff

Introduction: Complex Thinking in History

The assessment of high school history, which for a century has put high value on bits and pieces of information, faces a serious crisis in the age of Google (Osborne, 2003). There are ever more bits, ever easier to access, worth less and less. The teaching of history in general, and its assessment in particular, confronts a glut of information. In other school subjects, the shift toward the assessment of complex thinking is desirable; in history it is inescapable. But defining a target construct of complex thinking in history—historical thinking—is itself a complex task.

The idea of a target construct comprising cognition and learning captures history educators' quest over the past three decades to define historical thinking in a way that both expresses the discipline's modes of understanding and provides a guide to performances that can be rated as more or less competent or powerful. The term "historical thinking" names the target of that quest more accurately than does "complex thinking in history," as it conveys the distinctive nature of the questions, methods, and products of work in the field: "historical thinking" involves something other than applying generic "complex thinking" to the study of the past.

Efforts to define historical thinking have a widely recognized origin in Denis Shemilt's *History 13–16: Evaluation Study* (1980).[1] The Schools Council History Project, the target of that study, posited a series of "second order" or procedural concepts, including change, evidence, and historical accounts, which shape the practice of history, as opposed to substantive concepts like revolution, president, or civil rights that historians use in writing about the past. At the same time, Shemilt's ability to test *progression* in students' handling of second-order concepts provided a means for history educators to move beyond mere *aggregation* of more factual information as a measure of historical learning. British educational authorities attempted to build a model of the progression into the National Curriculum Attainment Targets, but the researchers whose work they built upon roundly criticized their efforts:

> Under no circumstances is it valid to report levels [of progression] to parents as "measures" of individual attainment or progress, to set levels as targets for individual pupils or colleagues, or to use levels as a basis for grade predictions or value-added calculations.
>
> (Lee & Shemilt, 2003)

In part, their objection stemmed from the small and provisional empirical research base available at that time that had contributed to the articulation of progression levels. Nevertheless, the definition of advancement in history learning as a progression in the mastery of second-order concepts has gained appeal internationally (VanSledright & Limon, 2006; Wineburg, 1996). Variations have appeared in national projects in the United States (National History Standards), Canada (The Historical Thinking Project), and Australia (National Curriculum). Moreover, most of the concepts (evidence, cause, change, significance, and empathy—called "perspective taking" by some) are universally accepted. VanSledright (2013) has parsed historical thinking into a further category (beyond substantive and procedural concepts) to include "strategic practices," most of which are subsumed under the second-order concept "evidence" in the British and Canadian models.

Currently, there are two important variants of the definition of a cognition and learning model for history education as progression in second-order concepts. Sam Wineburg, the preeminent history education researcher in the United States, has advocated for the notion that reading historical texts is central to the discipline, and competence in reading texts, both as evidence and accounts, should therefore be the starting point in the teaching, learning, and assessment of historical thinking. This approach has the elegance of fitting well with concerns about literacy across the curriculum (National Governors Association Center for Best Practices, 2010), while helping to define competencies specific to the discipline.

The second variant addresses the applications, the social and civic aims of history education, or what might be termed the uses and abuses of history, as a component of history education (MacMillan, 2008). Following Michael Oakshott (1983), the British pioneers held that this lay outside the discipline of history, and therefore it should remain outside the purview of history education. North American educators, with a strong tradition of social studies and citizenship education, resisted the British line of thinking. As a result, an influential Canadian list of second-order historical thinking concepts includes "the ethical dimension," which considers how history can inform contemporary life and what obligations, if any, historical sacrifices and injustices bear on the present (http://www.historicalthinking.ca). The ethical dimension presents special challenges for assessment, since there is disagreement among historians and philosophers of history as to the kinds of lines that can be drawn between past and present: how and where does one consider the ethos of past times to preclude judgments of (say) heroism and criminality, right and wrong, good and bad; and, alternatively, how and when do "universal" criteria apply (e.g., Fay, 2004)?

A similar dimension appears in the new Quebec curriculum as a citizenship "competency" of being able to understand contemporary issues in historical perspective. Quebec has had some difficulty with designing assessments that would capture this competency and which teachers would find useful and comprehensible. And it appears in the Swedish national curriculum as "historical consciousness," understanding the conditions of contemporary life both as the contingent product of historical forces and past decisions, and as the launching ground for the future.[2] Swedish history education scholars are currently designing assessments to measure these understandings.

The impetus for large-scale, high-stakes standardized testing across subject areas and disciplinary competencies, particularly powerful in the current American educational landscape, has driven a search for valid and reliable assessments of complex historical thinking that would meet the demands of this environment. We turn now to a survey of that landscape, particularly as it affects history and social studies. In the next five sections below, we first describe assessment of history learning in the context of accountability. This is followed up with a discussion of challenges in designing assessments of historical thinking and presentation of an evidence-centered assessment design approach for addressing these challenges. Key assessments that have a great impact on both teaching and assessment of history learning, end-of-course (EOC) assessments, *Advanced Placement* (AP), *International Baccalaureate* (IB), and the *National Assessment of Educational Progress* (NAEP) are described as part of the landscape of history assessment. This is followed up with a discussion of two assessment projects—Historical Assessments of Thinking (HAT) and Historical Thinking Assessment Tool (HTAT)—that have aimed to meet the challenges of assessment of historical thinking. Central to any assessment of complex thinking is validity of inferences from the assessment. We propose an evidence-centered design (ECD) approach to validating inferences from assessments of historical thinking and elaborate on methods and issues using examples from previous research.

History Assessments and the Quest for Accountability

The reauthorization of the Elementary and Secondary Education Act (ESEA) in 2001 (known as No Child Left Behind, NCLB) heralded a new paradigm of accountability in U.S. public education. In brief, to receive federal funding, states were required to assess all students in particular grades and subjects. The results of these assessments are being used to monitor progress of all students toward achieving proficiency. The intent of the law was laudable and reform-minded: to ensure that *all* students—minorities, low SES, English language learners, and students with disabilities—were held to high standards (given the opportunity to learn), and schools, local education agencies (LEAs), and states would be held accountable. Limitations of the law included the unrealistic goal of requiring 100 percent proficiency by 2014 and lack of common standards and assessments across states (see http://www2.ed.gov/nclb/landing.jhtml for more information on NCLB). These limitations were mitigated somewhat by the passage of the 2009 American Recovery and Reinvestment Act (ARRA) and the 2012 ESEA Waiver process. The ARRA funded over four billion dollars' worth of competitive grants known as Race to the Top (RTTT). States were eligible for the federal dollars only by committing to college-readiness standards (46 states and the District of Columbia have adopted the Common Core Learning Standards), common assessments and proficiency standards (e.g., Partnership for the Assessment of Readiness for College and Careers and the Smarter-Balanced Assessment Consortium), and a comprehensive educator effectiveness program that included a performance evaluation system based in part on student test scores. Two years later, the ESEA Waiver had similar requirements.

Under NCLB, states were required to test all students in each of the grades 3–8 annually in English language arts and mathematics and test all students once in elementary, middle, and high school in science. No social studies or history assessments were required as part of NCLB, and many educators considered this a signal of social studies and history being of lower priority than the other subjects. The National Council for Social Studies has voiced concern about the "erosion" of social studies in U.S. education,[3] and the National Council for History Education has voiced concern that history educators will not prevail if they are forced to compete with other subjects for funding.[4]

Currently, there are three major forces driving the use of standardized history/social studies assessments in U.S. schools:

- Both the RTTT applications and the ESEA Waiver encouraged educator performance evaluation systems to incorporate student test scores.
- The inclusion of literacy for history/social studies in the Common Core standards (currently adopted by most states).
- The continued requirement of demonstrated history/social studies competency as part of high school graduation requirements.

As a result of these factors, many states are redesigning their existing history/social studies assessments to align with Common Core standards, implementing new statewide history/social studies assessments. In some states, LEAs are developing their own assessments. For example, New York State has announced the redesign of their New York State Learning Standards in Social Studies, Global Studies Regents Exam, and U.S. History Regents Exam to incorporate Common Core literacy standards.

The Common Core Standards for Literacy in History and Social Studies require in-depth analysis of primary and secondary texts (see Appendix A for the ten anchor standards for grades 9–10). Most history assessments like AP and NAEP rely heavily on selected-response questions in addition to constructed-response (e.g., essay) questions, as selected-response questions are more economical to score and enhance reliability. Assessment designers will need to figure out ways to design assessments that do not fall prey to the long-standing criticism that selected-response questions only measure declarative knowledge. One design approach that helps mitigate against this tendency is the inclusion of rich stimuli (e.g., primary and secondary documents, maps, political cartoons, charts and graphs, etc.) followed by a set of items. However, such an approach extends testing time and reduces reliability in comparison to the same number of discrete selected-response items. Nonetheless, to adequately assess the Common Core standards, assessment designers will need to consider adopting contemporary approaches to assessment design that have explicit processes for addressing deeper levels of cognition than factual recall and simple reasoning.

Working in this environment, it is useful to articulate the dilemmas and contradictions, as the idealized assessment of complex historical thinking runs up against the constraints that are endemic to large-scale, high-stakes testing. The jury is still out as to whether this encounter will have a happy ending.

Designing Assessments of Historical Thinking

The design of assessments of historical thinking faces several significant challenges. The most obvious is the nature of the relationship between what is often confusingly called historical "content," or the declarative knowledge about events, people, and places of the past, and historical thinking. For instance, an analysis of historical causation is not possible without an understanding of the people, conditions, and events involved. Generic rules and algorithms (e.g., "Consider both underlying and immediate causes") must be taught and assessed in the context of specific historical events. One approach is to supply the needed information as a component of the assessment. Another is to recognize that knowledge and thinking go hand in hand and abandon the artificial attempt to isolate historical thinking. The Stanford History Education Group (2013) lists three assessment design principles, all of which focus on this problem of "content":

- Good assessments balance knowledge of content and historical thinking.
- Good assessments ask students to apply content knowledge rather than reproduce it.
- Good assessments require students to consider content in ways that require thought, judgment, and deep understanding.

Of course, these are easy to say and difficult to put into practice. The second factor that makes assessment of historical thinking challenging is the difficulty in designing tasks that engage students in complex thinking. The nature of the target construct creates significant assessment design challenges. A growing body of research focuses on assessment tasks with targeted cognitive components and difficulty levels (Ferrara & Chen, 2011; Gorin & Embretson, 2006; Huff & Ferrara, 2010; Sato, 2011). This research has demonstrated the difficulties involved in capturing complex thinking (Baxter & Glaser, 1998; Ferrara & Chen, 2011; Glaser & Baxter, 2002). In this context, cognitive targets, based on expert judgments, are no more than hypotheses about what the items may assess. For example, empirical investigations conducted by Ferrara et al. (2004, 2005) found significant mismatches between targeted and actual cognitive processes of test items. Predicting a simpler characteristic of items—such as item difficulty based on item features evaluated by experts—could only account for 25–50 percent of the variance in item p-values (Ferrara, Svetina, Skucha, & Murphy, 2011).

These challenges in designing assessments that include targets related to complex historical thinking draw attention to a need for (1) an assessment design process that takes into account construct complexity and (2) empirical evidence of constructs captured by the assessment. As discussed in previous chapters (Haertel et al., this volume), ECD (Mislevy, Steinberg, & Almond, 2002) has been proposed as a principled approach to designing assessments of complex constructs. ECD is a model-based approach to assessment design with three components (Ercikan, 2006; Ercikan & Seixas, 2011; Haertel et al., this volume; Mislevy et al., 2002; Pellegrino, Chudowsky, & Glaser, 2001). The *cognition and learning model* includes the description of progression and development in and definition of the target constructs; the *task model* identifies how tasks need to be designed to assess different construct components and levels; and the *evidence model* specifies how student performance should be evaluated and interpreted in relation to the targeted constructs. The key difference between ECD and typical assessment design approaches is a requirement in ECD for clear and explicit description of how tasks and the evaluation and interpretation of task performance should be related to the target constructs. This requirement encourages and supports the design of tasks and assessments that are aligned with intended target inferences.

Before exploring further how ECD might be employed to address key challenges of assessment design, we review the current state of large-scale history assessment.

The Current Landscape of History Assessments

As mentioned previously, the prevalence of EOC assessments has increased over the past decade; as a result, when considering the current landscape of history assessments, it is critical to consider EOC history assessment. The variety of history standards endorsed across the United States has resulted in a variety of statewide assessments.[5] In November 2008, the National History Center released a "Statement on State History Assessments." Specifically, the history assessment programs for six states (California, Illinois, Kansas, Massachusetts, New York, and Virginia) were independently reviewed in detail to form the basis of the National History Center's statement. A review of the history assessment programs from each of these six states reveals just how different EOC history assessment is across the states. For example, Kansas has U.S. History and World History assessments comprising only selected-response items and are administered in grades 6, 8, and high school (Bruner, 2008), whereas Massachusetts has a mixed-format history assessment (selected-response and constructed-response items) for sophomores in high school (Cohen, 2008). Although the current landscape for EOC history assessment contains great variety and lacks consistency across states, the future of EOC history assessments is linked to the assessment of the Common Core State Standards.

In addition to state EOC assessment, history assessment has been part of three key large-scale programs in the United States. These are the AP, IB, and NAEP. The first two are used for making high-stakes decisions for individual students, whereas NAEP is used to monitor educational outcomes for policy purposes. However, all three are widely used, generally highly regarded, and have the potential to influence both teaching and other assessments in history. The topics, knowledge, and skills covered in these assessments, as well as how they are assessed, influence how history is taught and tested. In the sections below, we review what kinds of history learning these assessments focus on and how the assessments are conducted.

AP History Assessments

The College Board's AP program offers college-level courses and corresponding examinations to high school students in 34 subject areas. The AP courses and exams are intended to prepare high school students for success in their college courses. There are three AP options within the history domain: AP U.S. History, AP European History, and AP World History. These three history courses are designed to be comparable to introductory college-level courses. The course descriptions for AP U.S. History, AP European History, and AP World History provide

Table 10.1 Themes Covered in the Three AP History Course Options

AP U.S. History	AP European History	AP World History
American Diversity American Identity Culture Demographic Changes Economic Transformations Environment Globalization Politics and Citizenship Reform Religion Slavery and Its Legacies in North America War and Diplomacy	Intellectual and Cultural History Political and Diplomatic History Social and Economic History	Interaction between Humans and the Environment Development and Interaction of Cultures State-Building, Expansion, and Conflict Creation, Expansion, and Interaction of Economic Systems Development and Transformation of Social Cultures

the historical themes and topic outlines for each of these courses (College Board, 2012a, 2012b, 2012c, 2012d, 2012e, 2012f). The themes covered in the three AP history course options are shown in Table 10.1. The AP World History curriculum framework was recently redesigned and emphasizes nine complex historical thinking skills which can be grouped into four overarching historical thinking skills (see Table 10.2 and College Board, 2012e, for an abbreviated summary of the historical thinking skills definitions), in addition to the five course themes shown in Table 10.1.

The AP exams are summative assessments with a 55-minute selected-response item section and a 130-minute constructed-response item section. The AP U.S. History and AP European History exams contain 80 selected-response items, whereas AP World History contains only 70 selected-response items. Within the constructed-response item section, all three exams begin with a document-based question (DBQ) and follow with two standard essay questions.

Currently, the AP program is engaged in a redesign effort for the AP history courses. An important goal of the redesign is to reduce the breadth and increase the depth of what is taught and assessed (College Board, 2012e) and, consequently, the AP assessments are moving away from factual recall and targeting deeper, more complex thinking. Specific goals of the redesigned AP history courses are as follows: (1) support the use of historical thinking skills, (2) articulate clear learning outcomes for the students, (3) encourage a flexible approach to teaching content, (4) encourage multiple approaches to teaching, and (5) reflect college-level expectations. The first redesigned AP history course (U.S. History) and the corresponding exam will be launched during the 2014–2015 academic year.[6]

The four common historical thinking skills are stated in the domain models for AP U.S. History, AP European History, and AP World History. The definitions of these four historical thinking skills and their sub-skills are shown in Table 10.2. Every item developed for these assessments of the three redesigned AP history courses is designed to align with at least one of the historical thinking skills, and each exam is designed to cover all historical thinking skills. The new history exams will contain 36 selected-response items (all of which are set-based items with a stimulus), four short answer questions, one DBQ, and one long essay. These new exams will still be administered as summative assessments in May.

IB History Assessments

The IB offers three international academic programs and one career certificate to students from ages 3 to 19 (International Baccalaureate, 2012a, 2012b, 2012c, 2012d, 2012e). There is

Table 10.2 Historical Thinking Skills in the Domain Model for Redesigned AP History Courses and Exams

Historical Thinking Skills	*Definition*
Skill #1: Crafting Historical Arguments from Historical Evidence	
Historical argumentation	Ability to define and frame a question about the past and to address that question by constructing an argument
Appropriate use of relevant historical evidence	Ability to identify, describe, evaluate, and use evidence about the past from diverse sources (written documents, works of art, archeological artifacts, oral traditions, and other primary sources), with respect to content, authorship, purpose, format, and audience
Skill #2: Chronological Reasoning	
Historical causation	Ability to identify, analyze, and evaluate multiple cause-and-effect relationships in a historical context, distinguishing between the long term and proximate
Patterns of continuity and change over time	Ability to recognize, analyze, and evaluate the dynamics of historical continuity and change over periods of time of varying lengths, as well as relating these patterns to larger historical processes or themes
Periodization	Ability to describe, analyze, evaluate, and construct models of historical periodization that historians use to categorize events into discrete blocks and to identify turning points, recognizing that the choice of specific dates favors one narrative, region, or group over another narrative, region, or group; therefore, changing the periodization can change a historical narrative
Skill #3: Comparison and Contextualization	
Comparison	Ability to describe, compare, and evaluate, in various chronological and geographical contexts, multiple historical developments and perspectives within one society and one or more developments across or between different societies
Contextualization	Ability to connect historical developments to specific circumstances in time and place and to broader regional, national, or global processes
Skill #4: Historical Interpretation and Synthesis	
Interpretation	Ability to describe, analyze, evaluate, and create diverse interpretations of the past—as revealed through primary and secondary historical sources—by analyzing evidence, reasoning, contexts, points of view, and frames of reference
Synthesis	Ability to arrive at meaningful and persuasive understandings of the past by applying all the other historical thinking skills, by drawing appropriately on ideas from different fields of inquiry or disciplines, and by creatively fusing disparate, relevant (and perhaps contradictory) evidence from primary sources and secondary works

the Primary Years Programme for students from ages 3 to 12, the Middle Years Programme (MYP) for students between ages 11 and 16, and the Diploma Programme (DP) for students between ages 16 and 19. These programs are interdisciplinary, and history is one subject area that may be part of a student's program, particularly within the MYP and the DP. The MYP is designed to encourage students to develop critical thinking skills, which are necessary for a study of history, and prepare them for the DP (International Baccalaureate, 2012b). The humanities course in the MYP is where students are first exposed to a range of historical sources and communication of historical knowledge. The historical concepts introduced during the MYP humanities course become more focused and specialized during the DP. There are four aims of the history course within the DP: (1) promote an understanding of history as a discipline, including the nature and diversity of its sources, methods, and interpretations, (2) encourage an understanding of the present through critical reflection upon the past, (3) encourage an understanding of the impact of historical developments at national, regional, and international levels, and (4) develop an awareness of one's own historical identity through the study of the historical experiences of different cultures. Components of the history course include "History and Europe and the Islamic world" and "20th century world history" (International Baccalaureate, 2012b).

The IB program utilizes a portfolio assessment model for its programs. That is, a collection of various assessments and tasks are used to evaluate a student's knowledge, skills, abilities, and progress over time. Assessment for the MYP comprises ongoing evidence-producing activities (e.g., examinations, problem-solving activities, organized debates), as well as a final assessment based on oral, written, and practical work at the end of the program. During the final year, a personal project is conducted. The final assessment is criterion-referenced, and students receive a score of 1 to 7 for each subject and for the personal project. Similarly, the DP comprises ongoing assessments and a final criterion-referenced assessment. However, with the DP, the examinations are more formal. At the end of the DP program, students complete written examinations in each of their courses.

National Assessment of Educational Progress

NAEP is a national survey of achievement. Its group-level assessment goals generate different constraints than the other assessments we have discussed, which are reported at the individual level. In history, NAEP assesses the U.S. history knowledge and thinking of students in grades 4, 8, and 12. The assessment is developed according to a framework developed by the National Assessment Governing Board and is organized around three components: *Themes in U.S. History*, *Periods of U.S. History*, and *Ways of Knowing and Thinking about U.S. History*. The following four themes in U.S. History are used to organize the framework as well as for reporting student knowledge and thinking: (1) change and continuity in American democracy: ideas, institutions, events, key figures, and controversies; (2) the gathering and interactions of peoples, cultures, and ideas; (3) economic and technological changes and their relation to society, ideas, and the environment; and (4) the changing role of America in the world. Each of the themes is assessed in each of the eight periods starting from 1607 to present.

NAEP identifies and defines the cognitive processes of historical knowing and thinking about U.S. history in two broad categories: (1) historical knowledge and perspective and (2) historical analysis and interpretation (NAGB, 2010). Historical knowledge and perspectives are defined as (1) knowing and understanding people, events, concepts, themes, movements, contexts, and historical sources; (2) sequencing events; (3) recognizing multiple perspectives and seeing an era or movement through the eyes of different groups; and (4) developing a general conceptualization of U.S. history. Historical analysis and interpretation is defined as (1) explaining issues and identifying historical patterns; (2) establishing cause-and-effect relationships; (3) finding value statements; (4) establishing significance; (5) applying historical knowledge and weighing evidence to draw sound conclusions; (6) making defensible generalizations; and (7) rendering insightful accounts of the past. Each of the four themes in each period includes items assessing historical knowledge and perspective, as well as historical analysis and interpretation.

The assessment uses both selected-response (50 percent) and constructed-response (50 percent) items to assess these domains. The historical knowledge and perspective cognitive domain assesses students' ability to identify and define specific factual information, themes, movements, and general principles operating in U.S. history as well as deducing meaning and comprehending patterns. The items assessing this domain may ask students to:

- name, recognize, list, identify, and give examples of people, places, events, concepts, and movements;
- place events, phenomena, and outcomes in a chronological framework and construct and label historical periods;
- define historical themes and give examples of the ways themes relate to specific factual information;
- describe the past from the perspectives of various men and women of the time; explain the perspective of an author of a primary source document; describe different perspectives related to a historical issue or event; and
- summarize the contributions of individuals and groups to U.S. history; summarize the meaning of historical sources, such as original documents, speeches, cartoons, artifacts, photos, art, music, architecture, literature, drama, dance, popular culture, biographies, journals, folklore, historic sites and places, and oral history narratives; and link these people and sources to general themes. (NAGB, 2010, p.42)

Historical analysis and interpretation assesses students' ability to make value judgments about historical information, weigh evidence, synthesize information, apply knowledge, make judgments, formulate generalizations, and draw conclusions. Students are asked to:

- specify and explain cause-and-effect relationships and connect contemporary events to their origins in the past;
- categorize information and develop strategies for organizing a large body of facts;
- examine multiple causes of historical developments;
- explain points of view, biases, and value statements in historical sources;
- determine the significance of people, events, and historical sources;
- weigh and judge different views of the past as advanced by historical figures themselves, historians, and present-day commentators and public figures;
- demonstrate that the interpretation and meaning of the past are open to change as new information and perspectives emerge;
- develop sound generalizations and defend these generalizations with persuasive arguments;
- make comparisons and recognize the limitations of generalizations; and
- apply knowledge, draw conclusions, and support those conclusions with convincing evidence. (NAGB, 2010, p. 43)

Student competencies are reported on the four scales that correspond to the four themes. Scale scores as well as achievement-level scores (Basic, Proficient, Advanced) are reported for the nation as well as by state.

Meeting the Challenges of Assessment of Historical Thinking

In the sections below, we describe two assessments, HAT and HTAT. Unlike the large-scale, standardized assessments surveyed above, neither is designed as an EOC test for a prescribed curriculum. Their illustrative value arises, rather, as products of assessment design that place models of complex historical cognition and learning central to assessment task design (which evokes student demonstrations of cognition and learning). Moreover, the design of HTAT employed the ECD approach, adapted to the assessment of historical thinking.

Historical Assessments of Thinking

Wineburg and his research team have recently developed history assessments which they called "Beyond the Bubble" (Stanford History Education Group, 2013). Following the Common Core State Standards, these assessments relegate second-order concepts to a supporting role and, instead, focus on historical reading skills: students being able to "analyse primary and secondary sources, cite textual evidence, consider the influence on an author's perspective, corroborate different sources, and develop written historical arguments" (Breakstone, Smith, & Wineburg, 2013, p. 53). In a number of recent presentations and publications, they have highlighted the pitfalls and problems of the selected-response item format (e.g., Breakstone et al., 2013; Wineburg, Smith, & Breakstone, 2012). Indeed, the name of their assessment website, "Beyond the Bubble," is a reference to the rejection of the "bubbles" that are critical to machine scoring of selected responses. The Stanford team has been more explicit about the parameters for the task model than they have been about a model for history cognition and learning. Perhaps they rightly assume that there is widespread agreement on using evidence to support a historical argument, sourcing, contextualization, and corroboration as basic components of historical literacy. They highlight the alignment of their tasks with the Common Core State Standards.

The emphasis, then, is upon the task model, building upon the rejection of selected-response items. They recognize the value of the AP-type DBQ, which demands extended essays in response to multiple primary source documents. However, they argue that the DBQ tests multiple competencies in a single summative task, placing a heavy cognitive burden on both test takers and scorers. Their tasks, requiring 10 minutes to complete and only moments to score, target a specific element of historical literacy and together provide a set of formative assessments that a teacher might use to, among other purposes, prepare students for the DBQ.

A particular assessment usually comprises one or two documents (often visual), one or two questions, and a requirement that students justify the answers to the questions. The assessment usually targets one or two elements of historical literacy. Scoring rubrics and sample student responses were developed, revised, and validated with student focus groups, think-aloud interviews as students completed the assessments, and piloting with larger samples. At present, there is a large bank of short assessments of American history made freely available and, thus, facilitating replication as well as further research and development (https://beyondthebubble.stanford.edu/).

Historical Thinking Assessment Tool

In this section, we describe how the three-model approach in ECD was applied to developing HTAT by Ercikan, Seixas, Gibson, and Lyon-Thomas (2012; Figure 10.1).

Cognition and Learning Model

The cognition and learning model for the assessment targeted three widely recognized second-order historical thinking concepts (Seixas, 2009): (1) using primary source evidence (*Evidence*); (2) taking historical perspectives (*Perspective*); and (3) understanding the ethical dimension of historical interpretations (*Ethical*). Using primary source evidence refers to finding, selecting, contextualizing, and interpreting sources for a historical argument. Taking historical perspectives involves understanding that the "past is a foreign country," with its different social, cultural, intellectual, and even emotional contexts that shaped people's lives and actions and reading sources with due consideration of the conditions and worldviews at the time when they were created. Understanding the ethical dimension of historical interpretations requires

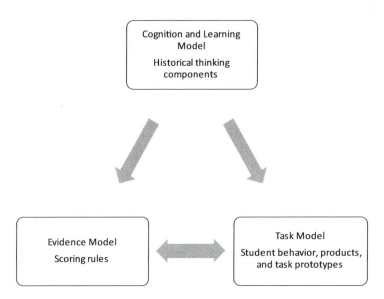

Figure 10.1 Construct, task, and evidence models.

understanding how we, in the present, judge actors in different circumstances in the past, when and how crimes and sacrifices of the past have consequences today, and what obligations we have today in relation to those consequences.[7] The selection of these three concepts was based on the priority given to them in history classes and limitations in the number of tasks that could be included in a single assessment that could be administered in schools (Seixas & Ercikan, 2011).

Task Model

The next design step in the assessment was to devise task prototypes that would elicit the intended behaviors and products. The intended student behavior and products, together with the task prototypes, constituted the *task model*. The topic used in the assessment was the internment of Ukrainian-Canadians during the First World War, events that had not been addressed in the eleventh-grade 20th-century Canadian history course, though it fell within its broad chronological and topical contents. Thus, all of the factual information that students would need in order to demonstrate competency in historical thinking was provided. This was done in three ways: through "background information" on the internment displayed on an introductory page, consisting of basic facts, dates, and numbers; second, through five document excerpts (approximately 100 words each); and finally, through brief contextualizing captions for each of the excerpts, giving the author, author's position, and date. A confounding variable in assessing historical thinking is the extent to which generic reading and writing skills—antecedent to the discipline-specific reading and writing skills—are required for demonstrating competency in any history assessment task. All documents were edited so that they would not be difficult for the majority of students to read.

As part of the cognition and learning model, the researchers enumerated the cognitive demands of the three second-order concepts. They then wrote one to three questions (a mixture of short constructed response and selected response) for each of the document excerpts, in order to elicit evidence of students' mastery of those demands. In answering these questions, students were expected to demonstrate understanding of how to make justifiable inferences about primary source evidence (cognitive demands of the construct "using primary source evidence"). They were expected to present explanations for the different perspectives presented in the documents and make inferences about authors' motivations after considering their positions, purposes, and contexts (cognitive demands of the construct "historical perspective taking"). The final two questions, both eliciting constructed response paragraphs, asked students to consider the different documents they read before making ethical judgments about Ukrainian internment. The first asked whether internment was justified; the second, whether the Canadian government owed an apology, recognition, or compensation to descendants. In responding to these two final questions, students were expected to demonstrate their ability to make ethical judgments about a historical act, taking into account the temporal distance between now and then (cognitive demands of the construct "the ethical dimension of history").

The instrument employs a particular approach to the use of documents. Like the AP DBQ (as is common in history assessment practice at upper levels), it includes multiple primary source documents, presenting different perspectives in relation to a particular historical incident. But rather than asking students to demonstrate their interpretation of the entire set of documents in a single large essay, shorter questions follow each of the documents. This allows for the inclusion of documents with a range of difficulties with respect to interpreting historical sources. It also fosters a cumulative understanding of the historical situation, as students encounter successive documents. Finally, by including multiple related but independently scored items, the instrument's reliability is enhanced—an important consideration in view of the fixed test time.

The selection of different item types (e.g., selected-response, short-answer, or performance-based) must include consideration of which formats are best suited for assessing the targeted construct. Selection is complicated by the other constraints, such as broad content domain coverage and limited testing time. HTAT included a variety of item types: selected-response, short constructed response, and two one-paragraph constructed-response questions that served as summative items. Most posed cognitive demands related to at least two of the three second-order historical thinking concepts: it proved difficult, and unnecessary, to separate them in item construction. There is evidence that selected-response item types have limitations in capturing complex historical thinking (Breakstone et al., 2013; Reich, 2009). HTAT provided further evidence that selected-response and constructed-response items captured somewhat different constructs, with constructed-response tasks having a closer relationship to the target construct. On the other hand, previous research indicated a high level of person-by-task interaction in science performance assessments (Shavelson, Baxter, & Gao, 1993), which implies serious limitations in measurement accuracy for assessments comprising a small number of performance-based or constructed-response items.

The decision to include selected-response tasks in HTAT was to increase the number of tasks that could be administered in a short period of time and thereby enhance measurement precision. Six selected-response tasks resulted in a very small increase in reliability from .67 to .71. Furthermore, item response theory (IRT)-based analyses also demonstrated that selected-response tasks contributed very little to the overall measurement accuracy. There was stronger evidence of historical thinking from student verbalizations for constructed-response tasks than for selected-response tasks. Exploratory factor analysis provided further evidence that selected-response tasks were measuring a somewhat different construct. First, all selected-response tasks primarily loaded onto a second factor. Second, the variance accounted for by the tasks with a one-factor model increased from 37 percent to 44 percent when the selected-response tasks were dropped from the factor analysis. Even though the increase in variance accounted for is not very big, the fact that this occurred when the number of tasks was reduced indicates that a somewhat different construct is being measured by the selected-response tasks. Whether this was due to flawed questions or a problematic question type deserves further study.

Evidence Model

The evidence model, that is, the evaluation and interpretation of evidence of competency with respect to the cognition and learning model, was guided by the definition of the construct, the cognitive demands, and the tasks. The first step in developing criteria for evaluating student responses to tasks was the identification of rules for extracting evidence that students demonstrated the intended cognitive demands, behaviors, and products. These rules were then refined to take into account both the specifics of the tasks and the types of responses students were expected to provide (Figure 10.1). More detailed information about cognitive demands and task prototypes for each historical thinking component is presented in Appendix A. In Appendix B, we present sample tasks and scoring rules from HTAT.

The evaluation of inferences in the evidence model which includes scoring of student responses in relation to the targeted construct requires both the evaluation of the scoring rules used to convert observations to scores as well as the implementation of the scoring rules (Ercikan, 2002). This evaluation needs to include expert judgments of appropriateness and adequacy of the scoring rules and be supported with empirical evidence. In addition to reviews by historical thinking experts, the scorer consistency provided empirical evidence of consistent interpretation of the scoring rules, thereby supporting accuracy of implementation of the scoring rules. The relationship between the resulting scores with the construct was investigated through examining the relationship between scores and the overall targeted construct—historical thinking—using IRT-based modeling.

Making inferences about student competencies is part of the evidence model. These inferences were examined by investigating whether the scores resulting from interpretation of student performances on tasks in the assessment provided an accurate and consistent measurement of historical thinking. This included investigating psychometric properties of the assessment tasks and scores, how the tasks were related to each other, whether the assessment lent itself to creating a single historical thinking scale, the level of measurement accuracy provided by the assessment, and the evidence that the tasks engaged students in historical thinking and scores are indicators of historical thinking. Internal consistency provided evidence regarding the degree to which the tasks in the assessment provided consistent measurement of historical thinking. The factor analysis provided evidence of how the tasks were related to each other and whether a unitary historical thinking scale could be constructed. IRT-based modeling of responses enabled estimation of the measurement accuracy provided by the assessment for students at different ability levels. Think-aloud protocols (TAPs) provided cognitive evidence of the assessment engaging students in historical thinking, thereby supporting the interpretation that scores are indicators of students' levels of competence. Both the psychometric and cognitive validity evidence supporting interpretations in the evidence model are described in the following section.

Validation in ECD

The key issue for any assessment is the extent to which it fulfills its intended purposes. Kane (2013) describes an argument-based approach to validation that involves two kinds of arguments, an interpretive and a validation argument. This approach to validation requires making intended inferences explicit at the outset to conduct evaluations of the adequacy of the evidence required to support the intended inferences. There are direct parallels between this approach to validation and ECD-based assessment design. ECD also requires intended inferences from assessments to be made explicit and the assessment design to be directly guided by these inferences. In particular, ECD "provides language, concepts, and knowledge representations for designing and delivering educational assessments, all organized around the evidentiary argument an assessment is meant to embody" (Mislevy, 2007, p. 1). The evaluation of the desired inference that scores from the assessment are accurate indicators of students' history knowledge and thinking involves the examination of: (1) the relationship between the target construct(s) and the tasks; (2) the connection between the tasks and interpretation of performances on the tasks; and (3) the degree to which interpretation of performances in relation to the target constructs is supported by evidence. In the sections below, we discuss each of these evaluation processes in relation to assessments of historical thinking in general, drawing upon examples from the validation of HTAT.

The Connection between Tasks and the Constructs: Validity by Design

The degree of construct representation is central to the validity of inferences from an assessment. Messick (1989) argued that the two main threats to validity are construct underrepresentation and construct-irrelevant variance. Thus, one component of the validation argument examines the degree to which the assessment tasks capture the target constructs (e.g., AERA, APA, & NCME, 1999). To this end, it is imperative to understand the cognitive processes used by students in responding to the tasks, which in turn depend on the connections between the constructs and the task models. Although validation certainly requires gathering evidence after the test is developed and scores are generated, it is equally important to gather evidence for the validity argument in the early phases of assessment design before scores are generated—and while there may still be an opportunity to modify the tasks or even the overall design. This is especially true for claims involving historical thinking skills that are drawn from a hypothesized cognitive model. Therefore, how the construct model guided task design and development is an important first step in the validity argument.

Second, evidence from the interactions of students with tasks, in particular the cognitive processes in which they engage in, constitutes another important source of validity evidence. In educational research, the most commonly used methods for gathering data about student cognitive processes are different types of TAPs. TAPs require participants to verbalize their thoughts while they are engaged in an educational activity (Ericsson & Simon, 1993). They have been used to examine students' knowledge structures and cognitive processes while they are engaged in solving a problem, interpreting a chart, or completing an activity (Leighton & Gierl, 2007). TAPs have been used to investigate cognitive processes in a variety of domains such as chemistry (Kozma, Chin, Russell, & Marx, 2000), history (Wineburg, 1991), science (Ercikan et al., 2010; Roth, 2003, 2009), language learning (Camps, 2003; Gu, Guangwei, & Zhang, 2005), writing (Ransdell, 1995), mathematics (Gallagher & De Lisi, 1994; Gierl, 1997; Martiniello, 2008; Schoenfeld, 2007), and reading (Fukkink, 2005; Pressley & Afflerbach, 1995; Wolfe & Goldman, 2005).

In assessment validation, TAPs provide evidence for examining students' understanding of test questions; whether specific words, phrases, and sentence structures create confusion or difficulty for students; and how their proficiency in the test language affects their formulation of solutions and responses (Ercikan et al., 2010). These protocols have also been used for broader validity investigations such as examining the cognitive demands of tasks and especially the degree to which the tasks make the intended cognitive demands (Ferrara et al., 2003, 2004, 2005; Ferrara & Chen, 2011); for examining validity of assessments for different populations such as English language learners and students with disabilities (Sato, 2011); construct validation (e.g., Hamilton, Nussbaum, & Snow, 1997; Katz, Bennett, & Berger, 2000); test construction (e.g., Embretson & Gorin, 2001; Tatsuoka, 1990); and for testing hypotheses about sources of differential item functioning (Ercikan et al., 2010).

TAPs can be conducted early in the task design phase to begin gathering such validity evidence, as well as to inform the design of the tasks. In task development, there is generally an underlying hypothesis about what the task is assessing and what is required of the student, with respect to content knowledge and skills, to respond appropriately to the task. However, without evidence that a student is interacting with the task in the intended manner, one can only speculate that the underlying hypothesis is correct.

For example, consider an item writer who is creating an item intended to assess reasoning in historical causation. How is the item writer to know that the item elicits evidence relevant to this reasoning? In the absence of data, the validity argument rests only on theoretical arguments and, perhaps, data from other assessments. If the item writer's implicit model is incorrect, validity may be seriously threatened. Specifically, in the words of Leighton (2004), "If test items are being systematically misunderstood, this would mean that (a) the assessment is eliciting content understandings and processes other than what was intended, or (b) the inferences drawn from the scores are inaccurate, or both" (p. 8).

Recent research by Kaliski, France, Huff, and Thurber (2010) demonstrated how TAPs can be conducted during item development for history assessments to gather cognitive validity evidence. Specifically, Kaliski et al. conducted TAPs with AP World History items that were being piloted for the redesigned exam along with current AP World History items. This allowed for comparison of students' verbalizations when they took items intended to assess complex historical thinking to those when they responded to items that assess factual recall. The transcribed verbal reports from the students were coded by two researchers for historical thinking skills (i.e., those described in Table 10.2). The degree of alignment between the intended historical thinking skill for the item and the coded historical thinking skill in the verbal report was examined to determine whether or not the items were functioning as intended. The results showed that complex historical thinking was elicited by the new item types, thus contributing to validity evidence for the redesigned exams.

Ercikan et al. (2012) used TAPs to investigate the cognitive processes students employed in responding to HTAT. For each task, key historical thinking competencies and cognitive demands were identified. These competencies and cognitive demands guided the identification of evidence of students' engagement in historical thinking in their verbalizations. Evidence of the construct being tapped by tasks can be considered from both task and student viewpoints. When students engage with a task, there are two factors that affect whether the task assesses the intended constructs. The first relates to item features and the second to student characteristics, including their cognitive development, language, and culture. Tasks need to be designed to engage students in cognitive processes that are targeted by the learning and cognition model. On the other hand, even when a task is successful in doing this for some students, it may not for others (e.g., those for whom the task may be too difficult). Furthermore, evidence obtained from student verbalizations of the expected cognitive engagement with a task is affected by a third factor: student verbalizations can be impacted by students' ability and willingness to monitor and communicate their thinking processes.

In the Ercikan et al. (2012) research, student verbalizations were interpreted from both the task and student points of view, with these three factors in mind. Students were expected to demonstrate evidence and perspective competencies on a select set of nine tasks. There was a great degree of variability of evidence of these competencies across the nine tasks. Overall, TAPs provided strong evidence that the great majority of the students engaged in historical thinking. On some items, smaller proportions of students' verbalizations included evidence of historical thinking. As indicated by previous research, while students' verbalizations may provide evidence of their engagement in historical thinking, lack of such evidence in verbalizations does not necessarily imply that they were not engaging in historical thinking.

The Connection between Evidence and Tasks and Constructs

The evidence model governs how relevant data are extracted from the student work product and then linked to the cognition and learning model. The interpretations of student responses to tasks using a set of scoring rules constitute the data used to evaluate the assessment claims. These data are transformed into evidence with respect to the target constructs using the evidence model. This model includes how student responses to individual tasks are interpreted using a scoring rubric, as well as how the evidence is accumulated across tasks in forming an overall score. The evaluation of the inferences from observations requires both careful analysis of the scoring rules used to convert observations to scores as well as the quality of implementation of the scoring rules. Inter-rater reliability can provide evidence of consistent interpretation of the scoring rules, thereby supporting accuracy of implementation.

There are several factors that should be considered in the interpretation of student responses in relation to the target construct (i.e., in the evidence model). The student performance is the outcome of an interaction between the student and the assessment. In addition to student competencies relevant to the assessment, such as their history knowledge and historical thinking, other student characteristics, properties of the assessment, and the assessment context can all affect the student response. Here we discuss (1) cognitive and non-cognitive demands of the assessment tasks that are *not* the intended targets of the assessment (i.e., construct-irrelevant factors) and (2) opportunities for students to learn the competencies targeted by the assessment.

Engaging students in complex thinking in history typically requires them to read and interpret historical documents, similar to the way a historian engages with the past. In order to assess student competencies identified in the construct, tasks need (1) to require history knowledge and thinking that goes beyond simple reading comprehension and (2) not to place cognitive demands that inappropriately jeopardize students' chances of demonstrating their history knowledge and thinking. The first can happen if students can respond to questions by simply using their reading comprehension and generic reasoning skills that are not particular to historical thinking. The second can happen when the reading comprehension requirement is unnecessarily so high that students who have not attained that skill level are disadvantaged. Minimizing construct-irrelevant factors in the design stage of the assessment is an essential aspect of achieving validity by design. However, construct-irrelevant factors, such as complex reading requirements, may be necessary, such as in upper grade levels of history education, for engaging students with authentic historical primary resources. Minimizing construct-irrelevant variance due to reading competency requirements involves (1) identifying ways of designing tasks with lower levels of reading complexity, (2) making such requirements explicit, and (3) taking the effect of these additional cognitive requirements into account in interpreting student responses.

Inferences from assessments that do not suffer from construct-irrelevant variance still may not be valid with respect to students' cognitive competencies. Whether students have had opportunities to learn (OTLs) the targeted competencies also affects interpretations of student performance. OTLs have been discussed as an aspect of validity of assessments in previous research (Burstein et al., 1995; McDonnell, 1995). However, it gains further salience when the assessment involves complex thinking. As discussed above, historical thinking involves both declarative knowledge as well as procedural knowledge. Assessment designers have to make decisions about whether historical thinking must be assessed within a content domain or whether it can be assessed independent of content knowledge. In the absence of a uniform curriculum, students cannot be expected to have similar declarative content knowledge about specific periods or topics. Such differential OTL content knowledge in turn affects the degree to which students can demonstrate their historical thinking competencies on tasks which also require specific content knowledge. In order to minimize the limitations induced by differential OTLs, tasks can be designed to provide all the necessary content knowledge to students. This was the approach taken in HTAT where all the factual knowledge students needed for answering questions on the assessment were presented to them in a six-point "background information" page and five excerpts from original source documents related to the Ukrainian internment. In a time-limited summative assessment context, this strategy may not be feasible. Another option, as in AP, is to offer a choice of topics students can select. These topics will need to cover a range of topics students are expected to know in a curriculum in the targeted grade to allow choice for students.

The evidence model not only includes how student responses to tasks are interpreted in relation to the cognition and learning model but also accumulation of evidence across tasks which produces an overall score intended to reflect students' overall competencies. Most large-scale assessments of educational learning outcomes in North America support such interpretations by assigning student scores to achievement levels, with corresponding achievement-level descriptors (ALDs; Ercikan & Julian, 2002; Ercikan & McCreith, 2002). ALDs are defined as descriptions of what students should know and be able to do within each performance category. In an ECD framework, ALDs are directly related to two elements that constitute the basis of the assessment framework: the claims about student proficiency that are the objectives of the assessment and statements that describe the observable in student work that provide evidence for such claims. These claims and evidence statements are typically established during the cognition and learning model development phase.

ALDs for each performance category are essential for supporting valid score interpretations when the purpose of an assessment is to reliably classify students into performance categories (e.g., AP exams). In ECD, the ALDs play a more prominent role in assessment design, task model design, and item development than in conventional approaches to assessment design. ALDs, as one of the artifacts from the domain modeling (i.e., cognition and learning model) phase of ECD, are strongly related to claims and evidence statements and are direct inputs into the task models (e.g., Plake, Huff, & Reshetar, 2010). For example, as part of the AP redesign project for World History, U.S. History, and European History, ALDs are being developed to describe what students know and can do for AP scores 1, 2, 3, 4, and 5. These ALDs are developed and refined prior to and during item development and are used during standard-setting procedures to inform where to set cut scores. See Appendix C for an example of ALDs that were used during a standard-setting workshop for AP World History in June 2012. Score interpretations are strengthened when ALDs are carefully constructed and then used to directly inform task models and item development (e.g., Bejar, Braun, & Tannenbaum, 2007; Schneider et al., 2010; see the following paragraph for a description of approaches for validating ALDs). When ECD is the assessment design framework, ALDs are directly informed by student work because of the critical role of evidence statements. Evidence statements describe the observable evidence in student work that become either part of the task model or one of the targets of measurement (Huff, Alves, Pellegrino, & Kaliski, 2013), which strengthens the validity of the score interpretations.

Whether or not the assessment design team is working within an ECD framework, ALDs should be carefully developed and refined throughout the test design process (e.g., Egan, Schneider, & Ferrara, 2011; Huff & Plake, 2010; Schneider et al., 2010). More specifically, ALDs should not only serve as the primary input in setting performance standards, but also to inform and guide item writing during the development of the assessment framework. Finally, after the assessment is administered and students have been classified into performance categories, empirical validation studies can be conducted to inform the final ALDs that are then used for score reporting. In other words, during this final phase, the intended score interpretation statements in ALDs about what students should know and can do in each performance category are empirically supported by the test scores, producing valid score interpretations. Various approaches exist for validating ALDs, but they generally can be considered as approaches that are grounded in scale-anchoring methodologies (e.g., Beaton & Allen, 1992; Chajewski & Kaliski, 2013; Reshetar et al., 2013a, 2013b; Sinharay, Haberman, & Lee, 2011). These methodologies require operational exam data as well as cut scores that are used to classify students on the exam. Psychometric methodologies (e.g., IRT; Chajewski & Kaliski, 2013) can be employed to classify items into performance levels. At this point, since both items and examinees are classified into performance levels, workshops involving subject matter experts can be conducted to review the alignment between what ALDs say students know and can do and what the empirical item classifications imply that students know and can do.

Discussion

This chapter emphasizes the importance of including historical thinking in assessments of history learning, describes challenges to including such complex thinking in large-scale assessments, and presents examples of designing and validating assessments of historical thinking. In any assessment, decisions about different aspects of the assessment involves trade-offs with regard to what is assessed and how it is assessed. These include how many and what types of assessment tasks should be included given the kinds of score reporting and interpretation intended (Ercikan & Julian, 2002). It also includes decisions about emphasizing declarative knowledge in specific history topics and periods versus complex historical thinking (Ercikan & Seixas, 2011). These trade-offs affect the accuracy and generalizability of claims (Ercikan & Roth, 2009, 2011) and should be guided by the purposes and uses of assessments. Two cornerstones of our discussion are ECD and the importance given to validation. Both of these gain heightened importance and value in assessing complex thinking such as historical thinking. In assessment design, close connections among construct and cognition, task, and evidence models are central to making valid inferences from assessments. Cognitive evidence from both the student and task perspectives can play an important role in supporting validity arguments about these connections.

Although ECD is a flagship approach for developing assessments, successful implementation can be a challenge, and one should consider several cautions and caveats about ECD before jumping in and beginning this rigorous model-based approach to assessment design. Hendrickson and colleagues (2013) recently described recommendations for implementing ECD and lessons learned from their recent experiences implementing ECD in the AP program. The four primary challenges described by Hendrickson et al. are: (1) integrating learning theory into assessment design, (2) identifying the appropriate levels of specificity with which to document the claims and evidence, (3) developing and evaluating task models, and (4) strategically incorporating iteration into the design process. At the heart of these challenges is accepting the iterative nature of ECD and realizing that, as progress is made moving forward in the ECD phases, it is often necessary to revisit previous phases to ensure that the best quality assessment is being developed. ECD can be time-consuming and resource-intensive, but the end result of having an evidence-centered assessment is worth it. Recognizing these challenges prior to beginning implementation of ECD should pay off.

Designing assessments of historical thinking using ECD is resource-intensive, complex work that must be executed within the fiduciary, operational, and political constraints of the particular testing program. A few common constraints faced by testing programs include the lack of: operational flexibility or financial resources to dedicate more than a perfunctory amount of time to design before starting item development; resources—in terms of funds and/or time—to score multiple extended constructed responses; or operational or political flexibility to extend student testing time to incorporate additional stimuli (e.g., selections from primary and secondary sources) and/or additional constructed responses. In addition, developing or adapting a cognition and learning model to inform assessment design; developing claims, evidence, and task models; developing ALDs and using them to inform design decisions; and conducting TAPs are typically considered "nice to have" rather than necessary steps in assessment design and development (see Schmeiser & Welch, 2006, for a description of a typical approach to assessment design). Assessment designers and historians who think it is essential to the quality of the assessment to commit the substantial human capital, time, and funds to these endeavors for a large-scale assessment program may encounter any range of resistance from the decision-makers (Hendrickson, Ewing, Kaliski, & Huff, 2013; Huff, Steinberg, & Matts, 2010). As such, compromises that fall short of the recommendations made here but still improve the assessment of historical thinking should be considered. For example, a testing program may not have the resources to fully implement ECD but may have the resources to articulate in fine detail task and item specifications that help ensure that the target of measurement is not simply declarative historical knowledge.

As noted earlier, the current state of affairs in regard to developing history assessments that assess the Common Core Standards for Literacy in History and Social Studies is both promising and challenging. Developing these assessments will require test developers, teachers, learning scientists, and psychometricians to collaborate in thinking outside the box in order to develop innovative history assessments. Given the existing evidence of the limitations of selected-response item types in assessing historical thinking, test developers will need to incorporate and utilize rich stimuli and write selected-response questions in different ways than they are commonly done in order to assess the historical thinking skills called for in the Common Core State Standards. Furthermore, these item types cannot be assumed to be measuring the intended complex thinking without cognitive evidence. Innovative item types that truly engage students in historical thinking, including some of the examples discussed in this chapter, should be considered as central to Common Core State Standards assessments. This endeavor is not going to be easy, but if implemented successfully, the results will be a huge success for history assessment in the United States. An ECD approach to designing these new assessments might be the solution, but we must embrace the iterative nature of ECD to make this work and not shy away from contemporary and innovative approaches to assessment design.

Appendix A: Common Core Anchor Standards for Literacy and Social Science, Grades 9–10

ANCHOR STANDARDS FOR READING

Key Ideas and Details

1 Cite specific textual evidence to support analysis of primary and secondary sources, attending to such features as the date and origin of the information.
2 Determine the central ideas or information of a primary or secondary source; provide an accurate summary of how key events or ideas develop over the course of the text.
3 Analyze in detail a series of events described in a text; determine whether earlier events caused later ones or simply preceded them.

Craft and Structure

4 Determine the meaning of words and phrases as they are used in a text, including vocabulary describing political, social, or economic aspects of history/social studies.
5 Analyze how a text uses structure to emphasize key points or advance an explanation or analysis.
6 Compare the point of view of two or more authors for how they treat the same or similar topics, including which details they include and emphasize in their respective accounts.

Integration of Knowledge and Ideas

7 Integrate quantitative or technical analysis (e.g., charts, research data) with qualitative analysis in print or digital text.
8 Assess the extent to which the reasoning and evidence in a text support the author's claims.
9 Compare and contrast treatments of the same topic in several primary and secondary sources.

Range of Reading and Level of Text Complexity

10 By the end of grade 10, read and comprehend history/social studies texts in the grades 9–10 text complexity band independently and proficiently.

Text Types and Purposes

1 Write arguments focused on discipline-specific content.
2 Write informative/explanatory texts, including the narration of historical events, scientific procedures/experiments, or technical processes.

Production and Distribution of Writing

3 Produce clear and coherent writing in which the development, organization, and style are appropriate to task, purpose, and audience.
4 Develop and strengthen writing as needed by planning, revising, editing, rewriting, or trying a new approach, focusing on addressing what is most significant for a specific purpose and audience.
5 Use technology, including the Internet, to produce, publish, and update individual or shared writing products, taking advantage of technology's capacity to link to other information and to display information flexibly and dynamically.

Research to Build and Present Knowledge

6 Conduct short as well as more sustained research projects to answer a question (including a self-generated question) or solve a problem; narrow or broaden the inquiry when appropriate; synthesize multiple sources on the subject, demonstrating understanding of the subject under investigation.
7 Gather relevant information from multiple authoritative print and digital sources, using advanced searches effectively; assess the usefulness of each source in answering the research question; integrate information into the text selectively to maintain the flow of ideas, avoiding plagiarism and following a standard format for citation.
8 Draw evidence from informational texts to support analysis, reflection, and research.

Range of Writing

9 Write routinely over extended time frames (time for reflection and revision) and shorter time frames (a single sitting or a day or two) for a range of discipline-specific tasks, purposes, and audiences.

Appendix B

Table B.1 Cognitive Demands for Evidence and the Task Prototypes

Cognitive Demands	Student Behaviors and Products Eliciting Competency	Task
1 Understanding how history is an interpretation based on inferences from primary sources; understands that traces, relics, and records (primary sources) are not necessarily accounts	Makes justifiable inferences from primary sources (both traces and accounts) Distinguishes between accounts and traces (primary sources)	Presented with an account and a trace: "What can you learn from these? How are they different?"
2 Being able to ask questions that turn primary sources into evidence for an argument or an account	Formulates questions to interpret a source Interprets relevant information in support or against an argument	Presented with a primary source, write two questions that this source would help to answer. [Alternatively], presented with a series of the questions, which would the source help to answer?

(Continued)

Table B.1 (Continued)

	Cognitive Demands	Student Behaviors and Products Eliciting Competency	Task
3	Reading sources in view of the conditions and worldviews at the time when it was created (contextualization)	Articulates the role of material conditions (including technologies) and worldviews (context of the source) in interpreting events, actions, and motivations	Presented with sources from situations foreign to our own (e.g., sultans killing their brothers, witches being burned, child labor), explain actions in terms of belief systems and conditions
4	Inferring purposes of sources' authors/creators as well as their assumptions (sourcing)	Authors' purposes and assumptions are taken into account when interpreting sources	Presented with source(s), and basic information about the author's background, use both to identify purposes and assumptions of the author
5	Validating inferences from a single source with inferences from other sources and expressing degrees of certainty (corroboration)	Validity of inferences	Presented with a single source and questions, what other documents/sources would help to corroborate inferences/interpretations?

Table B.2 Cognitive Demands for Historical Perspective Taking and the Task Prototypes

	Cognitive Demands	Student Behaviors and Products Eliciting Competency	Task
1	Recognizes the depths of difference between current beliefs, values, and motivations (worldviews) and those of earlier peoples	Explains the thinking of past actors, which appears bizarre or ignorant by today's standards, in terms of the circumstances of the time in which they lived	Write a paragraph explaining what motivated and justified people in … [e.g., going to war; burning witches; human sacrifice; child labor; feats of endurance; arranged marriages]
2	Explains the perspectives of people in the past in their historical context (see Evidence #3)	See #1	See #1
3	Makes factually accurate, evidence-based interpretations of the beliefs, values, and motivations of people in the past, but recognizes limitations of our understanding	Uses primary sources to develop hypotheses about the beliefs, etc. of people in the past. Assesses the degree of certainty and factors unaccounted for	Given a variety of primary sources (visual and/or print or artifactual), provide an explanation of [action or decision by individual or group]. Explain what sources or information would add strength to your explanation
4	Distinguishes various perspectives among historical actors	Contrasts the perspectives of two or more groups *within* the same historical period	Given two (or more) primary sources from different sides of a historical conflict, explain the positions of the two (or more) groups/people

Table B.3 Cognitive Demands for the Ethical Dimension and Task Prototypes

Cognitive Demands	Student Behaviors and Products Eliciting Competency	Task
Student understanding	"Understanding" restated in terms of what a student can do	Task (note: most of these assume prior knowledge and study of the period)
1 Recognizes implicit and/or explicit ethical stances in historical narratives in a variety of media (e.g., film, museum exhibits, books)	Identifies states, institutions, groups, and individuals on which history writers, through their arguments and narratives (in a variety of media), make judgments, positive and negative, ethical and unethical, progressive and regressive Analyzes for ethical judgments at the levels of a) word choice, b) inclusion and omission, c) narrative structure, d) (for visual sources) visual composition	Note: is this just a reading skill? Given a text passage or film clip ("Heritage Minutes" are ideal, for an easy exercise) identify the author's heroes and villains (individuals, groups, states) and how they are constructed and presented through the narrative
2 Makes reasoned ethical judgments about actions of people in the past, recognizing the historical context in which they were operating	Note: this depends on prior "perspective-taking" study of the groups involved, but goes beyond it: Analyzes "criminal" actions in the light of norms of the times. Could the actor have known better; were any others acting differently; what were the opportunities for alternative actions?	Presented with evidence of actions (from an era they have studies), that would be considered unjust today, make an ethical judgment, using criteria (constraints and opportunities for the actor; see left)
3 Assesses fairly the implications for today of sacrifices and injustices in the past (e.g., reparations, monuments, remembrance)	Builds an argument for or against the imposition of reparations (or other measures) for a historical injustice, based on considerations of a) collective responsibility, b) benefits and deficits to respective present-day descendants	Presented with a dilemma about the putting in place (or eliminating) some form of restitution/remembrance, consider various options and support a choice with considerations of a) and b) (left)
4 Uses historical accounts to inform judgments and action on current issues, recognizing the limitations of any direct "lessons" from the past	Identifies historical roots of contemporary problems Justifies analogies between current issues and historical issues through appropriate use of detail. Expresses the limits of analogies through further detail	Provided with the historical antecedent to a contemporary problem, explore the similarities, differences, and lessons that could be drawn, through appropriate use of detail

Appendix B: Sample Tasks and Scoring Rules from HTAT

Document 1: Attitudes toward Ukrainians in 1899

An interview with Reverend Father Moris in the Calgary *Daily Herald*, January 27, 1899:
As for the Galicians [Ukrainians] I have not met a single person in the whole of the North West who is sympathetic towards them. They are, from the point of view of civilization, 10 times

(Continued)

(Continued)

lower than the Indians. They have not the least idea of sanitation. In their personal habits and acts, [they] resemble animals, and even in the streets of Edmonton, when they come to market, men, women, and children would, if unchecked, turn the place into a common sewer.

1   What was Father Moris' view of Galicians?
   a   Most people in the North West are prejudiced against them.
   b   They are uncivilized and unclean.
   c   They are superior to Indians.
   d   Further Galician immigration should be encouraged.
2   This source would be useful for a historian today, because it:
   a   Describes the personal habits of Galician immigrants to Canada.
   b   Compares how Galicians and Indians lived at this time.
   c   Reveals the attitudes of some Canadians towards Galician immigrants to Canada.
   d   Helps to understand conditions on the streets of Edmonton.

Document 2: American Report on the Internment of Enemy Aliens in Canada

Under the terms of the 1907 Hague Convention, neutral governments were permitted to inspect the treatment of prisoners of war being held in enemy camps. American government representative G. Willrich reported on prisoners of war being held in a Canadian internment camp, December 29, 1916:

The prisoners in Canadian Internment Camps came to the Dominion [of Canada] as peaceful emigrants and the great majority of them at least have been good, law abiding residents. ... In other words, these men now held as prisoners ... are good, sturdy, inoffensive men, able and willing to work, most of them desirous of becoming [wanting to become] Canadian citizens. ... There is no doubt in my mind that, at the present moment, the great majority of the prisoners ... could safely be returned to their homes and families, and that such return would be more profitable to Canada in the end. ...

1   Mr. Willrich describes the Ukrainian prisoners as good, law abiding residents. In one sentence explain why Mr. Willrich describes Ukrainians so differently from Father Moris (Document 1).
2   How does this source contribute to your understanding of the internment camps?

Scoring rules

Task 1: Choice b is assigned 1, others assigned 0
Task 2: Choice c is assigned 1, others assigned 0
Task 4:

   2   Student presents an explanation for the perspective of Willrich or Father Moris and their motivations, in light of their positions, purposes, and contexts, based on the documents
   1   Student identifies why there is a difference but does not fully explain their answer
   0   Incorrect or no answer

Task 5:

   2   Response indicates awareness that the information presented in the document is an interpretation of conditions by the author

1 The information presented in the document is taken as "true"; the student's response does not indicate awareness that the information presented in the document is only one author's interpretation (see note below for exceptions)

0 No answer or wrong answer

Appendix C: Example ALDs Used in AP World History Standard Setting

AP 5—*Performance Level Descriptor for World History*

Argumentation and Use of Evidence

1 Constructs a persuasive historical argument accounting for conflicting historical evidence
2 Consistently analyzes primary sources using most of the following elements: audience, point of view, format, and argument
3 Recognizes possible limitations of evidence used to support historical arguments

Chronological Reasoning

4 Evaluates the interaction of multiple causes and effects in world history
5 Explains historical patterns of continuity and change over time with similar depth of complexity for both
6 Evaluates alternative models of periodization in world history

Comparison and Contextualization

7 Explains an appropriate world historical comparison using more than one of the following: geography, chronology, and different societies or within one society, and evaluates their significance
8 Investigates multiple ways in which specific historical phenomena relate to broader regional, national, or global processes

Interpretation and Synthesis

9 Articulates how models of historical interpretation change over time
10 Creates a persuasive understanding of the past by using multiple historical thinking skills and disparate evidence from primary and secondary sources

AP 4—*Performance Level Descriptor for World History*

Argumentation and Use of Evidence

1 Constructs an historical argument substantiated with relevant evidence
2 Appropriately analyzes primary sources using some of the following elements: audience, point of view, format, and argument
3 Analyzes relevant historical evidence to support an argument

Chronological Reasoning

4 Explains causes and effects in world history
5 Differentiates between short-term and long-term causes and effects

6   Explains historical patterns of continuity and change over time and connects them to global processes
7   Explains different models of periodization in world history
8   Demonstrates detailed knowledge of chronology in world history

Comparison and Contextualization

9   Explains an appropriate world historical comparison using one of the following: geography, chronology, and different societies or within one society
10 Explains how specific historical phenomena relate to broader regional, national, or global processes

Interpretation and Synthesis

11 Explains how historians use evidence to construct historical interpretations
12 Critically evaluates diverse historical interpretations
13 Employs different disciplinary perspectives to address historical questions
14 Identifies connections between different historical contexts, including the present

AP 3—Performance Level Descriptor for World History

Argumentation and Use of Evidence

1   Articulates a plausible historical claim or argument as appropriate with limited evidence
2   Identifies the context and purpose in primary sources
3   Identifies relevant historical evidence to support a claim or an argument
4   Distinguishes between primary and secondary sources

Chronological Reasoning

5   Distinguishes between cause and effect
6   Identifies basic causes and effects in world history
7   Identifies historical patterns of both continuity and change over time
8   Distinguishes between different models of periodization in world history
9   Demonstrates basic knowledge of chronology in world history

Comparison and Contextualization

10 Articulates an appropriate world historical comparison
11 Accurately identifies a relationship between specific historical phenomena and regional, national, or global processes

Interpretation and Synthesis

12 Identifies different historical interpretations of an historical event or process
13 With direction, employs different disciplinary perspectives to address historical questions
14 With direction, identifies connections between different historical contexts, including the present

AP 2—Performance Level Descriptor for World History

Argumentation and Use of Evidence

1   Makes an implausible claim not supported by the evidence
2   Misinterprets the context or purpose in primary sources

3   Misinterprets historical sources and misuses evidence
4   Usually confuses primary and secondary sources

Chronological Reasoning

5   Confuses cause and effect
6   May recall basic causes or effects, but not both
7   Identifies historical patterns of either continuity or change over time, but not both
8   Demonstrates basic awareness of periodization in world history
9   Demonstrates incomplete knowledge of chronology in world history

Comparison and Contextualization

10   Articulates a world historical comparison but does so incorrectly or inappropriately for the task
11   Makes vague or incorrect generalizations about relationships between historical phenomena and regional, national, or global processes

Interpretation and Synthesis

12   Misunderstands historical interpretations
13   With direction, recognizes different disciplinary perspectives but incorrectly employs them to address historical questions
14   Incorrectly identifies connections between different historical contexts, including the present

AP 1—Performance Level Descriptor for World History

Argumentation and Use of Evidence

1   Does not make historical claims or arguments
2   Does not address the context or purpose of primary sources
3   Does not connect facts to historical claims
4   Confuses primary and secondary sources

Chronological Reasoning

5   Cannot recall basic causes or effects
6   Does not identify historical patterns of continuity or change over time
7   Lacks basic awareness of periodization in world history
8   Lacks basic knowledge of chronology in world history

Comparison and Contextualization

9   Recalls relevant information but makes no direct comparison
10   Recalls relevant information without relating historical phenomena to regional, national, or global processes

Interpretation and Synthesis

11   Lacks awareness of the concept of historical interpretation
12   Makes no attempt to connect different historical contexts or employ different disciplinary perspectives to address historical questions

Notes

1 This discussion initially applies to developments in the English language. There was a separate development in German history education (e.g., Rüsen, von Borries, & Pandel, 1991), with very little exchange between the two, until very recent years. The Netherlands (Grever, de Bruijn, & von Boxtel, 2012; Wilschut, 2012), Sweden (Eliasson, Alven, Rosenlund, & Rudnert, 2012), and Canada (Duquette, 2012; Seixas, 2004) have led efforts to bridge the two schools of thought.
2 This links to the German tradition, Ruesen's disciplinary matrix (Lee, 2004), and Wilschut's (2012) imperative of time.
3 http://www.socialstudies.org/positions/nclbera
4 http://www.nche.net/advocacy
5 The movement toward various statewide EOC assessments in the United States contrasts with a variety of other arrangements. For example, there is a national curriculum in Australia, matched with state assessments; provincial curricula but few provincewide examinations in Canada; and national curriculum and assessment in Sweden and the UK.
6 In the 2011–2012 academic year, the redesigned course was launched for AP World History; however, the corresponding redesigned exam for AP World History has not yet been launched.
7 http://www.historicalthinking.ca

References

American Educational Research Association (AERA), American Psychological Association (APA), & National Council on Measurement in Education (NCME). (1999). *Standards for educational and psychological testing.* Washington, DC: AERA.

Baxter, G., & Glaser, R. (1998). Investigating the cognitive complexity of science assessments. *Educational Measurement: Issues and Practice, 17*, 37–45.

Beaton, A. E., & Allen, N. L. (1992). Interpreting scales through scale anchoring. *Journal of Educational Statistics, 17*, 191–204.

Bejar, I., Braun, H. I., & Tannenbaum, R. J. (2007). A prospective, predictive, and progressive approach to standard setting. In R. Lissitz (Ed.), *Assessing and modeling cognitive development in school: Intellectual growth and standard setting.* Maple Grove, MN: JAM Press.

Breakstone, J., Smith, M., & Wineburg, S. (2013). Beyond the bubble in history/social studies assessments. *Phi Delta Kappan, 94*(5), 53–57.

Bruner, M. (2008). *Assessing history in Kansas.* Retrieved September 14, 2015 from http://national historycenter.org/wp/wp-content/uploads/2008/11/brunerpaper.pdf

Burstein, L., McDonnell, L. M., Van Winkle, J., Ormseth, T., Mirocha, J., & Guiton, G. (1995). *Validating national curriculum indicators* (DRU-1086-NSF). Santa Monica, CA: RAND.

Camps, J. (2003). Concurrent and retrospective verbal reports as tools to better understand the role of attention in second language tasks. *International Journal of Applied Linguistics, 13*, 201–221.

Chajewski, M., & Kaliski, P. (2013). *Item selection methodology for validation of scale score performance level descriptors.* Paper presented at the annual meeting of the National Council on Measurement in Education, San Francisco, CA.

Cohen, S. (2008). *What form should tests take? Disagreement over assessment in Massachusetts.* Retrieved September 14, 2015 from http://nationalhistorycenter.org/wp/wp-content/uploads/2008/11/cohenpaper.pdf

College Board. (2012a). *AP central course descriptions.* Retrieved September 14, 2015 from http://apcentral.collegeboard.com/apc/public/courses/descriptions/index.html

College Board. (2012b). *AP United States history: Course description.* Retrieved September 14, 2015 from http://apcentral.collegeboard.com/apc/public/repository/ap-us-history-course-description.pdf

College Board. (2012c). *AP European history course description.* Retrieved September 14, 2015 from http://apcentral.collegeboard.com/apc/public/repository/ap-european-history-course-description.pdf

College Board. (2012d). *AP world history course and exam description.* Retrieved September 14, 2015 from http://apcentral.collegeboard.com/apc/public/repository/AP_WorldHistoryCED_Effective_Fall_2011.pdf

College Board. (2012e). *Historical thinking skills.* Retrieved September 14, 2015 from http://advancesinap.collegeboard.org/historical-thinking

College Board. (2012f). *Advances in AP history.* Retrieved September 14, 2015 from http://advancesinap.collegeboard.org/history

Duquette, C. (2012). *The connection between historical thinking and historical consciousness: Proposition of a new taxonomy.* Paper presented at the Assessment of Historical Thinking Conference, Toronto, ON.

Egan, K. L., Schneider, M. C., & Ferrara, S. (2011). The 6D framework: A validity framework for defining proficient performance and setting cut scores for accessible tests. In S. N. Elliott, R. J. Kettler, P. A. Beddow, & A. Kurz (Eds.), *Handbook of accessible achievement tests for all students* (pp. 275–292). New York, NY: Springer.

Eliasson, P., Alven, F., Rosenlund, D., & Rudnert, J. (2012). *Historical consciousness in Sweden.* Paper presented at the Assessment of Historical Thinking Conference, Vancouver, BC.

Embretson, S. E., & Gorin, J. S. (2001). Improving construct validity with cognitive psychology principles. *Journal of Educational Measurement, 38,* 343–368.

Ercikan, K. (2002). Scoring examinee responses for multiple inferences: Multiple-scoring in assessments. *Educational Measurement: Issues and Practice, 21,* 8–15.

Ercikan, K. (2006). Developments in assessment of student learning and achievement. In P. A. Alexander & P. H. Winne (Eds.), *American Psychological Association, division 15, handbook of educational psychology* (2nd ed., pp. 929–953). Hillsdale, NJ: Lawrence Erlbaum Associates.

Ercikan, K., Arim, R., Law, D., Domene, J., Gagnon, F., & Lacroix, S. (2010). Application of think loud protocols for examining and confirming sources of differential item functioning identified by expert reviews. *Educational Measurement: Issues and Practice, 29*(2), 24–35.

Ercikan, K., & Julian, M. (2002). Classification accuracy of assigning student performance to proficiency levels: Guidelines for assessment design. *Applied Measurement in Education, 15,* 269–294.

Ercikan, K., & McCreith, T. (2002). Effects of adaptations on comparability of test items and test scores. In D. Robitaille & A. Beaton (Eds.), *Secondary analysis of the TIMSS results: A synthesis of current research* (pp. 391–407). Dordrecht, the Netherlands: Kluwer Academic Publishers.

Ercikan, K., & Roth, W.-M. (2009). *Generalizing from educational research: Beyond qualitative and quantitative polarization.* New York, NY: Routledge.

Ercikan, K., & Roth, W.-M. (2011). Constructing data. In C. Conrad & R. Serlin (Eds.), *Sage handbook for research in education* (2nd ed., pp. 219–245). Thousand Oaks, CA: Sage Publications.

Ercikan, K., & Seixas, P. (2011). Assessment of higher order thinking: The case of historical thinking. In G. Scraw & D. H. Robinson (Eds.), *Assessment of higher order thinking skills* (pp. 245–261). Charlotte, NC: Information Age Publishing.

Ercikan, K., Seixas, P., Lyons-Thomas, J., & Gibson, L. (2012). *Designing and validating an assessment of historical thinking using evidence centered assessment design.* Paper presented at the American Educational Research Association, Vancouver, BC.

Ericsson, K. A., & Simon, H. A. (1993). *Protocol analysis: Verbal reports as data* (Rev. ed.). Cambridge, MA: The MIT Press.

Fay, B. (Ed.). (2004). Historians and ethics: A short introduction to the theme issue. *History and Theory, 43*(4), 1–2.

Ferrara, S., & Chen, J. (2011). *Evidence for the accuracy of item response demand coding categories in think aloud verbal transcripts.* Paper presented at the annual meeting of the American Educational Research Association, New Orleans, LA.

Ferrara, S., Duncan, T. G., Freed, R., Velez-Paschke, A., McGivern, J., Mushlin, S., . . . Westphalen, K. (2004). *Examining test score validity by examining item construct validity: Preliminary analysis of evidence of the alignment of targeted and observed content, skills, and cognitive processes in a middle school science assessment.* Paper presented at the annual meeting of the American Educational Research Association, San Diego, CA.

Ferrara, S., Duncan, T. G., Freed, R., Velez-Paschke, A., McGivern, J., Mushlin, S., . . . Westphalen, K. (2005). *Comparing the achievement constructs targeted and achieved in a statewide middle school science assessment.* Paper presented at the annual meeting of the National Council on Measurement in Education, Montreal, Canada.

Ferrara, S., Duncan, T. G., Perie, M., Freed, R., McGivern, J., & Chilukuri, R. (2003). *Item construct validity: Early results from a study of the relationship between intended and actual cognitive demands in a middle school science assessment.* Paper presented in S. Ferrara (Chair), *Cognitive and Other Influences on Responding to Science Test Items: What Is and What Can Be*, a symposium conducted at the annual meeting of the American Educational Research Association, Chicago, IL.

Ferrara, S., Svetina, D., Skucha, S., & Davidson, A. (2011). Test design with performance standards and achievement growth in mind. *Educational Measurement: Issues and Practice, 30*, 3–15.

Fukkink, R. G. (2005). Deriving work meaning from written context: A process analysis. *Learning and Instruction, 15*, 23–43.

Gallagher, A. M., & De Lisi, R. (1994). Gender differences in Scholastic Aptitude Test: Mathematics problem solving among high-ability students. *Journal of Educational Psychology, 86*(2), 204–211.

Gierl, M. J. (1997). Comparing cognitive representations of test developers and students on a mathematics test with Bloom's taxonomy. *Journal of Educational Research, 91*(1), 26–32.

Glaser, R., & Baxter, G. P. (2002). Cognition and construct validity: Evidence for the nature of cognitive performance in assessment situations. In H. I. Braun & D. N. Jackson (Eds.), *The role of constructs in psychological and educational measurement* (pp. 179–227). Mahwah, NJ: Lawrence Erlbaum Associates.

Gorin, J. S., & Embretson, S. E. (2006). Item difficulty modeling of paragraph comprehension items. *Applied Psychological Measurement, 30*(5), 394–411.

Grever, M., de Bruijn, P., & von Boxtel, C. (2012). Negotiating historical distance: Or, how to deal with the past as a foreign country in heritage education. *Paedagogica Historica, 48*(6), 873–887.

Gu, P. Y., Guangwei, H., & Zhang, L. J. (2005). Investigating language learner strategies among lower primary school pupils in Singapore. *Language and Education, 19*, 281–303.

Hamilton, L. S., Nussbaum, E. M., & Snow, R. E. (1997). Interview procedures for validating science assessments. *Applied Measurement in Education, 10*, 181–200.

Hendrickson, A., Ewing, M., Kaliski, P., & Huff, K. (2013). Evidence-centered design: Recommendations for implementation and practice. *Journal of Applied Testing and Technology, 14*, 27.

Huff, K., Alves, C., Pellegrino, J., & Kaliski, P. (2013). Using evidence centered design task models in automatic item generation. In M. Gierl & T. Haladyna (Eds.), *Automatic item generation.* New York, NY: Informa UK Limited.

Huff, K., & Ferrara, S. (2010, June). *Frameworks for considering item response demands and item difficulty.* Presentation at the Council of Chief State School Officers National Conference on Large-Scale Assessment, Detroit, MI.

Huff, K., & Plake, B. S. (2010). Innovations in setting performance standards for K–12 test-based accountability. *Measurement, 8*, 130–144.

Huff, K., Steinberg, L., & Matts, T. (2010). The promises and challenges of implementing evidence-centered design in large scale assessment. *Applied Measurement in Education, 23*, 310–324.

International Baccalaureate. (2012a). *Academic programmes and certificates.* Retrieved September 14, 2015 from http://www.ibo.org/general/what.cfm

International Baccalaureate. (2012b). *History subject outline.* Retrieved September 14, 2015 from http://www.ibo.org/en/programmes/diploma-programme/curriculum/individuals-and-soci eties/history

International Baccalaureate. (2012c). *The IB Diploma Programme.* Retrieved September 14, 2015 from http://www.ibo.org/diploma/index.cfm

International Baccalaureate. (2012d). *History.* Retrieved September 14, 2015 from http://www.ibo. org/diploma/curriculum/group3/history.cfm

International Baccalaureate. (2012e). *Establish an IB policy that recognizes achievement within the IB Diploma Programme.* Retrieved September 14, 2015 from http://www.ibo.org/globalassets/ publications/recognition/model-policy-overview-en.pdf

Kaliski, P., France, M., Huff, K., & Thurber, A. (2010). *Using think aloud interviews in evidence-centered assessment design for the AP World History exam.* Paper presented at the annual conference of the American Educational Research Association, Denver, CO.

Kane, M. (2013). Validity and fairness in the testing of individuals. In M. Chatterji (Ed.), *Validity and test use: An international dialogue on educational assessment, accountability and equity* (pp. 1–250). Bingley, UK: Emerald Group Publishing Limited.

Katz, I. R., Bennett, R. E., & Berger, A. E. (2000). Effects of response format on difficulty of SAT-Mathematics items: It's not the strategy. *Journal of Educational Measurement, 37,* 39–57.

Kozma, R., Chin, E., Russell, J., & Marx, N. (2000). The roles of representations and tools in the chemistry laboratory and their implications for chemistry learning. *The Journal of the Learning Sciences, 9,* 105–143.

Lee, P. (2004). Understanding history. In P. Seixas (Ed.), *Theorizing historical consciousness* (pp. 129–164). Toronto, ON: University of Toronto Press.

Lee, P., & Shemilt, D. (2003). A scaffold not a cage: Progression and progression models in history. *Teaching History, 113,* 13–23.

Leighton, J. P. (2004). Avoiding misconception, misuse, and missed opportunities: The collection of verbal reports in educational achievement testing. *Educational Measurement: Issues and Practice, 23,* 6–15.

Leighton, J. P., & Gierl, M. J. (2007). Verbal reports as data for cognitive diagnostic assessment. In J. P. Leighton & M. J. Gierl (Eds.), *Cognitive diagnostic assessment for education: Theory and applications* (pp. 146–172). New York, NY: Cambridge University Press.

MacMillan, M. (2008). *The uses and abuses of history.* Toronto, ON: Viking Canada.

Martiniello, M. (2008). Language and the performance of English-language learners in math word problems. *Harvard Educational Review, 78*(2), 333–368.

McDonnell, L. M. (1995). Opportunity to learn as a research concept and a policy instrument. *Educational Evaluation and Policy Analysis, 17*(3), 305–322.

Messick, S. (1989). Meaning and values in test validation: The science and ethics of assessment. *Educational Researcher, 18*(2), 5–11.

Mislevy, R. J. (2007). Validity by design. *Educational Researcher, 36*(8), 463–469.

Mislevy, R. J., Steinberg, L. S., & Almond, R. G. (2002). On the structure of educational assessments. *Measurement: Interdisciplinary Research and Perspectives, 1,* 3–63.

National Assessment Governing Board (NAGB). (2010). *U.S. history framework for the 2010 National Assessment of Educational Progress.* Washington, DC: NAGB.

National Governors Association Center for Best Practices/Council of Chief State School Officers. (2010). *Common Core State Standards for English language arts and literacy in history/social studies, science, and technical subjects.* Washington, DC: National Governors Association Center for Best Practices/Council of Chief State School Officers.

National History Center. (2008). *Statement on state history assessments.* Retrieved September 14, 2015 from http://nationalhistorycenter.org/tag/assessment

Oakshott, M. (1983). *On history.* London: Basil Blackwell.

Osborne, K. (2003). Teaching history in schools: A Canadian debate. *Journal of Curriculum Studies, 35*(5), 585–626.

Pellegrino, J., Chudowsky, N., & Glaser, R. (Eds.). (2001). *Knowing what students know: The science and design of educational assessment.* Washington, DC: National Academies Press.

Plake, B. S., Huff, K., & Reshetar, R. (2010). Evidence-centered assessment design as a foundation for achievement-level descriptor development and for standard setting. *Applied Measurement in Education, 23*(4), 342–357.

Pressley, M., & Afflerbach, P. (1995). *Verbal protocols of reading: The nature of constructively responsive reading.* Hillsdale, NJ: Lawrence Erlbaum Associates, Inc.

Ransdell, S. (1995). Generating thinking-aloud protocols: Impact on the narrative writing of college students. *American Journal of Psychology, 108,* 89–98.

Reich, G. (2009). *What are we measuring?* Paper presented at the annual meeting of the American Educational Research Association, New Orleans, LA.

Reshetar, R., Kaliski, P., Chajewski, M., Marsh, R., Chuah, S., Coleman, C., & Plake, B. (2013a, April). *Performance level descriptor validation studies for four advanced placement program® (AP®) mixed-format exams.* Paper presented at the annual meeting of the American Educational Research Association, San Francisco, CA.

Reshetar, R., Kaliski, P., Plake, B., Lionberger, K., & Chajewski, M. (2013b, April). *A performance level descriptor (PLD) validation study for the advanced placement program® (AP®) environmental science examination.* Paper presented at the annual meeting of the National Council on Measurement in Education, San Francisco, CA.

Roth, W.-M. (2003). Gesture-speech phenomena, learning and development. *Educational Psychologist*, 38, 249–263.

Roth, W.-M. (2009). Limits to general expertise: A study of in- and out-of-field graph interpretation. In S. P. Weingarten & H. O. Penat (Eds.), *Cognitive psychology research developments* (pp. 1–38). Hauppauge, NY: Nova Science.

Rüsen, J., von Borries, B., & Pandel, H.-J. (Eds.). (1991). *Geschichtsbewußtsein empirisch (Historical consciousness—An empirical approach)* (Vol. 7). Pfaffenweiler: Centaurus.

Sato, E. (2011, March). *Cognitive interviews of English language learners and students with disabilities and features contributing to item difficulty: Implications for item and test design.* Paper presented at the annual meeting of the American Educational Research Association, New Orleans, LA.

Schmeiser, C. B., & Welch, C. J. (2006). Test development. In R. L. Brennan (Ed.), *Educational measurement* (4th ed., pp. 307–354). Westport, CT: Praeger Publishers.

Schneider, M. C., Huff, K. L., Egan, K. L., Tully, M., & Ferrara, S. (2010). *Aligning achievement level descriptors to mapped item demands to enhance valid interpretations of scale scores and inform item development.* Paper presented at the annual conference of the American Educational Research Association, Denvert, CO.

Schoenfeld, A. H. (2007). Problem solving in the United States, 1970–2008: Research and theory, practice and politics. *International Journal of Mathematics Education*, 39, 537–551.

Seixas, P. (2004). Introduction. In P. Seixas (Ed.), *Theorizing historical consciousness* (pp. 3–20). Toronto, ON: University of Toronto Press.

Seixas, P. (2009). A modest proposal for change in Canadian history education. *Teaching History*, 137, 26–31.

Seixas, P., & Ercikan, K. (2011). Historical thinking in Canadian schools. *Canadian Journal of Social Research*, 4(1), 31–41.

Seixas, P., Ercikan, K., Gibson, L., & Lyons-Thomas, J. (2012). *Assessing historical thinking: Challenges and possibilities.* Paper presented at the American Educational Research Association, Vancouver, BC.

Shavelson, R., Baxter, G. P., & Gao, X. (1993). Sampling variability of performance assessments. *Journal of Educational Measurement*, 30, 215–232.

Shemilt, D. (1980). *History 13–16: Evaluation study.* Edinburgh, Scotland: Holmes McDougall.

Sinharay, S., Haberman, S. J., & Lee, Y.-H. (2011). When does scale anchoring work? A case study. *Journal of Educational Measurement*, 48, 61–80.

Stanford History Education Group. (2013). *Assessing 21st century skills with Library of Congress documents.* Retrieved February 10, 2013 from http://beyondthebubble.stanford.edu

Tatsuoka, K. K. (1990). Toward an integration of item-response theory and cognitive error diagnosis. In N. Frederiksen, R. Glaser, A. Lesgold, & M. Shafto (Eds.), *Diagnostic monitoring of skill and knowledge acquisition* (pp. 453–488). Hillsdale, NJ: Erlbaum.

VanSledright, B. (2013). *Assessing historical thinking and understanding: Innovative designs for new standards.* New York, NY and London, UK: Routledge.

VanSledright, B., & Limon, M. (2006). Learning and teaching social studies: A review of cognitive research in history and geography. In P. A. Alexander & P. H. Winne (Eds.), *Handbook of educational psychology* (pp. 545–571). Mahwah, NJ: Lawrence Erlbaum Associates.

Wilschut, A. (2012). *Images of time: The role of historical consciousness in learning.* Charlotte, NC: Information Age Publishing.

Wineburg, S. S. (1991). On the reading of historical texts: Notes on the breach between school and academy. *American Educational Research Journal*, 28, 495–519.

Wineburg, S. S. (1996). The psychology of learning and teaching history. In D. C. Berliner & R. C. Calfee (Eds.), *Handbook of educational psychology* (pp. 423–437). New York, NY: Macmillan.

Wineburg, S. S., Smith, M., & Breakstone, J. (2012). New directions in assessment: Using Library of Congress sources to assess historical understanding. *Social Education*, 76(6), 290–293.

Wolfe, M. B. W., & Goldman, S. R. (2005). Relations between adolescents' text processing and reasoning. *Cognition and Instruction*, 23, 467–502.

11 Assessing the Life Sciences

Using Evidence-Centered Design for Accountability Purposes

Geneva D. Haertel, Terry P. Vendlinski,
Daisy Rutstein, Angela DeBarger, Britte H. Cheng,
Cindy Ziker, Christopher J. Harris, Cynthia D'Angelo,
Eric B. Snow, Marie Bienkowski, and
Liliana Ructtinger

For over a decade, educators have been confronted by urgent demands for evidence of improved instruction and increased student learning. This same era has yielded sobering evidence that U.S. students' proficiency and enthusiasm for learning, especially STEM learning, had flagged (National Research Council, 2005a, 2007, 2011a). Opfer, Nehm, and Ha (2012) summarize the state of assessment practice in the life sciences:

> Assessments of student knowledge and reasoning patterns play a central role in science teaching. At their most effective, assessment instruments provide valid and reliable inferences about student conceptual progress, thereby facilitating guidance in targeting instruction and evaluating instructional efficacy (NRC, 2001). Despite their high potential however, assessment instruments for content-rich domains, such as biology, often lack validity in even the narrow sense described by Linn, Baker, and Dunbar (1991)—that is, the ability to independently predict outcomes on real-world assessments (e.g., teacher-developed achievement test). At their least effective, instruments may yield contradictory or false inferences about student knowledge, misconceptions, or reasoning processes (Nehm & Schonfeld, 2008). For some content areas—such as students' understanding of evolutionary processes—there are still remarkably few tools available for validly assessing students' progress.
>
> (Nehm, 2006, pp. 1–2)

In response to these criticisms, assessment experts have incorporated new understandings about learning and cognition, previously unimagined technologies, and developments in the statistical methods needed to model and score complex, "hard-to-assess" psychological constructs (Mislevy, Steinberg, Almond, Haertel, & Penuel, 2003). Despite the many advances that bear directly on the theoretical underpinnings and practical aspects of assessments for accountability purposes, most operational, large-scale assessments have not kept pace. Even though educators are aware of the need to assess "deeper" domain-specific content (Alonzo & Gotwals, 2012; Carver, 2006) and have viewed numerous illustrations of technology-enhanced, innovative item and task formats (Quellmalz & Pellegrino, 2009; Quellmalz, Timms, & Buckley, 2010), many current large-scale assessments still depend on traditional approaches for the design, development, presentation, and measurement of student performances. Because large-scale assessments involve multiple, complex operations—new technologies, innovative design tools, rigorous psychometric procedures, and the dynamics of widespread administration, delivery, scoring, and reporting—many testing companies need time to replace their existing resources and tools to implement the newer forms.

Over the past five years, the nation has invested considerable resources in educational reform (e.g., development of the Common Core State Standards [CCSS] and the aligned summative assessment systems; the Next Generation Science Standards [NGSS]). In conjunction with emerging performance standards, these reforms require, among other things, that students demonstrate higher level knowledge of content and the ability to apply this knowledge in domain-specific contexts, including STEM-related domains. Inferring whether students are able to marshal the knowledge and skills needed to meet these standards requires assessment systems designed to support inferences about "hard-to-assess" constructs that are valid for all students.

In particular, large-scale assessments used for accountability purposes are designed primarily to determine whether students within a jurisdiction (i.e., local, district, or statewide system) who have completed a course of study have attained the necessary level of competence to apply the knowledge and skills specified in the curriculum. This information is intended to serve the needs of policymakers at all levels, as well as parents and the public at large. Results of these assessments can also support improvement of educational systems and programs, identify gaps in performance among particular populations, and inform decisions regarding the allocation of resources among local educational authorities.

These assessments are required to implement the measurement of increasingly complex constructs and contribute information for high-stakes decisions. Consequently, the validity of the inferences made from the assessment data must be technically defensible and capable of withstanding legal scrutiny. The rigor required and the desire to make credible, comparable inferences across states led the U.S. government to support the formation of two national multi-state assessment consortia (the Smarter Balanced Assessment Consortium and the Partnership for Assessment of Readiness for College and Careers). The use of evidence-centered design (ECD) was identified as a design approach by both consortia as a means of designing assessments with the necessary technical qualities.

The ECD approach confers the following seven benefits on the development of large-scale accountability measures:

1   comprehensive, defensible validity arguments that directly relate the abilities and skills to be assessed to observations of what students can do and to the features of tasks that elicit those performances;
2   increased construct validity by identifying and reducing sources of construct-irrelevant variance;
3   efficient, scalable design of tasks that measure "hard-to-assess" complex constructs through the elicitation of evidence of "deep knowledge" and skills;
4   a structure that allows the integration of other design frameworks, such as Universal Design for Learning (UDL), 21st-century skills (e.g., communication, collaboration, information, media, technology, and problem solving), and learning progressions;
5   guidelines to identify item types that exploit technology and are best aligned to the purposes of the assessment and the focal knowledge, skills, and abilities (KSAs) to be addressed;
6   reusable design documents that can be used to efficiently generate new items and tasks (i.e., clones and variants) and reduce costs for future design and development; and
7   specifications of rendering and delivery of technology-enhanced assessment items and tasks.

The design of assessments aligned to the NGSS requires the same level of attention to validity that ECD imparts to the CCSS assessments. The importance of inferential validity for the decisions based on these increasingly complex and costly assessments—and the ramifications of these decisions—requires the federal government, states, and test vendors to take note of the benefits conferred by ECD on designing a new era of assessments for accountability purposes.

In the next section, we will characterize the state of assessment practices in the life sciences from an ECD perspective.

In this chapter, we describe the use of ECD as a systematic method to guide assessment development so that a coherent validity argument underlies the inferences made on the basis of student performance. The chapter sets forth, for both assessment experts and science educators, examples of the logic and the validity arguments needed to support the design and development of life science measures that document the knowledge, skills, and practices that students have attained at the end of their educational experiences.

In the first section, using ECD as a guide to the articulation of valid assessment arguments, the five layers of the ECD work process are described, including a detailed description of a Design Pattern used to conceptualize the assessment of model-based reasoning. In the second section, which focuses on designing and developing Interactive Computer Tasks (ICTs) to assess life science content and practices, background on ICTs is provided along with an example of a Design Pattern created for the measurement of photosynthesis and experimental design skills. The third section, measuring "hard-to-assess" life science constructs, describes the design of measures for three such constructs: model-based reasoning, systems thinking, and computational thinking in the life sciences. The fourth section, developing large-scale life science assessments for "hard-to-assess" populations, presents the refinement of state science assessment items using ECD processes with special attention to the modification of the items for use with students with disabilities. The fifth section, implications for the use of assessment results for the purposes of accountability, includes a discussion of the role of the NGSS, the technical qualities required for large-scale assessments, the need to address measurement bias, the importance of consequential validity, and the use of achievement level descriptors (ALDs). The influence of ECD is addressed in each of these sections. The concluding section identifies the challenges and benefits of using ECD for the development of large-scale accountability measures in the life sciences.

Using ECD to Guide the Articulation of Valid Assessment Arguments for Accountability Purposes

Although there are many approaches to ECD, in this chapter the ECD approach used is the one presented in the chapter "General Introduction to Evidence-Centered Design" (this volume). That chapter describes the five layers of ECD. Table 11.1 is a customization of these layers for the purpose of life science assessment. While the first two layers of work (i.e., Domain Analysis and Domain Modeling) can be tailored to the life sciences, layers 3, 4, and 5 (i.e., Conceptual Assessment Framework [CAF], Assessment Implementation, and Assessment Delivery) are common to all content domains.

ECD Layer 1: Domain Analysis in the Life Sciences

As the first layer of work, Domain Analysis involves gathering domain-specific knowledge and organizing it in ways that will help the assessment designer conceptualize the new assessment. Assessment designers in the life sciences draw on the information contained in this layer to identify the relevant KSAs, the representational forms that are commonly used, best instructional practices in the life sciences that may influence how students solve certain assessment tasks (e.g., conduct particular scientific procedures or calculate indices of scientific phenomena), and key features of situations encountered in life science investigations.

Most of the information in Domain Analysis is gathered from extant documents and examples. It represents a compilation of the knowledge, skills, practices, and forms that are in current use. In constructing a large-scale summative assessment in the life sciences, designers might draw on the National Science Education Standards (NRC, 1996), the NGSS (2013),

Table 11.1 Five Layers of ECD Applied to Life Science Assessment

Layer	Role	Key Entities	Selected Knowledge Representations
Domain Analysis	Gather substantive information about the life science domain of interest that has implications for assessment; how knowledge is constructed, acquired, used, communicated	Life science domain concepts, terminology, tools used in life science investigations, knowledge representations commonly used in the life science community, kinds of analyses conducted, situations of use, patterns of interaction	Representational forms and symbol systems used in the life science domain (e.g., diagrams of form and function of particular species, Punnett squares, food webs, phylogenetic trees, DNA/RNA, Codon table, computer program interfaces, life science content standards, life science concept maps)
Domain Modeling	Express assessment argument in narrative form based on information from Domain Analysis	Specifications of life science knowledge, skills, or other attributes to be assessed; features of situations that can evoke evidence; kinds of performances that convey evidence	Design Patterns; "big ideas" in life science such as evolution or photosynthesis; Toulmin and Wigmore diagrams for assessment arguments; assessment blueprints, ontologies, generic rubrics
CAF	Express assessment argument in structures and specifications for tasks and tests, evaluation procedures, measurement models	Student, evidence, and task models; student, observable, and task variables; rubrics; measurement models; test assembly specifications; task templates and task specifications	Algebraic and graphical representations of measurement models; task templates and task specifications; item generation models; generic rubrics; algorithms for automated scoring
Assessment Implementation	Implement assessment, including presentation-ready tasks and calibrated measurement models	Task materials (including all materials, tools, affordances); pilot-test data to hone evaluation procedures and fit of measurement models	Coded algorithms for rendering tasks, interacting with examinees and evaluating work products; tasks as displayed; IMS/QTI representation of materials; APIP formats for presenting assessment materials for students with disabilities; ASCII files of item parameters
Assessment Delivery	Coordinate interactions of students and tasks: task- and test-level scoring; reporting	Tasks as presented; work products as created; scores as evaluated	Renderings of materials; numerical and graphical summaries for individuals and groups; specifications for results files

Source: Adapted from Mislevy and Haertel, 2006.

Science Framework for the 2011 National Assessment of Educational Progress (NAEP; NAGB, 2010), and individual state life science standards and benchmarks. In addition, key publications of the National Research Council (NRC) such as *Taking Science to School: Committee on Science Learning, Kindergarten through Eighth Grade* (NRC, 2007), *Learning Science through Computer Games and Simulations* (NRC, 2011a), *Successful STEM Education: A Workshop Summary* (NRC, 2011b), *Systems for State Science Assessment* (NRC, 2006), *America's Lab Report: Investigations in High School Science* (NRC, 2005b), and *How Students Learn: History, Mathematics, and Science in the Classroom* (NRC, 2005c) provide information that could contribute to a comprehensive Domain Analysis. The Domain Analysis is the resource used to develop the Design Patterns in the Domain Modeling layer. For an example of a Domain Analysis conducted for the purpose of creating Design Patterns and Task Templates in the area of systems thinking, see *Large Scale Assessment Teaching Report 7* (Cheng, Ructtinger, Fujii, & Mislevy, 2010). For other examples, see the "General Introduction to Evidence-Centered Design" (this volume).

ECD Layer 2: Domain Modeling in the Life Sciences

In the Domain Modeling layer, the assessment designer begins to specify the assessment argument in narrative form using the information organized in the Domain Analysis layer. The narrative comprises one or more Design Patterns that clarify what content and skills are to be assessed, what evidence needs to be observed, what work products students need to complete as part of the assessment, and the rationale for why it is important to do so (Mislevy, Hamel, et al., 2003). Key attributes of Design Patterns in the life sciences are briefly described below. Two Design Patterns, *Observational Investigation* and *Experimental Investigation*, accompanied by detailed descriptions of their development, can be reviewed at Colker et al. (2010) and Mislevy et al. (2009), respectively. (These Design Patterns appear in Appendices A and E, respectively, in Chapter 5 of this volume.) For a description of a life science Design Pattern that integrates science content and practices, see DeBarger and Snow (2010). Appendix A is their Design Pattern titled "Model Use and Interdependence among Living Systems." It will be used to discuss the key attributes of Design Patterns for the life sciences.

Rationale

The attribute Rationale, included in the "Model Use and Interdependence among Living Systems" Design Pattern, is composed of an overview and a description of how the construct that is the focus of the Design Patterns is used in educational practice. These two aspects of the rationale provide background for what the assessment will measure. In addition, the rationale highlights the kinds of knowledge and skills that students will need to demonstrate to provide evidence of the construct being measured. The rationale for this Design Pattern is drawn from research in science education and philosophy of science (Gentner & Stevens, 1983; Hestenes, Wells, & Swackhamer, 1992; Johnson-Laird, 1983; Stewart & Hafner, 1994).

The overview presented in the "Model Use and Interdependence among Living Systems" Design Pattern indicates that this Design Pattern supports developing tasks that require students to reason through the structures, relationships, and processes of ecological models. As part of the Principled Assessment Designs in Inquiry Project (Mislevy & Haertel, 2006), a suite of Design Patterns was developed associated with the scientific practice of modeling. Seven different Design Patterns were created representing the range of assessment activities that students might be expected to demonstrate when modeling scientific phenomena. The seven Design Patterns included Model Formation, Model Use, Model Elaboration, Model Articulation, Model Evaluation, Model Revision, and Model-Based Inquiry. In assessing modeling of ecological phenomena, several modeling activities may be incorporated into the same assessment task. For example, the use of ecological models is often assessed in combination with the formation of ecological models. Many assessment tasks that address evaluation and revision of ecological models also involve activities that require model use.

The second part of the Design Pattern rationale focuses on the use of the Design Patterns. In the "Model Use and Interdependence among Living Systems" Design Pattern, scientific models are abstracted schemas. In psychology, a schema is a cognitive framework that supports an individual's organization and interpretation of information. These schemas involve entities and the relationships among them and can be used across a range of situations. Ecological models that show, for example, predator–prey relationships, the flow of energy, or the recycling of matter are instances of scientific models in life science. Scientific procedures can be carried out within the model to support inferences about the schema which is represented in the assessment task. Students must be able to use these models to reason about processes and interdependencies in living systems.

Focal KSAs

All Design Patterns are organized around Focal KSAs. The Design Pattern "Model Use and Interdependence among Living Systems" (Appendix A) will be used to illustrate the key steps in this layer. It reflects the "life science as inquiry" stance taken in the National Science Education Standards (NRC, 1996). Focal KSAs are the targeted knowledge and skills the assessment is intended to measure. An example of a Focal KSA from this Design Pattern is "ability to use an ecological model to explain the relationships among populations and communities." A second example is "ability to use an ecological model to explain how energy changes form in a food web."

Additional KSAs

Assessment task designers must specify which KSAs are the targets of inference for the assessment (i.e., constructs relevant with respect to validity) and which KSAs are not (i.e., construct irrelevant) and might result in invalid inferences. If an assessment task is intended to test the knowledge of Boyle's law, as well as the ability to formulate a model in an investigation, both the content knowledge about the gas laws and the skills of model formation are targets of inference. Additional KSAs (AKSAs) that assessment designers do not want to include as targets of inference are those which introduce alternative explanations for poor performance. Such AKSAs would invalidate the claim the assessment designer wants to make about what students know and can do. Examples of AKSAs from the "Model Use and Interdependence among Living Systems" Design Pattern include "knowledge of how to use and interpret required modeling tool(s) (e.g., online state assessment interface, STELLA and ESIS)." Another AKSA is "knowledge of required symbolic representations associated with procedures (e.g., chemical equations, mathematical notation)." These AKSAs are prerequisite knowledge for successful performance on the assessment tasks created using this Design Pattern, but are not the targets of measurement.

Potential Observations

Potential Observations are used to highlight the qualities of a performance that contains evidence relevant to the Focal KSAs. There can be many Potential Observations in a Design Pattern. Two examples of Potential Observations in this Design Pattern are "high quality explanation of how communities and populations represented in an ecological model interact." The second example is "accurate completion and description of a flow chart showing how energy flows in an ecological model." Each of these Potential Observations would be associated with particular Focal KSAs. An assessment task designer would use these Potential Observations in conjunction with their associated Focal KSAs in item writing.

Characteristic Features

Characteristic Features of assessment tasks are intended to elicit evidence about Focal KSAs. For example, a task designer using this Design Pattern might build an assessment task around the predator–prey relationships. Examinees would be presented with a real-world situation in which data had been collected about the prevalence of predators and prey for each of 10 successive years. This ecological model would also include indications of events that occurred over the 10-year cycle showing the pattern of relationships between the two interdependent populations over time. Such a model might be a characteristic feature of assessment tasks designed to elicit evidence about the Focal KSA "ability to use an ecological model to explain the relationships among populations and communities." Another Characteristic Feature appropriate to this Design Pattern would be the inclusion of questions in the assessment tasks that require students to reason through the relationships in the ecological model.

Variable Features

Most often, Variable Features of assessment tasks can be used to alter the difficulty of the assessment being designed. Other Variable Features can be used to support AKSAs, which without support would lead to alternative explanations for student performance. Some Variable Features can make designers aware of ways to match features of tasks with the characteristics of students, including their interests, prior knowledge, and background experience. An example of a Variable Feature in this Design Pattern is the type of ecological model used and the complexity of that model. Another Variable Feature would be the amount of background presented about the ecological model.

Potential Work Products

Assessment designers use Work Products to capture performances. In this Design Pattern, the following Work Products were identified: selected responses, procedures, constructed models, essays, and drawings. Any of these might be used to capture student work. In the case of an ICT, the Work Product might be a trace of actions the student followed in solving the assessment task.

Potential Rubrics

Potential Rubrics are the scoring rules for evaluating Work Products.

ECD Layer 3: The CAF in the Life Sciences

The Student, Evidence, and Task Models comprise the CAF (Messick, 1994; Mislevy & Haertel, 2006; Mislevy, Steinberg, & Almond, 2003). See Figure 5.1 in Chapter 5 (this volume) for a schematic representation of the relationships among the models. Each model has its own internal logic and structures, which are linked through the use of Student Model Variables, Observable Variables, Work Products, and Task Model Variables. These models are used in assessment design, regardless of the content domain being assessed. These models require specification of assessment task features, measurement models, and stimulus materials used in item and task presentation. The specification of these models constitutes the "nuts and bolts" of the technical requirements for the assessment that will guide its implementation and delivery in the content domain of interest.

In the Principled Assessment for Design in Inquiry (PADI) online assessment design system, the assessment designer uses Task Templates to specify these requirements. Appendix B is the summary page of a Task Template that could be used to design a large-scale life science accountability assessment to measure student inquiry about ecological systems. When designing high-stakes assessments, the precise specification of the Student, Evidence, and Task Models is essential. The alignment among the targets of the assessment (Student Model), the evidence collected (Evidence Model), and the task features (Task Model) preserve the structural validity of the assessment being developed and their coherence must be reviewed. When using ECD to design high-stakes assessments, the use of both Design Patterns and Task Templates is a desirable practice. Some of the more detailed objects the template contains are discussed below.

Student Model

The Student Model represents the student proficiencies to be measured. The number, nature, and granularity of these proficiencies and the way they interrelate are determined by the purpose of the assessment—a single student model variable to characterize students' overall proficiency or a multidimensional model of conducting inquiry in the life sciences, as part of an annual statewide test. In Appendix B, a two-dimensional student model is specified in order to track aspects of both content knowledge in ecological systems and inquiry skills such as making hypotheses, generating explanations, and analyzing and interpreting data.

Task Model

The Task Model describes an assessment setting in which students say, do, or make something to provide evidence. In designing the Task Model in "Model-Based Reasoning in Ecosystems Task Template," the assessment designer specified several task model variables, including the complexity of the problem, the number of organisms in the ecological system, and the type of ecosystem. A Work Product or Products were identified to capture students' performances. In this Summary Task Template, the assessment designer decided to capture student work using image-enhanced selected response, brief and extended constructed response, an ICT that includes dynamically generated tables and graphs that students produce and then describe using text, implicit logging of students' problem-solving attempts, and a drawing of a food web. These Work Products can be used with different assessment tasks generated from the same Task Model.

Simulations of science phenomena can be used to assess the science content and inquiry processes covered in state and national science frameworks. An example of a life sciences ICT that is aligned to state and national science frameworks is illustrated using one of the SimScientists assessment tasks developed at WestEd. In the SimScientists program, the assessment designers developed simulation-based, curriculum-embedded, and unit benchmark assessments for the middle school topic "ecosystems." These science simulations were later integrated into a balanced state science assessment system. (The National Research Council [2001] describes a balanced assessment system as a system of nested assessments, within a content domain, that is comprehensive, coherent, and provides continuous coverage of the content being assessed.) The SimScientists assessments represent a transition from testing discrete factual content to a focus on "connected knowledge structures that organize concepts and principles into crosscutting features of all systems—components, interactions, and emergent behaviors—and the inquiry practices used to investigate them" (Quellmalz, Timms, Silberglitt, & Buckley, 2012, p. 371). Designing complex technology-enhanced tasks can also be supported through the specification of the CAF.

In particular, the design of the Task Model helps identify the presentation environment that students will encounter. Specifically, in the SimScientists' population model simulation for ecosystems, students identify the starting values of one or more organisms and watch a set of icons that reveal the size of the population over time, as it increases, decreases, and reaches equilibrium. Students also watch the generation of a population curve and use a data tool to determine the size of the population at specific points on the curve. This assessment task is presented to the students as a series of synchronized representations. Students control the representations through their interactions with the computer and demonstrate inquiry practices such as making predictions, designing experiments to test their predictions, interpreting results of their experiments, making observations, drawing conclusions, and evaluating their predictions. To demonstrate these inquiry skills, students' Work Products need to be specified. In the SimScientists simulation, Work Products include students selecting from a choice of responses, altering the values of variables in the simulation, drawing arrows to relate interactions in the system, drawing a food web, and typing explanations of the tasks. Once specified, these Work Products can be reused in other science tasks with different contexts and topics. Decisions about the Characteristic and Variable Features in the Task Model are guided by the output of Domain Modeling.

Evidence Model

An Evidence Model bridges the Student Model and the Task Model. The Evidence Model consists of two components: the evaluation and the measurement components. For a complete description of the components of the Evidence Model, see "General Introduction to Evidence-Centered Design" (this volume). The evaluation component explains how features of the student work are used to obtain values for the Observable Variables and how they will be evaluated. Evaluation procedures may be algorithms for automated scoring procedures or rubrics used by trained scorers. The measurement component specifies how the evidence generated by the evaluation component will be assembled and combined to generate one or more student scores. Evidence Models can be developed to guide the scoring and interpretation of discrete items (that may be aggregated) and item bundles, such as those described by Kennedy (2005).

ECD helps in overall test assembly by requiring the specification of rules that govern the mix of item types, content of informational passages, numbers of items that use figures, abstract versus concrete concepts, sentence complexity, and many other task features. Statistical features of items such as their difficulty are also taken into account. Test forms are constructed and assembled to match the same targeted distributions of item difficulties and to represent the task features as specified in the test assembly rules.

Assessing students' abilities to conduct scientific investigations requires the modeling of interdependencies among several components of investigations (e.g., posing a question, designing an investigation, selecting tools and procedures, collecting data, analyzing and interpreting data, and drawing a conclusion). Using student performances from each of these components, the assessment designer may conceptualize a score which represents one of several multi dimensional constructs in which science content knowledge is crossed with scientific inquiry and practices. For example, an assessment designer can model the conditional dependencies between tasks intended to measure students' abilities to make scientific claims and their abilities to provide explanations about scientific phenomena in a modular way (Gotwals & Songer, 2006). Using the BioKIDS PADI Task Templates (see "General Introduction to Evidence-Centered Design," this volume, for an example of a BioKIDS Summary Task Template), assessment designers are able to create novel complex tasks but, importantly, know ahead of time how to score them. The use of the CAF and the specification of the Student, Evidence, and Task Models reduces the cost of assessment design, especially the design of ICTs, through the careful specification of technology requirements prior to rendering the tasks and through the reuse of assessment arguments, structures, processes, and materials specified in the CAF.

ECD Layer 4: Assessment Implementation in the Life Sciences

The Assessment Implementation layer of ECD involves the construction and preparation of all of the operational elements specified in the CAF. Assessment implementation includes authoring tasks, finalizing scoring rubrics and automated scoring rules, estimating the parameters in measurement models, and producing fixed test forms or algorithms for assembling tailored tests. Following the ECD approach requires specifying these implementation processes and is especially useful in science where complex interrelated procedures and processes need to be assessed (Scalise & Gifford, 2006). The past decade has seen many new types of assessment tasks, including ICTs, hands-on tasks, video game-based assessments, and computer simulations. It has also witnessed a rise in interest in integrating science content and practice. The demand to use new assessments in new ways requires careful attention to, and specification of, the processes needed to produce valid assessments. ECD supplies a language, tools, and structure for fulfilling these demands.

ECD Layer 5: Assessment Delivery in the Life Sciences

The Assessment Delivery layer structures students' interactions with tasks, the evaluations of their performances, and the generation of feedback and reports. Assessments can be delivered using a diverse set of modalities, including conventional paper–pencil assessments, portfolio assessments, hands-on tasks, ICTs, simulations, and game-based assessments. The delivery requirements must be considered in light of the need to ensure that the inferences based on the assessment are accurate and auditable. ECD supports these new delivery modalities and, because of the likelihood that science assessments will exploit these new means of delivery, attention to delivery specifications becomes an even more important step in the process.

As assessments of life science evolve toward computer-based delivery, automated scoring will become an increasingly critical part of the development process. Assessments generally require the selection and presentation of items and tasks, the scoring of responses, and the aggregation of these scored responses into a summary score. Almond, Steinberg, and Mislevy (2002) proposed a four-process architecture for the delivery of assessments. The four processes identified are Activity Selection, Presentation, Response Processing, and Summary Scoring. The contributions and the interactions among these four processes and their use during the delivery of the assessment are discussed. By articulating these processes in a modular fashion, the coherence among the assessment's purpose, design, and delivery is encouraged. When designing an adaptive technology-enhanced assessment, the use of an ECD process should facilitate devising scoring algorithms that can be readily deployed to make scoring and reporting processes more efficient than non-computer-based assessments. During Response Processing, specific data and algorithms (e.g., rubrics and solution data) are required to extract and evaluate the student's Work Products. Rubrics and solution data are referred to as Evidence Rule Data. During the Summary Scoring process, the student's evaluated responses are summarized based on Weight of Evidence Parameters. These parameters (i.e., scoring weights, conditional probabilities, and psychometric parameters) are used to create and update a student's Scoring Record.

When designing assessments that are computer-based, the four-process model confers efficiency. For example, the four-process model may specify the use of scoring algorithms and procedures that extract and evaluate student performances and automatically generate and update students' score reports. A useful source for understanding the Delivery layer of ECD is Williamson, Mislevy, and Bejar's (2006) volume titled *Automated Scoring of Complex Tasks in Computer-Based Testing*. This volume describes a variety of methods for designing automated scoring systems for complex constructed response tasks and compares them to human scoring alternatives.

Designing and Developing ICTs to Assess Life Science Content and Practices for Accountability Purposes

ECD is well suited to support the design of a wide variety of life science items and tasks. It can be used to design and develop both selected and constructed response items, whether or not they are stand-alone, discrete items, or items integrated within a larger assessment task. ECD can also be used to design scenario-based tasks that measure multi-step, complex performances, as well as hands-on tasks that involve manipulation of actual scientific tools and laboratory procedures. Information in the ECD design documents can help an item writer identify and create a narrative context for scenario-based tasks, select the most appropriate item format, align the item or task with the KSAs of interest, identify Characteristics and Variable Features to be included in tasks, generate response options for selected response items, and create rubrics for constructed response items. A large research literature has been compiled describing different kinds of science items, their strengths and weaknesses, and their technical qualities. The remainder of this section addresses the current challenge of harnessing technology to design and develop ICTs for use in science assessment.

As stated above, assessment designers are increasingly using ICTs for the purposes of formative and summative K–12 science assessment (Quellmalz & Pellegrino, 2009). The emergence of ICTs drew on the early foundational work of Mills, Potenza, Fremer, and Ward (2002), who recognized that computer-based technologies could be used in the assessment of knowledge and skills that were not easily examined using other delivery modes. Although ICTs have been administered more frequently over the past five to ten years, recent improvements in the speed and power of computers and reductions in the cost of designing and developing such tasks have made the presentation and delivery of ICTs increasingly feasible. ICTs are now used in licensure, certification, and admission tests, as well as in measures of domain-specific learning in K–12. An increasing number of large-scale, high-stakes, statewide testing programs are now employing ICTs. Science ICTs have been successfully used in such programs and are currently being piloted in the science scales of NAEP and the Programme for International Student Assessment, as well as literacy, numeracy, and problem solving in the Programme for the International Assessment of Adult Competencies (PIAAC). Advances in item and task design and psychometrics are required to ensure that the validity of the inferences drawn from ICTs is as defensible as inferences drawn from traditional forms of assessment. The proper use of ECD can address such challenges.

Bennett, Persky, Weiss, and Jenkins (2007) provided assessment designers with early examples of how problem solving could be assessed in technology-rich environments through the use of ICTs. They illustrated the "look and feel" of such tasks by producing prototypes, including the "Hot Air Balloon Task" which demonstrated the affordances of ICTs. More recently, the U.S. Department of Education issued a Solicitation for NAEP Science Interactive Computer Task Development (2011). In this solicitation, ICTs are described as "[engaging] students in problem-solving and inquiry tasks to assess complex science understandings and practices" (p. 2). The NAEP Science Framework (National Assessment Governing Board, 2010) identifies four types of ICTs—information search and analysis, empirical investigation, simulation, and concept mapping—and six situations in which ICTs confer advantages over other types of assessment formats. These situations include:

- observing scientific phenomena that cannot be easily observed in real time;
- modeling of scientific phenomena that cannot be easily observed because they are too small or too large;
- working in environments that are hazardous or disorderly;
- conducting repeated complex experiments in a limited amount of time;
- searching the Internet or other resource documents that are similar to those required in real-world tasks; and
- manipulating objects or symbolic materials virtually rather than requiring a physical laboratory set-up with actual equipment and real-time protocols.

Consistent with the NAEP framework, the four types of ICTs (i.e., information search and analysis, empirical investigation, simulation, and concept mapping) could be used in a single ICT task, or each type of ICT could be its own assessment task. ICTs can determine whether a student can solve a problem or conduct an inquiry, and be designed to track fine-grained process data, that documents the steps the student takes to solve the task as well (Chung & Baker, 2003). ICTs can be effectively used in both formative and summative assessments. They are suitable for use in formal classroom settings, workplaces, and informal learning contexts, including after-school programs and museums.

Over the past decade, psychometricians have explored the use of Bayesian networks for modeling the assessment data yielded by ICTs (Almond, DiBello, Moulder, & Zapata, 2007; Levy & Mislevy, 2004; West et al., 2010). For additional background on science ICTs, see Clarke-Midura, Mayrath, and Dede (2012), Mayrath, Clarke-Midura, Robinson, and Schraw (2012), Quellmalz and Pellegrino (2009), Quellmalz et al. (2012), and Zoanetti (2010).

Some educational researchers may not yet be acquainted with the use of telemetric data as a means of assessing student performances in simulations. A substantial amount of the early work using telemetric data focused on the measurement of engagement and cognitive processing (e.g., attention, rapidity of cognitive processing) rather than higher level, domain-specific problem solving, including model-based reasoning, systems thinking, and design within constraints. The analysis of telemetry, for the purposes of summative assessments of learning, is now being explored, and several probability-based approaches have yielded promising results (Mislevy et al., 2015). These include (1) Recency-weighting of evidence using models that do not accommodate change by fading the influence of past data; (2) Bayesian Model Tracing (Baker, Corbett, & Aleven, 2008); (3) Dynamic Bayes Nets with latent student modeling variables as Hidden Markov Models (Ting, Phon-Amnuaisuk, & Chong, 2008); and (4) periodic updating of higher level models when student modeling takes place in hierarchies (Kimball, 2008). It is anticipated that higher level, domain-specific modeling will be possible using telemetric data in combination with the probability-based methodologies identified above. These methods can be used to support the collection and analysis of simulation data in any domain and for multiple purposes.

In the following section, we will describe the design and development of a life science ICT using the ECD process.

Design and Development of the Marigold Life Science ICT for Summative Purposes

The Marigold ICT assesses a middle school student's life science content knowledge and the ability to use that knowledge in designing, conducting, and analyzing results from an experimental investigation. The content includes a student's knowledge of the process by which plants use energy, water, and minerals to grow. The science inquiry includes a student's ability to design, conduct, and analyze results from an experiment.

The Marigold ICT begins with each student creating a model that shows the inputs and outputs of photosynthesis. The ICT then prompts the student to design and conduct an experiment that investigates how the amount of light and water affects the growth of a marigold. Each student must identify a hypothesis, describe how to test the hypothesis, design the experiment by picking levels of variables, and interpret the results of the experiment. As a student progresses through the task, he or she is asked to explain his or her reasoning at numerous points in the investigation.

The initial question facing the assessment designer was whether an ICT is a more appropriate task format to measure a student's ability to design an experiment about photosynthesis than other task formats which may be less costly to develop. A second question was how to integrate scientific practices used in an experiment with life science content. While these questions are not unique to the design of ICTs, they are common in the design of extended tasks. A scenario-based ICT typically requires the use of several assessment items in order to measure several Focal KSAs, each of which may be associated with scientific content alone or with scientific content integrated with scientific practices. It is usually a challenge to design sets of items that can fulfill the multiple requirements associated with the assessment of these KSAs.

A related challenge was the development of the narrative structure that underlies the assessment task. For ICTs, it is important that the task presents a coherent, engaging story that is grade level-appropriate. One of the obvious strengths of using ICTs is the immediate appeal of the rich, graphical interface that is presented to students and the interactivity of the assessment tasks. The age-appropriateness, artistic quality, and comprehensibility of the ICT storyline, however, are critical determinants of the degree to which a student can engage in the task and perform at levels commensurate with their knowledge and skills (Clark & Martinez-Garza, 2012). Design Pattern attributes can be used to specify the narrative structure of the ICT, and Task Model Variables can be used to guide the design of the tasks. Among the narrative structures that have been used to support life science ICTs are (1) cause and effect; (2) investigation; (3) change over time; (4) general to specific or whole to parts; (5) specific to general or parts to whole; and (6) topic with examples. The narrative chosen for the purposes of an accountability assessment would need to be aligned to a specific component or aspect of the state or district assessment framework.

A final challenge in designing ICTs for large-scale accountability purposes is student accessibility. In addition to standard accessibility issues (e.g., perceptual and expressive capabilities including low vision, color blindness, poor eye–hand coordination, physical disabilities such as cerebral palsy resulting in an inability to manipulate input devices), technology introduces another layer of demands that can interfere with a student's ability to perform at his or her full potential. For example, a student may lack familiarity with the graphical interface, scrolling, and technology-enhanced item formats (e.g., drag-and-drop formats, dropdown menus, dynamic graphing tools), or he or she may lack knowledge and skill in using different technology devices and platforms.

Testing companies have introduced test accommodations and modifications in response to the need to provide fair testing practices for all students. Test developers and state and district assessment specialists have struggled to identify workable and clear definitions that distinguish between accommodations and modifications. For illustrative purposes, we present three commonly used testing accommodations (i.e., tests taken orally, use of large print, and extended time on test) and five modifications (i.e., outline in place of essay, Picture Communication Symbols [rebus], alternative books and materials, spelling support from a computer, and questions reworded with simpler language). There has been considerable discussion about the use of accommodations and modifications in assessments (AERA, APA, & NCME, 2014). Some educators and assessment designers believe that the use of modifications reduces the expectations of students, could increase gaps in learning, and adversely affects student performance in construct-relevant ways. Therefore, many states have included in their student Individualized Education Programs one or more accommodations and limited modifications.

Some large-scale assessments are beginning to incorporate principles of UDL to make assessments accessible to a wider range of students, including English language learners and those with disabilities. These assessments often make use of a combination of accommodations and UDL principles. With assessments that address accountability issues, the particular use of accommodations, modifications, and UDL principles must conform to the guidelines specified by the state in which the assessment will be used.

As is the case with ECD, one goal of implementing UDL principles into learning and assessment environments is to minimize construct-irrelevant variance (Almond et al., 2010; Cameto, Haertel, DeBarger, & Morrison, 2010). In designing ICTs, assessment designers have to be attentive to the additional demands computer-based technologies place on students. In particular, the designers of science ICTs that are accessible to all students have to consider the use of audio presentation, refreshable Braille, American Sign Language, calculators, and writing tools such as spell check, grammar check, speech-to-text, word prediction, and text-to-speech for proofreading. Large-scale science assessments often make use of complicated diagrams that need to be clearly labeled. In some cases, students with disabilities may require that these diagrams be orally described or the assessment may need to provide "mouse-over" or "hover" capabilities to provide students with perceptual limitations an opportunity to use such diagrams appropriately. Because many science items involve rich presentations with pictures, diagrams, animations, and charts, assessment designers should be familiar with the technology features available to support students with disabilities.

Applying ECD to Design and Development the Marigold ICT

In the following paragraphs, the five layers of work that comprise the ECD process are described in relation to the design and development of the Marigold ICT. (See Rutstein, 2013 for a complete description of the design and development process.)

Domain Analysis

The Marigold task was based on the life science content and practices that are specified in the NAEP Science Assessment Framework (National Assessment Governing Board, 2010). The NAEP life science content statements and Science Inquiry Principles comprise the Domain Analysis layer of the ECD process. Thus, when an assessment designer has an assessment framework or set of learning objectives, he or she may decide no additional organizational work need be done at the Domain Analysis level.

Domain Modeling

When the Marigold task was being designed, the Design Pattern for *Experimental Investigation* already had been generated.

Typically, Design Patterns focus on processes, practices, and skills relevant to a domain, but do not specify content, so that they can be applied for many purposes. However, the decision to integrate processes, practices, and skills with domain content is driven by the needs of the assessment designers. A decision had to be made as to whether the KSAs in the "Experimental Investigation Design Pattern" (Appendix C) should include science content or not. While integrating the content and the practice into one Design Pattern makes the Design Pattern more specific (and therefore not as applicable in as many situations), it does help ensure that items and tasks that are developed will measure practice in the context of a specific content area. In the case of Marigold, the decision was made to use the "Experimental Investigation Design Pattern" without modification. The Design Pattern itself remained content-independent, and content expertise in life science was drawn from the life science content statements found in the NAEP Science Framework for 2011.

Conceptual Assessment Framework

A Summary Task Template was created as part of the Marigold assessment design process. A Summary Task Template specifies an overview of the presentation of the task as well as information on Characteristic and Task Model Variables (see Appendix D). The Student, Evidence, and Task Models were specified. A two-dimensional Student Model was developed that included nodes representing constructs associated with science content (i.e., knowledge of photosynthesis) and nodes representing constructs associated with inquiry skills. The Evidence Model included measurement models that bundle items such as those that can be analyzed using the Multidimensional Random Coefficient Multinomial Logit Model (Adams, Wilson, & Wang, 1997; Wilson & Adams, 1995). The narrative structure field in the Design Pattern provides guidance for item writers on how to structure the assessment task in order to increase the coherence of its storyline. For Marigold, the "investigation" narrative structure was chosen.

Assessment Implementation

The writers of the Marigold task were able to use the Focal KSAs, Potential Observations, Potential Work Products, Narrative Structures, and Characteristic and Variable Features, as well as AKSAs provided in the Experimental Investigation Design Pattern, to guide their item writing. In addition, they drew on the life science content statements to contextualize the Focal KSAs of interest. Although the Marigold ICT addresses both life science content and practice, the individual items used in the task focus on either content or inquiry. Items were then aligned to specific Focal KSAs in the Design Pattern and/or specific content statements to ensure their content validity.

Below are two Focal KSAs (Fk) that were drawn from the Experimental Investigation Design Pattern and used in the Marigold task:

1 Fk4: Ability to identify, generate, or evaluate a prediction/hypothesis that is testable with a simple experiment.
2 Fk6: Ability to recognize that at a basic level an experiment involves manipulating one variable and measuring the effect on (or value of) another variable.

Potential Observations enabled the assessment designers to envision the student responses that they wanted the new items to elicit with respect to the Focal KSAs or content statements being assessed. Below are two Potential Observations (Po) that were selected for use in the Marigold ICT:

1 Po6: Accuracy in identifying variables (other than the treatment variables of interest) that should be controlled (held constant) or made equivalent (e.g., through random assignment).
2 Po12: Generate a prediction/hypothesis that is testable with a simple experiment.

Potential Work Products helped to determine which type of items and technologies were most likely to elicit the Potential Observations. Below are two Potential Work Products (Pw) that were selected for use in the Marigold ICT:

1   Pw7: Interactive tables—Students fill in values in a table.
2   Pw2: Constructed response—Students generate their response given a prompt.

The Characteristic and Variable Features were intended to help item writers determine what task features should be specified and which task features could be varied while still measuring the construct of interest. Below are examples of two Characteristic and Variable Features used in the Marigold ICT:

CHARACTERISTIC FEATURES (CF)

1   Cf2: Presentation of situation of scientific interest where variables can be (or have been) practically altered to address a causal prediction.
2   Cf5: Presentation of observed result from an experiment requiring the development of explanations, conclusions, or models.

VARIABLE FEATURES (VF)

1   Vf4: Ease or difficulty with which the treatment (independent variable) can be manipulated.
2   Vf6: The number of variables investigated and the complexity of their interrelationships.

The AKSAs that were used in designing Marigold included those related to UDL features. These AKSAs were specified in the Design Pattern and were used to identify sources of construct-irrelevant variance that might interfere with task performance. Below are two examples of AKSAs that were used in the Student Model associated with the design of the Marigold ICT. The first AKSA (familiarity with…) was selected to ensure that students who were not familiar with particular illustrations of how an experiment in the life sciences is depicted would have both textual and pictorial representations of each concept. The second AKSA was the need for sufficient short-term memory capacity. In the Marigold task, a student has to generate an experimental hypothesis and then use that hypothesis repeatedly to design their experiments. To support the need for short-term memory, a static presentation of the student's experimental hypothesis appears at the top of each computer screen.

1   Familiarity with representational forms (e.g., pictures, maps, and graphs).
2   Student needs based on UDL cognitive category (in the Marigold task, the UDL category that includes short-term memory capacity is referred to as "cognitive").

Appendix E includes the graphical interface for each item in the task.

Table 11.2 describes the assessment situations and items presented in the Marigold ICT task. The first column, "assessment situation," presents the component of the assessment task each student encounters. The second column, "nature of the construct being assessed," indicates whether the constructs being assessed during the particular assessment situation are associated with life science content or the inquiry process. The third column, "content knowledge or inquiry skill assessed," provides a description of the particular photosynthesis content or the science inquiry process being assessed. The fourth column, "item type," describes the format of the item being presented (e.g., selected response, constructed response); and the fifth column, "type of technology," indicates which technology enhancement (e.g., animation, drag and drop, dropdown menu, text box) is used to present the particular item.

Assessment Delivery

The Marigold ICT was designed to be delivered by computer as part of a large-scale assessment task. When such tasks are designed, the Evidence Model, including rubric development and the

Table 11.2 Description of the Assessment Situations, Constructs, Knowledge and Skills, Item Types, and Types of Technology Presented in the Marigold ICT

Assessment Situation	Nature of the Construct Being Assessed	Content Knowledge or Inquiry Skill Assessed	Item Type	Type of Technology
Introduction to the task	None	None	None	Animation
Create photosynthesis model	Life science content	Knowledge of the process of photosynthesis	Selected response	Drag and drop
Design and conduct an experiment and predict results	Life science content	Knowledge of what plants need to grow	Selected response	Drop down menu
	Knowledge of inquiry	Knowledge of variables	Constructed response	Text box
	Knowledge of inquiry	Knowledge of hypotheses	Selected response with multiple selection	Radio buttons
	Knowledge of inquiry	Knowledge of control variables	Selected response paired with a constructed response	Radio buttons Text box
	Knowledge of life science content	Knowledge of plant growth	Constructed response	Text box
	Inquiry skill	Ability to create a prediction	Constructed response	Text box
	Inquiry skill	Ability to design an experiment	Selected response	Interactive table
Explain, interpret, and generalize results	Inquiry skill	Ability to explain an experimental design	Constructed response	Question prompt branches depending on inputs from the student Text box
	Inquiry skill	Ability to interpret results of tables generated by student	Selected response Constructed response	Results and prompt shown depending on inputs from student Radio buttons Text box
	Inquiry skill	Ability to generalize from results of an experiment	Selected response Constructed response	Radio button Text box

specification of a measurement model, must be provided. Since Marigold is a single task that was intended to be incorporated within a life science assessment, the measurement model and scoring were not specified for the purposes of this chapter.

Benefits of ECD for Design and Development of Life Science ICTs

There are several benefits to using the ECD process. One is that the alignment among the items, the task, and the Focal KSAs is made explicit. This supports the inferential validity of the task by making clear what the task measures. The use of AKSAs also helps identify possible sources of construct-irrelevant variance and helps the task developer to minimize this variance, which again supports the validity of the assessment argument. The linkages among the Student Model, Evidence Model, and Task Model support the argument that the task is designed to elicit evidence about the construct(s) of interest.

An additional benefit of the ECD process is that it facilitates task development. Having a list of technology features that could be incorporated into the task makes it easier to develop items that take advantage of the interactive nature of ICTs. Design Patterns also list the requirements of the task and identify decisions required of a task developer. In ICTs, the narrative structure attribute provides information that can help the developer to create an engaging storyline. Information in the Design Pattern can be further elaborated in a Task Template to provide guidance for future item development.

A final benefit is the efficiency gained by reuse of an existing Design Pattern. The Marigold task was designed as a variant of an ICT task in Physical Science, referred to as the Pinball Car Race. For Pinball, the same Design Pattern, Experimental Investigation, was used, but applied to a different content area (force and motion). The development of the Marigold ICT took less time than the development of Pinball, as the same Design Pattern and a similar task structure was used.

Measuring "Hard-to-Assess" Life Science Constructs

"Hard-to-assess" constructs in the life sciences refer to those skills and abilities that go beyond the narrow set of competencies that have been the chief focus of many statewide K–12 science assessments. In the past few years, some educators have used the term "deeper learning" to refer to skills that are associated with (1) thorough understanding of core content, (2) ability to think critically and solve complex problems, (3) work collaboratively, (4) communicate effectively, (5) engage in self-directed learning, and (6) incorporate feedback (Alliance for Excellent Education, 2011). In response to the emergence of these new competencies, a flurry of interest has developed around the measurement of deeper learning.

The NRC is developing new standards and guidance for assessments that will measure challenging content and practices in science. These newly articulated science content standards and practices are defined and described in the *Framework for K–12 Science Education* (NRC, 2012), and the assessment framework is articulated in the NGSS (2013). The "hard-to-assess" science constructs include model-based reasoning, design under constraints, causation versus correlation, and systems thinking. Likewise, the computer science standards developed by the Computer Science Teachers Association and the National Education Technology Standards have stimulated interest in the development of measures of such constructs as computational thinking, a "hard-to-assess" construct in the computer sciences.

In the following section, we will describe the use of ECD as a means of measuring "hard-to-assess" constructs in modeling, systems thinking, and computational thinking.

Designing Assessments of Modeling in Life Sciences

The *Framework for K–12 Science Education* (NRC, 2012), as the principal guide for developing the new national K–12 science standards, asserts that proficiency in science requires using and applying knowledge in the context of scientific practice. According to this science-as-practice perspective (Duschl, 2008; Harris & Salinas, 2009; Lehrer & Schauble, 2006), when students have opportunities to use scientific practices to develop and apply their ideas, they deepen their conceptual understanding of content, as well as their understanding of how to do science.

The NGSS are very different from the previous generation of science standards in that they emphasize integrating core ideas in science with scientific practices in the form of performance expectations. The assessment development work described below aims to provide insight into how content and practice may be integrated in the design, implementation, and scoring of science assessments in a summative context (DeBarger, Penuel, & Harris, 2013; Harris et al., 2012).

This section describes the design of assessment tasks that measure the scientific practice of modeling. The backdrop for these design tasks is an efficacy study of the Project-Based Inquiry Science (PBIS) middle school curriculum comprising project-based inquiry science units in life, physical, and earth sciences across sixth, seventh, and eighth grades. Since PBIS curricular units are project-based (Krajcik & Blumenfeld, 2006), students investigate phenomena and apply concepts to answer a driving question or address a design challenge. The driving question or design challenge typically targets a core idea in science, and activities within a unit provide students with multiple occasions for engaging in a range of scientific practices, such as constructing explanations and developing and using models. In this way, the design of the PBIS curriculum anticipates where the science education field is headed—teaching a few core ideas and integrating them seamlessly with scientific practices.

Design Challenges

Few existing curriculum-embedded classroom assessments or large-scale assessment items explicitly elicit students' understanding of both content and practice as they are defined in the NRC framework and NGSS. A focus on modeling is an especially appropriate example of a "hard-to-assess" construct, requiring the integration of content and practice—it illustrates what is "new" and challenging in the NGSS. Central to the work of scientists, modeling is essential for the development of disciplinary knowledge. A notable shift required by the NGSS is that students should be able to construct, refine, critique, and use models to predict and explain phenomena in a given scientific discipline.

The NGSS identifies performance expectations that include assessable components of a given science topic reflecting an intersection of a core idea and scientific practices. These expectations may include boundary statements that identify limits to the level of understanding or context appropriate for a grade level and clarification statements that offer additional detail and examples. Performance expectations, however, do not provide sufficient detail to create an assessment. An example of an NGSS performance expectation in Ecosystems-Interactions, Energy, and Dynamics is presented below:

> Students who demonstrate understanding can:
>
> **5-LS2-1.** Develop a model to describe the movement of matter among plants, animals, decomposers, and the environment. [Clarification Statement: Emphasis is on the idea that matter that is not food (air, water, decomposed materials in soil) is changed by plants into matter that is food. Examples of systems could include organisms, ecosystems, and the Earth.] [Assessment Boundary: Assessment does not include molecular explanations.] (http://www.nextgenscience.org/5ls2-ecosystems-interactions-energy-dynamics)

In assessment task design, it is also important to consider the kinds of conceptual models and evidence that a student will encounter; grade level-appropriate contexts for assessing the performance expectations; options for task design features; and types of evidence that will reveal levels of student understanding and skills.

Using ECD in the Design Process

In this context, ECD was used as a strategy to articulate an assessment argument that unpacks performance expectations into an interrelated set of learning goals, describes the kinds of tasks and situations that would elicit evidence relevant to those goals, and demonstrates how particular performances can generate such evidence. An important first step in the ECD process was to construct a Design Pattern to articulate the argument underlying the design of the assessment tasks. In this instance, the intent was to elicit students' ability to engage in the practice of modeling. Design Patterns specify the student model, the kinds of observations that could provide evidence about acquisition of a Focal Knowledge or Skill, and the Characteristic and Variable Features of task situations that allowed students to provide this evidence (Mislevy, Hamel, et al., 2003). The Design Pattern (see Appendix F) made more explicit the knowledge and skills associated with the practice of modeling, elaborated the task and activity features intended to elicit such knowledge and skills, as well as provided concrete examples of student behaviors or performances that would demonstrate evidence of a student's ability with respect to the practice of modeling.

As shown in Appendix F, four Focal KSAs (Fks) were identified:

1   Fk1: Ability to construct a model and use the model to explain a phenomenon.
2   Fk2: Ability to construct a model and use the model to make a prediction about a phenomenon.
3   Fk3: Ability to compare a model to a real-world phenomenon (to evaluate the quality of the model).
4   Fk4: Ability to use a given model to make a prediction about a phenomenon.

The Design Pattern also provided Potential Observations that illustrate examples of student responses that would count as evidence relevant to each Focal KSA. For instance, to demonstrate proficiency on Fk1, the student should be able to demonstrate qualities drawn from all four of the Potential Observations (Pos) in this Design Pattern:

1   Po1: Given a brief real-world scenario describing an observable phenomenon, student applies scientific concepts appropriately to construct a model (using drawings and words) that explains why the phenomenon occurs.
2   Po2: Given a brief real-world scenario describing an observable phenomenon, student applies scientific concepts appropriately to construct a model (using drawings and words) and uses the model to make an accurate prediction about the phenomenon.
3   Po3: Given a model, student accurately describes similarities and differences between the model and a phenomenon.
4   Po4: Given a model, student uses the model to make an accurate prediction about a phenomenon.

For these Potential Observations, proficiency with respect to Focal KSAs requires that a student incorporate core ideas as she develops and uses models, expressing her responses in connected prose, graphs, or drawings.

The link between the content and practice of modeling is documented in the Design Pattern's fourth Characteristic Feature:

1   Cf4: All items must elicit core ideas as defined in the framework or NGSS.

The Characteristic Features also help to further delineate features of items and characteristics of models that would be used in items.

The Variable Features in Appendix F highlight ways that items can vary, yet still address Focal KSAs. For example, using this Design Pattern, items will vary with respect to:

1   Vf1: Drawing required: (1) none; (2) add to existing picture; (3) construct model from scratch.
2   Vf2: Complexity of scientific concept(s) to be modeled.
3   Vf3: Format of "real-world" phenomenon presented: (1) image, (2) data, (3) text, (4) combination.
4   Vf4: Core idea/component idea targeted in model.

Variable Features thus embody the ways that content and practice are linked. Variable Features also help to distinguish among different features of models, for example whether models address phenomena at the micro- or macro-level. In this way, Variable Features can affect difficulty and discrimination and highlight elements of crosscutting concepts from the NRC framework that should be considered in assessment design. In addition, the amount of time that the assessment task requires is affected by the Variable Features that are selected.

The Design Pattern makes clear that items should be designed to provide evidence of the conceptual model a student uses when thinking about a scientific phenomenon. Therefore, several items require a student to construct a model using drawings and writing to support an explanation of a phenomenon or justify a prediction about a phenomenon. A single rubric was designed for each constructed-response item that distinguishes among levels of sophistication with respect to both content knowledge and modeling. For complete credit in the most complex items, a student must construct drawings, explanations, and/or predictions that include scientifically accurate content knowledge and describe how her representation/drawing of the phenomenon helps to explain it.

How ECD Enhances the Quality of Items

There are few examples of the development of assessment items that measure students' ability to apply learning through the scientific practices identified in the NRC framework and NGSS. This study, conducted by DeBarger, Penuel, Harris, and Kennedy (2015), documents—for assessment developers and science educators alike—the logic and the validity argument underlying the development of the modeling assessments that simultaneously elicit these core ideas.

Using ECD to incorporate rigorous theoretical and empirically grounded perspectives, as well as to organize and systematize design and development, enabled the production of a coherent set of assessments to examine a student's abilities to engage with core science ideas through models. The assessments are coherent in the sense that they are built upon a logical argument that promoted consistency in the design of tasks and rubrics and the interpretation of student performances. ECD's language, representational forms, and unified perspective provided a framework to better measure scientific practices. At every layer of test development, ECD facilitated the recognition and exploitation of efficiencies from reuse and compatibility. While the items generated had a specific purpose in the project's efficacy study, the Design Pattern has been adapted for other assessment situations. The assessment argument specified in this example, which links both science content and practice, is applicable in both summative and formative assessment contexts.

Designing Assessments of Systems Thinking in Life Sciences

Many scientific phenomena can be conceptualized as systems of interdependent processes and parts. In life sciences, systems underlie core ideas such as understandings of ecosystems and interdependence and relationships among organisms—including the balance of predator and prey populations, structure and function of living systems, and adaptation and evolution across time. These can be studied as a group of interacting components as well as a macro-phenomenon that is the collective outcome of those interactions. The recent framework for K–12 Science Education and the NGSS identify "systems and systems models" as one of seven crosscutting concepts that provide a means of connecting ideas across science content areas into a "coherent scientifically-based view of the world" (NRC, 2012). Fluency in using systems is now seen as an essential foundation for scientific literacy and the preparation of students for scientific careers. The NGSS framework lists a set of guiding principles for how the crosscutting concepts, like systems and systems models, should be used instructionally, and these have implications for assessment design.

For example, a systems perspective provides a language that scientists and science students can use as a means to analyze and communicate about a variety of phenomena (Goldstone & Wilensky, 2008). Systems models provide useful tools that enable students and scientists to recognize how multiple factors interact and predict patterns of change over time. One benefit of a systems approach is that crosscutting concepts provide a common vocabulary for science and engineering (NRC, 2012).

The use of systems models provides a means to align topics across the science curriculum and assist students in developing an understanding of core ideas and practices in science and engineering. Because systems models use crosscutting concepts, they can be presented in a variety of contexts and thereby build a student's familiarity with science (NRC, 2012). Two key competencies that students are expected to develop across grade levels include (1) appreciating that phenomena can be modeled as interacting systems, and (2) understanding the characteristics of systems more broadly. It is important to be able to assess these proficiencies. Practically speaking, adoption of the NGSS will make assessment of systems necessary.

The design of assessments of systems thinking serves as a model for a process which can be applied to the design of assessments of other "hard-to-assess" constructs in summative and formative contexts.

Design Challenges

As with all "hard-to-assess" constructs, designers face four challenges when designing assessments of systems thinking. First, they must identify the appropriate competencies to be assessed. The relevant background knowledge needed to design a task in this area is substantial and ranges across many domains. The systems domain is itself quite complex and there are few seminal resources to help designers define key constructs. Second, designers must identify age- or grade-appropriate competencies in this domain. Given the complex and emerging nature of this domain as a topic of instruction, identifying grade-appropriate competencies can be difficult. Third, there is the challenge posed by the complex relationships between systems thinking and the content or context in which the task is situated; the interplay of required and necessary (but not focal) knowledge is a particularly difficult measurement challenge. Fourth, complex constructs such as those associated with systems, modeling, and computational thinking are hard to assess because the tasks that can elicit evidence of these competencies typically must be embedded in rich contexts.

Scalise (2012) argues that developing tasks for "hard-to-assess" constructs requires adequate time, materials, and context. Complex constructs need to be assessed in rich environments so that claims made about a student's abilities are warranted. Short, discrete, multiple-choice items can provide information about a student's understanding of systems; however, with such items the system must be presented in sufficient detail to provide the test takers with enough information and "sense" of the system and associated phenomena to arrive at a solution. In order to understand the task setting, the student must be given more time than is typically allotted for answering traditional multiple-choice items. Scenario-based tasks, which more readily can present a complex setting, are able to link multiple items to one framing context—thus using a student's time and cognitive resources more efficiently. Additionally, it has been argued that some more complex competencies, such as the ability to identify crucial qualitative or quantitative values of a system, require iterative use of a system model (de Jong & van Joolingen, 1998). Iterative use of a model is not ideally incorporated as part of a single discrete item. Scenario-based tasks that present multiple items are themselves challenging to design as they must provide a coherent storyline to link each item, adding to the set of challenges facing an assessment designer.

Using ECD in the Design Process

Three of the five layers of ECD are highlighted in this example of the design and development of a scenario-based task that measures systems thinking in the life sciences. The three layers of ECD that most informed this development process were Domain Analysis, Domain Modeling, and Assessment Implementation. When designing summative assessments, the designer must keep in mind several constraints common to accountability measures. For example, the amount of time available for the administration of the task, the need to provide clear directions that do not require intervention during the test administration process, and the use of scaffolds to support student performance in non-construct relevant ways. In particular, scaffolds such as the use of glossaries, providing guidance regarding the sequence of steps used in solving a problem, and highly detailed diagrams of scientific phenomena must be construct-irrelevant. The impact of these constraints on the designer using ECD is reflected in the specification of the characteristic and variable task features to be included in the assessment task.

DOMAIN ANALYSIS

An extensive literature review revealed a core set of understandings about systems that could anchor assessment design. This literature review comprised the Domain Analysis layer of the ECD process (Cheng et al., 2010).

DOMAIN MODELING

The student competencies identified in the review as crucial to systems thinking were then expressed as a set of Focal KSAs in a Design Pattern, comprising the Domain Modeling layer of ECD. The Focal KSAs or core competencies in the Systems and System Models domain are shown in Appendix G. Focal KSA4 illustrates the complexity of the domain of systems and makes clear the difficulty encountered by assessment designers as they try to operationalize such constructs.

1   Fk4: The ability to predict or interpret the outcome of an input (change) to the system.

This Focal KSA was identified in the literature of science instruction. The literature review suggested that a student's knowledge of systems is often compartmentalized, which makes the system difficult to understand as a whole and commonalities across systems difficult to recognize. In addition, components and interactions of systems often are taught as two separate pieces of knowledge, with most instruction focusing on the structural aspects of a system (Liu & Hmelo-Silver, 2009). This can make it difficult for students to reason about a whole system since they lack the knowledge of how the structure and functions of the different parts of a system interact to produce the behavior of the whole system. For example, high school students may learn about the role of oxygen in the respiration of food but be unable to link this to their knowledge of the flow of matter and energy in ecosystems (Hogan & Weathers, 2003). Because this ability was so often reported in the literature, it was deemed "core" and included among the Focal KSAs (Cheng et al., 2010). Focal KSAs were organized according to appropriate grade-bands in line with the NGSS guiding principle that knowledge of systems should increase in complexity and sophistication across grade levels.

KSAs that influence a student's ability to respond successfully to assessment tasks, but were not deemed Focal Knowledge and Skills for all of the items that could be generated using the Systems and System Models Design Pattern, were included as AKSAs. The most obvious Ak is the content knowledge required to examine a particular system, such as knowledge that an organism named in a representation is a type of fish, or knowledge that the region where this ecosystem is found is a wetlands habitat (see the complete list of Aks below). Ak1 is the content knowledge required to examine a particular system.

1   Ak1: Knowledge of components/structure of the system (content knowledge).
2   Ak2: Knowledge of the interactions in the system.
3   Ak3: Knowledge of crucial values.
4   Ak4: Knowledge of time scales operating in system.
5   Ak5: Ability to interpret the representation of the system.
6   Ak6: Scientific reasoning.
7   Ak7: Knowledge of the nature of models (e.g., physical, formulas, three-dimensional).
8   Ak8: Metacognitive skills.
9   Ak9: Knowledge of the representation of the system model (i.e., food web).

Assigning "content knowledge" as an Ak is not in conflict with the spirit of the NGSS since this Design Pattern is articulated in a way that facilitates the assessment of science practice in many content domains. In this case, the integration of content and practice would be implemented at the CAF layer of ECD using Task Templates and, therefore, is not represented in the Systems and System Models Design Pattern presented here. Alternatively, integration of content and practice can be articulated at the Design Pattern level if the content in the systems is to be assessed as a Focal Skill along with the science practice. An example of such a Design Pattern is presented in Appendix A.

Task Model Variables are another important set of design considerations. These variables include Characteristic Features, Variable Features, and Narrative Structures to be incorporated into potential tasks associated with a particular Design Pattern. As mentioned above, because scenario-based tasks are often more appropriate to assess systems thinking, a Characteristic Feature of tasks designed to assess the understanding of a system requires the use of a scenario or context. Cf2 is a Characteristic Feature from the Systems and System Models Design Pattern that exemplifies this design consideration:

1   Cf2: Task scenario: The situation presenting task prompt, scientific content, or context.

A Variable Feature prompts designers to consider which task features will be presented to students. From the Systems and System Models Design Pattern, we present three examples of Variable Features:

1   Vf1: Number of system components.
2   Vf2: Number of relationships presented (given to student versus student-generated).
3   Vf3: Type of relationship that is the target of the task.

When designing scenario-based items, the storyline of the task is crucial to the coherence of the set of items that comprise the task. Thus, the Design Pattern articulates several Narrative Structures that could be selected by the designer as they create a scenario-based task to assess systems thinking. Narrative Structures may include, for example, cause and effect, change over time, or investigation. See Appendix G for a list of Narrative Structures that could be used to structure systems thinking scenario-based assessment tasks.

ASSESSMENT IMPLEMENTATION

In this layer of ECD, a scenario-based task, referred to as the Burmese Python, was authored using the Systems and System Models Design Pattern described above. Each of the three items in the Burmese Python task is presented in Appendix H along with the Focal KSA it is designed to measure. In this task, a student is first provided with background information about the ecosystem in Everglades National Park. This contextual information will support the student in reasoning about a food web model (see Figure 1, Appendix H). A student is then asked to examine the food web in light of the growing presence of an invasive species, the Burmese Python, which is a predator in the ecosystem. Assessing a student's ability to reason about a particular system aligns to the NGSS framework guiding principle that crosscutting concepts should not be assessed separately from practices or core ideas.

In the item shown in Appendix H, Figure 2, the student is required to have knowledge of the food web representation being used to convey information about the Everglades ecosystem. A student who is not familiar with food webs as a representational form and is unable to conclude that the information provided includes both organisms as well as the relationships among them (e.g., predator–prey relationships) would be less likely to demonstrate his or her ability to make a prediction about the ecosystem. (See FKSA4 which is associated with Figure 2.) Assessment designers may choose to minimize the impact of the knowledge of the food web representation (see Ak9 below) by providing information about food webs that a student can use to successfully complete the task.

1   Ak9: Knowledge of the representation of the system model (i.e., food web).

Alternatively, designers may decide to integrate the Focal KSA—Fk4, ability to make a prediction—with knowledge of life science and knowledge of food webs as part of the CAF layer of ECD. In this case, the assessment designer would assess both the life science content associated with the predator–prey relationships in the Florida Everglades and knowledge of the food web representation.

Figure 3 in Appendix H is an example of how technology can tighten the alignment between a Work Product (creation of a food web) and the Focal KSA being measured. In Figure 3, a student is expected to identify the structure of the Florida Everglades food web after the Burmese Python has invaded the ecosystem. Technology provides a student with the capability to manipulate the food web in a constrained manner. If students were required to create a food web from scratch in a paper–pencil format, then extensive time would be required and they would likely produce highly variable responses that would be difficult to score fairly. The use of the drag-and-drop technology permits a student's knowledge of the structure of the food web to be easily expressed and scored, which is likely to increase both the content validity and reliability of the task.

Figure 4 provides an example of how a student can be provided with relevant background information including text passages and graphical displays that must be integrated in response to a multiple-choice question.

How ECD Enhances the Quality of Items

ECD can support the design of complex, rich, and coherent scenario-based tasks that assess both science understanding and practices. An ECD approach is well suited to support the design of most constructs, particularly "hard-to-assess" and new and emerging constructs. ECD helps designers to identify, in advance, the relevant features of the Work Product and how they will be evaluated. The example presented above demonstrates how an ECD-based design process can be used to design families of tasks that measure constructs in a manner consistent with the NGSS framework.

Designing Assessments of Computational Thinking in Life Sciences

Computational thinking can be broadly viewed as the reasoning skills needed to master and apply algorithmic thinking, pattern recognition, abstraction, decomposition, and other computational techniques to problems in a wide range of fields (e.g., see NRC, 2010; Wing, 2008). Over the past decade, there has been a growing focus on the concept of computational thinking both within computer science (e.g., Astrachan, Hambrusch, Peckham, & Settle, 2009) and outside computer science in education (e.g., Grover & Pea, 2013), the liberal arts (e.g., Adams, 2008), and the life sciences (e.g., Noble, 2002; Priami, 2007, 2009; Qin, 2009). In fact, computational biology and bioinformatics, which arguably arose from the integration of computational thinking and the life sciences, is currently one of the fastest-growing areas for innovation and development in the United States. A high school assessment task that blends computational thinking and biology might include creating and applying simple algorithms to large-scale data sets in order to predict the likelihood of disease occurrence or species proliferation or extinction.

To date, limited attention has been placed on the measurement of computational thinking learning outcomes. This is partly because no single specification of the organizing concepts and principles in the computational thinking domain (including the underlying knowledge, skills, and other attributes) has been constructed (and accepted) by STEM practitioners. This leaves open the question of what essential KSAs comprise computational thinking and how to assess them. Additionally, computational thinking can be seen as an integration of computer science content/concepts with problem solving and inquiry skills; as such, computational thinking can be considered a "hard-to-assess" construct.[1]

An ECD approach is well suited to create summative assessments that support valid inferences about computational thinking practices. Specifically, Snow and his associates (Rutstein, Snow, & Bienkowski, 2014; Snow, Bienkowski, & Rutstein, 2014; Snow, Rutstein, & Bienkowski, 2014) are creating and validating unit and summative assessments designed to measure seven computational thinking practices based on the Exploring Computer Science (ECS) curriculum:

1   analyze the effects of development in computing,
2   design and implement creative solutions and artifacts,
3   apply abstractions and models,
4   analyze computational work,
5   connect computation with other disciplines,
6   communicate thought processes and results, and
7   work effectively in teams.

Using ECD in the Design Process

The ECD approach is especially helpful when the knowledge and skills to be measured must be embedded in complex, multistep performances such as those required in computational thinking. Much of the work on the assessment of computational thinking to date has focused on the conceptualization required to organize the domain and begin the development of Design Patterns that can model the families of tasks needed to assess competencies in this area.

To organize this content domain for assessment purposes, computer science concepts and inquiry behaviors must be identified. A Domain Analysis conducted in this area as part of the Principled Assessments of Computational Thinking (PACT) project included a literature review, examination of computer science standards, and a review of computer science curricula (Snow, Bienkowski, et al., 2014). The computer science concepts of interest included practices such as applying abstractions and models. The computational thinking practices of interest drew on the contributions of Bybee et al.'s (1990) five Es of inquiry behavior: engage, explore, evaluate, explain, and elaborate.

DOMAIN MODELING

Previous research has shown that Design Patterns can be leveraged at strategic points in the assessment design and development process to improve both efficiency and validity (Snow et al., 2010). Thus, the PACT project created Design Patterns for each of the seven computational thinking practices identified in the ECS curriculum. Appendix I presents a preliminary Design Pattern that includes an Overview, Focal KSAs, Potential Observations, and Potential Work Products. The PACT project leverages the Computational Thinking Practice Design Patterns in at least two ways: (1) to support task writing across multiple groups of stakeholders, such as teachers, computer science faculty, and professional item writing staff; and (2) to promote integration of the formative, unit-level assessments and the culminating, summative assessment.

Benefits of ECD Approach

Developers of computational thinking tasks, whether they are teachers, computer science faculty, or professional item writers, can use Design Patterns to create tasks that address the same underlying computational thinking practices in terms of common Focal KSAs and Characteristic Features of tasks. Different choices can be made regarding AKSAs, Variable Features of tasks, Work Products, and Potential Observations associated with a student's performance. Focal KSAs at different grain sizes may be required for formative and summative inferences. Having common and explicit Design Patterns is likely to enhance the instructional validity and the evidentiary value of the assessment tasks.

Developing Life Science Assessments for "Hard-to-Assess" Populations

Much of the practice of ECD should be focused on the identification of sources of construct-irrelevant variance that can result in faulty interpretations of scores (Mislevy et al., 2013). Assessment design choices that are not carefully thought through can result in test items that employ unfamiliar language and syntax, incorporate poorly understood social and cultural item contexts and task stimuli, as well as modes of representations (visual, oral, behavioral) that can be systematically biased against sub-groups with limited access to those modalities. Fairness in the assessment situation requires that task contexts be equally familiar, appropriate, and accessible to all students, minimizing bias against particular groups by making the assessment designer aware of the many kinds of AKSAs that can contribute to faulty inferences about students' assessment performances. Achieving this degree of fairness is a "tall order"; however, this is an important and worthy goal that assessment designers need to keep in mind and try to achieve during the test development process.

The 1999 and 2014 editions of the Standards for Educational and Psychological Testing (AERA, APA, & NCME) recognized fairness as a fundamental issue of test validity. The Standards specifically address the incorporation of UDL principles as a means for developing tests that are fair to all examinees. An ECD-based assessment design process is able to incorporate UDL principles in order to build "fair" assessments and provide all students (those with and without disability) with an opportunity to perform at their best in large-scale accountability assessments. The infusion of UDL into the assessment design process from the outset is critical to minimizing accessibility barriers and minimizing construct-irrelevant variance.

This section describes the use of ECD to refine a set of large-scale science assessment items from an annual statewide assessment. As part of the Principled Science Assessment Design for Students with Disabilities project, funded by the U.S. Department of Education, a multidisciplinary team worked with representatives from four State Departments of Education assessment offices (Haertel, DeBarger, Villalba, Hamel, & Colker, 2010). The project sought to redesign a set of 21 multiple-choice middle school science assessment items. The items were taken from a pool of large-scale science assessment items from one of the participating states. These items were selected from a list of practice items that were used to prepare students for the upcoming annual state assessment. The items were selected to comprise a test that reflected a typical end-of-year summative science assessment. Students in the sample had not used these practice items in preparing for their annual statewide science assessment.

Design Challenges

This project explored the impact of non-relevant assessment task demands on students with learning disabilities, including attention deficit hyperactivity disorder and mild forms of cognitive impairment. Students with learning disabilities are often challenged with mild cognitive disabilities (e.g., reading, memory, aphasia) but also often have to contend with perceptual and expressive challenges. Students who are identified as learning-disabled are instructed and tested with general education students; they make up 41 percent of those students receiving special education services (U.S. Department of Education, 2007). The needs of these students are quite diverse, making it difficult to identify assessment design principles that can serve their needs, as well as those of the general education population.

Universal Design for Learning

UDL helps to meet the challenges of diversity by providing flexible assessment materials, techniques, and strategies (Dolan, Rose, Burling, Harms, & Way, 2007), including three guiding principles that address critical aspects of assessments. The first principle, to provide multiple means of representation, addresses the ways in which information can be presented in an assessment. The second principle is to provide multiple means of action and expression. This principle focuses on providing multiple ways in which a student can interact with content and express an answer or solution to a problem. Providing multiple means of engagement is the third principle, addressing the ways in which a student engages in the assessment activity (Rose & Meyer, 2002, 2006; Rose, Meyer, & Hitchcock, 2005). Using the general guidance provided by these principles, six categories of task demands have been identified as related to successful performance on assessment tasks. These six categories are not the measurement constructs of interest; they are student needs that should be supported during the assessment so that a student's performance is not unduly influenced by these construct-irrelevant capabilities. The six categories of student needs are: (1) using language and text; (2) interpreting data representations, graphics, and images; (3) accessing background knowledge and cognitive processes; (4) establishing task goals and monitoring progress; (5) managing information and resources; and (6) accessing working memory. During the ECD process, these six categories of needs are identified as AKSAs and are coupled with Variable Features that can be used by the assessment developer to provide supports in the items/tasks to mitigate sources of construct-irrelevant variance.

Using ECD in the Design Process

Three of the five layers of the ECD process were used in the redesign of the large-scale science assessment items. The work accomplished in these layers is described below.

Domain Modeling

PADI Design Patterns were created for knowledge and skills associated with NSES science content and inquiry standards (NRC, 1996). In this second layer of ECD, Focal KSAs were identified and Design Patterns were then used to create the Student, Evidence, and Task Models needed at the CAF layer of ECD.

Conceptual Assessment Framework

In the CAF, AKSAs, including irrelevant task demands, were reviewed and redesign strategies were conceptualized. The AKSAs were categorized using the six UDL categories. Each of the six categories of AKSAs was then linked to a set of Variable Features that might be used in the redesign of the task to reduce construct-irrelevant task demands. A particular set of Variable Features was incorporated into the redesign of each of the 21 items.

ASSESSMENT IMPLEMENTATION

After the redesign process, the revised item was implemented in an online version of the large-scale accountability assessment in science. To illustrate this implementation process, the revision of the food web item is described below.

Benefits of ECD Approach

The life science items selected for redesign represent three common life science objectives: (1) classification of organisms and living systems, (2) structure and function of living systems, and (3) processes of living systems. Items that address these objectives may require declarative knowledge of particular organisms or living systems in addition to knowledge of the relationships among them and the ability to use formal knowledge representations to communicate about those relationships. Items that assess a student's understanding of relationships among organisms, for example, may depend on scientific terminology and familiarity with specific organisms or ecosystems. A lack of this background knowledge may make it more difficult for a student to demonstrate knowledge of general concepts, relationships, and processes targeted in the Focal KSA. In response to this need for background knowledge, a typical food web item was modified to reduce demands related to background knowledge, language, and text. A description of the food web item is presented below. The Design Pattern that guided the redesign of the food web item is found in Appendix A.

Sample Revised Item: Food Web

The food web item is designed to assess both a student's knowledge of the movement of energy through an ecosystem, as well as a student's ability to use a representational format to analyze and interpret data. The item presents a food web that shows the interrelationships of different organisms in an ecosystem. The student is directed to indicate the result of a change in one part of the food web ecosystem by selecting from one of four response options. Employing the model shown in Appendix A, the item's features were analyzed in terms of both ECD and UDL principles. This analysis identified item revisions that would potentially minimize sources of construct-irrelevant variance, thereby increasing accessibility for all students.

The Focal KSA assessed in the food web item is:

1   Fk1: Ability to use an ecological model to explain the relationships among populations and communities.

Multiple AKSAs were identified in the food web item, Ak1 through Ak21. These can be found in the Design Pattern in Appendix A. Ak16 through Ak21 are the six UDL categories described above. Below are two AKSAs, Ak1 and Ak16, that were identified as considerable sources of construct-irrelevant variance in the original item (UDL categories are represented in square brackets). These AKSAs were used to guide the item revision process. The food web item was revised to support background knowledge and language and text demands.

1   Ak1: Knowledge of entities (e.g., plants and animals) represented in the ecological model [Background Knowledge Task Demand].
2   Ak16: Linguistic: vocabulary and symbols, syntax and underlying structure, English language proficiency, decoding and fluency [Language and Text Task Demand].

Variable features linked to the two AKSAs were selected as ways in which the item could be revised to reduce construct-irrelevant variance. First, a student unfamiliar with the particular organisms named in the food web item would be at a potential disadvantage in answering the item correctly, since she would not be able to utilize prior knowledge about whether the animal was a consumer or a producer. Adding graphics to depict each of the organisms supports a student's ability to identify each organism's general characteristics and thereby assist the student's identification of the consumer relationships represented in the food web. In addition, the use of images reduced reading demand by minimizing unnecessary scientific terminology. Additionally, the stem of the original item contained a complex syntactic construction. A student with a weak grasp of English would be at a disadvantage. This language was refined to deliver the same instructions to the student without compromising the construct of interest.

The original and revised items were presented to a current Director of Science Assessment for a state department of education and a former Director of Assessment for a second state. These science assessment experts provided a review of item content. In particular, whether the FKSA in the revised items had been altered as a result of the ECD and UDL revision process. Their feedback was addressed to ensure that the FKSA for both versions of the item was identical. Any concerns expressed by the experts were resolved to their satisfaction, indicating that the item KSA had indeed remained the same.

Performance of Food Web Item

The field testing of the original and revised food web item took place in three schools in the winter of 2012. Preidentification of students ensured that both general education and students with a high-incidence learning disability would be adequately represented in the sample. Each student participated in two online testing sessions approximately one month apart. Sessions were designed so that a student would receive both the revised and original version of the items balanced for order of presentation (e.g., for any given item, some students received the revised item in the first [or second] session and the original item in the second [or first] session).

Table 11.3 presents case counts, average gain, standard deviations, and an *F*-test between summary statistics of the performances of the general education students and students with disabilities for the food web item. The average gain in performance for the 37 general education students was 0.054 (score of the revised item minus the score on the original item). The average gain for the students with disabilities was 0.304. The difference between the two groups was significant, favoring the students with disabilities ($p = 0.018$). It is worth noting that the gains indicated are benefits of the UDL-infused item for students in both populations. However, the gain for students with disabilities is significantly higher than the gains for general education students, indicating that the UDL-based revisions removed task demands that disproportionately affect students with learning disabilities.

The project developed and implemented an ECD process by which assessment designers can integrate UDL into large-scale assessments for accountability purposes. Results from an exemplar set of 21 UDL-enhanced, large-scale test items were analyzed. Field test results indicate that by using this new process, assessment designers could systematically identify and reduce construct-irrelevant variance from items, thereby increasing the likelihood that more valid inferences could be drawn about a student's knowledge and skills.

The food web item revision presented above details how life science objectives can be better addressed using an ECD process that integrates principles of UDL for both general education students and students with learning disabilities, in conjunction with evidence from other sources of construct validity, in this case the expert reviews of the item revisions. Although the refinement of the item improved accessibility for students with disabilities, analyses of student performances on the remaining items had mixed results. Only 10 of the 21 UDL-enhanced assessment items demonstrated improved performance for students with disabilities when compared to the performance of regular education students on the same items. Therefore, the ECD process, as illustrated in the food web item, should not be interpreted as evidence that designing items with attention to UDL will always produce results that confirm the differential boost hypothesis (i.e., that "a fair accommodation increases the test scores of students with disabilities more than those of students without disabilities"; Cawthon, Ho, Patel, Potvin, & Trundt, 2009, p. 2). The field test results demonstrated that, in some cases, redesigned items enhanced the validity of the inferences about a student's performance by removing distracting information and item features, allowing for a more precise measure of what a student knows and can do. In particular, by having experts review the revised and original items to ensure that the item Focal KSA was not altered by the revision process, findings cannot be interpreted as the result of a change in the construct being measured for the students with disabilities. In some of these cases, the performance of students with disabilities did not increase more than the performance of students in regular education classrooms. Thus, these items, while having been revised to reduce sources of error addressed by UDL, did not confirm the differential boost hypothesis. Thus, performance on the items could be attributed to factors not related to the UDL principles addressed in this project.

Table 11.3 Gains of Scores on the Food Web Item (0 = incorrect, 1 = correct)

	n	*Average Gain*	*SD*	*ANOVA (One-Way)*
General education student gain	37	0.05	0.33	$F(1,58) = 5.88$, $p = 0.028$
Special education student gain	23	0.30	0.47	

Implications for Accountability in the Life Science Assessments

All assessments designed for accountability purposes have to withstand legal scrutiny, which requires evidence and backing for the claims about what a student knows and can do. Such high-stakes assessments have an impact on a variety of stakeholders—states, districts, students, parents, and teachers—and require the collection and analysis of substantial quantitative data to support their claims. The focus of this chapter has been on the use of life science accountability measures for states, K–12 schools, and students, whereas the impact of such assessments on teachers is briefly considered in the discussion of challenges at the end of this chapter.

Much attention has been paid in the last two decades to the design of legislation, such as NCLB, IDEA, and the Race to the Top initiative, which have used assessments as a lever for educational reform and social change. Assessment accountability systems were developed at the federal, state, and local levels to support these reforms.

In 2013–2014, two articles in *Education Week* identified a list of challenges that impede the implementation of the accountability measures used to assess the NGSS (Heitin, 2014; Sparks, 2013). Both articles indicated that the pace of adoption for the NGSS was slower than that for the CCSS. The reduced pace of adoption has been attributed in part to a concern that it is straining the capacity of districts and schools to implement the needed reforms in curriculum and instruction associated with mathematics and English language arts, so that taking on additional new standards and assessments in science may be a "challenge too far."

In this section, accountability issues associated with life science assessments are discussed. These include:

1   Limited adoption of the NGSS across states: At the time of the *Education Week* articles, only eight states included the NGSS in their assessment and accountability systems (California, Delaware, Kansas, Kentucky, Maryland, Rhode Island, Vermont, and the District of Columbia). The fact that most states have not yet adopted the NGSS means that the science assessments used for accountability purposes will differ among the states. Thus, no common science assessment can be used to compare student performance. The lack of adoption of the NGSS coupled with the absence of a common measure of complex science content and practices results in insufficient information to inform federal policymakers about the status of what U.S. students know and can do in the sciences.

2   Lack of instructional time: Students must have an opportunity to learn the new science content and practices specified in the NGSS before educators can draw valid inferences from the assessments targeted to measure those standards. Due to an emphasis on mathematics and English language arts, instructional time for deeper learning in science has been limited. Until more instructional time is devoted to the content described in the NGSS, the value of science assessment accountability systems targeted to those standards will be minimized.

3   Limited capacity of states to implement assessments of complex science practices: Substantial expertise in science assessment is required to interpret measures of complex science practices. States have limited capacity to provide the professional development needed to advance the expertise of their internal assessment development staff in this area.

4   Lack of professional development for teachers: Professional development must be designed to improve instruction in more challenging science content and practices. Without adequate opportunities to learn how to teach the NGSS, teachers will not have sufficient knowledge about how to integrate these standards in their instructional activities and prepare students for science accountability assessments.

The issues raised in the *Education Week* articles point to the complexities encountered when implementing accountability systems focused on the NGSS. High-stakes science assessments are costly to design—both because of the complexity of the content and practices being assessed and because of the many technical demands placed on these tests.

The evidence needed to support claims, warrants, and inferences based on accountability measures takes many forms and applies to assessments in all content domains. There are four topics central to the quality of the validity evidence required of accountability measures: (1) kinds of quantitative data needed to substantiate the technical qualities (reliability and validity) of the assessments; (2) differential item functioning (DIF) as revealed by patterns of performance on the assessment items for different subpopulations of test takers; (3) intended and unintended consequences of the use of the assessment; and (4) use of Achievement Level Descriptors (ALDs) to support standard setting, score interpretation, and use. The types of evidence yielded by such investigations are necessary to construct a valid assessment argument.

Technical Qualities

A peer review process associated with the technical qualities of statewide assessments for accountability purposes has been implemented by the U.S. Department of Education for more than a decade (Erpenbach, Forte-Fast, & Potts, 2003). This review process (typically referred to as peer review) requires that the validity and reliability of assessments be documented. This documentation typically includes:

- evidence of alignment of items and tasks with standards and benchmarks;
- results of cognitive laboratories documenting that assessment items and tasks elicit evidence of the construct being measured;
- results of pilot tests that indicate that test items and tasks perform at accepted industry standards using psychometric data such as *p*-values, item information curves, difficulty and discrimination indices, point-biserial correlations, etc.;
- evidence of the assessment's reliability including coefficients of internal consistency, inter-rater reliabilities, test–retest reliabilities, and generalizability studies; and
- evidence from studies to establish adequate construct representation.[2]

Peer review impels test developers to collect such evidence and present it in a manner that is open to examination and analysis by external assessment experts. The use of ECD as a test development process neither diminishes the need for empirical evidence nor reduces the standards of performance required in terms of the assessment's reliability and validity.

Assessment/Measurement Bias

One of the important qualities of an assessment used for accountability is its freedom from measurement bias. Measurement bias or DIF occurs when individuals from different subpopulations (e.g., English language learners vs. native English speakers, males vs. females, low vs. medium vs. high levels of socioeconomic status, test takers using computer vs. test takers using paper-based versions of assessment) with approximately the same latent ability or skill have a different probability of giving a particular response on a test item or task (Embretson & Reise, 2000; Popham, 2012). Analytic procedures frequently used to detect item biases or DIF were reviewed by Dorans and Holland (1992), Osterlind and Everson (2009), and Steinberg and Thiessen (2006). These include the Mantel–Haenszel approach (Mantel & Haenszel, 1959) and item response theory-based methods including the Rasch model. In addition, the use of logistic regression to determine measurement bias was reviewed by Swaminathan and Rogers (1990).

When providing documentation of the extent of measurement bias, it is insufficient to report simply that items function differently for groups; there must be a theoretical justification of why this occurs. Thus, evidence of DIF does not directly translate into an assessment being characterized as "unfair." There are situations in which a subpopulation would be expected to perform differently on particular assessment items, and assessment developers must account for differential performance in terms of explanatory theories and arguments. In cases where no such explanations can be provided, assessment items or tasks that exhibit DIF may need to be revised or omitted from the assessment. Thus, DIF analyses are used as a tool for item and assessment revision in combination with theory-based reasoning about the observed patterns of performance by subgroups. Assessment developers need to examine the magnitude of DIF in order to know whether the difference among the groups is important.[3]

In addition to the use of DIF, review committees can be used to examine items and tasks for use of language and illustrations that are stereotypical or offensive. While following the systematic processes of ECD should eliminate most sources of construct-irrelevant variance or extraneous material from each item, the use of pejorative terms, insensitive references, and demeaning illustrations requires careful attention during sensitivity reviews.

Consequential Validity

During the past two decades, the concept of validity has been extended to include both the intended and unintended consequences of test use (AERA, APA, & NCME, 1999). Any test designed for accountability purposes, including those in the life sciences, should take into account empirical evidence about its consequences, in particular its effect on decisions about social policy. A common example of consequential validity is the narrowing of a school's curriculum to exclude learning content that is not assessed (Chudowsky & Behuniak, 1997; Koretz, Barron, Mitchell, & Stecher, 1996).

The grading, selection, placement, and certification of different subpopulations can be disparately impacted by sources of invalidity such as construct underrepresentation or construct-irrelevant variance. Differential item performance is another source of invalidity. To address these sources of invalidity, the *Standards for Educational and Psychological Testing* (AERA, APA, & NCME, 1999) advises assessment designers and developers to "set forth clearly how test scores are intended to be interpreted and used. The population(s) for which a test is appropriate should be clearly delimited, and the construct that the test is intended to assess should be clearly described" (p. 17). It is well understood that no assessment is valid for all purposes or for use with all populations. Each recommended use needs to be validated, and the manner and context in which the test scores are to be used need to be carefully described. In cases where subpopulations are impacted disparately and negative social consequences accrue, the test items need to be further examined for evidence of construct-irrelevant variance and plausible rival hypotheses need to be investigated. This understanding is further explicated by the Standard below.

Standard 13.1 from the *Standards for Educational and Psychological Testing* asserts:

> When educational testing programs are mandated by school, district, state or other authorities, the ways in which test results are intended to be used should be clearly described. It is the responsibility of those who mandate the use of tests to monitor their impact and to identify and minimize potential negative consequences. Consequences resulting from the uses of the test, both intended and unintended, should also be examined by the test user.

The success of many educational reform policies depends on the proper use of assessment scores. Thus, curriculum and instructional reforms in all subject areas, including the life sciences, typically require careful examination of the assessments used to determine the impact of the reform. The effectiveness of standards-based accountability systems, in particular, requires the examination of the consequential validity of the assessments in use. Such studies permit deeper understanding of whether improved student performance on an assessment is associated with meaningful improvements in student achievement and learning (Borko & Stecher, 2001; McDonnell & Choisser, 1997; Stecher, Barron, Chun, & Ross, 2000).

Achievement Level Descriptors

Test authorizers and test developers are accountable for providing not only evidence of an assessment's reliability and validity but also information on the appropriate use of the assessment's results. The ECD process makes explicit the network of inferences regarded as the interpretive argument. Kane developed the concept of an interpretive argument as part of understanding the validity of an assessment. He (1992, p. 1) asserts:

> Validity is associated with the interpretation assigned to test scores rather than with the test scores or the test. The interpretation involves an argument leading from the scores to score-based statements or decisions, and the validity of the interpretation depends on the plausibility of this interpretive argument. The interpretive arguments associated with most test-score interpretations involve multiple inferences and assumptions. An explicit recognition of the inferences and assumptions in the interpretive argument makes it possible to identify the kinds of evidence needed to evaluate the argument. Evidence for the inferences and assumptions in the argument supports the interpretation, and evidence against any part of the argument casts doubt on the interpretation.

The claims and warrants that are developed during the item and task design in ECD can be used to support the development of ALDs and have the potential for use in standard setting for score interpretation. ALDs may serve to "contextualize" the standard-setting methodology that links cut scores and examinee performances in relation to ALDs (Plake, Huff, & Reshetar, 2010, p. 343). ALDs that are based on ECD need to be grounded in the assessment designer's conceptualization and analysis of the construct being assessed, as well as actual evidence from student performances that illustrate what students know and can do. Some ALDs are based largely on the perceptions and beliefs of educational stakeholders about what students can do at the various levels of performance. ECD has been identified for application in three standard-setting methodologies, such as the bookmark standard setting method (Mitzel, Lewis, Patz, & Green, 2001), the dominant profile judgment method (Plake, Hambleton, & Jaeger, 1997), and a predetermined performance category classification method (Bejar, Braun, & Tannenbaum, 2007). ALDs can be used in all content domains including the life sciences.

Conclusions

This chapter has described the theory and practices of ECD as applied to the assessment of the life sciences for accountability purposes. Several implementations of the use of ECD have been presented. They provide (1) "real-world" descriptions of how the ECD design processes are applied, (2) several examples of Design Patterns and Summary Task Templates, and (3) brief descriptions of how the ECD processes affect the development and revision of items, tasks, and/or assessments.

Challenges

The use of ECD has been implemented in the design of several large-scale life science assessments intended for accountability purposes. Several challenges have been identified and are discussed below.

There is a need to measure "hard-to-assess" constructs in the life sciences, including the knowledge and skills associated with science content, life science practices, and interdependent phases of inquiry. The measurement of these constructs requires probing a student's reasoning for evidence of deep knowledge and skills, including his or her ability to explain scientific phenomena, critique and evaluate the processes used in scientific studies (experimental and observational), understand epistemic practices, synthesize and compare ideas, and display and interpret data. The measurement of scientific processes is particularly challenging because of the interdependencies among phases of scientific investigations during the inquiry process. To measure understanding of science content and practices requires capturing not only the correctness of a student's performance on an item or task but also the sequence of processes and skills used to arrive at an answer, explanation, prediction, or conclusion. ECD is well suited to meeting these demands.

Technology-enhanced items in scenario-based formats may be a solution to several of the measurement challenges associated with the life sciences. Current technologies provide numerous approaches to presenting complex stimuli such as diagrams, tables, dynamic graphs, and micro-worlds involving simulations and animations. These types of stimuli are widely used in life science instruction and assessment. Technology is able to capture a student's response "step-by-step" as he or she progresses through the phases of a scientific investigation. For example, technology can capture the refinement of an experimental design that a student creates to test a hypothesis. Technology-enhanced items can capture the subsequent modifications in the design as a result of the data collected during the simulated investigations initiated by the student. In addition, advances in capturing a student's digital literacy can be used to better understand if a student is able to collect background information needed to conduct a scientific investigation. Simulated search procedures can be used to document a student's ability to conduct an effective web-based search to gather scientifically relevant information, to synthesize information from several multimedia sources, and to draw conclusions from these various information resources. ECD requires specification of task features and is an appropriate approach for delineating these complex interdependent items and tasks.

Another challenge in the design of life science accountability measures is the need for comprehensive, defensible validity arguments. The validity argument must relate the abilities and skills to be assessed in the life sciences to observations of what students can do and to the features of the tasks that elicit those performances. This is especially important when considering the use of these assessments for the purpose of teacher evaluation at the school or district level. In ECD, the systematic test development process, including a domain analysis based on relevant content standards and specification of KSAs, ensures that the construct to be measured has been properly delineated. This process helps guarantee that teachers are being held accountable for content and practices that are aligned to a standards-based argument. In the case of the life sciences, the NGSS or a state's science standards provide a basis for this argument.

ECD, when followed systematically, produces design documents (i.e., Design Patterns and Task Templates) as part of the design process. These Design Patterns and Task Templates are treated as "living documents" and are refined and updated as the assessment is modified over the years. The Design Patterns and Task Templates are reusable and generative. They can be used to modify the surface features of items while maintaining the same deep structure (i.e., assessment argument) used to help establish the validity of the interpretation of item and task scores. The use of Design Patterns and Task Templates contributes to ECD's ability to produce large-scale assessments efficiently. Nevertheless, there is a steep learning curve for assessment designers and developers who are new to ECD. Experience suggests that most assessment designers are able to successfully implement these processes with guidance from those experienced with ECD. Even after participating in a single ECD-based assessment design and development process, most designers understand the fundamental processes sufficiently to be able to contribute expertise in the codesign process. With more exposure to the method, designers are able to refine their practice and increase their efficiency and quality of work. It is the case, however, that substantial upfront costs (time and money) are associated with the initial creation and production of Design Patterns and Task Templates and the items and tasks that are subsequently produced. As a team of assessment designers grows in expertise, these upfront costs are reduced in new assessment development. Some of these cost reductions are also the result of decisions about how comprehensively the ECD process should be implemented. In many instances, new Domain Analyses and Student, Evidence, and Task Models can be reused with minor refinements; thus, the ECD process can be shortened.

In the last two decades, value-added methods have attracted considerable attention because of their potential applicability for accountability purposes. These methods represent a major challenge to consumers of accountability measures in all content areas. An accessible introduction to value-added models (VAMs) is provided by Douglas Harris (Harris & Wingarten, 2011) in his book *Value-Added Measures in Education: What Every Educator Needs to Know*. Harris explains the concept of value-added in terms of the practical realities of the classroom. He identifies the significant limitations of VAMs. He clearly explains sources of imprecision, including the flaws that exist in the models themselves. Finally, he discusses the trade-offs that have to be addressed in using VAMs in education policy. Below, more specific issues concerning VAMs are addressed.

VAMs are complex statistical models designed to estimate the relative contributions of teachers, schools, or programs to student test performance, including scores from life science assessments. According to Braun, Chudowsky, and Koenig (2010, pp. 4–5),

> These models address such questions as "How did the contribution of school X (or teacher X) to student improvement compare with that of the average school (or teacher)?" Or equivalently, "How much of the change in student performance can be attributed to students attending one school (or one teacher's class) rather than another?" To isolate school, teacher, or program effects, at least two years of students' test scores is taken into account, sometimes along with other student and school-level variables, such as poverty, family background, or quality of school leadership. With some models, the value-added estimate for a school or a teacher is the difference between the observed improvement of the students and the expected improvement (after taking account of differences among students that might be related to their academic achievement).

The most prominent examples of value-added analyses are those associated with the Education Value-Added Assessment System, which was first implemented in Tennessee and subsequently used in Ohio, Pennsylvania, and school districts throughout the United States (Betebenner & Linn, 2009). The attraction of such analyses in an era of accountability was promoted by the availability of funds from the U.S. Department of Education's Teacher Incentive Fund grants, that supported building sustainable teacher and principal performance-based compensation systems. In addition, guidance for Race to the Top (2009, p. 37809) applications required states to be:

> Differentiating teacher and principal effectiveness based on performance: … The extent to which the State, in collaboration with its participating LEAs, has a high quality plan and ambitious yet achievable annual targets to (a) determine an approach to measuring student growth (as defined in this notice); (b) employ rigorous, transparent, and equitable processes for differentiating the effectiveness of teachers and principals using multiple rating categories that take into account data on student growth (as defined in this notice) as a significant factor; (c) provide to each teacher and principal his or her own data and rating; and (d) use this information when making decisions.

Though the rationale for applying VAMs may be well intentioned, there are a number of concerns that have surfaced in recent years that require caution (Braun, Chudowsky, & Koenig, 2010). These concerns include uses and possible consequences, measurement issues, and analytic issues. Each of these categories is addressed below:

Uses and Possible Consequences

- When used in high-stakes situations, the reliability and validity of value-added estimates are not sufficient to support high-stakes decisions.
- When used in accountability systems, they are likely to result in unintended consequences as well as intended consequences for teachers, administrators, and students.
- Attributions of successful teaching may be associated with a single teacher's performance when the success is really a product of team teaching.

Measurement Issues

- Value-added estimates are based on test scores that are incomplete measures of student achievement, which can result in limited or misleading information about school, teacher, or program effectiveness.
- Test scores are susceptible to measurement error at the individual and aggregate level, which contributes to uncertainty in the value-added estimates.
- If the assumption underlying the value-added analyses is based on the use of a regression model with an equal-interval scale, it is likely that most tests will not meet this requirement and violate the assumption of the VAM.
- While some VAMs require vertically linked test score scales (test scores from different grades are linked to a common scale so that students' scores from different grades can be compared directly), it is unlikely that science assessments which are often subdomain-specific (e.g., life science, earth science, and physical science) would be vertically linked.

Analytic Issues

- Biased estimates of school and program effects can occur due to type of model and number and the statistical characteristics of the predictor variables that are included.
- Instability in the value-added estimates from small sample sizes may result in biased estimates of teacher or school effects that fluctuate substantially from year to year due not only to changes in teacher performance but also to changes in context (e.g., school leadership, student mobility).
- Data quality can be negatively impacted by missing or inaccurate data, resulting in bias from measurement error.
- Increasing the complexity of a VAM may account for more of the factors that influence effectiveness, but may obscure the interpretation of the model.

Edward Haertel (2013) delivered an invited lecture at Educational Testing Service titled "Reliability and Validity of Inferences about Teachers Based on Student Test Scores." In the paper that accompanied the lecture, Haertel addresses the use of VAMs as a means of translating student test scores into teacher effectiveness estimates and devotes much of the paper to describing an interpretative argument, as defined by Michael Kane (2006), for teacher VAM scores. He concludes that VAMs "have been seriously oversold and some specific applications have been very unwise" (p. 4). Haertel's conclusions concur with those expressed by Braun, Chudowsky, and Koenig (2010) that a VAM may claim a modest role in teacher evaluation but only if used in association with other information and in a local context where teachers and school administrators have autonomy in their decision making and interpretation of the teacher effectiveness estimates. Haertel's (2013, pp. 23–24) primary conclusion follows:

> My first conclusion should come as no surprise: Teacher VAM scores should emphatically *not* be included as a substantial factor with a fixed weight in consequential teacher personnel decisions. The information they provide is simply not good enough to use in that way. It is not just that the information is noisy. Much more serious is the fact that the scores may be systematically biased *for* some teachers and *against* others, and major potential sources of bias stem from the way our school system is organized. No statistical manipulation can assure fair comparisons of teachers working in very different schools, with different students, under different conditions. One cannot do a good enough job of isolating the signal of teacher effects from the massive influences of students' individual aptitudes, prior educational histories, out-of-school experiences, peer influences and differential summer learning loss, nor can one adequately adjust away the varying academic climates of different schools. Even if acceptably small bias from all these factors *could* be assured, the resulting scores would still be highly unreliable and overly sensitive to the particular achievement test employed. Some of these concerns can be addressed, by using teacher scores averaged across several years of data, for example. But the interpretive argument is a *chain* of reasoning, and every proposition in the chain must be supported. Fixing one problem or another is not enough to make the case.

The cautions regarding the use of VAMs apply to all summative achievement tests, including those in the sciences. The use of ECD alone, while it can strengthen the alignment of the items and tasks on the assessment to the construct being measured, is insufficient in itself to eliminate the many limitations surrounding the use of VAMs.

Benefits

Practical experience based on numerous implementations of ECD in large-scale science assessment for accountability purposes suggests a number of key benefits that flow from a rigorous, systematic ECD design approach. The most valued benefits are described below.

ECD is an ecumenical process—it can support the design of a wide range of assessments. It can be used to design formative, summative, classroom-based, large-scale, diagnostic, interim, benchmark, placement, certification, capstone, and exit examinations. ECD-based assessments can be founded on any psychological or theoretical base (e.g., cognitive science, trait psychology, stimulus-response theory, situational perspective). Any type of item or task can be designed using ECD, including selected response, constructed response, hands-on-performance tasks, ICTs, essays, drawings, cloze procedures, simulations, and game-based assessments. Items and tasks can be designed for individual or group administration. Items can be designed to be answered individually or as a collaborative process. The ECD design process supports the articulation of item stems, task prompts, rubrics, response options, and distractors for a wide range of assessment types and formats; thus, it is a worthwhile investment for assessment designers building accountability measures.

An ECD framework is able to support the integration of other design frameworks, such as UDL, 21st-Century Skills, and learning progressions. The attributes and key features required of assessment items and tasks aligned with these other frameworks can be incorporated within the ECD framework. When an ECD process does not serve as the overarching design framework during the development process, there is a danger that the assessment designers will layer the attributes of the other frameworks without attention to the underlying structure of the assessment argument. This can result in KSAs, observations, and task models which are often aligned to only one of the frameworks. The task models in such situations often become very complex. Thus, one of the most valuable benefits of using an ECD framework is its capacity to serve as an overarching, superordinate framework which can coordinate several subordinate frameworks.

Using ECD, designers spend considerable time during the assessment development process identifying and reducing sources of construct-irrelevant variance in assessment items and tasks. This increases the likelihood that the inferences drawn from test scores about what a child can say or do are more likely to be valid. The mechanism used to identify and reduce sources of construct-irrelevant variance occurs primarily in the articulation of KSAs and AKSAs. As AKSAs are identified, the assessment designer is presented with guidance as to which KSAs are needed for successful performance, but are not the targets of the assessments. Once the AKSAs have been identified, the designer can make a decision whether to support the knowledge or skills or to remove the requirements for these abilities from the assessment items and tasks. The designer can also decide how the Task Model and Variable Features may need to be modified to achieve valid inferences. ECD's capability to identify sources of construct-irrelevant variance is particularly important in the design of assessments for students with disabilities, English language learners, and young children in all content areas, including the life sciences.

In conclusion, if assessment practice is to play a constructive role in enhancing student learning in the 21st century, then a principled approach to design and development is essential. ECD provides such guidance.

Appendix A: Model Use and Interdependence among Living Systems Design Pattern

Model Use and Interdependence Among Living Systems | Design Pattern 2299

Title	[Edit]	Model Use and Interdependence Among Living Systems
Overview	[Edit]	This design pattern supports developing tasks that require students to reason through the structures, relationships, and processes of ecological models. Use of ecological models is often combined with the formation of ecological models in tasks. Many tasks that address evaluation and revision of ecological models also involve the use of these models.
Use	❶ [Edit]	U1. Scientific models are abstracted schemas involving entities and relationships, meant to be useful across a range of particular circumstances. Procedures within the model space can be carried out to support inferences about the situation beyond what is immediately observable. Ecological models that, for example, show predator-prey relationships, the flow of energy, and the recycling of matter are instances of scientific models in life science. Students must be able to use these models to reason about processes and interdependencies in living systems.
Focal knowledge, skills, and abilities	❶ [Edit]	Fk1. Ability to use an ecological model to explain the relationships among populations and communities details
		Fk2. Ability to use an ecological model to explain similarities and differences among types of interdependent relationships (e.g., predator/prey vs. parasite/host vs. producer/consumer/decomposer) details
		Fk3. Ability to use an ecological model to explain how populations in an ecosystem are dependent on biotic and abiotic resources details
		Fk4. Ability to use an ecological model to explain how producers make, use, and store food details
		Fk5. Ability to use an ecological model to explain how energy changes form in a food web details
		Fk6. Ability to use an ecological model to explain how the amount of matter stays the same as it is transferred between organisms and their physical environment details
Additional knowledge, skills, and abilities	❶ [Edit]	Ak1. Knowledge of entities (e.g., plants and animals) represented in the ecological model details
		Ak2. Knowledge of different ecological models (e.g., food webs, water cycle) details
		Ak3. Understanding that when two entities are related or interdependent, manipulating one will affect the other
		Ak4. Knowledge of how to use and interpret required modeling tool(s) (e.g., online state assessment interface, STELLA, ESIS) details
		Ak5. Knowledge of required symbolic representations associated procedures (e.g., chemical equations, mathematical notation)
		Ak6. Familiarity with task type (e.g., materials, protocols, expectations)
		Ak7. Knowledge of what a population is details
		Ak8. Knowledge of what a community is details
		Ak9. Knowledge of what an ecosystem is details
		Ak10. Ability to recognize whether an ecosystem is stable details
		Ak11. Ability to distinguish between biotic and abiotic resources in an ecological model details
		Ak12. Ability to recognize producers in a food web details
		Ak13. Ability to recognize consumers in a food web details

		🖫Ak14. Ability to recognize decomposers in a food web <u>details</u>
		🖫Ak15. Ability to determine interdependencies in a model by holding constant some entities while varying others <u>details</u>
		Ak16. Language and text . Vocabulary and symbols . Syntax and underlying structure . English-language proficiency . Decoding text or math notation
		Ak17. Graphic images . Decoding charts, graphs or images . Illustrating key concepts non-linguistically
		Ak18. Cognitive . Background knowledge . Concepts and categories . Information-processing strategies . Memory and transfer
		Ak19. Goals and monitoring . Goal and expectation setting . Goal maintenance and adjustment . Planning and sequencing steps in a process . Monitoring progress
		Ak20. Managing information and resources
		Ak21. Working memory

Potential observations	❶ [<u>Edit</u>]	🖫Po1. High quality explanation of how communities and populations represented in an ecological model interact. <u>details</u>
		🖫Po2. High quality explanation of how one or more interdependent relationships represented in an ecological model are similar to or different from other interdependent relationships represented in the model. <u>details</u>
		🖫Po3. High quality explanation of how populations represented in an ecological model are dependent on the biotic and abiotic resources shown in the model. <u>details</u>
		🖫Po4. High quality explanation of how producers make, use, and store food in an ecological model. <u>details</u>
		🖫Po5. High quality explanation of how energy represented in an ecological model, such as a food web, changes form. <u>details</u>
		🖫Po6. High quality explanation of how the amount of matter stays the same as it is transferred between the organisms and components of the physical environment shown in an ecological model. <u>details</u>
		🖫Po7. Accurate completion and description of a flow chart showing how energy flows in an ecological model
		🖫Po8. Accurate completion and description of a flow chart showing how matter flows in an ecological model

Potential work products	❶ [<u>Edit</u>]	Pw1. Selection of hypotheses, predictions, retrodictions, explanations, and/or missing elements of real world situation
		Pw2. Constructed hypotheses, predictions, retrodictions, explanations, and/or missing elements of real world situation, via: Creation of one or more representational forms; Filling in given, possibly partially filled in, representational forms. <u>details</u>
		Pw3. Intermediate products developed in selection/construction of hypotheses, predictions, explanations, and/or missing elements
		Pw4. Written/oral explanation of the hypotheses, predictions, explanations, and/or missing elements. <u>details</u>
		Pw5. Trace of actions taken in solution
		Pw6. Talk- aloud of solution.

		Pw7. Critique of a given solution
		Pw8. Completion and description of a flow chart showing how energy flows in an ecological model.
		Pw9. Completion of a flow chart showing how matter flows in an ecological model.
		Pw10. Description of how producers in an ecological system use the energy from sunlight to make sugars from carbon dioxide and water in a process called photosynthesis.
Potential rubrics	❸ [Edit]	
Characteristic features	❸ [Edit]	Cf1. Ecological model represents a real-world situation
		Cf2. Presentation of at least one ecological model appropriate to the situation
		Cf3. Questions require students to reason through the schema and relationships in the model
Variable features	❸ [Edit]	Vf1. Problem context/ Type of ecological model details
		Vf2. Complexity of model details
		Vf3. Relative stability of ecological model (should this be part of complexity? AHD) details
		Vf4. Use of visual and linguistic supports in model details
		Vf5. Model provided to or generated by student details
		Vf6. Data provided to or generated by student details
		Vf7. Degree of scaffolding provided details
		Vf8. Complexity of situation NOT SURE WHAT THIS MEANS (AHD)
		Vf9. Complexity of reasoning required details
		Vf10. Presentation of background about the ecological model details
		Vf11. Provision of definitions of terminology relevant to ecological model details
		Vf12. Provision of descriptions of entities in an ecological model details
		Vf13. Model use isolated vs. in the context of a larger investigation details
		Vf14. Group work or individual work details
Narrative structure	❸ [Edit]	Cause and effect. An event, phenomenon, or system is altered by internal or external factors.
		Change over time. A sequence of events is presented to highlight sequential or cyclical change in a system.
		General to Specific or Whole to Parts. A general topic is initially presented followed by the presentation of specific aspects of the general topic.
		Specific to general and Parts to whole. Specific characteristics of a phenomenon are presented, culminating in a description of the system or phenomenon as a whole.
National educational standards	❸ [Edit]	NSES 8ASI1.3. Use appropriate tools and techniques to gather, analyze, and interpret data. The use of tools and techniques, including mathematics, will be guided by the question asked and the investigations students design. The use of computers for the collection, summary, and display of evidence is part of this standard. Students should be able to access, gather, store, retrieve, and organize data, using hardware and software designed for these purposes.
		NSES 8ASI1.4. Develop descriptions, explanations, predictions, and models using evidence. Students should base their explanation on what they observed, and as they develop cognitive skills, they should be able to

differentiate explanation from description, providing causes for effects and establishing relationships based on evidence and logical argument. This standards requires a subject knowledge base so the students can effectively conduct investigations, because developing explanations establishes connections between the content of science and the contexts within which students develop new knowledge.

NSES 8ASI1.5. Think critically and logically to make the relationships between evidence and explanations. Thinking critically about evidence includes deciding what evidence should be used and accounting for anomalous data. Specifically, students should be able to review data from a simple experiment, summarize the data, and form a logical argument about the cause-and-effect relationships in the experiment. Students should begin to state some explanations in terms of the relationship between two or more variables.

Unifying Concepts 1.2 - Evidence, models, and explanation. Scientific explanations incorporate existing scientific knowledge and new evidence from observations, experiments, or models into internally consistent, logical statements. As students develop and as they understand more science concepts and processes,their scientific explanations should more frequently include a rich scientific knowledge base, evidence of logic, higher levels of analysis, greater tolerance of criticism and uncertainty, and a clearer demonstration of the relationship between logic, evidence, and current knowledge.

Unifying Concepts 1.3 - Constancy, change, and measurement. Some properties of objects and processes are characterized by constancy, other by change. These may include properties of materials, position of objects, motion, and form and function of systems. Interactions within and among systems result in changes which can be quantified. Different systems of measurement are used for different purposes. Scale includes understanding that different characteristics, properties, or relationships within a system might change as its dimensions are increased or decreased. Rate involves comparing one measured quantity with another measured quantity.

Unifying Concepts 1.1 - Systems, order, and organization. The goal of this standard is to think and analyze in terms of systems.

State standards	❶ [Edit]	
State benchmarks	❶ [Edit]	MCA III: 6.1.3.4.1. Determine and use appropriate safe procedures, tools, measurements, graphs and mathematical analyses to describe and investigate natural and designed systems in a physical science context.

MCA III: 7.4.2.1.1. Identify a variety of populations and communities in an ecosystem and describe the relationships among the populations and communities in a stable ecosystem.

MCA III: 7.4.2.1.2. Compare and contrast predator/prey, parasite/host and producer/consumer/decomposer relationships.

MCA III: 7.4.2.1.3. Explain how the number of populations an ecosystem can support depends on the biotic resources available as well as abiotic factors such as amount of light and water, temperature range and soil composition.

MCA III: 7.4.2.2.1. Recognize that producers use the energy from sunlight to make sugars from carbon dioxide and water through a process called photosynthesis. This food can be used immediately, stored for later use, or used by other organisms.

MCA III: 7.4.2.2.2. Describe the roles and relationships among producers, consumers and decomposers in changing energy from one form to another in a food web within an ecosystem.

MCA III: 7.4.2.2.3. Explain that the total amount of matter in an ecosystem remains the same as it is transferred between organisms and their physical environment, even though its form and location change. For example: Construct a food web to trace the flow of matter in an ecosystem

I am a kind of	❶ [Edit]	

These are kinds of me	❸ [Edit]	
These are parts of me	❸ [Edit]	
Templates	❸ [Edit]	
Exemplar tasks	❸ [Edit]	
Online resources	❸ [Edit]	
References	❸ [Edit]	R1. Stewart, J., & Hafner, R. (1994). R2. Johnson-Laird (1983) R3. Gentner & Stevens (1983) R4. Hestenes, Wells, & Swackhamer (1992)

Tags [Add Tag]

(No tags entered.)

Appendix B: Model-Based Reasoning in Ecosystems Task Template

Model-based Reasoning in Ecosystems | Template 2713

[| Permit | Delete | View: View (vertical)]

Title	[Edit]	Model-based Reasoning in Ecosystems
Overview	[Edit]	A template for model-based reasoning ecosystems-related assessments designed for accountability purposes. The assessment activities include animations and simulations of ecosystems.
Type	❶ [Edit]	[View]
Student Model Summary	❶ [Edit]	SM1. The student model provides information about student proficiencies on science inquiry and life science content knowledge dimensions associated with ecosystems.
Student Models	❶ [Edit]	Model-based Reasoning in Ecosystems: 2D Student Model. Two-dimensional student model with Life Science and Inquiry student model variables. The life science content focuses on ecosystems. The inquiry dimension of the model addresses the use of model-based reasoning in ecosystems.
Measurement Model Summary	❶ [Edit]	MM1. Items have measurement models which include dichotomous multiple-choice models, others are bundles with both multiple choice and open-ended models
Evaluation Procedures Summary	❶ [Edit]	EP1. Dichotomous responses and partial credit responses. Scoring of some work products may be automated.
Work Product Summary	❶ [Edit]	WP1. Response formats include selected response, brief and extended constructed response, drawing (e.g., arrows in a food web), and implicit logging of students' problem solving attempts, drag-and-drop, (e.g., fish and plants in a food web), position of sliders to control variables in simulation, dynamically generated tables and graphs.
Task Model Variable Summary	❶ [Edit]	TM1. TMVs allow the designer to adjust the complexity of the problem (e.g., number of apex predators in food web), number of fish and plants in food web, and surface features of the assessment (e.g., type of ecosystem).
Template-level Task Model Variables	❶ [Edit]	Amount of Data. The number of data points presented to students in graphs, tables and maps.
		Content knowledge required (simple.mod.complex). This variable represents the amount of content knowledge needed to bring to the task in order to solve the problem correctly
		Data Representation Format. The format of data as it is presented to students (bar graph, line graph, scatter plot, map, data table, pie chart).
		Level of scaffolding for content. The level of scaffolding for content within a given task or activity
		Level of scaffolding for inquiry. the level of scaffolding for carrying out a scientific investigation within a given task of activity
		Number of Organisms in Simulated Ecosystem (Run-Time). The number of organisms students choose to include in their investigations of the ecosystem.
		Number of Tries (ETA Simulation). The number of times student is allowed to enter information and run the simulation.
		Representational Format of Simulation. The type of simulation presented to students.
		Simulation Manipulation Methods. Methods to manipulate the simulation

		(e.g., sliders, drag and drop, text entry).
		Time to Destination (ETA Simulation). Time it takes for object to reach its destination (seconds or hours). This TMV refers to the time reported to students, not the actual running time of the animation.
		Types of Organisms in Simulated Ecosystem (Developer). Types of organisms in the simulated ecosystem as determined by assessment developer(s).
Task Model Variable Settings	❸ [Edit]	[View]
Materials and Presentation Requirements	❸ [Edit]	Ma1. Internet connection Ma2. Java
Template-level Materials and Presentation	❸ [Edit]	
Materials and Presentation Settings	❸ [Edit]	[View]
Activities Summary	❸ [Edit]	AS1. An ecosystem is presented as an animation and as a simulation. Students must observe the animation and answer questions based on their observations. Students manipulate parameters of the simulation (e.g., ratio of predator to prey) to investigate the relationships among organisms in the ecosystem.
Activities	❸ [Edit]	Observe and Classify Organisms. This activity involves answering questions based on observations of an animation of an ecosystem. Create Food Web. This activity involves answering questions based on observations of an animation of an ecosystem. Make Predictions Based on Observations or Food Web. This activity involves answering questions based on observations of an animation of an ecosystem. Make and Test Predictions Using Simulation. This activity involves manipulating a simulation of an ecosystem to answer questions about the relationships among the organisms represented in the simulation. The simulation is set with default parameters for each organism, and students can manipulate these parameters to investigate their predictions. Investigate Species Competition. This activity involves manipulating a simulation of an ecosystem to answer questions about the relationships among the organisms represented in the simulation. Students will use the simulation to introduce a new species that competes for resources with species in the existing and stable ecosystem.
Tools for Examinee	❸ [Edit]	Tf1. Computer with internet access
Exemplars	❸ [Edit]	
Educational Standards	❸ [Edit]	NSES 8ASI1.3. Use appropriate tools and techniques to gather, analyze, and interpret data. The use of tools and techniques, including mathematics, will be guided by the question asked and the investigations students design. The use of computers for the collection, summary, and display of evidence is part of this standard. Students should be able to access, gather, store, retrieve, and organize data, using hardware and software designed for these purposes. NSES 8ASI1.4. Develop descriptions, explanations, predictions, and models using evidence. Students should base their explanation on what they observed, and as they develop cognitive skills, they should be able to differentiate explanations from descriptions, providing causes for effects and

establishing relationships based on evidence and logical argument. This standards requires a subject knowledge base so the students can effectively conduct investigations, because developing explanations establishes connections between the content of science and the contexts within which students develop new knowledge.

NSES 8ASI1.5. Think critically and logically to make the relationships between evidence and explanations. Thinking critically about evidence includes deciding what evidence should be used and accounting for anomalous data. Specifically, students should be able to review data from a simple experiment, summarize the data, and form a logical argument about the cause-and-effect relationships in the experiment. Students should begin to state some explanations in terms of the relationship between two or more variables.

NSES 8ASI1.6. Recognize and analyze alternative explanations and predictions. Students should develop the ability to listen and to respect the explanations proposed by other students. They should remain open to and acknowledge different ideas and explanations, be able to accept the skepticism of others, and consider alternative explanations.

NSES 8ASI1.7. Communicate scientific procedures and explanations. With practice, students should become competent at communicating experimental methods, following instructions, describing observations, summarizing the results of other groups, and telling other students about investigations and explanations.

NSES 8ASI1.8. Use mathematics in all aspects of scientific inquiry. Mathematics is essential to asking and answering questions about the natural world. Mathematics can be used to ask questions; to gather, organize, and present data; and to structure convincing explanations.

NSES 8ASI1.1. Identify questions that can be answered through scientific investigations. Students should develop the ability to refine and refocus broad and ill-defined questions. An important aspect of this ability consists of students' ability to clarify questions and inquiries and direct them toward objects and phenomena that can be described, explained, or predicted by scientific investigations. Students should develop the ability to identify their questions with scientific ideas, concepts, and quantitative relationships that guide investigation.

Design Patterns	❶ [Edit]	MBR TR-3: Model Formation. This design pattern generates tasks in which students create a model of some real-world phenomenon or abstracted structure, in terms of entities, structures, relationships, processes, behaviors, etc.
		Scientific Reasoning. This design pattern concerns a scientific problem to solve or investigate. Do they effectively plan a solution strategy, carry out that strategy, monitor their own performance, and provide coherent explanations?
		Interpretation of Dynamic Graphs. Students are provided with a model in which they can manipulate model parameters and view the results in graph format (provided in a technology that allows instant redraws after parameter manipulations). This design pattern will assess how well students can manipulate the parameters and draw conclusions about the underlying phenomena.
I am a kind of	❶ [Edit]	
These are kinds of me	❶ [Edit]	
These are parts of me	❶ [Edit]	
Online resources	❶ [Edit]	
References	❶ [Edit]	

Tags [Add Tag]

Appendix C: Experimental Investigation Design Pattern Used for Marigold Task

Title	[Edit]	Experimental Investigation (used for the Marigold task)
Overview	[Edit]	This design pattern supports the writing of storyboards and items that address scientific reasoning and process skills in experimental investigations. In experimental investigations, it is necessary to manipulate one or more of the variables of interest and to control others while testing a prediction or hypothesis. This contrasts with observational investigations, where variables typically cannot be manipulated. This design pattern may be used to generate groups of tasks for science content strands amenable to experimentation. details
Use	❶ [Edit]	U1. This design pattern supports the construction of tasks that address experimental investigations - that is, investigations where experimental methods are appropriate (as compared with investigations where only observations of phenomena are possible). In order for students to have a well-rounded understanding of the scientific method, they need to be familiar with the context and methods of experimental investigations.
Focal knowledge, skills, and abilities	❶ [Edit]	Fk1. Ability to distinguish between experimental and observational methodology
		Fk2. Ability to recognize that when a situation of scientific interest includes aspects that can be altered or manipulated practically, it is suitable for experimental investigation details
		Fk3. Ability to recognize that the purpose of an experiment is to test a prediction/hypothesis about a causal relationship details
		Fk4. Ability to identify, generate, or evaluate a prediction/hypothesis that is testable with a simple experiment
		Fk5. Ability to plan and conduct a simple experiment step-by-step given a prediction or hypothesis
		Fk6. Ability to recognize that at a basic level, an experiment involves manipulating one variable and measuring the effect on (or value of) another variable details
		Fk7. Ability to identify variables of the scientific situation (other than the ones being manipulated or treated as an outcome) that should be controlled (i.e. kept the same) in order to prevent misleading information about the nature of the causal relationship details
		Fk8. Ability to recognize variables that are inconsequential in the design of an experiment details
		Fk9. Ability to recognize that steps in an experiment must be repeatable to dependably predict future results
		Fk10. Ability to recognize that random assignment to treatment conditions (i.e. levels of the independent variable) is an important way to rule out alternative explanations for a causal relationship details
		Fk11. Ability to interpret or appropriately generalize the results of a simple experiment or to formulate conclusions or create models from the results
Additional knowledge, skills, and abilities	❶ [Edit]	Ak1. Content knowledge (may be construct relevant) details
		Ak2. Prerequisite knowledge from earlier grades details
		Ak3. Prerequisite experience assessing or conducting component steps of an investigation details
		Ak4. Ability to collect, organize, analyze, and present data details

		Ak5.	Familiarity with representational forms (e.g., graphs, maps) details
		Ak6.	Student needs based on UDL categories may be included (Perceptive, Expressive, Language and Symbols, Cognitive, Executive Functioning, Affective)
Potential observations	❶ [Edit]	Po1.	Accuracy in identifying situation suitable for experimental investigation
		Po2.	Plausibility of a measurable research question being raised
		Po3.	Plausibility of hypothesis as being testable by a simple experiment
		Po4.	Plausibility/correctness of design for a simple experiment
		Po5.	Correct identification of independent and dependent variables
		Po6.	Accuracy in identifying variables (other than the treatment variables of interest) that should be controlled (held constant) or made equivalent (e.g., through random assignment).
		Po7.	Plausability/correctness of steps to take in the conduct of an experiment
		Po8.	Plausibility of plan for repeating an experiment
		Po9.	Correctness of recognized data patterns from experimental data
		Po10.	Plausibility/correctness of interpretation/explanation of experimental results
		Po11.	Accuracy in critiquing the experimental design, methods, results, and conclusions of others
		Po12.	Generate a prediction/hypothesis that is testable with a simple experiment
Potential work products	❶ [Edit]	Pw1.	Selected response - students select the response (or responses) from a provided set details
		Pw2.	Constructed Response - students must generate their response given a prompt
		Pw3.	Drag and Drop - students drag and drop objects around the screen
		Pw4.	Dynamic branching - students are provided different choices depending on which option they select.
		Pw5.	Hot spots - students can move the cursor around the screen and an event happens when they click or move their curser
		Pw6.	Simulation - students can interact with a simulation, by providing inputs
		Pw7.	Interactive graphs - students can generate or manipulate graphs details
		Pw8.	Highlighting - students can highlight parts of the screen details
Potential rubrics	❶ [Edit]		
Characteristic features	❶ [Edit]	Cf1.	Focus on Nature of Science (Strand I in MCA) benchmarks that relate to experimental investigations at the appropriate grade level
		Cf2.	Presentation of situation of scientific interest where variables can be (or have been) practically altered to address a causal prediction details
		Cf3.	Presentation of situation requiring the design or conduct of a controlled experiment details
		Cf4.	Presentation or representation of an experimental design
		Cf5.	Presentation of observed result from an experiment requiring the development of explanations, conclusions, or models details
Variable features	❶ [Edit]	Vf1.	Content (strand) context details

Vf2. Which one of multiple phases of experimental investigation will be addressed

Vf3. Qualitative or quantitative investigation or a combination

Vf4. Ease or difficulty with which the treatment (independent) variable can be manipulated

Vf5. Are manipulated variables given or to be determined?

Vf6. The number of variables investigated and the complexity of their interrelationships details

Vf7. Number of variables that need to be controlled to unambiguously study the relationship between the manipulated variable and the outcome variable details

Vf8. Length of time over which the experiment must be conducted in order to study the potential impact of the treatment variable

Vf9. Data representations details

Vf10. Variable features may be added to support student needs associated with UDL categories (Perceptual - Screen presentation will include variable font size, Option for altering screen contrast, Option for magnification or zoom, Optional text-to-speech; Expressive - Range of response options required (radio buttons, drag and drop), Range of student support for producing response (speech-to-text); Language and Symbols - Provision of multiple representations of symbols (linguistic labels for symbols, define abbreviations, etc.), Provide definitions of non-construct relevant terminology, Use of studentsÃ¢?? dominant language; Cognitive - Use of a concept map, Use of a response template, Use of context to heighten salience, Highlighting key terms and ideas; Executive Functioning - Breaking task into manageable units, Icons to encourage thinking and reflection, On-screen progress monitoring; Affective - Use of scenario or real-world context to heighten engagement, Age-appropriate materials
-Interactive narrative (gaming), Affirmation of participation

Narrative structure	❶ [Edit]	Cause and effect. An event, phenomenon, or system is altered by internal or external factors.
		Investigation. A student or scientist completes an investigation in which one or more variables may be observed or manipulated and data are collected
		Change over time. A sequence of events is presented to highlight sequential or cyclical change in a system.
National educational standards	❶ [Edit]	NSES 8ASI1.1. Identify questions that can be answered through scientific investigations. Students should develop the ability to refine and refocus broad and ill-defined questions. An important aspect of this ability consists of students' ability to clarify questions and inquiries and direct them toward objects and phenomena that can be described, explained, or predicted by scientific investigations. Students should develop the ability to identify their questions with scientific ideas, concepts, and quantitative relationships that guide investigation.
		NSES 8ASI1.2. Design and conduct a scientific investigation. Students should develop general abilities, such as systematic observation, making accurate measurements, and identifying and controlling variables. They should also develop the ability to clarify their ideas that are influencing and guiding the inquiry, and to understand how those ideas compare with current scientific knowledge. Students can learn to formulate questions, design investigations, execute investigations, interpret data, use evidence to generate explanations, propose alternative explanations, and critique explanations and procedures.
		NSES 8ASI1.3. Use appropriate tools and techniques to gather, analyze, and interpret data. The use of tools and techniques, including mathematics, will be guided by the question asked and the investigations students design. The use of computers for the collection, summary, and display of evidence

is part of this standard. Students should be able to access, gather, store, retrieve, and organize data, using hardware and software designed for these purposes.

NSES 8ASI1.4. Develop descriptions, explanations, predictions, and models using evidence. Students should base their explanation on what they observed, and as they develop cognitive skills, they should be able to differentiate explanation from description, providing causes for effects and establishing relationships based on evidence and logical argument. This standards requires a subject knowledge base so the students can effectively conduct investigations, because developing explanations establishes connections between the content of science and the contexts within which students develop new knowledge.

NSES 8ASI1.5. Think critically and logically to make the relationships between evidence and explanations. Thinking critically about evidence includes deciding what evidence should be used and accounting for anomalous data. Specifically, students should be able to review data from a simple experiment, summarize the data, and form a logical argument about the cause-and-effect relationships in the experiment. Students should begin to state some explanations in terms of the relationship between two or more variables.

NSES 8ASI1.6. Recognize and analyze alternative explanations and predictions. Students should develop the ability to listen and to respect the explanations proposed by other students. They should remain open to and acknowledge different ideas and explanations, be able to accept the skepticism of others, and consider alternative explanations.

NSES 8ASI1.7. Communicate scientific procedures and explanations. With practice, students should become competent at communicating experimental methods, following instructions, describing observations, summarizing the results of other groups, and telling other students about investigations and explanations.

State standards	❶ [Edit]
State benchmarks	❶ [Edit]
I am a kind of	❶ [Edit]
These are kinds of me	❶ [Edit]
These are parts of me	❶ [Edit]
Templates	❶ [Edit]
Exemplar tasks	❶ [Edit]
Online resources	❶ [Edit]
References	❶ [Edit]

Tags [Add Tag]

(No tags entered.)

Appendix D: Task Template for Designing and Conducting an Experiment about Photosynthesis

Task Template for designing and conducting an experiment about photosynthesis | Template 2347		[Permit | Delete | View: View (vertical)]
Title	[Edit]	Task Template for designing and conducting an experiment about photosynthesis
Overview	[Edit]	This task template provides details around a scenario-based ICT task designed to measure experimental investigation within the life sciences context.
Type	❸ [Edit]	[View]
Student Model Summary	❸ [Edit]	SM1. The student model provides information about student proficiencies on experimental investigation and life science content dimensions associated with photosynthesis
Student Models	❸ [Edit]	Experimental Investigation in Photosynthesis: 2D student model. Two-dimensional student model with life science and experimental investigation student model variables. The life science content focuses on knowledge of photosynthesis. The experimental investigation dimension focuses on the design and interpreting results from an experiment.
Measurement Model Summary	❸ [Edit]	MM1. Items have measurement models which include dichotomous multiple-choice models, others are bundled with both multiple choice and open-ended models.
Evaluation Procedures Summary	❸ [Edit]	EP1. Dichotomous responses and partial credit responses. Scoring of some work products may be automated. Scores will be developed for content as well as for experimental investigation. The experimental investigation would include both knowledge and skills.
Work Product Summary	❸ [Edit]	WP1. Response formats would include some of the following: selected response, brief and extended constructed response, drawing, implicit logging of students' problem solving attempts, drag-and-drop, hot-spots, dynamically generated tables and graphs, position of sliders to control variables in simulation and highlighting.
Task Model Variable Summary	❸ [Edit]	TM1. TMVs allow the designer to adjust the complexity of the problem (e.g., number of variables in the experiment, how easy the results are to interpret, the relationship between the data and the hypothesis), and the type of plant(s) used.
Template-level Task Model Variables	❸ [Edit]	Amount of Data. The number of data points presented to students in graphs, tables and maps.
		Cognitive complexity. The overall cognitive complexity of a task, including the numbers of variables and data tranformations per activity
		Content knowledge required (simple,mod,complex). This variable represents the amount of content knowledge needed to bring to the task in order to solve the problem correctly
		Data Representation Format. The format of data as it is presented to students (bar graph, line graph, scatter plot, map, data table, pie chart).
		Level of scaffolding for content. The level of scaffolding for content within a given task or activity
		Level of scaffolding for inquiry. the level of scaffolding for carrying out a scientific investigation within a given task of activity
		Number of items to be included/time allotted for the task .
		Technology Features to be allowed. (Individual activities might have additional requirements/limitations with relation to the type of technology features that can be included)

Task Model Variable Settings	❶ [Edit] [View]	
Materials and Presentation Requirements	❶ [Edit]	Ma1. Internet connection Ma2. Browser requirements
Template-level Materials and Presentation	❶ [Edit]	1) The overall scenario should be presented to the student. 2) Specific content questions should be presented to the student. 3) Students should be presented/asked to generate the hypothesis that will be tested in the task. 4) Students will be asked to contribute to the design of the experiment. 5) Students will presented with an opportunity to conduct the experiment (optional). 6) Students will be provided the results of their experiment. 7) Students will be asked to interpret/reflect on the results of their experiment. 8) Students will be given an opportunity to re-design, and re-run their experiment (steps 4-7) (Optional). 9) Students will be asked to draw a conclusion from their experiment. 10) Students will be provided with a closure to their task.
Materials and Presentation Settings	❶ [Edit] [View]	
Activities Summary	❶ [Edit]	AS1. The task begins with each student creating a model that shows the inputs and outputs of photosynthesis. The task then prompts the student to design and conduct an experiment that examines how variables (e.g., amount of water, amount of light) affect the growth of plants. Each student must identify or generate a hypothesis, describe how to test the hypothesis, design the experiment by picking levels of variables, and interpret the results of the experiment. As the assessment task progresses, the student is asked to explain her reasoning at numerous points in the investigation.
Activities	❶ [Edit]	Scenario presentation. The overall scenario, including the goal of the task, is presented to the student. Content questions. This activity involves answering questions related to the content measured in the task. There may also be content questions associated with the inquiry process (e.g., knowledge of what it means to control a variable, what is a dependent variable) Generating a hypothesis. This activity involves students generating a hypothesis related to the scenario that was provided. Designing an Experiment. This activity has students determining which variables to use and what the settings should be for these variables. Conducting an Experiment. This activity might involve students running a simulation of the experiment. Students may be asked to record data from the simulation. The simulation is set with default parameters and students may be able to manipulate these parameters to investigate their predictions. Interpreting Results from an Experiment. This activity asks students to interpret results. Concluding from an Experiment. This activity has students relating their interpretations back to the hypothesis for the experiment and possibly generalizing the results. Closing of the task. This activity provides students with a short summary of the task and indicates that the task is over.

Tools for Examinee	❶ [Edit]	Tf1. Computer with internet access
Exemplars	❶ [Edit]	
Educational Standards	❶ [Edit]	NSES 8ASI1.1. Identify questions that can be answered through scientific investigations. Students should develop the ability to refine and refocus broad and ill-defined questions. An important aspect of this ability consists of students' ability to clarify questions and inquiries and direct them toward objects and phenomena that can be described, explained, or predicted by scientific investigations. Students should develop the ability to identify their questions with scientific ideas, concepts, and quantitative relationships that guide investigation.

NSES 8ASI1.2. Design and conduct a scientific investigation. Students should develop general abilities, such as systematic observation, making accurate measurements, and identifying and controlling variables. They should also develop the ability to clarify their ideas that are influencing and guiding the inquiry, and to understand how those ideas compare with current scientific knowledge. Students can learn to formulate questions, design investigations, execute investigations, interpret data, use evidence to generate explanations, propose alternative explanations, and critique explanations and procedures.

NSES 8ASI1.3. Use appropriate tools and techniques to gather, analyze, and interpret data. The use of tools and techniques, including mathematics, will be guided by the question students asked and the investigations students design. The use of computers for the collection, summary, and display of evidence is part of this standard. Students should be able to access, gather, store, retrieve, and organize data, using hardware and software designed for these purposes.

NSES 8ASI1.4. Develop descriptions, explanations, predictions, and models using evidence. Students should base their explanation on what they observed, and as they develop cognitive skills, they should be able to differentiate explanation from description, providing causes for effects and establishing relationships based on evidence and logical argument. This standards requires a subject knowledge base so the students can effectively conduct investigations, because developing explanations establishes connections between the content of science and the contexts within which students develop new knowledge.

NSES 8ASI1.5. Think critically and logically to make the relationships between evidence and explanations. Thinking critically about evidence includes deciding what evidence should be used and accounting for anomalous data. Specifically, students should be able to review data from a simple experiment, summarize the data, and form a logical argument about the cause-and-effect relationships in the experiment. Students should begin to state some explanations in terms of the relationship between two or more variables.

NSES 8ASI1.6. Recognize and analyze alternative explanations and predictions. Students should develop the ability to listen and to respect the explanations proposed by other students. They should remain open to and acknowledge different ideas and explanations, be able to accept the skepticism of others, and consider alternative explanations.

NSES 8ASI1.7. Communicate scientific procedures and explanations. With practice, students should become competent at communicating experimental methods, following instructions, describing observations, summarizing the results of other groups, and telling other students about investigations and explanations. |
| **Design Patterns** | ❶ [Edit] | Experimental Investigation (used for the Marigold task). This design pattern supports the writing of storyboards and items that address scientific reasoning and process skills in experimental investigations. In experimental investigations, it is necessary to manipulate one or more of the variables of interest and to control others while testing a prediction or hypothesis. This contrasts with observational investigations, where variables typically cannot be manipulated. This design pattern may be used to generate groups of tasks for science content strands amenable to experimentation. |

I am a kind of	❸ [Edit]
These are kinds of me	❸ [Edit]
These are parts of me	❸ [Edit]
Online resources	❸ [Edit]
References	❸ [Edit]

Tags [Add Tag]

(No tags entered.)

Appendix E: Storyboard for Marigold ICT

In your science class, you have been learning about the process by which plants grow.

One student, Charlie, said that the marigold flowers that are growing inside his house are smaller than the marigolds in the garden outside.

The class discusses why this might be the case. With their teacher they decide to investigate the factors that affect the growth of marigolds.

Click the play button to watch the animation showing a marigold growing.

Animation of a Marigold growing

Play

Once you click next you can not go back ⇨

In your science class, you learned about the process by which plants produce sugar.

The sugar is combined with minerals in the soil to produce the fats, proteins and carbohydrates needed for plants to grow.

1. Drag the words on the left into either the inputs or outputs box to show the process by which plants produce sugar. You may put multiple words into each box. Not all words will be used.

Carbon Dioxide

Light

Nitrogen

Oxygen

Pollen

Sugar

Water

Inputs

⇨

Outputs

Once you click next you can not go back ⇨

The class discusses what <u>factors</u> might affect the difference in the growth of <u>marigolds</u> grown inside compared to those grown outside. They came up with the following list:

- Amount of light available
- Amount of noise in the environment
- Temperature of the environment
- Amount of water
- The number of people who walk by the plants

2. Pick two <u>factors</u> you think would have the most affect on the growth of the <u>marigold</u>. Explain your choices.

Factor 1:__[Drop down menu]_____

Factor 2 :__[Drop down menu]_____

Explanation:

Once you click next you can not go back ⇨

Charlie wanted to set up an experiment that would examine how the **amount of light** and the **amount of water** would affect the growth of a marigold.

The class decided to use the <u>factors</u> Charlie suggested. They then discussed how to design their experiment. The science teacher said that the first step was deciding on their hypothesis.

3. Which of the following are scientific hypotheses about the growth of a <u>marigold</u> that could be tested. Pick **ALL** that apply.

a. All <u>marigolds</u> like water.
b. The more frequently the <u>marigold</u> is watered, the faster it will grow.
c. The set up of an experiment measuring growth of a <u>marigold</u> should include an indoor environment and an outdoor environment.
d. More light makes <u>marigolds</u> happier, and happier <u>marigolds</u> grow taller.
e. <u>Marigolds</u> with more light and more water will grow larger.

Once you click next you can not go back ⇨

The class decided to test the following hypothesis: <u>Marigolds</u> with more light and more water will grow larger.

Next the class designed the experiment. The class read about marigolds. They found the following information:

- <u>Marigolds</u> can start as seeds or <u>seedlings</u>
- <u>Marigolds</u> need to be planted in soil
- <u>Marigolds</u> need water
- <u>Marigolds</u> need light
- <u>Marigolds</u> can be compared using the height of the longest stem
- <u>Marigolds</u> can be compared using the weight of the entire plant.

4a. From the list of variables, select two independent variables to test the hypothesis above.

- ○ Amount of water
- ○ Height of the longest stems
- ○ Type of soil used
- ○ Weight of the <u>marigold</u>
- ○ Exposure to light

4b. From the list of variables, select the dependent variable to test the hypothesis above.

- ○ Number of <u>seedlings</u> planted
- ○ Type of soil used
- ○ Weight of the <u>marigold</u>
- ○ Exposure to light

	Once you click next you can not go back	⇨

The hypothesis being tested is: : <u>Marigolds</u> with more light and more water will grow larger.

The class plants several <u>marigold seedlings</u> and varies the exposure to light and the amount of water they receive. They will run the experiment for 4 weeks.

For the experiment the class can use:

- 6 planter boxes with grow lights
- 36 <u>marigold seedlings</u>
- Two different types of soil
- Space in the back of the classroom (no outdoor space was available to use)
- Watering can and water

5. One student, Joanne, said that the class needed to make sure that all of the planter boxes have the same type of soil in them. David said that since they are not testing how the type of soil will affect the plant, the type of soil used does not matter.

a. Who do you agree with?
- ❑ Joanne
- ❑ David

b. Explain your answer.

	Once you click next you can not go back	⇨

The hypothesis being tested is: Marigolds with more light and more water will grow larger.

The class decided to use the following levels of each variable:

Amount of water: 3 levels

	Mon	Tues	Wed	Thurs	Fri
5 cups a week	🐛	🐛	🐛	🐛	🐛

	Mon	Tues	Wed	Thurs	Fri
2 cups a week	🐛			🐛	

	Mon	Tues	Wed	Thurs	Fri
1 cup a week	🐛				

Exposure to light: 2 levels

A grow light for 24 hours — 24 hours

A grow light for 3 hours — 3 hours

The class is going to weigh the seedlings before planting them. After 4 weeks the marigolds will be removed from the planter box, dried, and weighed again.

6. Assuming that marigolds with more light and more water will grow larger, **compare** the expected weight of the marigolds that are given
- 5 cups of water a week and exposed to 24 hours of grow light a day

with the marigolds that are given
- 1 cup of water a week and exposed to 3 hours of grow light a day.

The hypothesis is: Marigolds with more light and more water will grow larger.

7. Design the class experiment to test the hypothesis.

- For each planter box, pick:
  - How many hours per day the grow light is on,
  - The amount of water per week
  - The number of seedlings to be planted in each box

	Number of hours the grow light is on per day	Amount of water per week	Number of seedlings to plant
Planter Box 1	o 3 hours o 24 hours	o 1 cup o 2 cups o 5 cups	o 2 seedlings o 4 seedlings o 6 seedlings
Planter Box 2	o 3 hours o 24 hours	o 1 cup o 2 cups o 5 cups	o 2 seedlings o 4 seedlings o 6 seedlings
Planter Box 3	o 3 hours o 24 hours	o 1 cup o 2 cups o 5 cups	o 2 seedlings o 4 seedlings o 6 seedlings
Planter Box 4	o 3 hours o 24 hours	o 1 cup o 2 cups o 5 cups	o 2 seedlings o 4 seedlings o 6 seedlings
Planter Box 5	o 3 hours o 24 hours	o 1 cup o 2 cups o 5 cups	o 2 seedlings o 4 seedlings o 6 seedlings
Planter Box 6	o 3 hours o 24 hours	o 1 cup o 2 cups o 5 cups	o 2 seedlings o 4 seedlings o 6 seedlings

	Number of hours the grow light is on per day	Amount of water per week	Number of seedlings to plant
Planter Box 1	o 3 hours o 24 hours	o 1 cup o 2 cups o 5 cups	o 2 seedlings o 4 seedlings o 6 seedlings
Planter Box 2	o 3 hours o 24 hours	o 1 cup o 2 cups o 5 cups	o 2 seedlings o 4 seedlings o 6 seedlings
Planter Box 3	o 3 hours o 24 hours	o 1 cup o 2 cups o 5 cups	o 2 seedlings o 4 seedlings o 6 seedlings
Planter Box 4	o 3 hours o 24 hours	o 1 cup o 2 cups o 5 cups	o 2 seedlings o 4 seedlings o 6 seedlings
Planter Box 5	o 3 hours o 24 hours	o 1 cup o 2 cups o 5 cups	o 2 seedlings o 4 seedlings o 6 seedlings
Planter Box 6	o 3 hours o 24 hours	o 1 cup o 2 cups o 5 cups	o 2 seedlings o 4 seedlings o 6 seedlings

The hypothesis is: Marigolds with more light and more water will grow larger.

8. Explain why your design is a good way to test your hypothesis. If you want to change your design you may go back to the previous question and change the settings on the variables.

You may go back to change your settings

The results of the experiment that the class did are shown below.

The average weight gain of the marigolds planted in each box in milligrams (mg)

Box	Average weight gain (mg per plant)
Box 1: 6 seedlings Watered: 5 cups Grow light: 3 hrs	53
Box 2: 6 seedlings Watered: 2 cups Grow light: 3 hrs	68
Box 3: 6 seedlings Watered: 1 cup Grow light: 3 hrs	60
Box 4: 6 seedlings Watered: 5 cups Grow light: 24 hrs	66
Box 5: 6 seedlings Watered: 2 cups Grow light: 24 hrs	88
Box 6: 6 seedlings Watered: 1 cup Grow light: 24 hrs	86

9. Compare the results from box 1 to box 4, box 2 to box 5, and box 3 to box 6. What can you say about how the number of hours the grow light is on affects the growth of marigolds?
a. The more hours the grow light was on the **more** the marigolds grew.
b. The more hours the grow light was on the **less** the marigolds grew.

10. Explain your answer.

Once you click next you can not go back

The results of the experiment that the class did are shown below

The combined weight of the marigolds planted in each box in milligrams (mg)

Box	Average weight gain (mg per plant)
Box 1: 6 seedlings Watered: 5 cups Grow light: 3 hrs	53
Box 2: 6 seedlings Watered: 2 cups Grow light: 3 hrs	68
Box 3: 6 seedlings Watered: 1 cup Grow light: 3 hrs	60
Box 4: 6 seedlings Watered: 5 cups Grow light: 24 hrs	66
Box 5: 6 seedlings Watered: 2 cups Grow light: 24 hrs	88
Box 6: 6 seedlings Watered: 1 cup Grow light: 24 hrs	86

11. Compare the results from box 1 to box 2 and box 3. Compare the results from box 4 to box 5 and box 6. What can you say about how the amount of water affects the growth of marigolds?
a. Giving the marigolds 5 cups of water a week resulted in the greatest average weight gain. Giving the marigolds 2 cups of water a week resulted in the greatest average weight gain.
b. Giving the marigolds 1 cup of water a week resulted in the greatest average weight gain.

12. Explain your answer.

The hypothesis is: Marigolds with more light and more water will grow larger.

The combined weight of the marigolds planted in each box in milligrams (mg)

Box	Average weight gain (mg per plant)
Box 1: 6 seedlings Watered: 5 cups Grow light: 3 hrs	53
Box 2: 6 seedlings Watered: 2 cups Grow light: 3 hrs	68
Box 3: 6 seedlings Watered: 1 cup Grow light: 3 hrs	60
Box 4: 6 seedlings Watered: 5 cups Grow light: 24 hrs	66
Box 5: 6 seedlings Watered: 2 cups Grow light: 24 hrs	88
Box 6: 6 seedlings Watered: 1 cup Grow light: 24 hrs	86

13. You found that the more hours the grow light was on the _fill In from 8_ the marigold grew, and that giving the marigold _fill in from 10__ of water a week would result in the largest growing marigolds. Which of the following is true?
❏ These results **support** my hypothesis
❏ These results **contradict** my hypothesis
❏ These results **do not provide information** about my hypothesis

14. Explain your answer:

After another few weeks of observation, it was decided that using a grow light 24 hours and giving the marigolds 2 cups of water a week produced the greatest change in weight.

15. Can these results be generalized to roses?

_____ Yes _____ No

Explain your answer

Once you click next you can not go back

Thank you for helping figure out how to set up marigold garden.

Appendix F: Developing and Using Models Design Pattern

					Permit	Delete	View	View (vertical)

Title	[Edit]	Developing and Using Models v2
Overview	[Edit]	This design pattern describes targeted knowledge, skills and abilities (KSAs) for developing and using models at the middle school level. The design pattern also articulates task features and examples of observable student behaviors that provide evidence of students' ability to develop and use models.
Focal Knowledge, Skills, and Abilities	❶ [Edit]	FK1. Ability to construct a model and use the model to explain a phenomenon FK2. Ability to construct a model and use the model to make a prediction about a phenomenon FK3. Ability to compare a model to a real world phenomenon (to evaluate the quality of the model) FK4. Ability to use a given model to make a prediction about a phenomenon
Rationale	❶ [Edit]	R1. According to the Framework for K-12 Science Education (p. 3-8), "Conceptual models allow scientists and engineers to better visualize and understand a phenomenon under investigation or develop a possible solution to a design problem").... Scientists use models...to represent their current understanding of a system (or parts of a system) under study, to aid in the development of questions and explanations, and to communicate ideas to others."
Additional Knowledge, Skills, and Abilities	❶ [Edit]	AK1. Knowledge that a model explains or predicts AK2. Knowledge that a model explains or predicts AK3. Ability to construct a response in drawing or writing
Potential observations	❶ [Edit]	Po1. Given a brief real-world scenario describing an observable phenomenon, student applies scientific concepts appropriately to construct a model (using drawings and words) that explains why the phenomenon occurs. Po2. Given a brief real-world scenario describing an observable phenomenon, student applies scientific concepts appropriately to construct a model (using drawings and words) and uses the model to make an accurate prediction about the phenomenon. Po3. Given a model, student accurately describes similarities and differences between the model and a phenomenon. Po4. Given a model, student uses the model to make a prediction about a phenomenon.
Potential work products	❶ [Edit]	Pw1. Drawing of a model Pw2. Constructed response
Potential rubrics	❶ [Edit]	Pr1. Rubrics must simultaneously distinguish among levels of sophistication with respect to both content knowledge and modeling.
Characteristic features	❶ [Edit]	Cf1. All items must prompt students to make connections between observed phenomenon or evidence and reasoning underlying the observation/evidence. Cf2. All phenomenon for which a model is developed must be observable (e.g., difference in temperature as a substance is heated, an erupting volcano) or fit available evidence. Cf3. Models provided in stimulus materials must illustrate a process or why

		a phenomenon exists (e.g., image of volcanoes over hot spot must include hot spot and direction of plate movement).
	Cf4.	All items must elicit core ideas as defined in the Framework for K-12 Science Education.
Variable features ❶ [Edit]	Vf1.	Drawing required: (1) none; (2) add to existing picture; (3) construct model from scratch
	Vf2.	Complexity of scientific concept(s) to be modeled...Can we handle this with grade band (i.e., whether concepts align to "by grade 5," "by grade 8," or "by grade 12" grade band statements in the Framework?
	Vf3.	Format of "real-world" phenomenon presented: (1) image, (2) data, (3) text, (4) combination
	Vf4.	Core idea/component idea targeted in model
	Vf5.	Function of the model: (1) to explain a mechanism underlying a phenomenon; (2) to predict future outcomes; (3) to describe a phenomenon; (4) to generate data that inform how the world works
	Vf6.	Scale: Macro (observable scale); Micro (very small, unobservable)...do we need an option for super-macro / too large to observe (i.e., plate tectonics)
I am a kind of ❶ [Edit]		
These are kinds of me ❶ [Edit]		
These are parts of me ❶ [Edit]		
Educational standards ❶ [Edit]		From Framework for K-12 Science Education: Practice 2: Developing and Using Models. By grade 12, students should be able to: 1. Construct drawings or diagrams as representations of events or systems--for example, to draw a picture of an insect with labeled features, to represent what happens to the water in a puddle as it is warmed by the sun, or to represent a simple physical model of a real-world object and use it as the basis of an explanation or to make predictions about how the system will behave in specified circumstances. 2. Represent and explain phenomena with multiple types of models--for example,represent molecules with 3-D models or with bond diagrams--and move flexibly between model types when different ones are most useful for different purposes. 3. Discuss the limitations and precision of a model as the representation of a system, process, or design and suggest ways in which the model might be improved to better fit available evidence or better reflect a design's specifications. Refine a model in light of empirical evidence or criticism to improve its quality and explanatory power. 4. Use (provided) computer simulations or simulations developed with simple simulation tools as a tool for understanding and investigating aspects of a system, particularly those not readily visible to the naked eye. 5. Make and use a model to test a design, or aspects of a design, and to compare the effectiveness of different design solutions.
Templates ❶ [Edit]		
Exemplar tasks ❶ [Edit]		
Online resources ❶ [Edit]		
References ❶ [Edit]	R1.	http://www.nap.edu/cat...

Tags [Add Tag]

Appendix G: Systems and System Models Design Pattern

Systems and System Models | Design Pattern 2300			| | Permit | Delete | View: View (vertical) ⬍ |

Title	[Edit]	Systems and System Models
Overview	[Edit]	This design pattern supports the writing of storyboards and items that address systems thinking, including complex systems. Systems are characterized as interacting component or parts. Tasks typically require multi-step causal reasoning and the consideration of the effects of multiple concepts or factors. The prevalence of scientific phenomena that can be conceptualized as systems suggests the development of a design pattern that supports the design of tasks that target systems thinking across domains and grade levels. details
Use	❶ [Edit]	U1. Because systems thinking is relevant in any content domain, this design pattern identifies common aspects of students' systems thinking that are applicable across domains and grade levels. Aspects of systems thinking are described more fully in 'Details' associated with design pattern attributes and in these examples, interactions between general systems thinking and particular content domains are described.
		Reasoning about systems develops along a learning progression spanning the school years. As such, components of the design pattern are labeled to reflect the expected stage of introduction for these concepts. This categorization is intended to reflect current practice as evidenced in literature, but does not suggest a developmental pathway (i.e. what students should be expected to understand as determined by age).
		For example, an important form of systems thinking, reasoning about emergent system outcomes (a dimension of complexity), is typically associated with high school science and beyond (see details link).
		Grade Level Categorization: U: upper elementary H: high school C: college and above details
Focal knowledge, skills, and abilities	❶ [Edit]	Fk1. [U] Ability to identify the structure of the system (including interactions and outcomes) details
		Fk2. [H] Knowledge of types of system interactions details
		Fk3. [H] Knowledge of the types of outcomes details
		Fk4. [U] Ability to predict or interpret the outcome of an input (change) to the system
		Fk5. [U] Ability to identify crucial qualitative or quantitative values details
		Fk6. [H] Knowledge of dimensions of complexity details
		Fk7. [H] Knowledge of the impact of time scales on systems details
		Fk8. [H] Knowledge of the ubiquity of systems and their arbitrary bounds. details
		Fk9. [C] Ability to relate the scope of system and scope of reasoning. details
		Fk10. [U] Ability to use systems to conduct investigations (including reasoning across multiple systems and/or real-world phenomena) details
Additional knowledge, skills, and abilities	❶ [Edit]	Ak1. Knowledge of components/structure of the system (content knowledge) details
		Ak2. Knowledge of the interactions in the system details
		Ak3. Knowledge of crucial values
		Ak4. Knowledge of time scales operating in system
		Ak5. Ability to interpret the representation of the system details
		Ak6. Scientific Reasoning details
		Ak7. Knowledge of the nature of models (e.g., physical, formulas, 3D) details

		Ak8.	Metacognitive Skills details
		Ak9.	Knowledge of the representation of the system model (i.e., food web).
Potential observations	❶ [Edit]	Po1.	Student accurately identifies components, interactions, dimensions of complexity or outcomes of a system details
		Po2.	Student correctly labels the components, interactions, dimensions of complexity or outcomes of a system
		Po3.	Student accurately describes the components, interactions, dimensions of complexity or outcomes of a system
		Po4.	Student generates an accurate representation of the system (components, interactions, dimensions of complexity or outcomes)
		Po5.	Student correctly states or identifies a predicted outcome based on system input or state change
		Po6.	Student correctly states or identifies the results of an inquiry (i.e. the evaluation of a system as a representation of phenomenon)
Potential work products	❶ [Edit]	Pw1.	Student labels components, interactions, dimensions of complexity or outcomes of a system (e.g., physical, diagram)
		Pw2.	Multiple-choice or other selection of components, interactions, dimensions of complexity or outcomes of a system details
		Pw3.	Multiple-choice or other selection of whole system representations
		Pw4.	Figural Response: Drag-and-drop of name or label of components, interactions, dimensions of complexity or outcomes of a system details
		Pw5.	Generated text of names or labels of components, interactions, dimensions of complexity or outcomes of a system
		Pw6.	Generated representation of system or part of system including multiple components or interactions (components, interactions, dimensions of complexity or outcomes of a system)
		Pw7.	Student states or identifies a predicted outcome of system input or state change
		Pw8.	Student states or identifies the results of an inquiry (i.e. the evaluation of a system as a representation of phenomenon)
Potential rubrics	❶ [Edit]	Pr1.	Dichotomous: Correct/Incorrect
		Pr2.	Partial Credit (Identification of System Components) details
Characteristic features	❶ [Edit]	Cf1.	Representation of system (labeled image (e.g. pond ecosystem), concept map, text, equation, etc.)
		Cf2.	Task scenario: the situation presenting task prompt, scientific content or context details
Variable features	❶ [Edit]	Vf1.	Number of system components
		Vf2.	The number of relationships presented (given) vs. student generated
		Vf3.	Type of relationship that is the target of the task
		Vf4.	Prior content knowledge presented/required
		Vf5.	Scaffolds to help students understand that there are multiple interdependent levels within a system details
		Vf6.	Scaffolds to structure metacognitive reasoning details
		Vf7.	Embedded support for vocabulary details
Narrative structure	❶ [Edit]		Cause and effect. An event, phenomenon, or system is altered by internal or external factors.
			Change over time. A sequence of events is presented to highlight sequential or cyclical change in a system.
			Investigation. A student or scientist completes an investigation in which one or more variables may be observed or manipulated and data are collected
			Specific to general and Parts to whole. Specific characteristics of a phenomenon are presented, culminating in a description of the system or phenomenon as a whole.
			Topic with Examples. A given topic is presented using various examples to highlight the topic.

<u>General to Specific or Whole to Parts</u>. A general topic is initially presented followed by the presentation of specific aspects of the general topic.

National educational standards [Edit]	<u>NSES 8ASI1.1</u>. Identify questions that can be answered through scientific investigations. Students should develop the ability to refine and refocus broad and ill-defined questions. An important aspect of this ability consists of students' ability to clarify questions and inquiries and direct them toward objects and phenomena that can be described, explained, or predicted by scientific investigations. Students should develop the ability to identify their questions with scientific ideas, concepts, and quantitative relationships that guide investigation.

<u>NSES 8ASI1.4</u>. Develop descriptions, explanations, predictions, and models using evidence. Students should base their explanation on what they observed, and as they develop cognitive skills, they should be able to differentiate explanation from description, providing causes for effects and establishing relationships based on evidence and logical argument. This standards requires a subject knowledge base so the students can effectively conduct investigations, because developing explanations establishes connections between the content of science and the contexts within which students develop new knowledge.

<u>NSES 8ASI1.5</u>. Think critically and logically to make the relationships between evidence and explanations. Thinking critically about evidence includes deciding what evidence should be used and accounting for anomalous data. Specifically, students should be able to review data from a simple experiment, summarize the data, and form a logical argument about the cause-and-effect relationships in the experiment. Students should begin to state some explanations in terms of the relationship between two or more variables.

<u>NSES 8ASI1.6</u>. Recognize and analyze alternative explanations and predictions. Students should develop the ability to listen and to respect the explanations proposed by other students. They should remain open to and acknowledge different ideas and explanations, be able to accept the skepticism of others, and consider alternative explanations.

<u>Unifying Concepts 1.1 - Systems, order, and organization</u>. The goal of this standard is to think and analyze in terms of systems.

<u>Unifying Concepts 1.3 - Constancy, change, and measurement</u>. Some properties of objects and processes are characterized by constancy, other by change. These may include properties of materials, position of objects, motion, and form and function of systems. Interactions within and among systems result in changes which can be quantified. Different systems of measurement are used for different purposes. Scale includes understanding that different characteristics, properties, or relationships within a system might change as its dimensions are increased or decreased. Rate involves comparing one measured quantity with another measured quantity.

<u>Unifying Concepts 1.4 - Evolution and equilibrium</u>. The general idea of evolution is that the present arises from materials and forms of the past. Equilibrium is a physical state in which forces and changes occur in opposite and off-setting directions. Interacting units of matter tend toward equilibrium states in which the energy is distributed as randomly and uniformly as possible.

State standards [Edit]	
State benchmarks [Edit]	<u>MCA III: 4.1.2.1.1</u>. Describe the positive and negative impacts that the designed world has on the natural world as more and more engineered products and services are created and used. Item Specifications -Items may require students to classify impacts as positive, negative or both -Designed products and services are limited to those that are familiar to a grade 4 student, such as an aluminum can, plastic bag, plastic bottle or bicycle

<u>MCA III: 6.1.2.1.1</u>. Identify a common engineered system and evaluate its impact on the daily life of humans. For example: Refrigeration, cell phone or automobile. Item Specifications Ã¢‚¬Â¢ Items are limited to engineered machines, structures, processes and systems that would be equally accessible to middle level students in all socio-economic groups

<u>MCA III: 6.1.2.1.2</u>. Recognize that there is no perfect design and that new technologies have consequences that may increase some risks and decrease others. For example: Seat belts and airbags. Item Specifications ÃƒÂ¢Ã‚¬Ã‚¢ Items are limited to engineered machines, structures, processes and systems that would be equally accessible to middle level students in all socio-economic groups

<u>MCA III: 6.1.2.1.3</u>. Describe the trade-offs in using manufactured products in terms of features, performance, durability and cost. Item Specifications Ã¢‚¬Â¢ Items are limited to engineered machines, structures, processes

and systems that would be equally accessible to middle level students in all socio-economic groups Ã¢â‚¬Â¢ Items may include differences between an incandescent lightbulb and a compact fluorescent or the differences between using a pen versus a pencil

MCA III: 6.1.2.1.4. Explain the importance of learning from past failures, in order to inform future designs of similar products or systems. For example: Space shuttle or bridge design. Item Specifications - Items will include any necessary background knowledge about the system that failed - Items may be based on actual case studies of past engineering failures

MCA III: 6.1.2.2.1. Apply and document an engineering design process that includes identifying criteria and constraints, making representations, testing and evaluation, and refining the design as needed to construct a product or system that solves a problem. For example: Investigate how energy changes from one form to another by designing and constructing a simple roller coaster for a marble. Item Specifications - Items may require students to evaluate the feasibility of the representations, recognize the iterative nature of the design process, identify potential design changes or identify criteria and constraints - Items assessing this benchmark may also assess benchmark 8.1.3.3.3

MCA III: 6.1.3.1.2. Distinguish between open and closed systems.

MCA III: 6.1.3.1.1. Describe a system in terms of its subsystems and parts, as well as its inputs, processes and outputs. Item Specifications Ã¢â‚¬Â¢ Items are limited to designed or natural systems related to grades 6Ã¢â‚¬â€œ8 benchmarks in physical science, life science or Earth science content standards Ã¢â‚¬Â¢ Items may require students to label the components of a system

MCA III: 6.1.3.4.1. Determine and use appropriate safe procedures, tools, measurements, graphs and mathematical analyses to describe and investigate natural and designed systems in a physical science context.

MCA III: 7.1.3.4.1. Use maps, satellite images and other data sets to describe patterns and make predictions about natural systems in a life science context. For example: Use online data sets to compare wildlife populations or water quality in regions of Minnesota.

MCA III: 7.1.3.4.2. Determine and use appropriate safety procedures, tools, measurements, graphs and mathematical analyses to describe and investigate natural and designed systems in a life science context.

MCA III: 8.1.3.4.1. Use maps, satellite images and other data sets to describe patterns and make predictions about local and global systems in Earth science contexts. For example: Use data or satellite images to identify locations of earthquakes and volcanoes, ages of sea floor, ocean surface temperatures and ozone concentration in the stratosphere.

MCA III: 8.1.3.4.2. Determine and use appropriate safety procedures, tools, measurements, graphs and mathematical analyses to describe and investigate natural and designed systems in Earth and physical science contexts.

MCA III: 8.1.1.2.1. Use logical reasoning and imagination to develop descriptions, explanations, predictions and models based on evidence.

I am a kind of	❶ [Edit]
These are kinds of me	❶ [Edit]
These are parts of me	❶ [Edit]
Templates	❶ [Edit]
Exemplar tasks	❶ [Edit]
Online resources	❶ [Edit]
References	❶ [Edit]

Tags [Add Tag]

(No tags entered.)

Appendix H: Storyboard for the Burmese Python Assessment Task

Scene 1

BACKGROUND:

Everglades National Park is a large, warm, wetlands habitat in Florida.

In the last decade a new snake, the Burmese python, has invaded the Florida Everglades ecosystem. Starting in the 1990s, pet owners began to release pythons into the Everglades. This large snake thrives in warm and wet habitats, and was the top predator in its native habitat in southeast Asia.

Scene 2

BACKGROUND:

The food web for the Everglades includes many types of animals such as fish, birds, reptiles, insects, and mammals. Some of the Everglades animals are threatened species.

Scientists in Florida have recorded the content of pythons' stomachs to include, mammals, birds, and reptiles.

QUESTION:

Based on the python's diet, why will an increase in the python population in the Florida Everglades have a large effect on the food web?

- ⊚ Because pythons eat birds, all of the water birds would disappear
- ⊚ [Because pythons eat many animal species, they compete at multiple levels of the food web]
- ⊚ Because the python eats fish, the raccoon wouldn't have enough to eat and their population would decrease
- ⊚ Because pythons compete with alligators, the population of turtles would increase

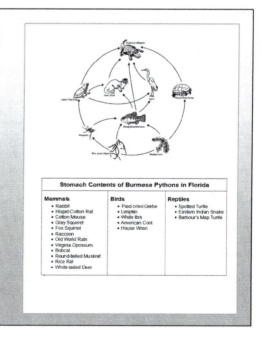

Stomach Contents of Burmese Pythons in Florida

Mammals	Birds	Reptiles
• Rabbit	• Pied-billed Grebe	• Spotted Turtle
• Hispid Cotton Rat	• Limpkin	• Eastern Indian Snake
• Cotton Mouse	• White Ibis	• Barbour's Map Turtle
• Gray Squirrel	• American Coot	
• Fox Squirrel	• House Wren	
• Raccoon		
• Old World Rats		
• Virginia Opossum		
• Bobcat		
• Round-tailed Muskrat		
• Rice Rat		
• White-tailed Deer		

Scene 3

BACKGROUND:

The Burmese python is now present in the Florida Everglades ecosystem. These pythons have been observed to have the same diet as the alligator.

QUESTION:
Drag the plant and animal icons below to show how the Everglades food web would look if you add the Burmese Python.

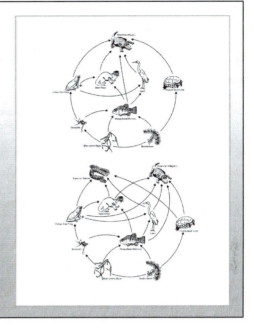

Scene 4

BACKGROUND:
Everglades park rangers estimate the size of the python population based on the number of pythons they find or capture. Over the past ten years, park rangers have seen a change in the number of Burmese pythons that they find annually.

QUESTION:
Form a conclusion about the Burmese Python population from the data shown in *Yearly Numbers of Recovered Pythons in Everglades National Park* and Surrounding Areas and select the option that best represents your conclusion.

- The number of pythons was stable until 2001 and then increased through 2007
- The number of pythons doubled every year
- The python population reached its limits in 2007
- Starting from 2004, the number of pythons began to level off.

Which of these is a plausible reason for the increase in the python population in the Everglades?
- ◎ Availability of many different types of prey;
- ◎ Presence of deep water;
- ◎ Availability of many types of grasses
- ◎ A large mosquito

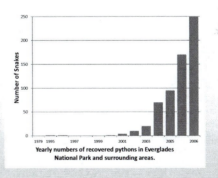

Yearly numbers of recovered pythons in Everglades National Park and surrounding areas.

Appendix I: Partial Design Pattern. Computational Thinking Practice: Analyze the Effects of Developments in Computing

Design Pattern Attribute	Attribute Content
Overview	This Design Pattern supports the development of tasks in which students show that they understand the range of problems to which computers and computing can be applied. They will demonstrate an understanding of how the forms that computers can take (including robotics) and their user interfaces affect usability. They will show an understanding of how computing has enabled innovations in various disciplines and in society as a whole, and at the same time has given rise to ethical questions. They will also demonstrate a broad understanding of "intelligent" machines.
Focal Knowledge, Skills, and Attributes (Focal KSAs) *What knowledge, skills, and other attributes should be measured?*	<ul><li>Ability to explain and give examples of the concepts of computer and computing.</li><li>Ability to describe the uses for computer hardware components.</li><li>Ability to identify a variety of electronic devices that contain computational processors.</li><li>Ability to choose appropriate hardware components for various types of users.</li><li>Ability to differentiate between ranking-based search engines and social bookmarking (collaborative) search engines.</li><li>Ability to describe a variety of Web 2.0 applications.</li><li>Ability to explain how computers are used for communications.</li><li>Ability to explain the implications of various forms of data exchange on social interactions.</li><li>Ability to explain how computers can be used as tools for visualizing data, modeling and design, and art.</li><li>Ability to explain the effects of computing on society within economic, social, and cultural contexts.</li><li>Ability to explain how the Internet facilitates global communication.</li><li>Ability to compare the positive and negative impacts of technology on culture (e.g., social networking, delivery of news and other public media, and intercultural communication).</li><li>Ability to describe current models of computer intelligence and learning.</li></ul>
Potential Observations *What behaviors or performances count as evidence of the knowledge, skills, and other attributes being measured?*	<ul><li>Ability to explain and give examples of the concepts of computer and computing.<ul><li>PO: Accuracy of explanation of the concept of a computer.</li><li>PO: Accuracy of explanation of the concept of computing.</li><li>PO: Correctness of examples used to represent the concepts of a computer and computing.</li></ul></li><li>Ability to describe the uses for computer hardware components.<ul><li>PO: Correctness of the description of the use(s) for a computer hardware component.</li></ul></li><li>Ability to identify a variety of electronic devices that contain computational processors.<ul><li>PO: Correctness of identification of an electronic device(s) that contains a computational processor.</li></ul></li><li>Ability to choose appropriate hardware components for various types of users.<ul><li>PO: Correctness of selection of hardware components for different types of users.</li></ul></li></ul>

- Ability to differentiate between ranking-based search engines and social bookmarking (collaborative) search engines.
  - PO: Accuracy of the explanation of the differences between ranking-based search engines and social bookmarking search engines (relate to IR).
- Ability to describe a variety of Web 2.0 applications.
  - PO: Correctness of description of Web 2.0 applications.
- Ability to explain how computers are used for communications.
  - PO: Accuracy of explanation of how computers are used for communications.
- Ability to explain the implications of various forms of data exchange on social interactions.
  - PO: Accuracy of explanation of the implications of various forms of data exchange.
- Ability to explain how computers can be used as tools for visualizing data, modeling and design, and art.
  - PO: Accuracy of explanation of how computers can be used as tools for visualizing data, modeling and design, and art.
- Ability to explain the effects of computing on society within economic, social, and cultural contexts.
  - PO: Accuracy of explanation of effect(s) of computing in economic, social, and cultural contexts.
- Ability to explain how the Internet facilitates global communication.
  - PO: Correctness of explanation of how the Internet can facilitate global communication.
- Ability to compare the positive and negative impacts of technology on culture (e.g., social networking, delivery of news and other public media, and intercultural communication).
  - PO: Correctness of description of positive impacts of technology on culture.
  - PO: Correctness of description of current models of computer intelligence and learning.
  - PO: Correctness of description of negative impacts of technology on culture.
  - PO: Accuracy of explanation comparing the positive and negative impacts of technology in culture.
  - Ability to describe current models of computer intelligence and learning.

Potential Work Products
What tasks or situations elicit the desired behaviors or performances?

- Ability to explain and give examples of the concepts of a computer and computing.
  - PW: Explanation of the concept of a computer.
  - PW: Explanation of the concept of computing.
  - PW: Description of examples that represent the concepts of a computer and computing.
- Ability to describe the uses for computer hardware components.
  - PW: Description of the use(s) for a computer hardware component.
- Ability to identify a variety of electronic devices that contain computational processors.
  - PW: Identification of electronic device(s) that contain a computational processor.

(Continued)

Design Pattern Attribute	Attribute Content
	• Ability to choose appropriate hardware components for various types of users.
	o PW: List matching hardware components to different types of users.
	• Ability to differentiate between ranking-based search engines and social bookmarking (collaborative) search engines.
	o PW: Explanation of the difference between ranking-based search engines and social bookmarking search engines.
	• Ability to describe a variety of Web 2.0 applications.
	o PW: Description of Web 2.0 applications.
	• Ability to explain how computers are used for communications.
	o PW: Explanation of how computers are used for communications.
	• Ability to explain the implications of various forms of data exchange on social interactions.
	o PW: Explanation of the implications of various forms of data exchange.
	• Ability to explain how computers can be used as tools for visualizing data, modeling and design, and art.
	o PW: Explanation of how computers can be used as tools for visualizing data, modeling and design, and art.
	• Ability to explain the effects of computing on society within economic, social, and cultural contexts.
	o PW: Explanation of effect(s) of computing in economic, social, and cultural contexts.
	• Ability to explain how the Internet facilitates global communication.
	o PW: Explanation of how the Internet can facilitate global communication.
	o Ability to compare the positive and negative impacts of technology on culture (e.g., social networking, delivery of news and other public media, and intercultural communication).
	o PW: Description of positive impacts of technology on culture.
	o PW: Description of negative impacts of technology on culture.
	o PW: Explanation comparing the positive and negative impacts of technology in culture.
	• Ability to describe current models of computer intelligence and learning.
	o PW: Description of current models of computer intelligence and learning.
ECS Unit Description	UNIT 1—Human–Computer Interaction In this unit students are introduced to the concepts of a computer and computing while investigating the major components of computers and the suitability of these components for particular applications. Students will experiment with Internet search techniques, explore a variety of websites and web applications, and discuss issues of privacy and security.

Fundamental notions of Human–Computer Interaction (HCI) and ergonomics are introduced. Students will learn that "intelligent" machine behavior is not "magic" but is based on algorithms applied to useful representations of information, including large data sets. Students will learn the characteristics that make certain tasks easy or difficult for computers, and how these differ from those that humans characteristically find easy or difficult. Students will gain an appreciation for the many ways in which computing-enabled innovation has had an impact on society, as well as for the many different fields in which they are used. Connections among social, economic, and cultural contexts will be discussed.

ECS Unit Objectives	**UNIT 1—Human–Computer Interaction** • Analyze the characteristics of hardware components to determine the applications for which they can be used. • Use appropriate tools and methods to execute Internet searches which yield requested data. • Evaluate the results of web searches and the reliability of information found on the Internet. • Explain the differences between tasks that can and cannot be accomplished with a computer. • Analyze the effects of computing on society within economic, social, and cultural contexts. • Communicate legal and ethical concerns raised by computing innovation. • Explain the implications of communication as data exchange.

ECS Unit Topics
(presented in recommended instructional sequence)
	UNIT 1—Human–Computer Interaction
	• Explore the concepts of a computer and computing.
	  o Explain and give examples of the concepts of a computer and computing.
	
	• "Demystify" and learn the function of the parts of a personal computer. Learn the terminology of hardware components necessary for the purchase of a home computer.
	  o Describe the uses for computer hardware components.
	  o Choose hardware components for various types of users.
	
	• Explore the World Wide Web and search engines. Experiment with a variety of search techniques, Internet resources, and Web 2.0 applications. Evaluate websites.
	  o Perform searches and explain how to refine searches to retrieve better information.
	  o Identify resources for finding information in addition to ranking-based search engines.
	  o Differentiate between ranking-based search engines and social bookmarking (collaborative) search engines.
	  o Use a variety of Web 2.0 applications.
	  o Develop and use a rubric to evaluate websites.
	
	• Examine the implications of data on society and how computers are used for communications.
	  o Explain how computers are used for communications.
	  o Recognize various forms of communication as data exchange.
	  o Describe the implications of data exchange on social interactions.
	  o Consider privacy of data that they create.

(Continued)

(Continued)

Design Pattern Attribute	Attribute Content
	• Explore how computers are used as a tool for visualizing data, modeling and design, and art in the context of culturally situated design tools. ○ Explain how computers can be used as tools for visualizing data, modeling and design, and art. ○ Identify mathematical connections in the output of the tools. ○ Edit an image using Photoshop. • Explore the idea of intelligence—especially as it relates to computers. Explore what it means for a machine to "learn." Discuss whether computers are intelligent or whether they only behave intelligently. ○ Explain the idea of intelligence especially as it relates to computers. ○ Explain what it means for a machine to "learn." ○ Discuss whether computers are intelligent or whether they only behave intelligently.

Acknowledgments

Research findings and assessment tasks described in this chapter were supported by the National Science Foundation under grants REC-0129331 (PADI Implementation Grant) and DRL-0733172 (An Application of Evidence-Centered Design to State Large-Scale Science Assessment), and a grant from the Institute of Education Sciences, U.S. Department of Education, R324A070035 (Principled Assessment Science Assessment Designs for Students with Disabilities).

We are grateful to Robert Mislevy at Educational Testing Service; Cathleen Kennedy and Mark Wilson at the BEAR Assessment Center, University of California, Berkeley; Nancy Songer, University of Michigan; Kathy Long at the Lawrence Hall of Science, University of California, Berkeley; Paul Nichols and Robert Dolan at Pearson; and David Rose and Elizabeth Murray at CAST for their participation and expertise in our project work. We also recognize the contributions of several anonymous reviewers for helpful suggestions on this chapter.

Disclaimer

Any opinions, findings, and conclusions or recommendations expressed in this material are those of the authors and do not necessarily reflect the views of the National Science Foundation or the Institute of Education Sciences, U.S. Department of Education.

Notes

1 For another perspective on how computational thinking skills are being defined, see the OECD's summary of assessment domains in PIAAC's Survey of Adult Skills (http://www.oecd.org/site/piaac/Summary%20of%20assessment%20domains%20in%20the%20Survey%20of%20Adult%20Skills.pdf). In particular, the definition and information about problem solving in technology-rich environments provides additional context for the computational thinking constructs described in this section.
2 See Crocker and Algina (1986), Miller, Linn, and Gronlund (2012), and Osterlind (2013) for comprehensive information on item analysis statistics and technical qualities of assessments that are used to provide evidence of a test's psychometric properties.
3 The magnitude of DIF present can be evaluated using procedures such as the STD P-DIF index (Dorans & Holland, 1993) which specifies levels of DIF considered problematic and worthy of investigation.

References

Adams, J. B. (2008). Computational science as a twenty-first century discipline in the liberal arts. *Journal of Computing Sciences in Colleges, 23*(5), 15–23.

Adams, R., Wilson, M., & Wang, W. (1997). The multidimension random coefficients multinomial logit model. *Applied Psychological Measurement, 21*(1), 1–23.

Alliance for Excellent Education. (2011, July). *Policy brief: Assessing deeper learning*. Washington, DC: Alliance for Excellent Education.

Almond, P., Winter, P., Cameto, R., Russell, M., Sato, E., Clarke-Midura, J., . . . Lazarus, S. (2010). Technology-enabled and universally designed assessment: Considering access in measuring the achievement of students with disabilities—A foundation for research. *The Journal of Technology, Learning and Assessment, 10*(5), 1–52.

Almond, R. G., DiBello, L. V., Moulder, B., & Zapata, D. (2007). Modeling diagnostic assessments with Bayesian networks. *Journal of Educational Measurement, 44*(4), 341–359.

Almond, R. G., Steinberg, L. S., & Mislevy, R. J. (2002). Enhancing the design and delivery of assessment systems: A four-process architecture. *Journal of Technology, Learning, and Assessment, 1*(5), 1–63.

Alonzo, A., & Gotwals, A. (2012). Introduction: Leaping into learning progressions in science. In A. Alonzo, & A. Gotwals (Eds.), *Learning progressions in science: Current challenges and future directions* (pp. 3–12). Rotterdam, The Netherlands: Sense Publishers.

American Educational Research Association (AERA), American Psychological Association (APA), & National Council on Measurement in Education (NCME). (1999). *The standards for educational and psychological testing*. Washington, DC: AERA.

AERA, APA, & NCME. (2014). *The standards for educational and psychological testing*. Washington, DC: AERA.

Astrachan, O., Hambrusch, S., Peckham, J., & Settle, A. (2009). *The present and future of computational thinking*. Paper presented at the Proceedings of the 40th ACM Technical Symposium on Computer Science Education, Chatanooga, TN.

Baker, R. S., Corbitt, A., & Aleven, V. (2008, June 23–27). More accurate student modeling through contextual estimation of slip and guess probabilities in Bayesian knowledge tracing. In B. P. Woolf, E. Almeur, R. Nkambou, & S. Lajoie (Eds.), *Intelligent tutoring systems* (pp. 406–415). Proceedings of the 9th International Conference on Intelligent Tutoring Systems, ITS 2008, Montreal, Canada.

Bejar, I. I., Braun, H., & Tannenbaum, R. (2007). A prospective, predictive and progressive approach to standard setting. In R. W. Lissitz (Ed.), *Assessing and modeling cognitive development in school: Intellectual growth and standard setting* (pp. 1–30). Maple Grove, MN: JAM Press.

Bennett, R. E., Persky, H., Weiss, A., & Jenkins, F. (2007). *Problem-solving in technology-rich environments: A report from the NAEP Technology-Based Assessment Project* (NCES-2007-466). Washington, DC: U.S. Department of Education, National Center for Education Statistics. Retrieved August 7, 2014 from http://nces.ed.gov/pubsearch/pubsinfo.asp?pubid=2007466

Betebenner, D. W., & Linn, R. L. (2009, December). *Growth in student achievement: Issues of measurement, longitudinal data analysis, and accountability*. Paper presented at the Exploratory Seminar: Measurement Challenges Within the Race to the Top Agenda, Austin, TX.

Borko, H., & Stecher, B. M. (2001, April). *Looking at reform through different methodological lenses: Survey and case studies of the Washington State education reform*. Paper presented as part of a symposium at the annual meeting of the American Educational Research Association, Seattle, WA.

Braun, H., Chudowsky, N., & Koenig, J. (Eds.). (2010). *Getting value out of value-added: Report of a workshop*. Washington, DC: The National Academies Press.

Bybee, R. W., Buchwald, C. E., Crissman, S., Heil, D. R., Kuerbis, P. J., Matsumoto, C., & McInerney, J. D. (1990). *Science and technology education for the middle years: Frameworks for curriculum and instruction*. Washington, DC: The National Center for Improving Science Education, The Network, Incorporated; Colorado Springs, CO: Biological Sciences Curriculum Study.

Cameto, R., Haertel, G., DeBarger, A. H., & Morrison, K. (2010). *Applying evidence-centered design to alternate assessments in mathematics for students with significant cognitive disabilities (alternate assessment design—Mathematics technical report 1)*. Menlo Park, CA: SRI International.

Carver, S. M. (2006). Assessing for deep understanding. In R. K. Sawyer (Ed.), *Cambridge handbook of the learning sciences*. New York, NY: Cambridge University Press.

Cawthon, S. W., Ho, E., Patel, P. G., Potvin, D. C., & Trundt, K. M. (2009). Multiple constructs and effects of accommodations on accommodated test scores for students with disabilities. *Journal of Practical Assessment Research and Evaluation, 14*(18), 1–9.

Cheng, B. H., Ructtinger, L., Fujii, R., & Mislevy, R. (2010). *Assessing systems thinking and complexity in science (large-scale assessment technical report 7)*. Menlo Park, CA: SRI International.

Chudowsky, N., & Behuniak, P. (1997, March). *Establishing consequential validity for large-scale performance assessments*. Paper presented at the annual meeting of the National Council of Measurement in Education, Chicago, IL.

Chung, G. K. W. K., & Baker, E. L. (2003). An exploratory study to examine the feasibility of measuring problem-solving processes using a click-through interface. *The Journal of Technology, Learning and Assessment, 2*(2), 1–30.

Clark, D. B., & Martinez-Garza, M. (2012). Prediction and explanation as design mechanics in conceptually-integrated digital games to help players articulate the tacit understandings they build through gameplay. In C. Steinkuhler, K. Squire, & S. Barab (Eds.), *Games, learning, and society: Learning and meaning in the digital age* (pp. 279–305). Cambridge, UK: Cambridge University Press.

Clarke-Midura, J., Mayrath, M., & Dede, C. (2012). Thinking outside the bubble: Virtual performance assessments for measuring inquiry learning. In M. Mayrath, J. Clarke-Midura, & D. Robinson (Eds.), *Technology-based assessment for 21st century skills: Theoretical and practical implications from modern research*. New York, NY: Springer-Verlag.

Colker, A. M., Liu, M., Mislevy, R. J., Haertel, G., Fried, R., & Zalles, D. (2010). *A design pattern for experimental investigation (large-scale assessment technical report 8)*. Menlo Park, CA: SRI International.

Crocker, L., & Algina, J. (1986). *Introduction to classical and modern test theory*. Orlando, FL: Holt, Rinehart and Winston.

DeBarger, A., Penuel, W. R., Harris, C. J., & Kennedy C. A. (2015). Building an assessment to design and use next generation science assessments in efficacy studies of curriculum interventions. *American Journal of Evaluation*. doi: 10.1177/1098214015581707

DeBarger, A. H., & Snow, A. (2010). *Design pattern on model use in interdependence among living systems (large-scale assessment technical report 13)*. Menlo Park, CA: SRI International.

de Jong, T., & van Joolingen, W. R. (1998). Scientific discovery learning with computer simulations of conceptual domains. *Review of Educational Research, 68*(2), 179–201.

Dolan, R. P., Rose, D. H., Burling, K., Harms, M., & Way, D. (2007, April). *The universal design for computer-based testing framework: A structure for developing guidelines for constructing innovative computer-administered tests*. Paper presented at the National Council on Measurement in Education Annual Meeting, Chicago, IL.

Dorans, N. J., & Holland, P. W. (1992). *DIF detection and description: Mantel-Haenszel and standardization*. Princeton, NJ: Educational Testing Service.

Dorans, N. J., & Holland, P. W. (1993). DIF detection and description: Mantel-Haenszel and standardization. In P. W. Holland & H. Wainer (Eds.), *Differential item functioning* (pp. 35–66). Hillsdale, NJ: Lawrence Erlbaum.

Duschl, R. A. (2008). Science education in three-part harmony: Balancing conceptual, epistemic, and social learning goals. *Review of Research in Education, 32*, 268–291.

Embretson, S. E., & Reise, S. P. (2000). *Item response theory for psychologists*. Mahwah, NJ: Lawrence Erlbaum.

Erpenbach, W. J., Forte-Fast, E., & Potts, A. (2003). *Statewide educational accountability under NCLB: Central issues arising from an examination of state accountability workbooks and US Department of Education reviews under the No Child Left Behind Act of 2001*. Washington, DC: The Council of Chief State School Officers.

Gentner, D., & Stevens, A. L. (Eds.). (1983). *Mental models*. Hillsdale, NJ: Lawrence Erlbaum.

Goldstone, R. R., & Wilensky, U. (2008). Promoting transfer by grounding complex systems principles. *Journal of the Learning Sciences, 17*(4), 465–516.

Gotwals, A. W., & Songer, N. B. (2006). *Cognitive predictions: BioKIDS implementation of the PADI assessment system* (PADI Technical Report 10). Menlo Park, CA: SRI International.

Grover, S., & Pea, R. (2013). Computational thinking in K–12: A review of the state of the field. *Educational Researcher, 42*(1), 38–43.

Haertel, E. (2013). *Reliability and validity of inferences about teachers based on student test scores.* Princeton, NJ: ETS.

Haertel, G., DeBarger, A. H., Villalba, S., Hamel, L., & Colker, A. M. (2010). *Integration of evidence-centered design and universal design principles using PADI, an online assessment design system* (PADI Technical Report 3). Menlo Park, CA: SRI International.

Harris, C. J., Penuel, W. R., DeBarger, A., Moorthy, S., Snow, E., Lundh, P., . . . Krajcik, J. S. (2012, April). *Developing linked learning assessments and observation protocols aligned to the framework for K–12 science education.* Paper presented at the annual meeting of the American Educational Research Association, Vancouver, Canada.

Harris, C. J., & Salinas, I. (2009). Authentic science learning in primary and secondary classrooms. In M. I. Saleh & M. S. Khine (Eds.), *Fostering scientific habits of mind: Pedagogical knowledge and best practices in science education* (pp. 125–144). Rotterdam, The Netherlands: Sense Publishers.

Harris, D., & Wingarten, R. (2011). *Value-added measures in education: What every educator needs to know.* Cambridge, MA: Harvard Education Press.

Heitin, L. (2014). Common science standards slow to catch on in states. *Education Week, 33*(19), 6.

Hestenes, D., Wells, M., & Swackhamer, G. (1992). Force concept inventory. *The Physics Teacher, 30*, 141–166.

Hogan, K., & Weathers, K. C. (2003). Psychological and ecological perspectives on the development of systems thinking. In A. R. Berkowitz, C. H. Nilon, & K. S. Hollweg (Eds.), *Understanding urban ecosystems: A new frontier for science and education* (pp. 233–260). New York, NY: Springer.

Johnson-Laird, P. N. (1983). *Mental models: Toward a cognitive science of language, inference and consciousness.* Cambridge, MA: Harvard University Press.

Kane, M. T. (1992). An argument-based approach to validity. *Psychological Bulletin, 112*(3), 527–535. doi:10.1037/0033-2909.112.3.527

Kane, M. T. (2006). Validation. In R. L. Brennan (Ed.), *Educational measurement* (4th ed., pp. 17–64). Washington, DC: American Council on Education.

Kennedy, C. (2005). *Constructing PADI measurement models for the BEAR Scoring Engine* (PADI Technical Report 7). Menlo Park, CA: SRI International.

Kimball, R. (2008). *The Microsoft data warehouse toolkit: With SQL server 2008 R2.* Indianapolis, IN: Wiley.

Koretz, D. M., Barron, S., Mitchell, K. J., & Stecher, B. M. (1996). *Perceived effects of the Kentucky instructional results information system* (Report Number MR-792-PCT/FF). Santa Monica, CA: RAND Corporation.

Krajcik, J. S., & Blumenfeld, P. C. (2006). Project-based learning. In R. K. Sawyer (Ed.), *Cambridge handbook of the learning sciences* (pp. 317–333). New York, NY: Cambridge University Press.

Lehrer, R., & Schauble, L. (2006). Scientific thinking and science literacy: Supporting development in learning in contexts. In W. Damon, R. M. Lerner, K. A. Renninger, & I. E. Sigel (Eds.), *Handbook of child psychology* (6th ed., Vol. 4). Hoboken, NJ: Wiley.

Levy, R., & Mislevy, R. J. (2004). Specifying and refining a measurement model for a computer-based interactive assessment. *International Journal of Testing, 4*, 333–369.

Linn, R., Baker, E. L., & Dunbar, S. B. (1991). Complex performance-based assessment: Expectations and validation criteria. *Educational Researcher, 20*(8), 15–21.

Liu, L., & Hmelo-Silver, C. E. (2009). Promoting complex systems learning through the use of conceptual representations in hypermedia. *Journal of Research in Science Teaching, 46*(9), 1023–1040.

Mantel, M., & Haenszel, W. (1959). Statistical aspects of the analysis of data from retrospective studies of disease. *Journal of the National Cancer Institute, 22*, 229–248.

Mayrath, M., Clarke-Midura, J., Robinson, D., & Schraw, G. (2012). *Technology-based assessment for 21st century skills: Theoretical and practical implications for modern research.* New York, NY: Springer-Verlag.

McDonnell, L. M., & Choisser, C. (1997, September). *Testing and teaching: Local implementation of new state assessments* (CSE Technical Report 442). National Center for Research on Evaluation, Standards, and Student Testing (CRESST), Center for the Study of Evaluation (CSE), Graduate School of Education and Information Studies, University of California, Los Angeles, CA.

Messick, S. (1994). The interplay of evidence and consequences in the validation of performance assessments. *Educational Researcher, 23*(2), 13–23.

Miller, M. D., Linn, R. L., & Gronlund, N. E. (2012). *Measurement and assessment in teaching* (11th ed.). London, UK: Pearson.

Mills, C. N., Potenza, M. T., Fremer, J. J., & Ward, W. L. (2002). *Computer-based testing: Building the foundation for future assessments.* Mahwah, NJ: Lawrence Erlbaum.

Mislevy, R. J., & Haertel, G. D. (2006). Implications of evidence-centered design for educational testing. *Educational Measurement: Issues and Practice, 25*(4), 6–20.

Mislevy, R. J., Haertel, G. D., Cheng, B. H., Ructtinger, L., DeBarger, A., Murray, E., . . . Vendlinski, T. (2013). A "conditional" sense of fairness in assessment. *Educational Research and Evaluation, 19*(2–3), 121–140.

Mislevy, R. J., Hamel, L., Fried, R., Gaffney, T., Haertel, G., Hafter, A., . . . Wenk, A. (2003). *Design patterns for assessing science inquiry* (PADI Technical Report 1). Menlo Park, CA: SRI International. Also presented at the American Education Research Association (AERA) in April, 2003.

Mislevy, R. J., Liu, M., Cho, Y., Fulkerson, D., Nichols, P., Zalles, D., . . . Hamel, L. (2009). *A design pattern for observational investigation assessment tasks* (Large-Scale Assessment Technical Report 2). Menlo Park, CA: SRI International. Retrieved August 7, 2014 from http://ecd.sri.com/down loads/ECD_TR2_DesignPattern_for_ObservationalInvestFL.pdf

Mislevy, R. J., Oranje, A., Bauer, M. I., von Davier, A., Corrigan, S., DiCerbo, K., & John, M. (2015). Psychometrics and game-based assessment. In F. Drasgow (Ed.), *Technology and testing: Improving educational and psychological measurement.* Madison, WI: National Council on Measurement in Education.

Mislevy, R. J., Steinberg, L. S., & Almond, R. G. (2003). On the structure of educational assessments. *Measurement: Interdisciplinary Research and Perspectives, 1,* 3–67.

Mislevy, R. J., Steinberg, L. S., Almond, R. G., Haertel, G. D., & Penuel, R. (2003). *Leverage points for improving educational assessment* (PADI Technical Report 2). Menlo Park, CA: SRI International.

Mitzel, H. C., Lewis, D. M., Patz, R. J., & Green, D. R. (2001). The Bookmark procedure: Psychological perspectives. In G. J. Cizek (Ed.), *Setting performance standards: Concepts, methods, and perspectives* (pp. 249–281). Mahwah, NJ: Lawrence Erlbaum.

National Assessment Governing Board (NAGB). (2010). *The science framework for the 2011 National Assessment of Educational Progress.* Washington, DC: U.S. Department of Education.

National Research Council (NRC). (1996). *National science education standards.* Washington, DC: National Academies Press.

NRC. (2001). *Knowing what students know: The science and design of educational assessment.* Washington, DC: National Academies Press.

NRC. (2005a). *Rising above the gathering storm: Energizing and employing America for a brighter economic future.* Washington, DC: National Academies Press.

NRC. (2005b). *America's lab report: Investigations in high school science.* Washington, DC: National Academies Press.

NRC. (2005c). *How students learn: History, mathematics, and science in the classroom.* Washington, DC: National Academies Press.

NRC. (2006). *Systems for state science assessments.* Washington, DC: National Academies Press.

NRC. (2007). *Taking science to school: Learning and teaching science in grades K–8.* Washington, DC: National Academies Press.

NRC. (2010). *Report of a workshop on the scope and nature of computational thinking.* Washington, DC: National Academies Press.

NRC. (2011a). *Learning science through computer games and simulations.* Washington, DC: National Academies Press.

NRC. (2011b). *Successful STEM education: A workshop summary.* Washington, DC: National Academies Press.

NRC. (2012). *A framework for K–12 science education: Practices, crosscutting concepts, and core ideas.* Washington, DC: National Academies Press.

Nehm, R. H. (2006). Faith-based evolution education? *BioScience, 56*(8), 638–639.

Nehm, R. H., & Schonfeld, L. S. (2008). Measuring knowledge of natural selection: A comparison of the CINS, an open-response instrument, and an oral interview. *Journal of Research in Science Teaching, 45*(10), 1131–1160.

NGSS. (2013). *Next generation science standards.* Retrieved August 7, 2014 from http://www.next-genscience.org/next-generation-science-standards

Noble, D. (2002). The rise of computational biology. *Nature Reviews Molecular Cell Biology, 3,* 459–463.

Opfer, J. E., Nehm, R. H., & Ha, M. (2012). Cognitive foundations for science assessment design: Knowing what students know about evolution. *Journal of Research in Science Teaching, 49*(6), 744–777.

Osterlind, S. J. (2013). *Constructing test items.* Boston, MA: Kluwer Academic Publishers.

Osterlind, S. J., & Everson, H. T. (2009). *Differential item functioning* (2nd ed.). Thousand Oaks, CA: Sage Publications.

Plake, B. S., Hambleton, R. K., & Jaeger, R. M. (1997). A new standard setting method for performance assessments: The dominant profile judgment method and some field test results. *Educational and Psychological Measurement, 57,* 400–411.

Plake, B. S., Huff, K., & Reshetar, R. (2010). Evidence-centered assessment design as a foundation for achievement level descriptor development and for standard setting. *Applied Measurement in Education, 23*(4), 342–357.

Popham, W. J. (2012). *Assessment bias: How to banish it* (2nd ed.). Boston, MA: Pearson.

Priami, C. (2007). Computational thinking in biology. In C. Priami (Ed.), *Transactions on computational systems biology VIII* (Vol. 4780, pp. 63–76). New York, NY: Springer-Verlag.

Priami, C. (2009). Algorithmic systems biology. *Communications of the ACM, 52*(5), 80–88.

Qin, H. (2009). *Teaching computational thinking through bioinformatics to biology students.* Paper presented at the Proceedings of the 40th ACM Technical Symposium on Computer Science Education, Chatanooga, TN.

Quellmalz, E. S., & Pellegrino, J. W. (2009). Technology and testing. *Science, 323,* 75–79.

Quellmalz, E. S., Timms, M. J., & Buckley, B. C. (2010). *The promise of simulation-based science assessment: The Calipers Project* (SimScientists Technical Report Series). San Francisco, CA: WestEd.

Quellmalz, E. S., Timms, M. J., Buckley, B. C., Davenport, J., Loveland, M., & Silberglitt, M. D. (2012). 21st century dynamic assessment. In M. Mayrath, J. Clarke-Midura, D. Robinson, & G. Schraw (Eds.), *Technology-based assessment for 21st century skills: Theoretical and practical implications for modern research.* New York, NY: Springer-Verlag.

Quellmalz, E. S., Timms, M. J., Silberglitt, M. D., & Buckley, B. C. (2012). Science assessments for all: Integrating science simulation into balanced state science assessment systems. *Journal of Research in Science Teaching, 49*(3), 363–393.

Race to the Top (RTTP), 74 Fed. Reg. 37,803 (July 29, 2009).

Rose, D. H., & Meyer, A. (2002). *Teaching every student in the digital age: Universal design for learning.* Alexandria, VA: ASCD.

Rose, D. H., & Meyer, A. (2006). *A practical reader in universal design for learning.* Cambridge, MA: Harvard Educational Press.

Rose, D. H., Meyer, A., & Hitchcock, C. (2005). *The universally designed classroom: Accessible curriculum and digital technologies.* Cambridge, MA: Harvard Education Press.

Rutstein, D. (2013, April 2–6). *ICT development and variant development.* Paper presented at the annual meeting of the National Council of Measurement in Education, San Francisco, CA.

Rutstein, D., Snow, E., & Biekowski, M. (2014). *Computational thinking practices: Analyzing and modeling a critical domain in computer science education.* Paper presented at the annual meeting of the American Educational Research Association (AERA), Philadelphia, PA.

Scalise, K. M. (2012, May 7–8). *Using technology to assess hard-to-measure constructs in the Common Core State Standards and to expand accessibility.* Paper prepared for an Invited Research Symposium on Technology Enhanced Assessments, Washington, DC. Retrieved August 7, 2014 from http://www.k12center.org/rsc/pdf/session1-scalise-paper-2012.pdf

Scalise, K. M., & Gifford, B. (2006). Computer-based assessment in e-learning: A framework for constructing "intermediate constraint" questions and tasks for technology platforms. *Journal of Technology, Learning, and Assessment, 4*(6), 1–45.

Snow, E., Bienkowski, M., & Rutstein, D. (2014). *Design patterns for computational thinking practices* (PACT Technical Report 1). Menlo Park, CA: SRI International.

Snow, E., Fulkerson, D., Feng, M., Nichols, P., Mislevy, R., & Haertel, G. (2010). *Leveraging evidence-centered design in large-scale test development* (Large-Scale Assessment Technical Report 4). Menlo Park, CA: SRI International.

Snow, E., Rutstein, D., & Bienkowski, M. (2014). *Leveraging design patterns for developing assessments for exploring computer science* (PACT Technical Report 2). Menlo Park, CA: SRI International.

Sparks, S. D. (2013). Challenges predicted for next-generation science tests, challenges envisioned for next-generation science tests. *Education Week, 33*(6), 6.

Stecher, B., Barron, S., Chun, T., & Ross, K. (2000). *The effects of the Washington state education reform on schools and classrooms* (CSE Technical Report 525). Los Angeles, CA: National Center for Research on Evaluation, Standards, and Student Testing.

Steinberg, L., & Thissen, D. (2006). Using effect sizes for research reporting: Examples using item response theory to analyze differential time functioning. *Psychological Methods, 11*(4), 402–415.

Stewart, J., & Hafner, R. (1994). The problem solving literature in the biology education. In D. Gable (Ed.), *Handbook of research on science teaching and learning*. Riverside, NJ: Macmillan.

Swaminathan, H., & Rogers, H. J. (1990). Detecting differential item functioning using logistic regression procedures. *Journal of Educational Measurement, 27*, 361–370.

Ting, C. Y., Phon-Amnuaisuk, S., & Chong, Y. K. (2008). Modeling and intervening across time in scientific inquiry exploratory learning environment. *Journal of Educational Technology & Society, 11*(3), 239–258.

U.S. Department of Education. (2011). *Solicitation for NAEP science interactive computer task (ICT) development*. Washington, DC: U.S. Department of Education.

U.S. Department of Education, Office of Special Education Programs, Data Analysis System (DANS). (2007, July 15). *Children with disabilities receiving special education under Part B of the Individuals with Disabilities Education Act* (OMB #1820–0043).

West, P., Rutstein, D., Mislevy, R. J., Liu, J., Choi, Y., Levy, R., . . . Behrens, J. T. (2010, August). *A Bayesian network approach to modeling learning progressions and task performance* (CRESST Report 776). National Center for Research on Evaluation, Standards, and Student Testing, Graduate School of Education and Information Studies, UCLA, Los Angeles, CA.

Williamson, D. M., Mislevy, R. J., & Bejar, I. I. (Eds.). (2006). *Automated scoring of complex tasks in computer-based testing*. Mahwah, NJ: Lawrence Erlbaum.

Wilson, M., & Adams, R. J. (1995). Rasch models for item bundles. *Psychometrika, 60*, 181–198.

Wing, J. (2008). Computational thinking and thinking about computing. *Philosophical Transactions of the Royal Society A: Mathematical, Physical and Engineering Sciences, 366*(1881), 3717–3725.

Zoanetti, N. (2010). Interactive computer based assessment tasks: How problem-solving process data can inform instruction. *Australian Journal of Educational Technology, 26*(5), 585–606.

12 Assessing Physical and Earth and Space Science in the Context of the NRC Framework for K–12 Science Education and the Next Generation Science Standards

Nathaniel J. S. Brown, Scott S. Maderer, and James Wood

This chapter describes current practices and future trends in large-scale science assessment in the United States. Particular emphasis is placed on how the design and implementation of science assessment could respond to the challenges presented by the 2012 National Research Council (NRC) report, *A Framework for K–12 Science Education: Practices, Crosscutting Concepts, and Core Ideas*, and the 2013 Next Generation Science Standards (NGSS). The NRC framework and the NGSS call for major changes in how science is taught in elementary through high school. Building on a growing consensus in the science education community, these documents downplay the importance of mastering disconnected science facts and narrowly defined inquiry skills and instead recommend the development over many years of deeply integrated conceptual understanding and authentic scientific practice. As has been discussed by others (Gorin & Mislevy, 2013; Pellegrino, 2013; Pellegrino, Wilson, Koenig, & Beatty, 2014), these framework and standards documents, in presenting a new vision of science education, present major challenges to states looking to design or revise large-scale science assessment systems to support accountability programs.

In this chapter, we first provide an overview of current large-scale science assessment practices in the United States, noting a recent trend toward adopting more end-of-course (EOC) exams for accountability purposes. We then describe the challenges presented by the NRC framework and the NGSS for developers of large-scale science assessments in an era of accountability. First, we focus on the design of assessment systems and the constraints involved in gathering reliable information about students, teachers, and schools with respect to the demanding breadth and depth of the new standards. Then, we turn to the design of individual assessments, describing a particular approach to principled assessment design—construct modeling—that is well suited to measuring student progress as students develop the deeper understandings and more sophisticated practices required by the new standards.

Throughout, specific examples are given of how construct specifications, items design, and scoring procedures can be adapted to meet these challenges. The content of these examples is Physical Science and Earth and Space Science, but these design considerations are also relevant to Life Science. (For a complementary perspective that focuses on evidence-centered design [ECD] as it applies to Life Science, see Haertel et al., Chapter 11 of this volume.) Likewise, while the emphasis is on large-scale assessment to support accountability, most of the issues raised in this chapter with respect to the design of individual science assessments are equally relevant to the design of classroom science assessments to support teaching and learning.

Current Practices and Future Trends in Large-Scale Science Assessment

Currently in the United States, large-scale assessment of science occurs much less frequently than mathematics and English language arts (ELA), but much more frequently than any other subject. At the state level, this reflects the priorities of the No Child Left Behind Act of 2001 (NCLB), which mandates yearly testing of mathematics and ELA from grade 3 to grade 8 and at least once during grades 10–12, but only mandates testing of science at least three times during K–12 education—once during grades 3–5, once during grades 6–9, and once during grades 10–12. As of the 2013–2014 school year,[1] a majority of states (69 percent) assess science only three times, the federally mandated minimum.

Assessment of science in high school presents a particular challenge compared to earlier grades because of the flexibility of the curricular sequence: not all students take the same science courses in the same order. As Biology courses are taken by more students than Physics, Chemistry, and Earth and Space Science, many states use high school science assessments that predominantly or exclusively cover Life Science content, with Physical and Earth and Space Science assessed much less frequently. On the grades 10–12 NCLB assessments, all states assess Life Science, while only just over half assess Physical Science (59 percent) and Earth and Space Science (55 percent). By point of contrast, on the grades 3–5 NCLB assessments, all states assess Physical and Earth and Space Science in addition to Life Science, and in grades 6–9, the vast majority of states assess Physical Science (98 percent), Earth and Space Science (94 percent), and Life Science (96 percent).

Mirroring current practice for the NCLB assessments, states that have high school graduation requirements that include minimum assessment scores assess science less frequently than mathematics and ELA, and among the sciences, Life Science is assessed most frequently. Of the 26 states requiring minimum assessment scores to graduate, half include a science requirement. Of the 13 states with science requirements, 10 include a Life Science requirement, 4 include a Physical Science requirement, 4 include an Earth and Space Science requirement, and 3 leave the choice of science up to the individual student.

A recent trend changing the landscape of large-scale science assessment in the United States is the increasing adoption of course-specific assessments that are administered at the end of a course, to support an increased emphasis on standardized assessment-based student and teacher accountability. EOC exams are designed to deal with the flexibility of the curricular sequence in high school and aim to measure student learning and/or teacher effectiveness at the most appropriate time: immediately after the relevant content has been taught and learned. A single schoolwide annual assessment, as is the model in the lower grades, makes it more difficult to link the achievement of high school students to their enrollment in particular courses or their instruction by particular teachers. As more states implement or expand their student and teacher accountability programs, driven in part by federal initiatives like the NCLB and the Race to the Top competitive grants, EOC exams are becoming more popular.

At the same time, there has been an effort to have EOC exams serve multiple purposes, rather than allowing the number of science assessments facing high school students to proliferate. As one example, half of the states (47 percent) are reporting EOC results to satisfy their NCLB requirements to assess science during grades 10–12. Only a small number of states (12 percent) currently administer parallel sets of science assessments: one schoolwide assessment that meets the NCLB requirements and a set of EOC exams that is used for other purposes. There has also been a trend toward replacing high school exit exams with minimum required scores on EOC exams. Of the 13 states with science assessment-based graduation requirements, 8 base those requirements on minimum EOC exam scores rather than a separate graduation exam.

This desire to use EOC exams for multiple purposes has led to a larger number of Life Science EOC exams than Physical and Earth and Space Science EOC exams. Because both the NCLB assessments and high school graduation exams are administered to all students and because not all students are required to take Chemistry, Physics, or Earth and Space Science, there have been many more Biology EOC exams developed: a majority of states have an EOC Biology exam (61 percent), while far fewer have an EOC Chemistry exam (24 percent), an EOC Physics exam (16 percent), an EOC Earth and Space Science exam (8 percent), and/or an EOC Physical Science exam (6 percent). The number of EOC science exams is rapidly increasing: in the 2011–2012 school year, the number of states with EOC exams in Biology (45 percent), Chemistry (14 percent), Physics (12 percent), Earth and Space Science (8 percent), and/or Physical Science (2 percent) was considerably smaller (Zinth, 2012).

At present, the primary functions of state science EOC exams are satisfying NCLB requirements and contributing to high school graduation requirements. Other accountability purposes are becoming more prevalent, however. With respect to student accountability, seven states require (and two recommend) that science EOC exam results be integrated into the final student grade for the course, with weights ranging from 15 percent to 30 percent. With respect to teacher accountability, 19 states are developing or have implemented teacher evaluation systems that take into account data on student growth as a requirement of receiving Race to the Top funds. Of these 19 states, 14 have science EOC exams that can be used as part of the evaluation of high school science teachers. The ability of EOC exams to simultaneously satisfy NCLB requirements, replace high school graduation exams, and support standardized assessment-based student and teacher accountability systems has provided a strong incentive for states to create new EOC exams in science.

Because of the increasing adoption of more EOC exams and the recent release of the NRC framework and the NGSS, most states are currently developing, considering developing, or redesigning large-scale science assessments, particularly in Physical and Earth and Space Science. As they plan the design and implementation of these new assessments, many states are expected to consider the recommendations of the NRC framework, whether or not they decide to fully adopt the NGSS. Given the expected impact of these documents on large-scale science assessment, we next describe four major shifts in form and content embodied by the NRC framework and the NGSS, in comparison to current state science standards. Each of these shifts has implications for the design of both state assessment systems and individual science assessments, which we discuss in later sections.

New Expectations for Science Standards

Existing state science standards, with their emphasis on the mastery of discrete, grade-specific facts and concepts, and the acquisition of low-level process-based skills decontextualized from real-world problems and solutions, are perceived as failing to prepare high school graduates to enter and succeed in science, technology, and engineering careers (Carnegie Corporation of New York & Institute for Advanced Study, 2007). Over the last decade, a consensus has emerged that standards for science education must change in fundamental ways; we characterize this consensus as involving four major shifts:

1   A shift away from knowing many individual pieces of scientific knowledge and toward understanding a small number of core ideas and concepts.
2   A shift away from mastering simple ideas and skills and toward making grade-appropriate progress toward deeper understanding and more sophisticated practice.
3   A shift away from separately learning science concepts and inquiry skills and toward integrating understanding and practice.
4   A shift away from acquiring narrowly defined, decomposed inquiry skills and toward engaging in a wider range of more authentic scientific practices.

Standards documents and assessment frameworks of the last decade have incorporated some of these shifts to varying degrees, notably the 2009 NAEP Science Framework (National Assessment Governing Board, 2008) and the Science College Board Standards for College Success (College Board, 2009), both of which embrace an integrated approach to content and practice. Drawing on these previous documents, and strongly influenced by the American Association for the Advancement of Science (AAAS) Project 2061, the National Science Teachers Association (NSTA) 2009 Anchors project, and the learning progression movement in science education (NRC, 2007), the NRC, in partnership with NSTA, AAAS, Achieve, Inc., and the Carnegie Corporation of New York, developed *A Framework for K–12 Science Education: Practices, Crosscutting Concepts, and Core Ideas* (2012). The NRC framework fully embraces the four shifts above, recommending that science standards should emphasize the increasing sophistication of a small number of core ideas over many years and an integrated approach to content and authentic scientific practice.

In an effort to implement the recommendations of the NRC framework, a consortium of 26 lead state partners, led by Achieve, Inc., developed the NGSS (NGSS Lead States, 2013a). As lead state partners, these states have stated their intention to give serious consideration to adopting and assessing the standards and to develop implementation plans to serve as models for all states. The NGSS have met with pushback from some corners, but even if the standards are not widely adopted, the influence of the NRC framework is considerable; at the time of this writing, in addition to the 13 states that have formally adopted the standards, many more are developing their own standards that are consistent with the recommendations of the NRC framework. In the discussions that follow, we focus on the NGSS because they exemplify an attempt to fully implement the recommendations of the NRC framework. The issues we raise, however, are relevant for science assessments aligned with any new science standards that are consistent with the trends described above.

The NGSS are written as performance expectations (PEs), which are meant to be "assessable statements of what students should know and be able to do" (NGSS Lead States, 2013d, p. 1). An example of a grade 3 Physical Science PE, given the identifier 3-PS2-1, is: "Plan and conduct an investigation to provide evidence of the effects of balanced and unbalanced forces on the motion of an object" (NGSS Lead States, 2013a). While PEs are not assessment tasks in and of themselves, they have been written with assessment in mind and are intended to be clear statements of the abilities for which students should be held accountable. Indeed, one can imagine the text of each PE being used as the stem for an open-ended performance assessment item, with a fair amount of scaffolding added to define the task, but without much further modification.

Notably, most PEs are accompanied by Clarification Statements and/or Assessment Boundaries, explicit statements about appropriate and inappropriate assessment task design. For example, 3-PS2-1 is accompanied by a Clarification Statement that suggests specific materials and experimental set-ups that could be designed into an item assessing this PE: "Examples could include an unbalanced force on one side of a ball can make it start moving; and, balanced forces pushing on a box from both sides will not produce any motion at all" (NGSS Lead States, 2013a). Likewise, 3-PS2-1 is accompanied by an Assessment Boundary that sets limits on what an item should require of the student: "Assessment is limited to one variable at a time: number, size, or direction of forces. Assessment does not include quantitative force size, only qualitative and relative. Assessment is limited to gravity being addressed as a force that pulls objects down" (NGSS Lead States, 2013a). Together, the Clarification Statements and Assessment Boundaries provide information for assessment developers to help craft specific assessment tasks based on the PEs.

Rather than identifying stand-alone skills or concepts, each PE draws on and integrates a science and engineering practice (SEP), one or more disciplinary core ideas (DCIs), and one crosscutting concept (CC). For example, 3-PS2-1 draws on one SEP (Practice 3: Planning and Carrying out Investigations), two DCIs (PS2.A: Forces and Motion; and PS2.B: Types of Interactions), and one CC (Concept 2: Cause and Effect). Moreover, each of these elements is part of an explicit progression describing how learning develops over time.[2] Indeed, the NGSS make the logic of progressions a central organizing feature, articulating a sequence of Grade Band Endpoints that describes the levels of understanding or practice that are expected by the ends of grades 2, 5, 8, and 12. These progressions, based on the framework and illustrated in the appendices of the NGSS, show how each SEP, DCI, and CC can be introduced in a meaningful way at the K–2 level and develop in sophistication over the years.

Impact of the New Standards on the Design of Assessment Systems

As described above, the NRC framework and the NGSS reflect a dramatic reimagining of the foundations of K–12 science education, embodying a growing consensus that four major shifts are required in how science is taught and learned. These changes likewise imply four major shifts in how competency in science should be assessed:

1   A shift away from assessing many individual pieces of scientific knowledge and toward assessing a small number of core ideas and concepts.
2   A shift away from assessing mastery of simple ideas and skills and toward assessing grade-appropriate progress toward deeper understanding and more sophisticated practice.
3   A shift away from separately assessing science concepts and inquiry skills and toward integrating understanding and practice in assessment tasks.
4   A shift away from assessing narrowly defined, decomposed inquiry skills and toward assessing a wider range of more authentic scientific practices.

These shifts have implications for the design of both individual science assessments and state science assessment systems. The latter is the focus of this section.

The first shift, the need to focus on a small number of core ideas, may seem to imply that the number of standards has decreased, but this is not the case. In fact, this shift is driven in part by the desire to greatly expand the presence of Earth and Space Science in the standards and the recognition that such an addition would be unreasonable without a corresponding reduction elsewhere. The NRC framework and the NGSS emphasize Life Science, Physical Science, and Earth and Space Science in roughly equal thirds across all grade levels. Although this balance is similar to the traditional balance in elementary school and middle school, it represents a dramatically increased focus on Earth and Space Science in high school, akin to the addition of an entire year of coursework (Wysession, 2013). To accommodate this increased focus, the number of physics and chemistry topics has been reduced in the standards, allowing the introduction of new topics focused on Earth and Space Science without expanding the overall number of topics. The result is a characterization of scientific domains (Life Science, Physical Science, and Earth and Space Science) that is different from the one traditionally used to structure high school science courses (biology, physics, and chemistry).

Although some high schools are expected to respond to the increased emphasis on Earth and Space Science by adding a fourth course on Earth and Space Science to the usual biology, physics, and chemistry course offerings, the majority of high schools are expected to eventually switch to one of three modified three-course maps described in the NGSS (NGSS Lead States, 2013c).

The first modified three-course map, and the one recommended by the NGSS, is called the Conceptual Progressions Model. This map proposes three new courses that mix and integrate material traditionally taught in separate science courses. The first course in this sequence covers mostly Physical Science topics, with some related Earth and Space Science topics. The second course covers mostly Life Science topics, with some related Physical Science topics. The third and final course in this sequence covers mostly Earth and Space Science topics, with some related Life Science topics. This model is said to be more efficient, require less reteaching of concepts and teaching of concepts out of their natural order, and better support the development of concepts that are cross-disciplinary.

Recognizing the major differences between the recommended Conceptual Progressions Model and current practice, the NGSS also describe two other modified three-course maps. These maps are designed to minimize disruption to existing curricula and methods of teacher preparation at the cost of less-than-maximal student learning. The Science Domains Model merges physics and chemistry into a single Physical Science course, with separate courses covering Earth and Space Science and Life Science. The Modified Science Domains Model divides the new Earth and Space Science standards among traditional biology, physics, and chemistry courses.

If different high schools within a state adopt different course maps, they will be teaching the content of the standards in different courses. This will complicate the development of science EOC exams for the state. One possible approach is to develop parallel sets of EOC exams, one set for each modified course map. A benefit of this approach is that the assessments would be aligned with the curriculum, and students and teachers will be evaluated on the full range of topics covered by each course. A drawback is that having parallel sets of EOC exams would complicate direct comparisons across students and teachers, as they would be responsible for learning and teaching different material. A second possible approach is to develop assessments that only cover the standards common to the courses in different course maps. For example, under this approach, a Physical Science EOC exam would cover only those Physical Science standards that are taught in both the Physical Science course from the Science Domains Model and the mostly Physical Science first course in the Conceptual Progression Model. Likewise, an Earth and Space Science EOC exam would cover only those Earth and Space Science standards that are taught in both the Earth and Space Science course from the Science Domains Model and the mostly Earth and Space Science third course in the Conceptual Progression Model. A benefit of this approach is that it would allow more straightforward comparisons among students and teachers working in the different course sequences, although selection bias would likely be a concern in interpretation. A drawback is that many standards would not be assessed at all, and these orphan standards would be unlikely to receive the same level of attention in the classroom as the standards that are assessed (Koretz & Hamilton, 2006; Koretz, McCaffrey, & Hamilton, 2001).

The second shift, the need to assess grade-appropriate progress toward deeper understanding and more sophisticated practice, highlights the need to situate and interpret student achievement within progressions of learning over multiple years. Minimally, this might be accomplished through traditional standard-setting procedures, in which the Grade Band Endpoints described in the NRC framework are used as the basis for defining the cut-offs between proficiency levels for a particular grade. Students could also be associated with levels of the progression based on their responses to particular items (Pollack, Atkins-Burnett, Rock, & Weiss, 2005) or, more ambitiously, using psychometric modeling (Briggs & Alonzo, 2012; Diakow, Torres Irribarra, & Wilson, 2013).

Looking across grades, the progressions of the NRC framework may suggest the use of vertical scaling (Kolen & Brennan, 2014). At the high school level, the independent nature of the subject matter in each science course has been a major hurdle for the vertical scaling of EOC exams. With a shift to a more integrated approach, such as that recommended by the Conceptual Progression Model course map, vertical scaling could become possible for states in which course maps are chosen at the state level. Despite this new possibility, we would caution that vertical scaling often rests on unexamined and questionable assumptions (Briggs, 2013). Moreover, there is no a priori reason to believe that a progression should be associated with a single scale; the relationship between scales and progressions may be complex (Wilson, 2009).

The third shift, the need to assess the multi-dimensional learning represented by the multiple progressions in the new standards, is related to a common issue in assessment design: the choice of how many constructs or subscales to measure (Haberman & Sinharay, 2010; Sinharay, 2010; Sinharay, Haberman, & Puhan, 2007). In theory, each of the progressions modeled in the standards could be measured in one assessment system, but this would require a large number of items to produce reliable scale scores for each dimension. A comprehensive Physical Science assessment system, for example, would include 8 SEPs, 13 Physical Science DCIs, and 7 CCs. A well-designed item based on a PE could simultaneously gather evidence of at least three of these progressions (one SEP, one or more DCI, and one CC), but a large number of items would still be necessary to cover all of the progressions, far more than could be administered to one student given constraints on testing time and student fatigue. At the school or district level, matrix sampling could likely be used to produce reliable estimates, with only a small proportion of the total item set administered to each student. However, at the student and teacher levels, a trade-off will need to be managed between the number of subscales reported and the reliability of the scale scores.

One possible approach would be for an assessment to sample from the progressions described in the NGSS, only assessing a subset of the SEPs, DCIs, and CCs, similar to how existing state assessments sample from the state standards. However, unless this sampling is carefully controlled, so that all progressions have an equal probability of appearing on a given year's assessment, reallocation of teaching is likely to occur, perhaps inflating test scores over time (Koretz & Hamilton, 2006; Koretz et al., 2001).

Another possible approach would be to abandon the goal of producing reliable measures of each dimension, opting instead to report one or a few composite scores with high reliability (but ambiguous meaning due to the conflation of many separate progressions), coupled with a detailed profile of student learning that is less reliable (due to the small number of items measuring each dimension). This approach is similar to that taken by the major assessment inventories, such as the Stanford 10, Terra Nova 3, and the Iowa Test of Basic Skills. One could imagine, for example, a state assessment system that reports five composite scores at a given grade level: Physical Science DCIs, Earth and Space Science DCIs, Life Science DCIs, Science and Engineering Practices, and Cross-Cutting Concepts.

In practice, there will always be a tension between measuring a small number of subscales with greater reliability and measuring a large number of subscales with less reliability. The appropriate balance for a particular assessment will depend on many factors. For example, there may be more of an emphasis on coverage for diagnosing and placing individual students in courses or programs, while there may be more of an emphasis on reliability for high-stakes decisions surrounding teacher and school evaluation.

Finally, the fourth shift, the need to assess a wider range of more authentic science practices, will likely require a renewed interest and investment in alternative item formats, including open-ended constructed-response, technology-enhanced, computer-based, and hands-on tasks. Of course, the ability of these performance-based items to assess more sophisticated practices comes at the cost of increased time and resources spent on development, administration, and/or scoring, and a potential negative impact on reliability (Messick, 1994; Shavelson, Baxter, & Pine, 1992). A later section discusses the need for these alternative item formats to assess the science practices called for in the standards and provides an extended account of the issues faced by one state as they developed and implemented simulation-based items in their state assessment system.

It appears likely that the NRC framework and the NGSS present too many challenges to be met successfully by a single end-of-year assessment for the purposes of accountability. The need for items that take longer to administer and the need to assess multiple dimensions of learning implies that no single assessment could provide reliable coverage of a reasonable subset of standards. For this reason, it is expected that states will need to develop a robust system of science assessments to serve the needs of accountability, in which the results from end-of-year tests are supplemented by other sources, including large-scale formative or diagnostic tests as well as district-supervised, teacher-developed classroom assessments (Pellegrino et al., 2014). While coordinating these different assessments and integrating their results presents a new set of challenges, a system of this scope is likely to be necessary to reliably assess a sufficiently broad range of the standards.

Impact of the New Standards on the Design of Individual Assessments

In addition to its impact on the design of state assessment systems, the structure of the new standards has important implications for the design of individual science assessments as well. Because of the extent and the specificity of this structure, we believe the development of new science assessments consistent with the standards will require a principled approach to assessment design. In the next section, we describe a particular approach to principled assessment design, called *construct modeling*, that is well suited to the development of science assessments consistent with the four major shifts in form and content embodied by the NRC framework and the NGSS. We then discuss these shifts in more detail and give specific examples of how these shifts will affect the design of science assessments.

Construct Modeling: A Principled Approach to Assessment Design

Principled assessment design refers to the development of an assessment with an explicit argument for how evidence will be gathered and interpreted that bears on the underlying knowledge, skills, and processes that the assessment is intended to address. Such an argument should include (a) a model of cognition, (b) tasks that elicit observations of student performance, and (c) methods of interpretation that connect the performance outcomes to the model of cognition (NRC, 2001). ECD, as described in other chapters in this volume, is an example of principled assessment design, and resources exist that discuss the application of ECD to the development of science assessments (e.g., Haertel et al., Chapter 11 of this volume; Quellmalz, Davenport, & Timms, 2012).

The approach to principled assessment design described here is called *construct modeling* (Brown & Wilson, 2011; Wilson, 2005), which has been used to develop several curriculum-based science assessment systems measuring both conceptual understanding and scientific practices in elementary, middle, and high school (Black, Wilson, & Yao, 2011; Lehrer, Kim, Ayers, & Wilson, 2014; Scalise, Claesgens, Wilson, & Stacy, 2006; Wilson & Sloane, 2000). Construct modeling is similar to ECD in its focus on developing an evidentiary chain of reasoning linking task design and scoring procedures to an underlying model of cognition. Construct modeling is unique, however, in its adoption of a particular progression-based model of cognition that defines the expected, qualitative levels of understanding or sophistication that students are likely to pass through on their way from intuition to expertise. For this reason, we believe construct modeling is particularly well suited for measuring the progression-based competencies defined by the NGSS.

Expanding upon the NRC (2001) model, the practice of assessment can be characterized as a cyclical process involving four steps (Brown & Wilson, 2011). In this model, illustrated in Figure 12.1, a cycle of assessment is the process by which a *question* about a student is answered, asking how much of one or more latent variables—representing, for example,

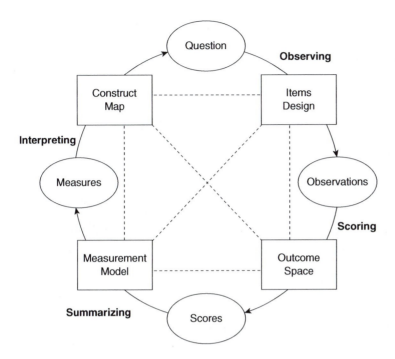

Figure 12.1 The four building blocks involved in construct modeling, each mediating one of the four steps of assessment.

Source: Brown, Nagashima, Fu, Timms, and Wilson (2010).

abilities, aptitudes, or proficiencies—they possess. The four steps in the cycle are (1) *observing*: eliciting performances assumed to depend upon the latent variable(s), leading to a set of *observations*; (2) *scoring*: categorizing different observed performances and assigning them relative value, or *scores*; (3) *summarizing*: combining the values of the individual performances to yield *measures* or *estimates* of each latent variable; and (4) *interpreting*: using the measures of the latent variable(s) to answer the *question*. Although the measures—the reported scale scores—are often thought of as the results of an assessment, the cycle of assessment is not complete until these numbers are interpreted, answering the question of how much of the latent variable(s) the student possesses, either relative to other students (as in norm referencing) or to descriptive criteria (as in criterion referencing).

Construct modeling involves the design, implementation, and evaluation of four building blocks termed the *construct map*, the *items design*, the *outcome space*, and the *measurement model* (Wilson, 2005). Each of these building blocks is designed to (a) mediate and provide structure for one of the four steps in a cycle of assessment, (b) reflect a single, meaningful latent variable or construct, and (c) be consistent with the other building blocks (Figure 12.1). Together, the building blocks form a coherent system of assessment that embodies the necessary evidentiary argument connecting a model of cognition, tasks, and methods of interpretation.

Construct modeling begins by creating a construct map that describes the expected, qualitative levels of understanding or sophistication that students may pass through on their way from intuition to expertise.[3] Examples of construct maps are given in the following sections (see, for example, Figures 12.5 and 12.23). The construct map is used to guide the design of the items so that the observations are most likely to be useful, informative, and easily interpretable with respect to the latent proficiency. Outcome spaces are then developed that describe in detail the qualitatively different kinds of student responses that can be elicited by the items and map these categories of responses to the levels of the construct map. In doing so, outcome spaces are tools that facilitate the process of scoring—categorizing and valuing—student responses, ensuring that scores are meaningfully related to the latent proficiency. The scored response data is then scaled using item response modeling.

Throughout the process of assessment development, the construct map serves as the foundation, representing the explicit model of cognition about which the assessment is designed to gather evidence. As described above, each PE in the NGSS draws on at least three proficiencies: a SEP, one or more DCIs, and a CC. In the construct modeling approach, each of these proficiencies and their associated progressions could be modeled with a construct map.

In the following sections, we return to the four fundamental shifts in the form and content of science standards recommended by the NRC framework and embodied by the NGSS, providing specific examples of the ways that construct modeling can be used to guide the design of items and scoring procedures that are consistent with these shifts. Many of the examples of items and scoring guides in the following sections are from the 2005, 2009, and 2011 NAEP Science Assessments. Note that we do not use these examples because they are particularly bad offenders. Indeed, the opposite is true: NAEP items are some of the best publicly available examples of large-scale science assessment items in the United States, representing a high standard of quality. Moreover, as mentioned above, the 2009 NAEP Science Framework (National Assessment Governing Board, 2008) made early progress in implementing some of the above shifts (Fu, Raizen, & Shavelson, 2009) and was one of several source documents used in the development of the NRC framework. The items we have selected are not meant to represent NAEP items in general, but are used instead to illustrate common issues in the design of items and scoring procedures without resorting to invented strawmen.

A Shift from Facts to Core Ideas

The first foundational shift in the new standards is a reduction in emphasis on items that simply measure students' knowledge of science facts. As the NRC framework argues, people can acquire such facts easily in the information age, and it is therefore more important to assess whether a student has the core ideas needed to evaluate and select reliable sources of scientific information than whether they already possess that information:

> The continuing expansion of scientific knowledge makes it impossible to teach all the ideas related to a given discipline in exhaustive detail during the K–12 years. But given the cornucopia of information instantly available today, an important role of science education is not to teach "all the facts" but rather to prepare students with sufficient core knowledge so that they can later acquire additional information on their own.
>
> (NRC, 2012, pp. 30–31)

As an example of the difficulty involved in separating knowledge of science facts and understanding of core ideas in assessment items, consider the item in Figure 12.2, from the 2005 NAEP Science Assessment.

To get a full score on this item, the student needs to indicate both an understanding of the core idea of "stored energy" (described in the NRC framework in DCI PS3.A: Definitions of Energy) and knowledge of the particular way that a hamburger stores energy. Notably, to get a partially correct score on this item, a response needs to only indicate one of these two things; that is, responses that only indicate knowledge of a science fact receive the same score as responses that only indicate understanding of the concept.

3. Is a hamburger an example of stored energy? Explain why or why not.

_____

_____

_____

_____

_____

Score & Description
Complete Student response indicates "yes" and states that a hamburger contains fat (grease), protein, carbohydrate, and nutrients and gives some indication of energy transfer. OR Student response indicates "yes" and traces the energy through the food chain. **Partial** Student response indicates "yes" and states that a hamburger contains fat (grease), protein, carbohydrates, and nutrients. OR Student response indicates "yes" and states that transfer of energy takes place. OR Student response indicates "yes" and states that food is energy/meat is energy/meat contains energy. **Unsatisfactory/Incorrect** Student demonstrates no understanding of the concept of stored energy by answering "no," or answers "yes" and gives no or an incorrect or irrelevant response.

Figure 12.2 An item assessing both knowledge of science facts and understanding of core ideas.

Source: U.S. Department of Education, Institute of Education Sciences, National Center for Education Statistics, National Assessment of Educational Progress, 2005 Science Assessment.

There are many relevant science facts that pertain to this item, including that hamburgers are a source of protein; hamburgers are generally high in fat; food energy can be stored as carbohydrates, proteins, and fats; fats have a higher density of energy storage than carbohydrates and proteins; and carbohydrates and proteins have 4 cal/g while fats have 9 cal/g. One difficulty facing assessment developers is that these facts are very tempting to use as the basis for assessment items. They are falsifiable and lend themselves easily to writing multiple-choice items. Focusing on core ideas, however, is trickier. Not all the implications of a core idea are always immediately clear, so it can be more difficult to define an exhaustive outcome space a priori.

As an example of this latter difficulty, consider the second response in Figure 12.3 ("Yes, because it just sits there & does nothing"), provided by NAEP as an example of an Unsatisfactory/ Incorrect response. This response, while sarcastic, is arguably correct. Stored energy is defined as energy stored in a gravitational, electric, or magnetic field. While the item writers were expecting a response that refers to energy stored in an electric field ("chemical energy" or "food energy" is energy stored in the electric fields surrounding atoms and molecules), this response refers to energy stored in a gravitational field ("potential energy"). Because the hamburger is not described as being in motion ("it just sits there & does nothing"), the student may have understood that it must be an example of stored energy rather than motion energy ("kinetic energy").

Unsatisfactory/Incorrect—Student Response

A hamburger is not an example
for stored energy because
when you eat a hamburger
makes you slow down all
of your energy

yes, because it just sits
there & does nothing.

Scorer comments:

The first response incorrectly states that a hamburger is not an example of stored energy. The second response states that a hamburger is an example of stored energy but provides an incorrect explanation.

Figure 12.3 Examples of unsatisfactory/incorrect student responses to the hamburger item (Figure 12.2).

Source: U.S. Department of Education, Institute of Education Sciences, National Center for Education Statistics, National Assessment of Educational Progress, 2005 Science Assessment.

Although it might be tempting to dismiss this example as either a poorly written item or a poorly designed scoring guide, there will always be a tension in item development between valuing conceptual understanding of the core idea and valuing knowledge of relevant science facts. Some students will demonstrate evidence of the former but not the latter, while others will demonstrate evidence of the latter but not the former. If these different types of evidence represent different levels of proficiency, they must be captured in the scoring guide. Importantly, the NRC framework values evidence of conceptual understanding of the core idea over evidence of knowledge of relevant science facts.

How might the scoring guide for the hamburger item be revised to better reflect this priority? Figure 12.4 shows three possible revised scoring guides. Scoring Guide 1 still values both the core idea and the science facts but prioritizes the former, while Scoring Guide 3 only values the core idea and ignores all evidence of knowledge of science facts. Scoring Guide 2 values knowledge of the science facts, but only at low levels of understanding.

Some assessment developers may be attracted to Scoring Guide 1, because it maximizes the information content of the item and will contribute more strongly to the reliability of the assessment. However, this increase in reliability may come at the cost of validity, if respondents who give evidence of scientific knowledge do not necessarily have more conceptual understanding than respondents who do not. For example, it is possible that some students who understand the core idea of stored energy would not be compelled to add to their response a description of how energy is stored in a hamburger, especially as the item stem does not ask for this additional information. Consequently, these students would receive only 2 points for their response, while other students with the same level of understanding would receive 3 points for including extra information about how a hamburger contains fat, protein, carbohydrates, and/or nutrients. Since these higher scores would not, in this case, actually indicate higher levels of understanding, the validity of this item would suffer, perhaps evidenced by a lower point-biserial correlation of the item scores with the total test scores when using this scoring guide compared to the others shown in Figure 12.4.

Scoring Guide 3 ignores all mention of the science facts and only rewards understanding of the core idea of stored energy. Because higher scores are unambiguously associated with having more

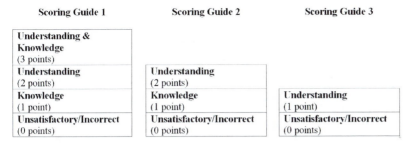

Scoring Guide 1   Scoring Guide 2   Scoring Guide 3

Understanding: Student response gives some indication of energy transfer OR traces the energy through the food chain
Knowledge: Student response states that a hamburger contains fat (grease), protein, carbohydrate, and/or nutrients.
Unsatisfactory/Incorrect: Student demonstrates no understanding of the concept of stored energy by answering "no," or answers "yes" and gives no or an incorrect or irrelevant response.

Figure 12.4 Three possible revised scoring guides for the "hamburger" item, illustrating a trade-off between validity and reliability.

of the construct—in this case, conceptual understanding of the DCIs—Scoring Guide 3 is likely to show the strongest evidence of validity based on internal structure when included on an assessment aligned with the NGSS. This increase in validity, however, generally comes at the cost of reduced reliability. In the present example, which only distinguishes between two levels of understanding, the number of response options has been cut in half. (For scoring guides that distinguish between more levels of understanding, the effect of ignoring science facts would be mitigated.)

Scoring Guide 2 represents one possible compromise between maximizing validity or reliability. It is plausible that a student who cannot articulate a complete understanding of the core idea of stored energy may still recognize the relevance of fat, protein, carbohydrates, and/or nutrients with respect to getting energy from eating a hamburger. Consequently, while some students who mention these facts may simply be stating what they know about hamburgers in the hope that they will get some credit, other students who mention these facts may be demonstrating a nascent, incomplete, or not fully articulated understanding of the concept of stored energy. Therefore, differentiating these responses from Unsatisfactory/Incorrect responses and giving them partial credit may be warranted. That is to say, the benefit to reliability from increasing the number of response categories may outweigh the cost to validity from giving higher scores to some responses that may not indicate a greater understanding of the core construct by the student.

In practice, the question of which of the three suggested scoring guides best manages the trade-off between validity and reliability would be answered most convincingly by trying them each in separate analyses, comparing the relevant item statistics and reliability measures from each analysis, and making an informed decision. However, we expect that a scoring guide that values articulation of science facts only at low levels of understanding—as illustrated by Scoring Guide 2—will often manage the trade-off well.

A Shift from Grade Level-Appropriate Mastery to Progressions

The second foundational shift represented in the new standards is the explicit recognition that learning develops over time and can be characterized by progressions. As mentioned above, the NRC framework and the NGSS make the logic of progressions a central organizing feature, articulating a sequence of Grade Band Endpoints that describe the understanding that is expected by the end of grades 2, 5, 8, and 12 and showing how each core idea and practice can be introduced in a meaningful way at the K–2 level and develop in sophistication over the years.

This is a change from many other standards, including the Common Core State Standards, in which standards at the lower grade levels often consist of easier skills or understanding that younger children can master, making it plausible that they can provide a completely correct response. A shift from mastery of basic ideas to age-appropriate but incomplete (and often technically incorrect) understanding of core ideas presents several challenges for item design. It is much easier to design items around correct responses than it is to design items around partial understandings. Fully correct or fully incorrect propositions are straightforward to use in the design of selected-response or short constructed-response items, forming the bases of response options. In contrast, intermediate levels of understanding are more difficult to write in propositional form, making it more likely that items would require some level of open-ended construction or a way for the student to illustrate or show the effects of their partial understanding.

Likewise, scoring of items developed for measuring progressions can also be challenging. In theory, polytomously scored items are well suited to differentiating between levels of a progression, because each level of the progression can be associated with different scores. In practice, however, defining the middle scoring levels of a progression-based item can be considerably more challenging than for a traditional partial credit item. In partial credit scoring, a fully correct response garners the top score, a response that is completely wrong gets a zero score, and the middle scores consist of responses that have some, but not all, of the required components. In general, individual score points are assigned to individually correct components of a response. In traditional items, identifying the discrete components of a fully correct response is relatively straightforward. As an example, in the NAEP hamburger item (Figure 12.2), the middle score of 1 indicates the response contains either a description of how the hamburger stores energy or a description of energy transfer, but not both. In other items, middle scores may indicate a response that demonstrates some, but not all, of the required solution steps.

In contrast, for items targeting understanding of core ideas in science, it can be difficult to identify the individually correct components of a complete response. Take, for example, DCI ESS1.B: Earth and the Solar System, which includes the following:

> Earth and the moon, sun, and planets have predictable patterns of movement. These patterns, which are explainable by gravitational forces and conservation laws, in turn explain many large-scale phenomena observed on Earth.

> (NRC, 2012, p. 175)

These phenomena include the day/night cycle, the phases of the moon, and the seasons. A fully correct understanding of this core idea involves a scientifically accurate model of the solar system, and a fully incorrect understanding would most likely mean that the student does not recognize any of the relevant patterns of movement. But how should the middle score levels be defined? Which patterns are recognized first, and which phenomena are the easiest to understand, thereby reflecting a lower level of the construct? Which come later or are harder and, therefore, reflect a higher level of the construct? Designing the middle levels of a scoring guide is not as straightforward as conducting a task decomposition and instead requires an understanding of how learning progresses in this particular topic area. A well-developed scoring guide should reflect both a measure of the individual components that make up a full response and an understanding of how these components fit together into the progression for that topic and grade.

The progressions described in the NGSS are a necessary starting point for developing these scoring guides, but they are not sufficient. For DCI ESS1.B, the Grade Band Endpoints dealing specifically with the day/night cycle, the phases of the moon, and the seasons are illustrated in Table 12.1.

Table 12.1 Grade Band Endpoints for the Earth and Space Science Disciplinary Core Idea ESS1.B

Grade Band	Endpoint
End of grade 2	Seasonal patterns of sunrise and sunset can be observed, described, and predicted.
End of grade 5	The orbits of Earth around the Sun and of the Moon around Earth, together with the rotation of Earth about an axis between its north and south poles, cause observable patterns. These include day and night; daily and seasonal changes in the length and direction of shadows; phases of the Moon; and different positions of the Sun, Moon, and stars at different times of the day, month, and year.
End of grade 8	Earth's spin axis is fixed in direction over the short term but tilted relative to its orbit around the Sun. The seasons are a result of that tilt and are caused by the differential intensity of sunlight on different areas of Earth across the year.

Note: ESS1.B includes an understanding of additional phenomena: ocean tides, lunar and solar eclipses, and cycles of ice ages. For simplicity of presentation, these additional phenomena are omitted.

Source: Adapted from NRC (2012).

Note that the progression begins to identify the sequence in which components of the fully correct model are acquired. For example, the rotation of the earth on its axis is understood before the tilt of that axis is understood. Likewise, the progression begins to identify when different phenomena can be explained. For example, the day/night cycle is easier to understand than the cause of the seasons. But there are many details left unspecified. Is the orbit of the earth around the sun easier to understand than the orbit of the moon around the earth? Can the phases of the moon be explained before the day/night cycle?

Consequently, the framework that the progression provides must be expanded to fully capture the range of responses students may give. This more detailed description of how learning progresses is provided by a construct map. An example from Briggs, Alonzo, Schwab, and Wilson (2006), describing a progression of understanding of the earth and the solar system, is shown in Figure 12.5.

This construct map expands on the progression in several important ways. First, it identifies further components of the model that should be more completely understood by students and when those components are added to the model. For example, Level 3 is an intermediate step on the way to the grade 5 endpoint: students have acquired the understanding that the earth orbits the sun but have not acquired all the details of this motion, believing perhaps that the earth orbits the sun once a day.

Second, it identifies the common errors and misconceptions students may have at each level and identifies the new information that has been learned. For example, a student at Level 3 may believe that the earth's orbit causes the day/night cycle. Taken at face value, this is just one of hundreds of misconceptions students may have, and it can be hard to value such a response as anything other than simply wrong. The construct map, however, identifies this misconception with a specific level of understanding and associates it with the acquisition of a new, correct component of the scientifically accurate model: the fact that the earth orbits the sun.

One way that a construct map is a useful tool for assessment developers is by serving as a master scoring guide for any polytomously scored item dealing with that core idea. For example, the construct map in Figure 12.5 could be used to consistently interpret and score responses to any items dealing with the day/night cycle, the phases of the moon, or the seasons. It can even be used to improve the scoring guides of existing items by aligning them with the progression. For instance, consider the item shown in Figure 12.6 from the 2005 NAEP Science Assessment. The original scoring guide is in the classic partial credit style: three components of a fully correct

Level	Description
5 8th grade	Student is able to put the motions of the Earth and Moon into a complete description of motion in the Solar System which explains: • the day/night cycle • the phases of the Moon (including the illumination of the Moon by the Sun) • the seasons
4 5th grade	Student is able to coordinate apparent and actual motion of objects in the sky. Student knows that: • the Earth is both orbiting the Sun and rotating on its axis • the Earth orbits the Sun once per year • the Earth rotates on its axis once per day, causing the day/night cycle and the appearance that the Sun moves across the sky • the Moon orbits the Earth once every 28 days, producing the phases of the Moon COMMON ERROR: Seasons are caused by the changing distance between the Earth and Sun. COMMON ERROR: The phases of the Moon are caused by a shadow of the planets, the Sun, or the Earth falling on the Moon.
3	Student knows that: • the Earth orbits the Sun • the Moon orbits the Earth • the Earth rotates on its axis However, student has not put this knowledge together with an understanding of apparent motion to form explanations and may not recognize that the Earth is both rotating and orbiting simultaneously. COMMON ERROR: It gets dark at night because the Earth goes around the Sun once a day.
2	Student recognizes that: • the Sun appears to move across the sky every day • the observable shape of the Moon changes every 28 days Student may believe that the Sun moves around the Earth. COMMON ERROR: All motion in the sky is due to the Earth spinning on its axis. COMMON ERROR: The Sun travels around the Earth. COMMON ERROR: It gets dark at night because the Sun goes around the Earth once a day. COMMON ERROR: The Earth is the center of the universe.
1	Student does not recognize the systematic nature of the appearance of objects in the sky. Student may not recognize that the Earth is spherical. COMMON ERROR: It gets dark at night because something (e.g., clouds, the atmosphere, "darkness") covers the Sun. COMMON ERROR: The phases of the Moon are caused by clouds covering the Moon. COMMON ERROR: The Sun goes below the Earth at night.
0	No evidence or off-track

© WestEd, 2002

Figure 12.5 A construct map describing a progression of understanding of the earth and the solar system.

Source: Briggs, Alonzo, Schwab, and Wilson (2002). Developed by WestEd in conjunction with the BEAR Center at the University of California, Berkeley, with NSF support (REC-0087848). Reprinted with permission.

14. Sometimes the Moon looks like a full circle, sometimes it looks like a half circle, and sometimes it looks like a crescent. Explain why the Moon appears to be different shapes at different times. You may use labeled drawings in your explanation.

Score & Description
Complete Student explanation includes all the points given below. Student can provide a drawing correctly illustrating the phases of the Moon. • The Moon is visible because it reflects (or is illuminated by) sunlight. • The Moon revolves around the Earth. • The portion of the illuminated half of the Moon that is visible from Earth changes, thus making the Moon appear to change shape. **Partial** Student explains 1 or 2 aspects of the causes of the phases of the Moon without major misconceptions. **Unsatisfactory/Incorrect** Student does not correctly explain any aspect of the phases of the Moon, or explains aspects but includes major misconceptions.

Figure 12.6 An item assessing understanding of the earth and the solar system.

Source: U.S. Department of Education, Institute of Education Sciences, National Center for Education Statistics, National Assessment of Educational Progress, 2005 Science Assessment.

response have been identified and the middle score is assigned to responses demonstrating only one or two of these three components. In 2005, only 3 percent of national respondents received the fully correct score, and 18 percent received the middle score.

According to the construct map in Figure 12.5, however, these three components are not indicative of the same level of understanding. Notably, the orbit of the moon around the earth is a more basic component than the illumination of the moon by the sun, implying that a response mentioning only the moon's orbit should receive a lesser score. Moreover, the common misconception that the phases of the moon are caused by a shadow persists all the way up through Level 4. Consequently, as the presence of this misconception in a response could be consistent with a relatively sophisticated level of understanding, it would not be appropriate to automatically give a response mentioning this misconception the lowest possible score.

For this item, using the construct map as a master scoring guide would increase both its reliability, by increasing the available score levels from three to four and thereby increasing the information content, and its validity, by providing a consistent means of interpreting different student responses in a way that reflects what is known about how understanding progresses for this core idea.

Traditionally, polytomously scored items are also constructed-response items, which greatly increases the time and cost associated with scoring. An innovation in item design that has not yet seen widespread adoption is the ordered multiple-choice (OMC) item (Briggs et al., 2006). OMC items combine the ease of administration and scoring associated with multiple-choice items with the benefits of polytomous scoring. Once a construct map has been created for a core idea, the levels of the construct map can be used to generate the response options for an OMC item. Two items assessing the above construct map are shown in Figure 12.7, one appropriate for grade 5 and the other appropriate for grade 8. Note that each multiple-choice item permits multiple score levels, corresponding to the different levels of the construct map.

Item appropriate for fifth graders:

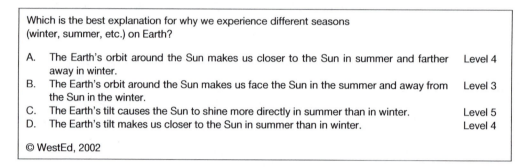

It is most likely colder at night because

A.	the Earth is at the furthest point in its orbit around the Sun.	Level 3
B.	the Sun has traveled to the other side of the Earth.	Level 2
C.	the Sun is below the Earth and the Moon does not emit as much heat as the Sun.	Level 1
D.	the place where it is night on Earth is rotated away from the Sun.	Level 4

© WestEd, 2002

Item appropriate for eighth graders:

Which is the best explanation for why we experience different seasons (winter, summer, etc.) on Earth?

A.	The Earth's orbit around the Sun makes us closer to the Sun in summer and farther away in winter.	Level 4
B.	The Earth's orbit around the Sun makes us face the Sun in the summer and away from the Sun in the winter.	Level 3
C.	The Earth's tilt causes the Sun to shine more directly in summer than in winter.	Level 5
D.	The Earth's tilt makes us closer to the Sun in summer than in winter.	Level 4

© WestEd, 2002

Figure 12.7 OMC items assessing understanding of the earth and the solar system, aligned with the construct map in Figure 12.5.

Source: Briggs, Alonzo, Schwab, and Wilson (2002). Developed by WestEd in conjunction with the BEAR Center at the University of California, Berkeley, with NSF support (REC-0087848). Reprinted with permission.

Because OMC items are polytomously scored, they usually have a larger information content and contribute more strongly to the reliability of the assessment than traditional multiple-choice items. At the same time, OMC items are easier to administer and cheaper to score than polytomously scored constructed-response items. Given these desirable properties, OMC items are well positioned to satisfy the needs of assessment designers attempting to implement the NGSS.

However, differentiating between levels of performance in a multiple-choice format can be difficult, because distractors that represent the performance of low-level students may stand out as obviously inferior when presented next to higher level performances. The use of computer-based items can help mitigate this by using multiple screens to present the distractors so that the advanced are shown only if the student demonstrates a minimum level of understanding. This is a type of adaptive testing where students respond to the same item but are exposed to different sets of response options.

An example of such an item from Scalise and Wilson (2008) is shown in Figure 12.8. The first screen presented to the student includes two response options that result in immediate scores but three response options that result in a new screen being presented, containing additional response options. Screen 2 contains response options that reflect a lower level of understanding, while Screen 3 contains response options that reflect a higher level of understanding. (In the original item, additional screens could be reached by students demonstrating the highest understanding.) By separating the response options in this way, response options containing technical terms, like "e density cloud," are not presented to low-ability students and are therefore less likely to be chosen simply because they sound correct.

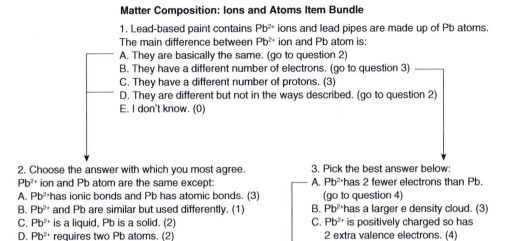

Matter Composition: Ions and Atoms Item Bundle

1. Lead-based paint contains Pb^{2+} ions and lead pipes are made up of Pb atoms. The main difference between Pb^{2+} ion and Pb atom is:
A. They are basically the same. (go to question 2)
B. They have a different number of electrons. (go to question 3)
C. They have a different number of protons. (3)
D. They are different but not in the ways described. (go to question 2)
E. I don't know. (0)

2. Choose the answer with which you most agree. Pb^{2+} ion and Pb atom are the same except:
A. Pb^{2+}has ionic bonds and Pb has atomic bonds. (3)
B. Pb^{2+} and Pb are similar but used differently. (1)
C. Pb^{2+} is a liquid, Pb is a solid. (2)
D. Pb^{2+} requires two Pb atoms. (2)

3. Pick the best answer below:
A. Pb^{2+}has 2 fewer electrons than Pb. (go to question 4)
B. Pb^{2+}has a larger e density cloud. (3)
C. Pb^{2+} is positively charged so has 2 extra valence electrons. (4)

Figure 12.8 An adaptive item assessing understanding of the composition of matter.

Source: Scalise and Wilson (2008). Reprinted courtesy of Lambert Academic Publishing.

A Shift from Isolated Knowledge and Skills to Integrated Knowledge and Practice

The third fundamental shift embodied in the new standards is the integration of scientific knowledge and practice. Rather than identifying stand-alone skills or concepts, each PE draws on and integrates a SEP, one or more DCIs, and one CC. Whereas most existing science assessment blueprints generally separate "inquiry" items from "conceptual" items, the NRC framework and other recent frameworks, including the 2009 NAEP framework (National Assessment Governing Board, 2008) and the 2009 College Board Standards for College Success (College Board, 2009), reject this dichotomy, explicitly intending that each PE be assessed as a holistic combination of content and practice.

The implications for assessment design are not as difficult to implement as may at first appear. The intent is not that inquiry items should be combined with conceptual items. Rather, this shift highlights that most, if not all, existing science assessment items are already combinations of a SEP and a DCI but also that often only one of these aspects is targeted at the appropriate grade level.

For example, traditional inquiry items that are designed to target the planning and conducting of an investigation, including the appropriate use of controlled variables, often involve very difficult scientific concepts. The assumption underlying this design decision is that the content should be equally unfamiliar to all respondents so as not to present an advantage to anyone. This is an effort to minimize construct-irrelevant variance, namely familiarity with the content. This is analogous to the choice of unfamiliar text passages in assessments of reading comprehension.

As an example, the item shown in Figure 12.9, from the 2005 NAEP Science Assessment, is a Scientific Investigation item intended to assess students' understanding of the importance of controlling variables in the design of an investigation. However, it inescapably involves some scientific concepts, as there is no such thing as a content-free scientific investigation. In particular, this item involves concepts from fluid dynamics and surface chemistry that a graduate student would find difficult. The grade 12 students taking this item are not expected to understand these concepts. Instead, the success of this item rests on the assumption that controlling variables

Oil is spilled onto the water from an ocean-going tanker. Investigators want to know whether wave motion will help disperse the oil. Design an experiment that they can carry out in a laboratory to find out whether wave motion will help disperse the oil. Describe the equipment they should use and the procedure they should follow.

Equipment:

_____

_____

_____

_____

_____

Procedure:

_____

_____

_____

_____

_____

_____

_____

_____

Figure 12.9 An inquiry item assessing controlled experiments with above-grade-level conceptual content.

Source: U.S. Department of Education, Institute of Education Sciences, National Center for Education Statistics, National Assessment of Educational Progress, 2005 Science Assessment.

when planning an investigation is a relatively context-free skill that can be acquired in one context and applied in new, unfamiliar contexts.

That this assumption was not met is reflected in the national results, where only 3 percent of grade 12 respondents mentioned the need for a controlled experiment in which the behavior of the oil is observed both in the presence and absence of waves. Contrast this grade 12 item with the grade 8 item from the 2009 NAEP Science Assessment shown in Figure 12.10, which involves grade-appropriate concepts from Newtonian mechanics. Although there are significant differences in item design that would tend to make this item easier—for example, the respondent is asked to critique an experimental set-up rather than design one from scratch—the difference in national performance is nonetheless striking, with 61 percent of grade 8 students mentioning the need to control the surface on which the experiments are conducted. Evidently, the understanding and application of controlled experiments that these grade 8 students demonstrate in a grade-appropriate conceptual context does not transfer seamlessly to the unfamiliar context faced by the grade 12 students.

Just as grade-inappropriate concepts can undermine an inquiry item, grade-inappropriate inquiry skills can undermine a conceptual item. However, while the most common problem for

Question refers to the following information.

Meg designs an experiment to see which of three types of sneakers provides the most friction.

She uses the equipment listed below.

    1. Sneaker 1
    2. Sneaker 2
    3. Sneaker 3
    4. Spring scale

She uses the setup illustrated below and pulls the spring scale to the left.

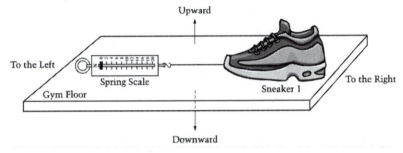

Meg tests one type of sneaker on a gym floor, a second type of sneaker on a grass field, and a third type of sneaker on a cement sidewalk. Her teacher is not satisfied with the way Meg designed her experiment. Describe one error in Meg's experiment.

_____

_____

_____

_____

Describe how Meg could improve the experiment to find out which of the three types of sneakers provides the most friction.

_____

_____

_____

_____

Figure 12.10 An inquiry item assessing controlled experiments with grade level-appropriate conceptual content.

Source: U.S. Department of Education, Institute of Education Sciences, National Center for Education Statistics, National Assessment of Educational Progress, 2009 Science Assessment.

inquiry items is that they are designed with content that is too difficult, the most common problem for conceptual items is that they are designed with practices that are too basic. For example, most conceptual items are designed to involve very basic scientific practices, such as predicting or explaining the behavior of a simplified model system. The assumption underlying this design decision is that the practice should be equally accessible to all respondents so as not to present a barrier to anyone. Again, the intention is to minimize construct-irrelevant variance, in this case unfamiliarity with complex or demanding scientific practices, such as using advanced mathematical or computational tools. In other words, the practice is chosen so that its difficulty does not "mask" the student's underlying conceptual understanding.

Although this design may be appropriate for assessing core ideas associated with lower grade bands, it places a cap on the sophistication of the core ideas that can be assessed at higher grade bands. For example, consider the two-dimensional, static, schematic modeling of macroscopic objects that occurs in force diagrams in typical paper-and-pencil physics assessments. When used in the context of an item like the grade 8 sneaker item (Figure 12.10), this simplified model is appropriate. However, it quickly reaches a ceiling with respect to the core ideas that it can support. The grade 12 item shown in Figure 12.11, from the 2009 NAEP Science Assessment, has reached that ceiling: it has supported basic quantification, requiring algebra to solve the mathematical form of Newton's second law, but the system remains two-dimensional, involves a single macroscopic object, and appears as a static schematic diagram.

This practice—using the force diagram model to explain and predict behavior—cannot easily support the assessment of more sophisticated understandings of Newton's second law, such as what happens in systems that involve forces acting in more than one dimension, forces that change over time, multiple objects, or objects that have internal structure. Some of these systems could be represented in static figures, but solutions would require more complicated mathematical formulations involving trigonometry, calculus, or differential equations. Some of these systems would be very difficult or impossible to represent in static figures. However, sophisticated computer models or simulations exist that can allow students to manipulate complex, dynamic systems and solve problems without relying on advanced mathematical formulations. (For examples in the context of large-scale science assessment, see Quellmalz, Timms, Silberglitt, & Buckley, 2012, and the Minnesota example below.) Using these computer models and simulations—one type of advanced practice required by the NGSS—students can demonstrate their higher level conceptual understandings in a way that is very difficult or impossible using the simplified, static models compatible with traditional paper-and-pencil assessments.

This difficulty is exacerbated in Earth and Space Science, in which many topics require a systems understanding that may not be assessable at all using simple practices such as the static, two-dimensional modeling illustrated in Figures 12.10 and 12.11. For example, in the previous section, the discussion of DCI ESS1.B: Earth and the Solar System focused on the K–8 region of the progression and construct map, covering the day/night cycle, the phases of the moon, and the seasons. Excluded from this discussion was the cycle of ice ages, which is a required topic at the high school level. However, understanding and explaining the ice age cycle requires sophisticated modeling and computation:

> Students mathematically and computationally apply Newtonian gravitational laws to the orbital motions of the solar system and analyze evidence to explain how changes in Earth's orbital parameters affect cyclic climate changes on Earth such as the repeating Ice Ages. This is not simplistic stuff.
>
> (Wysession, 2013, p. 18)

When test specifications or assessment blueprints create a false dichotomy between "conceptual" and "inquiry" items, neither conceptual understanding nor scientific practice is assessed well. Pairing grade level-appropriate content with simple, easily accessible practices places a low ceiling on the sophistication of the concepts that can be assessed. Pairing grade level-appropriate practices with difficult, unfamiliar content makes it hard for students to demonstrate the skills they possess. By explicitly pairing grade-appropriate DCIs with grade-appropriate SEPs, new standards like the NGSS offer a way forward. Rather than thinking of conceptual understanding as a source of construct-irrelevant variance affecting "inquiry" items, and familiarity with practices as a source of construct-irrelevant variance affecting "conceptual" items, the new standards consider both familiarity with practices and conceptual understanding as always construct-relevant.

3. The figure below shows a 2-kilogram (kg) object. A 10-newton (N) force pushes the object horizontally across a level flat surface. The frictional force that results from contact with the surface produces a 2-N force that opposes the direction of the object's movement.

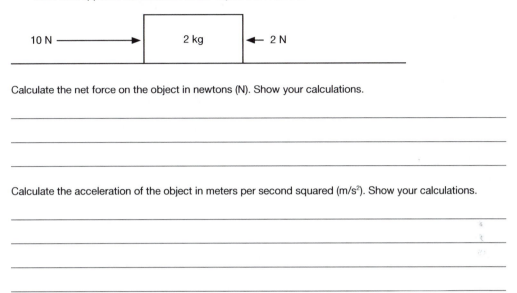

Calculate the net force on the object in newtons (N). Show your calculations.

_____

_____

_____

Calculate the acceleration of the object in meters per second squared (m/s²). Show your calculations.

_____

_____

_____

_____

Figure 12.11 A conceptual item constrained by below-grade-level scientific practice.

Source: U.S. Department of Education, Institute of Education Sciences, National Center for Education Statistics, National Assessment of Educational Progress, 2009 Science Assessment.

Indeed, the new standards define the construct to be assessed as neither context-free conceptual understanding nor content-free inquiry skills, but instead the application of conceptual understanding in the service of conducting scientific practice. To the extent that assessment developers design assessment tasks that align with the PEs described by the new standards, they can be confident that their tasks combine grade-appropriate practices and content, and that differences in proficiency among students can be interpreted as different amounts of construct-relevant skills and understandings.

A Shift from Narrowly Defined Inquiry Skills to Authentic Scientific Practices

The fourth foundational shift in the new standards is away from assessing narrowly defined, decomposed inquiry skills and toward assessing a wider range of more authentic scientific practices. Since the publication of the Benchmarks for Science Literacy (AAAS, 1993), many large-scale assessments have made an effort to develop and incorporate inquiry items, including some performance-based items. However, from the perspective of the framework and the NGSS, and as alluded to in the previous section, the scientific practices involved in these inquiry items have been rather simplistic and narrow. Traditionally, these items focus on specific, limited aspects of planning and carrying out investigations and analyzing and interpreting data.

Items that focus on planning and carrying out investigations include those assessing how to use simple measurement equipment, such as scales and graduated cylinders to measure mass or volume. Examples of these kinds of items from the 2005 NAEP Science Assessment are shown in Figures 12.12 and 12.13. The item in Figure 12.12 requires interpreting the analog read-out of a scale.

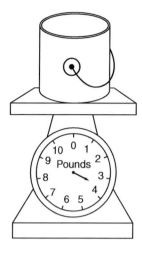

What does the can shown in the diagram weigh?

A. $1\frac{3}{4}$ pounds

B. $2\frac{3}{4}$ pounds

C. $3\frac{1}{2}$ pounds

D. $4\frac{1}{4}$ pounds

Figure 12.12 An inquiry item assessing the use of a scale.

Source: U.S. Department of Education, Institute of Education Sciences, National Center for Education Statistics, National Assessment of Educational Progress, 2005 Science Assessment.

Seventy percent of grade 4 students answered this item correctly. The item in Figure 12.13 requires using a graduated cylinder to measure the volume of a rock. Seventeen percent of grade 8 students and 31 percent of grade 12 students gave a completely correct response to this item.

Despite their relative difficulties, both items require the straightforward use of a simple piece of equipment to measure a single property of an object. According to the NGSS, this level of the Planning and Carrying Out Investigations practice is first associated with the K–2 grade band: "Make observations (firsthand or from media) and/or measurements to collect data that can be used to make comparisons" (NGSS Lead States, 2013b, p. 7). Importantly, however, individual PEs combine this practice with grade level-appropriate DCIs, so that measuring different properties appears at different grade levels. Thus, although scales and graduated cylinders are the staple of traditional inquiry items at all grade levels, most likely because assessment developers assume they can rely on students' familiarity with this equipment, the NGSS associate particular equipment with particular grade bands.

Specifically, the NGSS PEs (NGSS Lead States, 2013a) first mention measuring the volume of water in grade 4 in the service of understanding erosion (4-ESS2-1): "Make observations and/or measurements to provide evidence of the effects of weathering or the rate of erosion by

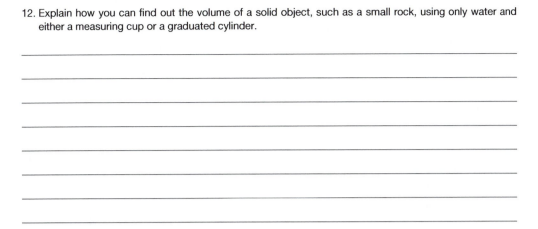

12. Explain how you can find out the volume of a solid object, such as a small rock, using only water and either a measuring cup or a graduated cylinder.

Figure 12.13 An inquiry item assessing the use of a graduated cylinder.

Source: U.S. Department of Education, Institute of Education Sciences, National Center for Education Statistics, National Assessment of Educational Progress, 2005 Science Assessment.

water, ice, wind, or vegetation." Likewise, the NGSS first mention measuring weight in grade 5 in the service of understanding the conservation of matter (PE 5-PS1-2): "Measure and graph quantities to provide evidence that regardless of the type of change that occurs when heating, cooling, or mixing substances, the total weight of matter is conserved." Finally, the NGSS only imply—but do not specifically mention—measuring the volume of an object by means of displacement at middle school in the service of understanding density (MS-PS1-2): "Analyze and interpret data on the properties of substances before and after the substances interact to determine if a chemical reaction has occurred."

At the same time, by grade 5, students are expected to measure properties using equipment that is much more sophisticated. For example, PE 5-PS1-3, "Make observations and measurements to identify materials based on their properties," specifically mentions color, hardness, reflectivity, electrical conductivity, thermal conductivity, response to magnetic forces, and solubility, while explicitly excluding density. Equipment that could measure properties like these include sensors that upload data to a computer; as costs come down, use of this equipment is becoming more common in science classrooms, although it is far from universal. This presents a problem for assessment developers, who must balance the NGSS mandate that assessments should incorporate these new practices with the reality that writing items involving such equipment will introduce construct-irrelevant variance due to the variability in their use in classrooms. Although it may be tempting to hold off on introducing new items until the use of this equipment becomes more widespread, assessment developers should be aware that omitting these types of items from the state assessment would likely prolong the delay in adopting this equipment in the classroom, as teachers will recognize that these practices are not being assessed. However, there is likely to be a middle ground: for example, an item could be written that describes someone using a thermal probe to gather temperature data, but that does not assume that students are familiar with the details of how to operate a thermal probe themselves.

As another example of the low-level and narrow approach in traditional inquiry items, items that focus on analyzing and interpreting data often require interpreting patterns in provided data tables. An example from the 2011 NAEP Science Assessment is shown in Figure 12.14. This item requires students to interpret the pattern of the data in the table in order to describe the relationship between two variables. Forty-three percent of grade 8 students gave either Partial or Complete responses to this item, reflecting an understanding of the relationship between the two variables.

Although interpreting a provided data table is one aspect of the SEP Analyzing and Interpreting Data, from the perspective of the NGSS it is both a low-level and narrow aspect of that practice, implying that its prevalence on large-scale assessments vastly overstates its importance. Just as the standards do for the DCIs, the NGSS identify progressions for each SEP that lay out the different elements and levels of the SEPs that find their way into the PEs (NGSS Lead States, 2013b). In the case of Analyzing and Interpreting Data, the element, "Analyze and interpret data to make sense of phenomena, using logical reasoning, mathematics, and/or computation," appears as the second of five elements at the grades 3–5 level and one of 24 elements making up the practice as it spans all four Grade Band Endpoints.

Notably, in contrast to interpreting provided data tables, the first element at the grades 3–5 level describes the ability to construct a data table: "Represent data in tables and/or various graphical displays (bar graphs, pictographs, and/or pie charts) to reveal patterns that indicate relationships." An item that assesses the ability to construct a data table, rather than simply interpreting an existing data table, would most likely require going beyond a static paper-and-pencil format to include features the respondent could manipulate (e.g., the Minnesota simulation item presented below). At higher grade levels, the use of data displays becomes even more sophisticated, moving beyond simple data tables to include displays and digital tools that can accommodate large data sets, identify linear and nonlinear relationships, identify temporal and spatial relationships, and fit functions to data sets. Again, these more sophisticated practices will likely require computer-based technology-enhanced item formats, such as those introduced in the 2013 PIAAC and planned for the 2015 PISA.

The NGSS provide progressions for all eight scientific and engineering practices described in the framework (NGSS Lead States, 2013b). These eight SEPs are listed below:

1   asking questions (for science) and defining problems (for engineering);
2   developing and using models;
3   planning and carrying out investigations;
4   analyzing and interpreting data;
5   using mathematics and computational thinking;
6   constructing explanations (for science) and designing solutions (for engineering);
7   engaging in argument from evidence;
8   obtaining, evaluating, and communicating information.

There are many aspects of these SEPs that have not been traditionally assessed in "inquiry" items, and some have never been assessed in a large-scale assessment context. However, a growing research base is providing examples of how these SEPs could be assessed. In the examples that follow, the eight SEPs are grouped together into three spheres of activity, as described in the NRC framework (NRC, 2012) and illustrated in Figure 12.15.

Investigating

The investigating sphere of activity includes SEPs 1 (Asking questions), 3 (Planning and carrying out investigations), 4 (Analyzing and interpreting data), and 5 (Using mathematics and computational thinking). These practices include not only the subset of practices traditionally associated with "inquiry" items as described above but also a wider range of more sophisticated skills.

Question refers to the following information.

Most soils are a mixture of particles of different sizes. Water moves through soil at different rates, depending largely on how much of each size particle makes up the soil. The table below shows the percentage of each size particle in five different soils (A, B, C, D, E) and the rate at which water moves through each of the soils.

RATE OF WATER MOVING THROUGH DIFFERENT SOILS

Soil	Percentage Largest Particles (%)	Percentage Medium-Sized Particles (%)	Percentage Smallest Particles (%)	Rate of Water Draining Through Soil (cm/hr)
A	100	0	0	21
B	85	10	5	6.1
C	40	40	20	1.3
D	20	65	15	0.69
E	0	0	100	0.05

Describe the relationship between the size of the soil particles and the rate at which water moves through the soil. Use the data in the table to support your answer.

_____

_____

_____

_____

_____

Figure 12.14 An inquiry item assessing the analysis of a provided data table.

Source: U.S. Department of Education, Institute of Education Sciences, National Center for Education Statistics, National Assessment of Educational Progress, 2011 Science Assessment.

The following is an example from the Minnesota state science assessments (part of the Minnesota Comprehensive Assessment—Series III) of how simulations have been used to support assessment of higher order investigating skills that go beyond interpreting precollected data displayed in tables. (For more examples of simulations in the context of large-scale science assessment, see Quellmalz et al., 2012.)

Minnesota started development of simulations that could be incorporated into their statewide science assessments in the fall of 2009. It began by defining the item and scoring characteristics of assessment tasks involving simulations:

Simulations are simply scenarios with a simulative scene embedded somewhere in it. Simulative scenes require students to manipulate variables and then view the results of a simulated situation. In the situation, students may (1) complete an investigation, (2) collect, record, and analyze data, and/or (3) influence the outcome of an event or phenomenon. These simulative scenes will support 2–4 items. There will be one task response item per simulation. A task response requires students to take an action in a simulative environment that generates a response based on the student action such as choosing variables to investigate a given question. The student action or generated response is scored rather than requiring students to transfer this understanding into a different format such as multiple-choice items.

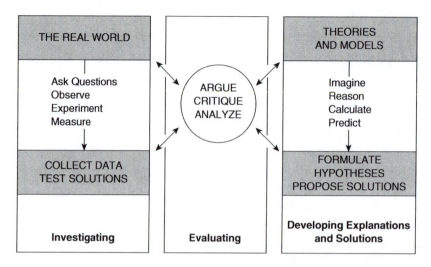

Figure 12.15 The three spheres of Science and Engineering Practice.

Source: Reprinted with permission from the National Academies Press, Copyright 2012, National Academy of Sciences. National Research Council. (2012). *A Framework for K-12 Science Education: Practices, Crosscutting Concepts, and Core Ideas.* Washington, D.C.: National Academies Press.

The decision to use task response items arose from a Minnesota state mandate that human-scored constructed-response items be eliminated from the Minnesota state assessments, both to allow for instantaneous scoring and reporting and to facilitate the move to computer adaptive testing. This mandate precluded the use of constructed-response items to accompany the simulations, asking students to, for example, explain why they chose particular variables or to explain the outcomes of the simulation. Instead, the actions that students took as they interacted with the simulation—for example, which variables were manipulated and in what order—had to be directly and automatically scorable.

The simulations are used to assess aspects of scientific practice that, in a classroom, would be done with a lab practical where a student must show proof of a particular skill such as setting up a controlled experiment or making observations. However, in order to justify putting limited resources into the development of simulations, each simulation needed to support not just a task response item assessing this higher order aspect of scientific practice but several other more traditional multiple-choice or technology-enhanced items assessing other content. For example, Figures 12.16–19 show a sequence of items linked to a simulation of water bottle rockets. First, background material is presented, and several lower level process skills are assessed (Figure 12.16). The simulation itself first appears in the second panel (Figure 12.17). This simulative scene allows students to select inputs and push *Start* to see an animation of the water bottle rocket. The data table is then populated with the selected inputs and the resulting outputs. At this point in the item sequence, the simulation is not used as an assessment item. Instead, it serves as additional context for the more traditional content items that follow. Finally, the simulation appears again in the third panel (Figure 12.18), where it forms the basis for the task response item. When the student clicks *Next*, the contents of the data table are taken as the student response and are automatically scored. The score is based on whether the student has successfully controlled for bottle type and air pressure while varying the amount of water in the rocket. The fourth panel (Figure 12.19) shows the simulative scene after two trials have been completed and the third trial is underway; the animation of the third trial is occurring and the data table is partially filled in.

Water bottle rockets are made by adding water to a bottle and pumping air into it. The flight time and height depend on the shape and the size of the water bottle rocket and the amounts of water and air you pump into the bottle.

Water

Air Pump

17

650 milliliters of water is put into the water bottle. Convert 650 milliliters to liters.

You can use the calculator to help you answer this question.

Use the keypad or type your answer in the box.

650 milliliters = [   ] liters

1	2	3
4	5	6
7	8	9
0		

Delete

Figure 12.16 Background material and traditional inquiry questions from a sequence of items based around a simulation of water bottle rockets.

Reprinted courtesy of the Minnesota Department of Education.

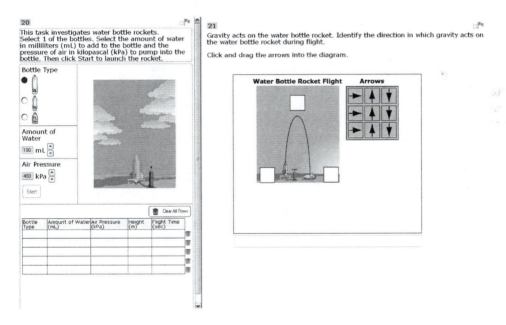

Figure 12.17 Simulation and traditional content questions from a sequence of items based around a simulation of water bottle rockets.

Reprinted courtesy of the Minnesota Department of Education.

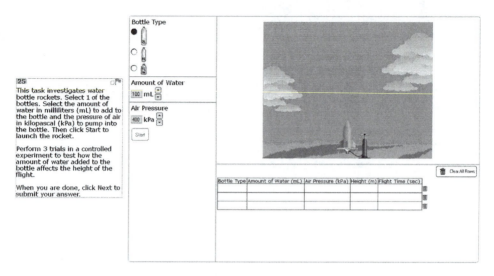

Figure 12.18 Simulation-based task response item (initial state) from a sequence of items based around a simulation of water bottle rockets.

Reprinted courtesy of the Minnesota Department of Education.

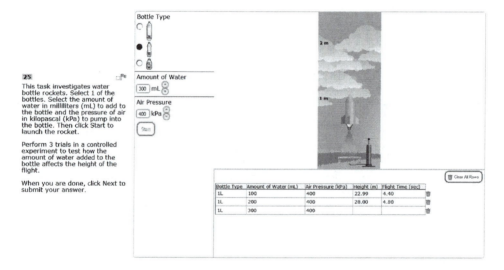

Figure 12.19 Simulation-based task response item (during use) from a sequence of items based around a simulation of water bottle rockets.

Reprinted courtesy of the Minnesota Department of Education.

During development of the simulation-based items, several issues emerged. The first issue was a tension between simulations that were flashy, exciting, and engaging and simulations that lent themselves to item generation and automatic scoring. Developers worked through many cycles, pursuing ideas for simulations that seemed promising but either did not have the supporting data to make them scientifically accurate, did not align to specific science benchmarks, or did not have enough appropriate (grade-level) variables to support the number and variety of assessment items that would be needed to justify the cost of development.

A second issue was limiting the scope of the assessment task to focus on the relevant aspect of scientific practice without introducing construct-irrelevant variance related to computer skills, or unrelated strategies like trial and error. For example, given this simulation, it would be natural to ask students to identify the best combination of inputs to make the water bottle rocket go the highest. However, while such a question would be productive and engaging in a formative or instructional environment, it would not be appropriate on a summative assessment as it would rely too heavily on trial and error and optimal search strategies.

Finally, a third issue that arises when using sequences of items like the one above is that the common stimulus material may introduce item dependence, which is a well-known and well-studied issue in the context of, for example, reading comprehension items that share a common stimulus in the form of a text passage. There are psychometric methods for detecting and accommodating item dependence, such as the use of item bundle or testlet models (for an overview, see Wainer, Bradlow, & Wang, 2007).

Developing Explanations

The developing explanations sphere of activity includes SEPs 2 (Developing and using models), 5 (Using mathematics and computational thinking), and 6 (Constructing explanations). These practices include the subset of practices traditionally associated with "conceptual" items as described above, but also include a wider range of more sophisticated skills. The following is an example of how more sophisticated models, not constrained by static, two-dimensional representations, could be incorporated into items to support assessment of higher-order explaining skills.

The Molecular Workbench is a collection of interactive molecular simulations developed by the Concord Consortium and available online (http://mw.concord.org/modeler/). Recently ported to and accessible on the Internet through a partnership with Google, the Molecular Workbench simulations are intended to be used in learning activities and are paired with formative assessment items that guide student exploration and experimentation. However, interactive simulations like these could also be incorporated into summative assessments.

As an example, consider the Molecular Workbench simulation of phase changes shown in Figure 12.20. The central pane shows a model of a substance made up of about 100 atoms. In addition to choosing whether the atoms of the substance are charged or neutral, there are two variables that can be adjusted by the student: Van der Waals attraction (the strength of the inter-molecular attraction) and temperature. By adjusting these variables and running the simulation, the substance can behave like a solid, liquid, or gas.

One item that could be constructed using this interactive simulation would be "Adjust the Van der Waals attraction and Temperature sliders until the substance behaves like a liquid." Such an item would be easy to score automatically, but would support a level of conceptual understanding beyond that revealed by static images. This is because a solid substance, when viewed dynamically, demonstrates several behaviors that students come to associate with static pictures of liquids and gases. For example, consider Figure 12.21, which shows a snapshot of the substance at a slightly higher temperature but still behaving as a solid. In this picture, the atoms in the main clump appear to be highly disordered, in a way that static pictures often use to characterize liquids. However, as watching the dynamic version illustrates, each atom is still highly constrained in its motion by its attraction to its neighbors and is not free to move about within the substance as in a liquid. While the substance in the picture looks like it is about to break apart, it is actually in the process of vibrating, an important behavior of solids that is hard to effectively illustrate in static pictures. Moreover, several atoms have broken free from the bulk of the substance and are traveling by themselves, in a way that static pictures often use to characterize gases. These atoms represent the solid's sublimated vapor, which is an important but often overlooked aspect of phase behavior.

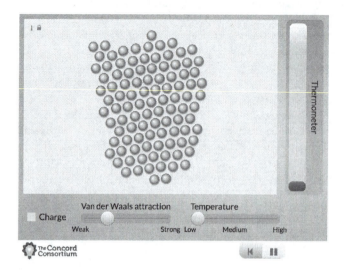

Figure 12.20 Molecular Workbench model of a chemical substance consisting of about 100 atoms, used to simulate phase changes.

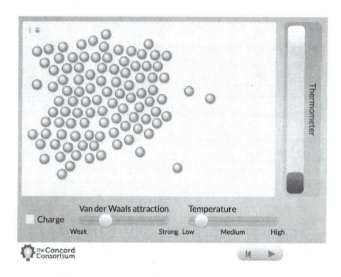

Figure 12.21 Molecular Workbench model of a chemical substance consisting of about 100 atoms, illustrating sophisticated concepts involved in phase changes.

Note: Screenshot images of "Charged and Neutral Atoms" Molecular Workbench interactive (concord.org/stem-resources/charged-and-neutral-atoms) used with permission from the Concord Consortium. Molecular Workbench (mw.concord.org) and "Charged and Neutral Atoms" are produced by the Concord Consortium (concord.org).

A dynamic simulation like this could support the assessment of more sophisticated conceptual understanding. Whereas traditional static pictures of solids, liquids, and gases can only illustrate intermolecular distance and, to a lesser extent, disorder, a dynamic simulation can illustrate relative ranges of motion characteristic of different phases. Simulations like these have the potential to support the assessment of the deeper understandings demanded by the new standards. However, in the absence of a strong research base, and with limited practical examples available, the addition of simulations to large-scale assessment will require considerable testing and some trial and error, as the Minnesota example above illustrates.

Evaluating

The evaluating sphere of activity includes SEPs 7 (Engaging in argument from evidence) and 8 (Obtaining, evaluating, and communicating information). These practices have rarely been assessed in large-scale assessments because they are difficult to meaningfully decompose and therefore appear to lend themselves better to performance assessments. However, the research literature contains several examples of successfully assessing these scientific practices in more traditional assessment formats, in ways that could be applied to large-scale science assessment.

As an example, the Evidence-Based Reasoning Assessment System (EBRAS; Brown, Furtak, Timms, Nagashima, & Wilson, 2010; Brown, Nagashima, Fu, Timms, & Wilson, 2010) was developed to assess evidence-based reasoning, a form of scientific argumentation. For the EBRAS, a model of evidence-based reasoning was developed by extending Toulmin's model of argumentation to include the use of scientific data and evidence. This model, called the Evidence-Based Reasoning Framework, is shown in Figure 12.22. The Evidence-Based Reasoning Framework is similar to a flowchart showing how two inputs, a premise and data, are processed through three distinct steps (analysis, interpretation, and application) to produce a claim as the output. In the study described below, the EBRAS was used to assess the validity, conceptual sophistication, and conceptual specificity of middle and high school students' evidence-based scientific reasoning on the topic of buoyancy. For the sake of brevity, we discuss here only the construct of validity.

As shown in Figure 12.23, a construct map was developed that examines the validity of the reasoning linking students' assumptions and their conclusions. As the term is used in formal logic, validity only describes whether the conclusions follow from the assumptions. It does not refer to the truthfulness of the assumptions. Therefore, an incorrect conclusion can still demonstrate validity as long as it follows logically from (incorrect) assumptions. Students' reasoning is described as *fully valid* when all of their conclusions follow from their assumptions. If the assumptions support some but not all of a student's conclusions, their reasoning is *partially valid*; this often occurs when students presume an additional, but unstated, assumption. If the conclusions contradict the assumptions, the reasoning is *invalid*. At the least valid end of the validity construct map, *no link* is apparent between the assumptions and conclusions; the assumptions are vague or not stated explicitly and therefore do not necessarily lead to the stated conclusion.

A key issue during the development of the assessment was how to meaningfully decompose the process of scientific argumentation into assessable tasks, without sacrificing the authenticity of the scientific practice. Based on extensive cognitive labs with students and pilot tests of potential item formats, it was determined that an appropriate and effective item template would present in the stimulus a single component from the Evidence-Based Reasoning Framework and require the student to apply a single process to produce or evaluate an adjacent component. For example, several of the items presented the student with data and asked them to summarize the data. In doing so, they would describe a piece of evidence via analysis. Other items might present the student with a rule (a scientific principle or law) and ask them to give examples of evidence that support that rule or to make a claim (e.g., predict an outcome) that would be consistent with that rule.

Because individual items using this template do not provide opportunities to observe students engaged in extended reasoning, items were clustered into sequences of three or four in which later items in the sequence build upon the student's responses to previous items. An example of an abbreviated item sequence is shown in Table 12.2. This sequence contains two

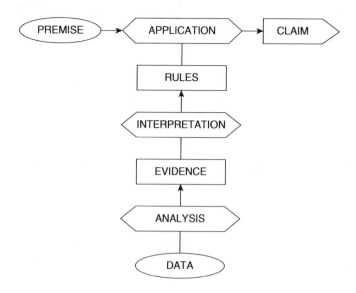

Figure 12.22 Evidence-Based Reasoning Framework, a model of scientific argumentation.
Source: Brown et al. (2010).

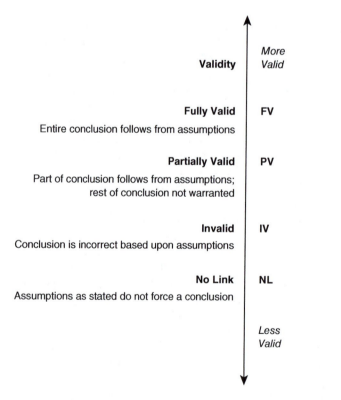

Figure 12.23 Construct map describing possible levels of the validity of students' scientific reasoning.
Source: Brown et al. (2010).

Table 12.2 Abbreviated Item Sequence Assessing a Multistep Process of Scientific Reasoning

Common stem		
Use the following information to answer Questions 3a and 3b.		
Here are some things that float in water:		
A A kitchen sponge		
B A plastic toy boat		
C An empty glass bottle		

Item	Prompt	Example response	Score
3a	What do these things have in common that causes them to float in water?	"They're all light."	FV
3b	Scientists require evidence to support their beliefs. Describe a specific thing you've seen, heard, or done that supports your belief that things float because of the reason you described in 3a.	"I float so anything smaller than me floats too. Except if it's really heavy."	PV

Note: The actual item sequence contained an additional follow-up question.

items, Items 3a and 3b, in which the second item explicitly references and builds upon the student's answer to the first item. First, in Item 3a, the student is presented with a claim about the behavior of three objects and asked to describe an assumption (premise) that could explain this claim. To answer, the student must implicitly or explicitly apply a rule. The item is not designed in a way to allow us to observe which rule is used, but the next item (Item 3b) requires the student to engage in further reasoning using that rule. Specifically, the student is asked to provide evidence supporting that rule. The item stem scaffolds the student to produce a response that allows the direct observation of how they interpret evidence in relation to a rule. (On the actual assessment, this item sequence contained an additional follow-up question targeting the use of counterevidence.)

The construct map shown in Figure 12.23 served as a master scoring guide for all the items on this assessment, allowing student responses to be evaluated using the levels specified in the construct map. Because the assessment items and scoring procedures were developed to be consistent with the construct map, the resulting scale scores demonstrated strong evidence of validity in addition to adequate reliability ($r = 0.88$).

Although the items developed for the EBRAS were human-scored, recent advances have made it possible to automate the scoring of such short, content-rich responses. A similar design philosophy could also be applied to develop selection items that could be automatically scored. An example would be to present students with several pieces of evidence and have them select the evidence that most validly supports a particular rule.

Conclusion

Large-scale assessment of Physical and Earth and Space Science is both rapidly expanding, as states develop new high school EOC exams to support student and teacher accountability programs, and dramatically shifting in form and content, as states respond to new expectations for science standards as exemplified by the NRC framework and the NGSS. These expectations reflect a dramatic reimagining of the foundations of K–12 science education and embody four major shifts in how competency in science should be assessed. As described in this chapter, these shifts will require major changes in the way assessment developers design both state science assessment systems and individual science assessments in order to validly and reliably assess the demanding breadth and depth of the new standards.

Addressing these challenges effectively will require the combined and concerted effort of content experts, teachers, assessment developers, and measurement experts, all working together to manage trade-offs between validity, reliability, usability, and utility. It will also require a principled approach to assessment design, of which construct modeling is a particularly well-suited example, given the progression-based nature of the NRC framework and the NGSS. However, principled does not mean orderly, and assessment development is best thought of not as a linear process but as the iterative refinement of a system. Each component of the system—the construct specification, the assessment tasks, the scoring procedures, and the measurement model—needs to be consistent with the other components and with the underlying model of cognition on which the assessment is based (Brown & Wilson, 2011). Indeed, the model of cognition is the foundation on which the entire system rests, providing needed focus, coherence, and the promise of validity. For all of the challenges they present, the new expectations of the NRC framework and the NGSS, including their embrace of explicit progressions of learning, present developers with a strong foundation on which science assessments can be constructed.

Notes

1 The data on current state assessment practice were collected in December 2013 and January 2014, by a search of the descriptions of science assessment frameworks, EOC exams, and high school graduation requirements on the Department of Education websites of the 50 states and the District of Columbia. The authors would like to thank Courtney Castle for her help in compiling these data.
2 The term "progressions" is used throughout this chapter rather than "learning progressions" to acknowledge the current debate surrounding the nature of learning progressions as universal descriptions of the necessary stages of cognitive development. To avoid implying this strong interpretation, "progressions" is used to suggest only an expected sequence of assessable proficiencies.
3 Note that it is not an assumption of construct modeling that all students will pass through all levels or that their patterns of growth will be similar. Construct modeling does not assume a particular growth model for learning or development. Instead, it assumes that the latent variable can be characterized as a continuous quantity, of which someone possesses a certain amount at a particular time. The levels of a construct map are not akin to Piagetian stages, but are merely qualitative descriptions of different amounts of the latent variable.

References

American Association for the Advancement of Science (AAAS). (1993). *Benchmarks for science literacy*. New York, NY: Oxford University Press.

Black, P., Wilson, M., & Yao, S. (2011). Road maps for learning: A guide to the navigation of learning progressions. *Measurement: Interdisciplinary Research and Perspectives, 9*, 1–52.

Briggs, D. C. (2013). Measuring growth with vertical scales. *Journal of Educational Measurement, 50*, 204–226.

Briggs, D. C., & Alonzo, A. C. (2012). The psychometric modeling of ordered multiple-choice item responses for diagnostic assessment with a learning progression. In A. C. Alonzo & A. W. Gotwals (Eds.), *Learning progressions in science: Current challenges and future directions*. Rotterdam, The Netherlands: Sense Publishers.

Briggs, D. C., Alonzo, A. C., Schwab, C., & Wilson, M. (2006). Diagnostic assessment with ordered multiple-choice items. *Educational Assessment, 11*(1), 33–63.

Brown, N. J. S., Furtak, E. M., Timms, M., Nagashima, S. O., & Wilson, M. (2010). The evidence-based reasoning framework: Assessing scientific reasoning. *Educational Assessment, 15*, 123–141.

Brown, N. J. S., Nagashima, S. O., Fu, A., Timms, M., & Wilson, M. (2010). A framework for analyzing scientific reasoning in assessments. *Educational Assessment, 15*, 142–174.

Brown, N. J. S., & Wilson, M. (2011). A model of cognition: The missing cornerstone of assessment. *Educational Psychology Review, 23*(2), 221–234.

Carnegie Corporation of New York & Institute for Advanced Study. (2007). *The opportunity equation: Transforming mathematics and science education for citizenship and the global economy.* Retrieved September 11, 2015 from https://www.carnegie.org/publications/the-opportunity-equation-transforming-mathematics-and-science-education-for-citizenship-and-the-global-economy

College Board. (2009). *Science college board standards for college success.* New York, NY: College Board.

Diakow, R., Torres Irribarra, D., & Wilson, M. (2013). Some comments on representing construct levels in psychometric models. In R. E. Millsap, L. A. van der Ark, D. M. Bolt, & C. M. Woods (Eds.), *New developments in quantitative psychology* (pp. 319–334). New York, NY: Springer.

Fu, A. C., Raizen, S. A., & Shavelson, R. J. (2009). The nation's report card: A vision of large-scale science assessment. *Science, 326,* 1637–1638.

Gorin, J. S., & Mislevy, R. J. (2013). *Inherent measurement challenges in the Next Generation Science Standards for both formative and summative assessment.* Princeton, NJ: K–12 Center at ETS.

Haberman, S. J., & Sinharay, S. (2010). Reporting of subscores using multidimensional item response theory. *Psychometrika, 75,* 209–227.

Kolen, M. J., & Brennan, R. L. (2014). *Test equating, scaling, and linking: Methods and practices* (3rd ed.). New York, NY: Springer.

Koretz, D., & Hamilton, L. S. (2006). Testing for accountability in K–12. In R. L. Brennan (Ed.), *Educational measurement* (4th ed., pp. 531–578). Westport, CT: American Council on Education/Praeger.

Koretz, D., McCaffrey, D., & Hamilton, L. (2001). *Toward a framework for validating gains under high-stakes conditions.* Los Angeles, CA: National Center for Research on Evaluation, Standards, and Student Testing.

Lehrer, R., Kim, M.-J., Ayers, E., & Wilson, M. (2014). Toward establishing a learning progression to support the development of statistical reasoning. In J. Confrey & A. Maloney (Eds.), *Learning over time: Learning trajectories in mathematics education.* Charlotte, NC: Information Age.

Messick, S. (1994). The interplay of evidence and consequences in the validation of performance assessments. *Educational Researcher, 23,* 13–23.

National Assessment Governing Board. (2008). *Science framework for the 2009 National Assessment of Educational Progress.* Washington, DC: U.S. Government Printing Office.

National Research Council (NRC). (2001). *Knowing what students know: The science and design of educational assessment.* Washington, DC: National Academies Press.

NRC. (2007). *Taking science to school: Learning and teaching science in grades K–8.* Washington, DC: National Academies Press.

NRC. (2012). *A framework for K–12 science education: Practices, crosscutting concepts, and core ideas.* Washington, DC: National Academies Press.

NGSS Lead States. (2013a). *Next Generation Science Standards: For states, by states.* Washington, DC: National Academies Press.

NGSS Lead States. (2013b). *Appendix F—Science and engineering practices in the NGSS.* Retrieved September 11, 2015 from http://www.nextgenscience.org/sites/ngss/files/Appendix%20F%20%20Science%20and%20Engineering%20Practices%20in%20the%20NGSS%20-%20FINAL%20060513.pdf

NGSS Lead States. (2013c). *Appendix K—Model course mapping in middle and high school for the Next Generation Science Standards.* Retrieved September 11, 2015 from http://www.nextgenscience.org/sites/ngss/files/Appendix%20K_Revised%208.30.13.pdf

NGSS Lead States. (2013d). *How to read the Next Generation Science Standards (NGSS).* Retrieved September 11, 2015 from http://www.nextgenscience.org/sites/ngss/files/How%20to%20Read%20NGSS%20-%20Final%208.19.13.pdf

Pellegrino, J. W. (2013). Proficiency in science: Assessment challenges and opportunities. *Science, 340*(6130), 320–323.

Pellegrino, J. W., Wilson, M. R., Koenig, J. A., & Beatty, A. S. (2014). *Developing assessments for the Next Generation Science Standards.* Washington, DC: National Academies Press.

Pollack, J., Atkins-Burnett, S., Rock, D., & Weiss, M. (2005). *Early childhood longitudinal study kindergarten class of 1998–99 (ECLS-K), psychometric report for the third grade* (NCES No. 2005–062). Washington, DC: U.S. Department of Education, National Center for Education Statistics.

Quellmalz, E. S., Davenport, J., & Timms, M. (2012, February). *21st century science assessments.* Paper presented at the annual meeting of the American Association for the Advancement of Science (AAAS), Vancouver, Canada.

Quellmalz, E. S., Timms, M. J., Silberglitt, M. D., & Buckley, B. C. (2012). Science assessments for all: Integrating science simulations into balanced state science assessment systems. *Journal of Research in Science Teaching, 49*(3), 363–393.

Scalise, K., Claesgens, J., Wilson, M., & Stacy, A. (2006). Contrasting the expectations for student understanding of chemistry with levels achieved: A brief case-study of student nurses. *Chemistry Education: Research and Practice, 7*(3), 170–184.

Scalise, K., & Wilson, M. (2008, March). *Bundle models for computer adaptive testing in e-learning assessment.* Paper presented at the annual meeting of the American Educational Research Association, New York, NY.

Shavelson, R. J., Baxter, G. P., & Pine, J. (1992). Performance assessments: Political rhetoric and measurement reality. *Educational Researcher, 21*, 22–27.

Sinharay, S. (2010). How often do subscores have added value? Results from operational and simulated data. *Journal of Educational Measurement, 47*, 150–174.

Sinharay, S., Haberman, S., & Puhan, G. (2007). Subscores based on classical test theory: To report or not to report. *Educational Measurement: Issues and Practice, 26*, 21–28.

Wainer, H., Bradlow, E. T., & Wang, X. (2007). *Testlet response theory and its applications.* Cambridge, UK: Cambridge University Press.

Wilson, M. (2005). *Constructing measures: An item response modeling approach.* Mahwah, NJ: Lawrence Erlbaum.

Wilson, M. (2009). Measuring progressions: Assessment structures underlying a learning progression. *Journal of Research in Science Teaching, 46*, 716–730.

Wilson, M., & Sloane, K. (2000). From principles to practice: An embedded assessment system. *Applied Measurement in Education, 13*(2), 181–208.

Wysession, M. E. (2013). The Next Generation Science Standards and the earth and space sciences. *Science Scope, 37*, 13–19.

Zinth, J. D. (2012). *End-of-course exams.* Denver, CO: Education Commission of the States.

13 Transforming Assessment in Mathematics

Introduction

Patricia A. Klag and Friedrich L. Kluempen

This is an exciting time in assessment—especially in mathematics—as the focus shifts to the implementation of the Common Core State Standards (CCSS) for Mathematics and the best way to measure students' understanding of the knowledge, practices, and skills mandated in the standards. The CCSS, published by the National Governors Association Center for Best Practices and the Council of Chief State School Officers (2010), stress the conceptual understanding of mathematics to complement the procedural skills required to prepare students for success in college and career. This chapter describes practical concerns surrounding the development of assessments in mathematics, with an emphasis on the CCSS. The focus is on high school mathematics. The discussion is couched in the context of Evidence-Centered Design (ECD). A brief description of the applicable features of ECD introduces some of the tensions that naturally arise during the design, development, and implementation of an assessment program. For a more complete treatment of ECD, see Mislevy, Steinberg, and Almond (2003)—who are the architects of ECD—or Haertel et al. (this volume). As with any design problem, the design of an assessment program is an exercise in optimization under constraints.

Following the brief discussion of the elements of ECD, the chapter presents a high-level overview of important topics in assessing mathematics, particularly those relating to the paradigm shift from past practices to meeting the expectations embodied by the CCSS. The overview is followed by a discussion of the tensions that arise during the design phase of an assessment program, highlighting some of the consequences of the transition to CCSS with respect to student learning and assessment and touching on some questions that arise from the announced goal to employ a computer-based administration model. A discussion of several issues to be considered during the development of item specifications, items, and tasks follows. One of the considerations specific to mathematics is the use of tools for problem solving (e.g., calculators). Here, the discussion points to some general issues and then delves into the tensions that the use of calculators introduces in the design of assessments and tasks, in contrast to their value in instruction and learning. In light of the trend toward computer-delivered tests, the chapter concludes with considerations of the interrelation between authenticity and validity, as well as the appropriate uses of technology.

Through the Lens of ECD

Developing assessments in mathematics presents a number of challenges. A well-designed assessment can provide an accurate and credible measure of students' knowledge, skills, and abilities. But when designed or implemented poorly, the link between the evidence collected and the intended inferences will be more tenuous. In particular, a central goal of any assessment is construct validity; that is, the test measures what it is intended to measure. The principal threats to validity are construct underrepresentation (some parts of the construct are not measured adequately) and construct-irrelevant variance (factors other than the intended construct that influence student performance) (Messick, 1995). Another goal of the assessment, especially in an ongoing program, is score reliability for individuals—that a test taker should receive relatively similar scores were she to take different forms of the test under the same conditions.

ECD can guide the development of an assessment program toward the goal of producing test scores that are based on evidence gathered to support the desired claims. As Mislevy, Almond, and Lukas (2004) wrote, "[ECD] provides a conceptual design framework for the elements of a coherent assessment" (p. 1), going on to state: "Designing assessment products in such a framework ensures that the way in which evidence is gathered and interpreted is consistent with the underlying knowledge and purposes the assessment is intended to address" (p. 2).

This chapter focuses on the practical, rather than theoretical, issues that arise when developing assessments in mathematics within a design framework informed by ECD. The theoretical framework provided by ECD is an excellent foundation for the assessment design but, as is often the case, what makes sense in theory is not always possible in practice.

The implementation of ECD for assessing individuals with respect to the CCSS begins with the claims the score user wants to make about test takers. At the highest level, the claim may be that students are college- and career-ready in mathematics (e.g., PARCConline, 2011; Smarter Balanced Assessment Consortium, 2012a). Underlying this claim are many subclaims that must be further delineated before test designers can determine what kind of evidence is required to support the claim. To conclude that a test taker is college- and career-ready, evidence must be gathered for a range of skills from procedural knowledge (e.g., fluency in multiplication) through conceptual understanding (e.g., analysis needed to create a model) and problem solving.

The focus then shifts to the next level; that is, the evidence needed to substantiate the claim that the student is indeed fluent in multiplication or is able to create a model to fit a data set. Related to this is the need to understand the characteristics of the test-taking population and how students in that population could provide that evidence. In the case of fluency of multiplication, for example, the fifth-grade student should be able to correctly solve a wide variety of multiplication problems. The type of evidence gathered for fourth graders, though, would differ in some ways.

What kinds of tasks can provide the required evidence? This is one of the greatest challenges in test design. For instance, a task that provides the best evidence for the CCSS mathematical practice (MP1)—"make sense of problems and persevere in solving them" (National Governors Association Center for Best Practices & Council of Chief State School Officers, 2010, p. 6)—might be more appropriate for a classroom exercise or project than a timed testing situation. The challenge is to design tasks that can assess the competency in the targeted standard under multiple constraints—development time and available testing time, mode of test delivery (computer-based or paper-and-pencil), ability to score the test efficiently and cost-effectively, etc.

In the example of multiplication fluency, the initial question concerns specification of the construct (i.e., What does fluency mean?). Is it the ability to solve a variety of problems correctly? Is it the ability to recall multiplication facts quickly? To test for the speed dimension of fluency, the assessment design could incorporate a timed section in which students must perform operations on single-digit and simple two-digit integers, and the total time needed to solve the problems contributes to the student's score. In testing the procedural aspect of fluency, the design could include problems that are not timed and are more complex; for example, multiplying two-digit with three- or four-digit numbers that either do or do not require regrouping. One further consideration that is noteworthy, and somewhat specific to mathematics assessments, is the use of technology for problem solving. The presence or absence of technology—ranging from ruler and compass to software packages—for a given task will affect not only the type of evidence that can be garnered but also its interpretation and must therefore be taken into account in the design phase.

These considerations, as well as clear statements about the nature of the evidence needed, all play a role in shaping the test specifications and test blueprints that guide the actual test development process and, thus, contribute to the validity of the test. In addition, test designers must also take into account factors that contribute to reliability, such as the number of questions, the response formats, time requirements, and psychometric characteristics.

A useful element of ECD is the development of task models. Task models "describe how to structure the kinds of situations we need to obtain the types of evidence needed for the evidence models" (Mislevy et al., 2004, p. 10). That is, task models provide the structure for a family of potential tasks. Well-developed task models can support the efficient generation of items that vary in terms of difficulty, cognitive complexity, and other characteristics in order to populate rich item pools. The design of task models requires decisions about task features such as item type (from a universe ranging from selected response to various types of constructed response), the inclusion of stimulus materials, and the mode of presentation (verbal, graphical, analytical, tabular). The decisions about task features are partially constrained by psychometric considerations (e.g., reliability), cost (e.g., scoring), and response time. For instance, for a given amount of testing time, the number of selected-response items that can be posed is greater than the number of constructed-response items. The number of questions posed, in turn, affects the amount and type of evidence generated.

Consider the example in Figure 13.1, which is modeled after a sample item from the Smarter Balanced Assessment (http://sampleitems.smarterbalanced.org/itempreview/ModernShell.aspx?config=SBAC\Content\EEProgressions3.json) (Smarter Balanced Assessment Consortium, 2012b). The task was designed to generate evidence for standard 8.EE.7a, which states, in part, "Give examples of linear equations in one variable with one solution, infinitely many solutions, or no solutions" (National Governors Association Center for Best Practices & Council of Chief State School Officers, 2010, p. 54). A task model for assessing the standard might include several item templates. These may contain both fixed and variable elements that can be employed to generate a variety of items that align to the standards. An item template for this "table-grid" item would specify the wording of the prompt as "For each [insert type of equation] in the table, select whether the equation has no solution, one solution, or infinitely many solutions." The types of functions that are appropriate to test with this template (e.g., linear, quadratic, exponential) would be specified as variable elements of the template and would be tied to the appropriate standard being assessed. The number of equations to be included as well as scoring rules would all be specified. In addition, the template can include a list, which could be expanded over time, of the forms of the equations that could be included in the task. Those forms might include:

$$ax + b = (c(ax + b))$$
$$ax = ax + b$$
$$a(x + b) = cx + b$$
$$a + b = ax + \frac{b}{x}$$

Finally, the template would indicate whether the coefficients a, b, and c must be whole numbers, integers, rational numbers, etc. The various features of the template—e.g., the types of numbers

For each equation in the table below, indicate whether the equation has no solution, one solution, or infinitely many solutions.

Equation	No Solution	One Solution	Infinitely Many Solutions
$3x + 5 = 3x - 5$			
$8(4x - 6) = 12x - 6$			
$5(3x + 6x + 7) = 9(5x + 5) - 10$			

Figure 13.1 Sample item measuring Standard 8.EE.7a.

used (integers versus fractions) and the structure of the equations (number of parameters, excluding equations with x in the denominator, etc.)—could be linked to different levels of difficulty on both theoretical and empirical grounds. If the linkages are reasonably accurate, then the template can be used to generate tasks that vary in difficulty depending on the choices of the fixed and variable elements. In subsequent uses of the model, the template could be updated based on data gathered from the administrations of previously generated instances of the tasks. For more on ECD and the use of task models, see Haertel et al. in this volume.

Good item development practices are based on clearly articulated objectives and specifications. It is often tempting to start item development early in the process (and sometimes development schedules necessitate this). The danger in this is that an item—even a very good item—will not necessarily provide the evidence needed to support the initial claim, or that time is spent trying to retrofit items to specifications rather than developing items directly to the specifications. Others assume that, with good task models, the items will "write themselves." Experienced item developers know this is rarely the case as, once the item writing process begins, tensions among the various requirements inevitably begin to emerge.

Use of ECD as a framework helps shift assessment development from more of an art toward more of a science. ECD can be especially helpful as the field transitions from more traditional assessments to more innovative ones that are called for by the CCSS and can assure greater psychometric consistency and construct validity. It is important to note, however, that when a testing program adheres to tightly defined task models for the sake of efficiency and consistency, an unintended consequence can be a decrease in variety among items and, ultimately, test forms. Some worry that innovation and creativity may be diminished and others are concerned with the possibility that the test can be gamed (Koretz, 2013). These risks can be mitigated by moving innovation to the task model and templates.

Transitioning to Common Core Assessments

We are at a crossroads in K–12 mathematics assessment in the United States. Two large, multi-state consortia have been formed to develop assessment systems that are intended to measure students' proficiency with respect to the CCSS, with a particular focus on college- and career-readiness. At the time of this writing, most states have joined either the Partnership for Assessment of Readiness for College and Careers (PARCC) or the Smarter Balanced Assessment Consortium. Also, most states and the District of Columbia are members of the testing consortia, while some states have either withdrawn their membership or never joined.

In July 2010, Achieve, Inc. published a comparison of the CCSS in mathematics with the mathematics standards for California and Massachusetts—two states that are considered leaders in mathematics education. The major findings were (Achieve, 2010):

- The CCSS are similarly rigorous to the California and Massachusetts standards. While all three describe similar content, the CCSS go beyond both sets of standards by identifying the level of content required of all students to graduate from high school and to be college- and career-ready.
- The CCSS are more coherent than the California and Massachusetts standards. The CCSS emphasize similar amounts of content in each grade level, but provide clearer and more precise progressions of learning across the grades.
- While there are a number of similarities between the CCSS and the California and Massachusetts standards, there are several key differences in coherence and focus which set the CCSS apart as a better set of standards.

Of particular note is the difference in rigor in the standards. The Achieve report states: "While the documents describe similar content, they nonetheless communicate different levels of rigor. The CCSS specifically define the knowledge and skills necessary for success in entry-level, credit-bearing courses and 21st century careers" (2010, p. 3). There is general agreement in the mathematics education community that the CCSS raise the bar for all students in terms of expectations to learn and do mathematics.

The National Council of Teachers of Mathematics, the National Council of Supervisors of Mathematics, the Association of State Supervisors of Mathematics, and the Association of Mathematics Teacher Educators released a joint public statement in support of the CCSS (NCTM, 2010):

> The release of the Common Core State Standards (CCSS) is a welcome milestone in the standards movement that began more than 20 years ago when the National Council of Teachers of Mathematics published Curriculum and Evaluation Standards for School Mathematics.... The CCSS provides the foundation for the development of more focused and coherent instructional materials and assessments that measure students' understanding of mathematical concepts and acquisition of fundamental reasoning habits, in addition to their fluency with skills. Most important, the CCSS will enable teachers and education leaders to focus on improving teaching and learning, which is critical to ensuring that all students have access to a high-quality mathematics program and the support that they need to be successful.
>
> Many aspects of the central elements of the CCSS echo the long-standing positions and principles of our organizations:
>
> - All students need to develop mathematical practices such as solving problems, making connections, understanding multiple representations of mathematical ideas, communicating their thought processes, and justifying their reasoning.
> - All students need both conceptual and procedural knowledge related to a mathematical topic, and they need to understand how the two types of knowledge are connected.
> - Curriculum documents should organize learning expectations in ways that reflect research on how children learn mathematics.

All students need opportunities for reasoning and sense making across the mathematics curriculum—and they need to believe that mathematics is sensible, worthwhile, and doable.

In preparation for the transition to assessments aligned to the CCSS, states are trying to align their existing item pools to the CCSS. However, it is not just a matter of seeing the extent to which the content "lines up." The Consortia are committed to developing assessments that measure student proficiencies with respect to the CCSS in a much more comprehensive and rigorous manner than is currently the case in regard to state standards.

Most state tests now rely heavily, or even exclusively, on traditional multiple-choice items that, typically, each measure a single concept or sub-standard. Some tests have a performance task section in which students must construct an answer, although, due to the cost of hand-scoring such tasks, some states have recently dropped constructed-response items in favor of machine-scored items. Tests that utilize computer delivery may include basic "technology-enhanced" items such as multiple-selection multiple-choice (where more than one option can be correct), and numeric entry. Items utilizing drag-and-drop response formats, hot spots, and graphing items are sometimes used.

The CCSS System Implementation Plan for California (California Department of Education, 2013, p. 2) states:

Although California's 1997 academic content standards and the CCSS for English-language arts and mathematics share many similarities in content and design, there are a number of notable differences between the two sets of standards.... The CCSS also focus on applying mathematical thinking to real world challenges, helping students develop a depth of understanding and ability to apply mathematics to novel situations.

To properly assess the standards, paper-and-pencil-delivered assessments are inadequate, since they limit the ways in which some concepts can be measured. Computer-based assessments support item types that enable students to provide more direct evidence of their understanding of mathematics concepts in machine-scorable ways. Consequently, both consortia plan to deliver assessments via computer in order to reap the advantages of computer delivery. These include cost-effective scoring, a reduction in the amount of time between administration and feedback to the teachers, and the availability of technology-enabled items that yield more direct evidence of student understanding. Appendix F of the Invitation to Negotiate for PARCC Item Development (2011, p. 30) states:

> The chief goal of technology enhancement is to measure a wider range of the standards in a cost-effective way.... Technology enhancements might be said to range from incremental to transformative. Incremental enhancements might include response formats that go beyond selected response—such as drag-and-drop, categorizing, ranking and sequencing, or single-number constructed response. Often, these formats have paper-based analogs. Truly transformative enhancements make possible what couldn't be done at all with paper: constructing shapes, testing conjectures numerically, running a simulation to correct a model, using a spreadsheet, winning a game, ... PARCC is also interested in technology enhancements that support wider accessibility (e.g., the ability to hover over words to see and/or hear their definition, etc.).

Sample items for the mathematics tests published by both consortia (CCSSToolBox, 2011; Smarter Balanced Assessment Consortium, 2012b) demonstrate the commitment to using technology-enhanced items. Furthermore, both consortia remain committed to the goal of incorporating transformative items over time.

Figure 13.2 shows one component of a sample high school task (CCSSToolBox, 2011) that involves reasoning about credit card interest and requires students to use a spreadsheet-like format to evaluate balances on a credit card. The task is intended to go beyond whether a student can solve a mathematical problem involving interest: "Students are expected to make sense of the contextual situation, extract and use mathematics to model the situation, answer mathematical questions, and then solve the problem within the context."

The task makes use of technology to scaffold the examinees' responses. That is, this part of the task presents several questions en route to the complete solution. Scaffolding has several advantages. It offers multiple entry points to the problem and, in the case of computer-administered assessments, it allows for computer scoring of some parts. In addition, students can receive partial credit for elements that would be scored as right or wrong with multiple-choice questions.

Figure 13.2 presents a static problem; that is, it presents the student with all of the information needed to answer the questions. Another category of computer-based test problems is dynamic, in which students must explore the scenario to uncover additional relevant information. Such problems require students to investigate, identify, control, and explain; thus, additional information about students' skills can be captured. For example, the PISA 2012 Problem Solving Framework includes problems in both of these categories (National Center for Education Statistics, 2013; OECD, 2013, p. 120).

Isabella's credit card

Isabella owes a balance of $300 on her credit card. She has stopped making purchases with the card, and she plans to make a $40 payment each month until her debt is paid and her credit card balance is $0. The monthly rate is 1.5%, and interest is added each month to the balance that remains.

Consider the spreadsheet. In a spreadsheet, each entry (cell) is referred to by its column letter and row number. For example, 260.00 is the entry in cell D2 of this spreadsheet.

	A	B	C	D	E
1	Month	Amount owed ($)	Monthly Payment ($)	Remaining amount owed after Payment ($)	Amount owed after 1.5% interest charge ($)
2	1	300.00	40.00	260.00	263.90
3	2	263.90	40.00		

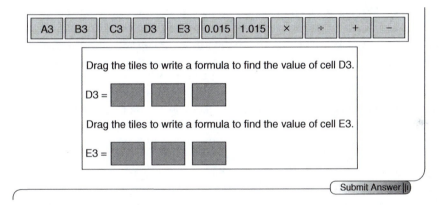

Drag the tiles to write a formula to find the value of cell D3.

D3 = ▨ ▨ ▨

Drag the tiles to write a formula to find the value of cell E3.

E3 = ▨ ▨ ▨

Submit Answer

Figure 13.2 Sample reasoning item from the CCSSToolBox.

Courtesy of PARCC.

Designing Assessments to Measure the CCSS

Designing an assessment to measure students' proficiencies with respect to the CCSS will involve a number of complexities specific to student readiness and the standards themselves. The tensions that arise will lead to design trade-offs among competing priorities. As with any design problem, the goal is optimization under the constraints presented by the assessment context. Using the ECD approach, the priorities are, generally speaking, the various claims to be made about the test takers. In the context of summative assessments, psychometric desiderata, total cost of the assessment, and examinee time are the most powerful constraints, while political considerations can also play a role.

In the near term, one of the challenges in measuring the CCSS is student readiness. Teachers are currently in the process of familiarizing themselves with the expectations and demands of the standards and developing appropriate pedagogical strategies. There will likely be gaps in preparedness for several years to come. The structure of the CCSS at the high school level—providing for topic coverage, rather than courses—gives rise to a further complication, as students may follow a traditional track or an integrated track. Further, the delivery of the curriculum may be a daily class over the course of a year or a block-scheduled delivery system that is either in or out of phase with the assessment cycle's timing. Test designs must account for variations in course and sequence, especially for midyear and interim assessments. In addition, designs must recognize that student preparedness will vary considerably and must ensure the capacity to gather sufficient information to measure students along the entire measurement scale, especially those at the lower end.

A further complication in this regard is the observation that high-stakes testing affects student and teacher behavior, most notably in what is taught in the classroom (Koretz, 2013). That is, after some rounds of testing and coaching, students—on average—adapt to idiosyncrasies in item presentation in relation to content as well as concentrations of content covered by the test. The result is that students perform better than their true ability. This phenomenon can be mitigated by broad content coverage and varied presentation, which will minimize the ability to predict question formats for specific content.

Another important design goal is to ensure fair assessment for particular subpopulations (e.g., English learners and students with disabilities). This entails eliminating, to the extent possible, the obstacles to a student in being able to demonstrate what they know and can do, that is, minimizing construct-irrelevant variance without undermining construct validity. In this regard, the careful application of ECD and the principles of Universal Design is essential (Chapter 5, this volume; Hansen & Mislevy, 2006; National Research Council, 2004).

The tension between enhanced construct representation and considerations of cost and the characteristics of the test-taking populations is readily apparent with many standards. For example, CCSS standard F-IF.C.7a (National Governors Association Center for Best Practices & Council of Chief State School Officers, 2010, p. 69) calls for the ability to graph a quadratic function. Although some aspects of this standard can be assessed by selected-response questions, requiring a student to actually construct a graph would be more construct-valid. With selected-response questions, the student can be asked questions about intercepts and extrema and to select the graph that best fits the given information from among a group of graphs. However, these approaches only serve to assess part of standard F-IF.C.7a. Fortunately, the introduction of computer-administered tests, together with advances in automated scoring, will greatly expand the range of response formats that can be machine-scored and will alter the balance between construct validity and cost/reliability, allowing for more comprehensive and deeper testing of standards (Bejar & Braun, 1994; Williamson, Mislevy, & Bejar, 2006).

As an illustrative example, consider the following standard on functions (National Governors Association Center for Best Practices & Council of Chief State School Officers, 2010, p. 70):

> **F-IF. 9** Compare properties of two functions each represented in a different way (algebraically, graphically, numerically in tables, or by verbal descriptions). For example, given a graph of one quadratic function and an algebraic expression for another, say which has the larger maximum.

A "traditional" question that would measure this standard is shown in Figure 13.3. The multiple-choice question is an efficient way to test whether a student understands the relationship between algebraic and graphical representations of functions. Students are "comparing" in the most basic of senses. As the CCSS are being implemented, though, assessment items and tasks that more truly provide evidence are being called for.

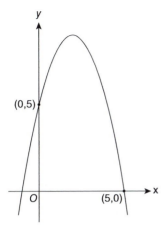

Which of the following could be the equation of the parabola shown above?

(A) $y = -x^2 - 4x + 5$

(B) $y = -x^2 + 4x + 5$

(C) $y = x^2 - 4x - 5$

(D) $y = x^2 + 4x + 5$

Figure 13.3 Sample item measuring CCSS Standard F-IF.9.

Now consider Figure 13.4, a sample task from PARCC for the same standard (2012). The task gauges understanding of several properties of the functions presented. Unlike a traditional multiple-choice question that is scored as right or wrong, the task allows for testing comparisons of values at greater depth, as well as awarding of partial credit, all in a machine-scorable format. While this item provides more direct testing of the standard and increased construct relevance, it also highlights the tensions that arise for testing students with disabilities and other subpopulations.

Figure 13.4, which provides greater information than a traditional multiple-choice item, is intended for computer delivery. An equivalent paper-and-pencil version would likely comprise a set of 4 three-choice items, each scored as right or wrong. Although a rough equivalence is certainly possible for this particular type of question, tasks that are more innovative in their use of technology present greater challenges for generating equivalents in the paper-and-pencil format. For example, an item that requires a student to draw a graph using graphing tools on a computer can be done without technology as a constructed response item for paper delivery, but then requires human scoring.

These examples highlight the need to consider score comparability in the design of a testing program in mathematics that is largely intended to be computer-delivered. It is not always feasible to have paper-and-pencil "equivalents" of items, so comparability at the item level may be difficult to achieve. It may be prudent to have item pools that can be used for both modes of delivery, with some items specifically excluded from paper forms.

If this approach is taken, analysis should be performed to confirm that the exclusion of items maintains the construct representation and construct validity. Separate standards for performance via computer delivery and paper delivery may be appropriate. This is an area where more research is needed.

SAMPLE ITEM

A portion of the graph of a quadratic function $f(x)$ is shown in the xy-plane. Selected values of a linear function $g(x)$ are shown in the table.

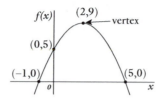

x	$g(x)$
–4	7
–1	1
2	–5
5	–11

For each comparison below, use the drop-down menu to select a symbol that correctly indicates the relationship between the first and the second quantity.

First Quantity	Comparison	Second Quantity
The y-coordinate of the y-intercept $f(x)$	▼	The y-coordinate of the y-intercept $g(x)$
$f(3)$	▼	$g(3)$
Maximum value of $f(x)$ on the interval $-5 \le x \le 5$	▼	Maximum value of $g(x)$ on the interval $-5 \le x \le 5$
$\dfrac{f(5) - f(2)}{5 - 2}$	▼	$\dfrac{g(5) - g(2)}{5 - 2}$

Figure 13.4 Sample PARCC item measuring CCSS Standard F-IF.9. Note: each drop-down menu contains the symbols >, <, and =.

Courtesy of PARCC.

Considerations in Developing Comprehensive Specifications for Tests of Mathematics

Generally speaking, comprehensive test specifications delineate content domain coverage, the range and frequency of different item types, and various psychometric desiderata. They also include a number of secondary requirements, typically related to the construct being measured or the context in which the assessment takes place. Although it is important to document the key characteristics of the test forms and the items that comprise them, it is often not possible to have every test form fully conform to all of the specifications, particularly the secondary ones. As a rule, content and statistical specifications are given highest priority.

In mathematics assessments, a comprehensive set of test specifications often considers such features as cognitive complexity and mathematical practices, available tools, the use of context, types of functions, and presentation modes. A brief discussion of each of these follows. Of course, how each feature is treated depends on the purpose of the test and other key features, as well as the test-taking population.

Large testing programs—with multiple administrations per year—and ongoing programs—with interest in longitudinal data—also need to consider form-to-form comparability. To ensure fairness to test takers, forms should be similar in both content and difficulty over time. The establishment and adherence to comprehensive test specifications can provide both guidance and structure to accomplish this goal. Although detailed content and statistical specifications are necessary for form comparability, they are not sufficient.

Cognitive Complexity

The difficulty of a test form is a function of several factors, including the content and the cognitive complexity of the items. A mathematics item of low complexity is one that involves recall of a fact or execution of a simple procedure. An item of high complexity may require students to apply and explain a concept or analyze and synthesize data. Item complexity is also influenced by factors such as the nature of the stimulus material (if any), the response mode, the extent of scaffolding, and the number of solution steps.

It is important to distinguish cognitive complexity from item difficulty. An item of low complexity can be difficult—that is, a low percentage of the testing population gives a correct response—if, for example, the question asks for recall of a concept that is unfamiliar or long forgotten. However, at the high end of the complexity spectrum, items are very likely to also be more difficult. Ideally, test specifications should include difficulty targets for items at different levels of complexity. This is particularly important if the population to be assessed has a wide range of knowledge and skills.

At the same time, there are a number of factors that constrain the designer's ability to control both cognitive complexity and item difficulty. Most critical in this regard are the target standards. Often the standards themselves, or the evidence statements for measuring the standards, have implicit cognitive complexity levels. Inasmuch as the CCSS mathematics standards call for more rigor and greater emphasis on critical thinking, the "natural" distribution of complexity is likely to be skewed toward the high end. Although, as noted above, complexity is not synonymous with difficulty, it is likely that the distribution of item difficulties will be centered at the high end of the underlying scale, resulting in greater errors of measurement at the lower end of the scale.

In the context of CCSS or other sets of rigorous standards, the need for accurate measurement along the ability continuum leads both to difficulties in the development of test specifications and to tensions in building test forms that conform to those specifications. Thus, it is important for item writers to understand the item features that contribute to both complexity and difficulty, in order to be able to construct test forms that can yield good evidence along the ability continuum without sacrificing construct representation. One strategy, for example, is the judicious use of scaffolding in an item. Scaffolding can offer weaker students an entry point into a problem and, thereby, yield useful data. However, this benefit may come at the expense of task authenticity.

Mathematical Practices

The mathematical practices delineated in the CCSS are as follows (National Governors Association Center for Best Practices & Council of Chief State School Officers, 2010, pp. 6–8):

MP1: Make sense of problems and persevere in solving them.

MP2: Reason abstractly and quantitatively.

MP3: Construct viable arguments and critique the reasoning of others.

MP4: Model with mathematics.

MP5: Use appropriate tools strategically.

MP6: Attend to precision.

MP7: Look for and make use of structure.

MP8: Look for and express regularity in repeated reasoning.

Detailed interpretations of the practices are included in the CCSS document, as is the charge that "Designers of … assessments … should all attend to the need to connect the mathematical practices to mathematical content in mathematics instruction" (National Governors Association Center for Best Practices & Council of Chief State School Officers, 2010, p. 8). Some aspects of the practices, such as the problem-solving facet of MP1, arise naturally in many test questions. Others need to be targeted more purposefully. For example, in MP5, the testing scenario must provide both appropriate questions and the required tool(s). Here again, it is useful to include target requirements for the applicable mathematical practices in the test specifications.

Both PARCC and Smarter Balanced have taken this charge into consideration in their design work, using the mathematical practices as the framework upon which the content rests. For example, the high-level claims for the Smarter Balanced assessments (2012a) clearly reflect the mathematical practices:

Claim #1—Concepts and Procedures
"Students can explain and apply mathematical concepts and interpret and carry out mathematical procedures with precision and fluency."

Claim #2—Problem Solving
"Students can solve a range of complex well-posed problems in pure and applied mathematics, making productive use of knowledge and problem solving strategies."

Claim #3—Communicating Reasoning
"Students can clearly and precisely construct viable arguments to support their own reasoning and to critique the reasoning of others."

Claim #4—Modeling and Data Analysis
"Students can analyze complex, real-world scenarios and can construct and use mathematical models to interpret and solve problems."

Use of Tools

Designers of mathematics assessments must consider the types of tools that students will be permitted, or even required, to use. Tools will depend to some extent on mode of administration. Some of the tools that have been used on mathematics assessments include calculators, rulers, fraction bars, pattern blocks, number cubes, and simulation tools. Tools are often intended for use with individual items. For example, on some tasks students are expected to demonstrate the ability to measure with a ruler, but not on other tasks where they are expected to use principles of geometry to find lengths on a figure. As the example implies, care needs to be taken that the availability of tools does not inappropriately affect the skills and knowledge being tested and, thus, change the construct being measured. With computer-delivered tests, access to tools can be regulated at the item level or the section level. In either case, student interaction with the tool can be recorded and analyzed. If the access is regulated on the section level, care must be taken that tools are not made available to students unintentionally. Tool availability should be consistent with the intent of the targeted standard(s) and should not introduce barriers for certain subpopulations.

The use of the above-mentioned tools is, in some sense, specific to mathematics assessments. Subjects such as science may present students with a virtual lab or hands-on tools to complete a performance-based task. And writing assessments may provide students with the typical word-processing tools. In mathematics, though, tools are often used for problem solving, and the development of items and tasks must be carefully considered based on whether students do or do not have tools available.

The fifth mathematical practice (MP5) in the CCSS calls for the application of appropriate tools in the course of problem solving. Per the standards, "tools might include pencil and paper, concrete models, a ruler, a protractor, a calculator, a spreadsheet, a computer algebra system, a statistical package, or dynamic geometry software" (National Governors Association Center for Best Practices & Council of Chief State School Officers, 2010, p. 7). The principles of ECD can assist in establishing policies for the use of tools and technologies in mathematics assessments. By and large, the knowledge and skills of selecting and appropriately using tools have not been measured. Paper-and-pencil assessments do not provide a mechanism to measure how students approach a problem and what tools they choose to use. Computer-delivered assessments can capture information on how students use online tools during the testing session. There is still work to be done on how to use this information.

In mathematics assessments, the most common tool is the calculator. Calculators have been permitted on assessments for decades, and the discussion below summarizes some of what has been learned about how to address the challenges in testing with calculators. Similar challenges, as well as some new ones, arise with newer tools, which are increasing in number and diversity. Calculator-use policies can take a number of approaches, as outlined below.

The Assessment Allows but Does Not Require the Use of a Calculator

In this scenario, students can decide whether or not to use (or even bring) a calculator. With this design, questions need to be accessible for students who do not use a calculator, and at the same time students with a calculator should not have a significant advantage on an item over students who do not. The type of calculator allowed must also be specified.

Consider CCSS standard A REI.D.11 (National Governors Association Center for Best Practices & Council of Chief State School Officers, 2010, p. 66): "Explain why the x-coordinates of the points where the graphs of the equations $y = f(x)$ and $y = g(x)$ intersect are the solutions of the equation $f(x) = g(x)$; find the solutions approximately." In the absence of technology, the functions and coefficients must be chosen carefully in order to facilitate the required arithmetic.

In Figure 13.5, the coefficients were chosen so that the resulting equation $x^2 - x - 2 = 0$ has integer solutions. While that is not strictly necessary in this example—the quadratic formula could have been used—the need for "nice" solutions does become a requirement in an applied problem where the resulting values are used for further calculations, for example when a question centers on finding the break-even point in a revenue model.

There are some questions for which a student using a calculator may have an advantage over a student who is not using a calculator. For example, the question presented in Figure 13.6 becomes trivial when even a basic four-function calculator is permitted.

Find all x-coordinates where the graphs of $y = x^2 - 1$ and $y = x + 1$ intersect.

Figure 13.5 Sample item measuring CCSS standard A REI.D.11.

Of the following fractions, which is least?

(A) $\dfrac{5}{16}$ (B) $\dfrac{5}{15}$ (C) $\dfrac{4}{16}$ (D) $\dfrac{4}{15}$

Figure 13.6 Sample question that is trivial when a calculator is permitted.

When a calculator is not permitted, a student with good number sense can quickly arrive at the correct answer by doing multiple comparisons and eliminating options, while the student who attempts to compare the fractions by computational methods will be at a disadvantage.

The Assessment Requires the Use of a Calculator

In this design scenario, decisions need to be made about whether the testing program will provide students with a calculator (either a physical calculator or one embedded in the software) or whether students will bring their own. Decisions also need to be made about the class of calculator that is permitted, whether basic four-function, scientific, graphing, or graphing with Computer Algebra System (CAS). When the design allows, there is an advantage to having students bring their own calculators—ones with which they are familiar—so that measurement is not confounded with familiarity with the calculator. This policy, though, raises concerns of equity—some students will have more sophisticated calculators than others. And some students may need to borrow calculators if they do not own one.

The class of calculator permitted on the assessment is a point of consideration. The advantage of a scientific calculator over a basic four-function calculator is the former's ability to evaluate trigonometric, exponential, and logarithmic functions. The next step, from scientific calculator to graphing calculator, is very significant. The graphing calculator allows for very different approaches to problem solving. For the example in Figure 13.5, the graphing calculator would permit a student to employ either a numerical solver or a graphing approach. In fact, one might argue that the example, as presented, is nearly devoid of reasoning with the use of a graphing calculator.

For graphing calculators, the distinction between a non-CAS and a CAS calculator becomes most apparent when a question requires algebraic manipulation. Take, for instance, the high school algebra standard on using "the structure of an expression to identify ways to rewrite it" (A SSE.A.2) (National Governors Association Center for Best Practices & Council of Chief State School Officers, 2010, p. 64), and consider the following examples.

The example in Figure 13.7 is rendered trivial by some graphing calculators and certainly by any CAS calculator. For the example, in Figure 13.8, a student using a CAS calculator will likely solve the equation for x and then modify that answer to get the value of $x - 3$. This approach circumvents the intention of the question, which is for the student to recognize the common factor of $(x - 3)$.

Another class of problems where the difference between a CAS and non-CAS calculator becomes apparent is the solving of systems of equations.

While non-CAS calculators have the ability to solve the system in Figure 13.9, it requires a sophisticated use of the calculator. The student would need to access the matrix algebra application and input the associated matrix there. An alternative method would be to graph the functions and find the x-coordinate of the point of intersection. For the student using a CAS

If $y(x-3) - (y+5)(x-3) = 12$, then $x =$

Figure 13.7 Sample item measuring CCSS standard A SSE.A.2.

If $y(x-3) - (y+5)(x-3) = 12$, then $x - 3 =$

Figure 13.8 Sample item measuring CCSS standard A SSE.A.2.

If $x = 9 - y$ and $8x = 10 - 3y$, what is the value of x?

Figure 13.9 Sample item that requires solving systems of equations.

Find the *x*-coordinate where the graphs of

$$y = 3,900 + \frac{200}{18} \cdot 3.70x \text{ and } y = 5,000 + \frac{200}{24} \cdot 3.70x \text{ intersect.}$$

Figure 13.10 Sample graphing calculator sensitive item in which the graphing utility should be turned off.

Tony is buying a used car. He will choose between two cars. The table below shows information about each car.

Car	Cost	Miles Per Gallon (MPG)	Estimated Immediate Repairs
Car A	$3200	18	$700
Car B	$4700	24	$300

Tony wants to compare the total costs of buying and using these cars.

- Tony estimates he will drive at least 200 miles per month.
- The average cost of gasoline per gallon in his area is $3.70.

Find the number of months after a purchase when the total accumulated cost of buying and using the Car A is the same as the cost of buying and using Car B.

Figure 13.11 Sample item in which the graphing utility can remain on. The item is an extension of sample 43052; Smarter Balanced, 2012b).

calculator, the solve command will do the job more readily. The caution is that permitting a variety of tools on the assessment will most likely lead to an uneven playing field.

As implied above, the disadvantage of having students supply their own calculators is lack of standardization—students have different levels of functionality available to them. Thus, test questions need to be crafted in a way that minimizes advantages of one model over another. With computer delivery, a built-in calculator can be supplied to the student. It is also possible to turn off certain features of the calculator on an item-by-item basis, if so desired. In one possible design scenario, the application/modeling problems appear in one section, allowing the full use of the calculator, while problems that test computational fluency appear in another section, where calculator use is limited. Consider the examples in Figures 13.10 and 13.11 above.

The mathematics involved in both examples is essentially the same. For the example given in Figure 13.11, the additional demand is the interpretation of the text. Here the test designers might allow the full use of the online graphing calculator. Once the student has extracted the relevant information, she is free to pursue one of several solution paths: a numeric solver or a solution via graphing and finding the point of intersection. But in the example in Figure 13.10, having these features available makes the task trivial.

The Assessment Prohibits All Technology

There may be instances in which it is desirable to prohibit technology, specifically calculators, on an assessment. For example, if computational fluency is part of the construct of the assessment, the evidence that is needed to support a claim that the student is fluent must be defined. Such evidence should show that students know their arithmetic facts and can perform simple operations without the use of a calculator. For paper-based testing, possible solutions are prohibiting all technology or introducing a two-part design—one part that restricts the use of

If $2x + y = 12$, then $10x + 5y =$

Figure 13.12 Sample item measuring CCSS standard A SSE.A.2.

technology and one part that permits it. If the larger purpose of the assessment is to measure the CCSS, then the preferable solution is a two-part assessment. On paper-based assessments or a computer-based test that uses hand-held technology, the administration becomes cumbersome, requiring the division of testing time into timed parts where students need to take out and put away the equipment.

When technology is permitted on a test, it is important that students are prepared to take the test with the technology. One of the more difficult tasks of the mathematics teacher is to instill the skill of deciding when the use of technology is helpful. In some cases, attempts by students to apply technology become a hindrance to problem solving. One area in which this is prevalent is in algebra where investigations are aimed at understanding the structure of expressions (A SSE.A.2). Consider the simple example in Figure 13.12. The key to this example is to see the common term $2x + y$ in the two expressions. The reflex for many students is to reach for a graphing calculator in the hope that it will aid in the solving of the problem. Students need to have a variety of experiences in using calculator technology in the classroom. They need to know *how* to use the technology. That is, the assessment should not be testing their ability to use a calculator rather than their ability to solve problems. They also need to know *when* to use technology; this is especially so in a timed testing situation.

As the example in Figure 13.12 shows, there are times when using a calculator will take more time and be more complicated than using mathematical reasoning. Students also need to know *where* in the solution of a problem to make use of the calculator. For example, if a question presents two possible models for growth in a population—one linear and one exponential—the use of the calculator should be determined by the questions that are asked. If the question is about end behavior, an understanding of linear and exponential functions suffices to say that the exponential model will show greater growth. If, on the other hand, the question focuses on small values of the variable, a calculator is necessary to compute and compare the predictions given by the models.

The goal of computer administration for the formative and summative assessments by the consortia lends itself well to the incorporation of computer algebra systems, spreadsheets, statistical packages, and geometry software. As with the discussion on calculators, the inclusion of these tools will provide better measurement when students are familiar with the functionality of the tools. Such familiarity can be ensured if the software is available to the teacher and students throughout the year. The study of statistics in particular should be helped greatly by the computer administration of assessments. When statistical software packages are not available, for example in paper-and-pencil administrations, the usual practice is to present small data sets. While such data sets have the advantage of being manageable for the calculator user, they are seldom rich enough to serve as the basis of good questions and they are often criticized as not representing authentic uses of statistics.

Context

Mathematics test questions can be roughly grouped into two categories: real life (items set in context) and abstract (items that are devoid of context). The context for real-life items ranges from minimal to very rich. Detailed test specifications should indicate the number of real-life items in a test form, as well as the nature of the contexts. Sometimes, the standard being measured naturally suggests that a real-life context is needed. In other cases, the standard may be measured with or without context. Items with settings in context often have a greater reading load and require the students to translate the words before performing the relevant mathematics. In order to ensure test form comparability, it is advisable to set a narrow range for the number of items on a form that include real-life context, keeping the total testing time in mind. Further delineation of the type of context may also be advisable in order to ensure form-to-form comparability.

Type of Function and Mode of Presentation

Test specifications should also offer guidelines for the types of mathematical functions to be used and the presentation of stimulus material. The types of functions that appear on the test are determined by course content. For high school courses, there is enough variety among algebraic, exponential, and trigonometric functions that a failure to set specific targets for each type of function can result in unbalanced test forms. For example, one assessment form targeting polynomial functions might largely consist of questions involving quadratics, while another form might have a preponderance of linear functions. The resulting difference in cognitive demand could be appreciable.

Content-information in mathematics items can be presented to students in a variety of ways, including verbally, graphically, tabularly, and analytically. Target distributions across modes of presentation help to ensure comparability, as well as the diversity that is sought by assessment designers for construct coverage. Similar to the discussion about context and function type, the different presentation modes for stimulus material carry distinct cognitive demands. While the level of demand depends on the individual examinee, care should be taken to ensure a variety of presentations so that particular test forms do not favor students who are more comfortable with a particular mode of presentation.

Technology Tools: An Aid to Learning, a Hindrance in Testing

The above discussion points out the distinction between learning with technology and testing with technology. Technology provides wonderful tools for exploration and knowledge building during the learning of mathematics; and the more powerful the technology, the greater the depth of the explorations that can be undertaken. Ideally, students benefit by having greater ownership of knowledge that they build themselves. For example, the relationship between functions $f(x)$ and $f(kx)$, where $k > 0$, can be explained in a lecture and demonstrated graphically by the teacher. When students are equipped with graphing technology, the teacher can instead ask "What is the relationship between the functions $f(x)$ and $f(kx)$, where $k > 0$?" and leave the students to investigate, which requires them to develop skills of abstraction and generalization along the route to new insights. Another benefit of technology is that students can be asked to solve problems that contain more realistic data that are not rigged for ease of arithmetic operations. Such benefits do not always readily carry over to assessments. Assessments that are standardized and timed do not easily allow for the measurement of some aspects of the CCSS Mathematical Practices. For example, students "make conjectures about the form and meaning of the solution and plan a solution pathway rather than simply jumping into a solution attempt," an aspect of the first Mathematical Practice (National Governors Association Center for Best Practices & Council of Chief State School Officers, 2010, p. 6) is best accomplished in an untimed setting. This is another example of a constraint that must be kept in mind during the design of tasks and assessments.

No discussion of tools and technology is complete without considering their impact on test security. The principal concern arises when the student supplies the technology which also has the capacity to store information or communicate wirelessly. So, for a paper-based assessment that allows the use of hand-held graphing calculators, the designers and administrators must wrestle with questions of security, both in terms of bringing information to the test (e.g., formulas and programs) and also carrying unauthorized information from the test administration environment. For situations where hand-held graphing calculators are permitted, possible security measures include clearing the memory of the calculator before the test, after the test, or both. Several calculator manufacturers are developing calculators with a "testing mode." The idea is to put the calculators in testing mode at the beginning of the assessment. The mode locks out certain functionalities of the calculator, including access to data stored in the memory. Once switched out of testing mode, which is triggered either manually or automatically via a timer, the data that was entered during the assessment is erased.

The College Board's Advanced Placement program has three courses in the mathematical sciences: Calculus AB, Calculus BC, and Statistics. Although these tests are given at paper-and-pencil administrations, the Advanced Placement program is notable as an example of a summative end-of-course testing program. The exams for the courses employ different design solutions with regard to the use of technology. The Statistics exam permits the use of graphing calculators throughout the exam, which comprises a multiple-choice section and a constructed-response section. The design solution for the Calculus exams utilizes a split design—both the multiple-choice and the constructed-response sections are broken into two parts, one that permits the use of a graphing calculator and the other that prohibits the use of a calculator. For both subjects, the paper-based administration model is driven by the size of the program and the relative lack of infrastructure to support computer-based assessments.

For specific courses, such as those in the Advanced Placement program, teachers' practices and opinions are influenced and impacted by testing policies with respect to the use of calculators. Some teachers may use spreadsheets and software packages available on computers and tablets in the classroom, while others may prefer to restrict the use of technology. However, testing policies regarding the use of technology can impact how mathematics is taught in the classroom in order to prepare students for the testing situation.

Tensions between Authenticity and Validity

The mission statement of the CCSS states that "the standards are designed to be robust and relevant to the real world, reflecting the knowledge and skills that our young people need for success in college and careers" (CCSSI, 2012). For high school mathematics, this comprises two areas: an ability to reason abstractly—understanding relationships and structure among mathematical objects—and an ability to reason from and within real-life settings.

The emphasis on engaging and interesting problems is particularly reflected in the prominence of scenario-based problems proposed for the high school assessment batteries of PARCC and Smarter Balanced. The expectation is that both consortia will include a substantial number of authentic mathematical challenges, that is, challenges that incorporate realistic settings and solution processes that require multiple steps.

Although the call for authenticity is very appealing, the move toward authenticity does give rise to a number of additional tensions that must be balanced. While context is necessary for authenticity, an unfamiliar context or an overly complex context can give rise to construct-irrelevant variance. Related to these concerns is the tension between a timed test and the time required to gain familiarity with the presented context. Furthermore, technical obstacles, such as limitations in a student's ability to navigate computer screens, may interfere with her ability to demonstrate mathematical competence. All of these tensions have the potential to reduce reliability and complicate scale maintenance. In summary, it is critical that threats to construct coverage, reliability, and construct validity are not introduced by the emphasis on authenticity in the assessments. See Messick (1994) for an excellent discussion on the tensions between authenticity and the aforementioned concepts in the context of performance assessments.

The following hypothetical example is a virtual tour of a context-rich problem that centers around reading and using bus schedules to plan a day trip into a city to see a musical. To proceed through the problem, the test taker must navigate through a series of computer screens that display different schedules along with information about the time and location of the musical. The test taker is presented with a lot of information—a picture of a bus and a bus schedule, a poster for the musical that gives the time of the musical performance and the location of the theater, a map of the city that shows where the bus stops—and needs to decide which pieces of information are relevant as she works through the different tasks asking which bus to take to the musical, shortest route from the bus stop to the musical, which bus to take after the musical, etc. The synthesis and extraction of data are, of course, critical to the authenticity of the task, but the test taker can get overwhelmed or distracted and not be able to actually get to the mathematics involved in solving the problems. Also, for some students, lack of an a priori familiarity with computing environments could present a possible source of construct-irrelevant variance. In addition, the context must be chosen carefully. This particular context might be criticized by some as not being familiar to test takers who live in rural areas. The item writer must select a scenario that is accessible to most test takers and presented in a way that minimizes possible confusion. Often this results in reduced authenticity.

For paper-based assessments, the same concerns regarding computer-based assessments apply with respect to processing information and reading load. In a computer environment, the processing of visual information can be managed in multiple ways; for example, tabs can be used to present different pieces of information, and these tabs can be available to the student throughout the task. In the paper-based environment, information must be presented linearly and generally requires processing of text. Nonetheless, concerns about possible construct-irrelevant variance must be kept in mind. The level of vocabulary and the complexity of the text have long been recognized as potential sources of construct-irrelevant variance. These concerns are compounded for English language learners, as well as student populations that require alternate test formats.

The use of authentic assessments also gives rise to a tension vis-à-vis the construct targets of the assessment. In particular, there should be sufficient opportunity for students to demonstrate competence for each construct. For example, the ability to model with mathematics is a targeted practice in the CCSS. If the assessment offers a single scenario to test this ability, a student's lack of familiarity with the provided context may present a significant impediment to completing the task successfully. Providing a sufficient number of tasks for each part of the construct mitigates this risk and has positive impact on reliability. Content coverage in a context-rich environment may necessitate a lengthy assessment or an assessment with parts given at different points in time. Of course, assessment length brings to the fore such factors as student fatigue, as well as cost and administrative scheduling difficulties.

Tensions Related to Item Specifications and Response Formats

There are a number of attributes to consider in providing item specifications. These include the fit to the evidence statement, content, and response format. It is important that there be clear guidance concerning how an evidence statement is to be measured. For example, for an evidence statement with multiple elements, item writers need to know whether items are restricted to target a single element or whether items must target all the elements. Additionally, item writers need to know the boundaries of the relevant content domain. An evidence statement about multiplication fluency needs to define the types of numbers to be used to test fluency (e.g., three-digit by two-digit whole numbers) and whether the items can include word problems or not, i.e., be strictly computational.

An important consideration in the design of an assessment is the response formats to be included. Multiple-choice questions have served assessment programs well over many decades and are still valuable for assessment. They are efficient to write, answer, and score, and they can provide a lot of information in a limited amount of testing time. They are, however, susceptible to a number of test-taking strategies.

When evaluating multiple-choice items, it is often not possible to know how students will interact with the items and whether the items are measuring the intended construct. Consider the example in Figure 13.13, which asks for the argument of a linear function with certain properties. To find a solution, the student can take any of the following approaches: (1) equate the expressions, solve the resulting linear equation for the variable, and then find the option that matches her solution (which is the likely intention of the question); (2) take each of the options and evaluate the function to see if the result is true for that value; or (3) use some deductive methods to eliminate some options. Approach 3 may occur when there is a discernible pattern in the options. In the given example, note that the negative of the key appears and the reciprocal of the key appears. Combining such pattern recognition with other features presented in the question may give the student sufficient confidence to choose the key without performing the calculations intended by the question. The possibility of employing such less desirable strategies can, and should, be minimized during the development of multiple-choice items by thoughtful choices for the options.

Computer delivery of assessments affords the opportunity to use a number of machine-scored response formats in mathematics that minimize the type of cueing described above. Some of the more common item types that are available to various assessments include multiple multiple-choice (students can select more than one correct answer from a list), numeric entry (students can enter a numeric answer from the keyboard), keyboard entry (students can enter a mathematics expression from the keyboard), drag-and-drop (students can select an object and classify it based on the context of the problem—see Figure 13.2), hot spots (students can highlight selectable parts of a diagram), table/grid (students can select relevant cells in a table to classify mathematical properties—see Figure 13.1), and dropdown menu (students can select options from dropdown menus to make sense of a problem—see Figure 13.4). Additionally, more complex item types might allow students to draw a graph or manipulate geometric figures. These item types, when used appropriately, can enhance the measurement of a construct and are further along the continuum with respect to authenticity.

Many of the more common item types described above are selected-response items. Exceptions are numeric and keyboard entry items, which are the simplest forms of constructed-response item types. Constructed-response items range from short responses, requiring as little as a single word or number, to extended responses that may be broken into several parts. The manner in which responses are captured also varies greatly. Some questions utilize technology, such as graphing functionality, while others capture responses in a text field or by some other mechanism.

The design of a constructed-response question must balance competing priorities. If the question is too broad, responses may not differentiate well among students. If the question is too directed, students' opportunities to demonstrate desired skills in reasoning and problem solving may be limited. For example, an extended constructed-response question about the proof of the Pythagorean theorem can be approached in a variety of ways. The question can be

If $f(x) = 2x + 3$, for what value of k does $f(k) = 8$?

(A) –2.5   (B) 0.4   (C) 1   (D) 2.5

Figure 13.13 Sample item that measures the understanding of the argument of a linear function.

stated as "Prove the Pythagorean theorem." Here, a correct response will give some evidence of mathematical practice MP3 and standard G SRT.B.4 (National Governors Association Center for Best Practices & Council of Chief State School Officers, 2010, pp. 6, 77). The drawback to such a broadly stated question is that an incorrect response may have little chance of earning any points. Furthermore, the lack of direction in the statement of the question presents a barrier to the student who has some knowledge of the material, but cannot get started. On the other hand, the question might be broken down into a number of parts that guide the student through the proof. This practice of scaffolding allows the student to demonstrate knowledge and provides several entry points to the problem. However, if too much guidance is provided by the presentation of the problem, there arises a danger of losing evidence of mathematical practice MP3 that calls for the student to construct arguments and communicate their reasoning.

Yet another consideration in this context is that extended constructed-response questions should be rich enough to earn points all along the score range. A question that, for example, has only four distinct steps or pieces to which points can be allocated may be a poor exemplar of a ten-point question. As a rule, the number of distinct steps in a problem should be aligned with the number of score points.

As shown above, thoughtful specifications of the attributes for items are an important contributor to the successful measurement of the claims for an assessment. Test specifications need to articulate the item types to be included in an assessment. With assessments that are given via computer, it is possible to include a wide variety of item types. Careful thought should be given to how many different types of interactions a student should encounter on a test, since each type of interaction adds to the cognitive load for the student. In order to make sure the test is measuring students' knowledge of mathematics and not familiarity with the item type, it is important that students have an opportunity to practice the different item types throughout the school year.

Technology

Lastly, the discussion focuses on the use of technology to deliver assessments. As noted throughout the chapter, innovation in assessment delivery platforms has opened the door to a more sophisticated testing experience. It allows test developers to incorporate more authentic assessments in mathematics (and other subjects), with the recognition that authenticity must be balanced with the overarching goal of a construct-valid test. It is critical that construct-irrelevant factors are not introduced in trying to measure the desired content.

Test designers should take care that technological enhancements do not introduce an unnecessary degree of construct-irrelevant variance. As a principle, the use of technology should allow better measurement of the construct. That is, it should provide avenues that allow the measurement of the construct in ways that are either limited or not possible without the technology. Consider the presentation of data—the most elementary application of technology—where the use of creative displays just for the sake of adding a visual can be a detriment. Perusing presentation of information online or in a newspaper quickly leads to examples of "chart junk": circle graphs embedded in rich graphics as a tree canopy, the bottom of a well, a piece of fruit, or deformed into the shape of a house; bar graphs where the bars are represented by pictures such as food items or sports equipment. All these embellishments are gratuitous, can get in the way of understanding the data presented, and can introduce mathematical infidelities as the reader interprets the ambiguities introduced to the data. In a similar fashion, care must be taken with the applications and simulations that will be incorporated into CCSS assessments with the goal of producing authenticity. For example, simulations should be used to enhance measurement. Consider a scenario that involves riding a bicycle. A simulation of someone riding a bicycle and showing how far she's traveled at a continuous speed does not really provide information that could not be presented in a paper-and-pencil item. However, a simulation in which students can change parameters such as speed, incline, wind resistance, etc., to explore the setting and draw conclusions, would be a more appropriate use of the technology.

Both PARCC (PARCConline, 2012) and the Smarter Balanced Assessment Consortium (California Department of Education, 2012) have expressed the goal to have as much as possible of their summative assessments machine-scored. As indicated in several places in this chapter, automated-scoring capabilities for constructed-response questions are not yet widely used in high-stakes, large-scale assessments. This is particularly true for extended written responses in mathematics that require the capacity to evaluate mathematical content—often when that content is presented by students with less-than-fully-developed written communication skills. There are a number of hurdles. Among them is having a student write and display mathematical notation in an online setting. Providing an interface for students to build mathematical expressions is a technical possibility via the use of available rendering engines and markup languages. Familiarizing students with such applications and ensuring their comfort with these tools is an obstacle that requires the availability of practice opportunities in the classroom. A student should not encounter the item types or tools for the first time in the assessment situation.

Conclusion

The assessment community is being challenged to create tests that more authentically measure students' abilities to do mathematics. Many assessment designers are embracing ECD methods or other principled approaches to design in order to fully specify the evidence needed to support desired claims regarding students' mathematical competencies. With those specifications in hand, decisions can be made about both item formats and aggregate test form characteristics.

Well-constructed multiple-choice items still have a place in assessment—they are cost-effective to write and score, and they contribute to test reliability. However, they are no longer sufficient; different item types that yield more direct evidence with respect to certain key competencies are required. The comprehensive assessment of the CCSS and mathematical practices requires students to demonstrate their ability to compute, draw, graph, and construct arguments. Item types that measure these competencies in a more targeted way often require students to construct responses or reason their way to a solution. Although the testing of these skills has been possible with paper-based assessments, the human scoring of such free-response items is costly and has led to the limited use of such items. The combination of computer-based administration and advances in automated scoring is facilitating machine scoring of a variety of formats. As the field transitions to online testing, the nature of the tensions in assessment design will change. Consequently, the next generation of assessments can incorporate more innovative item types that allow students to provide evidence of knowledge and skills in ways that can be machine-scored.

Although computer-based testing introduces new approaches to measuring constructs in the context of summative assessments of mathematics, it also generates some tensions that must be resolved. One such tension is the availability of powerful computational tools, such as statistical software packages and dynamic geometry applications, which represent a great advance over traditional calculators that have limited applicability to the domains of statistics and geometry. These technologies place a burden both on teachers, who must familiarize their students with the use of these tools, and test designers, who must consider when and how to employ a variety of tools to measure a broad range of skills. Other tensions may arise with the inclusion of tasks with high levels of authenticity, such as scenario-based tasks. In that case, there are concerns about equity and fairness with respect to opportunity to learn, especially familiarity with specific scenarios and the embedded tools. Test developers face a delicate balance in designing authentic tasks that are engaging, but that do not introduce construct-irrelevant features that interfere with students' ability to demonstrate their mathematical knowledge and skills.

The test design process cannot completely ignore the political realities that govern the focus on summative assessment and the use of these results for educator accountability. While the field is looking for next-generation assessments aligned to the Common Core, teachers are challenged to get up to speed on the standards themselves and to prepare students to succeed on the CCSS. There will likely be a lengthy transition period.

In summary, the design of summative assessments necessarily involves trade-offs and compromises between measurement goals, on the one hand, and operational considerations such as time, cost, and logistics, on the other. Ultimately, clients need to consult with score users and other stakeholders, as well as with content experts, assessment designers, psychometricians, and technical staff. A flexible, dynamic process following a principled assessment design approach can yield a high-quality assessment system.

References

Achieve. (2010). *Comparing the Common Core State Standards in mathematics to California and Massachusetts standards* (pp. 2–4). Washington, DC. Retrieved June 2014 from http://www.achieve.org/files/ComparingCCSSinMathematicstoMAandCAStandards.pdf

Bejar, I. I., & Braun, H. (1994). On the synergy between assessment and instruction: Early lessons from computer-based simulations. *Machine-Mediated Learning, 4,* 5–25.

California Department of Education. (2012). *SBAC e-mail update issue 22.* Retrieved June 2014 from http://web.archive.org/web/20130202151853/http://www.cde.ca.gov/ta/tg/sa/sbacupdate22.asp

California Department of Education. (2013). *Common Core State Standards system implementation plan for California.* Sacramento, CA. Retrieved June 2014 from http://www.cde.ca.gov/re/cc/documents/ccsssysimpplanforcaapr13.pdf

CCSSI. (2012). *Mission statement.* Retrieved June 2014 from http://www.corestandards.org/

CCSSToolBox. (2011). *Sample type II PARCC task from the mathematics Common Core toolbox.* Retrieved June 2014 from http://ccsstoolbox.agilemind.com/parcc/highschool_3829_1.html

Hansen, E. G., & Mislevy, R. J. (2006). Accessibility of computer-based testing for individuals with disabilities and English language learners within a validity framework. In M. Hricko (Ed.), *Online assessment and measurement: Foundations and challenges* (pp. 212–259). Hershey, PA: Information Science Publishing.

Koretz, D. (2013, December 5). *Adapting the practice of measurement to the demands of test-based accountability.* A working paper of the Education Accountability Project at the Harvard Graduate School of Education. Retrieved June 2014 from http://projects.iq.harvard.edu/files/eap/files/adapting_the_practice_of_measurement_12.5.13_wp_2.pdf

Messick, S. (1994). The interplay of evidence and consequences in the validation of performance assessments. *Educational Researcher, 23*(2), 13–23.

Messick, S. (1995). Validity of psychological assessment. *American Psychologist, 50*(9), 741–749.

Mislevy, R. J., Almond, R. G., & Lukas, J. F. (2004). *A brief introduction to evidence-centered design* (CSE Report 632). Los Angeles, CA: Center for Research on Evaluation, Standards, and Student Testing.

Mislevy, R. J., Steinberg, L. S., & Almond, R. G. (2003). On the structure of educational assessments. *Measurement: Interdisciplinary Research and Perspectives, 1,* 3–67.

National Center for Education Statistics. (2013). *PISA released assessment items.* Alexandria, VA: National Center for Education Statistics. Retrieved June 2014 from http://nces.ed.gov/surveys/pisa/releaseditems.asp

National Governors Association Center for Best Practices & Council of Chief State School Officers. (2010). *Common Core State Standards for Mathematics.* National Governors Association Center for Best Practices & Council of Chief State School Officers, Washington, DC.

National Research Council. (2004). *Keeping score for all: The effects of inclusion and accommodation policies on large-scale educational assessment.* Committee on Participation of English Language Learners and Students with Disabilities in NAEP and Other Large-Scale Assessments. Judith A. Koenig and Lyle F. Bachman, Editors. Washington, DC: National Academies Press.

NCTM. (2010). *Common Core State Standards joint statement.* Retrieved June 2014 from http://www.corestandards.org/assets/k12_statements/NCTM-NCSM-ASSM-AMTE-joint-statement.pdf

OECD. (2013). *PISA 2012 assessment and analytical framework: Mathematics, reading, science, problem solving and financial literacy.* Retrieved June 2014 from http://dx.doi.org/10.1787/9789264190511-en

PARCC. (2011). *Appendix F: Illustrations of innovative task characteristics.* Retrieved June 2014 from http://myflorida.com/apps/vbs/adoc/F28718_AppendixPagesITN201231PARCCItemDevelopmentFinal.pdf

PARCC. (2012). *Samples—Mathematics.* Retrieved June 2014 from http://web.archive.org/web/20150321001715/http://www.parcconline.org/samples/mathematics/high-school-functions

PARCConline. (2011). *Connections to the PARCC assessment.* Retrieved June 2014 from http://web.archive.org/web/20141030035541/http://www.parcconline.org/mcf/mathematics/connections-parcc-assessment

PARCConline. (2012). *PARCC item development FAQs.* Retrieved June 2014 from http://web.archive.org/web/20130911081011/http://www.parcconline.org/sites/parcc/files/PARCC%20Item%20Development%20ITN%20Summary%20-%2012-30-11.pdf

Smarter Balanced Assessment Consortium. (2012a). *Claims for the mathematics summative assessment.* Retrieved June 2014 from http://www.smarterbalanced.org/wordpress/wp-content/uploads/2012/09/Smarter-Balanced-Mathematics-Claims.pdf

Smarter Balanced Assessment Consortium. (2012b). *Sample items.* Retrieved June 2014 from http://sampleitems.smarterbalanced.org/itempreview/sbac/index.htm

Williamson, D. M., Mislevy, R. J., & Bejar, I. I. (2006). *Automated scoring of complex tasks in computer-based testing.* Mahwah, NJ: Lawrence Erlbaum.

Contributors

Marie Bienkowski is Deputy Director at the Center for Technology in Learning at SRI International, Menlo Park, California, USA.

Henry Braun is Boisi Professor of Education and Public Policy of the Educational Research, Measurement, and Evaluation Department in the Lynch School of Education, and Director of the Center for the Study of Testing, Evaluation, and Educational Policy at Boston College, USA.

Derek C. Briggs is Professor and Chair of the Research and Evaluation Methodology Program in the School of Education, University of Colorado, Boulder, USA.

Timothy S. Brophy is Professor of Music Education and Director of Institutional Assessment in the Office of the Provost and Senior Vice President for Academic Affairs at the University of Florida, USA.

Nathaniel J. S. Brown is Associate Research Professor of the Educational Research, Measurement, and Evaluation Department in the Lynch School of Education at Boston College, USA.

Katie Buckley is a senior analyst at Abt Associates, Inc., Cambridge, Massachusetts, USA.

Britte H. Cheng is a senior education researcher at the Center for Technology in Learning at SRI International, Menlo Park, California, USA.

Cynthia D'Angelo is an education researcher at the Center for Technology in Learning at SRI International, Menlo Park, California, USA.

Angela DeBarger is a program officer at Lucas Education Research, USA.

Charles DePascale is a senior associate at the National Center for the Improvement of Educational Assessment in Dover, New Hampshire, USA.

Kadriye Ercikan is Professor of Measurement, Evaluation, and Research Methodology, and Director of the Cross-Cultural Assessment & Research Methods in Education Research Lab, at the University of British Columbia, Canada.

Steve Ferrara is Vice President for Performance Assessment and Head, Center for Next Generation Learning and Assessment in Pearson's Research and Innovation Network, Washington, DC, USA.

Geneva D. Haertel is Director of Assessment Research and Design at the Center for Technology in Learning at SRI International, Menlo Park, California, USA.

Christopher J. Harris is a senior researcher in science education at the Center for Technology in Learning at SRI International, Menlo Park, California, USA.

Kristen Huff is Vice President for Research Strategy and Implementation at ACT, Inc., USA.

Pamela Kaliski is an associate psychometrician at the College Board, Newtown, Pennsylvania, USA.

Patricia A. Klag is General Manager of Assessment Development at Educational Testing Service, Princeton, New Jersey, USA.

Friedrich L. Kluempen is an assessment process specialist in the Research and Development Division at Educational Testing Service, Princeton, New Jersey, USA.

Suzanne Lane   is Professor of the Research Methodology Program, Department of Psychology in Education, University of Pittsburgh, USA.

Scott S. Maderer   is Senior Director in K–12 Assessment Development at Educational Testing Service, San Antonio, Texas, USA.

Margaret E. Malone   is Associate Vice President of World Languages and International Programs at the Center for Applied Linguistics, Washington, DC, USA.

Scott F. Marion   is Executive Director of the National Center for the Improvement of Educational Assessment in Dover, New Hampshire, USA.

Susan McGreevy-Nichols   is Executive Director of the National Dance Education Organization, Silver Spring, Maryland, USA.

Liliana Ructtinger   is a member of NSW Department of Education and Communities, Australia.

Daisy Rutstein   is an education researcher at the Center for Technology in Learning at SRI International, Menlo Park, California, USA.

F. Robert Sabol   is Professor of the Department of Art and Design in the College of Liberal Arts, Purdue University, USA.

Paul Sandrock   is Director of Education at the American Council on the Teaching of Foreign Languages, Alexandria, Virginia, USA.

Mary J. Schuttler   is Professor of Theatre Arts and Director of the undergraduate theatre education and masters in theatre education programs at the University of Northern Colorado, USA.

Peter Seixas   is Professor and Canada Research Chair at the University of British Columbia, Canada.

Scott C. Shuler   till recently served as an arts education consultant in the Connecticut State Department of Education and as president of the National Association for Music Education, USA.

Stephen G. Sireci   is Professor of Educational Policy, Research, and Administration, and Director of the Center for Educational Assessment, at the University of Massachusetts, Amherst, USA.

Eric B. Snow   is an education researcher at the Center for Technology in Learning at SRI International, Menlo Park, California, USA.

Amanda Soto   is a psychometrician at the National Board of Medical Examiners, Philadelphia, Pennsylvania, USA.

Terry P. Vendlinski   is a faculty member at Santa Monica College, Santa Monica, California, USA.

Denny Way is Senior Vice President of Psychometric & Research Services at Pearson, Inc., USA.

James Wood   is a science assessment specialist at Minnesota Department of Education, USA.

Louise Yarnall   is a senior research social scientist at the Center for Technology in Learning at SRI International, Menlo Park, California, USA.

Cindy Ziker   is a senior researcher at the Center for Technology in Learning at SRI International, Menlo Park, California, USA.

Reviewers

Courtney Bell is a managing senior research scientist at Educational Testing Service, USA.

Robert L. Brennan is Professor and Director of the Center for the Advanced Studies in Measurement and Assessment in the College of Education at the University of Iowa, USA.

Derek C. Briggs is Professor and Chair of the Research and Evaluation Methodology Program in the School of Education, University of Colorado, Boulder, USA.

Susan M. Brookhart is a consultant at Brookhart Enterprises, LLC, and a senior research associate at the Center for Advancing the Study of Teaching and Learning, Duquesne University, USA.

John A. Dossey is Distinguished Professor of Mathematics Emeritus at Illinois State University, USA.

Katherine Flanagan is an associate director at Massachusetts Department of Higher Education, USA.

Haley D. Freeman is Assistant Director of Test Development at Massachusetts Department of Elementary and Secondary Education, USA.

Amy Hendrickson is Senior Director of Psychometrics at the College Board, USA.

Joan Herman is Co-Director Emeritus of the National Center for Research on Evaluation, Standards, and Student Testing at the University of California, Los Angeles, USA.

Michael Kolen is a professor in the College of Education at the University of Iowa, USA.

Suzanne Lane is a professor in the Research Methodology Program, Department of Psychology in Education, University of Pittsburgh, USA.

Ric Leucht is a professor in the Department of Educational Research Methodology at the University of North Carolina, Greensboro, USA.

Roy Levy is an associate professor at T. Denny Sanford School of Social & Family Dynamics, Arizona State University, USA.

Judith Liskin-Gasparo is an associate professor in the Department of Spanish and Portuguese at the University of Iowa, USA.

Carol Myford is an associate professor in the Department of Education Psychology at the College of Education, University of Illinois at Chicago, USA.

James Pellegrino is Co-Director of the Learning Sciences Research Institute, Liberal Arts and Sciences Distinguished Professor, and Distinguished Professor of Education, University of Illinois at Chicago, USA.

Nancy Petersen is Vice President of ACT, Inc., USA.

Richard Shavelson is Professor Emeritus at the Graduate School of Education, Stanford University, USA.

Bruce VanSledright is a professor and coordinator of the PhD Strand in Elementary Education in the Department of Reading and Elementary Education, College of Education, University of North Carolina at Charlotte, USA.

Paula M. Winke   is an associate professor in the Department of Linguistics, Germanic, Slavic, Asian, and African Languages at Michigan State University, USA.

Rebecca Zwick   is Professor Emeritus in the Department of Education, Gevirtz School, Graduate School of Education, University of Santa Barbara, USA.

Index